U0602550

英国文论选

张中载　赵国新　编

外语教学与研究出版社
北京

图书在版编目 (CIP) 数据

英国文论选：汉、英 / 张中载，赵国新编. — 北京：外语教学与研究出版社，
2015.7
ISBN 978-7-5135-6454-0

I. ①英… II. ①张… ②赵… III. ①英语－阅读教学－高等学校－教材②英
国文学－文学欣赏 IV. ①H319.4：I

中国版本图书馆 CIP 数据核字 (2015) 第 190540 号

出 版 人　蔡剑峰
责任编辑　仲志兰
封面设计　李双双
出版发行　外语教学与研究出版社
社　　址　北京市西三环北路 19 号（100089）
网　　址　http://www.fltrp.com
印　　刷　中国农业出版社印刷厂
开　　本　650×980　1/16
印　　张　33
版　　次　2015 年 7 月第 1 版　2015 年 7 月第 1 次印刷
书　　号　ISBN 978-7-5135-6454-0
定　　价　69.00 元

购书咨询：（010）88819929　电子邮箱：club@fltrp.com
外研书店：http://www.fltrpstore.com
凡印刷、装订质量问题，请联系我社印制部
联系电话：（010）61207896　电子邮箱：zhijian@fltrp.com
凡侵权、盗版书籍线索，请联系我社法律事务部
举报电话：（010）88817519　电子邮箱：banquan@fltrp.com
法律顾问：立方律师事务所　刘旭东律师
　　　　　中咨律师事务所　殷　斌律师
物料号：264540001

推荐出版意见

张中载、赵国新两位教授编选的《英国文论选》是一部非常出色的英国文论读本。选材广泛，选目精当；从 17 世纪英国文学批评出现之际的佳作，到 20 世纪末具有的批评理论名篇，凡能反映英国文论主要特征、趋向的核心著述，基本收入在内。每篇选文之前都附有作者简介，这部分不仅概述了作者生平行谊，它更多地着墨于作者理论思想与批评要义，并紧密联系文学传统嬗变和时代思想风尚，使这部著作成为简要明了的英国文学批评史。每篇选文之后配有详尽的注释，有的篇章注释多达一百多条；注释不仅阐述了语言意义，还进行了思想探究，从中足见编者的认真态度与深厚学养。我认为这部文选达到了出版标准，特此推荐。

北京外国语大学英语学院教授　王丽亚
2013.12.3

推荐出版意见

　　《英国文论选》是国内的第二本英国文论选，与改前出版的英国文论选相比，它的学术含量更大。从选目来看，它绝不是相关英文文献的简单汇编，而是特从权衡的产物，入选篇章均为英国文学批评发展史各个阶段比较有代表性的作品，能够反映出英国文论的基本风貌和发展概况。作者简介和内容提要部分不仅介绍了作者生平和入选作品的基本内容，而且在很多方面进行了比较分析和思想发挥，体现出编者的独创见解。选文后附的很多注释，内容详尽，语言流畅，并概括了英文原句的大意，在很多地方，又不拘泥于原文，做出了重要评述和发挥。这些细节很能反映编者的深厚学养，也有利于读者们学。我认为这本文选已经达到学术出版水平，建议尽快出版。

北京师范大学外文学院教授　蒋红

2013.12.5

目 录

菲利普·锡德尼（1554—1586）

菲利普·锡德尼（1554—1586）出身贵族，是英国文艺复兴时期的著名学者、诗人、军人和朝臣。在牛津大学完成学业后曾周游欧洲大陆，回国后在伊丽莎白女王的朝廷为女王效力。他参加了英国和荷兰之间的战争，并担任佛兰德（Flanders）的卫成司令，直至去世。他是一个英勇善战的军人。据说在一次战役中他负伤，失血过多急需饮水、救护。在此危急关头，他却婉拒了为他提供的饮水和救护，而是把这两种能挽救他生命的急需品让给了比他军职低的战友。这一壮举使他成为英勇侠义之士的楷模。可惜他英年早逝，只活了短短的32年。

锡德尼生活的时代是英国历史上诗人辈出的时代。人们把1580年以后这一时期称为"黄金时代"。由于从文艺复兴发生较早的意大利引进了彼特拉克的十四行诗，英诗有了很大的发展，后来形成英国的十四行诗（或称莎士比亚十四行诗）。锡德尼一生写了一百多首十四行诗和其他诗体的诗篇，以及一部名为《爱星者和星星》（1580—1584）的诗集。他留给后人的是三部不朽之作：诗集《爱星者和星星》，一部长篇传奇故事《阿卡迪亚》（*Arcadia*, 1593，一部传奇式的著作，与作品同名的是古希腊一田园牧歌式的地区。后来文学家用 Arcadia 泛指任何有田园牧歌式淳朴生活的地方）和一篇文论《诗辩》。流芳百世的不仅是这些不朽之作，还有他崇高的人品。他在荷兰那次战役中英勇献身，留下"仁侠的楷模，风流的镜子"的美誉。

他的《阿卡迪亚》用散文和诗体写成，开创了英国的田园文学。在问世后的二百年中，它一直是英国的畅销书，对英国小说的发展有重大影响。

《诗辩》写成于1583年，1595年出版。它是英语文库中首部重要的文学批评论文。写《诗辩》的目的是要批驳清教徒牧师斯蒂温·戈森（Stephen Gosson）在他所写的《造谣学校》（*The School of Abuse*）中对诗的抨击。在《诗辩》中锡德尼批判了柏拉图在《理想国》中对诗人和诗品的错误论断。他说，正是这些错误的论断为清教徒提供了进攻诗的武器。

锡德尼从古希腊、罗马的文论家，诸如柏拉图、亚里士多德、贺拉斯、卡斯底维特罗等人那里汲取营养。要为诗辩护，他必须驳倒对诗的错误论断，例如诗浪费时间，诗是"谎言之母"，诗教恶等。他断言，在早期社会，诗是对民众进行教育的主要手段之一，对社会和文化施加积极的道德影响；而当时的诗人也备受尊敬。他引用贺拉斯的话，强调诗人用寓言给读者以教育和娱乐，创造一个高于现实世界的精神世界。

同柏拉图的观点相反，锡德尼认为诗人应该得到比哲学家和历史学家更高的地位。因为诗能以其趣味性促进人的道德，亦即诗有教化作用。他说："没有任何哲学教条能比阅读维吉尔的史诗更使人正直，"并说诗人"最先带来一切文明。"

内容提要

锡德尼首先提出，他决心为诗辩护，因为诗遭到不公正的待遇，甚至已经成为儿童的笑料。而在罗马社会的早期，诗人被视作与神学家和预言家一样，享有同样受尊敬的地位。古希腊人把写诗的人称作诗人。希腊文 *Poiein*（诗）是创作之意。因此，写诗的诗人就是一个创造者。锡德尼引用希腊的神话故事说安菲翁（Amphion）能用他的动人的诗打动石头，让石头自动地筑起底比斯城。诗人奥菲士（Orpheus）则能让动物聆听他的诗歌。诗人使语言成为科学的宝库。即便是对诗和诗人执有偏见的柏拉图也正是用诗的语言去打动雅典人。历史学家也必须用诗的语言叙述历史，并在历史中让历史人物运用诗的语言。在诗人的笔下，世界变得更美好。也就是说，诗人是一个美好世界的创造者。他说："大自然的世界是铜的，只有诗人才给予我们一个金的世界。"他认为艺术高于生活。

《诗辩》全文的中心思想就是诗人是创造者。柏拉图说诗人只是模仿者，诗人模仿的东西离真理甚远，必然会贻误青年，因此必须把诗人逐出他的"理想国"。锡德尼批驳了这一错误论断。在对诗进行分类后，他对诗的语言、文体、语法作了评论。

锡德尼指出，历史上曾经有过三种诗。一种诗是模仿上帝的美德，例如大卫创作的《诗篇》，所罗门创作的《雅歌》、《传道书》、《箴言》，摩西和底波拉创作的《颂歌》，以及《约伯记》等。第二种诗是用诗叙述各个学科，如历史、哲学、伦理道德、天文地理等。他说，这些用诗的语言来讨论哲学、历史、道德、天文的人是否可以称作是诗人，则应由语言学家去争论。第三种诗的创作者才是真正的诗人，这一类诗人的确是为了教育和怡情而进行模仿，他们最有见识，善于用最优美的语言让人们了解那个感动他们，并使他们向往的善行。

诗人也可以分为歌颂的、悲剧的、喜剧的、讽刺的、诙谐的、伤感的和田园的。

诗可以净化人的灵魂。锡德尼认为，人间的一切学问的目的就是德行，而诗人最能启发人的德行。诗人可以同时发挥历史学家和哲学家的功能。哲学家是艰深难懂的，诗人则用通俗动人的语言进行教育，因此可以称诗人为普及型的哲学家，《伊索寓言》就是最好的例证。

诗人优于历史学家，因为诗人不仅使人获得知识，并且能提高人的品行。他同时也为柏拉图辩解，说柏拉图当时反对诗和诗人只是因为当时的诗人对神持有错误的观点，因此毒害了青年的心灵。他指出，柏拉图在他的名著《伊安篇》(Ion) 中给予了诗很高的评价。

Sir Philip Sidney (1554—1586)

An Apology for Poetry

When the right virtuous Edward Wotton and I were at the Emperor's Court together, we gave ourselves to learn horsemanship of John Pietro Pugliano, one that with great commendation had the place of an esquire in his stable. And he, according to the fertileness of the Italian wit, did not only afford us the demonstration of his practice, but sought to enrich our minds with the contemplations therein which he thought most precious. But with none I remember mine ears were at any time more loaden, than when (either angered with slow payment, or moved with our learner-like admiration) he exercised his speech in the praise of his faculty. He said soldiers were the noblest estate of mankind, and horsemen the noblest of soldiers. He said they were the masters of war and ornaments of peace; speedy goers and strong abiders; triumphers both in camps and courts. Nay, to so unbelieved a point he proceeded, as that no earthly thing bred such wonder to a prince as to be a good horseman. Skill of government was but a *pedenteria*[1] in comparison. Then would he add certain praises, by telling what a peerless beast a horse was, the only serviceable courtier without flattery, the beast of most beauty, faithfulness, courage, and such more, that, if I had not been a piece of a logician before I came to him, I think he would have persuaded me to have wished myself a horse. But thus much at least with his no few words he drove into me, that self-love is better than any gilding to make that seem gorgeous wherein ourselves are parties. Wherein, if Pugliano's strong affection and weak arguments will not satisfy you, I will give you a nearer example of myself, who (I know not by what mischance) in these my not old years and idlest times having slipped into the title of a poet, am provoked to say something unto you in the defense of that my unelected vocation, which if I handle with more good will than good reasons, bear with me, since the scholar is to be pardoned that followeth the steps of his master. And yet I must say that, as I have just cause to make a pitiful defense of poor Poetry, which from almost the highest estimation of learning is fallen to be the laughing-stock of children, so have I need to bring some more available proofs, since the former is by no man barred of his deserved credit, the silly latter hath had even the names of philosophers used to the defacing of it, with great danger of civil war among the Muses.

And first, truly, to all them that professing learning inveigh against poetry may justly be objected, that they go very near to ungratefulness, to seek to deface that which, in the noblest nations and languages that are known, hath been the first light-giver to ignorance, and first nurse, whose milk by little and little enabled them to feed afterwards of tougher knowledges. And will they now play the hedgehog that, being received into the den, drove out his host, or rather the vipers, that with their birth kill their parents? Let learned Greece in any of her manifold sciences be able to show me one book before Musaeus, Homer, and Hesiod, all three nothing else but poets. Nay, let any history be brought that can say any writers were there before them, if they were not men of the same skill, as Orpheus[2], Linus[3], and some other are named, who, having been the first of that country that made pens deliverers of their knowledge to their posterity, may justly challenge to be called their fathers in learning, for not only in time they had this priority (although in itself antiquity be venerable) but went before them, as causes to draw with their charming sweetness the wild untamed wits to an admiration of knowledge, so, as Amphion was said to move stones with his poetry to build Thebes, and Orpheus to be listened to by beasts—indeed stony and beastly people. So among the Romans were Livius Andronicus[4], and Ennius[5]. So in the Italian language the first that made it aspire to be a treasure-house of science were the poets Dante[6], Boccaccio[7], and Petrarch[8]. So in our English were Gower[9] and Chaucer[10].

After whom, encouraged and delighted with their excellent foregoing, others have followed, to beautify our mother tongue, as well in the same kind as in other arts. This did so notably show itself, that the philosophers of Greece durst not a long time appear to the world but under the masks of poets. So Thales[11], Empedocles[12], and Parmenides[13] sang their natural philosophy in verses; so did Pythagoras[14] and Phocylides[15] their moral counsels; so did Tyrtaeus[16] in war matters, and Solon[17] in matters of policy: or rather, they, being poets, did exercise their delightful vein in those points of highest knowledge, which before them lay hid to the world. For that wise

Solon was directly a poet it is manifest, having written in verse the notable fable of the Atlantic Island, which was continued by Plato.

And truly, even Plato, whosoever well considereth shall find that in the body of his work, though the inside and strength were philosophy, the skin as it were and beauty depended most of poetry: for all standeth upon dialogues, wherein he feigneth many honest burgesses of Athens to speak of such matters, that, if they had been set on the rack, they would never have confessed them, besides his poetical describing the circumstances of their meetings, as the well ordering of a banquet, the delicacy of a walk, with interlacing mere tales, as Gyges' Ring[18], and others, which who knoweth not to be flowers of poetry did never walk into Apollo's garden.

And even historiographers (although their lips sound of things done, and verity be written in their foreheads) have been glad to borrow both fashion and perchance weight of poets. So Herodotus entitled his history by the name of the nine Muses; and both he and all the rest that followed him either stole or usurped of poetry their passionate describing of passions, the many particularities of battles, which no man could affirm, or, if that be denied me, long orations put in the mouths of great kings and captains, which it is certain they never pronounced. So that, truly, neither philosopher nor historiographer could at the first have entered into the gates of popular judgments, if they had not taken a great passport of poetry, which in all nations at this day, where learning flourisheth not, is plain to be seen, in all which they have some feeling of poetry. In Turkey, besides their law-giving divines, they have no other writers but poets. In our neighbor country Ireland, where truly learning goeth very bare, yet are their poets held in a devout reverence. Even among the most barbarous and simple Indians where no writing is, yet have they their poets, who make and sing songs, which they call *areytos*, both of their ancestors' deeds and praises of their gods—a sufficient probability that, if ever learning come among them, it must be by having their hard dull wits softened and sharpened with the sweet delights of poetry. For until they find a pleasure in the exercises of the mind, great promises of much knowledge will little persuade them that know not the fruits of knowledge. In Wales, the true remnant of the ancient Britons, as there are good authorities to show the long time they had poets, which they called bards, so through all the conquests of Romans, Saxons, Danes, and Normans[19], some of whom did seek to ruin all memory of learning from among them, yet do their poets, even to this day, last; so as it is not more notable in soon beginning than in long continuing. But since the authors of most of our sciences were the Romans, and before them the Greeks, let us a little stand upon their authorities, but even so far as to see what names they have given unto this now scorned skill.

Among the Romans a poet was called *vates*, which is as much as a diviner, foreseer, or prophet, as by his conjoined words *vaticinium* and *vaticinari* is manifest: so heavenly a title did that excellent people bestow upon this heart-ravishing knowledge. And so far were they carried into the admiration thereof, that they thought in the chanceable hitting upon any such verses great foretokens of their following fortunes were placed. Whereupon grew the word of *sortes Virgilianae*, when, by sudden opening Virgil's book, they lighted upon any verse of his making: whereof the histories of the emperors' lives are full, as of Albinus, the governor of our island, who in his childhood met with this verse, *Arma amens capio nec sat rationis in armis*;[20] and in his age performed it: which, although it were a very vain and godless superstition, as also it was to think that spirits were commanded by such verses—whereupon this word charms, derived of *carmina*, cometh—so yet serveth it to show the great reverence those wits were held in. And altogether not without ground, since both the Oracles of Delphos[21] and Sibylla's[22] prophecies were wholly delivered in verses. For that same exquisite observing of number and measure in words, and that high flying liberty of conceit proper to the poet, did seem to have some divine force in it.

And may not I presume a little further, to show the reasonableness of this word *vates*, and say that the holy David's Psalms are a divine poem? If I do, I shall not do it without the testimony of great learned men, both ancient and modern. But even the name Psalms will speak for me, which, being interpreted, is nothing but "songs"; then that it is fully written in meter, as all learned Hebricians[23] agree, although the rules be not yet fully found; lastly and principally, his handling his prophecy, which is merely poetical. For what else is the awaking his musical instruments, the often and free changing of persons, his notable *prosopopeias*[24], when he maketh you, as it were, see God coming in his majesty, his telling of the beasts' joyfulness, and hills' leaping, but a heavenly poesy, wherein almost he showeth himself a passionate lover of that unspeakable and everlasting beauty to be seen by the eyes of the mind, only cleared by faith? But truly now having named him, I fear me I seem to profane that holy name, applying it to poetry, which is among us thrown down to so ridiculous an estimation. But they that with quiet judgments will look a little deeper into it, shall find the end and working of it such, as, being rightly applied, deserveth not to be scourged out of the Church of God.

But now, let us see how the Greeks named it, and how they deemed of it. The Greeks called him "a poet", which name hath, as the most excellent, gone through other languages. It cometh of this word *poiein*, which is "to make": wherein, I know not whether by luck or wisdom, we Englishmen have met with the Greeks in calling him a *maker*: which name, how high and incomparable a title it is, I had rather were known by marking the scope of other sciences than by my partial allegation.

There is no art delivered to mankind that hath not the works of nature for his principal object, without which they could not consist, and on which they so depend, as they become actors and players, as it were, of what nature will have set forth. So doth the astronomer look upon the stars, and, by that he seeth, setteth down what order nature hath taken therein. So do the geometrician and arithmetician in their diverse sorts of quantities. So doth the musician in times tell you which by nature agree, which not. The natural philosopher thereon hath his name, and the moral philosopher standeth upon the natural virtues, vices, and passions of man; and "follow nature" (saith he) "therein, and thou shalt not err." The lawyer saith what men have determined; the historian what men have done. The grammarian speaketh only of the rules of speech; and the rhetorician and logician, considering what in nature will soonest prove and persuade, thereon give artificial rules, which still are compassed within the circle of a question according to the proposed matter. The physician weigheth the nature of a man's body, and the nature of things helpful or hurtful unto it. And the metaphysic, though it be in the second and abstract notions, and therefore be counted supernatural, yet doth he indeed build upon the depth of nature. Only the poet, disdaining to be tied to any such subjection, lifted up with the vigor of his own invention, doth grow in effect another nature, in making things either better than nature bringeth forth, or, quite anew, forms such as never were in nature, as the Heroes, Demigods, Cyclopes, Chimeras[25], Furies, and such like: so as he goeth hand in hand with nature, not enclosed within the narrow warrant of her gifts, but freely ranging only within the zodiac of his own wit.

Nature never set forth the earth in so rich tapestry as divers poets have done—neither with pleasant rivers, fruitful trees, sweet-smelling flowers, nor whatsoever else may make the too much loved earth more lovely. Her world is brazen, the poets only deliver a golden. But let those things alone, and go to man—for whom as the other things are, so it seemeth in him her uttermost cunning is employed—and know whether she have brought forth so true a lover as Theagenes[26], so constant a friend as Pylades[27], so valiant a man as Orlando[28], so right a prince as Xenophon's Cyrus[29], so excellent a man every way as Virgil's Aeneas. Neither let this be jestingly conceived, because the works of the one be essential, the other in imitation or fiction; for any understanding knoweth the skill of the artificer standeth in that idea or foreconceit of the work, and not in the work itself. And that the poet hath that idea is manifest, by delivering them forth in such excellency as he hath imagined them. Which delivering forth also is not wholly imaginative, as we are wont to say by them that build castles in the air; but so far substantially it worketh, not only to make a Cyrus, which had been but a particular excellency, as nature might have done, but to bestow a Cyrus upon the world, to make many Cyruses, if they will learn aright why and how that maker made him.

Neither let it be deemed too saucy a comparison to balance the highest point of man's wit with the efficacy of nature; but rather give right honor to the heavenly Maker of that maker, who, having made man to His own likeness, set him beyond and over all the works of that second nature[30]: which in nothing he showeth so much as in poetry, when with the force of a divine breath[31] he bringeth things forth far surpassing her doings, with no small argument to the incredulous of that first accursed fall of Adam[32], since our erected wit maketh us know what perfection is, and yet our infected will keepeth us from reaching unto it. But these arguments will by few be understood, and by fewer granted. Thus much (I hope) will be given me, that the Greeks with some probability of reason gave him the name above all names of learning. Now let us go to a more ordinary opening of him, that the truth may be more palpable: and so I hope, though we get not so unmatched a praise as the etymology of his names will grant, yet his very description, which no man will deny, shall not justly be barred from a principal commendation.

Poesy therefore is an art of imitation, for so Aristotle termeth it in his word *mimesis*, that is to say, a representing, counterfeiting, or figuring forth—to speak metaphorically, a speaking picture; with this end, to teach and delight. Of this have been three several kinds. The chief, both in antiquity and excellency, were they that did imitate the inconceivable excellencies of God. Such were David[33] in his Psalms; Solomon in his Song of Songs, in his Ecclesiastes, and Proverbs:[34] Moses and Deborah in their Hymns; and the writer of Job[35], which, beside other, the learned Emanuel Tremellius and Franciscus Junius do entitle the poetical part of the *Scripture*[36]. Against these none will speak that hath the Holy Ghost[37] in due holy reverence.

In this kind, though in a full wrong divinity, were Orpheus, Amphion, Homer in his *Hymns*, and many other, both Greeks and Romans, and this poesy must be used by whosoever will follow St. James's[38] counsel in singing psalms when they are merry, and I know is used with the fruit of comfort by some, when, in sorrowful pangs of their death-bringing sins, they find the consolation of the never-leaving goodness[39].

The second kind is of them that deal with matters, philosophical: either moral, as Tyrtaeus, Phocylides, and Cato[40]; or natural, as Lucretius[41] and Virgil's Georgics[42], or astronomical, as Manilius and Pontanus; or historical, as Lucan;[43] which who mislike, the fault is in their judgments quite out of taste, and not in the sweet food of sweetly uttered knowledge. But because this second sort is wrapped within the fold of the proposed subject, and takes not the course of his own invention, whether they properly be poets or no let grammarians dispute; and go to the third, indeed right poets, of whom chiefly this question ariseth, betwixt whom and these second is such a kind of difference as betwixt the meaner sort of painters, who counterfeit only such faces as are set before them, and the more excellent, who, having no law but wit, bestow that in colors upon you which is fittest for the eye to see, as the constant though lamenting look of Lucretia[44], when she punished in herself another's fault.

Wherein he painteth not Lucretia whom he never saw, but painteth the outward beauty of such a virtue. For these third be they which most properly do imitate to teach and delight, and to imitate borrow nothing of what is, hath been, or shall be; but range, only reined with learned discretion, into the divine consideration of what may be, and should be. These be they that, as the first and most noble sort may justly be termed *vates*, so these are waited on in the excellentest languages and best understandings, with the foredescribed name of poets; for these indeed do merely make to imitate, and imitate both to delight and teach, and delight to move men to take that goodness in hand, which without delight they would fly as from a stranger, and teach, to make them know that goodness whereunto they are moved: which being the noblest scope to which ever any learning was directed, yet want there not idle tongues to bark at them. These be subdivided into sundry more special denominations. The most notable be the heroic, lyric, tragic, comic, satiric, iambic, elegiac, pastoral, and certain others, some of these being termed according to the matter they deal with, some by the sorts of verses they liked best to write in; for indeed the greatest part of poets have appareled their poetical inventions in that numbrous kind of writing which is called verse—indeed but appareled, verse being but an ornament and no cause to poetry, since there have been many most excellent poets that never versified, and now swarm many versifiers that need never answer to the name of poets. For Xenophon, who did imitate so excellently as to give us *effigiem iusti imperii*, "the portraiture of a just empire," under name of Cyrus (as Cicero saith of him), made therein an absolute heroical poem.

So did Heliodorus in his sugared invention of that picture of love in *Theagenes and Chariclea*[45]; and yet both these writ in prose: which I speak to show that it is not rhyming and versing that maketh a poet—no more than a long gown maketh an advocate, who though he pleaded in armor should be an advocate and no soldier. But it is that feigning notable images of virtues, vices, or what else, with that delightful teaching, which must be the right describing note to know a poet by, although indeed the senate of poets hath chosen verse as their fittest raiment, meaning, as in matter they passed all in all, so in manner to go beyond them—not speaking (table talk[46] fashion or like men in a dream) words as they chanceably fall from the mouth, but peising each syllable of each word by just proportion according to the dignity of the subject.

Now therefore it shall not be amiss first to weigh this latter sort of poetry by his works, and then by his parts, and, if in neither of these anatomies he be condemnable, I hope we shall obtain a more favorable sentence. This purifying of wit, this enriching of memory, enabling of judgment, and enlarging of conceit, which commonly we call learning, under what name soever it come forth, or to what immediate end soever it be directed, the final end is to lead and draw us to as high a perfection as our degenerate souls, made worse by their clayey lodgings, can be capable of. This, according to the inclination of the man, bred many formed impressions. For some that thought this felicity principally to be gotten by knowledge and no knowledge to be so high and heavenly as acquaintance with the stars, gave themselves to astronomy; others, persuading themselves to be demigods if they knew the causes of things, became natural and supernatural philosophers; some an admirable delight drew to music; and some the certainty of demonstration to the mathematics. But all, one and other, having this scope—to know, and by knowledge to lift up the mind from the dungeon of the body to the enjoying his own divine essence. But when by the balance of experience it was found that the astronomer looking to the stars might fall into a ditch, that the inquiring philosopher might be blind in himself, and the mathematician might draw forth a straight line with a crooked heart, then, lo, did proof, the overruler of opinions, make manifest that all these are but serving sciences, which, as they have each a private end in themselves, so yet are they all directed to the highest end of the mistress-knowledge, by the Greeks called *architectonike*[47], which stands (as I think) in the knowledge of a man's self, in the ethic and politic consideration, with the end of well doing and not of well knowing only—even as the saddler's next end is to make a good saddle, but his farther end to serve a nobler faculty, which is horsemanship; so the horseman's to soldiery, and the soldier not only to have the skill, but to perform the practice of a soldier. So that, the ending end of all earthly learning being virtuous action, those skills, that most serve to bring forth that, have a most just title to be princes over all the rest. Wherein we can show the poet's nobleness, by setting him before his other competitors, among whom as principal challengers step forth the moral philosophers, whom, me thinketh, I see coming towards me with a sullen gravity, as though they could not abide vice by daylight, rudely clothed for to witness outwardly their contempt of outward things, with books in their hands against glory, whereto they set their names, sophistically speaking against subtlety, and angry with any man in whom they see the foul fault of anger. These men casting largesse as they go of definitions, divisions, and distinctions, with a scornful interrogative do soberly ask whether it be possible to find any path so ready to lead a man to virtue as that which teacheth what virtue is—and teacheth it not only by delivering forth his very being, his causes, and effects, but also by making known his enemy, vice (which must be destroyed), and his cumbersome servant, passion (which must be mastered), by showing the generalities that containeth it, and the specialities that are derived from it; lastly, by plain setting down, how it extendeth itself out of the limits of a man's own little world to the government of families, and maintaining of public societies.

The historian scarcely giveth leisure to the moralist to say so much, but that he, laden with old mouse-eaten records, authorizing himself (for the most part) upon other histories, whose greatest authorities are built upon the notable foundation of hearsay; having much ado to accord differing writers and to pick truth out of partiality; better acquainted with a thousand years ago than with the present age, and yet better knowing how this world goeth than how his own wit runneth; curious for antiquities and inquisitive of novelties; a wonder to young folks and a tyrant in table talk, denieth, in a great chafe, that any man for teaching of virtue, and virtuous actions, is comparable to him. "I am '*lux vitae, temporum magistra, vita memoriae, nuntia vetustatis,*'"&c.[48]

The philosopher (saith he)

teacheth a disputative virtue, but I do an active. His virtue is excellent in the dangerless Academy of Plato, but mine showeth forth her honorable face in the battles of Marathon, Pharsalia, Poitiers, and Agincourt[49]. He teacheth virtue by certain abstract considerations, but I only bid you follow the footing of them that have gone before you. Old-aged experience goeth beyond the fine-witted philosopher, but I give the experience of many ages. Lastly, if he make the song book, I put the learner's hand to the lute; and if he be the guide, I am the light.

Then would he allege you innumerable examples, conferring story by story, how much the wisest senators and princes have been directed by the credit of history, as Brutus, Alphonsus of Aragon, and who not, if need be? At length the long line of their disputation maketh a point in this, that the one giveth the precept, and the other the example.

Now, whom shall we find (since the question standeth for the highest form in the school of learning) to be moderator? Truly, as me seemeth, the poet; and if not a moderator, even the man that ought to carry the title from them both, and much more from all other serving sciences. Therefore compare we the poet with the historian, and with the moral philosopher; and, if he go beyond them both, no other human skill can match him. For as for the Divine, with all reverence it is ever to be excepted, not only for having his scope as far beyond any of these as eternity exceedeth a moment, but even for passing each of these in themselves.

And for the lawyer, though Jus be the daughter of justice, and justice the chief of virtues, yet because he seeketh to make men good rather *formidine poenae* than *virtutis amore*[50], or, to say righter, doth not endeavor to make men good, but that their evil hurt not others, having no care, so he be a good citizen, how bad a man he be: therefore, as our wickedness maketh him necessary, and necessity maketh him honorable, so is he not in the deepest truth to stand in rank with these who all endeavor to take naughtiness away, and plant goodness even in the secretest cabinet of our souls. And these four are all that any way deal in that consideration of men's manners, which being the supreme knowledge, they that best breed it deserve the best commendation.

The philosopher therefore and the historian are they which would win the goal, the one by precept, the other by example. But both, not having both, do both halt. For the philosopher, setting down with thorny argument the bare rule, is so hard of utterance, and so misty to be conceived, that one that hath no other guide but him shall wade in him till he be old before he shall find sufficient cause to be honest. For his knowledge standeth so upon the abstract and general, that happy is that man who may understand him, and more happy that can apply what he doth understand.

On the other side, the historian, wanting the precept, is so tied, not to what should be but to what is, to the particular truth of things and not to the general reason of things, that his example draweth no necessary consequence, and therefore a less fruitful doctrine.

Now doth the peerless poet perform both: for whatsoever the philosopher saith should be done, he giveth a perfect picture of it in someone by whom he presupposeth it was done; so as he coupleth the general notion with the particular example. A perfect picture I say, for he yieldeth to the powers of the mind an image of that whereof the philosopher bestoweth but a wordish description: which doth neither strike, pierce, nor possess the sight of the soul so much as that other doth.

· · ·

For conclusion, I say the philosopher teacheth, but he teacheth obscurely, so as the learned only can understand him; that is to say, he teacheth them that are already taught. But the poet is the food for the tenderest stomachs, the poet is indeed the right popular philosopher, whereof Aesop's tales give good proof: whose pretty allegories, stealing under the formal tales of beasts, make many, more beastly than beasts, begin to hear the sound of virtue from these dumb speakers.

· · ·

I conclude, therefore, that he excelleth history, not only in furnishing the mind with knowledge, but in setting it forward to that which deserveth to be called and accounted good: which setting forward, and moving to well doing, indeed setteth the laurel crown upon the poet as victorious, not only of the historian, but over the philosopher, howsoever in teaching it may be questionable.

For suppose it be granted (that which I suppose with great reason may be denied) that the philosopher, in respect of his methodical proceeding, doth teach more perfectly than the poet, yet do I think that no man is so much *philophilosophos*[51] as to compare the philosopher, in moving, with the poet.

And that moving is of a higher degree than teaching, it may by this appear, that it is well-nigh the cause and the effect of teaching. For who will be taught, if he be not moved with desire to be taught, and what so much good doth that teaching bring forth (I speak still of moral doctrine) as that it moveth one to do that which it doth teach? For, as Aristotle saith, it is not *gnosis* but *praxis*[52] must be the fruit. And how *praxis* cannot be, without being moved to practice, it is no hard matter to consider.

The philosopher showeth you the way, he informeth you of the particularities, as well of the tediousness of the way, as of the pleasant lodging you shall have when your journey is ended, as of the many by-turnings that may divert you from your way. But this is to no man but to him that will read him, and read him with attentive studious painfulness; which constant desire whosoever hath in him, hath already passed half the hardness of the way, and therefore is beholding to the philosopher but for the other half. Nay truly, learned men have learnedly thought that where once reason hath so much overmastered passion as that the mind hath a free desire to do well, the inward light each mind hath in itself is as good as a philosopher's book; seeing in nature we know it is well to do well, and what is well and what is evil, although not in the words of art which philosophers bestow upon us. For out of natural conceit the philosophers drew it; but to be moved to do that which we know, or to be moved with desire to know, *Hoc opus, hic labor est*[53].

Now therein of all sciences (I speak still of human, and according to the humane conceits) is our poet the monarch. For he doth not only show the way, but giveth so sweet a prospect into the way, as will entice any man to enter into it. Nay, he doth, as if your journey should lie through a fair vineyard, at the first give you a cluster of grapes, that, full of that taste, you may long to pass further. He beginneth not with obscure definitions, which must blur the margent[54] with interpretations, and load the memory with doubtfulness; but he cometh to you with words set in delightful proportion, either accompanied with, or prepared for, the well-enchanting skill of music;

and with a tale forsooth he cometh unto you, with a tale which holdeth children from play, and old men from the chimney corner. And, pretending no more, doth intend the winning of the mind from wickedness to virtue: even as the child is often brought to take most wholesome things by hiding them in such other as have a pleasant taste: which, if one should begin to tell them the nature of aloes or rhubarb they should receive, would sooner take their physic at their ears than at their mouth. So is it in men (most of which are childish in the best things, till they be cradled in their graves): glad they will be to hear the tales of Hercules[55], Achilles, Cyrus, and Aeneas; and, hearing them, must needs hear the right description of wisdom, valor, and justice; which, if they had been barely, that is to say philosophically, set out, they would swear they be brought to school again.

· · ·

Since then poetry is of all human learning the most ancient and of most fatherly antiquity, as from whence other learnings have taken their beginnings; since it is so universal that no learned nation doth despise it, nor no barbarous nation is without it; since both Roman and Greek gave divine names unto it, the one of *prophesying*, the other of *making*, and that indeed that name of *making* is fit for him, considering that whereas other arts retain themselves within their subject, and receive, as it were, their being from it, the poet only bringeth his own stuff, and doth not learn a conceit out of a matter, but maketh matter for a conceit; since neither his description nor his end containeth any evil, the thing described cannot be evil; since his effects be so good as to teach goodness and to delight the learners; since therein (namely in moral doctrine, the chief of all knowledges) he doth not only far pass the historian, but, for instructing, is well-nigh comparable to the philosopher, and, for moving, leaves him behind him; since the Holy Scripture (wherein there is no uncleanness) hath whole parts in it poetical, and that even our Savior Christ vouchsafed to use the flowers of it; since all his kinds are not only in their united forms but in their severed dissections fully commendable; I think (and think I think rightly) the laurel crown appointed for triumphing captains doth worthily (of all other learnings) honor the poet's triumph. But because we have ears as well as tongues, and that the lightest reasons that may be will seem to weigh greatly, if nothing be put in the counterbalance, let us hear, and, as well as we can, ponder, what objections may be made against this art, which may be worthy either of yielding or answering.

. . .

Now, that verse far exceedeth prose in the knitting up of the memory, the reason is manifest—the words (besides their delight, which hath a great affinity to memory) being so set as one word cannot be lost but the whole work fails; which accuseth itself, calleth the remembrance back to itself, and so most strongly confirmeth it. Besides, one word so, as it were, begetting another, as, be it in rhyme or measured verse, by the former a man shall have a near guess to the follower: lastly, even they that have taught the art of memory have showed nothing so apt for it as a certain room divided into many places well and thoroughly known. Now, that hath the verse in effect perfectly, every word having his natural seat, which seat must needs make the words remembered. But what needeth more in a thing so known to all men? Who is it that ever was a scholar that doth not carry away some verses of Virgil, Horace, or Cato, which in his youth he learned, and even to his old age serve him for hourly lessons? But the fitness it hath for memory is notably proved by all delivery of arts: wherein for the most part, from grammar to logic, mathematic, physic, and the rest, the rules chiefly necessary to be borne away are compiled in verses. So that, verse being in itself sweet and orderly, and being best for memory, the only handle of knowledge, it must be in jest that any man can speak against it. Now then go we to the most important imputations laid to the poor poets. For aught I can yet learn, they are these. First, that there being many other more fruitful knowledges, a man might better spend his time in them than in this. Secondly, that it is the mother of lies. Thirdly, that it is the nurse of abuse, infecting us with many pestilent desires, with a siren's sweetness drawing the mind to the serpent's tale of sinful fancy—and herein, especially, comedies give the largest field to ear (as Chaucer saith)—how both in other nations and in ours, before poets did soften us, we were full of courage, given to martial exercises, the pillars of manlike liberty, and not lulled asleep in shady idleness with poets' pastimes. And lastly, and chiefly, they cry out with an open mouth, as if they outshot Robin Hood[56], that Plato banished them out of his commonwealth[57]. Truly, this is much, if there be much truth in it. First, to the first, that a man might better spend his time is a reason indeed: but it doth (as they say) but *petere principium*[58]: for if it be, as I affirm, that no learning is so good as that which teacheth and moveth to virtue, and that none can both teach and move thereto so much as poetry, then is the conclusion manifest that ink and paper cannot be to a more profitable purpose employed. And certainly, though a man should grant their first assumption, it should follow (methinks) very unwillingly, that good is not good because better is better. But I still and utterly deny that there is sprung out of earth a more fruitful knowledge. To the second therefore, that they should be the principal liars, I answer paradoxically, but truly, I think truly, that of all writers under the sun the poet is the least liar, and, though he would, as a poet can scarcely be a liar. The astronomer, with his cousin the geometrician, can hardly escape, when they take upon them to measure the height of the stars.

注释

1. *pedenteria*：即英语的 pedantry。
2. Orpheus：奥菲士，诗人和歌手。希腊神话说他弹奏竖琴时，能让猛兽俯首，顽石点头。
3. Linus：古希腊音乐教师。
4. Livius Andronicus：利维亚斯·安德罗尼库斯（约前 280—约前 204），古罗马第一个诗人，首次将《奥德赛》译成拉丁文的诗体形式。
5. Ennius：恩尼乌斯（约前 239—约前 169），古罗马诗人和戏剧家，作品包括喜剧、悲剧及讲述罗马历史的史诗《编年记》（*Annals*）。
6. Dante：但丁，13 世纪至 14 世纪意大利诗人。《神曲》是他的传世之作。
7. Boccaccio：薄伽丘（Giovanni Boccaccio, 1313—1375），意大利文艺复兴时期著名作家，代表作为《十日谈》。
8. Petrarch：彼特拉克（Francesco Petrarch, 1304—1374），意大利文艺复兴时期的诗人、学者。他写的十四行诗被称为 Petrarchan Sonnet。
9. Gower：约翰·高尔（John Gower, 1330？—1408），14 世纪英国诗人。
10. Chaucer：乔叟（Geoffrey Chaucer, 1340？—1400），14 世纪英国诗人，《坎特伯雷故事集》（*Canterbury Tales*）是他的代表作。

11. Thales：泰利斯（约前 624—前 546）古希腊哲学家、数学家、天文学家。

12. Empedocsles：恩培多克勒（前 490—前 430），古希腊哲学家、诗人。

13. Parmenides：巴门尼德，公元前 6 世纪至 5 世纪希腊哲学家。他的许多哲学理论被完整地保存了下来。

14. Pythagoras：毕达哥拉斯，公元前 6 世纪希腊哲学家、数学家。

15. Phocylides：甫希里迪斯，与毕达哥拉斯同时代，希腊诗人。

16. Tyrtaeus：提尔泰奥斯，公元前 7 世纪希腊诗人。

17. Solon：梭伦（约前 638—约前 559），古雅典政治家、诗人。

18. Gyges 是公元前 7 世纪 Lydia 国王，他杀死了国王 Candaules 后成为国王。公元前 5 世纪希腊著名历史学家 Herodotus 有这样的叙述：Gyges 是国王 Candaules 手下一名得宠的战将。他年少时是个穷苦的牧羊人。有一天，他在一峡谷偶然得到一只神魔戒指。他只要戴上这只戒指，就能成为隐身人。Candaules 的皇后是绝色佳丽，国王为此深感骄傲。他为了炫耀他的妻子的美妙体态，坚持要 Gyges 隐身偷看皇后诱人的裸体。Gyges 从命，结果被皇后察觉。于是，皇后命令他在两者之间进行选择：要么自杀，要么杀死她的丈夫，夺取王位，娶她为妻。Gyges 选择了后者。柏拉图在《理想国》中说，Gyges 凭借神魔戒指赢得了王位和皇后，并说人若对自己的行动后果无所顾忌，就不可能有德行。

19. Normans：诺曼人，即公元 10 世纪定居诺曼底（Normandy，在法国西北部）的斯堪的纳维亚人。此处指 1066 年征服英国的诺曼人。

20. *Arma amens capio nec sat rationis in armis*：即 "Insane, I take arms, nor is there reason for arms." 引自《埃涅阿斯纪》（*Aeneid*），II。

21. Delphos：希腊地名。

22. Sibylla：罗马女预言家。

23. Hebrician：Hebrides 群岛的居民。Hebrides 群岛在苏格兰西岸近海。

24. *prosopopeia*：即英语的 personification。

25. Chimera：希腊神话中喷火的妖怪，上半身像狮，下半身像蛇，腰身像山羊。

26. Theagenes：爱情小说 *Theagenes and Chariclea* 中的男主人公。*Theagenes and Chariclea* 见注 45。

27. Pylades：皮拉得斯，希腊神话中人物。

28. Orlando：奥兰多，相传为查理大帝（Charlemagne, 742—814）的外

甥。他是许多浪漫故事的主人公。

29. Cyrus：居鲁士。此处指波斯王子 Cyrus the Younger（后继承王位）。他是色诺芬（Xenophon）笔下理想国王的典型。

30. that second nature：本段提到的 "the heavenly Maker" 指创造万物的上帝。"that maker" 指创造者诗人。上帝创造的人为 the first nature（第一自然），上帝创造的其他东西为 the second nature（第二自然）。

31. a divine breath：上帝创造万物时用的神气。

32. fall of Adam：基督教教义中人类始祖亚当的堕落。亚当违背上帝的命令，偷吃禁果，犯了罪，致使整个人类成为罪人。这就是所谓的"原罪"（Original Sin）。

33. David：大卫，为《诗篇》(Psalms) 的作者。Psalms，《圣经》中的《诗篇》。

34. Solomon in his Song of Songs ...and Proverbs：Solomon（所罗门）是大卫的儿子和继承者，古代以色列国王，以智慧著称。Song of Songs (《雅歌》)，亦作 Song of Solomon；Ecclesiastes (《传道书》)；Proverbs (《箴言》)。《圣经》中的《雅歌》、《传道书》和《箴言》相传均为所罗门所作。

35. Moses and Deborah ... Job：Moses（摩西），《圣经》中古代犹太人的首领。Deborah（底波拉），《圣经》中犹太女先知，昵称为 Debby。Job，《约伯记》，《圣经·旧约》中的一卷。约伯是上帝宠爱的人，他安贫乐道，又能忍耐，在任何情况下都对上帝忠心不移。

36. Emanuel Tremellius and Franciscus Junius ... the *Scripture*：Emanuel Tremellius 为 16 世纪犹太学者，他把《圣经》译成了拉丁文。*Scripture* 即《圣经》(*Holy Scripture*)。

37. Holy Ghost："圣灵"，亦作"上帝圣灵"，基督教基本信条三位一体中的第三位；其他二位是"圣父"、"圣子"。基督教认为上帝集圣父、圣子、圣灵于一身，即三位一体。

38. St. James：即圣雅各，耶稣十二门徒之一。《新约》中有《雅各书》。

39. never-leaving goodness：此处意为上帝的善良关怀与人类永存。

40. Cato：（小）加图（前 95—前 46），公元前 1 世纪罗马著名政治家。他反对凯撒和喀提林，在得知共和军战败后，愤而自杀。

41. Lucretius：卢克莱修（约前 94—前 55），古罗马诗人、哲学家，著有教谕诗《物性论》(On the Nature of Things).

42. Georgics：《农事诗集》，四卷共 2,000 行的长诗，是维吉尔（Virgil）

模仿希腊早期诗人赫西奥德（Hesiod）所写的《工作与时日》（*Works and Days*）的诗作。英国 17 世纪诗人德莱顿（John Dryden）称其是 "the best poem of the best poet"。

43. ... as Manilius and Pontanus ... as Lucan：Manilius, 公元 1 世纪罗马诗人，长诗 *Astronomica* 的作者。此诗共 5 卷，讨论天文学。Pontanus, 公元 15 世纪意大利诗人。Lucan 卢坎（39—65），生于西班牙的古罗马诗人，因反对罗马皇帝尼禄（Nero），被迫自杀。他是当时名扬全国的诗人、学者。

44. Lucretia：卢克丽霞，古罗马传说中的贞烈女子，她被强奸后自尽。

45. *Theagenes and Chariclea*：亦作 *Aethiopica*（《埃塞俄比亚人》），公元前 3 世纪希腊作家 Heliodorus 所写的一部爱情小说。也是古希腊保存下来的五部小说中的一部。故事叙述女祭司 Chariclea 与 Theagenes 相恋，两人来到了埃及。正当她要被作为牺牲品献给众神时，她被认出是国王的女儿。有情人终成眷属。

46. table talk：席间漫谈。

47. *architectonike*：即 architectonics，哲学中与知识的系统化有关的学科，亦称认识体系论。

48. 此句引自西塞罗（Cicero）所写的《论演说家》（*On the Orator*）。英译文是："The light of truth, the life of memory, the teacher of life, the messenger of antiquity."。

49. ... in the battles of Marathon, Pharsalia, Poitiers, and Agincourt：Battle of Marathon 发生在公元前 490 年。此役雅典人打败了入侵的波斯人，波斯死亡 6,400 人，雅典仅阵亡 192 人。Battle of Pharsalia 发生在公元前 48 年，庞培在此役中被凯撒打败。Battle of Poitiers 是 1337 至 1453 年英法之间的"百年战争"中的一次战役，发生在 1356 年。在该战役中英军以少胜多打败了法军。Battle of Agincourt, 1415 年发生在法国的 Agincourt（Pas de Calais），法军被英军打败。

50. 此句英译文为：through "fear of punishment" rather than through "love of virtue"。

51. *philophilosophos*：希腊文，意为哲学爱好者。

52. ...not *gnosis* but *praxis*：英译文是 not "knowledge" but "action"。

53. *Hoc opus, hic labor est.*：英译文是 "This is the work, this the labor." 引自《埃涅阿斯纪》。

54. margent：即 margin。在锡德尼时代，书页边的空白常用作记读书笔记。

55. Hercules：赫丘利，罗马神话中的大力神，希腊神话中称赫拉克勒斯（Heracles），以完成 12 项英雄业绩而闻名。据说，他曾经被要求在快乐与美德之间选择，前者提供声色犬马之娱，后者提供终生劳作与卓著美名。他毅然选择了后者。

56. Robin Hood：罗宾汉，12 世纪英国民间传说中家喻户晓的绿林好汉。他劫富济贫，为民除暴，深受民众的爱戴。

57. out of his commonwealth：即 out of his Republic，引自柏拉图的《理想国》（*Republic*）。

58. *petere principium*：即 "beg the question"。

培根　《学术的演进》

弗朗西斯·培根（1561—1626）

　　弗朗西斯·培根（1561—1626）是英国文艺复兴时期的一个杰出人才。他既是科学哲学家，又是散文家，还是杰出的律师。他21岁就被选为下院议员，官至大理院院长，封为勋爵。在英国文学史中，他是文学家中官位最显赫的人物。他又是出色的法官，在他65年的生涯中有45年从事法律工作。他对英国的科学、文化和文学的发展作出了举足轻重的贡献，却又因受贿被议会弹劾去职。他是一个优点和缺点都突出的人物，一个充满着矛盾的人物。英国著名诗人蒲柏称培根为"最聪明、最出色、最卑鄙的人。"所谓"卑鄙"，是因为他受了贿。马克思称他是"英国唯物主义的真正始祖"。本·琼森为他的口才所倾倒。在评论培根的演说时，他说道："若论说话干净，准确，有分量，最不空洞，最没有废话，谁也比不过他。"弥尔顿、伏尔泰、歌德等文学巨子对他都赞许备至。

　　他的贡献主要在两个方面：科学和文学。作为自然科学的哲学家，他与中世纪的经院派决裂，首次把自然科学分门别类，并用新的归纳法向传统的权威挑战，为现代实验科学开道。他所写的《学术的演进》（*The Advancement of Learning*，1605）和《新工具》（*Novum Organum*，1620）对科学作出了贡献。《学术的演进》指明了科学的正确思想方法和研究方法。《新工具》则痛斥"偶像"，亦即虚妄或错误的思想习惯，提出了归纳法这一崭新的研究方法。

　　培根又是一个杰出的散文家。他的《随笔》（*The Essays*）以其绝妙的散文为英国乃至世界的散文树立了楷模。他有科学家的准确性和逻辑性，律师和法官的雄辩，语言大师的清晰、生动的语言。他把这些优点融合在他的散文中，就形成了他特有的文体风格。他的文章气势宏伟雄浑，语言生动简约。他的多数作品都是用拉丁文写的，即便是原先用英语写的作品，他也译成了拉丁文，因为他认为拉丁文将会成为永存不朽的语言。

随笔是文艺复兴时期新涌现的一种文学形式。虽然 1580 年法国人蒙田（Montaigne）比培根早 17 年首次推出这一散文形式，但是培根的随笔却别具一格。蒙田的随笔悠然从容如流水，培根的随笔则庄严睿智，极富哲理，颇似古罗马哲学家、戏剧家塞内加（Seneca）的风格。培根是英国随笔的首创者，英国 18 世纪初的散文家如约瑟夫·艾迪生（Joseph Addison）和理查德·斯梯尔（Richard Steele）等都效仿他的随笔风格。

他写的《随笔》初版时仅有短文 10 篇，经过 1612 年、1625 年两次增补，最后收录短文 58 篇。这些文章的题材广泛，或谈处世之道，或议成功之秘诀，或说读书、婚姻、娱乐。无论是谈读书、美或高位，或探讨哲理，或议论人生，妙句警语处处可见，且文章短小精悍，甚多卓识，读来让人为之倾倒。他论述起来雄辩滔滔，却又反对舞文弄墨，更不因词害意。

内容提要

《学术的演进》写于 1605 年。此时，培根与詹姆士一世的关系密切。他以此文献给国王，目的是想以此唤起王室对科学发展的支持。此处摘录该文中的一部分，主要是谈诗。

培根首先对诗和历史作了区分。他认为诗享受极大的自由，因为诗不需要遵循任何自然法则；诗需要想象。历史必须客观地叙述事实，而诗却可以杜撰或虚构人物、事件和行为，并且比历史所叙述的人和事更生动、更有力。诗能给读者以高尚、道德和愉快，因此诗能起到纯洁人的心灵的作用。

他把诗分为三类。第一类是叙述性的，这类诗是对历史的模仿。第二类是描绘性的，它采用意象。第三类是隐喻性的或寓言式的，如《伊索寓言》。这三类诗又可分为神学诗和异教诗。他认为诗是学术的第三部分，在表达感情、激情、堕落、习俗等方面优于哲学，而在机智和雄辩方面也不比演说逊色。

他认为，历史和诗分属两个不同的领域。诗反映主观世界，而历史则反映客观世界。他说："诗能按人的愿望把事物的本质呈现给读者，而理性却让人遵循事物的本质。"培根同意锡德尼的观点，认为诗创造一个比现实世界更美好的世界，因为诗能表达人们的愿望，讲述人们的经历，给人以道德教诲，让人看到世界美好的一面。

Sir Francis Bacon (1561—1626)

The Advancement of Learning

Poesy is a part of learning in measure of words for the most part restrained, but in all other points extremely licensed, and doth truly refer to the imagination, which, being not tied to the laws of matter, may at pleasure join that which nature hath severed, and sever that which nature hath joined, and so make unlawful matches and divorces of things: "*Pictoribus atque poetis*, etc."[1] It is taken in two senses in respect of words or matter. In the first sense it is but a character of style, and belongeth to arts of speech, and is not pertinent for the present. In the latter, it is, as hath been said, one of the principal portions of learning, and is nothing else but feigned history, which may be styled as well in prose as in verse.

The use of this feigned history hath been to give some shadow of satisfaction to the mind of man in those points wherein the nature of things doth deny it, the world being in proportion inferior to the soul; by reason whereof there is agreeable to the spirit of man a more ample greatness, a more exact goodness, and a more absolute variety than can be found in the nature of things. Therefore, because the acts or events of true history have not that magnitude which satisfieth the mind of man, poesy feigneth acts and events greater and more heroical; because true history propoundeth the successes and issues of actions not so agreeable to the merits of virtue and vice, therefore poesy feigns them more just in retribution and more according to revealed providence; because true history representeth actions and events more ordinary and less interchanged, therefore poesy endueth them with more rareness and more unexpected and alternative variations: so as it appeareth that poesy serveth and confereth to magnanimity, morality, and to delectation. And therefore it was ever thought to have some participation of divineness, because it doth raise and erect the mind, by submitting the shows of things to the desires of the mind, whereas reason doth buckle and bow the mind unto the nature of things. And we see that by these insinuations and congruities with man's nature and pleasure, joined also with the agreement and consort it hath with music, it hath had access and estimation in rude times and barbarous regions, where other learning stood excluded.

The division of poesy which is aptest in the propriety thereof (besides those divisions which are common unto it with history, as feigned chronicles, feigned lives, and the appendices of history, as feigned epistles, feigned orations, and the rest) is into poesy narrative, representative, and allusive. The narrative is a mere imitation of history with the excesses before remembered, choosing for subject commonly wars and love, rarely state, and sometimes pleasure or mirth. Representative is as a visible history, and is an image of actions as if they were present, as history is of actions in nature as they are, that is past; allusive, or parabolical, is a narration applied only to express some special purpose or conceit: which latter kind of parabolical wisdom was much more in use in the ancient times, as by the fables of Aesop, and the brief sentences of the seven[2], and the use of hieroglyphics may appear. And the cause was for that it was then of necessity to express any point of reason which was more sharp or subtle than the vulgar in that manner, because men in those times wanted both variety of examples and subtlety of conceit: and as hieroglyphics were before letters, so parables were before arguments: and nevertheless now and at all times they do retain much life and vigor, because reason cannot be so sensible, nor examples so fit.

But there remaineth yet another use of poesy parabolical opposite to that which we last mentioned; for that tendeth to demonstrate and illustrate that which is taught or delivered, and this other to retire and obscure it: that is, when the secrets and mysteries of religion, policy, or philosophy, are involved in fables or parables. Of this in divine poesy we see the use is authorized. In heathen poesy we see the exposition of fables doth fall out sometimes with great felicity, as in the fable that the giants being overthrown in their way against the gods, the earth their mother in revenge thereof brought forth fame:

> *Illam terra parens ira irritata deorem,*
> *Extremam, ut perhibent, Caeo Enceladoque sororem*
> *Progenuit:*[3]

expounded that when princes and monarchs have suppressed actual and open rebels, then the malignity of people, which is the mother of rebellion, doth bring forth libels and slanders, and taxations of the states, which is of the same kind with rebellion, but more feminine: so in the fable that the rest of the gods having conspired to bind Jupiter, Pallas called Briareus[4] with his hundred hands to his aid, expounded that monarchies need not fear any curbing of their absoluteness by mighty subjects, as long as by wisdom they keep the hearts of the people, who will be sure to come in on their side: so in the fable that Achilles was brought up under Chyron the centaur[5], who was part a man and part a beast, expounded ingenuously, but corruptly, by Machiavelli[6] that it belongeth to the education and discipline of princes to know as well how to play the part of the lion in violence and the fox in guile, as of the man in virtue and justice. Nevertheless in many the like encounters, I do rather think that the fable was first and the exposition devised than that the moral was first and thereupon the fable framed. For I find it was an ancient vanity in Chrysippus[7] that troubled himself with great contention to fasten the assertions of the Stoics upon the fictions of the ancient poets: but yet that all the fables and fictions of the poets were but pleasure and not figure, I interpose no opinion. Surely of those poets which are now extant, even Homer himself (notwithstanding he was made a kind of scripture by the later schools of the Grecians) yet I should without any difficulty pronounce, that his fables had no such inwardness in his own meaning: but what they might have, upon a more original tradition, is not easy to affirm, for he was not the inventor of many of them. In this third part of learning which is poesy, I can report no deficience. For being as a plant that cometh of the lust of the earth, without a formal seed, it hath sprung up and spread abroad, more than any other kind: but to ascribe unto it that which is due for the expressing of affections, passions, corruptions and customs, we are beholding to poets more than to the philosophers' works, and for wit and eloquence not much less than to orators' harangues.

注释

1. "*Pictoribus atque poetis*, etc.": 英译文为："To painters and poets, etc.",引自贺拉斯(Horace)的《诗艺》(*Art of Poetry*)。
2. the seven: 公元前 6 世纪希腊的 7 位贤人(seven sages or Seven Wise

Men of Greece：Thales【泰利斯】, Solon【梭伦】, Bias【拜厄斯】, Pittacus【皮特克斯】, Periander【佩里安德】, Chilon【芝隆】and Cleobolus【克里奥波勒斯】）。

3. *Illam ...Progenuit.*：英译文为 "Angered by the Gods, Mother Earth, it is said, gave birth to the last one, sister to Caeus and Enceladus." 引自《埃涅阿斯纪》。

4. Jupiter, Pallas called Briareus...：Jupiter（朱庇特），罗马诸神中最高的神，即希腊神话中的宙斯（Zeus）。Pallas（帕拉斯），希腊神话中智慧女神雅典娜（Athena）的朋友。雅典娜无意中杀死了帕拉斯。为了纪念帕拉斯，她把自己的名字改为 Pallas Athena。Briareus（布里阿柔斯），亦作 Briareos，希腊神话中的百手巨人。

5. Chyron the centaur：希腊神话中的半人半马怪。

6. Machiavelli：马基雅弗利（Niccolò Machiavelli, 1469—1527），文艺复兴时期意大利政治哲学家。他主张为了国家的利益，政府可以采用各种不正当的手段。他的《君主论》一书最为有名。

7. Chrysippus：克律西帕斯，公元前 3 世纪希腊禁欲主义哲学家。

霍布斯 《对德文南特为〈冈迪伯特〉所写的序言的解说》

托马斯·霍布斯（1588—1679）

霍布斯是 17 世纪英国著名哲学家。在他同时代的英国人中，没有一个人在国外的名声比他高。凡是去英国访问的外国文人都希望能同这位有学识的人会晤。1647 年他被委任为威尔士亲王的数学导师。他曾把英国著名学者培根的一些英语随笔译成拉丁文，并笔录下培根的思想。他同培根一样，强调知识的实用价值。他关注的是人和自然，对人和自然界以外的抽象的超自然世界没有兴趣。与培根不同的是，他认为科学主要是演绎的，科学研究应该用演绎法和几何学示范法，而不是培根所主张的归纳法。

17 世纪英国资产阶级革命时，霍布斯因持有保王思想，并与王室过往甚密，唯恐身有不测，遂出走法国。在欧洲大陆，他与诸如伽利略、笛卡儿等著名学者均有交往。也正是在旅居欧洲大陆期间，由于研究欧几里得的《几何原本》，他首创演绎法。在法国，他同法国大数学家梅尔森和意大利物理学家伽利略讨论了运动中的物质问题。

他的哲学三部曲是：《论物体》（1655），从运动解释物质现象；《论人》（1658），阐述在人的认识和欲望中包含哪些特殊的肉体运动；《论公民》（1642），由上述观念推论人类的社会组织。他的名著《利维坦》（*Leviathan*）在巴黎写成，1651 年在伦敦出版，著作包括"论人"、"论国家"、"论基督教国家"和"论黑暗王国" 4 个部分。

作为一个思想家，他对人的哲学作出了贡献。他提出了利己主义心理学，成为功利学派的先驱。在政治理论方面，他首先剖析达到和平和安全所必需的条件，然后根据他的"社会契约论"，提出一个能够取得上述条件的理想国方案。他的"社会契约论"认为，为了使人摆脱悲惨的战争，使人因惧怕遭到惩罚而遵守和平协议和自然法则，必须建立一个使用武力、实施惩罚的权力机构或政府。个人应该把自己的权力交给他人或众人组成的机构，从而加入一种社会契约，以确保个人的平安。

他认为人的体能和智能是均等的。因此，人人均有机会达到自己的目的。当两个人追求同一物，而此物只能由一人得到时，个人为了自己的生存和享受，就不得不同人竞争，使参与竞争的一方成为不可信任的敌人。因此，霍布斯认为，人的天性是自私的。

他认为，人对权力、财富、知识和荣誉的追求使人产生激情。因此，人与人总是处于敌对状态，人的自身安全全靠自己的力量和智慧。于是就有了"人为人敌"的论断。但是，他又说，人同时具有激情和理智。激情使人与人处于敌对状态；理智又使人考虑到搏斗可能导致自身的死亡。为了自身的安全，人又需要和平。因此，必须制定出人人均需遵守的和平协议。人还必须遵循自然规律。在他所写的《利维坦》一书中，霍布斯列举了19条自然规律，其中最基本的一条是理智准则。根据这一准则，人人都必须为和平而奋斗。只有人人都遵守自然规律，人类才能共享和平。

霍布斯认为政府不是上帝的创造物，而是人的创造物。这就使他的政治理论彻底摆脱了宗教迷信。这一点是值得称道的。

他说，一切知识均源于人的感觉和经验，而感觉又源于物质的运动。当物体处于静止状态时，若无外力的推动，物体将永远处于静止状态。一旦物体开始运动，若无外力阻碍，物体将处于永恒运动状态。人的欲望正是为了保存自己而对客观世界物质运动所作出的反应。霍布斯认为，只有物质的东西才是可认识的，而认识世界则要靠人的经验。人不可能知道是否存在上帝，因为人未能亲身经验上帝的存在。

霍布斯的散文也很出众。他也是文学家，晚年以重新研究古典作品自娱。1675 至 1676 年，他出版了《奥德赛》和《伊利亚特》的英译本。

他是一个集哲学、政治学、物理学、文学于一身，多才多艺的杰出学者。

内容提要

先说明文章的标题。Sir William Davenant（1606—1668）出生于英国牛津，并在牛津大学求学。他是 17 世纪英国著名诗人和剧作家，1638 年获英国桂冠诗人称号。他曾积极支持查理一世，被封为爵士。Gondibert 是他创作的一部未完成的浪漫史诗；1650 年史诗的第 1 卷、第 2 卷和部分第 3 卷出版，1651 年完成其他部分。在结尾前，诗人已对自己的诗作感到厌倦，随之搁笔，使这部共有 1,700 诗节的史诗成为未完成的作品。这部浪漫史诗写的是 Gondibert 公爵的爱情故事。

霍布斯的《对德文南特为〈冈迪伯特〉所写的序言的解说》一文写于 1650 年。在这篇论文中霍布斯探讨了文学的主要文类，以及文学艺术创作和客观现实的关系。他认为文学要虚构，诗人要有想象力。但是虚构应有限度，不能太多地超越或违背客观现实。文学作品应该在文体上和谐、得体、前后一致。

他说，诗人写作的对象是生活在宫廷、城市和乡村这三个范围内的人。宫廷内的人均属有权有势者，对平民百姓施加巨大影响，故称其为英雄。城市喧嚣、熙攘、空气污浊，故城市生活和市民有颇多可讽刺之处。乡村宁静，有田园风光，民风淳朴。三种地域三类人，诗亦可据此分为三类：英雄诗、讽刺诗和田园诗。这三大类诗又可根据其表现形式的不同（或是叙述性的，或是戏剧性的），进而分为六类：一、叙述性的英雄诗，即史诗；二、戏剧性的英雄诗，即悲剧；三、讽刺性的叙述诗，即讽刺诗；四、戏剧性的叙述诗，即喜剧；五、叙述性的田园诗，即田园诗，亦即古时的牧歌；六、戏剧性的田园诗，即田园性喜剧。

诗起源于古希腊。古希腊人用诗的语言祭神。早在"诗人"这一称谓出现之前，诗这一文体就广为预言家、祭神者和法律所使用。赞美诗也采用诗体。

诗有韵律，能朗朗上口，且文体优雅。因此，诗常被用作歌词吟唱，用作戏剧的台词。

古时的诗人在人民中享有极高的声誉。在人民的眼中，诗人似神，是预言家，是人民心目中的精神权威。诗的语言也就如同神的语言，受到人民的崇敬。

时间和教育培养经验；经验产生记忆；记忆孕育判断力和想象力；想象力激发诗情。想象力能给诗人素材、灵感和意象。因此，想象力是诗人不可缺少的才能。

霍布斯探讨的一个重要问题是文学艺术和客观现实的关系。有人喜欢在文学作品中看到超越现实可能性的、过分夸张的虚构，如铁人、飞马、刺不透的盔甲等等。有人认为，诗的美就在于虚构的大胆。霍布斯认为，虚构应有一定的限度，不能超越客观现实，导致荒诞。

要使诗真实、自然，诗人必须做到两点：一、对所写的东西有深刻的了解；二、知识渊博。诗人对所写的东西了解深刻表现在他的诗表达清晰、贴切、有特色。这会使无知者和有知者均感满意。知识渊博则表现在表达新颖。新颖能赢得读者的赞赏，引起读者的好奇心，而好奇心又是获取知识不可缺少的条件。

Thomas Hobbes (1588—1679)

Answer to Davenant's Preface to Gondibert

SIR,

If to commend your poem I should only say, in general terms, that in the choice of your argument, the disposition of the parts, the maintenance of the characters of your persons, the dignity and vigor of your expression, you have performed all the parts of various experience, ready memory, clear judgment, swift and well-governed fancy, though it were enough for the truth, it were too little for the weight and credit of my testimony. For I lie open to two exceptions, one of an incompetent, the other of a corrupted witness. Incompetent, because I am not a poet; and corrupted with the honor done me by your preface. The former obliges me to say something, by the way, of the nature and differences of poesy.

As philosophers have divided the universe, their subject, into three regions, celestial, aerial, and terrestrial, so the poets (whose work it is, by imitating human life in delightful and measured lines, to avert men from vice and incline them to virtuous and honorable actions) have lodged themselves in the three regions of mankind, court, city, and country, correspondent in some proportion to those three regions of the world. For there is in princes and men of conspicuous power, anciently called heroes, a luster and influence upon the rest of men resembling that of the heavens, and an insincereness, inconstancy, and troublesome humor of those that dwell in populous cities, like the mobility, blustering, and impurity of the air; and a plainness, and though dull, yet a nutritive faculty in rural people, that endures a comparison with the earth they labor.

From hence have proceeded three sorts of poesy, heroic, scommatic[1], and pastoral. Every one of these is distinguished again in the manner of representation, which sometimes is narrative, wherein the poet himself relateth, and sometimes dramatic, as when the persons are every one adorned and brought upon the theater to speak and act their own parts. There is therefore neither more nor less than six sorts of poesy. For the heroic poem narrative, such as is yours, is called an epic poem. The heroic poem dramatic is tragedy. The scommatic narrative is satire, dramatic is comedy. The pastoral narrative is called simply pastoral, anciently bucolic; the same dramatic, pastoral comedy. The figure therefore of an epic poem and of a tragedy ought to be the same, for they differ no more but in that they are pronounced by one or many persons. Which I insert to justify the figure of yours, consisting of five books divided into songs, or cantos, as five acts divided into scenes has ever been the approved figure of a tragedy.

They that take for poesy whatsoever is writ in verse will think this division imperfect, and call in sonnets, epigrams, eclogues, and the like pieces, which are but essays and parts of an entire poem, and reckon Empedocles and Lucretius (natural philosophers) for poets, and the moral precepts of Phocylides, Theognis, and the quatrains of Pybrach and the history of Lucan, and others of that kind amongst poems, bestowing on such writers for honor the name of poets rather than of historians or philosophers. But the subject of a poem is the manners of men, not natural causes; manners presented, not dictated; and manners feigned, as the name of poesy imports, not found in men. They that give entrance to fictions writ in prose err not so much, but they err: for prose requireth delightfulness, not only of fiction, but of style, in which, if prose contend with verse, it is with disadvantage and, as it were, on foot against the strength and wings of Pegasus.

For verse amongst the Greeks was appropriated anciently to the service of their gods, and was the holy style, the style of the oracles, the style of the laws, and the style of men that publicly recommended to their gods the vows and thanks of the people, which was done in their holy songs called hymns, and the composers of them were called prophets and priests before the name of poet was known. When afterwards the majesty of that style was observed, the poets chose it as best becoming their high invention. And for the antiquity of verse, it is greater than the antiquity of letters. For it is certain Cadmus[2] was the first that from Phoenicia[3], a country that neighboreth Judea[4], brought the use of letters into Greece. But the service of the gods and the laws, which by measured sounds were easily committed to the memory, had been long time in use before the arrival of Cadmus there.

There is, besides the grace of style, another cause why the ancient poets chose to write in measured language[5], which is this. Their poems were made at first with intention to have them sung, as well epic as dramatic—which custom hath been long time laid aside, but began to be revived, in part, of late years in Italy—and could not be made commensurable to the voice or instruments in prose, the ways and motions whereof are so uncertain and undistinguished, like the way and motion of a ship in the sea, as not only to discompose the best composers, but also to disappoint sometimes the most attentive reader and put him to hunt counter for the sense. It was therefore necessary for poets in those times to write in verse.

The verse which the Greeks and Latins, considering the nature of their own languages, found by experience most grave, and for an epic poem most decent, was their hexameter, a verse limited not only in the length of the line, but also in the quantity of the syllables. Instead of which we use the line of ten syllables, recompensing the neglect of their quantity with the diligence of rhyme. And this measure is so proper for a heroic poem as without some loss of gravity and dignity it was never changed. A longer is not far from ill prose, and a shorter is a kind of whisking, you know, like the unlacing rather than the singing of a Muse. In an epigram or a sonnet a man may vary his measures, and seek glory from a needless difficulty, as he that contrived verses into the forms of an organ, a hatchet, an egg, an altar, and a pair of wings; but in so great and noble a work as is an epic poem, for a man to obstruct his own way with unprofitable difficulties is great imprudence. So likewise to choose a needless and difficult correspondence of rhyme is but a difficult toy, and forces a man sometimes for the stopping of a chink to say somewhat he did never think; I cannot therefore but very much approve your stanza, wherein the syllables in every verse are ten, and the rhyme alternate.

For the choice of your subject, you have sufficiently justified yourself in your preface. But because I have observed in Virgil, that the honor done to Aeneas and his companions has so bright a reflection upon Augustus Caesar and other great Romans of that time as a man may suspect him not constantly possessed with the noble spirit of those his heroes, and believe you are not acquainted with any great man of the race of Gondibert[6], I add to your justification the purity of your purpose, in having no other motive of your labor but to adorn virtue and procure her lovers, than which there cannot be a worthier design, and more becoming noble poesy.

In that you make so small account of the example of almost all the approved poets, ancient and modern, who thought fit in the beginning, and sometimes also in the progress of their poems, to invoke a Muse or some other deity that should dictate to them or assist them in their writings, they that take not the laws of art from any reason of their own but from the fashion of precedent times will perhaps accuse your singularity. For my part, I neither subscribe to their accusation, nor yet condemn that heathen custom otherwise than as accessory to their false religion. For their poets were their divines, had the name of prophets, exercised amongst the people a kind of spiritual authority, would be thought to speak by a divine spirit, have their works which they writ in verse (the divine style) pass for the word of God and not of man, and to be hearkened to with reverence. Do not our divines (excepting the style) do the same, and by us that are of the same religion cannot justly be reprehended for it? Besides, in the use of the spiritual calling of divines, there is danger sometimes to be feared from want of skill, such as is reported of unskillful conjurers, that mistaking the rites and ceremonious points of their art, call up such spirits as they cannot at their pleasure allay again, by whom storms are raised that overthrow buildings and are the cause of miserable wrecks at sea. Unskillful divines do oftentimes the like: for when they call unseasonably for zeal there appears a spirit of cruelty; and by the like error, instead of truth they raise discord; instead of wisdom, fraud; instead of reformation, tumult; and controversy instead of religion. Whereas in the heathen poets, at least in those whose works have lasted to the time we are in, there are none of those indiscretions to be found that tended to subversion or disturbance of the commonwealths wherein they lived. But why a Christian should think it an ornament to his poem, either to profane the true God or invoke a false one, I can imagine no cause but a reasonless imitation of custom, of a foolish custom, by which a man, enabled to speak wisely from the principles of nature and his own meditation, loves rather to be thought to speak by inspiration, like a bagpipe.

Time and education begets experience; experience begets memory; memory begets Judgment and Fancy[7]: Judgment begets the strength and structure, and Fancy begets the ornaments of a poem. The ancients therefore fabled not absurdly in making memory the mother of the Muses. For memory is the world (though not really, yet so as in a looking glass) in which the Judgment, the severer sister, busieth herself in a grave and rigid examination of all the parts of nature, and in registering by letters their order, causes, uses, differences, and resemblances; whereby the Fancy, when any work of art is to be performed, finds her materials at hand and prepared for use, and needs no more than a swift motion over them, that what she wants, and is there to be had, may not lie too long unespied. So that when she seemeth to fly from one Indies[8] to the other, and from heaven to earth, and to penetrate into the hardest matter and obscurest places, into the future and into herself, and all this in a point of time, the voyage is not very great, her self being all she seeks; and her wonderful celerity consisteth not so much in motion as in copious imagery discreetly ordered and perfectly registered in the memory, which most men under the name of philosophy have a glimpse of, and is pretended to by many that, grossly mistaking her, embrace contention in her place. But so far forth as the fancy of man has traced the ways of true philosophy, so far it hath produced very marvelous effects to the benefit of mankind. All that is beautiful or defensible in building, or marvelous in engines and instruments of motion, whatsoever commodity men receive from the observations of the heavens, from the description of the earth, from the account of time, from walking on the seas, and whatsoever distinguisheth the civility of Europe from the barbarity of the American savages, is the workmanship of Fancy but guided by the precepts of true philosophy. But where these precepts fail, as they have hitherto failed in the doctrine of moral virtue, there the architect, Fancy, must take the philosopher's part upon herself. He therefore that undertakes a heroic poem, which is to exhibit a venerable and amiable image of heroic virtue, must not only be the poet, to place and connect, but also the philosopher, to furnish and square his matter, that is, to make both body and soul, color and shadow of his poem out of his own store: which how well you have performed I am now considering.

Observing how few the persons be you introduce in the beginning, and how in the course of the actions of these (the number increasing) after several confluences they run all at last into the two principal streams of your poem, Gondibert and Oswald[9], methinks the fable is not much unlike the theater. For so, from several and far distant sources, do the lesser brooks of

Lombardy[10], flowing into one another, fall all at last into two main rivers, the Po and the Adice. It hath the same resemblance also with a man's veins, which, proceeding from different parts, after the like concourse insert themselves at last into the two principal veins of the body. But when I considered that also the actions of men, which singly are inconsiderable, after many conjunctures grow at last either into one great protecting power or into two destroying factions, I could not but approve the structure of your poem, which ought to be no other than such as an imitation of human life requireth.

In the streams themselves I find nothing but settled valor, clean honor, calm counsel, learned diversion, and pure love, save only a torrent or two of ambition, which, though a fault, has somewhat heroic in it, and therefore must have place in a heroic poem. To show the reader in what place he shall find every excellent picture of virtue you have drawn is too long. And to show him one is to prejudice the rest; yet I cannot forbear to point him to the description of love in the person of Birtha, in the seventh canto of the second book. There has nothing been said of that subject neither by the ancient nor modern poets comparable to it. Poets are painters: I would fain see another painter draw so true, perfect, and natural a love to the life, and make use of nothing but pure lines, without the help of any the least uncomely shadow, as you have done. But let it be read as a piece by itself, for in the most equal height of the whole the eminence of parts is lost.

There are some that are not pleased with fiction, unless it be bold, not only to exceed the work, but also the possibility of nature[11]: they would have impenetrable armors, enchanted castles, invulnerable bodies, iron men, flying horses, and a thousand other such things, which are easily feigned by them that dare. Against such I defend you (without assenting to those that condemn either Homer or Virgil) by dissenting only from those that think the beauty of a poem consisteth in the exorbitancy of the fiction. For as truth is the bound of historical, so the resemblance of truth is the utmost limit of poetical liberty[12]. In old time amongst the heathen such strange fictions and metamorphoses were not so remote from the articles of their faith as they are now from ours, and therefore were not so unpleasant. Beyond the actual works of nature a poet may now go; but beyond the conceived possibility of nature, never. I can allow a geographer to make in the sea a fish or a ship which by the scale of his map would be two or three hundred miles long, and think it done for ornament, because it is done without the precincts of his undertaking; but when he paints an elephant so, I presently apprehend it as ignorance, and a plain confession of *terra incognita*[13].

As the description of great men and great actions is the constant design of a poet, so the descriptions of worthy circumstances are necessary accessions to a poem, and being well performed are the jewels and most precious ornaments of poesy. Such in Virgil are the funeral games of Anchises[14], the duel of Aeneas and Turnus[15], etc.; and such in yours are "The Hunting," "The Bataile,[16]" "The City Mourning," "The Funeral," "The House of Astragon," "The Library," and "The Temple," equal to his, or those of Homer whom he imitated.

There remains now no more to be considered but the expression, in which consisteth the countenance and color of a beautiful Muse, and is given her by the poet out of his own provision, or is borrowed from others. That which he hath of his own is nothing but experience and knowledge of nature, and specially human nature, and is the true and natural color. But that which is taken out of books (the ordinary boxes of counterfeit complexion) shows well or ill, as it hath more or less resemblance with the natural, and are not to be used without examination unadvisedly. For in him that professes the imitation of nature, as all poets do, what greater fault can there be than to betray an ignorance of nature in his poem—especially having a liberty allowed him, if he meet with anything he cannot master, to leave it out?

That which giveth a poem the truth and natural color consisteth in two things, which are, to know well, that is, to have images of nature in the memory distinct and clear, and to know much. A sign of the first is perspicuity, property, and decency, which delight all sorts of men, either by instructing the ignorant or soothing the learned in their knowledge. A sign of the latter is novelty of expression, and pleaseth by excitation of the mind; for novelty causeth admiration, and admiration curiosity, which is a delightful appetite of knowledge.

There be so many words in use at this day in the English tongue, that though of *magnifique*[17] sound, yet (like the windy blisters of a troubled water) have no sense at all, and so many others that lose their meaning by being ill coupled, that it is a hard matter to avoid them; for having been obtruded upon youth in the schools by such as make it, I think, their business there (as 'tis expressed by the best poet) "with terms to charm the weak and pose the wise,"[18] they grow up with them, and, gaining reputation with the ignorant, are not easily shaken off.

To this palpable darkness I may also add the ambitious obscurity of expressing more than is perfectly conceived, or perfect conception in fewer words than it requires. Which expressions, though they have had the honor to be called strong lines, are indeed no better than riddles, and, not only to the reader but also after a little time to the writer himself, dark and troublesome.

To the property of expression I refer that clearness of memory by which a poet, when he hath once introduced any person whatsoever speaking in his poem, maintaineth in him to the end the same character he gave him in the beginning. The variation whereof is a change of pace that argues the poet tired.

Of the indecencies of a heroic poem the most remarkable are those that show disproportion either between the persons and their actions, or between the manners of the poet and the poem. Of the first kind is the uncomeliness of representing in great persons the inhuman vice of cruelty or the sordid vice of lust and drunkenness. To such parts as those the ancient approved poets thought it fit to suborn, not the persons of men, but of monsters and beastly giants, such as Polyphemus[19], Cacus[20], and the centaurs. For it is supposed a Muse, when she is invoked to sing a song of that nature, should maidenly advise the poet to set such persons to sing their own vices upon the stage, for it is not so unseemly in a tragedy. Of the same kind it is to represent scurrility or any action or language that moveth much laughter. The delight of an epic poem consisteth not in mirth, but admiration. Mirth and laughter is proper to comedy and satire. Great persons that have their minds employed on great designs have not leisure enough to laugh, and are pleased with the contemplation of their own power and virtues, so as they need not the infirmities and vices of other men to recommend themselves to their own favor by comparison, as all men do when they laugh. Of the second kind, where the disproportion is between the poet and the persons of his poem, one is in the dialect of the inferior sort of people, which is always different from the language of the court. Another is to derive the illustration of anything from such metaphors or comparisons as cannot come into men's thoughts but by mean conversation and experience of humble or evil arts, which the person of an epic poem cannot be thought acquainted with.

From knowing much, proceedeth the admirable variety and novelty of metaphors and similitudes, which are not possible to be lighted on in the compass of a narrow knowledge. And the want whereof compelleth a writer to expressions that are either defaced by time or sullied with vulgar or long use. For the phrases of poesy, as the airs of music, with often hearing become insipid, the reader having no more sense of their force than our flesh is sensible of the bones that sustain it. As the sense we have of bodies consisteth in change and variety of impression, so also does the sense of language in the variety and changeable use of words. I mean not in the affectation of words newly brought home from travail, but in new and withal significant translation to our purposes of those that be already received, and in farfetched but withal apt, instructive, and comely similitudes.

Having thus, I hope, avoided the first exception against the incompetency of my judgment, I am but little moved with the second, which is of being bribed by the honor you have done me by attributing in your preface somewhat to my judgment. For I have used your judgment no less in many things of mine, which coming to light will thereby appear the better. And so you have your bribe again.

Having thus made way for the admission of my testimony, I give it briefly thus: I never yet saw poem that had so much shape of art, health of morality, and vigor and beauty of expression as this of yours. And but for the clamor of the multitude, that hide their envy of the present under a reverence of antiquity, I should say further that it would last as long as either the *Aeneid* or *Iliad*, but for one disadvantage; and the disadvantage is this: The languages of the Greeks and Romans, by their colonies and conquests, have put off flesh and blood, and are become immutable, which none of the modern tongues are like to be. I honor antiquity, but that which is commonly called old time is young time. The glory of antiquity is due, not to the dead, but to the aged.

And now, while I think on it, give me leave with a short discord to sweeten the harmony of the approaching close. I have nothing to object against your poem, but dissent only from something in your preface sounding to the prejudice of age. 'Tis commonly said that old age is a return to childhood: which methinks you insist on so long, as if you desired it should be believed. That's the note I mean to shake a little. That saying, meant only of the weakness of body, was wrested to the weakness of mind by froward children, weary of the controlment of their parents, masters, and other admonitors. Secondly, the dotage and childishness they ascribe to age is never the effect of time, but sometimes of the excesses of youth, and not a returning to, but a continual stay with, childhood. For they that, wanting the curiosity of furnishing their memories with the rarities of nature in their youth, and pass their time in making provision only for their ease and sensual delight, are children still at what years soever, as they that coming into a populous city, never going out of their inn, are strangers still, how long soever they have been there. Thirdly, there is no reason for any man to think himself wiser today than yesterday, which does not equally convince he shall be wiser tomorrow than today. Fourthly, you will be forced to change your opinion hereafter when you are old; and in the meantime you discredit all I have said before in your commendation, because I am old already. But no more of this.

I believe, sir, you have seen a curious kind of perspective, where he that looks through a short hollow pipe upon a picture containing divers figures sees none of those that are there painted, but some one person made up of their parts, conveyed to the eye by the artificial cutting of a glass. I find in my imagination an effect not unlike it from your poem. The virtues you distribute there amongst so many noble persons represent in the reading the image but of one man's virtue to my fancy, which is your own, and that so deeply imprinted as to stay forever there, and govern all the rest of my thoughts and affections in the way of honoring and serving you to the utmost of my power, that am, sir,

Your most humble and obedient servant,

Thomas Hobbes.
Paris, January 10, 1650

注释

1. scommatic：讽刺性的。
2. Cadmus：卡德摩斯，希腊神话中底比斯城（Thebes）的创建者，后来成为底比斯的国王。
3. Phoenicia：腓尼基，叙利亚古国。
4. Judea：朱迪亚，今巴勒斯坦古地区。
5. in measured language：即 language in verse form。
6. Gondibert：冈迪伯特，指浪漫史诗《冈迪伯特》（*Gondibert*）中的主要人物 Duke Gondibert。
7. fancy：即 imagination。
8. Indies：此处指古印度和古印度周边地区。
9. Oswald：奥斯瓦尔德，指浪漫史诗《冈迪伯特》中的主要人物 Prince Oswald。
10. Lombardy：伦巴第区，地名，在意大利北部。
11. nature：指 reality。
12. poetical liberty：亦可称 poetical license，指写诗允许夸张，如唐诗中的 "白发三千丈" 等。
13. *terra incognita*：意为 undiscovered territory。
14. Anchises：安喀塞斯，希腊神话中的特洛伊王子。他同女神阿佛洛狄特（Aphrodite，即罗马神话中的维纳斯）相爱，生下埃涅阿斯（Aeneas）。
15. Turnus：特纳斯，罗马诗人维吉尔所写的史诗《埃涅阿斯纪》中的意大利英雄，在与埃涅阿斯战斗中被其杀死。
16. bataile：即 battle。
17. *magnifique*：意为 magnificent。
18. "with terms to charm the weak and pose the wise,"：引自 *Gondibert*。
19. Polyphemus：波吕斐摩斯，希腊神话中的独目巨人之一。
20. Cacus：凯卡斯，罗马神话中口能喷火的怪物。

德莱顿 《论戏剧诗》

约翰·德莱顿（1631—1700）

约翰·德莱顿是英国文艺复兴时代的文学名家，纵横穿梭于各门文类，集诗人、戏剧家、批评家、翻译家、散文家于一身。在诗歌领域，他是弥尔顿死后最伟大的英国诗人，1668 年荣膺桂冠诗人的头衔；在戏剧领域，他总共创作了 27 部作品，有悲剧、英雄悲剧、闹剧、悲喜剧、歌剧，几乎涉足全部戏剧题材，构成了王政复辟时代（1660—1688）戏剧创作的主流；在文学批评领域，他是英国第一位戏剧理论家和批评家，被称为"英国文学批评之父"（塞缪尔·约翰逊语）；他的散文简洁明朗，平易如话，议题有感而发，其流风余韵，延及 18 世纪；受崇古风气的熏染，他翻译过维吉尔、普鲁塔克等古罗马作家的名作，译笔晓畅，可读性强。

德莱顿出生在清教色彩浓厚的资产阶级家庭，毕业于剑桥大学的三一学院。他曾是英国革命的支持者，克伦威尔统治时期，他在革命政府中任职。克伦威尔去世之际，他同约翰·弥尔顿、安德鲁·马维尔一道出席葬礼。查理二世复辟之后，他改宗天主教，写诗称颂查理二世，批评英国国教。这种首鼠两端的投机行为，最为时人诟病。王政复辟时期，他获得桂冠诗人的称号；但是，1688 年"光荣革命"之后，这一头衔又被新政府剥夺。

德莱顿的作品主要写于王政复辟时代。查理二世从法国翩然而归，不仅带回来了奢靡的凡尔赛宫廷生活方式，也带回来了法兰西的新古典主义理念。在此之前，新古典主义风格已经出现在本·琼生的作品中；但是，本·琼生的新古典主义理念主要来自意大利。王政复辟之后，法国的新古典主义对英国文坛开始产生强劲而全面的影响。对于这套舶来的理论，德莱顿总体上赞成，但没有生吞活剥地接受或亦步亦趋地顶礼膜拜，而是始终保持一种批判式的认可。正因为这个原因，他的文学批评显得非常具有灵活性。法国新古典主义热衷于制定绝对的理论标准，例如"三一律"，敦促后人加以师法；德莱顿则无意去构建普遍性法则，而是有的放矢，品评和鉴赏具体作家的风格、具体作品的技巧。就此而言，他是实践型的批评家，而非理论型的批评家。他认为，在不同的国家，观众的禀性和需求不尽相同，作家的创作要因时因地、量体裁衣，切不可泥古不化、刻舟求剑。"诗人所面对的风尚、时代以及观众的性情大不相同，那些让古希腊人满意的作品不一定让英国观众满意"，这条论断挑战了法国新古典主义的一个重要观点，即在任何时空、任何文化中，人性都是恒定不变的。就某种程度而言，这条论断发出了现代读者反映批评的先声。他还给戏剧下了一个定义：戏剧是对人性公正而生动的描述。所谓公正，就是不偏不倚、如实地模仿描述，这就是亚里士多德提倡的艺术模仿自然的原则；然而，"生动"就要求剧作家要顾及观众的口味，这就很可能有悖于新古典主义的典范性原则（decorum）。

内容提要

本文选自德莱顿最有代表性的批评论作《论戏剧诗》。全文以四人对话形式展开，讨论当时英国文坛上的热门问题：古代戏剧与现代戏剧孰优孰劣，法国新古典主义戏剧理论对于当代英国戏剧是否具有指导意义，以及戏剧创作中可能涉及的一些具体问题。在第一个问题上，德莱顿基本上持有厚今薄古的态度；在第二个问题上，他认为法国新古典主义的三一律原则过于刻板，妨碍了戏剧内容的丰赡。

文中四位对话者的名字是尤吉涅斯（Eugius）、克里提斯（Crites）、利西迪亚斯（Lisideius）和尼安达（Neander），分别影射王政复辟时代的诗人查尔斯·塞克威尔（Charles Sackville）、罗伯特·霍华德（Robert Howard）、查尔斯·塞德利（Charles Sedley）以及德莱顿本人。据后来的学者推测，Neander 可能由希腊文中的 neo 和 andros 组合而成，意为 newman（新人）。这篇选文是尼安达在四人讨论中的发言。这种利用人名来影射个人主张的做法，在新古典主义时代屡见不鲜。

作者对莎士比亚的才能推崇备至，认为他在古今文学家当中才智最广博、悟性最强；他洞悉世间百态，行文运笔得心应手，浑然天成，毫无斧凿之痕；他写人状物栩栩如生，仿佛伸手可及。至于有人说莎士比亚学问不济，德莱顿反倒认为这是一种恭维，因为他的学问纯属天赐，无需借助书本之力；他只需借助自己的心智，即可洞察世态人情，而无需旁视他途。不过，莎士比亚的创作并非白璧无瑕、无可指责。在德莱顿看来，他的作品有时平淡无味，他的一些诙谐妙语（comic wit）有时沦为插科打诨，而一些严肃妙语又过于渲染、流于浮词虚饰。但不管怎么说，他总能以大手笔表现大题材，让二者珠联璧合，相得益彰；他信笔所至，总能远迈时贤。因此，伊顿公学的约翰·黑尔说，其他作家写过的题材，莎士比亚都能写，而且写得更好。在同时代的作家当中，有人在现今时代更受推崇，声誉在他之上；但是，在莎翁时代，比起弗莱彻和本·琼生这些人，人们更尊崇的是莎士比亚。查理一世在位时期，正值本·琼生的文名如日中天之际；但约翰·萨克灵和大部分朝臣都认为，莎士比亚胜过本·琼生。

德莱顿认为，在戏剧领域，琼生是最为博学、最有文学判断眼光的作家；他不仅严于察己，也严于察人。我们不能说他缺少文学才华（wit），只能说他珍惜这种才华而不肯滥用。他下笔极简，要言不烦，作品既成，无须修改。在他之前，妙语的运用、辞藻的遴选、个人癖性的描写，在戏剧界已屡见不鲜；但是，直到本·琼生横空出世，戏剧艺术才臻于完美。比起前人，他更能扬长避短。在他的作品中，很少发现描写男女求爱或震撼心灵的场面；他本人的文学才质过于阴沉忧郁，不能出色地做到这一点；而且，他也深知，在这方面，前人的成就已经达到了相当高的程度。他的专长在于描写人物的癖性，他喜欢表现工匠这样的人物。他谙熟古希腊古罗马作家的作品，并从中进行了大胆借鉴。两部直接以罗马故事为题材的悲剧中，他几乎引用和翻译了古罗马所有作家和史家的作品。这种公然剽窃的行径，他干起来毫不顾忌。他劫掠起作家，犹如帝王盘剥百姓，毫无惧色；以别人之所失，化为自己之所得。于是，在他笔下，古罗马时代的典章制度、礼仪风俗，悉数呈现在今人眼前；即便由时人执笔，也不见得在他之上。他行文刻意追求拉丁化，这在他的喜剧中表现得尤为明显。结果，他笔下的文字不符合英文的特色，读来不像英文，更像拉丁文。与莎士比亚相比，他以锤炼字句见长，而莎士比亚更有才华。莎士比亚相当于荷马，开风气之先，为后世的戏剧诗人效仿；本·琼生相当于维吉尔，为工巧细致的典范。他固然让人对他钦佩有加，但更让人心仪的则是莎士比亚。

John Dryden (1631—1700)

From An Essay of Dramatic Poesy

To begin, then, with Shakespeare. He was the man who of all modern, and perhaps ancient poets, had the largest and most comprehensive soul. All the images of nature[1] were still present to him, and he drew them, not laboriously, but luckily; when he describes anything, you more than see it, you feel it too. Those who accuse him to have wanted[2] learning, give him the greater commendation: he was naturally learned[3]; he needed not the spectacles of books to read nature; he looked inwards[4], and found her there. I cannot say he is everywhere alike[5]; were he so, I should do him injury to compare him with the greatest of mankind.[6] He is many times flat, insipid; his comic wit degenerating into clenches[7], his serious swelling into bombast. But he is always great, when some great occasion is presented to him; no man can say he ever had a fit subject for his wit,[8] and did not then raise himself as high as above the rest of poets,

Quantum lenta solent inter viburna cupressi.[9]

The consideration of this made Mr. Hales of Eton[10] say, that there was no subject of which any poet ever writ[11], but he would produce it much better done in Shakespeare; and however others are now generally preferred before him, yet the age wherein he lived, which had contemporaries with him Fletcher[12] and Jonson[13], never equalled them to him in their esteem: and in the last king's court[14], when Ben's reputation was at highest, Sir John Suckling[15], and with him the greater part of the courtiers, set our Shakespeare far above him.

Beaumont and Fletcher, of whom I am next to speak, had, with the advantage of Shakespeare's wit, which was their precedent, great natural gifts, improved by study: Beaumont especially being so accurate a judge of plays, that Ben Jonson, while he lived, submitted all his writings to his censure, and, 'tis thought, used his judgment in correcting, if not contriving, all his plots. What value he had for him, appears by the verses he writ to him[16]; and therefore I need speak no farther of it. The first play that brought Fletcher and him in esteem was their *Philaster*[17]: for before that, they had written two or three very unsuccessfully, as the like is reported of Ben Jonson, before he writ *Every Man in His Humor*[18]. Their plots were generally more regular than Shakespeare's, especially those which were made before Beaumont's death; and they understood and imitated the conversation of gentlemen much better; whose wild debaucheries, and quickness of wit in repartees, no poet before them could paint as they have done. Humor[19], which Ben Jonson derived from particular persons, they made it not their business to describe: they represented all the passions very lively, but above all, love. I am apt to believe the English language in them arrived to its highest perfection: what words have since been taken in, are rather superfluous than ornamental. Their plays are now the most pleasant and frequent entertainments of the stage; two of theirs being acted through the year for one of Shakespeare's or Jonson's: the reason is, because there is a certain gaiety in their comedies, and pathos in their more serious plays, which suit generally with all men's humors. Shakespeare's language is likewise a little obsolete, and Ben Jonson's wit comes short of theirs.

As for Jonson, to whose character I am now arrived, if we look upon him while he was himself (for his last plays were but his dotages[20]), I think him the most learned and judicious writer which any theater ever had. He was a most severe judge of himself, as well as others. One cannot say he wanted wit, but rather that he was frugal of it. In his works you find little to retrench or alter. Wit, and language, and humor also in some measure, we had before him; but something of art was wanting to the drama till he came. You seldom find him making love in any of his scenes, or endeavoring to move the passions; his genius was too sullen and saturnine[21] to do it gracefully, especially when he knew he came after those who had performed both to such a height. Humor was his proper sphere; and in that he delighted most to represent mechanic people[22]. He was deeply conversant in the ancients, both Greek and Latin, and he borrowed boldly from them: there is scarce a poet or historian among the Roman authors of those times whom he has not translated in *Sejanus* and *Catiline*[23]. But he has done his robberies so openly, that one may see he fears not to be taxed[24] by any law. He invades authors like a monarch; and what would be theft in other poets is only victory in him. With the spoils of these writers he so represents old Rome to us, in its rites, ceremonies, and customs, that if one of their poets had written either of his tragedies, we had seen less of it than in him. If there was any fault in his language, 'twas that he weaved it too closely and laboriously, in his comedies especially: perhaps, too, he did a little too much Romanise our tongue[25], leaving the words which he translated almost as much Latin as he found them: wherein, though he learnedly followed their language, he did not enough comply with the idiom of ours. If I would compare him with Shakespeare, I must acknowledge him the more correct poet, but Shakespeare the greater wit. Shakespeare was the Homer, or father of our dramatic poets; Jonson was the Virgil, the pattern of elaborate writing; I admire him, but I love Shakspeare.

注释

1. 这里的 nature，不专指自然界，而是泛指宇宙之间的事态万物。

2. wanted：缺少。

3. naturally learned：（他的学问）浑然天成，他无须读书即可洞悉世间百态。

4. looked inwards：反诸自心，无须旁视。

5. he is everywhere alike：他处处都对。

6. I should do him injury to compare him with the greatest of mankind：莎士比亚横绝古今，即便把他与人类最伟大的作家相比，那对他也是一种侮辱。意即，莎士比亚不可超越。

7. clenches：插科打诨。

8. no man can say he ever had a subject for wit：一旦莎士比亚找到与他的天才相称的题材，他的作品就会远迈时贤。wit 这里指天才，而非"诙谐妙语"。

9. 拉丁文，语出维吉尔的《牧歌》（Ecologues），意为"犹如低矮灌木丛中的翠柏"，类似汉语中的"鹤立鸡群"。

10. Mr. Hales of Eton: John Hales（1584—1656），伊顿公学的教师。

11. writ：write 的过去式；本文中的 poet，不单指诗人，而泛指"作家"。

12. Fletcher：弗莱彻（John Fletcher，1579—1625），英国詹姆士一世统治时期的著名剧作家，与弗朗西斯·博蒙特密切合作，创作剧本 10

余部，尤以悲喜剧见长，主要有《菲拉斯特》《少女的悲剧》等。

13. Jonson：琼生（Ben Jonson, 1572—1637），英国剧作家、诗人、评论家，剧作有《炼金术士》（*The Alchemist*）和《圣巴托罗缪市集》（*Bartholomew Fair*）等。

14. 指查理一世统治时期（1625—1649）。

15. Sir John Suckling：萨克林（1609—1642），英国诗人、廷臣。

16. 指本·琼生所作的箴言诗《致弗朗西斯·博蒙特》。

17. *Philaster*：《菲拉斯特》，弗莱彻与博蒙特合著的悲喜剧，讲述王子与美人恋爱的故事，情节复杂，悬念迭起，很受贵族和市民阶层的欢迎。菲拉斯特为剧中主人公的名字。

18. 本·琼生的"癖性喜剧"《人人高兴》（*Every Man in His Humor*, 1598）。故事大意为：老爱德华好管闲事，对小爱德华经常疑神疑鬼，唯恐他滥交匪人。剧中另有疑心极大的商人凯特利，唯恐自己年轻的妻子另觅情郎，误会由此而产生。经过一系列波折之后，真相终于大白，小爱德华爱的是凯特利的妹妹，最后有情人终成眷属。

19. humor：这里的 humor，既不是通常所说的"幽默"，也不是指"心情"，而是本·琼生所谓的"癖性"。本·琼生在《人人高兴》的序言中解释说，"当一个人被某种特性所控制，以至于他的情感、精神和力量都被指向某一特定方向，那么这种特性就可被称作'癖性'"。"癖性"一说来自中世纪生理学中著名的体液论。按照这种理论，人体有四种体液（humor），分别为血液、黏液、胆汁和忧郁液。如果四种体液比例协调，人的情绪就稳定平和；如果其中一种比例过高，则使人易怒、胆怯、多疑、嫉妒、贪婪。癖性喜剧挖苦和讽刺的就是具有上述特殊气质的人物。参见王佐良、何其莘《英国文艺复兴时期的文学史》。

20. 这里指的是本·琼生的一些晚期剧作，如《新闻批发客栈》（1629）和《一只桶的故事》（1633）。这些作品质量平庸，没有创新，并不成功。作者在句子中指出，这些失败之作表明，本·琼生的创作已呈现老迈疲态。

21. saturnine：阴沉、忧郁。

22. mechanic people：体力劳动者、工匠。

23. 这是琼生以罗马故事为题材的两部戏剧，分别作于 1603 和 1611 年。

24. taxed：受到惩罚。

25. romanise our tongue：使英语拉丁化。

亚历山大·蒲柏（1688—1744）

亚历山大·蒲柏是英国新古典主义诗人和批评家，出生在伦敦一个殷实的布商家庭，全家信奉天主教。当时英国天主教徒社会地位底下，政治上遭歧视，既不允许上大学，也不能出任公职。蒲柏12岁时脊柱患结核病，身体畸形，从此居家读书。他师从一位教士，学会了古希腊文和拉丁文；经过短期学习，又掌握了法文和意大利文，借以博览群典，追思古人的精神余韵。他少有诗才，16岁时即发表《田园诗》。经过王政复辟时期戏剧名家威廉·威彻利的引荐，进入伦敦的文人圈子。

1711年，蒲柏发表诗体论著《批评论》。全诗共700多行，妙语名句纷呈，有的已成为民谚，流传至今。例如，"天使惧怕涉足处，笨伯争先涌入"、"错误人难免，宽恕最可贵"。《批评论》让蒲柏一举成名，使他有机会结识当时的文坛要人艾迪生和斯梯尔，成为他们小圈子中的一员。1712年，在他们主办的杂志《旁观者》上，蒲柏发表了田园诗《弥赛亚》。同年，他还写出名作、长篇戏仿史诗《劫发记》，描写两个大家族之间的争执。事情起因很简单，一家的少爷偷剪了另一家小姐的一缕秀发，令对方羞恼不已，致使两家关系势如水火。蒲柏以游戏的笔法、滑稽的腔调夸张造势，把这一琐事无限放大，把两家的对立之势写得如同希腊诸邦与特洛伊之间那样剑拔弩张。这首诗讽刺了上流社会的空虚和无聊，也暴露了作者对这个珠光宝气的浮华世界的艳羡。1714年该诗再版，又增加了4章。

1713年，他发表《温莎森林》（*Windsor Forest*）一诗，颂扬安妮女王，深得托利党人的赏识，并因此结交了乔纳森·斯威夫特（属托利党）。此后，他与艾狄生（属辉格党）一行渐渐疏远。他与斯威夫特、讽刺作家约翰·盖伊（John Gay）等人结成"涂鸦社"（Scriblerus Club），讽刺世风，戏笑时政，发泄对辉格党政府的不满。从1715年到1720年，他以英雄双韵体的诗格陆续翻译出版了《伊利亚特》，声震文坛，好评如潮。不过，就精神气质和选词设句而言，这个译本与荷马原文相距甚远，带有更多时代的特色。后来，他又与人合作，译完了《奥德赛》，以求完璧。这套英译荷马史诗销路极好，蒲柏收益丰厚。从此，蒲柏经济上得以自立，摆脱了寒素和困窘之境，成为英国文学史上第一位职业作家。他用这笔收入在乡下置业筑园，尽享田园之趣。蒲柏的译作遭到艾狄生等人的嫉视和批评，他们暗助别人推出另一个译本，但新译本的质量、口碑和销路远不及蒲柏译本。

在此期间，蒲柏还花大力气，编订了一套 6 卷本的《莎士比亚全集》，于 1825 年出版。蒲柏毕竟不是莎学专家，难免谬误，遭致物议。著名莎学专家刘易斯·蒂博德（Lewis Theobald）写了一本小册子《恢复莎士比亚的本来面目》（*Shakespeare Restored*, 1726），对蒲柏多有指责。羞恼之下，蒲柏把蒂博德写进了他另一部讽刺名作《群愚史诗》（*Dunciad*），这首长诗嘲讽了伦敦的穷酸文人和书贾，以蒂博德为"群愚之王"。该诗第 1 卷于 1728 年问世，未署作者真名，在转年出版的增订本中，蒲柏又添加了大量脚注和附录。这样做一举双得，既戏仿了蒂博德琐碎的学院派考证作风，又透露出讽刺对象和事情本末。1743 年，他又补充了一卷，冠以《新群愚史诗》之名。第二年，经过增订和修补，4 卷全本《群愚史诗》问世。在新版本中，桂冠诗人锡伯（C. Cibber）取代蒂博德，成为主角，其讽刺范围也从文人和书贾扩展到整个英国社会。

蒲柏还著有多部诗体信札，例如《人论》（1733—1734），《道德论》（1731—1735），《仿贺拉斯诗札》等。其中最有影响的是《仿贺拉斯诗札》中《致阿巴斯诺特医生书》。阿巴斯诺特是"涂鸦社"同道，曾任安妮女王的御医。在这封自传性很强的诗札中，蒲柏极尽挖苦和讽刺之能事，对他的许多文坛宿敌，包括上文提到的艾狄生、锡伯、蒂博德等人，进行了丑化和抨击。

蒲柏去世后，诗名依旧兴盛不衰。到了 18 世纪末叶，随着浪漫主义诗歌兴起，他的声誉大不如从前。在时人眼里，他的诗作是人为的妙手所得，缺少自然的天成。例如，赫兹利特说他是讲究人工而非自然的诗人。马修·阿诺德代表了 19 世纪许多批评家的观点，他认为蒲柏的诗不是诗歌的经典，而是散文的经典。

但是，到了 20 世纪 20 年代，随着浪漫派诗风的衰落，蒲柏作品的许多优点又重新受到人们的重视。

内容提要

自 18 世纪初至中叶，英国文学史上的诸多名家，例如乔纳森·斯威夫特、约瑟夫·艾迪生、亚历山大·蒲柏等人，都笃信新古典主义的核心主张：模仿古希腊和古罗马的经典作家，遵循他们的批评法则，师法其作品所表现出的批评戒律。蒲柏的《批评论》更是英国新古典主义的理论体现。

《批评论》殊少新见，主要观点来自罗马时代的贺拉斯、法国的布瓦洛以及英国诗人约翰·德莱顿。即便是以诗论诗这种写作形式，也并非天下独步，在贺拉斯、布瓦洛、维达那里早有前例。只是它文采斐然，音调铿锵，妙语佳句连篇，英雄双韵体炉火纯青，臻于极致，让习见之论熠熠生辉，精彩纷呈。这正应了诗中的一句名言，"所思寻常有，妙笔则空前（what oft was thought, but ne'er so well expressed）"。其原因有多种：一则蒲柏尚古心思太重，无意作标新立异之论；二则抑扬格五音步诗律甚严，以它作诗论文无异于戴镣铐跳舞，形式严重束缚思想，论证说理不能系统深入，考辨事实无从自由展开；再则，蒲柏作此诗时，才 20 岁左右，对他不能期待过高。

《批评论》发表于 1711 年，至于在哪一年完成，说法不一；一般锁定在 1709 年，因艾迪生在《旁观者》杂志高度评价而声名远扬。贺拉斯的《诗艺》为其最主要范本，当然，蒲柏也提到了布瓦洛的《诗艺》。与前两者不同之处在于，《批评论》主要针对的是批评家而非作家。其中描述了古往今来诗人与批评家的对立，批评家谨守文学成规作为作品评判的准绳；诗人不愿受其束缚，随时准备破戒。

《批评论》大致可分为 3 部分。第 1 部分（（1—200 行）树立了古人的首要地位，最明显地表现在 181—200 行对古人的盛赞。第 2 部分（201—559 行）剖析了现代人的种种谬误。第 3 部分（560—744 行）提出改良的方案，并对文学批评史进行了简短回顾。

蒲柏告诫批评家要有自知之明，认清自己天赋之高下、鉴赏力的高低以及学问的深浅，谨慎为文，不要过犹不及，弄巧成拙。因为人的能力有局限，只能在某一方面出类拔萃。假如一个人记忆力过人，他的理解力必然不济；假若他的想象力突出，那他的记忆力必然很弱。一门学问只适合一种天才，艺术领域范围广大，而人的才智狭隘，只能专事某一局部领域。正确的批评态度是：深入了解古代作家的固有特征，熟悉他著作的情节、主题、目的，对那个时代的宗教、国情、时代精神了然于胸，才能放手去批评。至于作家，他应当公正地看待古人制定的原则。维吉尔曾发现，荷马和自然殊途同归。蒲柏进一步引申，模仿古人就是模仿自然。在古人的规则不及之处，诗人侥幸可以偏离常规；但是，这类破戒行为越少越好，而且，至少要找到先例作为破戒的托词。在 180—200 行，蒲柏盛赞古人的精神光焰万丈，永恒存在，泽被后代，为世人所景仰膜拜。

正如评论者所指出，《批评论》中的一些关键词意义繁多，往往让读者困惑不已。例如 nature 一词，有时候指客观世界，有时指人性，有时指事物的本质。art 一词也是如此，有时指人为创造的世界，对立于神造的世界；有时指技巧和手法，与创造性的本能相对立；有时指支配某种技巧的规则，与技巧本身相对立。当然，它还可以有最常见的意义，即艺术产品的总称。wit 的词义更加丰富，它可以表示鉴赏力、才智、妙语、天才、创造力，还可以指具备上述品质的个人——才子。蒲柏在使用这些关键术语时，并没有明确透露出其具体含义。当他说，nature 是 art 的来源、目的和考验的时候，他同时使用这两个词的多种含义，增强了文字意义的张力。

Alexander Pope (1688—1744)

An Essay on Criticism

'Tis hard to say, if greater Want[1] of Skill
Appear in *Writing* or in *Judging* ill;
But, of the two, less dang'rous is th' Offence,
To tire our *Patience,* than mis-lead our *Sense.*[2]
5 Some few in *that,* but Numbers err in *this,*
Ten Censure wrong for one who Writes amiss; [3]
A *Fool* might once *himself* alone expose,
Now *One* in *Verse* makes many more in *Prose.*[4]
'Tis with our *Judgments* as our *Watches,* none
10 Go just *alike,* yet each believes his own.
In *Poets* as true *Genius* is but rare, [5]
True *Taste* as seldom is the *Critick's* Share;
Both must alike from Heav'n derive their Light[6],
These *born* to Judge, as well as those to Write.
15 Let such teach others who themselves excell,
And *censure freely* who have *written well.*
Authors are partial to their *Wit*[7], 'tis true,
But are not *Criticks* to their *Judgment* too?
Yet if we look more closely, we shall find
20 Most have the *Seeds* of Judgment in their Mind;
Nature affords at least a *glimm'ring Light*;
The *Lines,* tho' touch'd but faintly, are drawn right.
But as the slightest Sketch, if justly trac'd,
Is by ill *Coloring* but the more disgrac'd,
25 So by *false Learning* is *good Sense* defac'd; [8]
Some are bewilder'd in the Maze of Schools[9],
And some made *Coxcombs*[10] Nature meant but *Fools.*
In search of *Wit*[11] these lose their *common Sense,*
And then turn Criticks in their own Defence.
30 Each burns alike, who can, or cannot write,[12]

Or with a *Rival's*, or an *Eunuch's* spite.

All *Fools* have still[13] an Itching to deride,

And fain *wou'd* be upon the *Laughing Side*;

If *Maevius*[14] Scribble in *Apollo's* spight,

35 There are, who *judge* still w*orse* than he can w*rite*.

Some have at first for *Wits*, then *Poets* past,

Turn'd *Criticks* next, and prov'd plain *Fools* at last;

Some neither can for *Wits*[15] nor *Criticks* pass,

As heavy Mules are neither *Horse* nor *Ass*.

40 Those half-learn'd Witlings, num'rous in our Isle,

As half-form'd Insects on the Banks of *Nile*,[16]

Unfinish'd Things, one knows not what to call,

Their Generation's so *equivocal*:

To tell 'em[17], wou'd a *hundred Tongues* require,

45 Or *one vain Wit's,* that might a hundred tire.

But *you* who seek to *give* and *merit* Fame,

And justly bear a Critick's noble Name,

Be sure *your self* and your own *Reach* to know,

How far your *Genius*, *Taste*, and *Learning* go; [18]

50 Launch not beyond your Depth, but be discreet,

And mark *that Point* where Sense and Dulness[19] *meet*.

Nature to all things fix'd the Limits fit,

And wisely curb'd proud Man's pretending Wit:

As on the *Land* while *here* the *Ocean* gains,

55 In *other Parts* it leaves wide sandy Plains;

Thus in the *Soul* while *Memory* prevails,

The solid Pow'r of *Understanding* fails; [20]

Where Beams of warm *Imagination* play,

The *Memory's* soft Figures melt away.

60 One *Science*[21] only will one *Genius* fit;

So v*ast* is Art,[22] so *narro*w Human Wit:

Not only bounded to *peculiar Arts*,

But oft in *those,* confin'd to *single Parts.*

Like Kings we lose the Conquests gain'd before,

65 By vain Ambition still to make them more:
    Each might his *sev'ral Province* well command,
    Wou'd all but stoop to what they *understand.*
    First follow NATURE[23], and your Judgment frame
    By her just Standard, which is still[24] the same: [25]

70 *Unerring Nature*, still divinely bright,
    One *clear, unchang'd* and *Universal* Light,
    Life, Force, and Beauty, must to all impart,[26]
    At once the *Source*, and *End*, and *Test* of *Art.*[27]
    Art from that Fund each *just Supply* provides,

75 Works *without Show*,[28] and *without Pomp* presides:
    In some fair Body thus th' informing Soul
    With Spirits feeds, with Vigor fills the whole,
    Each Motion guides, and ev'ry Nerve sustains;
    It self unseen, but in th'*Effects*, remains.

80 Some, to whom Heav'n in Wit has been profuse,
    Want as much more, to turn it to its use; [29]
    For *Wit*[30] and *Judgment* often are at strife,
    Tho' meant each other's Aid, like *Man* and *Wife.*
    'Tis more to *guide* than *spur* the Muse's Steed; [31]

85 Restrain his Fury, than provoke his Speed;
    The winged Courser, like a gen'rous[32] Horse,
    Shows most true Mettle when you *check* his Course.[33]
    Those RULES of old *discover'd*, not *devis'd*,
    Are *Nature* still, but *Nature Methodiz'd*; [34]

90 *Nature*, like *Liberty*,[35] is but restrain'd
    By the same Laws which first *herself* ordain'd.
    Hear how learn'd *Greece* her useful Rules indites,
    When to repress, and when indulge our Flights:
    High on *Parnassus* Top her Sons she show'd,

95 And pointed out those arduous Paths they trod,
    Held from afar, aloft, th' Immortal Prize,[36]
    And urg'd the rest by equal Steps to rise;
    Just *Precepts* thus from great *Examples* giv'n,

She drew from *them* what they deriv'd from *Heav'n*.[37]
100 The gen'rous Critick *fann'd* the *Poet's Fire*,
And taught the World, w*ith Reason* to *Admire*.
Then Criticism the Muse's Handmaid prov'd,
To dress her Charms, and make her more belov'd;
But following Wits from that Intention stray'd;
105 Who cou'd not win the Mistress, woo'd the Maid; [38]
Against the Poets *their own Arms* they turn'd,
Sure to hate most the Men from whom they *learn'd*.
So modern *Pothecaries*[39], taught the Art
By *Doctor's Bills*[40] to play the *Doctor's Part*,
110 Bold in the Practice of *mistaken Rules*,
Prescribe, apply, and call their *Masters Fools*.
Some on the Leaves[41] of ancient Authors prey,
Nor Time nor Moths e'er spoil'd so much as they:[42]
Some dryly plain, without Invention's Aid,
115 Write dull *Receits*[43] how Poems may be made:[44]
These leave the Sense, their Learning to display,
And those explain the Meaning quite away.[45]
You then whose Judgment the right Course wou'd steer,
Know well each ANCIENT's proper *Character*,
120 His *Fable*[46], *Subject*, *Scope*[47] in ev'ry Page,
Religion, Country, Genius of his *Age*:
Without all these at once before your Eyes,
Cavil you may, but never *Criticize*.
Be *Homer's* Works your *Study*, and *Delight*,
125 Read them by Day, and meditate by Night,
Thence form your Judgment, thence your Maxims bring,
And trace the Muses *upward* to their *Spring*; [48]
Still with *It self compar'd*, his *Text* peruse;
And let your *Comment* be the *Mantuan Muse*.[49]
130 When first young *Maro*[50] in his boundless Mind
A Work t' outlast Immortal *Rome* design'd,
Perhaps he seem'd *above* the Critick's Law,

And but from *Nature's Fountains* scorn'd to draw:[51]

But when t' examine ev'ry Part he came,

135 *Nature* and *Homer* were, he found, the *same*:

Convinc'd, amaz'd, he checks the bold Design,

And Rules as strict his labor'd Work confine,

As if the *Stagyrite*[52] o'erlook'd each Line.

Learn hence for Ancient *Rules* a just Esteem;[53]

140 To copy *Nature* is to copy *Them.*

Some Beauties yet, no Precepts can declare[54],

For there's a *Happiness*[55] as well as *Care*[56].

Musick resembles *Poetry*, in each

Are *nameless Graces* which no Methods teach,

145 And which, a *Master-Hand* alone can reach.

If, where the *Rules* not far enough extend,

(Since Rules were made but to promote their End)

Some Lucky LICENSE answers to the full

Th' Intent propos'd, *that License* is a *Rule.*[57]

150 Thus *Pegasus*, a nearer way to take,

May boldly deviate from the common Track.

Great Wits sometimes may *gloriously offend,*

And *rise* to *Faults* true Criticks *dare not mend*;

From *vulgar Bounds* with *brave Disorder* part,

155 And *snatch* a *Grace* beyond the Reach of Art,

Which[58], without passing thro' the *Judgment*, gains

The *Heart*, and all its End *at once* attains.

In *Prospects*, thus, some *Objects* please our Eyes,

Which *out of* Nature's *common Order* rise,

160 The shapeless *Rock*, or hanging *Precipice.*

But tho' the *Ancients* thus their *Rules* invade.

(As *Kings* dispense with *Laws* Themselves have made)

Moderns, beware! [59] Or if you must offend

Against the *Precept*, ne'er transgress its *End,*

165 Let it be *seldom,* and *compell'd by Need,*

And have, at least, *Their Precedent* to plead.

The Critick else proceeds without Remorse,

Seizes your Fame, and puts his Laws in force.[60]

I know there are,[61] to whose presumptuous Thoughts

170 Those *Freer Beauties*, ev'n in *Them*, seem Faults:

Some Figures *monstrous* and *mis-shap'd* appear,

Consider'd *singly*, or beheld too *near*,

Which, but *proportion'd* to their *Light*, or *Place*,

Due Distance *reconciles* to Form and Grace.[62]

175 A prudent Chief not always must display

His Pow'rs in *equal Ranks*, and *fair Array*,

But with th' *Occasion* and the *Place* comply,

Conceal his Force, nay seem sometimes to *Fly*.[63]

Those oft are *Stratagems* which *Errors* seem,

180 Nor is it *Homer Nods*, but *We* that *Dream*.[64]

Still green with Bays[65] each *ancient* Altar stands,

Above the reach of *Sacrilegious* Hands,

Secure from *Flames*, from *Envy's* fiercer Rage,

Destructive *War*, and all-involving *Age*.

185 See, from *each Clime* the Learn'd their Incense bring;

Hear, in *all Tongues* consenting *Paeans* ring![66]

In Praise so just, let ev'ry Voice be join'd,

And fill the *Gen'ral Chorus* of *Mankind*!

Hail *Bards*[67] *Triumphant*! born in *happier Days*;

190 *Immortal* Heirs of *Universal* Praise!

Whose Honors with Increase of Ages *grow*,

As Streams roll down, *enlarging* as they flow!

Nations *unborn* your mighty Names shall sound,

And Worlds applaud that must not yet be *found*!

195 Oh may some Spark of *your* Coelestial Fire

The last, the meanest of your Sons inspire,

(That on weak Wings, from far, pursues your Flights;

Glows while he *reads*, but *trembles* as he *writes*.)

To teach vain Wits[68] a Science *little known*,

200 T' *admire* Superior Sense, and *doubt* their own!

注释

1. want：缺点，不足。

2. 大意为：在二者当中，让读者误入歧途比让他们不忍卒读更危险。

3. 大意为：因为一个人写错，便有十个人发难。

4. 大意为：蠢材可能只有一次机会让自己现形；一首歪诗却产生许多拙劣的文章。

5. 大意为：这同我们判断力的关系犹如看手表，每块表上面的钟点都不相同，然而，大家只相信自己的手表。

6. light：眼力。

7. wit：写作的才华。

8. 这是名句，大意为：假学问损害真良知。

9. school：指某派批评。

10. coxbomb：自负的蠢材。

11. wit：才智。

12. 大意为：无论会不会写，各个都狂热不已。

13. still：总是。

14. Maevius：与贺拉斯同时代的一位拙劣诗人。

15. wit：才子。

16. 据说，古人认为早期的动物和昆虫产生于尼罗河两岸。

17. tell：数。

18. 这两行大意为：你应有自知之明，弄清楚自己的天才、鉴赏力和学问的水平如何。

19. dulness：即 dullness，意为"愚笨"。

20. 大意为：在个人的心灵中，如果记忆力好，理解力必然差。在以下两行，作者又列举了个人的想象力和记忆力之间的消长关系。

21. one science：一门学问。

22. 蒲柏在此暗用古希腊著名医生希波克拉底的箴言："生命短暂有限，而艺术（有时译为'学问'）永恒漫长，机会稍纵即逝，实验危险难测，判断不易作出。"

23. nature 一词含义甚广。这里兼指自然界、人类经验的总和，宇宙中秩序与和谐的原则。

24. still：总是。

25. 德莱顿曾写道，"因为自然亘古不变，绝不可能自相矛盾。"

26. Life, Force, and Beauty, must to all impart：必定赋予万物以生命、力量和美。

27. 大意为：自然既是艺术的源泉，又是艺术的目的，还是衡量艺术的标准。

28. 蒲柏在此暗用一句拉丁语名言：艺术不可炫技。

29. 大意为：有的人才华横溢，但是，他缺少更多的才华将其付诸使用。

30. *Wit*：这个词含义众多，见内容提要部分。

31. Steed：指古希腊神话中生有双翼的飞马珀加索斯（Pegasus），它奋蹄踏出泉水，传说诗人饮此泉水可获得灵感。

32. gen'rous：亢奋的。

33. 这句诗大意为：当你控制骏马的行进步伐，它才表现出真正的英雄气概。

34. 大意为：古人所发现的（并非人为设计的）种种规则，仍然算是自然的东西，只不过是经过条理化的自然。

35. liberty：蒲柏的手稿中写作 "monarchy"（王室）。

36. 大意为：在远处高举不朽的奖赏。

37. 大意为：她从伟大的榜样那里归纳出正确的戒律，而那些伟大的榜样则得之于天。

38. 这两行大意为：如果批评家让自己的才智违背了这种意愿（上两行所说的为诗歌服务），他就难赢得小姐（即诗歌）的芳心，只好求助于婢女（批评）。

39. pothecary：英语中的方言，意为"药剂师"。

40. doctor's bill：医生开的药方。

41. leaves：书页（leaf）的复数形式。

42. 在这两行中，蒲柏讽刺了那些专事名物训诂、琐碎考证的批评家，挖苦他们的破坏力超过蠹虫。

43. receit：药方。

44. 大意为：（有的批评家文字）枯燥无味，毫无新意，却开出单调的方子，教人如何写诗。

45. 这两行大意为：前一种批评家不顾见解，只顾卖弄学问，后者则曲解意义。

46. fable：情节。

47. scope：目的。

48. spring：即珀加索斯踏出的赫利孔山上的泉水。

49. Mantuan Muse：指维吉尔，他出生在 Mantua 附近。

50. Maro：指维吉尔。

51. 这几行大意为：维吉尔年轻的时候雄心万丈，想以一部作品比罗马更永垂不朽，他只从自然的源泉中汲取养分，无视批评家制定的戒律。

52. *Stagyrite*：指亚里士多德，Stagyra 是亚里士多德的出生地。

53. 大意为：要正确对待古人制定的规则。

54. declare：解释。

55. happiness：好运，快乐。

56. care：烦恼。

57. 这几行大意为：在诗律不及之处（因为制定规则就是为了强化规则的目的），要是破格之举侥幸满足了诗人的意图，那么这一破格之举便是规则。

58. which：指 grace。

59. 大意为：虽说古人可以如此破戒（犹如帝王取消钦定的法律），现代人则要小心对待。

60. 大意为：至少要找到先例作为破戒的借口，否则批评家就会毫不留情地施行他的规则批评你，使你的声誉受损。

61. I know there are：即 I know there are those（我知道有这样一些人）。

62. 这四行大意为：有的物体当你单独看或近看时，显得狰狞可怕，或者奇形怪状；如果把它们放到适当的背景和地点，适中的距离，就会显现出其外形与优雅。蒲柏在此借用了贺拉斯《诗艺》中的一段著名文字。贺拉斯说，有些绘画只可近观，而不可远看。这里的"light"相当于"context"（语境，背景）。

63. 这四行大意为：深谋远虑的领袖人物并不总是炫耀他的权势显赫，服饰华美，而是视场合与地点而定。他的威力藏而不露，有时似乎根本不存在。

64. 大意为：不是荷马打盹，而是我们在做梦。蒲柏在这里再次暗用贺拉斯的话。贺拉斯曾说过，"荷马也偶有失误"（I'm aggrieved when sometimes even excellent Homer nods）。

65. bay：月桂树，这里指诗人的声誉。

66. consenting：一致。Paean：派安赞歌，指古希腊对神，尤指对太阳神或月神的合唱赞美诗。

67. bard：泛指诗人。

68. wit：同注释 15。

伯克 《关于崇高美和秀丽美概念起源的哲学探讨》

埃德蒙·伯克（1729—1797）

　　埃德蒙·伯克是英国政治家、美学家，1729 年生于爱尔兰的都柏林，1750 年移居伦敦。1757 年在他 28 岁时发表了《关于崇高美和秀丽美概念起源的哲学探讨》这篇著名的论文，扬名国内外，引起狄德罗、康德、莱辛等著名学者的注意。1764 年，他当选为国会议员，1765 年进入下院。他积极参与乔治三世时代的宪法争论。当时，英国政治的一个关键问题是，究竟是由国王还是由国会控制行政部门。他在《关于目前不满情绪的根源》一文中指出，政府主要人选应由全国人民通过国会决定，不能按国王的个人意旨行事。就是在这篇文章中，他对"政党"一词作出了精辟的解释：政党是人们根据共同的原则联合组织的团体。

　　伯克主张英国放宽对爱尔兰议会、天主教徒和经济贸易的控制，并允许爱尔兰在立法上独立。他主张解除对美国的殖民统治，但是不主张美国独立。他对英国的东印度公司在印度的不善管理和所作所为提出了尖锐的批评，主张废除东印度公司对印度的管理。

　　这些都是伯克的政治观点中的可取之处。但是，他对 1789 年爆发的法国大革命却持反对态度，甚至要求政府不承认法国大革命后建立的新政权，鼓动英国政府对法国新政权发动战争。他不赞同法国大革命提出的"自由"和"平等"，这些又是他政治观点中的消极面。

　　他深受 17 世纪英国唯物主义哲学家约翰·洛克（John Locke，1632—1704）的经验主义的影响，认为人的知识源于感官的经验。因此，人们称伯克为经验主义者、唯物主义者。

　　他发表的重要论著有：《关于崇高美和秀丽美概念起源的哲学探讨》（1757），《关于目前不满情绪的根源》（1770），《法国革命论》（1790）。他的著名演说有：《论美洲的赋税》（1774），《论与殖民地的和解》（1775），《论福克斯先生的东印度法案》（1783）等。

内容提要

文章写于 1757 年，修订本于 1759 年出版。这里选的是《关于崇高美和秀丽美概念起源的哲学探讨》(修订本)中的 4 个部分：关于品位，关于崇高美(第 7 段)，关于秀丽美(第 10 段)，崇高美和秀丽美的比较(第 27 段)。

伯克依据洛克的经验主义理论，提出所有的知识均源于感官的经验；人们把从感官所得的简单的概念综合为复杂的概念。他认为，"想象"(或称"某种创造力")以两种方式发挥作用：一是按照感官接受事物的顺序和方法随意表现事物的意象；二是依据一个不同的次序把这些事物的意象用新的方式组合起来。他对是非、好坏、品位问题有很大的兴趣，探讨这些问题是否对所有人都有一个统一的标准，是否存在着逻辑问题等。

他认为事物的是非曲直、好与坏、品位、美与丑，对所有人说来，很可能有一个公认的标准。否则，人们又怎么去判断真善美和是非曲直，如何去判断什么是高尚，什么是自私。撒谎、欺骗、把自己的快乐建立在他人的痛苦上，这些都是人们所不齿的。把天鹅和鹅放在一起，人们会一致同意天鹅比鹅美。雄狮比雌狮美，雄孔雀比雌孔雀美，山间小溪比污浊的水沟美，这也是大家公认的。由此可见，品位在某些方面有一个公认的统一的标准。如果人类的品位没有固定的原则和标准，手艺人制作的手工艺品就不可能在市场上畅销，艺术家也就不可能画出对世人均有吸引力的作品。

然而，伯克认为，对品位作出界定却不是一件容易的事。他的界定是：品位是头脑在感受到有想象力的作品和优雅的艺术时对其作出的判断。他说，"所有感官的快感，无论是视觉，或是感官中最难以说清的品位力，对所有的人，不管社会地位高或低，有学识者或无学识者，都是一样的。"他说品位包括以下三个要素：一、能用感官感受到感官带来的主要快感(这里所说的感官的快感可以理解为：眼睛看到湖中的白天鹅，耳朵听到美妙的音乐，舌头尝到美味的菜肴，鼻子闻到花儿的芬芳时，人所产生的快感。伯克在这里强调的是感官的功能。)；二、想象力的运用(即想象力给人带来的快感)；三、能进行推理。

他强调感官的功能，认为感觉是产生思想和快感的基础。他认为，虽然人有相同的感官，但是人对客观事物的感受程度却并不相同，因为构成品位的感受力和判断力是因人而异的，而且差异很大。感受力的缺陷会造成品位的匮乏，而判断力的缺陷会导致错误的或低水平的品位。有的人感觉迟钝，即便是能给他人留下深刻印象的事物，在他心中也难以引起反响。

品位随着人的判断力的提高而提高，而判断力的提高则又靠知识的积累、专心和判断力的使用。在人的所有活动中，品位和判断力是融为一体的。不同的人有不同的喜恶。品位的统一必须依赖感觉的统一，而感觉实际上是多种多样的，因此品位也各异。

关于想象力，伯克说，因为想象力表现人的感觉，因此想象力与感觉是密不可分的。只有人感觉是好的东西，才会产生好的想象和意象。所以，人的想象如同人的感觉一样，是大致相同的。

他说，判断的任务是找出事物的区别所在。没有比较就没有鉴别，也就没有判断。判断力有缺陷会导致错误的审美结果，而这一缺陷往往源于一个人天生的理解力的欠缺，或者是因为缺乏适当的、良好的训练。对艺术品正确的判断亦可称为品位，这在很大程度上有赖于感觉的灵敏。灵敏的感觉、丰富的想象力和正确的思考是获得良好的品位所不可缺少的，而无知、漫不经心、偏见、轻率、轻浮和固执等等自然会影响对事物作出正确的判断，从而影响品位。

品位随着判断力的提高而提高。品位的提高还有赖于知识的扩充、对所鉴赏的事物的细心观察和品位的经常运用。

关于崇高的讨论开先河者是朗吉弩斯。在他之后是艾迪生、伯克、康德和叔本华。他们都撰文讨论了这个问题。伯克与朗吉弩斯对崇高的界定是不同的。

朗吉弩斯说，"崇高是绝妙的表达"，"崇高用在最合适的场合时，会以闪电般的光芒照亮四方，刹那间显示出一个雄辩家的全部威力。"他又说，崇高的思想才能产生崇高的作品，而崇高的作品则能净化人的灵魂。他认为崇高的语言有五个条件：庄严伟大的思想、强烈激动的感情、运用修辞的技巧、运用高雅的措词、整个篇章结构融为一体时所呈现的高贵与卓越。而这五条中首要的是作家本人必须具备高尚的人格和思想。他的名句是："崇高是伟大灵魂的反映。诗人的精神和他的修辞技巧是崇高的两大组成部分。"

伯克关于崇高美和秀丽美的论述受到朗吉弩斯的启发，但是他们的对象和侧重点不同。朗吉弩斯在论述崇高时，对象是诗人（作家），着重讨论在文学创作中如何使作品获得崇高美。伯克则从读者的主体美感经历出发，论述什么东西能在读者心中唤起崇高美。伯克对崇高的界定是：任何能引起痛苦的危险感的事物，或者说，任何可怕的事物，即是以在人心中引起像恐惧这样的强烈感情的事物，就是崇高。

他认为人最强烈的感情不是快乐，而是痛苦。他举例说，当人体遭受折磨时，痛苦在他的身上和心中所产生的作用比快感要强烈得多。正因为如此，一般说来，人们宁可死去，也不愿长期遭受痛苦的折磨。

如果把伯克关于崇高的界定同朗吉弩斯对崇高的界定作一比较，我们可以看出，朗吉弩斯的论述更可取，更有说服力。

关于秀丽美

伯克首先谈到激情，认为动物的激情源于性欲，而人却不同；人的激情具有社会性，比动物的激情要复杂得多。自然规律决定了男女之间的性爱。但是，不同于动物的是人在选择异性时，倾心于异性的身体美。人的美具有社会性。当我们看到异性的身体美时，我们会产生一种温柔和爱的感觉。我们希望接近具有秀丽美的身体，与之交往。

关于崇高美与秀丽美的比较

伯克认为崇高美与秀丽美有明显的差别。具有崇高美的物体恢宏，而具有秀丽美的东西娇小。秀丽美应是柔和、精美；崇高美应是粗糙、漫不经心。秀丽美避免恰当的线条；崇高美却喜好恰当的线条。秀丽美不应是晦涩的，崇高美则应是阴暗朦胧的。秀丽美应该轻巧、精致；崇高美则应是壮实，甚至宏大。秀丽美和崇高美的本质是不同的。崇高美源于痛苦，秀丽美则源于快感。崇高美和秀丽美各具特点，即便是把这些特点混为一体，也不能使其丧失各自的特点。

Edmund Burke (1729—1797)

A Philosophical Inquiry into the Origin of Our Ideas of the Sublime and Beautiful

Introduction of Taste

On a superficial view we may seem to differ very widely from each other in our reasonings, and no less in our pleasures: but, notwithstanding this difference, which I think to be rather apparent than real, it is probable that the standard both of reason and taste is the same in all human creatures. For if there were not some principles of judgment as well as of sentiment common to all mankind, no hold could possibly be taken either on their reason or their passions, sufficient to maintain the ordinary correspondence of life. It appears indeed to be generally acknowledged, that with regard to truth and falsehood there is something fixed. We find people in their disputes continually appealing to certain tests and standards, which are allowed on all sides, and are supposed to be established in our common nature. But there is not the same obvious concurrence in any uniform or settled principles which relate to taste. It is even commonly supposed that this delicate and aerial faculty, which seems too volatile to endure even the chains of a definition, cannot be properly tried by any test, nor regulated by any standard. There is so continual a call for the exercise of the reasoning faculty; and it is so much strengthened by perpetual contention, that certain maxims of right reason seem to be tacitly settled amongst the most ignorant. The learned have improved on this rude science, and reduced those maxims into a system. If taste has not been so happily cultivated, it was not that the subject was barren, but that the laborers were few or negligent; for to say the truth, there are not the same interesting motives to impel us to fix the one, which urge us to ascertain the other. And, after all, if men differ in their opinions concerning such matters, their difference is not attended with the same important consequences; else I make no doubt but that the logic of taste, if I may be allowed the expression, might very possibly be as well digested, and we might come to discuss matters of this nature with as much certainty, as those which seem more immediately within the province of mere reason. And, indeed, it is very necessary, at the entrance into such an inquiry as our present, to make this point as clear as possible; for if taste has no fixed principles, if the imagination is not affected according to some invariable and certain laws, our labor is likely to be employed to very little purpose; as it must be judged a useless, if not an absurd undertaking, to lay down rules for caprice, and to set up for a legislator of whims and fancies.

The term *taste*, like all other figurative terms, is not extremely accurate; the thing which we understand by it is far from a simple and determinate idea in the minds of most men, and it is therefore liable to uncertainty and confusion. I have no great opinion of a definition, the celebrated remedy for the cure of this disorder. For, when we define, we seem in danger of circumscribing nature within the bounds of our own notions, which we often take up by hazard or embrace on trust, or form out of a limited and partial consideration of the object before us, instead of extending our ideas to take in all that nature comprehends, according to her manner of combining. We are limited in our inquiry by the strict laws to which we have submitted at our setting out. *"Circa vilem patulumque morabimur orbem, /Unde pudor proferre pedem vetat aut operis lex."*[1]

A definition may be very exact, and yet go but a very little way towards informing us of the nature of the thing defined; but let the virtue of a definition be what it will, in the order of things, it seems rather to follow than to precede our inquiry, of which it ought to be considered as the result. It must be acknowledged that the methods of disquisition and teaching may be sometimes different, and on very good reason undoubtedly; but, for my part, I am convinced that the method of teaching which approaches most nearly to the method of investigation is incomparably the best; since, not content with serving up a few barren and lifeless truths, it leads to the stock on which they grew; it tends to set the reader himself in the track of invention, and to direct him into those paths in which the author has made his own discoveries, if he should be so happy as to have made any that are valuable.

But to cut off all pretense for caviling, I mean by the word *taste*, no more than that faculty or those faculties of the mind, which are affected with, or which form a judgment of, the works of imagination and the elegant arts. This is, I think, the most general idea of that word, and what is the least connected with any particular theory. And my point in this inquiry is, to find whether there are any principles, on which the imagination is affected, so common to all, so grounded and certain, as to supply the means of reasoning satisfactorily about them. And such principles of taste I fancy there are; however paradoxical it may seem to those, who on a superficial view imagine that there is so great a diversity of tastes, both in kind and degree, that nothing can be more indeterminate.

All the natural powers in man, which I know, that are conversant about external objects, are the senses; the imagination; and the judgment. And first with regard to the senses. We do and we must suppose, that as the conformation of their organs are nearly or altogether the same in all men, so the manner of perceiving external objects is in all men the same, or with little difference. We are satisfied that what appears to be light to one eye, appears light to another; that what seems sweet to one palate, is sweet to another; that what is dark and bitter to this man, is likewise dark and bitter to that; and we conclude in the same manner of great and little, hard and soft, hot and cold, rough and smooth; and indeed of all the natural qualities and affections of bodies. If we suffer ourselves to imagine, that their senses present to different men different images of things, this skeptical proceeding will make every sort of reasoning on every subject vain and frivolous, even that skeptical reasoning itself which had persuaded us to entertain a doubt concerning the agreement of our perceptions. But as there will be little doubt that bodies present similar images to the whole species, it must necessarily be allowed, that the pleasures and the pains which every object excites in one man, it must raise in all mankind, whilst it operates naturally, simply, and by its proper powers only; for if we deny this, we must imagine that the same cause, operating in the same manner, and on subjects of the same kind, will produce different effects; which would be highly absurd. Let us first consider this point in the sense of taste, and the rather as the faculty in question has taken its name from that sense. All men are agreed to call vinegar sour, honey sweet, and aloes bitter; and as they are all agreed in finding these qualities in those objects, they do not in the least differ concerning their effects with regard to pleasure and pain. They all concur in calling sweetness pleasant, and sourness and bitterness unpleasant. Here there is no diversity in their sentiments; and that there is not, appears fully from the consent of all men in the metaphors which are taken from the sense of taste. A sour temper, bitter expressions, bitter curses, a bitter fate, are terms well and strongly understood by all. And we are altogether as well understood when we say, a sweet disposition, a sweet person, a sweet condition and the like. It is confessed, that custom and some other causes have made many deviations from the natural pleasures or pains which belong to these several tastes; but then the power of distinguishing between the natural and the acquired relish remains to the very last. A man frequently comes to prefer the taste of tobacco to that of sugar, and the flavor of vinegar to that of milk; but this makes no confusion in tastes, whilst he is sensible that the tobacco and vinegar are not sweet, and whilst he knows that habit alone has reconciled his palate to these alien pleasures. Even with such a person we may speak, and with sufficient precision, concerning tastes. But should any man be found who declares, that to him tobacco has a taste like sugar, and that he cannot distinguish between milk and vinegar; or that tobacco and vinegar are sweet, milk bitter, and sugar sour; we immediately conclude that the organs of this man are out of order, and that his palate is utterly vitiated. We are as far from conferring with such a person upon tastes, as from reasoning concerning the relations of quantity with one who should deny that all the parts together were equal to the whole. We do not call a man of this kind wrong in his notions, but absolutely mad. Exceptions of this sort, in either way, do not at all impeach our general rule, nor make us conclude that men have various principles concerning the relations of quantity or the taste of things. So that when it is said, taste cannot be disputed, it can only mean, that no one can strictly answer what pleasure or pain some particular man may find from the taste of some particular thing. This indeed cannot be disputed; but we may dispute, and with sufficient clearness too, concerning the things which are naturally pleasing or disagreeable to the sense. But when we talk of any peculiar or acquired relish, then we must know the habits, the prejudices, or the distempers of this particular man, and we must draw our conclusion from those.

This agreement of mankind is not confined to the taste solely. The principle of pleasure derived from sight is the same in all. Light is more pleasing than darkness. Summer, when the earth is clad in green, when the heavens are serene and bright, is more agreeable than winter, when everything makes a different appearance. I never remember that anything beautiful, whether a man, a beast, a bird, or a plant, was ever shown, though it were to a hundred people, that they did not all immediately agree that it was beautiful, though some might have thought that it fell short of their expectation, or that other things were still finer. I believe no man thinks a goose to be more beautiful than a swan, or imagines that what they call a Friesland hen excels a peacock. It must be observed too, that the pleasures of the sight are not near so complicated, and confused, and altered by unnatural habits and associations, as the pleasures of the taste are; because the pleasures of the sight more commonly acquiesce in themselves; and are not so often altered by considerations which are independent of the sight itself. But things do not spontaneously present themselves to the palate as they do to the sight; they are generally applied to it, either as food or as medicine; and from the qualities which they possess for nutritive or medicinal purposes they often form the palate by degrees, and by force of these associations. Thus opium is pleasing to Turks, on account of the agreeable delirium it produces. Tobacco is the delight of Dutchmen, as it diffuses a torpor and pleasing stupefaction. Fermented spirits please our common people, because they banish care, and all consideration of future or present evils. All of these, together with tea and coffee, and some other things, have passed from the apothecary's shop to our tables, and were taken for health long before they were thought of for pleasure. The effect of the drug has made us use it frequently; and frequent use, combined with the agreeable effect, has made the taste itself at last agreeable. But this does not in the least perplex our reasoning; because we distinguish to the last the acquired from the natural relish. In describing the taste of an unknown fruit, you would scarcely say that it had a sweet and pleasant flavor like tobacco, opium, or garlic, although you spoke to those who were in the constant use of these drugs, and had great pleasure in them. There is in all men a sufficient remembrance of the original natural causes of pleasure, to enable them to bring all things offered to their senses to that standard, and to regulate their feelings and opinions by it. Suppose one who had so vitiated his palate as to take more pleasure in the taste of opium than in that of butter or honey, to be presented with a bolus of squills; there is hardly any doubt but that he would prefer the butter or honey to this nauseous morsel, or to any other bitter drug to which he had not been accustomed; which proves that his palate was naturally like that of other men in all things, that it is still like the palate of other men in many things, and only vitiated in some particular points. For in judging of any new thing, even of a taste similar to that which he had been formed by habit to like, he finds his palate affected in the natural manner, and on the common principles. Thus the pleasure of all the senses, of the sight, and even of the taste, that most ambiguous of the senses, is the same in all, high and low, learned and unlearned.

Besides the ideas, with their annexed pains and pleasures, which are presented by the sense; the mind of man possesses a sort of creative power of its own; either in representing at pleasure the images of things in the order and manner in which they were received by the senses, or in combining those images in a new manner, and according to a different order. This power is called imagination; and to this belongs whatever is called wit, fancy, invention, and the like. But it must be observed, that this power of the imagination is incapable of producing anything absolutely new; it can only vary the disposition of those ideas which it has received from the senses. Now the imagination is the most extensive province of pleasure and pain, as it is the region of our fears and our hopes, and of all our passions that are connected with them; and whatever is calculated to affect the imagination with these commanding ideas, by force of any original natural impression must have the same power pretty equally over all men. For since the imagination is only the representation of the senses, it can only be pleased or displeased with the images, from the same principle on which the sense is pleased or displeased with the realities; and consequently there must be just as close an agreement in the imaginations as in the senses of men. A little attention will convince us that this must of necessity be the case.

But in the imagination, besides the pain or pleasure arising from the properties of the natural object, a pleasure is perceived from the resemblance which the imitation has to the original: the imagination, I conceive, can have no pleasure but what results from one or other of these causes. And these causes operate pretty uniformly upon all men, because they operate by principles in nature, and which are not derived from any particular habits or advantages. Mr. Locke very justly and finely observes of wit, that it is chiefly conversant in tracing resemblances; he remarks, at the same time, that the business of judgment is rather in finding differences. It may perhaps appear, on this supposition, that there is no material distinction between the wit and the judgment, as they both seem to result from different operations of the same faculty of comparing. But in reality, whether they are or are not dependent on the same power of the mind, they differ so very materially in many respects, that a perfect union of wit and judgment is one of the rarest things in the world. When two distinct objects are unlike to each other, it is only what we expect; things are in their common way; and therefore they make no impression on the imagination: but when two distinct objects have a resemblance, we are struck, we attend to them, and we are pleased. The mind of man has naturally a far greater alacrity and satisfaction in tracing resemblances than in searching for differences: because by making resemblances we produce new images; we unite, we create, we enlarge our stock; but in making distinctions we offer no food at all to the imagination; the task itself is more severe and irksome, and what pleasure we derive from it is something of a negative and indirect nature. A piece of news is told me in the morning; this, merely as a piece of news, as a fact added to my stock, gives me some pleasure. In the evening I find there was nothing in it. What do I gain by this, but the dissatisfaction to find that I had been imposed upon? Hence it is that men are much more naturally inclined to belief than to incredulity. And it is upon this principle, that the most ignorant and barbarous nations have frequently excelled in similitudes, comparisons, metaphors, and allegories, who have been weak and backward in distinguishing and sorting their ideas. And it is for a reason of this kind, that Homer and the oriental writers, though very fond of similitudes, and though they often strike out such as are truly admirable, seldom take care to have them exact; that is, they are taken with the general resemblance, they paint it strongly, and they take no notice of the difference which may be found between the things compared.

Now as the pleasure of resemblance is that which principally flatters the imagination, all men are nearly equal in this point, as far as their knowledge of the things represented or compared extends. The principle of this knowledge is very much accidental, as it depends upon experience and observation, and not on the strength or weakness of any natural faculty; and it is from this difference in knowledge, that what we commonly, though with no great exactness, call a difference in taste proceeds. A man to whom sculpture is new, sees a barber's block, or some ordinary piece of statuary; he is immediately struck and pleased, because he sees something like a human figure; and, entirely taken up with this likeness, he does not at all attend to its defects. No person, I believe, at the first time of seeing a piece of imitation ever did. Some time after, we suppose that this novice lights upon a more artificial work of the same nature; he now begins to look with contempt on what he admired at first; not that he admired it even then for its unlikeness to a man, but for that general though inaccurate resemblance which it bore to the human figure. What he admired at different times in these so different figures, is strictly the same; and though his knowledge is improved, his taste is not altered. Hitherto his mistake was from a want of knowledge in art, and this arose from his inexperience; but he may be still deficient from a want of knowledge in nature. For it is possible that the man in question may stop here, and that the masterpiece of a great hand may please him no more than the middling performance of a vulgar artist; and this not for want of better or higher relish, but because all men do not observe with sufficient accuracy on the human figure to enable them to judge properly of an imitation of it. And that the critical taste does not depend upon a superior principle in men, but upon superior knowledge, may appear from several instances. The story of the ancient painter and the shoemaker is very well known. The shoemaker set the painter right with regard to some mistakes he had made in the shoe of one of his figures, which the painter, who had not made such accurate observations on shoes, and was content with a general resemblance, had never observed. But this was no impeachment to the taste of the painter; it only showed some want of knowledge in the art of making shoes. Let us imagine, that an anatomist had come into the painter's working room. His piece is in general well done, the figure in question in a good attitude, and the parts well adjusted to their various movements; yet the anatomist, critical in his art, may observe the swell of some muscle not quite just in the peculiar action of the figure. Here the anatomist observes what the painter had not observed; and he passes by what the shoemaker had remarked. But a want of the last critical knowledge in anatomy no more reflected on the natural good taste of the painter, or of any common observer of his piece, than the want of an exact knowledge in the formation of a shoe. A fine piece of a decollated head of St. John the Baptist[2] was shown to a Turkish emperor; he praised many things, but he observed one defect: he observed that the skin did not shrink from the wounded part of the neck. The sultan on this occasion, though his observation was very just, discovered no more natural taste than the painter who executed this piece, or than a thousand European connoisseurs, who probably would have made the same observation. His Turkish majesty had indeed been well acquainted with that terrible spectacle, which the others could only have represented in their imagination. On the subject of their dislike there is a difference between all these people, arising from the different kinds and degrees of their knowledge; but there is something in common to the painter, the shoemaker, the anatomist, and the Turkish emperor, the pleasure arising from a natural object, so far as each perceives it justly imitated; the satisfaction in seeing an agreeable figure; the sympathy proceeding from a striking and affecting incident. So far as taste is natural, it is nearly common to all.

In poetry, and other pieces of imagination, the same parity may be observed. It is true, that one man is charmed with *Don Belianis*[3], and reads Virgil coldly; whilst another is transported with the *Aeneid*, and leaves *Don Belianis* to children. These two men seem to have a taste very different from each other; but in fact they differ very little. In both these pieces, which inspire such opposite sentiments, a tale exciting admiration is told; both are full of action, both are passionate; in both are voyages, battles, triumphs, and continual changes of fortune. The admirer of *Don Belianis* perhaps does not understand the refined language of the *Aeneid*, who, if it was degraded into the style of the *Pilgrim's Progress*[4], might feel it in all its energy, on the same principle which made him an admirer of *Don Belianis*.

In his favorite author he is not shocked with the continual breaches of probability, the confusion of times, the offenses against manners, the trampling upon geography; for he knows nothing of geography and chronology, and he has never examined the grounds of probability. He perhaps reads of a shipwreck on the coast of Bohemia; wholly taken up with so interesting an event, and only solicitous for the fate of his hero, he is not in the least troubled at this extravagant blunder. For why should he be shocked at a shipwreck on the coast of Bohemia, who does not know but that Bohemia may be an island in the Atlantic Ocean? And after all, what reflection is this on the natural good taste of the person here supposed?

So far then as taste belongs to the imagination, its principle is the same in all men; there is no difference in the manner of their being affected, nor in the causes of the affection; but in the degree there is a difference, which arises from two causes principally; either from a greater degree of natural sensibility, or from a closer and longer attention to the object. To illustrate this by the procedure of the senses, in which the same difference is found, let us suppose a very smooth marble table to be set before two men; they both perceive it to be smooth, and they are both pleased with it because of this quality. So far they agree. But suppose another, and after that another table, the latter still smoother than the former, to be set before them. It is now very probable that these men, who are so agreed upon what is smooth, and in the pleasure from thence, will disagree when they come to settle which table has the advantage in point of polish. Here is indeed the great difference between tastes, when men come to compare the excess or diminution of things which are judged by degree and not by measure. Nor is it easy, when such a difference arises, to settle the point, if the excess or diminution be not glaring. If we differ in opinion about two quantities, we can recourse to a common measure, which may decide the question with the utmost exactness; and this, I take it, is what gives mathematical knowledge a greater certainty than any other. But in things whose excess is not judged by greater or smaller, as smoothness and roughness, hardness and softness, darkness and light, the shades of colors, all these are very easily distinguished when the difference is any way considerable, but not when it is minute, for want of some common measures, which perhaps may never come to be discovered. In these nice cases, supposing the acuteness of the sense equal, the greater attention and habit in such things will have the advantage. In the question about the tables, the marble-polisher will unquestionably determine the most accurately. But notwithstanding this want of a common measure for settling many disputes relative to the senses, and their representative the imagination, we find that the principles are the same in all, and that there is no disagreement until we come to examine into the preeminence or difference of things, which brings us within the province of the judgment.

So long as we are conversant with the sensible qualities of things, hardly any more than the imagination seems concerned; little more also than the imagination seems concerned when the passions are represented, because by the force of natural sympathy they are felt in all men without any recourse to reasoning, and their justness recognized in every breast. Love, grief, fear, anger, joy, all these passions have, in their turns, affected every mind; and they do not affect it in an arbitrary or casual manner, but upon certain, natural, and uniform principles. But as many of the works of imagination are not confined to the representation of sensible objects, nor to efforts upon the passions, but extend themselves to the manners, the characters, the actions, and designs of men, their relations, their virtues and vices, they come within the province of the judgment, which is improved by attention, and by the habit of reasoning. All these make a very considerable part of what are considered as the objects of taste; and Horace sends us to the schools of philosophy and the world for our instruction in them. Whatever certainty is to be acquired in morality and the science of life; just the same degree of certainty have we in what relates to them in works of imitation. Indeed it is for the most part in our skill in manners, and in the observances of time and place, and of decency in general, which is only to be learned in those schools to which Horace recommends us, that what is called taste, by way of distinction, consists: and which is in reality no other than a more refined judgment. On the whole, it appears to me, that what is called taste, in its most general acceptation, is not a simple idea, but is partly made up of a perception of the primary pleasures of sense, of the secondary pleasures of the imagination, and of the conclusions of the reasoning faculty, concerning the various relations of these, and concerning the human passions, manners, and actions. All this is requisite to form taste, and the groundwork of all these is the same in the human mind; for as the senses are the great originals of all our ideas, and consequently of all our pleasures, if they are not uncertain and arbitrary, the whole groundwork of taste is common to all, and therefore there is a sufficient foundation for a conclusive reasoning on these matters.

Whilst we consider taste merely according to its nature and species, we shall find its principles entirely uniform; but the degree in which these principles prevail, in the several individuals of mankind, is altogether as different as the principles themselves are similar. For sensibility and judgment, which are the qualities that compose what we commonly call a *taste*, vary exceedingly in various people. From a defect in the former of these qualities arises a want of taste; a weakness in the latter constitutes a wrong or a bad one. There are some men formed with feelings so blunt, with tempers so cold and phlegmatic, that they can hardly be said to be awake during the whole course of their lives. Upon such persons the most striking objects make but a faint and obscure impression. There are others so continually in the agitation of gross and merely sensual pleasures, or so occupied in the low drudgery of avarice, or so heated in the chase of honors and distinction, that their minds, which had been used continually to the storms of these violent and tempestuous passions, can hardly be put in motion by the delicate and refined play of the imagination. These men, though from a different cause, become as stupid and insensible as the former; but whenever either of these happen to be struck with any natural elegance or greatness, or with these qualities in any work of art, they are moved upon the same principle.

The cause of a wrong taste is a defect of judgment. And this may arise from a natural weakness of understanding (in whatever the strength of that faculty may consist), or, which is much more commonly the case, it may arise from a want of a proper and well-directed exercise, which alone can make it strong and ready. Besides, that ignorance, inattention, prejudice, rashness, levity, obstinacy, in short, all those passions, and all those vices, which pervert the judgment in other matters, prejudice it no less in this its more refined and elegant province. These causes produce different opinions upon everything which is an object of the understanding, without inducing us to suppose that there are no settled principles of reason. And indeed, on the whole, one may observe, that there is rather less difference upon matters of taste among mankind, than upon most of those which depend upon the naked reason; and that men are far better agreed on the excellence of a description in Virgil, than on the truth or falsehood of a theory of Aristotle.

A rectitude of judgment in the arts, which may be called a good taste, does in a great measure depend upon sensibility; because if the mind has no bent to the pleasures of the imagination, it will never apply itself sufficiently to works of that species to acquire a competent knowledge of them. But though a degree of sensibility is requisite to form a good judgment, yet a good judgment does not necessarily arise from a quick sensibility to pleasure; it frequently happens that a very poor judge, merely by force of a greater complexional sensibility, is more affected by a very poor piece, than the best judge by the most perfect; for as everything new, extraordinary, grand, or passionate, is well calculated to affect such a person, and that the faults do not affect him, his pleasure is more pure and unmixed; and as it is merely a pleasure of the imagination, it is much higher than any which is derived from a rectitude of judgment; the judgment is for the greater part employed in throwing stumbling blocks in the way of the imagination, in dissipating the scenes of its enchantment, and in tying us down to the disagreeable yoke of our reason: for almost the only pleasure that men have in judging better than others, consists in a sort of conscious pride and superiority, which arises from thinking rightly; but then this is an indirect pleasure, a pleasure which does not immediately result from the object which is under contemplation. In the morning of our days, when the senses are unworn and tender, when the whole man is awake in every part, and the gloss of novelty fresh upon all the objects that surround us, how lively at that time are our sensations, but how false and inaccurate the judgments we form of things! I despair of ever receiving the same degree of pleasure from the most excellent performances of genius, which I felt at that age from pieces which my present judgment regards as trifling and contemptible. Every trivial cause of pleasure is apt to affect the man of too sanguine a complexion: his appetite is too keen to suffer his taste to be delicate; and he is in all respects what Ovid[5] says of himself in love, "*Molle meum levibus cor est violabile telis,*

/Et semper causa est, cur ego semper amem."[6] One of this character can never be a refined judge; never what the comic poet calls *"elegans formarum spectator."*[7] The excellence and force of a composition must always be imperfectly estimated from its effect on the minds of any, except we know the temper and character of those minds. The most powerful effects of poetry and music have been displayed, and perhaps are still displayed, where these arts are but in a very low and imperfect state. The rude hearer is affected by the principles which operate in these arts even in their rudest condition; and he is not skillful enough to perceive the defects. But as the arts advance toward their perfection, the science of criticism advances with equal pace, and the pleasure of judges is frequently interrupted by the faults which are discovered in the most finished compositions.

Before I leave this subject, I cannot help taking notice of an opinion which many persons entertain, as if the taste were a separate faculty of the mind, and distinct from the judgment and imagination; a species of instinct, by which we are struck naturally, and at first glance, without any previous reasoning, with the excellences or the defects of a composition. So far as the imagination and the passions are concerned, I believe it true, that the reason is little consulted; but where disposition, where decorum, where congruity are concerned, in short, wherever the best taste differs from the worst, I am convinced that the understanding operates, and nothing else; and its operation is in reality far from being always sudden, or, when it is sudden, it is often far from being right. Men of the best taste by consideration come frequently to change these early and precipitate judgments, which the mind, from its aversion to neutrality and doubt loves to form on the spot. It is known that the taste (whatever it is) is improved exactly as we improve our judgment, by extending our knowledge, by a steady attention to our object, and by frequent exercise. They who have not taken these methods, if their taste decides quickly, it is always uncertainly; and their quickness is owing to their presumption and rashness, and not to any sudden irradiation, that in a moment dispels all darkness from their minds. But they who have cultivated that species of knowledge which makes the object of taste, by degrees and habitually attain not only a soundness but a readiness of judgment, as men do by the same methods on all other occasions. At first they are obliged to spell, but at last they read with ease and with celerity; but this celerity of its operation is no proof that the taste is a distinct faculty. Nobody, I believe, has attended the course of a discussion which turned upon matters within the sphere of mere naked reason, but must have observed the extreme readiness with which the whole process of the argument is carried on, the grounds discovered, the objections raised and answered, and the conclusions drawn from premises, with a quickness altogether as great as the taste can be supposed to work with; and yet where nothing but plain reason either is or can be suspected to operate. To multiply principles for every different appearance is useless, and unphilosophical too in a high degree.

This matter might be pursued much farther; but it is not the extent of the subject which must prescribe our bounds, for what subject does not branch out to infinity? It is the nature of our particular scheme, and the single point of view in which we consider it, which ought to put a stop to our researches.

Section VII

Of the Sublime

Whatever is fitted in any sort to excite the ideas of pain, and danger, that is to say, whatever is in any sort terrible, or is conversant about terrible objects, or operates in a manner analogous to terror, is a source of the sublime; that is, it is productive of the strongest emotion which the mind is capable of feeling. I say the strongest emotion, because I am satisfied the ideas of pain are much more powerful than those which enter on the part of pleasure. Without all doubt, the torments which we may be made to suffer, are much greater in their effect on the body and mind, than any pleasures which the most learned voluptuary could suggest, or than the liveliest imagination, and the most sound and exquisitely sensible body could enjoy. Nay I am in great doubt, whether any man could be found who would earn a life of the most perfect satisfaction, at the price of ending it in the torments, which justice inflicted in a few hours on the late unfortunate regicide in France[8]. But as pain is stronger in its operation than pleasure, so death is in general a much more affecting idea than pain; because there are very few pains, however exquisite, which are not preferred to death; nay, what generally makes pain itself, if I may say so, more painful, is, that it is considered as an emissary of this king of terrors. When danger or pain press too nearly, they are incapable of giving any delight, and are simply terrible; but at certain distances, and with certain modifications, they may be, and they are delightful, as we every day experience. The cause of this I shall endeavor to investigate hereafter.

Section X

Of Beauty

The passion which belongs to generation, merely as such, is lust only; this is evident in brutes, whose passions are more unmixed, and which pursue their purposes more directly than ours. The only distinction they observe with regard to their mates, is that of sex. It is true, that they stick severally to their own species in preference to all others. But this preference, I imagine, does not arise from any sense of beauty which they find in their species, as Mr. Addison[9] supposes, but from a law of some other kind to which they are subject; and this we may fairly conclude, from their apparent want of choice amongst those objects to which the barriers of their species have confined them. But man, who is a creature adapted to a greater variety and intricacy of relation, connects with the general passion, the idea of some social qualities, which direct and heighten the appetite which he has in common with all other animals; and as he is not designed like them to live at large, it is fit that he should have something to create a preference, and fix his choice; and this in general should be some sensible quality; as no other can so quickly, so powerfully, or so surely produce its effect. The object therefore of this mixed passion which we call love, is the beauty of the sex. Men are carried to the sex in general, as it is the sex, and by the common law of nature; but they are attached to particulars by personal beauty. I call beauty a social quality; for where women and men, and not only they, but when other animals give us a sense of joy and pleasure in beholding them (and there are many that do so), they inspire us with sentiments of tenderness and affection towards their persons; we like to have them near us, and we enter willingly into a kind of relation with them, unless we should have strong reasons to the contrary. But to what end, in many cases, this was designed, I am unable to discover; for I see no greater reason for a connection between man and several animals who are attired in so engaging a manner, than between him and some others who entirely want this attraction, or possess it in a far weaker degree. But it is probable, that providence did not make even this distinction, but with a view to some great end, though we cannot perceive distinctly what it is, as his wisdom is not our wisdom, nor our ways his ways.

Section XXVII

The Sublime and Beautiful Compared

On closing this general view of beauty, it naturally occurs, that we should compare it with the sublime; and in this comparison there appears a remarkable contrast. For sublime objects are vast in their dimensions, beautiful ones comparatively small; beauty should be smooth, and polished; the great, rugged and negligent; beauty should shun the right line, yet deviate from it insensibly; the great in many cases loves the right line, and when it deviates, it often makes a strong deviation; beauty should not be obscure; the great ought to be dark and gloomy; beauty should be light and delicate; the great ought to be solid, and even massive. They are indeed ideas of a very different nature, one being founded on pain, the other on pleasure; and however they may vary afterwards from the direct nature of their causes, yet these causes keep up an eternal distinction between them, a distinction never to be forgotten by any whose business it is to affect the passions. In the infinite variety of natural combinations we must expect to find the qualities of things the most remote imaginable from each other united in the same object. We must expect also to find combinations of the same kind in the works of art. But when we consider the power of an object upon our passions, we must know that when anything is intended to affect the mind by the force of some predominant property, the affection produced is like to be the more uniform and perfect, if all the other properties or qualities of the object be of the same nature, and tending to the same design as the principal; "If black, and white blend, soften, and unite, /A thousand ways, are there no black and white? "[10] If the qualities of the sublime and beautiful are sometimes united, does this prove, that they are the same, does it prove, that they are any way allied, does it prove even that they are not opposite and contradictory? Black and white may soften, may blend, but they are not therefore the same. Nor when they are so softened and blended with each other, or with different colors, is the power of black as black, or of white as white, so strong as when each stands uniform and distinguished.

注释

1. "*Circa vilem patulumque morabimur orbem，/ Unde pudor proferre pedem vetat aut operis lex.*"：意大利语，引自贺拉斯的《诗艺》。引语有错。英语译为："We shall linger with the low and open world, from which modesty and the law of work prevent our feet from moving."

2. St. John the Baptist：《圣经》中的施洗约翰。他在耶稣之前传道，劝人悔罪，后被斩首。

3. *Don Belianis*：全名为 *The Famous and Delectable History of Don Belianis of Greece*（《希腊贝里安尼斯先生著名趣事记》），1673 年出版的一部通俗小说，作者不可考。

4. *Pilgrim's Progress*：17 世纪英国作家约翰·班扬（John Bunyan）的名著，中译名为《天路历程》。

5. Ovid：奥维德（前 43—17），古罗马诗人，代表作为长诗《变形记》（*Metamorphoses*）。

6. "*Molle meum...semper amem.*"：引自奥维德所写的《古代名媛》（*Heroides*，意为 "letters of heroines"），引语有误。英译文是："My soft heart is vulnerable to light darts, and there is always a reason why I am always in love."

7. "*elegans formarum spectator*"：引自古罗马喜剧作家泰伦斯（Terence）所写的喜剧《阉奴》（*Eunuch*，即 *Eunuchus*），英译文是："a refined observer of forms"。

8. ... the late unfortunate regicide in France.：指法国人罗伯特·达米安（Robert Damiens，1715—1757）企图刺杀法国国王路易十五，后被折磨至死。

9. Mr. Addison：指约瑟夫·艾迪生（Joseph Addison, 1672—1719），英

国著名随笔作家，与斯梯尔（Richard Steele）一起创办了刊物《旁观者》（*The Spectator*, 1711—1714）。

10. "... are there no black and white？"：引自英国 18 世纪著名诗人亚历山大·蒲柏所写的《人论》（*An Essay on Man*）。引语有误。

《论品位的标准》

大卫·休谟（1711—1776）

大卫·休谟，苏格兰人，18 世纪英国政治学家、经验主义哲学家、历史学家和作家。他和当时的著名学者卢梭、亚当·斯密是好友。休谟去世后，他的自传由亚当·斯密安排出版。休谟是 18 世纪有重要影响的哲学家和经济学家，他对因果推理问题的批判启发了德国思想家康德创立"批判"哲学。他还推动了 19 世纪法国数学家和哲学家孔德提出实证哲学。他写的 6 卷本《英国史》（1754—1762）使他名扬英国。在 18 世纪的英国，他是哲学的象征。20 世纪中叶，英国的反形而上学家认为他是世界上少数几个杰出的哲学家之一。

休谟和伯克一样，深受 17 世纪英国哲学家约翰·洛克的影响。他把洛克的经验主义发展到绝对怀疑主义，认为一切观念均源于印象，任何有关事实的论证都是徒劳的。他写的《人类理解力研究》试图确定人类认识的原则。他认为，不可能有超越经验的关于任何事物的知识。作为经验主义者，他强调感觉和经验的重要性。他说："所有艺术的一般规则都建立在经验上，建立在人性共有的感情上。"

他把哲学看成是归纳的、实验的人性科学，是描述心灵是如何获得知识的。他认为，印象是感觉的终极材料，观念是这些材料的复合、变换、扩大或缩减。

作为政治经济学家，他反对商业制度，坚持金钱与财富的区别。

休谟很少专题论述艺术和美学原则。他的主要兴趣是人的心理活动。只是在心理活动同艺术发生关系时，他才议论艺术。18 世纪人们对读者和观众在欣赏文学和艺术时的心理活动表现出浓厚的兴趣。休谟的《论品位的标准》就是从心理学的角度探讨这个问题。他感兴趣的不是文学艺术作品本身应有的品质，而是读者应具备什么品质，才能欣赏文学艺术作品。

他还提出，时间可以改变人对文学艺术作品的评价，因为人的思想观念和道德观念、情趣和爱好是随着时间的推移发生变化的。不同年龄的人对文学作品的兴趣也不同：20 岁的青年人可能喜欢奥维德（Ovid）的作品；40 岁的中年人可能欣赏贺拉斯的作品；50 岁的人则可能爱读罗马历史学家塔西佗（Tacitus）的作品；而不同国度的人对文学艺术作品的欣赏程度和评价也不同。美国人不可能像法国人那样喜爱拉辛（Racine）。法国人不可能像英语国家的人民那样能理解和喜爱莎士比亚的作品。

休谟的文论强调读者的心理和经验，对古典的理性主义哲学的论点提出异议。《论品位的标准》是他写的著名文论。

他的主要哲学著作是《人性论》（1734—1737），书共分三卷。第一卷《论理智》（后改名为《人类理解力研究》，1748）阐明人的认识过程，描述观念的起源、空间和时间的观念，因果关系以及关于感觉的怀疑主义。第二卷为《论人的情感》。第三卷是《论道德》（后改名为《道德原则研究》，1751）。

内容提要

休谟首先提出，如同人对事物的看法不同，人的品位也是多种多样的，其差异也大相径庭。什么是美，什么是丑，各人的看法不尽相同，甚至有很大差异。人人都赞扬一篇文章的优雅、贴切、简练和气魄，批评文章中的空洞、浮夸和矫揉造作、冷漠无情、虚假的光彩夺目。就文章的总体而论，批评家的看法是一致的。但是在文章的具体方面，批评家的看法就不同了。在不同的时代，不同的国度，作家都一致赞扬仁义、高尚、谨慎、诚实，批评那些与此相反的品质，这说明人的情感是相同的。

有必要找出品位的标准，找出一种规则，使人的不同情感能协调一致，使大家对哪种情感可取，哪种情感不可取，有一个可以遵循的准则。人的判断与情感不同，对一个事物就可能有千百种不同的意见。但是，正确和公正的意见只可能有一个。难就难在如何找出并确定这一正确意见。情感则不同。一个物体可能引起人的千百种情感，这千百种情感都是合乎情理的。

美作为一种品质并不存在于物体本身，它存在于人的心目中。美是人看到物体时在心中油然而生的一种感受。某人在一个物体上看到的是丑陋，而另一个人看到的则是美。可见，人对美和丑的情感是不同的；审美标准是多极的，不稳定的。虽然休谟坚信确有普遍的情趣标准，但是他承认要找到真正的美和丑的标准是徒劳的。他说："我们徒劳地寻找可以用来调和各种矛盾情感的标准。"

诗中的美往往是建立在虚构、夸张、隐喻或歪曲诗的用词的原意之上。如果禁止使用任何富有想象力的诙谐妙语，刻意把每句话都写得像几何学那样准确，那是违背批评学的规律的。但是，虽然诗可以脱离准确的真实性，却不能超越艺术的规则。这种艺术规则或者是因为作者有天才，生来就掌握，或者是因为作者善于观察。

虽然艺术的一般规则是建立在经验和对人性共同情感的观察上，但是我们不能设想在所有情况下作家对这些规则都感到满意。人的感情受内心和外部环境的影响；它是十分纤细、微妙的。如果外部环境不好，或作者的心境不好，就会直接影响创作。因此，创作时既要有良好的外部环境，也要有良好的心境。所谓良好的心境就是平和的心绪，思想的集中，对审美对象的全神贯注。唯如此，才能发现物体的美。

有的作品的美能经久不衰，如荷马的史诗在两千多年前受到希腊人和罗马人的喜爱，至今在巴黎和伦敦仍是人们敬佩的杰作。世事沧桑，但岁月仍不能淹没他的伟大的作品的光彩。所以，真正的美是经得起时间的考验的。偏见和忌妒也不能抹杀美。

由此可见，尽管品位繁多，且变幻无常，但是什么值得赞扬，什么应该批评，总是有规可循的。

品位实为一种判断，而判断本质上是依靠经验而不是依赖理性。艺术的原则是建立在经验上的。是经验，而不是理性，告诉我们什么给我们带来愉快，什么给我们带来痛苦。这同判断正确与谬误不同。

要发现艺术的规则，读者和批评家必须依靠"人性共同的情感"。但是一个批评家的情感往往受到时间、地点和环境的影响。确定品位的标准，必须有"一种完全平和的心境"，亦即人的心境处于一种心平气和的状态。在这种心境中，人摆脱了盛怒、偏见，不迎合时尚。只有这样，人才能集中思想对鉴赏的物体进行仔细的品味，发挥自己的想象力。

要有情感，要对事物作出正确的判断，自然需要人的感官处于正常状态。发高烧的人尝不出香味；害黄疸病的人看不清颜色。就内心而言，缺乏想象力的人也不可能看到事物的美。味觉好，才能品味出混杂在一起的各种差别细微的味道。精神上的品位也一样。精神品位强的人一眼就能看出物体的美和丑。因此，完美的人必然具有完美的感觉和感情。

要能欣赏、判断美，就需要不断实践，即对不同类别的美进行比较。有比较才能鉴别。对各种美不进行比较的人是没有资格对美发表意见的。而批评家要正确地判断物体的美也必须不抱任何偏见。除了对美的载体进行检验和鉴别外，不让任何杂念进入自己的头脑。偏见对正确的判断具有破坏性，阻碍智力机能的运作，腐蚀我们的审美情感和审美力。

因此，虽然品位的原则是普遍的，对所有的人说来几乎都是一样的，但是极少有人有资格对所有的艺术作品都作出判断，或者能把他们的情感看作是美的标准。因为人的内心感受能力很难达到完美无缺的境地。如果批评家不敏锐，他就不能观察到许多细微的特点。如果他的判断力没有足够的实践，在判断时就会出现困惑和犹豫。如果不进行比较，那些毫无价值的美，甚至是缺陷而不是美，倒成了被赞美的对象。如果批评者有偏见，他所有的自然情感都会遭到破坏。如果感觉迟钝，他也不可能鉴赏美。因此，高超的批评家应具备以下特点：敏锐的观察力、实践、比较、无偏见和灵敏的感官。

这样的批评家哪里去找？休谟自己也难以作出回答。

品位的标准也并不像它看起来那样容易确定。

什么是美，什么是丑，其界限有时难以分清。原因有二：一是人的性情不同。二是不同的时代不同的国家有着不同的风俗习惯和规矩，因此对事物也就存在着不同的看法。虽然休谟坚信有普遍的品位标准，但是由于上述差异的存在，普遍的品位标准是难以找到的。他承认，某些审美的矛盾简直是不可能解决的。他举例说，年轻人血气方刚，自然易为温柔、性爱的形象所动。而年事较高者则喜欢哲学思考，考虑处世哲学和节制情欲。人的品位不同：有的人更喜爱崇高美，有的人更喜爱温柔美，有的人则喜欢开玩笑。批评家不能凭自己的喜好来判断优劣美丑。

David Hume (1711—1776)

Of the Standard of Taste

The great variety of taste, as well as of opinion, which prevails in the world, is too obvious not to have fallen under everyone's observation. Men of the most confined knowledge are able to remark a difference of taste in the narrow circle of their acquaintance, even where the persons have been educated under the same government, and have early imbibed the same prejudices. But those, who can enlarge their view to contemplate distant nations and remote ages, are still more surprised at the great inconsistence and contrariety. We are apt to call barbarous whatever departs widely from our own taste and apprehension: but soon find the epithet of reproach retorted on us. And the highest arrogance and self-conceit is at last startled, on observing an equal assurance on all sides, and scruples, amidst such a contest of sentiment, to pronounce positively in its own favor.

As this variety of taste is obvious to the most careless inquirer; so will it be found, on examination, to be still greater in reality than in appearance. The sentiments of men often differ with regard to beauty and deformity of all kinds, even while their general discourse is the same. There are certain terms in every language, which import blame, and others praise; and all men, who use the same tongue, must agree in their application of them. Every voice is united in applauding elegance, propriety, simplicity, spirit in writing; and in blaming fustian, affectation, coldness, and a false brilliancy: but when critics come to particulars, this seeming unanimity vanishes; and it is found, that they had affixed a very different meaning to their expressions. In all matters of opinion and science, the case is opposite: The difference among men is there oftener found to lie in generals than in particulars; and to be less in reality than in appearance. An explanation of the terms commonly ends the controversy; and the disputants are surprised to find, that they had been quarreling, while at bottom they agreed in their judgment.

Those who found morality on sentiment, more than on reason, are inclined to comprehend ethics under the former observation, and to maintain, that, in all questions, which regard conduct and manners, the difference among men is really greater than at first sight it appears. It is indeed obvious that writers of all nations and all ages concur in applauding justice, humanity, magnanimity, prudence, veracity; and in blaming the opposite qualities. Even poets and other authors, whose compositions are chiefly calculated to please the imagination, are yet found, from Homer down to Fénelon[1], to inculcate the same moral precepts, and to bestow their applause and blame on the same virtues and vices. This great unanimity is usually ascribed to the influence of plain reason; which, in all these cases, maintains similar sentiments in all men, and prevents those controversies, to which the abstract sciences are so much exposed. So far as the unanimity is real, this account may be admitted as satisfactory: but we must also allow that some part of the seeming harmony in morals may be accounted for from the very nature of language. The word *virtue*, with its equivalent in every tongue, implies praise; as that of *vice* does blame: And no one, without the most obvious and grossest impropriety, could affix reproach to a term, which in general acceptation is understood in a good sense; or bestow applause, where the idiom requires disapprobation. Homer's general precepts, where he delivers any such, will never be controverted; but it is obvious, that, when he draws particular pictures of manners, and represents heroism in Achilles and prudence in Ulysses[2], he intermixes a much greater degree of ferocity in the former, and of cunning and fraud in the latter, than Fénelon would admit of. The sage Ulysses in the Greek poet seems to delight in lies and fictions, and often employs them without any necessity or even advantage: But his more scrupulous son, in the French epic writer, exposes himself to the most imminent perils, rather than depart from the most exact line of truth and veracity.

The admirers and followers of the Alcoran[3] insist on the excellent moral precepts interspersed throughout that wild and absurd performance. But it is to be supposed, that the Arabic words, which correspond to the English, equity, justice, temperance, meekness, charity, were such as, from the constant use of that tongue, must always be taken in a good sense; and it would have argued the greatest ignorance, not of morals, but of language, to have mentioned them with any epithets, besides those of applause and approbation. But would we know, whether the pretended prophet had really attained a just sentiment of morals? Let us attend to his narration; and we shall soon find, that he bestows praise on such instances of treachery, inhumanity, cruelty, revenge, bigotry, as are utterly incompatible with civilized society. No steady rule of right seems there to be attained to; and every action is blamed or praised, so far only as it is beneficial or hurtful to the true believers.

The merit of delivering true general precepts in ethics is indeed very small. Whoever recommends any moral virtues, really does no more than is implied in the terms themselves. That people, who invented the word *charity*, and used it in a good sense, inculcated more clearly and much more efficaciously, the precept, "be charitable, " than any pretended legislator or prophet, who should insert such a maxim in his writings. Of all expressions, those, which, together with their other meaning, imply a degree either of blame or approbation, are the least liable to be perverted or mistaken.

It is natural for us to seek a standard of taste; a rule by which the various sentiments of men may be reconciled; at least, a decision afforded, confirming one sentiment, and condemning another.

There is a species of philosophy, which cuts off all hopes of success in such an attempt, and represents the impossibility of ever attaining any standard of taste. The difference, it is said, is very wide between judgment and sentiment. All sentiment is right; because sentiment has a reference to nothing beyond itself, and is always real, wherever a man is conscious of it. But all determinations of the understanding are not right; because they have a reference to something beyond themselves, to wit, real matter of fact; and are not always conformable to that standard. Among a thousand different opinions which different men may entertain of the same subject, there is one, and but one, that is just and true; and the only difficulty is to fix and ascertain it. On the contrary, a thousand different sentiments, excited by the same object, are all right: because no sentiment represents what is really in the object. It only marks a certain conformity or relation between the object and the organs or faculties of the mind; and if that conformity did not really exist, the sentiment could never possibly have being. Beauty is no quality in things themselves: it exists merely in the mind which contemplates them; and each mind perceives a different beauty. One person may even perceive deformity, where another is sensible of beauty; and every individual ought to acquiesce in his own sentiment, without pretending to regulate those of others. To seek the real beauty, or real deformity, is as fruitless an inquiry, as to pretend to ascertain the real sweet or real bitter. According to the disposition of the organs, the same object may be both sweet and bitter; and the proverb has justly determined it to be fruitless to dispute concerning tastes. It is very natural, and even quite necessary, to extend this axiom to mental, as well as bodily taste; and thus common sense, which is so often at variance with philosophy, especially with the skeptical kind, is found, in one instance at least, to agree in pronouncing the same decision.

But though this axiom, by passing into a proverb, seems to have attained the sanction of common sense; there is certainly a species of common sense which opposes it, at least serves to modify and restrain it. Whoever would assert an equality of genius and elegance between Ogibly and Milton,[4] or Bunyan and Addison, would be thought to defend no less an extravagance, than if he had maintained a molehill to be as high as Tenerife[5], or a pond as extensive as the ocean. Though there may be found persons, who give the preference to the former authors, no one pays attention to such a taste; and we pronounce without scruple the sentiment of these pretended critics to be absurd and ridiculous. The principle of the natural equality of tastes is then totally forgot, and while we admit it on some occasions, where the objects seem near an equality, it appears an extravagant paradox, or rather a palpable absurdity, where objects so disproportioned are compared together.

It is evident that none of the rules of composition are fixed by reasoning *a priori*[6], or can be esteemed abstract conclusions of the understanding, from comparing those habitudes and relations of ideas, which are eternal and immutable. Their foundation is the same with that of all the practical sciences, experience; nor are they anything but general observations, concerning what has been universally found to please in all countries and in all ages. Many of the beauties of poetry and even of eloquence are founded on falsehood and fiction, on hyperboles, metaphors, and an abuse or perversion of terms from their natural meaning. To check the sallies of the imagination, and to reduce every expression to geometrical truth and exactness, would be the most contrary to the laws of criticism; because it would produce a work, which, by universal experience, has been found the most insipid and disagreeable. But though poetry can never submit to exact truth, it must be confined by rules of art, discovered to the author either by genius or observation. If some negligent or irregular writers have pleased, they have not pleased by their transgressions of rule or order, but in spite of these transgressions: They have possessed other beauties, which were conformable to just criticism; and the force of these beauties has been able to overpower censure, and give the mind a satisfaction superior to the disgust arising from the blemishes. Ariosto[7] pleases; but not by his monstrous and improbable fictions, by his bizarre mixture of the serious and comic styles, by the want of coherence in his stories, or by the continual interruptions of his narration. He charms by the force and clearness of his expression, by the readiness and variety of his inventions, and by his natural pictures of the passions, especially those of the gay and amorous kind: And however his faults may diminish our satisfaction, they are not able entirely to destroy it. Did our pleasure really arise from those parts of his poem, which we denominate faults, this would be no objection to criticism in general: It would only be an objection to those particular rules of criticism, which would establish such circumstances to be faults, and would represent them as universally blamable. If they are found to please, they cannot be faults; let the pleasure, which they produce, be ever so unexpected and unaccountable.

But though all the general rules of art are founded only on experience and on the observation of the common sentiments of human nature, we must not imagine, that, on every occasion, the feelings of men will be conformable to these rules. Those finer emotions of the mind are of a very tender and delicate nature, and require the concurrence of many favorable circumstances to make them play with facility and exactness, according to their general and established principles. The least exterior hindrance to such small springs, or the least internal disorder, disturbs their motion, and confounds the operation of the whole machine. When we would make an experiment of this nature, and would try the force of any beauty or deformity, we must choose with care a proper time and place, and bring the fancy to a suitable situation and disposition. A perfect serenity of mind, a recollection of thought, a due attention to the object; if any of these circumstances be wanting, our experiment will be fallacious, and we shall be unable to judge of the catholic and universal beauty. The relation, which nature has placed between the form and the sentiment, will at least be more obscure; and it will require greater accuracy to trace and discern it. We shall be able to ascertain its influence not so much from the operation of each particular beauty, as from the durable admiration, which attends those works, that have survived all the caprices of mode and fashion, all the mistakes of ignorance and envy.

The same Homer, who pleased at Athens and Rome two thousand years ago, is still admired at Paris and at London. All the changes of climate, government, religion, and language, have not been able to obscure his glory. Authority or prejudice may give a temporary vogue to a bad poet or orator; but his reputation will never be durable or general. When his compositions are examined by posterity or by foreigners, the enchantment is dissipated, and his faults appear in their true colors. On the contrary, a real genius, the longer his works endure, and the more wide they are spread, the more sincere is the admiration which he meets with. Envy and jealousy have too much place in a narrow circle; and even familiar acquaintance with his person may diminish the applause due to his performances: but when these obstructions are removed, the beauties, which are naturally fitted to excite agreeable sentiments, immediately display their energy; and while the world endures, they maintain their authority over the minds of men.

It appears then, that, amidst all the variety and caprice of taste, there are certain general principles of approbation or blame, whose influence a careful eye may trace in all operations of the mind. Some particular forms or qualities, from the original structures of the internal fabric, are calculated to please, and others displease; and if they fail of their effect in any particular instance, it is from some apparent defect or imperfection in the organ. A man in a fever would not insist on his palate as able to decide concerning flavors; nor would one, affected with the jaundice, pretend to give a verdict with regard to colors. In each creature, there is a sound and defective state; and the former alone can be supposed to afford us a true standard of taste and sentiment. If, in the sound state of the organ, there be an entire or a considerable uniformity of sentiment among men, we may thence derive an idea of the perfect beauty; in like manner as the appearance of objects in daylight, to the eye of a man in health, is denominated their true and real color, even while color is allowed to be merely a phantasm of the senses.

Many and frequent are the defects in the internal organs which prevent or weaken the influence of those general principles, on which depends our sentiment of beauty or deformity. Though some objects, by the structure of the mind, be naturally calculated to give pleasure, it is not to be expected, that in every individual the pleasure will be equally felt. Particular incidents and situations occur, which either throw a false light on the objects, or hinder the true from conveying to the imagination the proper sentiment and perception.

One obvious cause, why many feel not the proper sentiment of beauty, is the want of that delicacy of imagination, which is requisite to convey a sensibility of those finer emotions. This delicacy everyone pretends to: everyone talks of it; and would reduce every kind of taste or sentiment to its standard. But as our intention in this essay is to mingle some light of the understanding with the feeling of sentiment, it will be proper to give a more accurate definition of delicacy, than has hitherto been attempted. And not to draw our philosophy from too profound a source, we shall have recourse to a noted story in *Don Quixote*[8].

"It is with good reason, " says Sancho[9] to the squire with the great nose, "that I pretend to have a judgment in wine: this is a quality hereditary in our family. Two of my kinsmen were once called to give their opinion of a hogshead, which was supposed to be excellent, being old and of a good vintage. One of them tastes it; considers it; and after mature reflection pronounces the wine to be good, were it not for a small taste of leather, which he perceived in it. The other, after using the same precautions, gives also his verdict in favor of the wine; but with the reserve of a taste of iron, which he could easily distinguish. You cannot imagine how much they were both ridiculed for their judgment. But who laughed in the end? On emptying the hogshead, there was found at the bottom, an old key with a leathern thong tied to it."

The great resemblance between mental and bodily taste will easily teach us to apply this story. Though it be certain that beauty and deformity, more than sweet and bitter, are not qualities in objects, but belong entirely to the sentiment, internal or external; it must be allowed, that there are certain qualities in objects, which are fitted by nature to produce those particular feelings. Now as these qualities may be found in a small degree, or may be mixed and confounded with each other, it often happens, that the taste is not affected with such minute qualities, or is not able to distinguish all the particular flavors, amidst the disorder, in which they are presented. Where the organs are so fine, as to allow nothing to escape them; and at the same time so exact as to perceive every ingredient in the composition: this we call delicacy of taste, where we employ these terms in the literal or metaphorical sense. Here then the general rules of beauty are of use; being drawn from established models, and from the observation of what pleases or displeases, when presented singly and in a high degree: and if the same qualities, in a continued composition and in a smaller degree, affect not the organs with a sensible delight or uneasiness, we exclude the person from all pretensions to this delicacy. To produce these general rules or avowed patterns of composition is like finding the key with the leathern thong; which justified the verdict of Sancho's kinsmen, and confounded those pretended judges who had condemned them. Though the hogshead had never been emptied, the taste of the one was still equally delicate, and that of the other equally dull and languid; but it would have been more difficult to have proved the superiority of the former, to the conviction of every bystander. In like manner, though the beauties of writing had never been methodized, or reduced to general principles; though no excellent models had ever been acknowledged; the different degrees of taste would still have subsisted, and the judgment of one man been preferable to that of another; but it would not have been so easy to silence the bad critic, who might always insist upon his particular sentiment, and refuse to submit to his antagonist. But when we show him an avowed principle of art; when we illustrate this principle by examples, whose operation, from his own particular taste, he acknowledges to be conformable to the principle; when we prove, that the same principle may be applied to the present case, where he did not perceive or feel its influence: he must conclude, upon the whole, that the fault lies in himself, and that he wants the delicacy, which is requisite to make him sensible of every beauty and every blemish, in any composition or discourse.

It is acknowledged to be the perfection of every sense or faculty, to perceive with exactness its most minute objects, and allow nothing to escape its notice and observation. The smaller the objects are, which become sensible to the eye, the finer is that organ, and the more elaborate its make and composition. A good palate is not tried by strong flavors; but by a mixture of small ingredients, where we are still sensible of each part, notwithstanding its minuteness and its confusion with the rest. In like manner, a quick and acute perception of beauty and deformity must be the perfection of our mental taste; nor can a man be satisfied with himself while he suspects, that any excellence or blemish in a discourse has passed him unobserved. In this case, the perfection of the man, and the perfection of the sense or feeling, are found to be united. A very delicate palate, on many occasions, may be a great inconvenience both to a man himself and to his friends: but a delicate taste of wit or beauty must always be a desirable quality; because it is the source of all the finest and most innocent enjoyments, of which human nature is susceptible. In this decision the sentiments of all mankind are agreed. Wherever you can ascertain a delicacy of taste, it is sure to meet with approbation; and the best way of ascertaining it is to appeal to those models and principles, which have been established by the uniform consent and experience of nations and ages.

But though there be naturally a wide difference in point of delicacy between one person and another, nothing tends further to increase and improve this talent, than practice in a particular art, and the frequent survey or contemplation of a particular species of beauty. When objects of any kind are first presented to the eye or imagination, the sentiment, which attends them, is obscure and confused; and the mind is, in a great measure, incapable of pronouncing concerning their merits or defects. The taste cannot perceive the several excellences of the performance; much less distinguish the particular character of each excellency, and ascertain its quality and degree. If it pronounces the whole in general to be beautiful or deformed, it is the utmost that can be expected; and even this judgment, a person, so unpracticed, will be apt to deliver with great hesitation and reserve. But allow him to acquire experience in those objects, his feeling becomes more exact and nice: he not only perceives the beauties and defects of each part, but marks the distinguishing species of each quality, and assigns it suitable praise or blame. A clear and distinct sentiment attends him through the whole survey of the objects; and he discerns that very degree and kind of approbation or displeasure, which each part is naturally fitted to produce. The mist dissipates, which seemed formerly to hang over the object: the organ acquires greater perfection in its operations; and can pronounce, without danger of mistake, concerning the merits of every performance. In a word, the same address and dexterity, which practice gives to the execution of any work, is also acquired by the same means, in the judging of it.

So advantageous is practice to the discernment of beauty, that, before we can give judgment on any work of importance, it will even be requisite, that that very individual performance be more than once perused by us, and be surveyed in different lights with attention and deliberation. There is a flutter or hurry of thought which attends the first perusal of any piece, and which confounds the genuine sentiment of beauty. The relation of the parts is not discerned: the true characters of style are little distinguished: the several perfections and defects seem wrapped up in a species of confusion, and present themselves indistinctly to the imagination. Not to mention, that there is a species of beauty, which, as it is florid and superficial, pleases at first; but being found incompatible with a just expression either of reason or passion, soon palls upon the taste, and is then rejected with disdain, at least rated at much lower value.

It is impossible to continue in the practice of contemplating any order of beauty, without being frequently obliged to form comparisons between the several species and degrees of excellence, and estimating their proportion to each other. A man, who has had no opportunity of comparing the different kinds of beauty, is indeed totally unqualified to pronounce an opinion with regard to any object presented to him. By comparison alone we fix the epithets of praise or blame, and learn how to assign the due degree of each. The coarsest daubing contains a certain luster of colors and exactness of imitation, which are so far beauties, and would affect the mind of a peasant or Indian with the highest admiration. The most vulgar ballads are not entirely destitute of harmony or nature; and none but a person, familiarized to superior beauties would pronounce their numbers harsh, or narration uninteresting. A great inferiority of beauty gives pain to a person conversant in the highest excellence of the kind, and is for that reason pronounced a deformity: as the most finished object, with which we are acquainted, is naturally supposed to have reached the pinnacle of perfection, and to be entitled to the highest applause. One accustomed to see, and examine, and weigh the several performances, admired in different ages and nations, can only rate the merits of a work exhibited to his view, and assign its proper rank among the productions of genius.

But to enable a critic the more fully to execute this undertaking, he must preserve his mind free from all prejudice, and allow nothing to enter into his consideration, but the very object which is submitted to his examination. We may observe, that every work of art, in order to produce its due effect on the mind, must be surveyed in a certain point of view, and cannot be fully relished by persons, whose situation, real or imaginary, is not conformable to that which is required by the performance. An orator addresses himself to a particular audience, and must have a regard to their particular genius, interest, opinions, passions, and prejudices; otherwise he hopes in vain to govern their resolutions, and inflame their affections. Should they even have entertained some prepossessions against him, however unreasonable, he must not overlook this disadvantage; but, before he enters upon the subject, must endeavor to conciliate their affection, and acquire their good graces. A critic of a different age or nation, who should peruse this discourse, must have all these circumstances in his eye, and must place himself in the same situation as the audience, in order to form a true judgment of the oration. In like manner, when any work is addressed to the public, though I should have a friendship or enmity with the author, I must depart from this situation; and considering myself as a man in general, forget, if possible, my individual being and my peculiar circumstances. A person influenced by prejudice, complies not with this condition; but obstinately maintains his natural position, without placing himself in that point of view, which the performance supposes. If the work be addressed to persons of a different age or nation, he makes no allowance for their peculiar views and prejudices; but, full of the manners of his own age and country, rashly condemns what seemed admirable in the eyes of those for whom alone the discourse was calculated. If the work be executed for the public, he never sufficiently enlarges his comprehension, or forgets his interest as a friend or enemy, as a rival or commentator. By this means, his sentiments are perverted; nor have the same beauties and blemishes the same influence upon him, as if he had imposed a proper violence on his imagination, and had forgotten himself for a moment. So far his taste evidently departs from the true standard; and of consequence loses all credit and authority.

It is well known, that in all questions, submitted to the understanding, prejudice is destructive of sound judgment, and perverts all operations of the intellectual faculties: it is no less contrary to good taste; nor has it less influence to corrupt out sentiment of beauty. It belongs to good sense to check its influence in both cases; and in this respect, as well as in many others, reason, if not an essential part of taste, is at least requisite to the operations of this latter faculty. In all the nobler productions of genius, there is a mutual relation and correspondence of parts; nor can either the beauties or blemishes be perceived by him, whose thought is not capacious enough to comprehend all those parts, and compare them with each other, in order to perceive the consistence and uniformity of the whole. Every work of art has also a certain end or purpose, for which it is calculated; and is to be deemed more or less perfect, as it is more or less fitted to attain this end. The object of eloquence is to persuade, of history to instruct, of poetry to please by means of the passions and the imagination. These ends we must carry constantly in our view, when we peruse any performance; and we must be able to judge how far the means employed are adapted to their respective purposes. Besides every kind of composition, even the most poetical, is nothing but a chain of propositions and reasonings; not always, indeed, the justest and most exact, but still plausible and specious, however disguised by the coloring of the imagination. The persons introduced in tragedy and epic poetry, must be represented as reasoning, and thinking, and concluding, and acting, suitably to their character and circumstances; and without judgment, as well as taste and invention, a poet can never hope to succeed in so delicate an undertaking. Not to mention, that the same excellence of faculties which contributes to the improvement of reason, the same clearness of conception, the same exactness of distinction, the same vivacity of apprehension, are essential to the operations of true taste, and are its infallible concomitants. It seldom, or never happens, that a man of sense, who has experience in any art, cannot judge of its beauty; and it is no less rare to meet with a man who has a just taste without a sound understanding.

Thus, though the principles of taste be universal, and, nearly, if not entirely the same in all men; yet few are qualified to give judgment on any work of art, or establish their own sentiment as the standard of beauty. The organs of internal sensation are seldom so perfect as to allow the general principles their full play, and produce a feeling correspondent to those principles. They either labor under some defect, or are vitiated by some disorder; and by that means, excite a sentiment, which may be pronounced erroneous. When the critic has no delicacy, he judges without any distinction, and is only affected by the grosser and more palpable qualities of the object: the finer touches pass unnoticed and disregarded. Where he is not aided by practice, his verdict is attended with confusion and hesitation. Where no comparison has been employed, the most frivolous beauties, such as rather merit the name of defects, are the objects of his admiration. Where he lies under the influence of prejudice, all his natural sentiments are perverted. Where good sense is wanting, he is not qualified to discern the beauties of design and reasoning, which are the highest and most excellent. Under some or other of these imperfections, the generality of men labor; and hence a true judge in the finer arts is observed, even during the most polished ages, to be so rare a character: strong sense, united to delicate sentiment, improved by practice, perfected by comparison, and cleared of all prejudice, can alone entitle critics to this valuable character; and the joint verdict of such, wherever they are to be found, is the true standard of taste and beauty.

But where are such critics to be found? By what marks are they to be known? How to distinguish them from pretenders? These questions are embarrassing; and seem to throw us back into the same uncertainty, from which, during the course of this essay, we have endeavored to extricate ourselves.

But if we consider the matter aright, these are questions of fact, not of sentiment. Whether any particular person be endowed with good sense and a delicate imagination, free from prejudice, may often be the subject of dispute, and be liable to great discussion and inquiry: But that such a character is valuable and estimable will be agreed in by all mankind. Where these doubts occur, men can do no more than in other disputable questions, which are submitted to the understanding: they must produce the best arguments, that their invention suggests to them; they must acknowledge a true and decisive standard to exist somewhere, to wit, real existence and matter of fact; and they must have indulgence to such as differ from them in their appeals to this standard. It is sufficient for our present purpose, if we have proved, that the taste of all individuals is not upon an equal footing, and that some men in general, however difficult to be particularly pitched upon, will be acknowledged by universal sentiment to have a preference above others.

But in reality the difficulty of finding, even in particulars, the standard of taste, is not so great as it is represented. Though in speculation, we may readily avow a certain criterion in science and deny it in sentiment, the matter is found in practice to be much more hard to ascertain in the former case than in the latter. Theories of abstract philosophy, systems of profound theology, have prevailed during one age: in a successive period, these have been universally exploded: their absurdity has been detected: other theories and systems have supplied their place, which again gave place to their successors: and nothing has been experienced more liable to the revolutions of chance and fashion than these pretended decisions of science. The case is not the same with beauties of eloquence and poetry. Just expressions of passion and nature are sure, after a little time, to gain public applause, which they maintain forever. Aristotle, and Plato, and Epicurus[10], and Descartes[11], may successively yield to each other: but Terence and Virgil maintain a universal, undisputed empire over the minds of men. The abstract philosophy of Cicero has lost its credit: the vehemence of his oratory is still the object of our admiration.

Though men of delicate taste be rare, they are easily to be distinguished in society, by the soundness of their understanding and the superiority of their faculties above the rest of mankind. The ascendant, which they acquire, gives a prevalance to that lively approbation, with which they receive any productions of genius, and renders it generally predominant. Many men, when left to themselves, have but a faint and dubious perception of beauty, who yet are capable of relishing any fine stroke, which is pointed out to them. Every convert to the admiration of the real poet or orator is the cause of some new conversion. And though prejudices may prevail for a time, they never unite in celebrating any rival to the true genius, but yield at last to the force of nature and just sentiment. Thus, though a civilized nation may easily be mistaken in the choice of their admired philosopher, they never have been found long to err, in their affection for a favorite epic or tragic author.

But notwithstanding all our endeavors to fix a standard of taste, and reconcile the discordant apprehensions of men, there still remain two sources of variation, which are not sufficient indeed to confound all the boundaries of beauty and deformity, but will often serve to produce a difference in the degrees of our approbation or blame. The one is the different humors of particular men; the other, the particular manners and opinions of our age and country. The general principles of taste are uniform in human nature: where men vary in their judgments, some defect or perversion in the faculties may commonly be remarked; proceeding either from prejudice, from want of practice, or want of delicacy; and there is just reason for approving one taste, and condemning another. But where there is such a diversity in the internal frame or external situation as is entirely blameless on both sides, and leaves no room to give one the preference above the other; in that case a certain degree of diversity in judgment is unavoidable, and we seek in vain for a standard, by which we can reconcile the contrary sentiments.

A young man, whose passions are warm, will be more sensibly touched with amorous and tender images, than a man more advanced in years, who takes pleasure in wise, philosophical reflections concerning the conduct of life and moderation of the passions. At twenty, Ovid may be the favorite author; Horace at forty; and perhaps Tacitus[12] at fifty. Vainly would we, in such cases, endeavor to enter into the sentiments of others, and divest ourselves of those propensities, which are natural to us. We choose our favorite author as we do our friend, from a conformity of humor and disposition. Mirth or passion, sentiment or reflection; whichever of these most predominates in our temper, it gives us a peculiar sympathy with the writer who resembles us.

One person is more pleased with the sublime; another with the tender; a third with raillery. One has a strong sensibility to blemishes, and is extremely studious of correctness: another has a more lively feeling of beauties, and pardons twenty absurdities and defects for one elevated or pathetic stroke. The ear of this man is entirely turned toward conciseness and energy; that man is delighted with a copious, rich, and harmonious expression. Simplicity is affected by one; ornament by another. Comedy, tragedy, satire, odes, have each its partisans, who prefer that particular species of writing to all others. It is plainly an error in a critic, to confine his approbation to one species or style of writing, and condemn all the rest. But it is almost impossible not to feel a predilection for that which suits our particular turn and disposition. Such preferences are innocent and unavoidable, and can never reasonably be the object of dispute, because there is no standard, by which they can be decided.

For a like reason, we are more pleased, in the course of our reading, with pictures and characters, that resemble objects which are found in our own age or country, than with those which describe a different set of customs. It is not without some effort, that we reconcile ourselves to the simplicity of ancient manners, and behold princesses carrying water from the spring, and kings and heroes dressing their own victuals. We may allow in general, that the representation of such manners is no fault in the author, nor deformity in the piece; but we are not so sensibly touched with them. For this reason, comedy is not easily transferred from one age or nation to another. A Frenchman or Englishman is not pleased with the *Andria*[13] of Terence, or *Clitia* of Machiavel[14]; where the fine lady, upon whom all the play turns, never once appears to the spectators, but is always kept behind the scenes, suitably to the reserved humor of the ancient Greeks and modern Italians. A man of learning and reflection can make allowance for these peculiarities of manners; but a common audience can never divest themselves so far of their usual ideas and sentiments, as to relish pictures which in no wise resemble them.

But here there occurs a reflection, which may, perhaps, be useful in examining the celebrated controversy concerning ancient and modern learning; where we often find the one side excusing any seeming absurdity in the ancients from the manners of the age, and the other refusing to admit this excuse, or at least, admitting it only as an apology for the author, not for the performance. In my opinion, the proper boundaries in this subject have seldom been fixed between the contending parties. Where any innocent peculiarities of manners are represented, such as those above mentioned, they ought certainly to be admitted; and a man, who is shocked with them, gives an evident proof of false delicacy and refinement. The poet's monument more durable than brass must fall to the ground like common brick or clay, were men to make no allowance for the continual revolutions of manners and customs, and would admit of nothing but what was suitable to the prevailing fashion. Must we throw aside the pictures of our ancestors, because of their ruffs and farthingales? But where the ideas of morality and decency alter from one age to another, and where vicious manners are described, without being marked with the proper characters of blame and disapprobation; this must be allowed to disfigure the poem, and to be a real deformity. I cannot, nor is it proper I should, enter into such sentiments; and however I may excuse the poet, on account of the manners of his age, I never can relish the composition. The want of humanity and of decency, so conspicuous in the characters drawn by several of the ancient poets, even sometimes by Homer and the Greek tragedians, diminishes considerably the merit of their noble performances, and gives modern authors an advantage over them. We are not interested in the fortunes and sentiments of such rough heroes: we are displeased to find the limits of vice and virtue so much confounded: and whatever indulgence we may give to the writer on account of his prejudices, we cannot prevail on ourselves to enter into his sentiments, or bear an affection to characters, which we plainly discover to be blamable.

The case is not the same with moral principles, as with speculative opinions of any kind. These are in continual flux and revolution. The son embraces a different system from the father. Nay, there scarcely is any man, who can boast of great constance and uniformity in this particular. Whatever speculative errors may be found in the polite writings of any age or country, they detract but little from the value of those compositions. There needs but a certain turn of thought or imagination to make us enter into all the opinions, which then prevailed, and relish the sentiments or conclusions derived from them. But a very violent effort is requisite to change our judgment of manners, and excite sentiments of approbation or blame, love or hatred, different from those to which the mind from long custom has been familiarized. And where a man is confident of the rectitude of that moral standard, by which he judges, he is justly jealous of it, and will not pervert the sentiments of his heart for a moment, in complaisance to any writer whatsoever.

Of all speculative errors, those, which regard religion, are the most excusable in compositions of genius; nor is it ever permitted to judge of the civility or wisdom of any people, or even of single persons, by the grossness or refinement of their theological principles. The same good sense, that directs men in the ordinary occurrences of life, is not harkened to in religious matters, which are supposed to be placed altogether above the cognizance of human reason. On this account, all the absurdities of the pagan system of theology must be overlooked by every critic, who would pretend to form a just notion of ancient poetry; and our posterity, in their turn, must have the same indulgence to their forefathers. No religious principles can ever be imputed as a fault to any poet, while they remain merely principles, and take no such strong possession of his heart, as to lay him under the imputation of bigotry or superstition. Where that happens, they confound the sentiments of morality, and alter the natural boundaries of vice and virtue. They are therefore eternal blemishes, according to the principle above mentioned; nor are the prejudices and false opinions of the age sufficient to justify them.

It is essential to the Roman Catholic religion to inspire a violent hatred of every other worship, and to represent all pagans, Mahometans[15], and heretics as the objects of divine wrath and vengeance. Such sentiments, though they are in reality very blamable, are considered as virtues by the zealots of that communion, and are represented in their tragedies and epic poems as a kind of divine heroism. This bigotry has disfigured two very fine tragedies of the French theater, *Polyeucte* and *Athalie*[16]; where an intemperate zeal for particular modes of worship is set off with all the pomp imaginable, and forms the predominant character of the heroes. "What is this, " says the sublime Joad to Josabet, finding her in discourse with Mathan,[17] the priest of Baal, "does the daughter of David speak to this traitor? Are you not afraid, lest the earth should open and pour forth flames to devour you both? Or lest these holy walls should fall and crush you together? What is his purpose?

Why comes that enemy of God hither to poison the air, which we breathe, with his horrid presence? " Such sentiments are received with great applause on the theater of Paris; but at London the spectators would be full as much pleased to hear Achilles tell Agamemnon[18], that he was a dog in his forehead, and a deer in his heart, or Jupiter threaten Juno[19] with a sound drubbing, if she will not be quiet.

Religious principles are also a blemish in any polite composition, when they rise up to superstition, and intrude themselves into every sentiment, however remote from any connection with religion. It is no excuse for the poet, that the customs of his country had burthened life with so many religious ceremonies and observances, that no part of it was exempt from that yoke. It must forever be ridiculous in Petrarch to compare his mistress Laura, to Jesus Christ. Nor is it less ridiculous in that agreeable libertine, Boccace, very seriously to give thanks to God Almighty and the ladies, for their assistance in defending him against his enemies.

注释

1. Fénelon：费奈隆（1651—1715），17 世纪法国牧师和作家。
2. Ulysses：尤利西斯，即奥德修斯（Odysseus），希腊神话中的英雄。荷马史诗《奥德赛》和《伊利亚特》中的主人公。
3. the Alcoran：即《古兰经》（*The Koran*），伊斯兰教经典。
4. Ogibly and Milton：John Ogibly（约翰·奥格尔比，1600—1676），英国诗人、翻译家。John Milton（约翰·弥尔顿，1608—1674），英国诗人、政论家。
5. Tenerife：特内里费岛，加那利群岛（the Canary Islands）中的最大岛。
6. *a priori*：即 *apriori*，拉丁文，意为 from what is before。
7. Ariosto：阿里奥斯托（Lodovico Ariosto, 1474—1533），意大利诗人，其代表作为《疯狂的奥兰多》（*Orlando Furioso*）。
8. *Don Quixote*：西班牙作家塞万提斯的长篇小说《堂吉诃德》。
9. Sancho：即桑丘·潘沙（Sancho Panza），堂吉诃德的侍从。他是与充满幻想和理想主义的堂吉诃德恰成对比的小说人物。
10. Epicurus：伊壁鸠鲁（前 341—前 270），希腊著名哲学家。
11. Descartes：笛卡尔（1596—1650），法国哲学家、数学家。

12 Tacitus：塔西佗，公元 1 世纪至 2 世纪罗马历史学家。

13. *Andria*：泰伦斯在公元前 166 年写的第一部喜剧。

14. *Clitia* of Machiavel：马基雅弗利所写的喜剧 *Clitia*。

15. Mahometan：即 Moslem。

16. *Polyeucte* and *Athalie*：*Polyeucte*（《波里耶克特》）是 17 世纪法国诗人、戏剧家高乃依（Corneille）的作品。*Athalie*（《雅塔丽亚》）是 17 世纪法国戏剧家拉辛的作品。

17. ....Joad to Josabet...Mathan：Joad, Josabet, Mathan 均为剧中人物。

18. Agamemnon：阿伽门农，特洛伊战争中希腊联军统帅，后为其妻所杀。

19. Juno：朱诺，罗马神话中主神朱庇特之妻。朱诺即希腊神话中的赫拉（Hera）。

约翰逊 《〈莎士比亚戏剧集〉序言》

塞缪尔·约翰逊（1709—1784）

塞缪尔·约翰逊，英国诗人、批评家、散文家、语言学家和辞典编写者。说起英国文学，可以载入史册的名家很是不少，但是有两个作家在英国文学史中却以耀眼的光辉流芳百世。他们就是莎士比亚和约翰逊。我国读者知莎士比亚者甚多，知约翰逊者少。他们两人是英国文人中被引用得最多的人。莎士比亚以其经久不衰的戏剧享誉全球，约翰逊则以其博学多才闻名于世。他写的散文气势宏伟，兼有拉丁散文的典雅和英语散文的雄健；而文字的朴素和精练、文章结构的整齐匀称又使其散文风格独具魅力。《致切斯特菲尔德伯爵书》（"Letter to Lord Chesterfield"）短短一封信就充溢着让人非背下来吟诵不足以尽兴的绝妙名句。

他单枪匹马用 8 年多时间编纂了《英语辞典》（*A Dictionary of the English Language*, 1755）。这部词典收词 4 万。它虽然不是英国的第一部辞典，但却以词义精确、文学引语丰富著称。它的缺点是有错误和偏见。这部辞典的出版是辞书编纂史上一件大事，出版后在英国引起轰动，并被奉为权威性的著作。

1738 年，约翰逊发表了他的第一篇长诗《伦敦》（"London"），用讽刺的笔调抨击英国政治的腐败和城市生活的罪恶，并为贫苦的文人鸣不平。1765 年，他编注的 8 卷本《莎士比亚戏剧集》（*The Plays of William Shakespeare*）出版。他对莎剧的版本校勘、字义疏证、故事渊源等都有新的研究成果。《〈莎士比亚戏剧集〉序言》（"Preface to Shakespeare"）是一篇公认的经典性论文。在这篇论文中，他否定了古典主义戏剧的"三一律"，指出莎士比亚打破了"三一律"，仍写出了不朽的杰作。约翰逊另一部卓越的作品是《诗人传》（*The Lives of the Most Eminent English Poets*，1779—1781，共 52 篇），其中包括对弥尔顿、德莱顿、蒲柏等重要诗人的评论。

约翰逊强烈反对战争，为穷人和被压迫者呐喊，反对欧洲殖民主义，为黑人和其他土著人民的权利呼吁。这是他政治思想的可贵之处。他反对古典主义的"三一律"及其他条规，主张依据作品自身的优缺点评断一部作品。他被称为20世纪"`新批评派"之父。

今人对约翰逊的了解，除了他的作品外，应归功于他的朋友、传记家詹姆斯·鲍斯韦尔（James Boswell，1740—1795）。他常常跟随约翰逊，手拿笔和笔记本，随时随地记录下约翰逊的讲话，写出了著名传记《塞缪尔·约翰逊传》（*The Life of Samuel Johnson*）。他对约翰逊推崇备至，称他为"英国文坛的大可汗"。

在文学批评上他的两个重要观点是：一、对文学作品的批评判断要首先考虑道德。二、诗人（作家）在作品中所表现的应该是具有普遍性的人的感受，而不是其特殊性。这两点主张引起后人不少争论。18世纪后期和19世纪初的浪漫派诗人就反对这一观点，认为道德批评论太狭隘。他们认为诗人应该表现诗人个人的特殊感受和经历。尽管约翰逊的理论不无欠缺之处，他在文学批评上的一些精辟见解却令后人十分钦佩。

内容提要

约翰逊的文学艺术观点是现实主义。他反对放纵想象。他关注文学作品的道德问题，认为现实主义作家比浪漫主义作家更需要关注道德，因为浪漫主义作家写的传奇体的文学作品原本就是作者杜撰的一些脱离现实的离奇故事。而现实主义作家的作品因为是表现现实，就应该有真实性和正确性。

《〈莎士比亚戏剧集〉序言》这一标题给人一个印象，似乎它只谈莎士比亚戏剧。其实，文章的内容涉及许多文学艺术的重大问题。例如作家究竟是表现具有普遍性的人的感受，还是表现其特殊性。这历来是批评家和文人所争论的问题。

他首先指出，人们习惯崇尚已经去世的作家的古老作品，并非因为这些作品出色，而是因为存在一种偏爱，以为凡是经历了岁月的考验仍能保存下来的作品，均是佳作。批评界争论的一个问题是批评家对活着的当代作家的作品吹毛求疵，而对古人所写的流传至今的作品则推崇备至。当一个作家在世时，我们用他的次作去评估他的写作能力；而一旦他作古，却又用他的佳作来评判他。文学作品是需要经历时间的考验的，因为只有在长时期的鉴赏、比较后，才能确定文学作品的真正价值。莎士比亚的作品就是一个很好的例证。

那么，究竟是什么东西使得莎士比亚如此长久地得到国人的喜爱呢？

一个重要的原因是他能在作品中表现有普遍性的东西。文学作品只有表现带普遍性的事物和人的感受时，才能受到众人的喜爱，并长期受到读者的喜爱。有的作品因其新奇，能取悦于一时，但不能经受时间的检验。

莎士比亚之所以能超越其他作家，正是因为他是一个表现事物和感情的普遍性的作家。他所表现的不是一时一地的风尚和奇特。别的作家在作品中表现的是人物的个人特点，而莎士比亚的作品表现的则是一类人的特点。正因为如此，他的作品才具有普遍的教育意义。他的作品不以华丽的词句取胜，而是以其深刻的寓言给人以启迪。有的剧院演出的戏剧中的人物是日常生活中少见的，用的语言也鲜为人知，叙述的事情也稀奇古怪。莎士比亚则不同，他用日常生活中简练、通俗的语言表现日常生活中的事。

莎士比亚的戏剧没有超人式的英雄人物，只有我们在日常生活中常见的人。剧中人物的言行就如同我们的言行。即便是剧中的角色是神或幽灵，其语言也是百姓生活中使用的语言。他有一种天才，能把遥远或生疏的事物写得平易近人，把不可思议的奇异事物写得通俗亲切。正因为如此，人们赞扬他的戏剧是生活的一面镜子。

他是既能写喜剧又能写悲剧的剧作家。这是古希腊、古罗马的剧作家所未能做到的。

这篇文章最重要的论点是："写作的目的是教诲；诗的目的是寓教于娱。"

后人把莎士比亚的戏剧分为喜剧、历史剧和悲剧。但是，他们并没有划分这三种戏剧的明确概念。按照他们的看法，剧中主要人物，即便是经历了许多苦难，只要结局欢乐，便是喜剧。而所谓悲剧，尽管剧中也不乏轻快的欢乐，只要是结局不幸，就是悲剧。所谓历史剧，只是按情节发生的年代顺序一一说来，虽然情节之间毫无关联。把《安东尼和克莉奥佩特拉》称作悲剧，把《理查二世》称作历史剧，是牵强附会的。历史剧和悲剧之间的界限并不清楚。

莎士比亚的戏剧融严肃和欢快于一体。因此，观众在看他的一台戏时，时而哀恸，时而欢快。他能驾驭观众的感情。

他不拘泥于创作上的条条框框，只是按自己的脾性，自然地、随心所欲地创作剧本，毫不费力地发挥自己的天才和创造性。他的作品像坚不可摧的岩石，在巨浪的冲击下始终巍然屹立。许多诗人的作品经受不起时间的考验，而莎士比亚的作品却能经久不衰。他的文体永远不过时；他的语言具有很强的生命力，因为它来自日常生活用语，不追求典雅，不标新立异，不追赶时髦。他是运用语言的大师，他的语言至今娓娓动听。他的对话虽有粗俗或难懂之处，却流畅、明白。

这些都是莎士比亚的作品的突出优点。但是，他的作品也并非完美无瑕。他的作品的缺陷也足以使其优点黯然失色。

第一个缺点是他在写剧本时似乎不考虑道德目的，为了剧情的需要牺牲德行。他所关注的是使观众或读者得到娱乐，而不是得到教诲。他的戏剧也有给人以教诲的箴言，但是这都是他随意写的，缺乏目的性。他未能正确地处理剧中的善与恶，是与非，有意识地激浊扬清。作家有义务伸张正义，使世界越来越美好。

另一个缺点是情节松散。莎士比亚似乎并未很好地设计剧本的情节。其实，只要他稍微用些心思，就能把剧情写得好些。显而易见，在他的许多剧本中，莎士比亚忽略了剧本后半部的写作。他急于求成，虎头蛇尾，不能做到善始善终。

第三个缺点是莎士比亚不考虑剧中情节的时间和地点，以至于将不同的国家和时代的习俗、机构和见解混淆在一个国家或一个时代，因此失去了可信性和可靠性。

他的喜剧性场景很少是出色的。当他的剧中人相互讥讽，说俏皮话时，他们的戏谑语是粗俗的，他们开的玩笑是下流的。剧中的绅士淑女缺乏优雅的气质，在外表和风度上几乎和小丑差不多。他叙述时颇多浮华、累赘之词。其实，诗体剧的叙述应该是越精练越好，否则势必拖延剧情的发展。有时所用语言和叙述的事物不吻合。琐碎的感情表露和粗俗的思想令人失望。

莎士比亚对双关语有一种强烈的癖好，处处滥用，也不管是否用得适当、确切、合理。双关语对他说来就如同一个男人爱上了埃及艳后克莉奥佩特拉；为了她，哪怕失去整个世界也心甘情愿。

关于"三一律"。莎士比亚的历史剧不存在"三一律"问题，而在他的其他剧本中，他遵循情节的统一。像亚里士多德所要求的那样，他的戏剧的情节有头、身、尾三部分。但是他却不在乎时间和地点的统一。主张时间和地点统一的人认为，延续几个月甚至几年的事情不可能在舞台上用三个小时表演完。观众坐在剧院里，而舞台上的大使却在短短的三小时内出差到一个遥远的国度，在那里会见国王，继而很快地回到国内。他们认为，那样的安排使观众感到剧情不真实，难以接受、相信。

上述观点其实是不正确的，因为观众脑子里很清楚：他们是在剧院里看戏，而戏是在小小的舞台上由演员表演的。因此，观众并不要求戏剧在时间和地点上的统一，也就不存在可信或不可信的问题。约翰逊说，莎士比亚是否知晓"三一律"，或者是他明知道，却有意不遵循这些规则，或者是由于无知偏离了这些规则，他不清楚。约翰逊认为，除了情节的统一需要遵循外，时间与地点的统一是没有必要的。

Samuel Johnson (1709—1784)

Preface to *Shakespeare*[1]

That praises are without reason lavished on the dead, and that the honors due only to excellence are paid to antiquity, is a complaint likely to be always continued by those, who, being able to add nothing to truth, hope for eminence from the heresies of paradox; or those, who, being forced by disappointment upon consolatory expedients, are willing to hope from posterity what the present age refuses, and flatter themselves that the regard which is yet denied by envy, will be at last bestowed by time.

Antiquity, like every other quality that attracts the notice of mankind, has undoubtedly votaries that reverence it, not from reason, but from prejudice. Some seem to admire indiscriminately whatever has been long preserved, without considering that time has sometimes cooperated with chance; all perhaps are more willing to honor past than present excellence; and the mind contemplates genius through the shades of age, as the eye surveys the sun through artificial opacity. The great contention of criticism is to find the faults of the moderns, and the beauties of the ancients. While an author is yet living we estimate his powers by his worst performance, and when he is dead, we rate them by his best.

To works, however, of which the excellence is not absolute and definite, but gradual and comparative; to works not raised upon principles demonstrative and scientific, but appealing wholly to observation and experience, no other test can be applied than length of duration and continuance of esteem. What mankind have long possessed they have often examined and compared; and if they persist to value the possession, it is because frequent comparisons have confirmed opinion in its favor. As among the works of nature no man can properly call a river deep, or a mountain high, without the knowledge of many mountains, and many rivers; so in the productions of genius, nothing can be styled excellent till it has been compared with other works of the same kind. Demonstration immediately displays its power, and has nothing to hope or fear from the flux of years; but works tentative and experimental must be estimated by their proportion to the general and collective ability of man, as it is discovered in a long succession of endeavors. Of the first building that was raised, it might be with certainty determined that it was round or square; but whether it was spacious or lofty must have been referred to time. The Pythagorean scale of numbers[2] was at once discovered to be perfect; but the poems of Homer we yet know not to transcend the common limits of human intelligence, but by remarking, that nation after nation, and century after century, has been able to do little more than transpose his incidents, new-name his characters, and paraphrase his sentiments.

The reverence due to writings that have long subsisted arise therefore not from any credulous confidence in the superior wisdom of past ages, or gloomy persuasion of the degeneracy of mankind, but is the consequence of acknowledged and indubitable positions, that what has been longest known has been most considered, and what is most considered is best understood.

The poet, of whose works I have undertaken the revision, may now begin to assume the dignity of an ancient, and claim the privilege of established fame and prescriptive veneration. He has long outlived his century, the term commonly fixed as the test of literary merit. Whatever advantages he might once derive from personal allusions, local customs, or temporary opinions, have for many years been lost; and every topic of merriment, or motive of sorrow, which the modes of artificial life afforded him, now only obscure the scenes which they once illuminated. The effects of favor and competition are at an end; the tradition of his friendships and his enmities has perished; his works support no opinion with arguments, nor supply any faction with invectives; they can neither indulge vanity nor gratify malignity; but are read without any other reason than the desire of pleasure, and are therefore praised only as pleasure is obtained; yet, thus unassisted by interest or passion, they have passed through variations of taste and changes of manners, and, as they devolved from one generation to another, have received new honors at every transmission.

But because human judgment, though it be gradually gaining upon certainty, never becomes infallible; and approbation, though long continued, may yet be only the approbation of prejudice or fashion; it is proper to inquire, by what peculiarities of excellence Shakespeare has gained and kept the favor of his countrymen.

Nothing can please many, and please long, but just representations of general nature. Particular manners, can be known to few, and therefore few only can judge how nearly they are copied. The irregular combinations of fanciful invention may delight a while, by that novelty of which the common satiety of life sends us all in quest; but the pleasures of sudden wonder are soon exhausted, and the mind can only repose on the stability of truth.

Shakespeare is above all writers, at least above all modern writers, the poet of nature; the poet that holds up to his readers a faithful mirror of manners and of life. His characters are not modified by the customs of particular places, unpracticed by the rest of the world; by the peculiarities of studies or professions, which can operate but upon small numbers; or by the accidents of transient fashions or temporary opinions: they are the genuine progeny of common humanity, such as the world will always supply, and observation will always find. His persons act and speak by the influence of those general passions and principles by which all minds are agitated, and the whole system of life is continued in motion. In the writings of other poets a character is too often an individual; in those of Shakespeare it is commonly a species.

It is from this wide extension of design that so much instruction is derived. It is this which fills the plays of Shakespeare with practical axioms and domestic wisdom. It was said of Euripides[3], that every verse was a precept; and it may be said of Shakespeare, that from his works may be collected a system of civil and economical prudence. Yet his real power is not shewn in the splendor of particular passages, but by the progress of his fable, and the tenor of his dialogue; and he that tries to recommend him by select quotations, will succeed like the pedant in Hierocles[4], who, when he offered his house to sale, carried a brick in his pocket as a specimen.

It will not easily be imagined how much Shakespeare excels in accommodating his sentiments to real life, but by comparing him with other authors. It was observed of the ancient schools of declamation, that the more diligently they were frequented, the more was the student disqualified for the world, because he found nothing there which he should ever meet in any other place. The same remark may be applied to every stage but that of

Shakespeare. The theater, when it is under any other direction, is peopled by such characters as were never seen, conversing in a language which was never heard, upon topics which will never rise in the commerce of mankind. But the dialogue of this author is often so evidently determined by the incident which produces it, and is pursued with so much ease and simplicity, that it seems scarcely to claim the merit of fiction, but to have been gleaned by diligent selection out of common conversation, and common occurrences.

Upon every other stage the universal agent is love, by whose power all good and evil is distributed, and every action quickened or retarded. To bring a lover, a lady and a rival into the fable; to entangle them in contradictory obligations, perplex them with oppositions of interest, and harass them with violence of desires inconsistent with each other; to make them meet in rapture and part in agony; to fill their mouths with hyperbolical joy and outrageous sorrow; to distress them as nothing human ever was delivered; is the business of a modern dramatist. For this probability is violated, life is misrepresented, and language is depraved. But love is only one of many passions; and as it has no great influence upon the sum of life, it has little operation in the dramas of a poet, who caught his ideas from the living world, and exhibited only what he saw before him. He knew, that any other passion, as it was regular or exorbitant, was a cause of happiness or calamity.

Characters thus ample and general were not easily discriminated and preserved, yet perhaps no poet ever kept his personages more distinct from each other. I will not say with Pope[5], that every speech may be assigned to the proper speaker, because many speeches there are which have nothing characteristical; but perhaps, though some may be equally adapted to every person, it will be difficult to find any that can be properly transferred from the present possessor to another claimant. The choice is right, when there is reason for choice.

Other dramatists can only gain attention by hyperbolical or aggravated characters, by fabulous and unexampled excellence or depravity, as the writers of barbarous romances invigorated the reader by a giant and a dwarf; and he that should form his expectations of human affairs from the play, or from the tale, would be equally deceived. Shakespeare has no heroes; his scenes are occupied only by men, who act and speak as the reader thinks that he should himself have spoken or acted on the same occasion. Even where the agency is supernatural the dialogue is level with life. Other writers disguise the most natural passions and most frequent incidents; so that he who contemplates them in the book will not know them in the world: Shakespeare approximates the remote, and familiarizes the wonderful; the event which he represents will not happen, but if it were possible, its effects would probably be such as he has assigned; and it may be said, that he has not only shewn human nature as it acts in real exigencies, but as it would be found in trials, to which it cannot be exposed.

This therefore is the praise of Shakespeare, that his drama is the mirror of life; that he who has mazed his imagination, in following the phantoms which other writers raise up before him, may here be cured of his delirious ecstasies, by reading human sentiments in human language, by scenes from which a hermit may estimate the transactions of the world, and a confessor predict the progress of the passions.

His adherence to general nature has exposed him to the censure of critics, who form their judgments upon narrow principles. Dennis[6] and Rymer[7] think his Romans not sufficiently Roman; and Voltaire[8] censures his kings as not completely royal. Dennis is offended, that Menenius[9], a senator of Rome, should play the buffoon; and Voltaire perhaps thinks decency violated when the Danish usurper is represented as a drunkard. But Shakespeare always makes nature predominate over accident; and if he preserves the essential character, is not very careful of distinctions superinduced and adventitious. His story requires Romans or kings, but he thinks only on men. He knew that Rome, like every other city, had men of all dispositions; and wanting a buffoon, he went into the senate house for that which the senate house would certainly have afforded him. He was inclined to shew a usurper and a murderer not only odious but despicable, he therefore added drunkenness to his other qualities, knowing that kings love wine like other men, and that wine exerts its natural power upon kings. These are the petty cavils of petty minds; a poet overlooks the casual distinction of country and condition, as a painter, satisfied with the figure, neglects the drapery.

The censure which he has incurred by mixing comic and tragic scenes, as it extends to all his works, deserves more consideration. Let the fact be first stated, and then examined.

Shakespeare's plays are not in the rigorous and critical sense either tragedies or comedies, but compositions of a distinct kind; exhibiting the real state of sublunary nature, which partakes of good and evil, joy and sorrow, mingled with endless variety of proportion and innumerable modes of combination; and expressing the course of the world, in which the loss of one is the gain of another; in which, at the same time, the reveler is hasting to his wine, and the mourner burying his friend; in which the malignity of one is sometimes defeated by the frolic of another; and many mischiefs and many benefits are done and hindered without design.

Out of this chaos of mingled purposes and casualties the ancient poets, according to the laws which custom had prescribed, selected, some the crimes of men, and some their absurdities; some the momentous vicissitudes of life, and some the lighter occurrences; some the terrors of distress and some the gaieties of prosperity. Thus rose the two modes of imitation, known by the names of tragedy and comedy, compositions intended to promote different ends by contrary means, and considered as so little allied, that I do not recollect among the Greeks or Romans a single writer who attempted both.

Shakespeare has united the powers of exciting laughter and sorrow not only in one mind, but in one composition. Almost all his plays are divided between serious and ludicrous characters, and, in the successive evolutions of the design, sometimes produce seriousness and sorrow, and sometimes levity and laughter.

That this is a practice contrary to the rules of criticism will be readily allowed; but there is always an appeal open from criticism to nature. The end of writing is to instruct; the end of poetry is to instruct by pleasing. That the mingled drama may convey all the instruction of tragedy or comedy cannot be denied, because it includes both in its alterations of exhibition and approaches nearer than either to the appearance of life, by shewing how great machinations and slender designs may promote or obviate one another, and the high and the low cooperate in the general system by unavoidable concatenation.

It is objected, that by this change of scenes the passions are interrupted in their progression, and that the principal event, being not advanced by a due gradation of preparatory incidents, wants at last the power to move, which constitutes the perfection of dramatic poetry. This reasoning is so specious, that it is received as true even by those who in daily experience feel it to be false. The interchanges of mingled scenes seldom fail to produce the intended vicissitudes of passion. Fiction cannot move so much, but that the attention may be easily transferred; and though it must be allowed that pleasing melancholy be sometimes interrupted by unwelcome levity, yet let it be considered likewise, that melancholy is often not pleasing, and that the disturbance of one man may be the relief of another; that different auditors have different habitudes; and that, upon the whole, all pleasure consists in variety.

The players, who in their edition[10] divided our author's works into comedies, histories, and tragedies, seem not to have distinguished the three kinds by any very exact or definite ideas.

An action which ended happily to the principal persons, however serious or distressful through its intermediate incidents, in their opinion, constituted a comedy. This idea of a comedy continued long amongst us; and plays were written, which, by changing the catastrophe, were tragedies today, and comedies tomorrow.

Tragedy was not in those times a poem of more general dignity or elevation than comedy; it required only a calamitous conclusion, with which the common criticism of that age was satisfied, whatever lighter pleasure it afforded in its progress.

History was a series of actions, with no other than chronological succession, independent on each other, and without any tendency to introduce or regulate the conclusion. It is not always very nicely distinguished from tragedy. There is not much nearer approach to unity of action in the tragedy of *Antony and Cleopatra*, than in the history of *Richard the Second*. But a history might be continued through many plays; as it had no plan, it had no limits.

Through all these denominations of the drama, Shakespeare's mode of composition is the same; an interchange of seriousness and merriment, by which the mind is softened at one time, and exhilarated at another. But whatever be his purpose, whether to gladden or depress, or to conduct the story, without vehemence or emotion, through tracts of easy and familiar dialogue, he never fails to attain his purpose; as he commands us, we laugh or mourn, or sit silent with quiet expectation, in tranquility without indifference.

When Shakespeare's plan is understood, most of the criticisms of Rymer and Voltaire vanish away. The play of *Hamlet* is opened, without impropriety, by two sentinels; Iago bellows at Brabantio's window,[11] without injury to the scheme of the play, though in terms which a modern audience would not easily endure; the character of Polonius[12] is seasonable and useful; and the grave-diggers themselves may be heard with applause.

Shakespeare engaged in dramatic poetry with the world open before him; the rules of the ancients were yet known to few; but public judgment was unformed; he had no example of such fame as might force him upon imitation, nor critics of such authority as might restrain his extravagance. He therefore indulged his natural disposition, and his disposition, as Rymer has remarked, led him to comedy. In tragedy he often writes, with great appearance of toil and study, what is written at last with little felicity; but in his comic scenes, he seems to produce without labor what no labor can improve. In tragedy he is always struggling after some occasion to be comic; but in comedy he seems to repose, or to luxuriate, as in a mode of thinking congenial to his nature. In his tragic scenes there is always something wanting, but his comedy often surpasses expectation or desire. His comedy pleases by the thoughts and the language, and his tragedy for the greater part by incident and action. His tragedy seems to be skill, his comedy to be instinct.

The force of his comic scenes has suffered little diminution from the changes made by a century and a half, in manners or in words. As his personages act upon principles arising from genuine passion, very little modified by particular forms, their pleasures and vexations are communicable to all times and to all places; they are natural, and therefore durable; the adventitious peculiarities of personal habits, are only superficial dies, bright and pleasing for a little while, yet soon fading to a dim tinct, without any remains of former luster; but the discriminations of true passion are the colors of nature; they pervade the whole mass, and can only perish with the body that exhibits them. The accidental compositions of heterogeneous modes are dissolved by the chance which combined them; but the uniform simplicity of primitive qualities neither admits increase, nor suffers decay. The sand heap by one flood is scattered by another, but the rock always continues in its place. The stream of time, which is continually washing the dissoluble fabrics of other poets, passes without injury by the adamant of Shakespeare.

If there be, what I believe there is, in every nation, a style which never becomes obsolete, a certain mode of phraseology so consonant and congenial to the analogy and principles of its respective language as to remain settled and unaltered; this style is probably to be sought in the common intercourse of life, among those who speak only to be understood, without ambition of elegance. The polite are always catching modish innovations, and the learned depart from established forms of speech, in hope of finding or making better; those who wish for distinction forsake the vulgar, when the vulgar is right; but there is a conversation above grossness and below refinement, where propriety resides, and where this poet seems to have gathered his comic dialogue. He is therefore more agreeable to the ears of the present age than any other author equally remote, and among his other excellencies deserves to be studied as one of the original masters of our language.

These observations are to be considered not as unexceptionably constant, but as containing general and predominant truth. Shakespeare's familiar dialogue is affirmed to be smooth and clear, yet not wholly without ruggedness or difficulty; as a country may be eminently fruitful, though it has spots unfit for cultivation: His characters are praised as natural, though their sentiments are sometimes forced, and their actions improbable; as the earth upon the whole is spherical, though its surface is varied with protuberances and cavities.

Shakespeare with his excellencies has likewise faults, and faults sufficient to obscure and overwhelm any other merit. I shall show them in the proportion in which they appear to me, without envious malignity or superstitious veneration. No question can be more innocently discussed than a dead poet's pretensions to renown; and little regard is due to that bigotry which sets candor higher than truth.

His first defect is that to which may be imputed most of the evil in books or in men. He sacrifices virtue to convenience, and is so much more careful to please than to instruct, that he seems to write without any moral purpose. From his writings indeed a system of social duty may be selected, for he that thinks reasonably must think morally; but his precepts and axioms drop casually from him; he makes no just distribution of good or evil, nor is always careful to show in the virtuous a disapprobation of the wicked; he carries his persons indifferently through right and wrong, and at the close dismisses them without further care, and leaves their examples to operate by chance. This fault the barbarity of his age cannot extenuate; for it is always a writer's duty to make the world better, and justice is a virtue independent on time or place.

The plots are often so loosely formed, that a very slight consideration may improve them, and so carelessly pursued, that he seems not always fully to comprehend his own design. He omits opportunities of instructing or delighting which the train of his story seems to force upon him, and apparently rejects those exhibitions which would be more affecting, for the sake of those which are more easy.

It may be observed, that in many of his plays the latter part is evidently neglected. When he found himself near the end of his work, and, in view of his reward, he shortened the labor to snatch the profit. He therefore remits his efforts where he should most vigorously exert them, and his catastrophe is improbably produced or imperfectly represented.

He had no regard to distinction of time or place, but gives to one age or nation, without scruple, the customs, institutions, and opinions of another, at the expense not only of likelihood, but of possibility. These faults Pope has endeavored, with more zeal than judgment, to transfer to his imagined interpolators. We need not wonder to find Hector quoting Aristotle,[13] when we see the loves of Theseus and Hippolyta[14] combined with the Gothic mythology of fairies. Shakespeare, indeed, was not the only violator of chronology, for in the same age Sidney, who wanted not the advantages of learning, has, in his, *Arcadia*, confounded the pastoral with the feudal times the days of innocence, quiet and security, with those of turbulence, violence, and adventure.

In his comic scenes he is seldom very successful, when he engages his characters in reciprocations of smartness and contests of sarcasm; their jests are commonly gross, and their pleasantry licentious; neither his gentlemen nor his ladies have much delicacy, nor are sufficiently distinguished from his clowns by any appearance of refined manners. Whether he represented the real conversation of his time is not easy to determine; the reign of Elizabeth is commonly supposed to have been a time of stateliness, formality and reserve; yet perhaps the relaxations of that severity were not very elegant. There must, however, have been always some modes of gaiety preferable to others, and a writer ought to choose the best.

In tragedy his performance seems constantly to be worse, as his labor is more. The effusions of passion which exigence forces out are for the most part striking and energetic; but whenever he solicits his invention, or strains his faculties, the offspring of his throes is tumor, meanness, tediousness and obscurity.

In narration he affects a disproportionate pomp of diction, and a wearisome train of circumlocution, and tells the incident imperfectly in many words, which might have been more plainly delivered in few. Narration in dramatic poetry is naturally tedious, as it is inactive, and obstructs the progress of the action; it should therefore always be rapid, and enlivened by frequent interruption. Shakespeare found it an encumbrance, and instead of lightening it by brevity, endeavored to recommend it by dignity and splendor.

His declamations or set speeches are commonly cold and weak, for his power was the power of nature; when he endeavored, like other tragic writers, to catch opportunities of amplification, and instead of inquiring what the occasion demanded, to show how much his stores of knowledge could supply, he seldom escapes without the pity or resentment of his reader.

It is incident to him to be now and then entangled with an unwieldy sentiment, which he cannot well express, and will not reject; he struggles with it awhile, and if it continues stubborn, comprises it in words such as occur, and leaves it to be disentangled and evolved by those who have more leisure to bestow upon it.

Not that always where the language is intricate the thought is subtle, or the image always great where the line is bulky; the equality of words to things is very often neglected, and trivial sentiments and vulgar ideas disappoint the attention, to which they are recommended by sonorous epithets and swelling figures.

But the admirers of this great poet have never less reason to indulge their hopes of supreme excellence, than when he seems fully resolved to sink them in dejection, and mollify them with tender emotions by the fall of greatness, the danger of innocence, or the crosses of love. He is not long soft and pathetic without some idle conceit, or contemptible equivocation. He no sooner begins to move, than he counteracts himself; and terror and pity, as they are rising in the mind, are checked and blasted by sudden frigidity.

A quibble is to Shakespeare, what luminous vapors are to the traveler; he follows it at all adventures; it is sure to lead him out of his way, and sure to engulf him in the mire. It has some malignant power over his mind, and its fascinations are irresistible. Whatever be the dignity or profundity of his disquisition, whether he be enlarging knowledge or exalting affection, whether he be amusing attention with incidents, or enhancing it in suspense, let but a quibble spring up before him, and he leaves his work unfinished. A quibble is the golden apple for which he will always turn aside from his career, or stoop from his elevation. A quibble, poor and barren as it is, gave him such delight, that he was content to purchase it, by the sacrifice of reason, propriety and truth. A quibble was to him the fatal Cleopatra for which he lost the world, and was content to lose it.

It will be thought strange, that, in enumerating the defects of this writer, I have not yet mentioned his neglect of the unities; his violation of those laws which have been instituted and established by the joint authority of poets and critics.

For his other deviations from the art of writing I resign him to critical justice, without making any other demand in his favor, than that which must be indulged to all human excellence; that his virtues be rated with his failings: but, from the censure which this irregularity may bring upon him, I shall, with due reverence to that learning which I must oppose, adventure to try how I can defend him.

His histories, being neither tragedies nor comedies, are not subject to any of their laws; nothing more is necessary to all the praise which they expect, than that the changes of action be so prepared as to be understood, that the incidents be various and affecting, and the characters consistent, natural, and distinct. No other unity is intended, and therefore none is to be sought.

In his other works he has well enough preserved the unity of action. He has not, indeed, an intrigue regularly perplexed and regularly unraveled: he does not endeavor to hide his design only to discover it, for this is seldom the order of real events, and Shakespeare is the poet of nature: but his plan has commonly what Aristotle requires a beginning, a middle, and an end; one event is concatenated with another, and the conclusion follows by easy consequence. There are perhaps some incidents that might be spared, as in other poets there is much talk that only fills up time upon the stage; but the general system makes gradual advances, and the end of the play is the end of expectation.

To the unities of time and place he has shown no regard; and perhaps a nearer view of the principles on which they stand will diminish their value, and withdraw from them the veneration which, from the time of Corneille, they have very generally received, by discovering that they have given more trouble to the poet, than pleasure to the auditor.

The necessity of observing the unities of time and place arises from the supposed necessity of making the drama credible. The critics hold it impossible, that an action of months or years can be possibly believed to pass in three hours; or that the spectator can suppose himself to sit in the theater, while ambassadors go and return between distant kings, while armies are levied and towns besieged, while an exile wanders and returns, or till he whom they saw courting his mistress, shall lament the untimely fall of his son. The mind revolts from evident falsehood, and fiction loses its force when it departs from the resemblance of reality.

From the narrow limitation of time necessarily arises the contraction of place. The spectator, who knows that he saw the first act at Alexandria, cannot suppose that he sees the next at Rome, at a distance to which not the dragons of Medea could, in so short a time have transported him; he knows with certainty that he has not changed his place, and he knows that place cannot change itself; that what was a house cannot become a plain; that what was Thebes[15] can never be Persepolis[16].

Such is the triumphant language with which a critic exults over the misery of an irregular poet, and exults commonly without resistance or reply. It is time therefore to tell him by the authority of Shakespeare, that he assumes, as an unquestionable principle, a position, which, while his breath is forming it into words, his understanding pronounces to be false. It is false, that any representation is mistaken for reality; that any dramatic fable in its materiality was ever credible, or, for a single moment, was ever credited.

The objection arising from the impossibility of passing the first hour at Alexandria, and the next at Rome, supposes, that when the play opens, the spectator really imagines himself at Alexandria, and believes that his walk to the theater has been a voyage to Egypt and that he lives in the days of Antony and Cleopatra. Surely he that imagines this may imagine more. He that can take the stage at one time for the palace of the Ptolemies[17], may take it in half an hour for the promontory of Actium[18]. Delusion, if delusion be admitted, has no certain limitation; if the spectator can be once persuaded, that his old acquaintance are Alexander and Caesar, that a room illuminated with candles is the plain of Pharsalia[19], or the bank of Granicus[20], he is in a state of elevation above the reach of reason, or of truth, and from the heights of empyrean poetry, may despise the circumscriptions of terrestrial nature. There is no reason why a mind thus wandering in ecstasy should count the clock, or why an hour should not be a century in that calenture of the brains that can make the stage a field.

The truth is, that the spectators are always in their senses, and know, from the first act to the last, that the stage is only a stage, and that the players are only players. They came to hear a certain number of lines recited with just gesture and elegant modulation. The lines relate to some action, and an action must be in some place; but the different actions that complete a story may be in places very remote from each other; and where is the absurdity of allowing that space to represent first Athens, and then Sicily[21], which was always known to be neither Sicily nor Athens, but a modern theater?

By supposition, as place is introduced, time may be extended; the time required by the fable elapses for the most part between the acts; for, of so much of the action as is represented, the real and poetical duration is the same. If, in the first act, preparations for war against Mithridates[22] are represented to be made in Rome, the event of the war may, without absurdity, be represented, in the catastrophe, as happening in Pontus[23]; we know that there is neither war, nor preparation for war; we know that we are neither in Rome nor Pontus; that neither Mithridates nor Lucullus[24] are before us. The drama exhibits successive imitations of successive actions; and why may not the second imitation represent an action that happened years after the first, if it be so connected with it, that nothing but time can be supposed to intervene? Time is, of all modes of existence, most obsequious to the imagination; a lapse of years is as easily conceived as a passage of hours. In contemplation we easily contract the time of real actions, and therefore willingly permit it to be contracted when we only see their imitation.

It will be asked, how the drama moves, if it is not credited. It is credited with all the credit due to a drama. It is credited, whenever it moves, as a just picture of a real original; as representing to the auditor what he would himself feel, if he were to do or suffer what is there feigned to be suffered or to be done. The reflection that strikes the heart is not, that the evils before us are real evils, but that they are evils to which we ourselves may be exposed. If there be any fallacy, it is not that we fancy the players, but that we fancy ourselves unhappy for a moment; but we rather lament the possibility than suppose the presence of misery, as a mother weeps over her babe, when she remembers that death may take it from her. The delight of tragedy proceeds from our consciousness of fiction; if we thought murders and treasons real, they would please no more.

Imitations produce pain or pleasure, not because they are mistaken for realities, but because they bring realities to mind. When the imagination is recreated by a painted landscape, the trees are not supposed capable to give us shade, or the fountains coolness; but we consider how we should be pleased with such fountains playing beside us, and such woods waving over us. We are agitated in reading the history of Henry the Fifth[25], yet no man takes his book for the field of Agincourt[26]. A dramatic exhibition is a book recited with concomitants that increase or diminish its effect. Familiar comedy is often more powerful in the theater, than in the page; imperial tragedy is always less. The humor of Petruchio[27] may be heightened by grimace; but what voice or what gesture can hope to add dignity or force to the soliloquy of Cato[28]?

A play read, affects the mind like a play acted. It is therefore evident, that the action is not supposed to be real; and it follows, that between the acts a longer or shorter time may be allowed to pass, and that no more account of space or duration is to be taken by the auditor of a drama, than by the reader of a narrative, before whom may pass in an hour the life of a hero, or the revolutions of an empire.

Whether Shakespeare knew the unities, and rejected them by design, or deviated from them by happy ignorance, it is, I think, impossible to decide, and useless to inquire. We may reasonably suppose, that, when he rose to notice, he did not want the counsels and admonitions of scholars and critics, and that he at last deliberately persisted in a practice, which he might have begun by chance. As nothing is essential to the fable, but unity of action, and as the unities of time and place arise evidently from false assumptions, and, by circumscribing the extent of the drama, lessen its variety, I cannot think it much to be lamented, that they were not known by him, or not observed: nor, if such another poet could arise, should I very vehemently reproach him, that his first act passed at Venice, and his next in Cyprus. Such violations of rules merely positive, become the comprehensive genius of Shakespeare, and such censures are suitable to the minute and slender criticism of Voltaire:

> *Non usque adeo permiscuit imis*
> *Longus summa dies, ut non, si voce Metelli*
> *Serventur leges, malint a Caesare tolli.*[29]

Yet when I speak thus slightly of dramatic rules, I cannot but recollect how much wit and learning may be produced against me; before such authorities I am afraid to stand, not that I think the present question one of those that are to be decided by mere authority, but because it is to be suspected, that these precepts have not been so easily received but for better reasons than I have yet been able to find. The result of my inquiries, in which it would be ludicrous to boast of impartiality, is, that the unities of time and place are not essential to a just drama, that though they may sometimes conduce to pleasure, they are always to be sacrificed to the nobler beauties of variety and instruction; and that a play, written with nice observation of critical rules, is to be contemplated as an elaborate curiosity, as the product of superfluous and ostentatious art, by which is shewn, rather what is possible, than what is necessary.

He that, without diminution of any other excellence, shall preserve all the unities unbroken, deserves the like applause with the architect, who shall display all the orders of architecture in a citadel, without any deduction from its strength; but the principal beauty of a citadel is to exclude the enemy; and the greatest graces of a play, are to copy nature and instruct life.

Perhaps what I have here not dogmatically but deliberately written, may recall the principles of the drama to a new examination. I am almost frightened at my own temerity; and when I estimate the fame and the strength of those that maintain the contrary opinion, am ready to sink down in reverential silence; as Aeneas withdrew from the defense of Troy, when he saw Neptune shaking the wall, and Juno heading the besiegers.[30]

注释

1.《〈莎士比亚戏剧集〉序言》是约翰逊为他所编的 8 卷《莎士比亚戏剧集》写的序言。此处选的是该序言的第一部分。

2. the Pythagorean scale of numbers：毕达哥拉斯数阶。毕达哥拉斯为公元前 6 世纪希腊哲学家、数学家。他的贡献是他提出在客观世界中和音乐中数的功能这一学说。他认为，数的形而上学观念和包括音乐与天文的实在，从根本上说，其本性是数学的。他的著名格言是："一切都是数"，即一切现存的事物最终均可归结为数的关系。

3. Euripides：欧里庇得斯（前 480—前 406），古希腊三大悲剧家之一。

4. Hierocles：希罗克里斯，公元 2 世纪埃及亚历山大城的哲学家。

5. Pope：这里指的是蒲柏 1725 年编的《莎士比亚戏剧集》序言中的观点。

6. Dennis：丹尼斯（John Dennis，1658—1734），英国诗人、文论家。这里指的是丹尼斯在《论莎士比亚的天才与著述》（*Essay on the Genius*

and Writings of Shakespeare，1713）中叙述的观点。

7. Rymer：托马斯·赖默（Thomas Rymer，1643—1713），英国小说家、剧作家。这里指他在《短评悲剧》（*A Short View of Tragedy*，1693）中叙述的观点。

8. Voltaire：伏尔泰，18 世纪法国著名文学家。他对莎士比亚的剧作颇多微词。这里指他在《论古今悲剧》（*Dissertation sur la tragédie ancienne et moderne*，1749）和《向欧洲各国呼吁》（*Appel à toute les nations de L'Europe*，1761）中所叙述的观点。

9. Menenius：阿格里帕（Menenius Agrippa，公元前 6 世纪古罗马元老院议员。有关内容见丹尼斯所写的《论莎士比亚的天才与著述》。

10. in their edition：指约翰·赫明（John Heminges）和亨利·康德尔（Henry Condell）1623 年合编的对开本《莎士比亚戏剧集》。

11. Iago...Brabantio's window：Iago（埃古）和 Brabantio（勃拉班修）均为莎士比亚著名悲剧《奥赛罗》（*Othello*）中的人物。

12. Polonius：波洛尼厄斯，莎士比亚著名悲剧《哈姆雷特》中的人物。

13. ...Hector quoting Aristotle：Hector（赫克托耳）是希腊神话中特洛伊国王普里阿摩斯（Priam）的长子，荷马史诗《伊利亚特》中的英雄人物。莎士比亚在他写的剧中让赫克托耳引用亚里士多德显然是违背了时间的顺序，因为后者比前者晚了许多年。此错出现在莎剧《特洛伊罗斯与克瑞西达》（*Troilus and Cressida*），II.ii.166—167。

14. Theseus：忒修斯，希腊神话中雅典的民族英雄。Hippolyta，希波吕忒，亦作 Hippolyte，希腊神话中女战士国（Amazon）的女皇。

15. Thebes：底比斯，古希腊东部一主要城市。在古希腊历史上，雅典、斯巴达和底比斯是希腊三个最重要的城市。而底比斯又是古希腊神话与传说中提及最多的一个城市。著名悲剧作家索福克勒斯（Sophocles）称这座城市为 "the only city where mortal women are the mothers of gods"。

16. Persepolis：波斯波利斯，古波斯帝国都城之一，其废墟在今伊朗设拉子附近。

17. the Ptolemies：埃及托勒密王（公元前 305 年至前 30 年埃及王朝的诸王）。

18. Actium：亚克兴角，古希腊西北部海岬。

19. Pharsalia：法萨利亚，古罗马地名。公元前 48 年夏凯撒在此击败庞培。

20. Granicus：格拉尼卡斯河，小亚细亚西北部的河流，公元前 334 年亚历山大大帝打败波斯人的战场。

21. Sicily：意大利的西西里岛。

22. Mithridates：米特拉达梯六世（Mithridates Ⅵ），本都王国（Pontus）国王（前120—前63），罗马的死敌。

23. Pontus：本都王国，在黑海南部小亚细亚。

24. Lucullus：卢卡拉斯（约前110—前56），古罗马将军兼执政官。

25. Henry the Fifth：亨利五世，英国国王（1413—1422）。

26. the field of Agincourt：阿让库尔战场。阿让库尔为法国北部城镇，1415年在英法百年战争（1337—1453）的一次战役中，英军在此击败法军。百年战争以法军最后战胜英军结束。法军夺取了除加来以外英国在法国境内的全部领地。

27. Petruchio：彼特鲁乔，莎士比亚戏剧《驯悍记》中一人物。

28. Cato：加图（前234—前149），古罗马政治家、作家。

29. 引自罗马诗人卢坎的史诗《法萨利亚》（*Pharsalia*，描写古罗马凯撒和庞培之间的内战）。英译文为："A long time has not so confused the highest and lowest that the laws made by Metellus may not wish to be overthrown by Caesar."

30. and Juno heading the besiegers：引自维吉尔的史诗《埃涅阿斯纪》。

杨格 《试论独创性文学作品》

爱德华·杨格（1683—1765）

英国诗人爱德华·杨格 1683 年出生于英格兰南部温切斯特附近的一个牧师家庭，曾就读于牛津大学，获法学博士学位。他早年从事戏剧和诗歌创作，由于缺乏舞台感，其作品很少上演。1721 年在特鲁里街（Drury Lane）剧院上演的《复仇》（The Revenge）为其代表剧作。自 1725 至 1728 年，他发表了一系列讽刺诗，很受尊崇，可惜时运不济，诗名反被小他 5 岁的蒲柏超过。也许正是这种瑜亮情结作祟的缘故，他感觉问鼎文坛无望，才进入教会，当上牧师，后来成为英王乔治二世的宫廷牧师，以善于布道著称。不过，这无助于他仕途的升迁。1730 年，他又到伦敦附近的乡下当牧师，优游林下而不废吟咏。无奈好景不长，在 10 年中，他接连经历了两次惨痛的家庭变故：女殇妻亡。此后，他的诗风愈加阴沉忧郁。1742 年，他发表了长篇悼亡诗《哀怨》（The Complaint, or Night Thoughts on Life, Death and Immortality），抒发内心的痛楚，寄托对妻女的哀思。该诗近万行，由 9 篇无韵素体诗组成，充满了宗教的气息、感伤的情绪和宇宙幻灭的意识。一经发表，声震文坛，也算是不幸之余酸楚的偏得。

在他晚年的作品中，最可称道的是他在 1759 年发表的长篇论文《试论独创性文学作品》，又名《致〈查尔斯·格兰迪森爵士〉作者书》（"To the Author of Sir Charles Grandison"）。《查尔斯·格兰迪森爵士》是 18 世纪英国小说家塞缪尔·理查森（Samuel Richardson）7 卷本长篇小说。塞缪尔·理查森为杨格文友，两人互通翰墨多年，切磋为文之道，理查森经常向他建言献策。早在 1757 年，理查森在致杨格的信中就提及此文，对原稿提出了修改意见。据某些文史学家考证，这篇文章源于作者和理查森两人对约瑟夫·沃顿（Joseph Warton）《论蒲柏的作品与天才》（"Essay on Genius and Writings of Pope"，1756）的探讨和交流，该文是题献给杨格的。沃顿在文中列举了当代诗人面临的种种挑战，其中很严重的一种就是诗歌想象力的衰退。他认为，在当代诗坛，近似于散文体的教谕诗一家独擅，而不见莎士比亚、弥尔顿那种气韵高昂、想象奔放的的崇高诗风。杨格的文章就是针对这种悲观论调而发的。不过，在批评新古典主义和标举"想象力"方面，二者声气相投，汇为蓄势待发的浪漫主义文论的涌动暗流。

当时英国文坛还是由新古典主义主宰，新古典主义前期巨子亚历山大·蒲柏虽已过世多年，但余威尚在；后期巨子塞缪尔·约翰逊也声名鹊起，虎视文坛。在这种情势之下，这样一篇批判新古典主义的末流和余弊、发浪漫主义先声的争鸣文章发表后，在国内引起的回应并不热烈，自然是意料之中。根据鲍斯韦尔的记载，塞缪尔·约翰逊以他惯用的口吻说，杨格把平常之见当做新鲜事物，委实让他吃惊。不过，它在国外却掀起了波澜。文章发表的第二年，德国就出了两种译本，推动了那里方兴未艾的"狂飙运动"。

不过，应当指出的是，虽说杨格不遗余力推举独创性，他的这种独创性观念却决非"独创"，与他相近的观点，早在50多年前就已经隐约浮现。早就有人说过，创造性天才比古典主义的模仿和训练更重要。可见"独创"委实不易，在人类思想的发展史上，延续与继承往往多于革命性断裂。

内容提要

爱德华·杨格生活的时代正是英国文学史上的新古典主义时代（1660—1780）。在文学领域，新古典主义是以古希腊、古罗马经典作家为典范的一套文学创作和批评原则，在17和18世纪主导法国文坛，指导当时法国的戏剧创作。高乃伊和拉辛的悲剧，莫里哀的喜剧都是新古典主义时代的产物。追根溯源，新古典主义肇始于16世纪意大利学者重新发现了一度失传的亚里士多德的《诗学》。亚里士多德的模仿论及对文学体裁的分类和贺拉斯在《诗艺》中阐发的风格与题材一致的原则及艺术兼顾教谕和娱乐的功能，主宰了新古典主义文学观。从更广阔的思想史的角度看，新古典主义体现了18世纪（所谓理性时代）的世界观和思想诉求，那就是侧重理想、明晰、节制、秩序和规范性。

英国的新古典主义以德莱顿为前导，斯威夫特、菲尔丁（Henry Fielding）、艾迪生、斯梯尔为主力，蒲柏集大成，塞缪尔·约翰逊为殿军。这一时期的主要作家大都崇尚传统，师法古希腊、古罗马文学大家，古罗马作家更是极力推崇的对象。在他们看来，古典作家已为后世确立和完善了主要文学体裁，文学并非笔墨游戏，而是一门严肃艺术，只有经过勤学苦练才能掌握其优异和精妙。因此，这一时期的作家都很刻苦，他们仔细揣摩古典作家的精神气度和行文运思，悉心模仿先贤的谋篇布局和遣词设句，力求恪守文学艺术的规则。新古典主义的核心论断就是，古人的创作已经登峰造极，不可逾越，今人的任务就是模仿他们。蒲柏在《批评论》（1711）中更是大胆放言，说模仿古人和模仿自然是一回事儿。

新古典主义在英国的兴衰流变与中产阶级的兴起关系重大。在整个 18 世纪，无论在人数还是政治力量上，英国中产阶级都迅速壮大，走在欧洲诸国的前列。随着闲暇时间增多、识字率提高，他们对文化品位的渴求也就益发强烈，服务于他们的文学市场也随之兴旺发达。《闲谈者》和《旁观者》这两本文学期刊应这个时运而异军突起。新古典主义的批评家们不失时机地承担起教化这些粗鄙无文之士的历史使命，文学研究成为提高读者文化品位、进行道德教育的重要手段。从德莱顿时代直到蒲柏过世，这一时期的批评家主要关注道德和社会问题，而非拟订批评方法论或者分析具体的文本。时移事异，到了 18 世纪后半叶，资产阶级读者群继续扩大，进一步改变了文学生产的性质。此时，他们已不再满足于被动接受贵族气息浓厚的高雅品位，而要求适合自己阅读习惯的作品。就作者方面而言，图书市场的扩大和新版权法的制定，促成贵族赞助制度的没落；作家的收入与市场需求挂钩，独立性增强，他们不再需要刻意逢迎某些贵族的喜好。文学批评的风气也发生了转变，批评家开始取悦于一般的读者大众，不再像过去那样专门迎合教育程度高的精英人物，不再强调古典学问的文雅标准，开始重视作品中所反映的个人生活体验。他们与新古典主义原则渐行渐远。文学的教化功能减弱，由娱乐和教谕兼顾转向偏重娱乐功能。虽说他们一时还不愿意完全放弃新古典主义的理念，但已经从追求秩序、雅致和规范转向寻求新的审美愉悦手段和新的天才标准。相应地，文学独创性得以突出和强调；为了达到独创目的，他们主张，作家应当充分发挥自己的才智，不落前人的窠臼，只以自然为师法对象，切不可对先贤的旧作亦步亦趋。到了 18 世纪中叶，新古典主义的模仿论在很大程度上已经成为因袭故智、盲目崇古的同义词，具有贬义。除了杨格之外，当时很多批评家，例如约瑟夫·沃顿（Joseph Warton）、托马斯·沃顿（Thomas Warton）等都关注独创性和天才的关系。杨格大胆宣告，独创性是评判作品高下的绝对标准。他的做法更加系统，也更全面。

在杨格看来，独创性是天才的首要标准。那些以模仿为能事的作家只不过是善于揣摩古人而已，只会重复原创，未能有所改进；独创性作品却会因拓展文学疆域而泽被后世。模仿不但无益，而且贻害不浅。它矫揉造作，还导致学术停滞，因为它鼓励作家"想的少写的多"。莎士比亚完全从自己的感受和思考出发，不像弥尔顿，他没有窒息自己天才的学问，因而是英国文学史上最伟大的作家。相形之下，蒲柏因为过分模仿古人、专事雕琢而难膺天才之誉。

杨格没有全然否定模仿，他把模仿分为两种：模仿自然和模仿其他作家。前者是独创，后者是因袭，他着力反对的是后者。他打了一个比方，独创性作品好比自然界的植物，它从天才的根茎中自动成长起来，模仿之作却是艺匠根据前人提供的材料制造出来的。他反对一味模仿古人，但也反对厚今薄古。对待古人正确的态度应该是，从他们的思想中汲取养料来丰富自己，不要让他们变成巨大的精神负担，从而泯灭自己的思想。读古人之书时，要让古人思想的魅力点燃自己的想象；写自家作品时，要调动自己的判断力，不让古人干扰自己的思想。要以古人的精神和趣味而不是材料来打造自己的作品，过分敬畏古人会使文学天才受到束缚，无法驰骋自己的想象，失去了写出杰作所需要的自由空间。需要指出的是，新古典主义者和杨格所使用的"自然"概念，含义大致相同。按照朱光潜在《西方美学史》中的说法，"新古典主义者所了解的'自然'并不是现实风景，也还不是一般感性世界，而是天生事物（'自然'在西文中的本义，包括人在内）的常理常情，往往特指人性。"

与学问相比，杨格更推重天才。他说天才就是一种神圣灵感，它好比身体天生的力量，学问好比辅助性武器装备。天才有童稚天才和晚熟天才之分。晚熟天才无须学问亦可成为伟人巨匠，如莎士比亚；童稚天才需要学问的滋养和哺育，如斯威夫特。在近代作家中，杨格最推崇莎士比亚，说他可以与古代最伟大的作家相提并论。莎士比亚读书不多，正因此，他的天才没有被学问窒息而光焰万丈。古典作品恰到好处地成为他独创思想的源头。相形之下，博学的本·琼生让学问窒息了自己的创造力。在戏剧创作上，他专事模仿古人，缺乏莎士比亚的原创精神。根据古罗马历史著作提供的素材写就的《喀提林》（*Cataline*）一剧，虽然也能博得时誉，但终究是梁下架屋，愈见其小。

　　除天赋之外，杨格还指出社会环境对文学成就的影响。人类的心智在各个时代难分高下，今人能力与古人不相上下，成就却难以比肩。这固然是因为维吉尔、贺拉斯等人天赋卓绝；另外，当时的社会氛围也功不可没。他们的文学活动得到了统治阶层的奖掖和一般民众的支持，因而成就了高不可攀的文学功业。

　　杨格的文章发表之后，许多批评家都接受了他的观点，把独创性当做评判文学的主要标准。威廉·达夫认为，莎士比亚因为不肯因袭古典形式，而高出侪辈作家，他是近世唯一具有独创性的作家。甚至新古典主义的重镇塞缪尔·约翰逊也以原创性为标准，来评判弥尔顿的《失乐园》。他的盖棺论定之语是，"它算不上最伟大的英雄诗，就因为不是第一部"。

　　杨格在很多地方与浪漫主义思想不期而合。他将独创性作品比作从天才的根茎中自发生长的植物，这种文学有机论正是后来的德国和英国浪漫主义诗人和评论家大力提倡的，尤其柯勒律治更是不遗余力加以宣扬。他对天才与灵感作用的强调与浪漫主义重视个人才能、主观精神声气相投。他对独创性和想象的论述，在浪漫主义那里有了长足发展。

Edward Young (1683—1765)

From "Conjectures on Original Composition"

I begin with *Original* Composition; and the more willingly, as it seems an original subject to me, who have seen nothing hitherto written on it: But, first, a few thoughts on Composition in general. Some are of opinion, that its growth, at present, is too luxuriant; and that the Press is overcharged. Overcharged, I think, it could never be, if none were admitted but such as brought their Imprimatur from *sound Understanding*, and the *Public Good*. Wit, indeed, however brilliant, should not be permitted to gaze self-enamored on its useless Charms, in that Fountain of Fame (if so I may call the Press), if beauty is all that it has to boast; but, like the first *Brutus*[1], it should sacrifice its most darling offspring to the sacred interests of virtue, and real service of mankind.

This restriction allowed, the more composition the better. To men of letters, and leisure, it is not only a noble amusement, but a sweet refuge; it improves their parts, and promotes their peace: It opens a back-door out of the bustle of this busy, and idle world, into a delicious garden of moral and intellectual fruits and flowers; the key of which is denied to the rest of mankind. When stung with idle anxieties, or teased with fruitless impertinence, or yawning over insipid diversions, then we perceive the blessing of a lettered recess. With what a gust do we retire to our disinterested, and immortal friends in our closet,[2] and find our minds, when applied to some favorite theme, as naturally, and as easily quieted, and refreshed, as a peevish child (and peevish children are we all till we fall asleep) when laid to the breast? Our happiness no longer lives on charity; nor bids fair for a fall, by leaning on that most precarious, and thorny pillow, another's pleasure, for our repose. How independent of the world is he, who can daily find new acquaintance, that at once entertain, and improve him, in the little world, the minute but fruitful creation, of his own mind?

These advantages *Composition* affords us, whether we write ourselves, or in more humble amusement peruse the works of others. While we bustle through the thronged walks of public life, it gives us a respite, at least, from care; a pleasing pause of refreshing recollection. If the country is our choice, or fate, there it rescues us from *sloth* and *sensuality*, which, like obscene vermin, are apt gradually to creep unperceived into the delightful bowers of our retirement, and to poison all its sweets. Conscious guilt robs the rose of its scent, the lily of its luster; and makes an *Eden* a deflowered, and dismal scene.

Moreover, if we consider life's endless evils, what can be more prudent, than to provide for consolation under them? A consolation under them the wisest of men have found in the pleasures of the pen. Witness, among many more, *Thucydides, Xenophon, Tully, Ovid, Seneca, Pliny* the younger,[3] who says *In uxoris infirmitate, & amicorum periculo, aut morte turbatus, ad studia, unicum doloris levamentum, confugio.*[4] And why not add to these their modern equals, *Chaucer, Rawleigh*[5], *Bacon, Milton, Clarendon,*[6] under the same shield, unwounded by misfortune, and nobly smiling in distress? [7]

Composition was a cordial to these under the frowns of fortune; but evils there are, which her smiles cannot prevent, or cure. Among these are the languors of old age. If those are held honorable, who in a hand benumbed by time have grasped the just sword in defence of their country; shall they be less esteemed, whose unsteady pen vibrates to the last in the cause of religion, of virtue, of learning?[8] Both these are happy in *this,* that by fixing their attention on objects most important, they escape numberless little anxieties, and that *tedium vitae*[9] which often hangs so heavy on its evening hours. May not this insinuate some apology for my spilling ink, and spoiling paper, so late in life?

But there are, who write with vigor, and success, to the world's delight, and their own renown. These are the glorious fruits where genius prevails. The mind of a man of genius is a fertile and pleasant field, pleasant as *Elysium*, and fertile as *Tempe;*[10] it enjoys a perpetual spring. Of that spring, *Originals* are the fairest flowers: *Imitations* are of quicker growth, but fainter bloom. *Imitations* are of two kinds; one of nature, one of authors: The first we call *Originals*, and confine the term *Imitation* to the second. I shall not enter into the curious enquiry of what is, or is not, strictly speaking, *Original*, content with what all must allow, that some compositions are more so than others; and the more they are so, I say, the better. *Originals* are, and ought to be, great favorites, for they are great benefactors; they extend the republic of letters, and add a new province to its dominion: *Imitators* only give us a sort of duplicates of what we had, possibly much better, before; increasing the mere drug of books, while all that makes them valuable, *knowledge* and *genius*, are at a stand.[11] The pen of an *original* writer, like *Armida's*[12] wand, out of a barren waste calls a blooming spring: Out of that blooming spring an *Imitator* is a transplanter of laurels, which sometimes die on removal, always languish in a foreign soil.

But suppose an *Imitator* to be most excellent (and such there are), yet still he but nobly builds on another's foundation; his debt is, at least, equal to his glory; which therefore, on the balance, cannot be very great. On the contrary, an *Original*, though but indifferent[13] (its *Originality* being set aside), yet has something to boast; it is something to say with him in *Horace*,

>   *Meo sum Pauper in aere;*[14]

and to share ambition with no less than *Caesar*[15], who declared he had rather be the first in a village, than the second at *Rome*.[16]

Still farther: An *Imitator* shares his crown, if he has one, with the chosen object of his imitation; an *Original* enjoys an undivided applause. An *Original* may be said to be of a v*egetable* nature; it rises spontaneously from the vital root of genius; it *grows*, it is not *made*: *Imitations* are often a sort of *manufacture* wrought up by those *mechanics*, *art*, and *labor*, out of pre-existent materials not their own.

Again: We read *Imitation* with somewhat of his languor, who listens to a twice-told tale: Our spirits rouse at an *Original*,[17] that is a perfect stranger, and all throng to learn what news from a foreign land: And though it comes, like an *Indian* prince, adorned with feathers only, having little of weight; yet of our attention it will rob the more solid, if not equally new: Thus every telescope is lifted at a new-discovered star; it makes a hundred astronomers in a moment, and denies equal notice to the sun. But if an *Original*, by being as excellent, as new, adds admiration to surprise, then are we at the writer's mercy; on the strong wing of his imagination, we are snatched from *Britain* to *Italy*, from climate to climate, from pleasure to pleasure; we have no home, no thought, of our own; till the magician drops his pen: And then falling down into ourselves, we awake to flat realities, lamenting the change, like the beggar who dreamt himself a prince.[18]

It is with thoughts, as it is with words; and with both, as with men; they may grow old, and die. Words tarnished, by passing through the mouths of the vulgar, are laid aside as inelegant, and obsolete. So thoughts, when become too common, should lose their currency; and we should send new metal to the mint, that is, new meaning to the press. The division of tongues at *Babel*[18] did not more effectually debar men from *making themselves a name* (as the Scripture speaks,) than the too great concurrence, or union of tongues will do for ever. We may as well grow good by another's virtue, or fat by another's food, as famous by another's thought. The world will pay its debt of praise but once; and instead of applauding, explode a second demand, as a cheat.[20]

If it is said, that most of the *Latin* classics, and all the *Greek*, except, perhaps, *Homer*, *Pindar*[21], and *Anacreon*[22], are in the number of *Imitators*, yet receive our highest applause; our answer is, that they though not *real*, are *accidental Originals*; the works they imitated, few excepted, are lost: They, on their father's decease, enter as lawful heirs, on their estates in fame: The fathers of our copyists are still in possession; and secured in it, in spite of *Goths*[23], and Flames, by the perpetuating power of the Press. Very late must a modern *Imitator's* fame arrive, if it waits for their decease.

An *Original* enters early on reputation: *Fame*, fond of new glories, sounds her trumpet in triumph at its birth; and yet how few are awakened by it into the noble ambition of like attempts? Ambition is sometimes no vice in life; it is always a virtue in Composition. High in the towering *Alps* is the fountain of the *Po*[24]; high in fame, and in antiquity, is the fountain of an *Imitator's* undertaking; but the river, and the imitation, humbly creep along the vale. So few are our *Originals*, that, if all other books were to be burnt, the lettered world would resemble some metropolis in flames, where a few incombustible buildings, a fortress, temple, or tower, lift their heads, in melancholy grandeur, amid the mighty ruin. Compared with this conflagration, old *Omar*[25] lighted up but a small bonfire, when he heated the baths of the Barbarians, for eight months together, with the famed *Alexandrian* library's inestimable spoils, that no prophane book might obstruct the triumphant progress of his holy *Alcoran* round the globe.

But why are *Originals* so few? Not because the writer's harvest is over, the great reapers of antiquity having left nothing to be gleaned after them; nor because the human mind's teeming time is past, or because it is incapable of putting forth unprecedented births; but because illustrious examples *engross*, *prejudice*, and *intimidate*. They *engross* our attention, and so prevent a due inspection of ourselves; they *prejudice* our judgment in favor of their abilities, and so lessen the sense of our own; and they *intimidate* us with the splendor of their renown, and thus under diffidence bury our strength. Nature's impossibilities, and those of diffidence lie wide asunder.[26]

Let it not be suspected, that I would weakly insinuate anything in favor of the moderns, as compared with antient authors; no, I am lamenting their great inferiority. But I think it is no *necessary* inferiority; that it is not from divine destination, but from some cause far beneath the moon.[27] I think that human souls, through all periods, are equal; that due care, and exertion, would set us nearer our immortal predecessors than we are at present; and he who questions and confutes this, will show abilities not a little tending toward a proof of that equality, which he denies.[28]

After all, the first antients had no merit in being *Originals*: They could *not* be *Imitators*. Modern writers have a *choice* to make; and therefore have a merit in their power. They may soar in the regions of *liberty*, or move in the soft fetters of easy *imitation*; and *imitation* has as many plausible reasons to urge, as *Pleasure* had to offer to *Hercules*. *Hercules* made the choice of an hero, and *so* became immortal.

Yet let not assertors of classic excellence imagine, that I deny the tribute it so well deserves. He that admires not antient authors, betrays a secret he would conceal, and tells the world, that he does not understand them. Let us be as far from neglecting, as from copying, their admirable compositions: Sacred be their rights, and inviolable their fame. Let our understanding feed on theirs; they afford the noblest nourishment; but let them nourish, not annihilate, our own. When we read, let our imagination kindle at their charms; when we write, let our judgment shut them out of our thoughts; treat even *Homer* himself as his royal admirer was treated by the cynic; bid him stand aside, nor shade our Composition from the beams of our own genius; for nothing *Original* can rise, nothing immortal, can ripen, in any other sun.[29]

Must we then, you say, not imitate antient authors? Imitate them, by all means; but imitate aright. He that imitates the divine *Iliad*, does not imitate *Homer*; but he who takes the same method, which *Homer* took, for arriving at a capacity of accomplishing a work so great. Tread in his steps to the sole fountain of immortality; drink where he drank, at the true *Helicon*[30], that is at the breast of nature: Imitate; but imitate not the *Composition*, but the *Man*. For may not this paradox pass into a maxim? *viz.*[31] "The less we copy the renowned ancients, we shall resemble them the more."

But possibly you may reply, that you must either imitate *Homer*, or depart from nature. Not so: For suppose you was to change place, in time, with *Homer*; then, if you write naturally, you might as well charge *Homer* with an imitation of you. Can you be said to imitate *Homer* for writing *so*, as you would have written, if *Homer* had never been? As far as a regard to nature, and sound sense, will permit a departure from your great predecessors; so far, ambitiously, depart from them; the farther from them in *similitude*, the nearer are you to them in *excellence*; you rise by it into an *Original*; become a noble collateral, not a humble descendant from them. Let us build our Compositions with the spirit, and in the taste, of the ancients; but not with their materials: Thus will they resemble the structures of *Pericles*[32] at *Athens*, which *Plutarch*[33] commends for having had an air of antiquity as soon as they were built. All eminence, and distinction, lies out of the beaten road; excursion, and deviation, are necessary to find it; and the more remote your path from the highway, the more reputable; if, like poor *Gulliver*[34] (of whom anon) you fall not into a ditch, in your way to glory.

What glory to come near, what glory to reach, what glory (presumptuous thought!) to surpass, our predecessors? And is that then in nature absolutely impossible? Or is it not, rather, contrary to nature to fail in it? Nature herself sets the ladder, all wanting is our ambition to climb. For by the bounty of nature we are as strong as our predecessors; and by the favor of time (which is but another round in nature's scale) we stand on higher ground. As to the *first*, were *they* more than men? Or are we less? Are not our minds cast in the same mould with those before the flood?[35] The flood affected matter; mind escaped. As to the *second*; though we are moderns, the world is an ancient; more ancient far, than when they, whom we most admire, filled it with their fame. Have we not their beauties, as stars, to guide; their defects, as rocks, to be shunned; the judgment of ages on both, as a chart to conduct, and a sure helm to steer us in our passage to greater perfection than theirs? And shall we be stopped in our rival pretensions to fame by this just reproof?

Stat contra, dicitque tibi tua pagina, fur es.[36]

It is by a sort of noble contagion, from a general familiarity with their writings, and not by any particular sordid theft, that we can be the better for those who went before us. Hope we, from plagiarism, any dominion in literature; as that of *Rome* arose from a nest of thieves?[37]

Rome was a powerful ally to many states; ancient authors are our powerful allies; but we must take heed, that they do not succor, till they enslave, after the manner of *Rome*. Too formidable an idea of their superiority, like a specter, would fright us out of a proper use of our wits; and dwarf our understanding, by making a giant of theirs. Too great awe for them lays genius under restraint, and denies it that free scope, that full elbowroom, which is requisite for striking its most masterly strokes. Genius is a master-workman, learning is but an instrument; and an instrument, though most valuable, yet not always indispensable. Heaven will not admit of a partner in the accomplishment of some favorite spirits; but rejecting all human means, assumes the whole glory to itself. Have not some, though not famed for erudition, *so* written, as almost to persuade us, that they shone brighter, and soared higher, for escaping the boasted aid of that proud ally?[38]

Nor is it strange; for what, for the most part, mean we by genius, but the power of accomplishing great things without the means generally reputed necessary to that end?[39] A *genius* differs from a *good understanding*, as a migician from a good architect; *that* raises his structure by means invisible; *this* by the skilful use of common tools. Hence genius has ever been supposed to partake of something divine. *Nemo unquam vir magnus fuit, sine aliquo afflatu divino.*[40]

Learning, destitute of this superior aid, is fond, and proud, of what has cost it much pains; is a great lover of rules, and boaster of famed examples: As beauties less perfect, who owe half their charms to cautious art, learning inveighs against natural unstudied graces, and small harmless inaccuracies, and sets rigid bounds to that liberty, to which genius often owes its supreme glory; but the no-genius its frequent ruin. For unprescribed beauties, and unexampled excellence, which are characteristics of *genius*, lie without the pale of *learning*'s authorities, and laws; which pale, genius must leap to come at them: But by that leap, if genius is wanting, we break our necks; we lose that little credit, which possibly we might have enjoyed before. For rules, like crutches, are a needful aid to the lame, though an impediment to the strong. A *Homer* casts them away; and, like his *Achilles*,

Jura negat sibi nata, nihil non arrogat,[41]

by native force of mind. There is something in poetry beyond prose-reason; there are mysteries in it not to be explained, but admired; which render mere prose-men infidels to their divinity. And here pardon a second paradox; *viz.* "*Genius* often then deserves most to be praised, when it is most sure to be condemned; that is, when its excellence, from mounting high, to weak eyes is quite out of sight."

If I might speak farther of learning, and genius, I would compare genius to virtue, and learning to riches. As riches are most wanted where there is least virtue; so learning where there is least genius. As virtue without much riches can give happiness, so genius without much learning can give renown. As it is said in *Terence, Pecuniam negligere interdum maximum est lucrum;*[42] so to neglect of learning, genius sometimes owes its greater glory. Genius, therefore, leaves but the second place, among men of letters, to the learned. It is their merit, and ambition, to fling light on the works of genius, and point out its charms. We most justly reverence their informing radius for that favor; but we must much more admire the radiant stars pointed out by them.

A star of the first magnitude among the moderns was *Shakespeare*; among the ancients, *Pindar*; who (as *Vossius*[43] tells us) boasted of his no-learning, calling himself the eagle, for his flight above it. And such genii as these may, indeed, have much reliance on their own native powers. For genius may be compared to the natural strength of the body; learning to the super-induced accouterments of arms: if the first is equal to the proposed exploit, the latter rather encumbers, than assists; rather retards, than promotes, the victory. *Sacer nobis inest Deus,*[44] says *Seneca*. With regard to the moral world, *conscience*, with regard to the intellectual, *genius*, is that god within. Genius can set us right in Composition, without the rules of the learned; as conscience sets us right in life, without the laws of the land: *This*, singly, can make us good, as men: *that*, singly, as writers, can, sometimes, make us great.

I say, sometimes, because there is a genius, which stands in need of learning to make it shine. Of genius there are two species, an earlier, and a later: or call them *infantine*, and *adult*. An adult genius comes out of nature's hand, as *Pallas*[45] out of *Jove's* head, at full growth, and mature: *Shakespeare's* genius was of this kind; on the contrary, *Swift* stumbled at the threshold, and set out for distinction on feeble knees.[46] His was an infantine genius; a genius, which, like other infants, must be nursed, and educated, or it will come to nought: Learning is its nurse, and tutor; but this nurse may overlay with an indigested load, which smothers common sense; and this tutor may mislead, with pedantic prejudice, which vitiates the best understanding: As too great admirers of the fathers of the church[47] have sometimes set up their authority against the true sense of Scripture; so too great admirers of the classical fathers have sometimes set up their authority, or example, against reason.[48]

. . .

Quite clear of the dispute concerning *ancient and modern learning*, we speak not of performance, but powers. The modern powers are equal to those before them; modern performance in general is deplorably short. How great are the names just mentioned? Yet who will dare affirm, that as great may not rise up in some future, or even in the present age? Reasons there are why talents may not *appear*, none why they may not *exist*, as much in one period as another. An evocation of vegetable fruits depends on rain, air, and sun; an evocation of the fruits of genius no less depends on externals. What a marvellous crop bore it in *Greece*, and *Rome*? And what a marvellous sunshine did it there enjoy? What encouragement from the nature of their governments, and the spirit of their people? *Virgil* and *Horace* owed their divine talents to Heaven; their immortal works, to men; thank *Maecenas*[49] and *Augustus*[50] for them. Had it not been for these, the genius of those poets had lain buried in their ashes. *Athens* expended on her theater, painting, sculpture, and architecture, a tax levied for the support of a war. *Caesar* dropped his papers when *Tully* spoke; and *Philip* trembled at the voice of *Demosthenes*[51]. And has there arisen but one *Tully*, one *Demosthenes*, in so long a course of years? The powerful eloquence of them both in one stream, should never bear me down into the melancholy persuasion, that several have not been born, though they have not emerged. The sun as much exists in a cloudy day, as in a clear; it is outward, accidental circumstances that with regard to genius either in nation, or age,

Collectas fugat nubes, solemque reducit.[52]

As great, perhaps, greater than those mentioned (presumptuous as it may sound) may, possibly, arise; for who hath fathomed the mind of man? Its bounds are as unknown, as those of the creation; since the birth of which, perhaps, not One has so far exerted, as not to leave his possibilities beyond his attainments, his powers beyond his exploits. Forming our judgments, altogether by what *has* been done, without knowing, or at all inquiring, what possibly *might* have been done, we naturally enough fall into too mean an opinion of the human mind. If a sketch of the divine *Iliad* before *Homer* wrote, had been given to mankind, by some superior being, or otherwise, its execution would, probably, have appeared beyond the power of man. Now, to surpass it, we think impossible. As the first of these opinions would evidently have been a mistake, why may not the second be so too? Both are founded on the same bottom; on our ignorance of the possible dimensions of the mind of man.

Nor are we only ignorant of the dimensions of the human mind in general, but even of our own. That a man may be scarce less ignorant of his own powers, than an oyster of its pearl, or a rock of its diamond; that he may possess dormant, unsuspected abilities, till awakened by loud calls, or stung up by striking emergencies, is evident from the sudden eruption of some men, out of perfect obscurity, into public admiration, on the strong impulse of some animating occasion; not more to the world's great surprise, than their own. Few authors of distinction but have experienced something of this nature, at the first beamings of their yet unsuspected genius on their hitherto dark Composition: The writer starts at it, as at a lucid meteor in the night;

is much surprised; can scarce believe it true. During his happy confusion, it may be said to him, as to Eve at the lake,

What there thou seest, fair creature, is thyself.[53]

Genius, in this view, is like a dear friend in our company under disguise; who, while we are lamenting his absence, drops his mask, striking us, at once, with equal surprise and joy. This sensation, which I speak of in a writer, might favor, and so promote, the fable of poetic inspiration: A poet of a strong imagination, and stronger vanity, on feeling it, might naturally enough realize the world's mere compliment, and think himself truly inspired. Which is not improbable; for enthusiasts of all kinds do no less.

Since it is plain that men may be strangers to their own abilities; and by thinking meanly of them without just cause, may possibly lose a name, perhaps a name immortal; I would find some means to prevent these evils. Whatever promotes virtue, promotes something more, and carries its good influence beyond the *moral* man: To prevent these evils, I borrow two golden rules from *ethics*, which are no less golden in *Composition*, than in life. 1. *Know thyself*; 2dly, *Reverence thyself*: I design to repay ethics in a future letter,[54] by two rules from rhetoric for its service.

1st. *Know thyself.* Of ourselves it may be said, as *Martial* says of a bad neighbor,

Nil tam prope, proculque nobis.[55]

Therefore dive deep into thy bosom; learn the depth, extent, bias, and full fort of thy mind; contract full intimacy with the stranger within thee; excite and cherish every spark of intellectual light and heat, however smothered under former negligence, or scattered through the dull, dark mass of common thoughts; and collecting them into a body, let thy genius rise (if a genius thou hast) as the sun from chaos; and if I should then say, like an *Indian, Worship it*, (though too bold) yet should I say little more than my second rule enjoins, (*viz.*) *Reverence thyself.*

That is, let not great examples, or authorities, browbeat thy reason into too great a diffidence of thyself: Thyself so reverence, as to prefer the native growth of thy own mind to the richest import from abroad; such borrowed riches make us poor. The man who thus reverences himself, will soon find the world's reverence to follow his own. His works will stand distinguished; his the sole property of them; which property alone can confer the noble title of an *author*; that is; of one who (to speak accurately) *thinks*, and *composes*; while other invaders of the press, how voluminous and learned soever, (with due respect be it spoken) only *read*, and *write*.[56]

This is the difference between those two luminaries in literature, the well-accomplished scholar, and the divinely-inspired enthusiast; the *first* is, as the bright morning star; the *second*, as the rising sun. The writer who neglects those two rules above will never stand alone; he makes one of a group, and thinks in wretched unanimity with the throng: Incumbered with the notions of others, and impoverished by their abundance, he conceives not the least embryo of new thought; opens not the least vista through the gloom of ordinary writers, into the bright walks of rare imagination, and singular design; while the true genius is crossing all public roads into fresh untrodden ground; he, up to the knees in antiquity, is treading the sacred footsteps of great examples, with the blind veneration of a bigot saluting the papal toe;[57] comfortably hoping full absolution for the sins of his own understanding, from the powerful charm of touching his idol's infallibility.

· · ·

Shakespeare mingled no water with his wine, lowered his genius by no vapid imitation. *Shakespeare* gave us a *Shakespeare*, nor could the first in ancient fame have given us more! *Shakespeare* is not their son, but brother; their equal; and that, in spite of all his faults. Think you this too bold? Consider, in those ancients what is it the world admires? Not the fewness of their faults, but the number and brightness of their beauties; and if *Shakespeare* is their equal (as he doubtless is) in that, which in them is admired, then is *Shakespeare* as great as they; and not impotence, but some other cause, must be charged with his defects. When we are setting these great men in competition, what but the comparative size of their genius is the subject of our inquiry? And a giant loses nothing of his size, though he should chance to trip in his race. But it is a compliment to those heroes of antiquity to suppose *Shakespeare* their equal only in dramatic powers;

therefore, though his faults had been greater, the scale would still turn in his favor. There is at least as much genius on the *British* as on the *Grecian* stage, though the former is not swept so clean; so clean from violations not only of the *dramatic*, but *moral* rule; for an honest heathen, on reading some of our celebrated scenes, might be seriously concerned to see, that our obligations to the religion of nature were canceled by Christianity.

Johnson[58], in the serious drama, is as much an imitator, as *Shakespeare* is an original. He was very learned, as *Sampson*[59] was very strong, to his own hurt: Blind to the nature of tragedy, he pulled down all antiquity on his head, and buried himself under it; we see nothing of *Johnson*, nor indeed, of his admired (but also murdered) ancients; for what shone in the historian is a cloud on the poet; and *Cataline* might have been a good play, if *Salust* had never writ.[60]

Who knows whether *Shakespeare* might not have thought less, if he had read more? Who knows if he might not have labored under the load of *Johnson's* learning, as *Enceladus* under *AEtna*?[61] His mighty genius, indeed, through the most mountainous oppression would have breathed out some of his inextinguishable fire; yet, possibly, he might not have risen up into that giant, that much more than common man, at which we now gaze with amazement, and delight. Perhaps he was as learned as his dramatic province required; for whatever other learning he wanted, he was master of two books, unknown to many of the profoundly read, though books, which the last conflagration alone can destroy; the book of nature, and that of man. These he had by heart, and has transcribed many admirable pages of them, into his immortal works. These are the fountain-head, whence the *Castalian* streams[62] of *original* composition flow; and these are often mudded by other waters, though waters in their distinct channel, most wholesome and pure: As two chemical liquors, separately clear as crystal, grow foul by mixture, and offend the sight. So that he had not only as much learning as his dramatic province required, but, perhaps, as it could safely bear. If *Milton* had spared some of his learning, his muse would have gained more glory, than he would have lost, by it.

注释

1. the first Brutus：布鲁图（Lucius Junius Brutus），古罗马传说中的人物。据说他在公元前 509 年将埃特鲁西暴君卢西乌斯·塔奎尼乌斯逐出罗马，建立罗马共和国。他的几个儿子参与塔奎尼乌斯的复辟阴谋，被他处死。

2. 这句话大意为：我们意兴盎然，退隐私室，与那些恬淡无私和永垂不朽的朋友们（指写作——编者按）神交。这一段的主要意思是：远离尘嚣，息影书斋，抛却俗世烦恼，潜心写作，足以怡情益智。

3. Thucydides：修昔底德，古希腊历史学家。Xenophon，色诺芬，古希腊将领、苏格拉底的学生，有著作多种。Tully，即 Marcus Tullius Cicero，西塞罗（19 世纪早期英国读者称他为 Tully）。Seneca，塞内加，古罗马哲学家、政治家和剧作家。Pliny the younger，小普林尼，罗马作家、执政官，以其 9 卷描述罗马帝国社会生活和私人生活的信札而著称。

4. 拉丁文，大意为"每当我的妻子健康不佳，朋友身患重病或奔赴黄泉，让我心神不安，我就躲进书房。这里是唯一能够慰籍我内心苦楚的地方。"

5. Rawleigh：罗利（Sir Walter Raleigh，约 1552—1618），英国探险家、作家、女王伊丽莎白一世的宠臣。著有《世界史》，以及散文、诗歌等。

6. Clarendon: 克拉伦登（Edward Hyde Clarendon，1609—1674），英国政治家、历史学家，英王查理二世枢密顾问官和大法官，著有《英国叛乱和内战史》（*The True Historical Narrative of the Rebellion and Civil War in England*）。

7. 此段大意为：古往今来，有多少智慧卓绝之士在笔墨生涯中找到了人生的慰藉。因此，在厄运当头之际，他们依然露出勇敢的微笑。

8. 这段话大意为：拿起正义之剑保家卫国之士与那些为了宗教、美德和学术而笔耕不辍的人同样应当得到尊重。

9. tedium vitae：拉丁文，大意为"生之倦怠"。

10. *Elysium*：极乐世界，古希腊神话中受神佑得福的逝者居住之地。*Tempe*，滕比河谷，希腊东北部的一条峡谷，在古典作品中，是肥沃溪谷的代称。

11. 这句话大意为：模仿只会重复已有的原创之作，而且很可能不及原创；它只会增加书籍的滞销，使创造书籍价值的知识和天才停滞不前。

12. Armida 是意大利文艺复兴后期诗人塔索（Tasso）的史诗《被解放的耶路撒冷》（"Jerusalem Delivered"）中法力高深的女妖。

13. though but indifferent：虽说平庸。

14. 拉丁文，大意是：我虽穷，可花的是自己的钱。

15. 即尤利乌斯·凯撒。

16. 相当于汉语"宁为鸡头，不为凤尾"。

17. 大意是：原创之作令我们精神为之一振，而模仿之作总引起我们的倦怠，就像同一个故事再听一遍。rouse，这里作 awaken 解。

18. 这段话大意为：只要是原创，即使分量有限，也会引起读者的注意；要是它优异与新颖兼擅，读者在惊奇之余又多上一分赞美。读者的思绪完全被作家的想象力所控制，情随物迁，任驰东西，直到那摄人魂魄的作品戛然而止，才恍然如黄粱梦断，若有所失。

19. Babel：通天塔。根据《圣经》的说法，起初，人类可以用同一种语言互相沟通。人类在巴比伦拟建通天塔上天，上帝怒其狂妄，使建塔人突然操不同语言，彼此无法沟通，通天塔因此未能建成。

20. 这句话大意是：世人只会首赞原创之作，对模仿之作，不仅不会再赞扬，反而会斥其为欺骗。

21. Pindar：品达（约前 518—约前 438），古希腊诗人，著有合唱琴歌、竞技胜利者颂等，保存至今的只有竞技胜利者颂 45 首。

22. Anacreon：阿那克里翁（约前 570—约前 480），古希腊宫廷诗人，所作的诗歌多以歌颂醇酒、妇人为主，其诗体被后人称为"阿那克里翁诗体"。

23. Goth：哥特人，日耳曼民族，多次侵扰罗马帝国，曾经劫掠罗马，焚毁书籍文物。

24. Po：波河，意大利北部的重要河流。

25. Omar：奥玛尔（约 581—644），全名为 Omar ibn al Khattab，阿拉伯帝国第二任哈里发（伊斯兰国家政教合一的领袖的尊号）。据说他的部队在北非亚历山大城之时，纵火焚烧了举世闻名的亚历山大图书馆。现已证明，此说系无稽之谈。在此之前，该馆已被焚烧多次，最近的一次在公元 391 年。

26. 本段大意为：古人显赫的文学功业让今人高山仰止，自信全失，扼杀了自己的创造力。

27. 古典学者托马斯·布莱克韦尔（Thomas Blackwell）在《荷马的生平与著述》（*An Inquiry into the Life and Writings of Homer*，1735）中臆断，天空的星体对天才和原创力有重要影响。

28. 这句话大意为：反对和驳斥这一点的人，所显示出的能力反倒倾向于他所否定的平等的证据。（这里的平等，指的是上文所说人类的心智在各个时代都是平等的。）

29. 这里说的是亚历山大大大帝（Alexander the Great，前356—前323）与希腊哲学家、犬儒派创始人第欧根尼（Diogenes，约前412—前323）之间对话的典故。亚历山大垂询对方有何求，第欧根尼却回答："且站到一边，不要挡着阳光。"

30. Helicon：赫利孔山，位于希腊中部。根据希腊神话，这里是希腊文艺女神缪斯居住的地方，这里的泉水给诗人灵感。

31. *viz*：拉丁文 *videlicet* 的缩略形式，"即"，通常读作 namely。

32. Pericles：伯里克利（前495—前429），雅典政治家，文治武功卓著。在他统治期间，雅典进入了鼎盛时期，兴建了许多庙宇和大型建筑物。

33. Plutarch：普卢塔克（约46—约120），古希腊传记作家、散文家，最主要著作为《希腊罗马名人比较列传》。

34. Gulliver：斯威夫特名著《格列佛游记》（*Gulliver's Travels*），的主人公。

35.《圣经》中所说的毁灭地球生灵的大洪水。

36. 出自古罗马诗人马提雅尔（Martial，约40—约104）的《碑铭体诗集》（*Epigrams*）。大意为：你的作品当面指控你是文贼。

37. 据说，罗马城的建立者罗穆卢斯（Romulus）早年为盗贼首领。

38. 这句话大意为：不也有一些人，他们并非博学多闻之士，其作品不也同样出色吗？这差不多能够说服我们，没有学问助一臂之力，他们更能大放异彩。

39. 这句话大意为：在大多数情况下，我们所认为的天才，是指完成丰功伟业的那种力量。天才之士在完成丰功伟业之时，并没有动用一般认为做此事所必需的手段。

40. 拉丁文，大意为：没有神圣的灵感，谁也成不了伟人。语出西塞罗。

41. 拉丁文，大意为：他否认法则是为他制定的，法则对他没有约束力。语出贺拉斯《诗艺》，与原文略有出入。

42. 这句话拉丁文大意为：有的时候，轻视金钱反倒是发财的最佳手段。

43. Vossius：福厄西斯（1577—1649），荷兰批评家、人文主义神学家。

44. 拉丁文，大意为：神明在我们内心。

45. Pallas：即希腊神话中的雅典娜，战争和智慧女神、艺术的保护神。据说她是从她父亲宙斯（罗马神话中为朱庇特，即 Jove）的脑袋里生出来的。

46. 这句话的大意是：斯威夫特刚执笔即受挫，追求声誉而根底不牢。斯威夫特最早写过品达体的颂诗，但很不成功。

47. fathers of the church：指 8 世纪以前创建教义的早期基督教作家，例如奥古斯丁。

48. 在以上四段当中，作者反复论证天才比学问更重要。

49. Maecenas：米西纳斯（前 70—前 8），罗马贵族、巨富，奥古斯都的密友和顾问、著名的文学赞助人，与诗人维吉尔、贺拉斯等友善。

50. Augustus，奥古斯都（前 63—14），原名屋大维，罗马帝国第一代皇帝，在位期间奖掖学术和文化。"奥古斯都"是罗马元老院封给他的尊号。

51. Demosthenes：狄摩西尼（前 384—前 322），希腊演说家，曾向雅典市民发表演说，反抗马其顿国王菲利普二世。

52. 拉丁文，出自维吉尔《埃涅阿斯纪》。大意为：他拨开层层乌云，重现天日。

53. 出自弥尔顿《失乐园》（"Paradise Lost"）第 4 篇，意为：你在那里看到的，美人，正是你自己。

54. 作者后来未写。

55. 拉丁文，大意为：与我们距离很近，又相隔甚远。

56. 作者在以上 4 段主要表达的意思是：人不可妄自菲薄，要认识自己、尊重自己，深入内心去捕捉灵感，激发智慧的火花，不要被先贤的伟大著作吓倒而丧失了信心。

57. 当时英国新教徒对天主教和天主教徒极为鄙视，故有此语。

58. 指本·琼生。

59.《圣经》中的力士参孙。相传他被绑在两根房柱之间，他奋力推倒了房柱，与敌人同归于尽。

60. 本·琼生的《悲剧》，取材于罗马历史学家萨卢斯特（Sallust）的《喀提林阴谋》（ *The Conspiracy of Catiline* ）。

61. *Enceladus*：希腊神话中的大力士巨人，向诸神挑战，失败后被压在西西里的埃特纳火山下。

62. Castalian streams：来自帕纳塞斯山（太阳神和文艺女神的灵地）的卡斯塔利亚泉水，喝到这里泉水的人会产生诗歌灵感。

《为女权辩护》

玛丽·沃尔斯通克拉夫特（1759—1797）

　　玛丽·沃尔斯通克拉夫特出生于伦敦的一个破落的资产阶级家庭，早年备尝生活的艰辛。她的父亲酗酒成性，几乎挥霍掉了祖上的遗产，打骂子女成为家常便饭。玛丽从十五岁开始就告别了正规教育，但她天分奇高，读书勤奋，依靠自学，掌握了法文、德文、丹麦文和意大利文。十九岁时便离开家庭，自谋生路，从事家庭教师等卑微职业。1784 年，她和好友在外地合办了一家学校，在那里结识了激进的思想家、不从国教派的著名人物理查德·普莱斯（Richard Price）。普莱斯是当地的教长，在一些青年作家中颇有影响，其中包括玛丽。此人的激进言论惹怒了英国现代保守主义的鼻祖埃德蒙·伯克；后者的名著《法国革命论》（*Reflections on the Revolution in France*）就是为驳斥普莱斯而写的。学校没有维持多久便告破产，但是，这段从教经历却催生了玛丽的第一部著作《论女孩的教育》（*Thoughts on the Education of Daughters*, 1786）。她在书中首次提出了许多有关女性教育的思想，例如，为已婚妇女提供素质教育，为女性提供更多的职业选择。这都是她早年生活切肤之痛的结晶。

　　为了谋生，她还跑到爱尔兰，在一个丑闻不断的贵族家庭做家庭教师。在此期间，她创作了长篇小说《玛丽》（*Mary, A Fiction*, 1788）。不知何因，玛丽突然被解雇，只身回到伦敦。她的才华得到出版商约瑟夫·约翰逊的激赏，应邀为新创刊的杂志《分析评论》（*Analytical Review*）写稿、做翻译。《玛丽》这部小说也由约翰逊安排出版。玛丽在伦敦还结识了许多著名的激进知识分子，例如法国革命的辩护士、《人权宣言》（*The Rights of Man*）的作者托马斯·潘恩（Thomas Paine）、画家亨利·弗塞利（Henry Fuseli）、政治哲学家威廉·葛德温（William Goldwin）以及诗人威廉·布莱克（William Blake）。1789 年的法国大革命让英国激进文人和思想家大受鼓舞，让保守主义者深为恐惧。埃德蒙·伯克在《法国革命论》中激烈反对这场革命。他的主要理由是，大革命带来的民主是文明社会的公敌，民主导致的群众暴政泯灭了人性。他异常恐惧法国革命中的民主观念和人权观念，积极捍卫传统、君主制和世袭贵族政体。为了驳斥伯克的观点，玛丽在 1790 年匿名出版了《为人权辩护》（*A Vindication of the Rights of Men*）。紧接着，她写出了自己最重要的著作《为女权辩护》。在这部女性主义奠基之作中，她主张：法国革命赋予男性的权利也应扩展到女性身上，女性也应像男性那样有权发展自己的能力；现存的法律使女性屈从于男性，这种状况应当改变；社会上认同的女性特征，例如温柔可爱、盲目顺从等等，并非女性与生俱有的，而是后天教育和社会舆论造成的。

就在写这本书期间，她爱上了画家、有妇之夫弗塞利。弗塞利的妻子竟然提出，三人可以共同生活。这让她十分惊恐，只身去了巴黎。法国革命时期的恐怖统治令她触目惊心，她对法国革命的热情逐渐降低。在巴黎，她爱上了一个美国商人，两人同居，育有一女。这位商人艳遇不断，令她异常苦恼，两次自杀未遂。结束了这段不幸的情事之后，她黯然返回伦敦，与戈德温不期而遇，随后二人同居。1797年，怀孕后，为了让新生儿获得合法权利，她与戈德温正式结婚。同年九月，她因产后并发症去世。她与戈德温所生的女儿就是后来诗人雪莱（Percy Bysshe Shelley）的妻子、赫赫有名的玛丽·雪莱（Mary Shelley）。

内容提要

选文出自《为女权辩护》。作者开篇伊始，即驳斥当时社会非常通行的一种见解：女子无才便是德；她进而明确主张，让女子获得美德和幸福的唯一道路是，承认她们像男人一样有自己的灵魂，不要一味地盲从社会舆论。男性经常抱怨女性行事愚蠢、卑躬屈节，其实这都是社会教育不良令女性无知无识的结果。女性从小就接受教导，并以母亲为典范，学习察言观色、行事圆滑、性情柔和、表面恭谨、恪守礼数，她们只有这样才能得到男人的呵护。

弥尔顿在《失乐园》中以亚当的口吻发表了人类应当彼此平等的见解，认为这是人类和谐与快乐的保证；但就在同一部著作之中，他又让夏娃处处屈从于亚当，并借用夏娃的口吻说，"上帝是你的法律，你是我的规范，不求甚解就是女人最美妙的知识，并因此而受到称赞"。

作者在此非常敏锐地发现了弥尔顿在人类平等和男女平等方面的内在矛盾。

女性身上的缺陷并非先天所有，实际上是后天所养成。作者认为，在当前的社会中，束缚女性的理智，折磨女性的感官机能，使她们处于被奴役地位，背后的原因多种多样，其中最为严重的是女性做事情没有条理性。这是社会教育不良的结果。与男性相比，女性接受的知识不像男性接受的知识那样具有条理性。她们在家庭和社会中总是处于从属地位，导致的结果便是，她们囿于家门，与人罕有交往，涉世不深。因此，她们获得的知识是零星、不成系统的。而且，对于女性来说，学习是一件次要的事情。在女性教育方面，智力的培养远不及体态的培养。在她们年轻之际，由于没有机会与同龄男性进行竞争，她们固有的才智变得迟滞起来。她们也得不到机会从事严肃认真的科学研究。即使她们天资聪颖，这种聪颖也被用到生活和举止容貌上了。

假如男女受到同样的教育，二者是没有任何区别的。在这方面，男性军人就是一个例证。他们年纪轻轻就被抛到社会上。此时，他们还没有充足的知识储备，还没有足够的理性判断力，只能从人们的谈话中获取肤浅的知识；知人论世都是偶然观察的产物，学养不足，而且未经理性判断的检验。他们只学到一套表面规矩，人云亦云，盲从权威。与女性一样，他们被教导成取悦于人的人。

作者是启蒙运动的信徒，推崇卢梭的才华，佩服他的许多见解；但是，卢梭的女性观却令她相当恼怒。卢梭崇尚人类平等观念，但是在他的小说《爱弥儿》中，却表现出与此相悖的女性观。小说的女主人公被描写成男性的情欲对象，一个风骚的奴隶，在恐惧心理的支配下发挥天生狡猾的才能。这就是在暗示：顺从是女性最先需要培养的品质。

Mary Wollstonecraft (1759—1797)

From *A Vindication of the Rights of Woman*

From *Chapter II.*

The Prevailing Opinion of a Sexual Character Discussed

To account for, and excuse the tyranny of man, many ingenious arguments have been brought forward to prove, that the two sexes, in the acquirement of virtue, ought to aim at attaining a very different character:[1] or, to speak explicitly, women are not allowed to have sufficient strength of mind to acquire what really deserves the name of virtue. Yet it should seem, allowing them to have souls, that there is but on way appointed by Providence to lead *mankind* to either virtue or happiness.

If then women are not a swarm of ephemeron triflers[2], why should they be kept in ignorance under the specious name of innocence? Men complain, and with reason, of the follies and caprices of our sex, when they do not keenly satirize our headstrong passions and groveling vices.—Behold, I should answer, the natural effect of ignorance! The mind will ever be unstable that has only prejudices to rest on, and the current will run with destructive fury when there are no barriers to break its force. Women are told from their fancy, and taught by the example of their mothers, that a little knowledge of human weakness, justly termed cunning, softness of temper, *outward* obedience, and a scrupulous attention to a puerile kind of propriety, will obtain for them the protection of man; and should they be beautiful, everything else is needless, for, at least, twenty years of their lives.

Thus Milton[3] describes our first frail mother[4]; though when he tells us that women are formed for softness and sweet attractive grace, I cannot comprehend his meaning, unless, in the true Mahometan[5] strain, he meant to deprive us of souls, and insinuate that we were beings only designed by sweet attractive grace, and docile blind obedience, to gratify the sense of man when he can no longer soar on the wing of contemplation.

How grossly do they insult us who thus advise us only to render ourselves gentle, domestic brutes! For instance, the winning softness so warmly, and frequently, recommended, that governs by obeying[6]. What childish expressions, and how insignificant is the being—can it be an immortal one? Who will condescend to govern by such sinister methods! "Certainly," says Lord Bacon[7], "man is of kin to the beasts by his body; and if he be not of kin to God by his spirit, he is a base and ignoble creature!" Men, indeed, appear to me to act in a very unphilosophical[8] manner when they try to secure the good conduct of women by attempting to keep them always in a state of childhood. Rousseau[9] was more consistent when he wishes to stop the progress of reason in both sexes, for if men eat of the tree of knowledge, women will come in for a taste;[10] but, from the imperfect cultivation which their understandings now receive, they only attain a knowledge of evil.

Children, I grant, should be innocent; but when the epithet is applied to men, or women, it is but a civil term for weakness. For if it be allowed that women were destined by Providence to acquire human virtues, and by the exercise of their understandings, that stability of character which is the firmest ground to rest our future hopes upon, they must be permitted to turn to the fountain of light, and not forced to shape their course by the twinkling of a mere satellite.[11] Milton, I grant, was of a very different opinion; for he only bends to the indefeasible right of beauty, though it would be difficult to render two passages which I now mean to contrast, consistent.[12] But into similar inconsistencies are great men often led by their senses.[13]

> "To whom thus Eve with *perfect beauty* adorn'd.
> My Author and Disposer, what thou bidst
> *Unargued* I obey; so God ordains;
> God is *thy law, thou mine*: to know no more
> Is woman's *happiest* knowledge and her *praise*."[14]

These are exactly the arguments that I have used to children; but I have added, your reason is now gaining strength, and, till it arrives at some degree of maturity, you must look up to me for advice—then you ought to think, and only rely on God.

Yet in the following lines Milton seems to coincide with me; when he makes Adam thus expostulate with his Maker.

"Hast thou not made me here thy substitute,

And these inferior far beneath me set?

Among *unequals* what society

Can sort, what harmony or true delight?

Which must he mutual, in proportion due

Giv'n and receiv'd; but in *disparity*

The one intense, the other still remiss

Cannot well suit with either, but soon prove

Tedious alike: of *fellowship* I speak

Such as I seek, fit to participate

All rational delight—"[15]

In treating, therefore, of the manners of women, let us, disregarding sensual arguments,[16] trace what we should endeavor to make them in order to co-operate, if the expression be not too bold, with the supreme Being[17].

By individual education, I mean, for the sense of the word is not preciously defined, such an attention to a child as will slowly sharpen the senses, form the temper, regulate the passions as they begin to ferment, and set the understanding to work before the body arrives at maturity; so that the man may only have to proceed, not to begin, the important task of learning to think and reason.

To prevent any misconstruction[18], I must add, that I do not believe that a private education can work the wonders which some sanguine writers have attributed to it. Men and women must be educated, in a great degree, by the opinions and manners of the society they live in. In every age there has been a stream of popular opinion that has carried all before it,[19] and given a family character, as it were, to the century. It may then fairly be inferred, that, whatever effect circumstances have on the abilities, every being may become virtuous by the exercise of its own reason; for if but one being was created with vicious inclinations, that is positively bad, what can save us from atheism?[20] Or if we worship a God, is not that God a devil?

Consequently, the most perfect education, in my opinion, is such an exercise of the understanding as is best calculated to strengthen the body and form the heart. Or, in other words, to enable the individual to attain such habits of virtue as will render it independent. In fact, it is a farce to call any being virtuous whose virtues do not result from the exercise of its own reason. This was Rousseau's opinion respecting men:[21] I extend it to women, and confidently assert that they have been drawn out of their sphere[22] by false refinement, and not by an endeavor to acquire masculine qualities. Still the regal homage[23] which they receive is so intoxicating, that till the manners of the times are changed, and formed on more reasonable principles, it may be impossible to convince them that the illegitimate power, which they obtain, by degrading themselves, is a curse, and that they must return to nature and equality, if they wish to secure the placid satisfaction that unsophisticated affections[24] impart. But for this epoch we must wait—wait, perhaps, till kings and nobles, enlightened by reason, and, preferring the real dignity of man to childish state, throw off their gaudy hereditary trappings: and if then women do not resign the arbitrary power of beauty—they will prove that they have less mind than man. [25]

I may be accused of arrogance; still I must declare what I firmly believe, that all the writers who have written on the subject of female education and manners from Rousseau to Dr. Gregory[26], have contributed to render women more artificial, weak characters, than they would otherwise have been; and, consequently, more useless members of society. I might have expressed this conviction in a lower key[27]; but I am afraid it would have been the whine of affection[28], and not the faithful expression of my feelings, of the clear result, which experience and reflection have led me to draw. When I come to that division of the subject, I shall advert to the passages that I more particularly disapprove of, in the works of the authors I have just alluded to; but it is first necessary to observe, that my objection extends to the whole purport of those books, which tend, in my opinion, to degrade one half of the human species[29], and render women pleasing at the expense of every solid virtue[30].

Though, to reason on Rousseau's ground, if man did attain a degree of perfection of mind when his body arrived at maturity, it might be proper, in order to make a man and his wife *one*[31], that she should rely entirely on his understanding; and the graceful ivy, clasping the oak that supported it, would form a whole in which strength and beauty would be equally conspicuous. But, alas! husbands, as well as their helpmates, are often only overgrown children; nay, thanks to early debauchery, scarcely men in their outward form[32]—and if the blind lead the blind, one need not come from heaven[33] to tell us the consequence.

Many are the causes that, in the present corrupt state of society, contribute to enslave women by cramping their understandings and sharpening their senses. One, perhaps, that silently does more mischief than all the rest,[34] is their disregard of order.

To do everything in an orderly manner, is a most important precept, which women, who, generally speaking, receive only a disorderly kind of education, seldom attend to with that degree of exactness that men, who from their infancy are broken into method, observe. This negligent kind of guess-work[35]—for what other epithet can be used to point out the random exertions of a sort of instinctive common sense, never brought to the test of reason?—prevents their generalizing matters of fact—so they do to-day, what they did yesterday, merely because they did it yesterday.

This contempt of the understanding in early life has more baneful consequences than is commonly supposed; for the little knowledge which women of strong minds attain, is, from various circumstances, of a more desultory kind than the knowledge of men, and it is acquired more by sheer observations on real life, than from comparing what has been individually observed with the results of experience generalized by speculation. Led by their dependent situation and domestic employments more into society, what they learn is rather by snatches; and as learning is with them, in general, only a secondary thing, they do not pursue any one branch with that persevering ardor necessary to give vigor to the faculties, and clearness to the judgment. In the present state of society, a little learning is required to support the character of a gentleman; boys are obliged to submit to a few years of discipline. But in the education of women, the cultivation of the understanding is always subordinate to the acquirement of some corporeal accomplishment; even while enervated by confinement and false notions of modesty, the body is prevented from attaining that grace and beauty which relaxed half-formed limbs never exhibit. Besides, in youth their faculties are not brought forward by emulation; and having no serious scientific study, if they have natural sagacity it is turned too soon on life and manners. They dwell on effects, and modifications, without tracing them back to causes; and complicated rules to adjust behavior are a weak substitute for simple principles.

As a proof that education gives this appearance of weakness to females, we may instance the example of military men, who are, like them, sent into the world before their minds have been stored with knowledge or fortified by principles. The consequences are similar, soldiers acquire a little superficial knowledge, snatched from the muddy current of conversation, and, from continually mixing with society, they gain, what is termed a knowledge of the world; and this acquaintance with manners and customs has frequently been confounded with a knowledge of the human heart. But can the crude fruit of casual observation, never brought to the test of judgment, formed by comparing speculation and experience, deserve such a distinction? Soldiers, as well as women, practise the minor virtues with punctilious politeness. Where is then the sexual difference, when the education has been the same? All the difference that I can discern, arises from the superior advantage of liberty, which enables the former to see more of life.

It is wandering from my present subject, perhaps, to make a political remark,[36] but, as it was produced naturally by the train of my reflections, I shall not pass it silently over.

Standing armies can never consist of resolute, robust men; they may be well disciplined machines, but they will seldom contain men under the influence of strong passions, or with very vigorous faculties. And as for any depth of understanding, I will venture to affirm, that it is as rarely to be found in the army as amongst women; and the cause, I maintain, is the same. It may be further observed, that officers are also particularly attentive to their persons, fond of dancing, crowded rooms, adventures, and ridicule[37]. Like the *fair* sex[38], the business of their lives is gallantry.—They were taught to please, and they only live to please. Yet they do not lose their rank in the distinction of sexes, for they are still reckoned superior to women, though in what their superiority consists, beyond what I have just mentioned, it is difficult to discover.

The great misfortune is this, that they both acquire manners before morals, and a knowledge of life before they have, from reflection, any acquaintance with the grand ideal outline of human nature. The consequence is natural; satisfied with common nature, they become a prey to prejudices, and taking all their opinions on credit, they blindly submit to authority. So that, if they have any sense, it is a kind of instinctive glance, that catches proportions, and decides with respect to manners; but fails when arguments are to be pursued below the surface, or opinions analyzed.

May not the same remark be applied to women? Nay, the argument may be carried still further, for they are both thrown out of a useful station by the unnatural distinctions established in civilized life. Riches and hereditary honors have made cyphers of women to give consequence to the numerical figure;[39] and idleness has produced a mixture of gallantry and despotism into society, which leads the very man who are the slaves of their mistresses to tyrannize over their sisters, wives, and daughters. This is only keeping them in rank and file, it is ture.[40] Strengthen the female mind by enlarging it, and there will be an end to blind obedience; but as blind obedience is ever sought for by power, tyrants and sensualists[41] are in the right when they endeavor to keep women in the dark, because the former only want slaves, and the latter a play-thing. The sensualist, indeed, has been the most dangerous of tyrants, and women have been duped by their lovers, as princes by their ministers, whilst dreaming that they reigned over them.

I now principally allude to Rousseau, for his character of Sophia[42] is, undoubtedly, a captivating one, though it appears to me grossly unnatural; however it is not the superstructure, but the foundation of her character, the principles on which her education was built, that I mean to attack; nay, warmly as I admire the genius of that able writer, whose opinion I shall often have occasion to cite, indignation always takes place of admiration, and the rigid frown of insulted virtue effaces the smile of complacency, which his eloquent periods[43] are wont to raise, when I read his voluptuous reveries. Is this the man, who, in his ardor for virtue, would banish all the soft arts of peace, and almost carry us back to Spartan discipline[44]? Is this the man who delights to paint the useful struggle of passion, the triumphs of good dispositions, and the heroic flights which carry the glowing soul out of itself?—How are these mighty sentiments lowered when he describes the pretty foot and enticing airs of his little favorite! But, for the present,

I waive the subject,[45] and, instead of severely reprehending the transient effusions of overweening sensibility, I shall only observe[46], that whoever has cast a benevolent eye on society, must often have been gratified by the humble mutual love, not dignified by sentiment, or strengthened by a union in intellectual pursuits. The domestic trifles of the day have afforded matters for cheerful converse[47], and innocent caresses have softened toils which did not acquire great exercise of mind or stretch of thought: yet, had not the sight of this moderate felicity excited more tenderness than respect? An emotion similar to what we feel when children are playing, or animals sporting[48], whilst the contemplation of the noble struggles of suffering merit[49] has raised admiration; and carried our thoughts to that world where sensation will give place to reason.

Women are, therefore, to be considered either as moral beings, or so weak that they must be entirely subjected to the superior faculties of men.

Let us examine this question. Rousseau declares that a woman should never, for a moment, feel herself independent, that she should be governed by fear to exercise her *natural* cunning, and made a coquettish slave in order to render her a more alluring object of desire, a *sweeter* companion to man, whenever he chooses to relax himself. He carries the arguments, which he pretends to draw from the indications of nature, still further, and insinuates that truth and fortitude, the corner stones of all human virtue, should be cultivated with certain restrictions, because, with respect to the female character, obedience is the grand lesson which ought to be impressed with unrelenting rigor[50].

What nonsense! When will a great man arise with sufficient strength of mind[51] to puff away the fumes which pride and sensuality have thus spread over the subject! If women are by nature inferior to men, their virtues must be the same in quality, if not in degree, or virtue is a relative idea; consequently, their conduct should be founded on the same principles, and have the same aim.

Connected with man as daughters, wives, and mothers, their moral character may be estimated by their manner of fulfilling those simple duties; but the end, the grand end of their exertions[52] should be to unfold their own faculties and acquire the dignity of conscious virtue. They may try to render their road pleasant; but ought never to forget, in common with man, that life yields not the felicity which can satisfy an immortal soul. I do not mean to insinuate, that either sex should be so lost in abstract reflections or distant views, as to forget the affections and duties that lie before them, and are, in truth, the means appointed to produce the fruit of life; on the contrary, I would warmly recommend them, even while I assert, that they afford most satisfaction when they are considered in their true, sober light.

Probably the prevailing opinion, the woman was created for man, may have taken its rise from Mose's poetical story[53]; yet, as very few, it is presumed, who have bestowed any serious thought on the subject, ever supposed that Eve was, literally speaking, one of Adam's ribs, the deduction must be allowed to fall to the ground;[54] or, only be so far admitted as it proves that man, from the remotest antiquity, found it convenient to exert his strength to subjugate his companion, and his invention to show that she ought to have her neck bent under the yoke, because the whole creation was only created for his convenience or pleasure.

Let it not be concluded that I wish to invert the order of things;[55] I have already granted, that, from the constitution of their bodies, men seem to be designed by Providence to attain a greater degree of virtue. I speak collectively of the whole sex; but I see not the shadow of a reason[56] to conclude that their virtues should differ in respect to their nature. In fact, how can they, if virtue has only one eternal standard? I must therefore, if I reason, consequentially, as strenuously maintain that they have the same simple direction, as that there is a God.

It follows then the cunning should not be opposed to wisdom, little cares to great exertions, or insipid softness, varnished over with the name of gentleness, to that fortitude which grand views alone can inspire.

I shall be told that woman would then lose many of her peculiar graces, and the opinion of a well known poet might be quoted to refute my unqualified assertion. For Pope has said, in the name of the whole male sex,

"Yet ne'er so sure our passion to create,
As when she touch'd the brink of all we hate."[57]

In what light this sally places men and women, I shall leave to the judicious to determine; meanwhile I shall content myself with observing, that I cannot discover why, unless they are mortal,[58] females should always be degraded by being made subservient to love or lust.

To speak disrespectfully of love is, I know, high treason against sentiment and fine feelings; but I wish to speak the simple language of truth, and rather to address the head than the heart. To endeavor to reason love out of the world, would be to out Quixote Cervantes[59], and equally offend against common sense; but an endeavor to restrain this tumultuous passion, and to prove that it should not be allowed to dethrone superior powers, or to usurp the scepter which the understanding should ever coolly wield, appears less wild.

Youth is the season for love in both sexes; but in those days of thoughtless enjoyment provision should be made for the more important years of life, when reflection takes place of sensation. But Rousseau, and most of the male writers who have followed his steps, have warmly inculcated that the whole tendency of female education ought to be directed to one point—to render them pleasing.

Let me reason with[60] the supporters of this opinion who have any knowledge of human nature, do they imagine that marriage can eradicate the habitude of life? The woman who has only been taught to please will soon find that her charms are oblique sunbeams, and that they cannot have much effect on her husband's heart when they are seen every day, when the summer is passed and gone. Will she then have sufficient native energy to look into herself for comfort, and cultivate her dormant faculties? or, is it not more rational to expect that she will try to please other men; and, in the emotions raised by the expectation of new conquests, endeavor to forget the mortification her love or pride has received? When the husband ceases to be a lover—and the time will inevitably come, her desire of pleasing will then grow languid, or become a spring of bitterness; and love, perhaps, the most evanescent of all passions, gives place to jealousy or vanity.

I now speak of women who are restrained by principle or prejudice; such women, though they would shrink from an intrigue with real abhorrence,[61] yet, nevertheless, wish to be convinced by the homage of gallantry that they are cruelly neglected by their husbands; or, days and weeks are spent in dreaming of the happiness enjoyed by congenial souls till their health is undermined and their spirits broken by discontent. How then can the great art of pleasing be such a necessary study? It is only useful to a mistress; the chaste wife, and serious mother, should only consider her power to please as the polish of her virtues, and the affection of her husband as one of the comforts that render her task less difficult and her life happier. But, whether she be loved or neglected, her first wish should be to make herself respectable, and not to rely for all her happiness on a being subject to like infirmities with herself.[62]

. . .

1792

注释

1. aim at attaining a very different character：以培养不同的性格为目的。
2. a swarm of ephemeron triflers：一群生命短促的小人物。
3. 即约翰·弥尔顿。
4. our first frail mother：指夏娃。弥尔顿在《失乐园》中讲述了人类如何堕落的故事。
5. 伊斯兰教徒。这句话暗示，伊斯兰教也否认妇女是有灵魂的。
6. governs by obeying：佯作服从姿态，以此来获取支配丈夫的权力。
7. 即弗朗西斯·培根。下面的引文出自培根的《论说文集》。
8. unphilosophical：不明智的。
9. 即卢梭（Jean-Jacques Rousseau, 1712—1778），法国启蒙思想家，文中有关卢梭的引文，多出自他的《爱弥儿》一书。
10. 即《旧约》创世纪第二、三章有关亚当和夏娃偷吃禁果的故事。
11. the fountain of light：太阳。the twinkling of a mere satellite：指月亮的微光。
12. 下面两段话（弥尔顿《失乐园》引文）的意思正相反。
13. 这句话暗含讽刺：大人物的见识经常前后矛盾。
14.（美艳无缺的夏娃对他表示：）

"我的创作者和安排者啊，你所
吩咐的，我都依从，从不争辩，

这是神定的。神是你的法律，

你是我的法律；此外不识不知，

这才是最幸福的知识，女人的美誉。"

（引文见《失乐园》第四卷 634—638 行，朱维之译）

15. "您不是造我在这儿做您的代言人，

把这些愚劣者遥遥放在我下面吗？

不平等之间，能有什么交际，

什么和谐，或真正的欢乐呢？

这要求互相平衡，互相授受。

但在不平衡的情况下，

这个张，那个驰，互不配合，

结果，二者不久便厌倦了。

我所说的和所寻求的友谊，

是能互相分享一切出于理性的

愉快……"

16. 大意为：不要从感官方面寻找依据。

17. the supreme Being：上帝。

18. misconstruction：误解。

19. that has carried all before it：势不可挡。

20. 大意为：只要一个人生而禀性邪恶，那么，我们就有充分的理由信奉无神论（按照基督教的说法，人是上帝造的，而上帝不可能造恶人）。

21. 大意为：这是卢梭对男人的看法。

22. they have been drawn out of their sphere：有违妇道，发生越轨行为。

23. regal homage：帝王般的荣誉。

24. unsophisticated affections：纯真的爱情（不是依靠工于心计而得到的）。

25. less mind than man：智力上不如男人。

26. Dr. Gregory：格里高利（John Gregory, 1724—1773），苏格兰医学家，著有《父亲给女儿的赠言》（*A Father's Legacy to His Daughters*）。沃尔斯通克拉夫特经常援引他的著作。

27. in a lower key：低调一点儿。

28. the whine of affection：嗔怪。

29. one half of the human species：人类的另一半，即妇女。

30. render women pleasing at the expense of every solid virtue：让女性牺牲美德，取悦于男性。

31. one：（融为）一体。

32. 大意为：由于他们早年纵情声色，淘虚了身体，他们现在的外表并无阳刚之气。

33. 即耶稣（Jesus）。

34. that silently does more mischief than all the rest：其中暗无声息、为害最甚的。

35. guess-work：下文所说的做事全凭某种本能性的常识。

36. 大意为：在这里发表政治性评论或许有些跑题。

37. ridicule：嘲弄人。

38. 这里指女性。

39.【作者原注】That is, women are merely zeroes（"ciphers"）to add to the family name, inflating its value but being nothing in themselves.

40. 大意为：这只会使她们（上文提到的 sisters, wives and daughters）恪守本分。

41. sensualist：好色之徒。

42. Sophia 是卢梭《爱弥儿》中的主人公。

43. eloquent periods：流畅的句子。

44. Spartan discipline："斯巴达式的规则"，指禁欲主义。

45. waive the subject：抛开这一话题。

46. observe：评论。

47. cheerful converse：愉快的交谈。

48. animals sporting：动物间的戏耍。

49. suffering merit：受苦受难的优秀人物。

50. unrelentling rigor：严格地。

51. with sufficient strength of mind：用强大的意志力。

52. their exertions：指的是 the exertions of "those simple duties"。

53. Mose's poetical story：指《圣经》中摩西的故事。

54. 大意为：这种推论注定不能成立。

55. 大意为：不要由此而得出结论说，我想把事情的顺序颠倒过来。

56. 大意为：但我找不到一点理由……

57. 这两句诗的大意为：一旦她们触怒我们，无法预料后果如何。

58. 大意为：除非她们死掉。

59. 大意为：说服世人抛弃爱情，就像从塞万提斯的作品中去掉堂吉诃德一样，是违反常规之举。

60. reason with：同……讲道理。

61. 大意为：尽管她们厌恶与男人私通。

62. a being subject to like infirmities with herself：与她有相同缺陷的男性。

威廉·华兹华斯（1770—1850）

威廉·华兹华斯于 1770 年出生于坎伯兰郡的考克茅斯，此地位于英格兰西北部风景秀丽的湖区。他幼年失怙，八岁左右即被送往湖区中部的一所文法学校读书，寄宿在当地农民家中。质朴的乡间生活，怡人的山光水色，良师的启发教导，对他日后形成崇尚自然的思想、清新俊朗的诗风有很大影响。1787 年，他进入剑桥大学深造。在学期间，他大量阅读古典作品，自学多门欧洲语言。在 1790 年的 9 月和 10 月，他与同学步行游历法国、瑞士和意大利。大革命爆发已届一年，但法国民众的激情炽烈，华兹华斯也成为共和派的热情支持者。1791 年，他大学毕业后再次赴法，结识了革命阵营中的温和派——吉伦特派。1793 年他出版了自己最早的两部诗集《黄昏信步》(*An Evening Walk*)和《景物素描集》(*Descriptive Sketches*)，诗中对法国革命多有赞颂。拿破仑上台后，对外扩张，战事连年不断，华兹华斯最终对法国革命产生幻灭感。

　　1795 年，一位钦佩其才、认同其政治观点的朋友去世之后留给他一笔不菲的遗产，使他得以心无旁骛，潜心创作。同年，在妹妹多萝西的陪同下，他离开了政治风暴的中心——伦敦，迁居多塞特郡的乡下，观察自然，探索人生，求得心灵的宁静。就是在这一年，华兹华斯兄妹初识柯勒律治。两年之后，他们与柯勒律治比邻而居，交往日密，相互激励，成为文坛上的一段佳话。1798 年 10 月，华兹华斯和柯勒律治匿名出版了《抒情歌谣集》，揭开了英国浪漫主义诗歌运动的帷幕，在英国诗歌发展史上产生了划时代的意义。这部短集收诗几十首，大部分是华兹华斯的作品；开篇之作是柯勒律治的《古舟子咏》("The Rime of the Ancient Mariner")，压卷之作是华兹华斯的《丁登寺》("Tintern Abbey")。1880 年问世的新版在内容上有所调整，增添了华兹华斯的几首新作，更重要的是，还增加了华兹华斯的序言。这篇自我辩护性质的序言系统地提出了华兹华斯的诗歌主张，成为英国浪漫主义的美学宣言，文学批评史上的名篇。华兹华斯在文中敦促诗人摆脱新古典主义的形式羁绊，摈弃华而不实的诗意辞藻，在日常生活中、尤其是在普通民众的生活中寻找诗歌题材和表达方式。

1798 年至 1799 年春，华兹华斯兄妹在德国小住了一段时期，在那里开始创作自传性长诗《序曲》（"The Prelude"），写出《露西》组诗（the Lucy poems）。回国后，他们定居格林斯米尔附近的"鸽庐"（Dove Cottage）。1802 年，他与旧日相识的女友玛丽·哈钦生结婚，同年开始创作代表作《不朽的征兆》（"Intimations of Immortality from Recollections of Early Childhood"）。几年之后，各种打击接踵而至：1805 年，他的弟弟约翰死于海难；1810 年，他与柯勒律治友情破裂，分道扬镳；1812 年，他的一子一女先后早殇。他的创作高峰已过，自1815 年后，不复有新的力作问世。不过，此时他在诗坛已经功成名就，驰誉国内。1843 年，他继骚塞之后荣膺桂冠诗人的称号，1850 年去世。

内容提要

浪漫主义肇始于 18 世纪末期的德国，尔后跨海西来，蔓延至英伦诸岛。德国古典唯心主义哲学家对浪漫主义产生了极大的推动作用，并与作家形成了良好的互动。德国浪漫主义者当中既有歌德和席勒这样的诗人，施莱格尔兄弟这样的批评家，还有康德、谢林这样的哲学家。德国浪漫主义文论后来专注理论，走向了抽象一途，诚非偶然。在英国浪漫主义文论家当中，只有柯勒律治的著述理论气息浓厚，这是受德国思潮影响的结果；其余人的行文风格明显还是英国式的，经验主义特征非常明显：着眼于具体的诗歌创作，就事论事，不作抽象的理论演绎。这一时期的浪漫主义批评大家，如华兹华斯、雪莱和济慈（John Keats），他们的文学批评都是基于个人的创作有感而发，或是替自己辩护，或是为自己总结。

《〈抒情歌谣集〉序》的核心内容体现在第六段，其大意为：集中所收诸诗，都是从日常生活当中遴选事件和情节；在叙述和描写之时，尽量选用人们在日常生活中实际使用的语言；与此同时，对这些寻常小事加以想象渲染，让它们以异乎寻常的方式呈现在读者的脑海中，这样做的目的是使它们变得生动有趣。从这些事件和情节当中切切实实地追查人性中的基本规律：即人们如何精神振奋，浮想联翩。诗中所选用的题材，一般都来自乡野村俗：因为，在这种环境之下，人们心中的强烈情感可以发展成熟，充分抒发，少受约束，而其语言会更加质朴有力；因为，在这种生活环境之下，人的各种基本情感极为单纯，思考起来更准确，表达起来更有力度。正因为田园生活中的各种习俗萌生于这些情感中，萌生于田园劳作的必要特性中，因此，它们就更容易为人理解，存在也更为持久；最后，在田园生活环境下，人的强烈情感与永恒的自然之美融为一体。这些诗歌之所以采用乡民的日常语言，就是因为，这些人时时刻刻与世界上最美好的东西交往沟通，而语言的精华即来源于此；因为他们的社会地位很低，他们的社交单纯狭窄而且一成不变，所以他们很少受到社会上种种虚荣行径的影响，他们表达情感和观点的方式不带做作的成分。这些日常经验和正常情感所产生的语言，比起诗人惯常使用的诗意辞藻，显得更具永久魅力，更富有哲理性。这类诗人总是认为，越是与人们共有的情感相抵牾，越是使用武断任性的表达法，以满足自己奇谲诡异的趣味和偏好，就越能给自己增光添彩。在这里，值得注意的是，乔叟作品中的那些动人篇章，使用的几乎都是澄澈透明的语言；时至今日，这样的语言依旧让人读得懂。

作者之所以如此强调诗歌语言应当质朴清新，意在反对新古典主义的末流专事雕琢、古意斑斓的诗风。作者还得出结论说，上乘诗作，除了有韵律之外，其用语与散文没有区别；在一首好诗当中，最有趣的诗行往往是用散文体语言写就的。他特意引用了喜欢堆砌典故的托马斯·格雷的一首十四行诗，用以说明，格雷力主严格区分诗意辞藻与散文语言；然而，在他的这篇作品中，唯一有价值的三行诗，恰恰是用明白如话的散文体写成的。华兹华斯对诗歌语言与散文语言之间关系的论述，在某种程度上预示了后来瑞恰慈（I. A. Richards）对诗歌语言和科学语言的区分辨析。华兹华斯对诗歌语言的探索，成为英国文论对浪漫主义文学的一大贡献。

Willam Wordsworth (1770—1850)

Preface to *Lyrical Ballads, with Pastoral and Other Poems*

(1802)

The first Volume of these Poems has already been submitted to general perusal[1]. It was published, as an experiment, which, I hoped, might be of some use to ascertain, how far, by fitting to metrical arrangement a selection of the real language of men in a state of vivid sensation, that sort of pleasure and that quantity of pleasure may be imparted[2], which a Poet may rationally endeavor to impart.

I had formed no very inaccurate estimate of the probable effect of those Poems; I flattered myself that they who should be pleased with them would read them with more than common pleasure: and, on the other hand, I was well aware, that by those who should dislike them they would be read with more than common dislike. The result has differed from my expectation in this only, that I have pleased a greater number, than I ventured to hope I should please.

For the sake of variety, and from a consciousness of my own weakness, I was induced to request the assistance of a Friend[3], who furnished me with the Poems of the ANCIENT MARINER, the FOSTER-MOTHER'S TALE, the NIGHTINGALE, and the Poem entitled LOVE. I should not, however, have requested this assistance, had I not believed that the Poems of my Friend would in a great measure have the same tendency as my own, and that, though there would be found a difference, there would be found no discordance in the colors of our style; as our opinions on the subject of poetry do almost entirely coincide.

Several of my Friends are anxious for the success of these Poems from a belief, that, if the views with which they were composed were indeed realized, a class of Poetry would be produced, well adapted to interest mankind permanently, and not unimportant in the multiplicity, and in the quality of its moral relations: and on this account they have advised me to prefix a systematic defence of the theory, upon which the poems were written. But I was unwilling to undertake the task, because I knew that on this occasion the Reader would look coldly upon my arguments, since I might be suspected of having been particularly influenced by the selfish and foolish hope of *reasoning* him into an approbation of these particular Poems:[4] and I was still more unwilling to undertake the task, because, adequately to display my opinions, and fully to enforce my arguments, would require a space wholly disproportionate to the nature of a preface. For to treat the subject with the clearness and coherence, of which I believe it susceptible, it would be necessary to give a full account of the present state of the public taste in this country, and to determine how far this taste is healthy or depraved; which[5], again, would not be determined, without pointing out, in what manner language and the human mind act and re-act on each other, and without retracing the revolutions, not of literature alone, but likewise of society itself. I have altogether declined to enter regularly upon this defence; yet I am sensible, that there would be some impropriety in abruptly obtruding upon the Public, without a few words of introduction, Poems so materially different from those, upon which general approbation is at present bestowed.

It is supposed, that by the act of writing in verse an Author makes a formal engagement that he will gratify certain known habits of association[6]; that he not only thus apprizes the Reader that certain classes of ideas and expressions will be found in his book, but that others will be carefully excluded. This exponent or symbol held forth by metrical language must in different areas of literature have excited very different expectations,[7] for example, in the age of Catullus, Terence, and Lucretius, and that of Statius or Claudian;[8] and in our country, in the age of Shakespeare and Beaumont and Fletcher, and that of Donne and Cowley,[9] or Dryden, or Pope. I will not take upon me to determine the exact import of the promise which by the act of writing in verse an Author, in the present day, makes to his Reader; but I am certain, it will appear to many persons that I have not fulfilled the terms of an engagement thus voluntarily contracted. [They who have been accustomed to the gaudiness and inane phraseology[10] of many modern writers, if they persist in reading this book to its conclusion, will, no doubt, frequently have to struggle with feelings of strangeness and awkwardness:

they will look round for poetry, and will be induced to inquire by what species of courtesy these attempts can be permitted to assume that title.[11]] I hope therefore the Reader will not censure me, if I attempt to state what I have proposed to myself to perform; and also, (as far as the limits of a preface will permit) to explain some of the chief reasons which have determined me in the choice of my purpose: that at least he may be spared any unpleasant feeling of disappointment, and that I myself may be protected from the most dishonorable accusation which can be brought against an Author, namely, that of an indolence[12] which prevents him from endeavoring to ascertain what is his duty, or, when his duty is ascertained, prevents him from performing it.

The principal object, then, which I proposed to myself in these Poems was to [chuse[13] incidents and situations from common life, and to relate or describe them, throughout, as far as was possible, in a selection of language really used by men; and, at the same time, to throw over them a certain coloring of imagination, whereby ordinary things should be presented to the mind in an unusual way; and, further, and above all, to make these incidents and situations interesting] by tracing in them, truly though not ostentatiously, the primary laws of our nature: chiefly, as far as regards[14] the manner in which we associate ideas in a state of excitement. Low and rustic life was generally chosen, because in that condition, the essential passions of the heart find a better soil in which they can attain their maturity, are less under restraint, and speak a plainer and more emphatic language; because in that condition of life our elementary feelings co-exist in a state of greater simplicity, and, consequently, may be more accurately contemplated, and more forcibly communicated; because the manners of rural life germinate from these elementary feelings; and, from the necessary character of rural occupations, are more easily comprehended; and more durable; and lastly, because in that condition the passion of men are incorporated with the beautiful and permanent forms of nature. The language, too, of these men is adopted (purified indeed from what appears to be its real defects, from all lasting and rational causes of dislike or disgust) because such men hourly communicate with the best objects from which the best part of language is originally derived; and because, from their rank in society and the sameness and narrow circle of their intercourse, being less under the influence of social vanity they convey their feelings and notions in simple and unelaborated expressions. Accordingly, such a language, arising out of repeated experience and regular feelings, is a more permanent, and a far more philosophical language, than that which is frequently substituted for it by Poets, who think that they are conferring honor upon themselves and their art, in proportion as they separate themselves from the sympathies of men, and indulge in arbitrary and capricious habits of expression, in order to furnish food for fickle tastes, and fickle appetites, of their own creations.[15]

I cannot, however, be insensible of the present outcry against the triviality and meanness both of thought and language, which some of my contemporaries have occasionally introduced into their metrical compositions; and I acknowledge that this defect, where it exists, is more dishonorable to the Writer's own character than false refinement or arbitrary innovation, though I should contend at the same time that it is far less pernicious in the sum of its consequences. From such verses the Poems in these volumes will be found distinguished at least by one mark of difference, that each of them has a worthy *purpose*. Not that I mean to say, that I always began to write with a distinct purpose formally conceived; but I believe that my habits of meditation have so formed my feelings, as that my descriptions of such objects as strongly excite those feelings, will be found to carry along with them a purpose.[16] If in this opinion I am mistaken, I can have little right to the name of a Poet. For all good poetry is the spontaneous overflow of powerful feelings: but though this be true, Poems to which any value can be attached, were never produced on any variety of subjects but by a man, who being possessed of more than usual organic sensibility, had also thought long and deeply. For our continued influxes of feeling are modified and directed by our thoughts, which are indeed the representatives of all our past feelings; and, as by contemplating the relation of these general representatives to each other we discover what is really important to men, so, by the repetition and continuance of this act[17], our feelings will be connected with important subjects, till at length, if we be originally possessed of much sensibility, such habits of mind will be produced, that, by obeying blindly and mechanically the impulses of those habits, we shall describe objects, and utter sentiments, of such a nature and in such connection with each other, that the understanding of the being to whom we address ourselves[18], if he be in a healthful state of association, must necessarily be in some degree enlightened, and his affections ameliorated.

· · ·

I will not suffer a sense of false modesty to prevent me from asserting,[19] that I point my Reader's attention to this mark of distinction, far less for the sake of these particular Poems than from the general importance of the subject. The subject is indeed important! For the human mind is capable of being excited without the application of gross and violent stimulants; and he must have a very faint perception of its beauty and dignity[20] who does not know this, and who does not further know, that one being is elevated above another, in proportion as he possesses this capability[21]. It has therefore appeared to me, that to endeavor to produce or enlarge this capability is one of the best services in which, at any period, a Writer can be engaged; but this service, excellent at all times, is especially so at the present day. For a multitude of causes, unknown to former times, are now acting with a combined force to blunt the discriminating powers of the mind, and unfitting it for all voluntary exertion to reduce it to a state of almost savage torpor.[22] The most effective of these causes are the great national events[23] which are daily taking place, and the encreasing accumulation of men in cities, where the uniformity of their occupations produces a craving for extraordinary incident, which the rapid communication of intelligence[24] hourly gratifies. To this tendency of life and manners the literature and theatrical exhibitions of the country have conformed themselves. The invaluable works of our elder writers, I had almost said the works of Shakespeare and Milton, are driven into neglect by frantic novels[25], sickly and stupid German Tragedies[26], and deluges of idle and extravagant stories in verse. When I think upon this degrading thirst after courageous stimulation, I am ashamed to have spoken of the feeble effort with which I have endeavored to counteract it; and, reflecting upon the magnitude of the general evil, I should be oppressed with no dishonorable melancholy, had I not a deep impression of certain inherent and indestructible qualities of the human mind,[27] and likewise of certain powers in the great and permanent objects that act upon it, which are equally inherent and indestructible; and did I not further add to this impression a belief, that the time is approaching when the evil will be systematically opposed, by men of greater powers, and with far more distinguished success.

Having dwelt thus long on the subjects and aim of these Poems, I shall request the Reader's permission to apprize him of a few circumstances relating to their *style*, in order, among other reasons, that I may not be censured for not having performed what I never attempted. [The Reader will find that personifications of abstract ideas really occur in these volumes; and, I hope, are utterly rejected as an ordinary device to elevate the style,[28] and raise it above prose. I have proposed to myself to imitate, and, as far as is possible, to adopt the very language of men; and assuredly such personifications do not make any natural or regular part of that language. They are, indeed, a figure of speech occasionally prompted by passion, and I have made use of them as such, but I have endeavored utterly to reject them as a mechanical device of style, or as a family language which Writers in meter seem to lay claim to by prescription.[29]] I have wished to keep my Reader in the company of flesh and blood,[30] persuaded that by so doing I shall interest him. I am, however, well aware that others who pursue a different track may interest him likewise; I do not interfere with their claim, I only wish to prefer a different claim of my own. There will also be found in those volumes little of what is usually called poetic diction; I have taken as much pains to avoid it as others ordinarily take to produce it; this I have done for the reason already alleged, to bring my language near to the language of men, and further, because the pleasure which I have proposed to myself to impart is of a kind very different from that which is supposed by many persons to be the proper object of poetry. I do not know how, without being culpably particular, I can give my Reader a more exact notion of the style in which I wished these poems to be written than by informing him that I have at all times endeavored to look steadily at my subject, consequently, I hope that there is in these Poems little falsehood of description, and that my ideas are expressed in language fitted to their respective importance. Something I must have gained by this practice, as it is friendly to one property of all good poetry, namely good sense; but it has necessarily cut me off from a larger portion of phrase and figures of speech which from father to son have long been regarded as the common inheritance of Poets. I have also thought it expedient to restrict myself still further, having abstained from the use of many expressions, in themselves proper and beautiful, but which have been foolishly repeated by bad Poets, still such feelings of disgust are connected with them as it is scarcely possible by any part of association to overpower. [31] If in a Poem there should be found a series of lines, or even a single line, in which the language, though naturally arranged, and according to the strict laws of meter, does not differ from that of prose, there is a numerous class of critics, who, when they stumble upon these prosaisms[32], as they call them, imagine that they have made a notable discovery, and exult over the Poet as a man ignorant of his own profession[33]. Now these men would establish a canon of criticism which the Reader will conclude he must utterly reject, if he wishes to be pleased with these volumes.[34] And it would be a most easy task to prove to him, that not only the language of a large portion of every good poem, even the most elevated character,[35] must necessarily, except with reference to the meter, in no respect differ from that of good prose, but likewise that some of the most interesting parts of the best poems will be found to be strictly the language of prose, when prose is well written. The truth of this assertion might be demonstrated by innumerable passages from almost all the poetical writings, even of Milton himself. I have not space for much quotation; but, to illustrate the subject in a general manner, I will here adduce a short composition of Gray[36], who was at the head of those, who, by their reasonings, have attempted to widen the sepace of separation betwixt Prose and Metrical composition, and was more than any other man curiously elaborate in the structure of his own poetic diction.

> In vain to me the smiling mornings shine,
> And reddening Phoebus[37] lifts his golden fire:
> The birds in vain their amorous descant join[38],
> Or cheerful fields resume their green attire.
> These ears, alas! for other notes repine; [39]
> *A different object do these eyes require*[40];
> *My lonely anguish melts no heart but mine*;
> *And in my breast the imperfect joys expire*[41];

Yet morning smiles the busy race[42] to cheer,

And new-born pleasure brings to happier men;

The fields to all their wonted tribute bear; [43]

To warm their little loves the birds complain.

I fruitless mourn to him that cannot hear,

And weep the more because I weep in vain.

It will easily be perceived that the only part of this Sonnet which is of any value is the lines printed in Italics: it is equally obvious, that, except in the rhyme, and in the use of the single word "fruitless" for fruitlessly,[44] which is so far a defect, the language of these lines does in no respect differ from that of a prose.

[By the foregoing quotation I have shewn that the language of Prose may yet be adapted to Poetry; and I have previously asserted that a large portion of the language of every good poem can in no respect differ from that of good Prose. I will go further. I do not doubt that it may be safely affirmed, that there neither is, nor can be, any essential difference between the language of prose and metrical composition.] We are fond of tracing the resemblance between Poetry and Painting,[45] and, accordingly, we call them Sisters: but where shall we find bonds of connection sufficiently strict to typify the affinity betwixt metrical and prose composition? They both speak by and to the same organs; the bodies in which both of them are clothed may be said to be of the same substance, their affections are kindred, and almost identical, not necessarily differing even in degree; Poetry[46] sheds no tears 'such as Angels weep,'[47] but natural and human tears; she can boast of no celestial Ichor[48] that distinguishes her vital juices from those of prose; the same human blood circulates through the veins of them both.

If it be affirmed that rhyme and metrical arrangement of themselves constitute a distinction which overturns what I have been saying on the strict affinity of metrical language with that of prose, and paves the way for other artificial distinctions which the mind voluntarily admits;[49] [I answer that the language of such Poetry as I am recommending is, as far as is possible, a selection of the language really spoken by men; that this selection, wherever it is made with true taste and feeling, will of itself form a distinction far greater than would at first be imagined, and will entirely separate the composition from vulgarity and meanness of ordinary life; and, if meter be superadded thereto, I believe that a dissimilitude[50] will be produced together sufficient for the gratification of a rational mind. What other distinction would we have? Whence is it to come? And where is it to exist? Not, surely, where the poet speaks through the mouths of his characters: it cannot be necessary here, either for elevation of style, or any of its supposed ornaments; for, if the Poet's subject be judiciously chosen, it will naturally, and upon fit occasion, lead him to passions the language of which, if selected truly and judiciously, must necessarily be dignified and variegated, and alive with metaphors and figures. I forebear to speak of an incongruity which would shock the intelligent Reader, should the poet interweave any foreign splendor of his own[51] with that which the passion naturally suggests: it is sufficient to say that such addition is unnecessary. And, surely, it is more probable that those passages, which with propriety abound with metaphors and figures, will have their due effect, if, upon other occasions where the passions are of a milder character, the style also be subdued and temperate.

But, as the pleasure which I hope to give by the Poems I now present to the Reader must depend entirely on just notions upon this subject[52], and, as it is in itself of the highest importance to our taste and moral feelings, I cannot content myself with these detached remarks.[53] And if, in what I am about to say, it shall appear to some that my labor is unnecessary, and that I am like a man fighting a battle without enemies, I would remind such persons that, whatever may be the language outwardly holden by men,[54] a practical faith in the opinions which I am wishing to establish is almost unknown.[55] If my conclusions are admitted, and carried as far as they must be carried if admitted at all, our judgments concerning the works of the greatest Poets both ancient and modern will be far different from what they are at present, both when we praise, and when we censure: and our moral feelings influencing, and influenced by these judgments will, I believe, be corrected and purified.

Taking up the subject, then, upon general grounds, I ask what is meant by the word Poet? What is a Poet? To whom does he address himself? And what language is to be expected from him? He is a man speaking to men:

a man, it is true, endued with more lively sensibility, more enthusiasm, and tenderness, who has a greater knowledge of human nature, and a more comprehensive soul, than are supposed to be common among mankind; a man pleased with his own passions and volitions, and who rejoices more than other men in the spirit of life that is in him; delighting to contemplate similar volitions and passions as manifested in the goings-on of the Universe, and habitually impelled to create them where he does not find them. To these qualities he has added a disposition to be affected more than other men by absent things as if they were present; an ability of conjuring up in himself passions, which are indeed far from being the same as those produced by real events, yet (especially in those parts of the general sympathy which are pleasing and delightful) do more nearly resemble the passions produced by real events, than any thing which, from the motions of their own minds merely, other men are accustomed to feel in themselves; whence, and from practice,[56] he has acquired a greater readiness and power in expressing what he thinks and feels, and especially those thoughts and feelings which, by his own choice, or from the structure of his own mind, arise in him without immediate external excitement.

But, whatever portion of this faculty we may suppose even the greatest Poet to possess, there cannot be a doubt but that the language which it will suggest to him, must, in liveliness and truth, fall far short of that which is uttered by men in real life,[57] under the actual pressure of those passions, certain shadows of which the Poet thus produces, or feels to be produced, in himself. However exalted a notion we would wish to cherish of the character of a Poet,[58] it is obvious, that, while he describes and imitates passions, his situation is altogether slavish and mechanical, compared with the freedom and power of real and substantial action and suffering. So that it will be the wish of the Poet to bring his feelings near to those of the persons whose feelings he describes, nay, for short spaces of time perhaps, to let himself slip into an entire delusion, and even confound and identify his own feelings with theirs; modifying only the language which is thus suggested to him, by a consideration that he describes for a particular purpose, that of giving pleasure. Here, then, he will apply the principle on which I have so much insisted, namely, that of selection; on this he will depend for removing what would otherwise be painful or disgusting in the passion; he will feel that there is no necessity to trick out or elevate nature: and, the more industriously he applies this principle, the deeper will be his faith that no words, which his fancy or imagination can suggest, will be to be compared with those which are in the emanations of reality and truth.

But it may be said by those who do not object to the general spirit of these remarks, that, as it is impossible for the Poet to produce upon all occasions[59], language as exquisitely fitted for the passion as that which the real passion itself suggests, it is proper that it should consider himself as in the situation of a translator, who deems himself justified when he substitutes excellences of another kind for those which are unattainable by him; and endeavors occasionally to surpass his original, in order to make some amends for the general inferiority to which he feels that he must submit. But this would be to encourage idleness and unmanly despair. Further, it is the language of men who speak of what they do not understand;[60] who talk of Poetry as a matter of amusement and idle pleasure; who will converse with us as gravely about a *taste* for Poetry, as they express it, as if it were a thing as indifferent as a taste for Rope-dancing, or Frontiniac or Sherry[61]. Aristotle, I have been told, hath said, that Poetry is the most philosophic of all writing:[62] it is so: its object is truth, not individual and local, but general, and operative; not standing upon external testimony, but carried alive into the heart by passion; truth which is its own testimony, which gives strength and divinity to the tribunal[63] to which it appeals, and receives them from the same tribunal. Poetry is the image of man and nature. The obstacles which stand in the way of fidelity of the Biographer and Historian, and of their consequent utility,[64] are incalculably greater than those which are to be encountered by the Poet who has an adequate notion of the dignity of his art. The Poet writes under one restriction only, namely, that of the necessity of giving immediate pleasure to a human Being possessed of that information which may be expected from him, not as a lawyer, a physician, a mariner, an astronomer or a natural philosopher, but as a Man. Except this one restriction, there is no object standing between the Poet and the image of things; between this, and the Biographer and Historian there are a thousand.

Nor let this necessity of producing immediate pleasure be considered as a degradation of the Poet's art. It is far otherwise. It is an acknowledgement of the beauty of the universe, an acknowledgement the more sincere, because it is not formal, but indirect; it is a task light and easy to him who looks at the world in the spirit of love: further, it is a homage paid to the native and naked dignity of man, to the grand elementary principle of pleasure, by which he knows, and feels, and lives, and moves. We have no sympathy but what is propagated by pleasure: I would not be misunderstood; but wherever we sympathize with pain it will be found that the sympathy is produced and carried on by subtle combinations with pleasure. We have no knowledge, that is, no general principles drawn from the contemplation of particular facts, but what has been built up for pleasure, and exists in us by pleasure alone. The Man of Science[65], the Chemist and Mathematician, whatever difficulties and disgusts they may have had to struggle with, know and feel this. However painful may be the objects with which the Anatomist's knowledge is connected, he feels that his knowledge is pleasure, [66] and where he has not pleasure he has no knowledge. What then does the Poet? He considers man and the objects that surround him as acting and re-acting upon each other, so as to produce an infinite complexity of pain and pleasure; he considers man in his own nature and in his ordinary life as contemplating this with a certain quantity of immediate knowledge, with certain convictions, intuitions, and deductions which by habit become of the nature of intuitions[67], he considers him as looking upon this complex scene of ideas and sensations, and finding every where objects that immediately excite in him sympathies which, from the necessities of his nature, are accompanied by an overbalance of enjoyment.

To this knowledge which all men carry about with them, and to these sympathies in which without any other discipline than that of our daily life we are fitted to take delight, the Poet principally directs his attention. [68] He considers man and nature as essentially adapted to each other, and the mind of man as naturally the mirror of the fairest and most interesting qualities of nature. And thus the Poet, prompted by this feeling of pleasure which accompanies him through the whole course of his studies, converses with general nature with affections akin to those, which, through labor and length of time, the Man of Science has raised up in himself, by conversing with those particular parts of nature which are the objects of his studies. The knowledge both of the Poet and the Man of Science is pleasure; but the knowledge of the one[69] cleaves to us as a necessary part of our existence, our natural and unalienable inheritance; the other is a personal and individual acquisition, slow to come to us, and by no habitual or direct sympathy connecting us with our fellow-beings. The Man of Science seeks truth as a remote and unknown benefactor; he cherishes and loves it in his solitude: the Poet, singing a song in which all human beings join with him, rejoices in the presence of truth as our visible friend and hourly companion. Poetry is the breath and finer spirit of all knowledge; it is the impassioned expression which is in the countenance of all Science. Emphatically may it be said of the Poet, as Shakespeare hath said of man, 'that he looks before and after.'[70] He is the rock of defence of human nature; an upholder and preserver, carrying every where with him relationship[71] and love. In spite of difference of soil and climate, of language and manners, of laws and customs, in spite of things silently gone out of mind and things violently destroyed, the Poet binds together by passion and knowledge the vast empire of human society, as it is spread over the whole earth, and over all time. The objects of the Poet's thoughts are every where; though the eyes and senses of man are, it is true, his favorite guides, yet he will follow wheresoever he can find an atmosphere of sensation in which to move his wings. Poetry is the first and last of all knowledge—it is immortal as the heart of man. If the labors of Men of Science should ever create any material revolution, direct or indirect, in our condition, and in the impressions which we habitually receive, the Poet will sleep then no more than at present,[72] but he will be ready to follow the steps of the Man of Science, not only in those general indirect effects, but he will be at his side, carrying sensation into the midst of the objects of the Science itself. The remotest discoveries of the Chemist, the Botanist, the Mineralogist, will be as proper objects of the Poet's art as any upon which it can be employed,[73] if the time should ever come when these things shall be familiar to us, and the relations under which they are contemplated by the followers of these respective Sciences shall be manifestly and palpably material to us as enjoying and suffering beings. If the time should ever come when what is now called Science, thus familiarized to men, shall be ready to put on, as it were, a form of flesh and blood, the Poet will lend his divine spirit to aid the transfiguration, and will welcome the Being thus produced, as a dear and genuine inmate of the household of man.[74] It is not, then, to be supposed that any one, who holds that sublime notion of Poetry which I have attempted to convey, will break in upon the sanctity and truth of his pictures by transitory and accidental ornaments[75], and endeavor to excite admiration of himself by arts, the necessity of which must manifestly depend upon the assumed meanness of his subject.

What I have thus far said applies to Poetry in general; but especially to those parts of composition where the Poet speaks through the mouths of his characters; and upon his point it appears to have such weight that I will conclude, there are few persons of good sense, who would not allow that the dramatic parts of composition are defective, in proportion as they deviate from the real language of nature, [76] and are colored by a diction of the Poet's own, either peculiar to him as an individual Poet, or belonging simply to Poets in general, to a body of men who, from the circumstance of their compositions being in meter, it is expected will employ a particular language.

It is not, then, in the dramatic parts of composition that we look for this distinction of language; but still it may be proper and necessary where the Poet speaks to us in his own person and character. To this I answer by referring my Reader to the description which I have before given of a Poet. Among the qualities which I have enumerated as principally conducing to form a Poet, is implied nothing differing in kind from other men, but only in degree. The sum of what I have there said is, that the Poet is chiefly distinguished from other men by a greater promptness to think and feel without immediate external excitement, and a greater power in expressing such thoughts and feelings as are produced in him in that manner.[77] But these passions and thoughts and feelings are the general passions and thoughts and feelings of men. And with what are they connected? Undoubtedly with our moral sentiments and animal sensations, and with the causes which excite these; with the operations of the elements and the appearances of the visible universe; with storm and sun-shine, with the revolutions of the seasons, with cold and heat, with loss of friends and kindred, with injuries and resentments, gratitude and hope, with fear and sorrow. These, and the like, are the sensations and objects which the Poet describes, as they are the sensations of other men, and the objects which interest them. The Poet thinks and feels in the spirit of the passions of men. How, then, can his language differ in any material degree from that of all other men who feel vividly and see clearly? It might be *proved* that it is impossible. But supposing that this were not the case, the Poet might then be allowed to use a peculiar language when expressing his feelings for his own gratification, or that of men like himself. But poets do not write for Poets alone, but for men. Unless therefore we are advocates for that admiration which depends upon ignorance, and that pleasure which arises from hearing what we do not understand, the Poet must descend from this supposed height, and, in order to excite rational sympathy, he must express himself as other men express themselves. To this it may be added, that while he is only selecting from the real language of men, or, which amounts to the same thing, composing accurately in the spirit of such selection, he is treading upon safe ground, and we know what we are to expect from him. Our feelings are the same with respect to meter; for, as it may be proper to remind the Reader,] the distinction of meter is regular and uniform, and not like that which is produced by what is usually called poetic diction, arbitrary, and subject to infinite caprices upon which no calculation whatever can be made. In the one case, the Reader is utterly at the mercy of the Poet respecting what imagery or diction he may choose to connect with the passion, whereas, in the other, the meter obeys certain laws, to which the Poet and Reader both willingly submit because they are certain, and because no interference is made by them with the passion but such as the concurring testimony of ages has shewn to heighten and improve the pleasure which co-exist with it.[78]

注释

1. perusal: 阅读。
2. impart: 传达，表达。
3. 指诗集的合作者塞缪尔·柯勒律治。
4. reasoning him into an approbation of these particular poems: 通过讲道理诱使读者认可这部诗集中收录的作品。
5. which 指的是上文提到的 "公众的阅读趣味健康或堕落的情况"。

6. habits of association：联想习惯。

7. 大意为：韵文语言的这种表现手法在不同的文学领域一定会引起不同的期待。

8. 文中列举的均为古罗马诗人。

9. John Donne（1572—1631）：英国诗人、玄学派诗歌代表，写有情诗、讽刺诗、宗教诗、布道文等。Abraham Cowley（1618—1667）：英国诗人。

10. the gaudiness and inane phraseology：辞藻华丽、空洞。

11. by what species of courtesy these attempts can be permitted to assume that title：到底是出于何种礼貌，才把这些东西称作诗？

12. indolence：懒惰。

13. chuse：chose。

14. regards：关于。

15.【作者原注】It is worthwhile here to observe that the effecting parts of Chaucer are almost always expressed in language pure and universally intelligible even to this day.

16. 大意为：但是，我认为，我的思考习惯塑造了我的情感。每当我描写那些激起我的强烈情感的东西时，我的描写就会带有一定的目的性。

17. this act 指的是前面所说的 contemplating the relation of these general representatives to each other。

18. the being to whom we address ourselves：我们的读者。

19. 大意为：我决不会因为故作谦虚而不肯正面说出……

20. have a very faint perception of its beauty and dignity：无法充分领会人的心灵的优美和高贵。

21. this capability：指的是人变得兴奋起来的能力。

22. 大意为：过去鲜为人知的许多因素现在正在合力削弱人的鉴别能力，使人的头脑变得像野蛮人的头脑一样麻木。这里的 it 指代 mind。

23. 指法国革命和拿破仑战争。

24. the rapid communication of intelligence：迅速传播的新闻。

25. 指当时社会上风行的哥特小说。

26. 指同时代的德国闹剧。

27. 大意为：当我想起这股邪恶势力力大无穷之时，若不是我深感人类的心灵天生具有某些不可毁灭的品质，我就要被那可耻的忧郁给压倒了。

28. "are utterly rejected..." 的 主 语 是 上 文 中 的 "personifications of abstract ideas"。

29. 大意为：拟人手法的使用，不应成为常例，只能在诗人激情迸发之际偶尔为之，我就这样用过；但我决不会把它们当做表现风格的机械手段，或诗人必须使用的行规语言。

30. keep my reader in the company of flesh and blood：让读者读到有血有肉（真实、不做作）的作品。

31. 大意为：我也认为，我应当进一步约束自己，不要使用某些词句。这些词句本身并无不当之处，而且还很漂亮，但是，由于屡经劣等诗人愚蠢因袭，如今读来却令人作呕。读者再怎么发挥联想艺术，也无法驱走这种令人生厌的感觉。

32. prosaisms：散文化的词句。

33. ignorant of his own profession：对自己的本行一窍不通。

34. 大意为：如果读者喜欢这些诗，就会反对那帮批评家所确立的一套批评标准。

35. even the most elevated character：这里指的可能是史诗。

36. Gray：格雷（Thomas Gray，1716—1771），英国"墓园派"诗人。引文出自他的 "Sonnet on the Death of Mr. Richard West"。West 是诗人的同学、好友，格雷在给他的信中写道，"趋时的语言绝不是诗的语言"（The language of the age is never the language of poetry）。华兹华斯在此特地选中格雷的诗歌，剖析其中的日常语言，颇有擒贼先擒王之意。

37. Phoebus：太阳神福玻斯。

38. amorous descant join：欢乐地合唱情歌。

39. notes：歌声。repine：抱怨。

40. these eyes："我的"眼睛。

41. expire：消逝。

42. busy race：繁忙的人们。

43. 大意为：田野给人们带来了常见的礼物。

44. 按照华兹华斯的意思，格雷这里应该用 fruitlessly, 而不应该用 fruitless。因为前者为副词，可以修饰动词 mourn；后者为形容词，不能修饰动词。

45. 在华兹华斯之前，探讨过诗歌与绘画关系的名作主要有贺拉斯的《诗艺》、锡德尼的《诗辩》、蒲柏的《批评论》、莱辛的《拉奥孔》、约翰逊的《漫游者》等等。

46. 作者在原注中说明，这里使用 "poetry"，是与散文相对立的韵文。

47. 大意为："天使哭泣"，语出弥尔顿《失乐园》卷 1 第 620 行。

48. ichor：灵液，希腊神话中所说的在神的脉络中流动的液体。

49. 下文括号中的内容（9 段）为初版所没有，是 1802 年版中后加的。

50. dissimilitude：不同之处。

51. foreign splendor of his own：诗人自己制造出来的那种外在的富丽堂皇。

52. just notions upon this subject：有关这一问题的正确理解。

53. these detached remarks：这些题外话。

54. 大意为：不管人们怎么评论我。

55. 大意为：我要确立的这些看法眼下几乎无人知晓。

56. 大意为：由于他经常实践……

57. in liveliness and truth：在生动性和真实性方面；fall far short of：比不上。

58. 大意为：不论我们怎么推崇诗人的品质。

59. upon all occasions：随时随地。

60. 大意为：说这种话的人是在说自己并不真正懂得的事物。

61. 文中出现的 Frontiniac 和 Sherry，都是酒的名称。

62. 诗更有哲理性。这是亚里士多德在《诗学》中的著名论断。

63. tribunal：法庭。

64. 大意为：传记作家和历史学家在体现自己作品的忠实性进而体现其实用性而遇到的重重困难。

65. 可能指英国化学家戴维（Humphrey Davy，1778—1829）。

66. 大意为：不管解剖学家的知识是怎样与解剖对象的痛苦联系在一起，他仍然为自己掌握了解剖知识而感到愉快。

67. by habit become of the nature of intuitions：因习惯而成直觉。

68. "To this knowledge... we are fitted to take delight"：动词不定式短语，是 "directs his attention" 的宾语。

69. the knowledge of the one：其中一种知识。

70. 语出《哈姆雷特》。

71. relationship：友情。

72. 大意为：诗人只是一时沉睡。

73. 大意为：化学家、植物学家和矿物学家的那些罕见的发现，就像一切可以入诗的题材一样，将成为诗人的写作对象。

74. 大意为：如果有那么一天，现在所谓的科学能够为人所熟知，仿佛变成一个有血有肉的生命，那么诗人一定凭借他神圣高洁的精神玉成其事，把它当做相亲相近的一家人来欢迎。

75. transitory and accidental ornaments：难以经久流传和无关紧要的浮词虚饰。

76. 大意为：凡是有识之士无不同意，诗歌是否完美无瑕取决于诗人是否脱离现实生活中鲜活的语言。

77. 大意为：诗人与众人不同之处是，他无需直接的外部刺激就能敏捷思索、感悟，且能更有力表现由此而产生的思想和情感。

78. but such as the concurring testimony of ages has shown to heighten and improve the pleasure which co-exist with it：正如各个时代的思想和感情共同证明的，（韵律遵守的法则）有助于提高和改进伴随着激情的愉悦。

塞缪尔·泰勒·柯勒律治（1772—1834）

英国大诗人、批评家和哲学家塞缪尔·泰勒·柯勒律治 1772 年出生在英格兰西南德文郡的一个牧师家庭。他幼年即喜好文学，经常沉溺于文学世界中，认同于其中的要角；他因想象力非凡，而有神童之誉。他 9 岁丧父，被亲属送进基督教会创办的慈幼学校。在校期间，他熟读希腊、罗马文学，热衷启蒙哲学，一度萌生无神论思想，但教师的鞭打责罚又使之消失于无形之中。19 岁时，就学于剑桥大学耶稣学院，因债务缠身，在大学三年级时自动辍学；化名加入龙骑兵，混迹行伍。不久被家人发现，送回剑桥。不过，他还是没有完成学业，就在 1794 年 12 月再别剑桥。在这一年的 6 月，柯勒律治曾访问牛津，遇到罗伯特·骚塞（Robert Southey），两人一见如故，相互引为知己。他们合作写出历史剧《罗伯斯庇尔的失败》（*The Fall of Robspierre*），但从未能上演。他们还萌生了一个极为大胆的乌托邦设想：在美国的宾夕法尼亚买一块荒地，带上少数人，远离邪恶的社会，创建一个人人平等的柏拉图式共和国。这个梦想很快破灭，柯勒律治唯一的收获是，他娶了骚塞未婚妻的姐姐。

1795 年他初识威廉·华兹华斯；此后两人过往甚密，开始了思想和创作上的合作，创造了英国文学史上的一段佳话。此时柯勒律治精力旺盛，思想开阔，热情奔放。因感时伤世而思想消沉的华兹华斯受他乐观情绪的感染，重新振作起来，转向生机盎然的大自然去寻找诗歌的素材。从 1797 年开始，两人策划《抒情歌谣集》，转年 7 月，他们匿名出版了这部具有划时代意义的作品。《抒情歌谣集》收录诗歌 23 首，华兹华斯 19 首，柯勒律治 4 首。《〈抒情歌谣集〉序》成为英国文学浪漫主义的宣言书，古典主义的墓志铭。从 1797 年仲夏至 1798 年底，两人关系最为融洽；这也是柯勒律治诗歌创作的高峰，他的传世名篇《古舟子咏》（"The Rime of the Ancient Mariner"）和《忽必烈汗》（"Kubla Khan"）就是写于此时。他们两人分工明确：华兹华斯发掘和描摹日常生活中的凡人琐事，赋予它们新颖的魅力，唤起读者神奇的感受；柯勒律治以神秘事物为题材，以自然逼真的人物和环境描写为手段，使读者在阅读中暂时放弃其不信任感，创建所谓诗的真实。

1798 年 9 月，柯勒律治抛妻别子，追随华兹华斯兄妹，东渡大海，游学德国。他在德国呆了 10 个月，广泛接触了德国唯心主义哲学家康德（Immanuel Kant）、谢林（Friedrich Wilhelm Joseph von Schelling）和浪漫派文学家施莱格尔兄弟（August Wilhelm von and Friedrich von Schlegel）、席勒（Johann Christoph Friedrich von Schiller）等人的论著，并将这些德国思想的精华介绍给英国读者。德国思想对他影响极深，使他在评论中自觉地将文学分析同这些思辨因素结合起来，赋予文学批评以哲学基础；他的重要文学批评观念，例如"想象说"、"有机论"均有日耳曼的渊源。或许正因为这一点，有人说他是英语世界第一位具有现代意义的批评家。

自德国返回伦敦后，他翻译了席勒的《华伦斯坦》（*Wallenstein*），参与编辑《晨报》（*The Morning Post*），还打算写一本论形而上学的巨著，可惜未果。1800 年，他与华兹华斯兄妹一道移居湖区（Lake District）。此时他又移情别恋，爱上华兹华斯未婚妻的妹妹萨拉·哈钦森（Sara Hutchinson），这在《爱情》（"Love"）（1799）等诗中有所反映。他吸鸦片也已成瘾，到了无法自拔的境地。他开始编辑整理自己的《日记》（*Notebook*）。《日记》记载了他对自己生活、写作以及梦想的种种精思熟虑，是他最具传世价值和最有感染力的著作之一。

1804 年柯勒律治只身出国，此行主要目的是恢复健康和重振事业。在马耳他，他给英国总督当了两年秘书，后来又游历西西里和意大利。1807 年与妻子分手。1808 年，柯勒律治抱病作了一系列有关诗歌和戏剧的演讲。在后来的 10 年中，他不时举行演讲，听众中有拜伦（George Gordon Byron）和济慈。这些演讲被后人辑录成《关于莎士比亚演讲集》（*Shakespearian Criticism*）。柯勒律治提出了莎剧"有机形式"理论以及从内在心理出发塑造人物等理论，体现了谢林所说的无意识因素在艺术中的作用以及施莱格尔的戏剧批评对他的深刻影响。

在萨拉·哈钦森的襄助下，他创办了周刊《友人》（*The Friend*）。很多文章都出自他本人之手，孕育了他后来那些成熟的哲学批评的萌芽。这本内容涵盖文学、宗教、政治的综合性期刊，只出了 28 期便告终结。柯勒律治与华兹华斯发生争吵，关系破裂。从 1811 到 1814 年，柯勒律治身体状况极差，精神恍惚，常有轻生弃世的念头。在 1813—

1814 年冬天，柯勒律治恢复了对基督教的信仰，公开承认自己吸毒，并接受治疗，慢慢恢复写作。1815 年，从 6 月到 9 月，他口述自己最重要的评论著作《文学生涯》。这本书直到 20 世纪还有重大影响。新批评家对此书用力甚勤，他们从中梳理出柯勒律治著名的"想象说"、"有机论"以及他的诗歌调和观。这本书有急就章的性质，体裁不一，内容驳杂，包括生平自述、哲学见解、文学理论、具体的作品分析，还有对华兹华斯的回忆。这与他本人倡导体系、讲求方法和符合逻辑等主张大相异趣。不过，书中也经常闪现一些识力透彻的名句，颇有启发的评判，显示出作者的苦心孤诣和英才天纵。

自 1816 年起，直到他 1834 年辞世，柯勒律治一直在青年医生詹姆斯·吉尔曼（James Gillman）家中休养和接受治疗。在青年浪漫派那里，柯勒律治的名声已是如日中天。他周围有一群门徒和崇拜者，卡莱尔（Thomas Carlyle）以他为"圣贤"，兰姆（Charles Lamb）说他是"受了轻伤的大天使。"作诗之余，他还经常演讲，随时发表文学和哲学见解。

他晚年的作品当中，更见思想功力的是那些社会批评和宗教批评论著。他的《世俗布道》（*Lay Sermons*）（1816, 1817）探讨了改良与道德责任问题；《政教宪法》（*On the Constitution of Church and State*）中提出，他理想中的统治阶级是"文士阶层"（clerisy）。这一概念，不仅为 19 世纪的马修·阿诺德（Matthew Arnold）和查尔斯·纽曼（Charles Newman）所接受，也为 20 世纪的雷蒙·威廉斯（Raymond Williams）所乐道；20 世纪的文学批评偶尔流露出他的思想遗风。

在政治思想上，他既有保守主义的成分，又有激进的内容。他尊崇传统，强调社会的有机属性，偏爱历史所形成的固有道德秩序。他反对自由主义者在资本主义发展中奉行的自由放任政策。他主张，政府应对工厂主加以管理，政府应扶持教育，提高公民的道德和知识。他的思想影响贯穿 19 世纪，成为英国托利党开明派的哲学依据。他竭力反对无政府性质的个人主义和唯利主义，就此而言，他是保守的。然而，他的宗教思想却是激进的，他主张建立一个新型的民族教会；这个教会不是由教士领导，而是由全社会成员中选拔出的精英人士"知识阶层"来领导。他主张的基督教是自由主义性质的，以个人良知而不是以教义或礼仪为根基。

内容提要

康德是浪漫派文学理论的一个重要思想源头,浪漫派所标举的"想象"这个口号与康德的认识论渊源深厚。康德的认识论彻底推翻了笛卡尔(René Descarte)、霍布斯(Thomas Hobbes)和洛克(John Locke)以来那种消极被动的感知学说。洛克在《论人类的理解力》(*An Essay Concerning Human Understanding*)中提出,人的大脑好似一块白板(tabula rasa)任由经验在上面书写。大脑要做的,就是把当前所有感觉储存在记忆中,一经需要,即调出来加以回忆;大脑将当前的感觉材料与过去储存的感觉材料加以联系和比较,形成一些简单观念,再联系和比较这些比较简单的观念,形成比较复杂的观念。然而,有人却对此说提出疑问:大脑中的形象果真对应某一外在之物吗?精神性的内在世界与物质性的外在世界真的是这样截然对立吗?

与洛克的认识论不同,康德的认识论强调人在认识外界事物过程中的主观建构作用。康德认为,外部世界由许多自在之物(noumena)组成。对于这些自在之物的存在,我们并没有明确的认识,权且加以承认。当自在之物作用于我们的感觉之时,大脑就积极活动起来,将这些感觉材料加工成为各种"再现之物"。首先,这些材料被打上我们自己的印记,以及时间和空间的标识(依康德之见,时间和空间体现的都是人为的精神特征,而非物质性特征);然后,经过康德所谓解释力诸范畴,标出其数量、质量、内容和关系等。这样一来,自在之物就完全进入大脑之中;呈现出来的就是现象,即我们心目中的世界。康德认为,这一现象世界不是给定的,而是我们有意识地通过富有成效的想象这一加工系统创造出来的。因为人的大脑含有的机制大体相同,所以,我们对自在之物的感知比较一致,方式大体相同。外部世界的种种特征在我们看来似乎客观真实,虽说它们主要是大脑主观运作的结果。

康德颠覆了客观现实的客观性:我们所体验的世界总是带有我们主观创造的成分。这个新视角瓦解了"模仿"和"想象"的对应。在整个18世纪,对于"想象"的界定,主要依靠将其对立于"模仿"。"想象"意味着发明和编造新事物,"模仿"则逼真地复制客观现实。文学想象力的倡导者从康德思想中汲取了力量。谢林说,无意地创造了现实世界的想象,却有意识地创造了理想的艺术世界。谢林还提出第一位想象力(primary imagination)与第二位想象力(secondary imagination)

的区分，这个区分又出现在柯勒律治《文学生涯》第 13 章。

柯勒律治写道，"我认为，第一位的想象力是一切人类知觉的活力和原动力，它是无限的'我存在'中的永恒的创造行为在有限的心灵中的重复。"这里，"我存在"语出《圣经》，指上帝；"有限的心灵"指人类。柯勒律治所谓第一位的想象力，就是康德所说"富有成效的想象力"，它是我们在每一个有意识的瞬间创造出知觉世界的精神能力。正如上帝创造自在之物，人类创造出现象。第一位的想象力既是上帝在永恒的创造行动中体现的"活力"，也是每一个人所具有的创造力。如果说第一位的想象力与一般的知觉有关，它是我们体现现实世界的能力；第二位的想象力则是第一位想象力的"回声"。第一位的想象力是在我们无意为之的情况下创造出知觉世界的，第二位的想象力却与"自觉的意识"（conscious will）共存，至少在一定程度对它作出了反应。第二位的想象力发挥作用的性质无异于第一位的想象力，它只在程度上和发挥作用的方式上与前者有别。它"溶化、分解和分散"知觉世界，从而创建另外一个世界。换言之，它至少将知觉世界重新塑造为一个更为理想的和更完整的画面。这个溶解和再创造的过程越彻底，所产生的艺术形式就越别出心裁；这一过程越不彻底，所产生的艺术就越贴近现实。另外，柯勒律治还将想象与幻想（fancy）严格区分开来，反映出他与 18 世纪新古典主义之间的距离。塞缪尔·约翰逊在他的《英语词典》（1765）中将"幻想"当做"想象"的定义之一。在柯勒律治看来，幻想是比较低级的活动，因为它完全在习见的知觉世界内发挥作用，不会像第二位的想象力那样创造一个新的知觉世界，它只同"固定和有限的东西"打交道。蒲柏和约翰逊等新古典主义的批评家认为，除了莎士比亚这样的文学天才不受文学规范束缚之外，其他人都要师法古人，勤学苦练。在柯勒律治看来，诗人写出有创造性的作品确是丰富的想象力使然；这种想象力可详加分析，其来源却神秘莫测。

在第 14 章中，柯勒律治主要讲述了两方面的内容：诗歌与散文体作品的区别；诗的来源。

就表面形式而言，诗歌因其谨守格律、用韵严整而与散文体作品泾渭分明。就目的和内容而言，诗歌的直接目的为获取快乐（pleasure）而非传播真理、记录事实，从而有别于科学和历史。然而，柯勒律治又提出另一个疑问：假若一本散文体小说改写成韵文体，它就能成为诗歌吗？按照表面形式去判断，它似乎算得上，然而它缺乏真正的诗歌应有的神韵。在真正的诗歌中，形式与内容、结构与属性是密切相关的。所以说，诗必须是一个整体，各个组成部分相互支持、互为解释，且比例协调，配合并支持韵律分布的目的和既有的影响。

柯勒律治在这一章中还极力标举天才和想象在诗歌创作中的重要性。他说出了英国浪漫主义的一句名言："诗是什么？这无异于在问诗人是什么？"他认为诗产生于作诗的天才，作诗的天才维护并润饰了诗人头脑中的形象、思想和情感。而诗才以良知为躯体，幻想为服饰，运动为生命，想象为灵魂。想象力在意志和理解力的推动下，在它们的暗中控制之下，调和了许多对立的东西：同一和殊异，一般和具体，观念与形象，个别与典型，新感觉与老事物，不寻常的情绪与不寻常的秩序，理智与情感。而且，它在调和天然与人工的关系时，依然让艺术从属于自然，形式从属于内容，我们对诗人的钦佩从属于我们对诗的感应。

Samuel Taylor Coleridge (1772—1834)

From *Biographia Literaria*

Chapter 13

The IMAGINATION then I consider either as primary, or secondary. The primary IMAGINATION I hold to be the living Power and prime Agent of all human Perception, and as a repetition in the finite mind of the eternal act of creation in the infinite I AM.[1] The secondary I consider as an echo of the former, co-existing with the conscious will, yet still as identical with the primary in the *kind* of its agency, and differing only in *degree*, and in the *mode* of its operation. It dissolves, diffuses, dissipates, in order to re-create; or where this process is rendered impossible, yet still at all events it struggles to idealize and to unify. It is essentially *vital*, even as all objects (*as* objects) are essentially fixed and dead.

Fancy, on the contrary, has no other counters to play with, but fixities and definites. The Fancy is indeed no other than a mode of Memory emancipated from the order of time and space; and blended with, and modified by that empirical phenomenon of the will, which we express by the word CHOICE. But equally with the ordinary memory it must receive all its materials ready made from the law of association.

· · ·

From Part II

Canto 14

During the first year that Mr. Wordsworth and I were neighbors,[2] our conversations turned frequently on the two cardinal points of poetry, the power of exciting the sympathy of the reader by a faithful adherence to the truth of nature, and the power of giving the interest of novelty by the modifying colors of imagination. The sudden charm, which accidents of light and shade, which moon-light or sun-set diffused over a known and familiar landscape, appeared to represent the practicability of combining both. These are the poetry of nature. The thought suggested itself (to which of us I do not recollect) that a series of poems might be composed of two sorts. In one, the incidents and agents were to be, in part at least, supernatural; and the excellence aimed at was to consist in the interesting of the affections by the dramatic truth of such emotions, as would naturally accompany such situations, supposing them real. And real in *this* sense they have been to every human being who, from whatever source of delusion, has at any time believed himself under supernatural agency. For the second class, subjects were to be chosen from ordinary life; the characters and incidents were to be such, as will be found in every village and its vicinity, where there is a meditative and feeling mind to seek after them, or to notice them, when they present themselves.[3]

In this idea orginated the plan of the "Lyrical Ballads; " in which it was agreed, that my endeavors should be directed to persons and characters supernatural, or at least romantic; yet so as to transfer from our inward nature a human interest and a semblance of truth sufficient to procure for these shadows of imagination that willing suspension of disbelief for the moment, which constitutes poetic faith[4]. Mr. Wordsworth, on the other hand, was to propose to himself as his object, to give the charm of novelty to things of every day, and to excite a feeling analogous to the supernatural, by awakening the mind's attention from the lethargy of custom, and directing it to the loveliness and the wonders of the world before us; an inexhaustible treasure, but for which in consequence of the film of familiarity and selfish solicitude we have eyes, yet see not, ears that hear not, and hearts that neither feel nor understand.[5]

With this view I wrote the "Ancient Mariner," and was preparing among other poems, the "Dark Ladie," and the "Christabel," in which I should have more nearly realized my ideal, than I had done in my first attempt. But Mr. Wordsworth's industry had proved so much more successful, and the number of his poems so much greater,[6] that my compositions, instead of forming a balance, appeared rather an interpolation of heterogeneous matter[7]. Mr. Wordsworth added two or three poems written in his own character, in the impassioned, lofty, and sustained diction, which is characteristic of his genius. In this form the "Lyrical Ballads" were published; and were presented by him, as an *experiment*,[8] whether subjects, which from their nature rejected the usual ornaments and extra-colloquial style of poems in general, might not be so managed in the language of ordinary life as to produce the pleasurable interest, which it is the peculiar business of poetry in impart.[9] To the second edition he added a preface of considerable length; in which notwithstanding some passages of apparently a contrary import, he was understood to contend for the extension of this style to poetry of all kinds, and to reject as vicious and indefensible all phrases and forms of style that were not included in what he (unfortunately, I think, adopting an equivocal expression) called the language of *real* life. From this preface, prefixed to poems in which it was impossible to deny the presence of original genius, however mistaken its direction might be deemed, arose the whole long continued controversy.[10] For from the conjunction of perceived power with supposed heresy I explain the inveteracy and in some instances, I grieve to say, the acrimonious passions, with which the controversy has been conducted by the assailants.

Had Mr. Wordsworth's poems been the silly, the childish things, which they were for a long time described as being; had they been really distinguished from the compositions of other poets merely by meanness of language and inanity of thought; had they indeed contained nothing more than what is found in the parodies and pretended imitations of them; they must have sunk at once, a dead weight, into the slough[11] of oblivion, and have dragged the preface along with them. But year after year increased the number of Mr. Wordsworth's admirers. They were found too not in the lower classes of the reading public, but chiefly among young men of strong sensibility and meditative minds; and their admiration (inflamed perhaps in some degree by opposition) was distinguished by its intensity, I might almost say, by its *religious fervor*. These facts, and the intellectual energy of the author, which was more or less consciously felt, where it was outwardly and even boisterously denied, meeting with sentiments of aversion to his opinions, and of alarm at their consequences, produced an eddy of criticism, which would of itself have borne up the poems by the violence, with which it whirled them round and round. With many parts of this preface in the sense attributed to them and which the words undoubtedly seem to authorise,

I never concurred; but on the contrary objected to them as erroneous in principle, and as contradictory (in appearance at least) both to other parts of the same preface, and to the author's own practice in the greater number of the poems themselves.[12] Mr. Wordsworth in his recent collection has, I find, degraded this prefatory disquisition to the end of his second volume, to be read or not at the reader's choice.[13] But he has not, as far as I can discover, announced any change in his poetic creed. At all events, considering it as the source of a controversy, in which I have been honored more than I deserve, by the frequent conjunction of my name with his, I think it expedient to declare once for all, in what points I coincide with his opinions, and in what points I altogether differ.[14] But in order to render myself intelligible I must previously, in as few words as possible, explain my ideas, first, of a POEM; and secondly, of POETRY itself, in *kind*, and in *essence*.

The office of philosophical *disquisition* consists in just *distinction*; while it is the privilege of the philosopher to preserve himself constantly aware, that distinction is not division. In order to obtain adequate notions of any truth, we must intellectually separate its distinguishable parts; and this is the technical *process* of philosophy. But having so done, we must then restore them in our conceptions to the unity, in which they actually co-exist; and this is the *result* of philosophy. A poem contains the same elements as a prose composition; the difference therefore must consist in a different combination of them, in consequence of a different object proposed. According to the difference of the object will be the difference of the combination[15]. It is possible, that the object may be merely to facilitate the recollection of any given facts or observations by artificial arrangement; and the composition will be a poem, merely because it is distinguished from prose by meter, or by rhyme, or by both conjointly. In this, the lowest sense, a man might attribute the name of a poem to the well known enumeration of the days in the several months;

> "Thirty days hath September,
>
> April, June, and November," etc.

and others of the same class and purpose. And as a particular pleasure is found in anticipating the recurrence of sounds and quantities, all compositions that have this charm superadded, whatever be their contents, *may* be entitled poems.

So much for the superficial *form*. A difference of object and contents supplies an additional ground of distinction.[16] The immediate purpose may be the communication of truths; either of truth absolute and demonstrable, as in works of science; or of facts experienced and recorded, as in history. Pleasure, and that of the highest and most permanent kind, may *result* from the *attainment* of the end; but it is not itself the immediate end. In other works the communication of pleasure may be the immediate purpose; and though truth, either moral or intellectual, ought to be the *ultimate* end, yet this will distinguish the character of the author, not the class to which the work belongs. Blest indeed is that state of society, in which the immediate purpose would be baffled by the perversion of the proper ultimate end; in which no charm of diction or imagery could exempt the Bathyllus even of an Anacreon, or the Alexis of Virgil, from disgust and aversion![17]

But the communication of pleasure may be the immediate object of a work not metrically composed; and that object may have been in a high degree attained, as in novels and romances. Would then the mere superaddition of meter, with or without rhyme, entitle *these* to the name of poems? The answer is, that nothing can permanently please, which does not contain in itself the reason why it is so, and not otherwise.[18] If meter be superadded, all other parts must be made consonant with it. They must be such, as to justify the perpetual and distinct attention to each part, which an exact correspondent recurrence of accent and sound are calculated to excite. The final definition then, so deduced, may be thus worded. A poem is that species of composition, which is opposed to works of science, by proposing for its *immediate* object pleasure, not truth; and from all other species (having *this* object in common with it) it is discriminated by proposing to itself such delight from the *whole*, as is compatible with a distinct gratification from each component *part*.

Controversy is not seldom excited in consequence of the disputants attaching each a different meaning to the same word; and in few instances has this been more striking, than in disputes concerning the present subject.[19] If a man chooses to call every composition a poem, which is rhyme, or measure, or both, I must leave his opinion uncontroverted. The distinction is at least competent to characterize the writer's intention. If it were subjoined, that the whole is likewise entertaining or affecting, as a tale, or as a series of interesting reflections, I of course admit this as another fit ingredient of a poem, and an additional merit. But if the definition sought for be that of a *legitimate* poem, I answer, it must be one, the parts of which mutually support and explain each other; all in their proportion harmonizing with, and supporting the purpose and known influences of metrical arrangement. The philosophic critics of all ages coincide with the ultimate judgement of all countries, in equally denying the praises of a just poem, on the one hand, to a series of striking lines or distichs[20], each of which absorbing the whole attention of the reader to itself disjoins it from its context, and makes it a separate whole, instead of a harmonizing part; and on the other hand, to an unsustained composition, from which the reader collects rapidly the general result unattracted by the component parts. The reader should be carried forward, not merely or chiefly by the mechanical impulse of curiosity, or by a restless desire to arrive at the final solution; but by the pleasureable activity of mind excited by the attractions of the journey itself. Like the motion of a serpent, which the Egyptians made the emblem of intellectual power;[21] or like the path of sound through the air; at every step he pauses and half recedes, and from the retrogressive movement collects the force which again carries him onward. *Precipitandus est liber spiritus,*[22] says Petronius Arbiter most happily. The epithet, *liber,* here balances the preceding verb; and it is not easy to conceive more meaning condensed in fewer words.

But if this should be admitted as a satisfactory character of a poem, we have still to seek for a definition of poetry. The writings of PLATO, and Bishop TAYLOR[23], and the Theoria Sacra of BURNET[24], furnish undeniable proofs that poetry of the highest kind may exist without meter, and even without the contradistinguishing objects of a poem. The first chapter of Isaiah[25] (indeed a very large proportion of the whole book) is poetry in the most emphatic sense: yet it would be not less irrational than strange to assert, that pleasure, and not truth, was the immediate object of the prophet. In short, whatever *specific* import we attach to the word, poetry, there will be found involved in it, as a necessary consequence, that a poem of any length neither can be, or ought to be, all poetry. Yet if a harmonious whole is to be produced, the remaining parts must be preserved *in keeping* with the poetry; and this can be no otherwise effected than by such a studied selection and artificial arrangement, as will partake of *one*, though not a *peculiar*, property of poetry.[26] And this again can be no other than the property of exciting a more continuous and equal attention, than the language of prose aims at, whether colloquial or written.[27]

My own conclusions on the nature of poetry, in the strictest use of the word, have been in part anticipated in the preceding disquisition on the fancy and imagination. What is poetry? is so nearly the same question with, what is a poet? that the answer to the one is involved in the solution of the other. For it is a distinction resulting from the poetic genius itself, which sustains and modifies the images, thoughts, and emotions of the poet's own mind. The poet, described in *ideal* perfection, brings the whole soul of man into activity, with the subordination of its faculties to each other, according to their relative worth and dignity.[28] He diffuses a tone, and spirit of unity, that blends, and (as it were) *fuses*, each into each, by that synthetic and magical power, to which we have exclusively appropriated the name of imagination. This power, first put in action by the will and understanding, and retained under their irremissive,[29] though gentle and unnoticed, control (*laxis effertur habenis*[30]) reveals itself in the balance or reconciliation of opposite or discordant qualities: of sameness, with difference; of the general with the concrete; the idea, with the image; the individual, with the representative; the sense of novelty and freshness, with old and familiar objects; a more than usual state of emotion, with more than usual order; judgment ever awake and steady self-possession, with enthusiasm and feeling profound or vehement; and while it blends and harmonizes the natural and the artificial, still subordinates art to nature; the manner to the matter; and our admiration of the poet to our sympathy with the poetry. "Doubtless," as Sir John Davies[31] observes of the soul (and his words may with slight alteration be applied, and even more appropriately to the poetic IMAGINATION)—

> Doubtless this could not be, but that she turns
> Bodies to spirit by sublimation strange,

As fire converts to fire the things it burns,

As we our food into our nature change.

From their gross matter she abstracts their forms,

And draws a kind of quintessence from things;

Which to her proper nature she transforms

To bear them light, on her celestial wings.

Thus does she, when from individual states

She doth abstract the universal kinds;

Which then re-clothed in divers names and fates

Steal access through our senses to our minds.

Finally, GOOD SENSE is the BODY of poetic genius, FANCY its DRAPERY, MOTION its LIFE, and IMAGINATION the SOUL that is every where, and in each; and forms all into one graceful and intelligent whole.

注释

1. 语出《旧约·出埃及记》第3章14节："神对摩西说:'我是自有永有的'（ I AM THAT I AM）"。

2. 1797—1798年柯勒律治与华兹华斯在英格兰西南部居住，住处相距不远。

3. 在《抒情歌谣集》的酝酿和策划过程中，柯勒律治和华兹华斯各有分工。柯勒律治处理超自然性质的题材，诱使读者暂时对其信以为真，从而打动他们的感情；华兹华斯则以日常生活中的凡人琐事为题材，通过真实描写自然而然激起读者同情的力量。这里所提到两种诗即是他们各自努力的方向。作者在下一段进一步具体说明了他们各自的任务。

4. 大意为：使读者暂时放弃常识，相信超自然题材的真实性。

5. 见《旧约·以赛亚书》第6章9—10节。柯勒律治称华兹华斯的方法是"唤醒人们的注意力，使之不再关注那些催人欲睡的习见之物，指引人们去关注眼前美丽的东西和奇妙的东西；眼前这个世界是一种永不枯竭的宝藏，可是由于对它太熟悉和师心自用，我们对它睹若无物，听若罔闻，在心灵上对它既无感受，也无从理解。"

6. 《抒情歌谣集》第 1 版收诗 23 首，其中华兹华斯 19 首，柯勒律治 4 首。

7. 大意为：华兹华斯先生作品的数量比我的要多，致使我的作品不但未能与其保持平衡，反倒像凭空插入的异物。

8. 《抒情歌谣集》第 1 版的广告说明："集中收录的绝大多数作品可被视为尝试之作。作者写这些诗主要是想弄清楚，社会中下层阶级的日常语言究竟在多大程度上可适用于诗歌以达到娱人目的。"

9. 大意为：一般说来，就诗的特性而言，反对追求藻饰和优雅文风的那些题材，经过日常生活中语言的处理，可否产生那种娱乐的情趣，也就是诗歌本身应当产生的那种娱乐情趣。

10. 围绕华兹华斯诗歌理论和创作实践而出现的一场争议，尤见批评家弗朗西斯·杰弗里（Francis Jeffrey）在《爱丁堡评论》（*Edinburgh Review*）上发表的一些敌视文字。

11. slough：泥淖。

12. 华兹华斯认为，《抒情歌谣集》中他本人的诗作，并不含有"通常所谓诗歌用语"；相反，他以日常生活中人们真正用于交谈的语言入诗。柯勒律治对此持有异议：华兹华斯诗中许多词语固然为常见之词，然而这些词语在诗中的排列和组合却是日常交谈中不常见的。他认为华兹华斯诗歌用词最具个性化和特点，这些个性化很强的用语，既不同于传统的诗歌用语，也不同于日常语言的平凡特征。

13. 在 1815 年出版的两卷本《诗集》中，华兹华斯以《抒情歌谣集》的序言为附录，加一篇新的序言和"附录性"文字。

14. 大意为：不管怎么说，既然《抒情歌谣集》序言被当做争议的来源，而又因为我的名字与华兹华斯经常并列而获得过分的殊荣，我认为，应当干脆一次说明白，我在哪些方面与他见解一致，在哪些方面与他完全不同。

15. 大意为：目的不同，组合也就不同。

16. 目的与内容的不同也是诗与散文区别的基础。

17. 大意为：在某种社会环境中，直接的目的会因为颠倒了终极目的而无法实现，这真是天佑；在这样的社会里，无论诗歌用词或意象如何魅力十足，也无法使阿那克里翁笔下的巴塞鲁斯、维吉尔笔下的阿莱克西斯不受人们的厌恶。
维吉尔的《牧歌》第二首内容为牧羊人克里顿向男奴阿莱克西斯倾诉相思之情。巴塞鲁斯为萨摩斯岛的美少年，古希腊抒情诗人阿那克里翁为他写了好几首颂诗。

18. 柯勒律治文集的编者曾经引用塞缪尔·约翰逊的话："要想抵得住恶毒的攻击，经得住时间的考验，本身就得含有某种原创性的发展原则（*Rambler*，No.154, 1751）。"

19. 大意为：争议通常是因争论双方对于同一个词的意义各执己见而引起的；这种争议也发生在诗的定义上，其激烈程度也实属罕见。

20. distich：自成一段的两行诗。在希腊和拉丁文诗歌中，这类对句通常不押韵。

21. 大意为：就像古埃及人视蛇的运动为智慧力量的象征。

22. 拉丁文，大意为：自由的精神必须加以催促。源自古罗马作家佩特罗尼乌斯的小说《萨蒂利孔》（*Satyricon*）。liber 意为"自由的"。

23. Bishop TAYLOR：即杰里米·泰勒（Jeremy Taylor, 1613—1667），英国基督教圣公会教士、作家，他的布道深得柯勒律治推许。

24. BURNET：伯内特（Thomas Burnet, 1635—1715），英国传教士，著有《地球的神圣理论》（*Telluris Theoria Sacra*）。

25. Isaiah：即《以赛亚书》。

26. 大意为：然而，如果产生一个和谐的整体，其余部分必须与诗保持一致；这只能通过精心的选择和人为的编排才能做到，从而具有诗的一种属性，虽说还不是诗独有的属性。

27. 大意为：这就是那种较之散文语言（无论是口头形式还是书面形式的）能够激起读者更持久、更均等的注意力的属性。

28. 大意为：在理想中完美状态下的诗人，带动了人的整个灵魂，让灵魂的各种能力根据它们的相对价值和尊贵地位彼此从属制约。

29. irremissive：不松懈的。

30. *laxis effertur habenis*：拉丁文，大意为：用松松的缰绳激发它。

31. Sir John Davies：约翰·戴维斯（1569—1626），英国诗人。以下这段引文出自他的诗作《汝应自知》（*Nosce Teipsum*，1599），引文略有出入。这首诗探讨了灵魂的不朽和特征这一主题。

珀西·比希·雪莱（1792—1822）

　　珀西·比希·雪莱，自弥尔顿以来最激进的英国诗人，1792 年出生于苏塞克斯郡一个饶有资产的乡绅家庭。他的祖父为准男爵（这一封号是授予平民的，可世袭），其父为国会议员。在孩童时代，雪莱即表现出敏感好动、富于想象的精神气质。在伊顿公学就读期间，因强烈反抗教师体罚学生、学长欺侮学弟等陋规，而得到"疯雪莱"和"伊顿的无神论者"等蔑称。这段学校生活令他相当不快，不过，令他颇感欣慰的是，家中还有一群姐妹崇拜他的才华和博学，这充实了他的情感空间。他私下写了一部哥特式恐怖小说，与妹妹合作出了一本诗集。

　　在这一时期，他熟读了百科全书派学者和休谟的著作，英国空想社会主义前驱威廉·戈德温的《政治正义论》（*Enquiry Concerning Political Justice*）更是他的案头必备，对他的政治思想的影响极大；可以说，早在成年之前，他就在认真思考历史、命运和人类的种种谬误。在牛津就学期间，他又大量阅读了一些激进思想家，例如托马斯·潘恩、孔多塞等人的著作。他在穿着打扮和言论举止上也有意偏离正统，挑战流俗。1811，他与大学好友 T. J. 霍格（T. J. Hogg）印了一本惊世骇俗的小册子《无神论的必要性》（*The Necessity of Atheism*），引起了一场轩然大波，结果双双被牛津开除。接下来，他与期盼"浪子回头"的父亲发生争执，又自我放逐于家门之外。同年，他本着浪漫的侠义精神，与倾心于他的哈丽特·威斯布鲁克（Harriet Westbrook）私奔；雪莱自称，"这是意志的行动，不是情欲的冲动"。哈丽特是一位退休的咖啡店老板的女儿，时年 16 岁。两人在爱丁堡成婚后，开始了 3 年左右颠沛流离的生活。在爱尔兰，他发表了《告爱尔兰人民书》（*An Address to the Irish People*, 1812）支持他们的民族解放事业。他还与自己精神导师、远在伦敦的戈德温通信，交换意见。在此期间最能反映其政治思想的长诗《麦布女王》（*Queen Mab*, 1813）猛烈攻击王室、战争、商业和宗教，赞美共和论、自由恋爱、无神论和素食主义。

1814 年，雪莱与哈丽特关系恶化，婚姻关系名存实亡，虽有挚友托马斯·皮考克（Thomas Peacock）的悉心相劝，雪莱还是撇下哈丽特和两个孩子，与戈德温的女儿玛丽私奔，还带走了玛丽的异母妹妹简。玛丽是戈德温与大才女玛丽·沃尔斯通克拉夫特的女儿。他们三人游历了经过革命战争浩劫的法国、瑞士和德国，饱受了舟车困顿之苦，囊中匮乏之羞。这段梦幻般的旅途上的种种情况在他未完成的小说《刺客》（The Assassins, 1814）中有所反映，亦可见于他们共同编订的日记《六周纪行》（A Six Weeks Tour, 1817）。

回到伦敦后，他创作的长诗《复仇者》（Alastor），第一次引起公众的注意和大量的评论。1816 年，他在瑞士与拜伦泛舟日内瓦湖。此时，玛丽·雪莱也开始动笔写作《弗兰肯斯坦》（Frankenstein）。就在是年秋天，哈丽特自沉河水。雪莱与玛丽正式结婚。为了争夺他与玛丽所生一对儿女的抚养权，雪莱与老岳丈对簿公堂，惨遭败诉。这段时期他与李·亨特（Leigh Hunt）、济慈、赫兹利特（William Hazlitt）等自由派文人情好日密。他的长诗《伊斯兰的反叛》（The Revolt of Islam）于 1817 年出版，诗中的莱昂（Laon）和情人西丝娜（Sythna）为无政府主义者，为雪莱和玛丽的化身。雪莱讴歌这两个为了信仰而献身的人物，他们不甘平淡的生活，幻想着轰轰烈烈的业绩，去挑战布满荆棘的险恶命运。

由于债务缠身、健康恶化和社会舆论的压力，雪莱携家远遁意大利，至死未返英伦。1819 年春，动笔写他的传世名作《解放了的普罗米修斯》（Prometheus Unbound）。这一年他连遭不幸：幼女病死威尼斯，幼子病死罗马，玛丽·雪莱精神崩溃。不过，在他一生短暂的创作生涯中，这一年却最为多产。他完成了四幕剧《解放了的普罗米修斯》（翌年出版）；作政治长诗《暴政的假面游行》（The Mask of Anarchy），抗议英国政府镇压群众集会；他预言新社会即将来临的《西风颂》也于是年秋杀青。这些诗作大都是有感而发，受到欧洲政治事件的促动；即便几首纯粹的抒情诗，例如《致云雀》（"To a Skylark"）和《云》（"The Cloud", 1820）也与政治态势有关。1819 年，他还完成了诗体悲剧《钦契》（The Cenci），此剧直到 100 多年后才在巴黎上演。雪莱生前并非诗名卓著，身后才享尽荣光。他在世时，诗作很难在英国出版，即使出版，销售也不尽如人意。身在异国他乡的雪莱为此十分沮丧，不时发出知音难觅之慨。

从 1820 年到 1821 年，他写了几篇政论和文论，其中包括传世名篇《改良的哲学观》（A Philosophical View of Reform）和《为诗一辩》。在前一篇文章中，雪莱就英国所面临的自由、革命和改良等问题，发表成熟和缜密的论断，是对他在 1817—1820 年间写就的那些政治诗歌的思想说明。1821 年，因惊悼济慈英年早逝，雪莱写了《阿多尼斯》（Adonais）一诗以示缅怀。他以希腊美神阿多尼斯喻济慈，期许他在永恒的美丽世界中复活。雪莱夫人则说，这是一首自挽诗；的确，雪莱向来喜欢在情感的幻想世界中遁世隐身。此时，希腊如火如荼的独立战争又令他血脉偾张，一气完成了他的最后一部诗体剧《希腊》（Hellas）。

1822 年 8 月，雪莱乘船拜访侨居利沃那的拜伦和李·亨特，返航途中遭遇风暴，不幸罹难。雪莱的诗歌充盈着缥缈的神韵和清逸的气息，令人回味无穷，没有济慈那种幽怨缠绵的低沉声调，也没有拜伦那种激情似火有时又抑郁哀伤的风格。在政治上，雪莱颇具理想和抱负，他的政治见解中固然有书生论政的不切实际，也有后来被证实的惊人预见。例如，他在 1817 年小册中发表的对议会改革的见解，托利党人在 1867 年通过。马修·阿诺德说他是"美丽而无用的天使"，而 19 世纪另一位批评大家丹麦的格奥尔格·勃兰克斯（Geong Brandes）则认为，"他的生命后来对人类思想解放产生的影响，要比 1792 年 8 月（雪莱出生之月）在法国发生的任何历史事件都更具有深远意义。"

内容提要

雪莱身后诗名之盛，非他生前所能想见。他玲珑剔透的抒情诗、极富浪漫色彩的行迹最令读者心仪。可是，这种印象也多少掩盖了雪莱本人博学多闻、通览古今的一面。雪莱生前广泛涉猎希腊、罗马的文学和哲学及启蒙思想家的著述，甚至对当代自然科学也有浓厚兴趣。他从希腊文翻译柏拉图和荷马的著作，从拉丁文翻译斯宾诺莎（Spinoza），从西班牙文翻译卡尔德隆（Caldrón），从德文翻译歌德（Gothe），从意大利文翻译但丁，甚至还翻译过一些阿拉伯文的片断。写作《为诗一辩》一文之时，他正在翻译柏拉图的《会饮篇》（Symposium）。

《为诗一辩》是为了回应托马斯·皮考克《诗歌的四个时代》（The Four Ages of Poetry）而写的论战性文字，被认为是他最出色的文章。也许因为受到意大利历史哲学家乔万尼·维科（Giovanni Vico）历史循环论的启发——维科认为，人类社会要经过"神祇时代"、"英雄时代"、"凡人时代"三个历史阶段，如此循环不已——皮考克以戏谑的口吻将诗歌发展历程依次分为四个阶段：铁的时代，诗风质朴粗野，以民间歌谣和传奇故事为主要创作形式，相对应的社会历史形态是原始蛮荒时期和中世纪时代；黄金时代是公元前 5 世纪的雅典和文艺复兴时期的欧洲，在此期间，创作天才大放异彩，以大型史诗和悲剧为主要创作形式；接下来是文人勃发喷张的创作想象受到制约、讲求师法的白银时代，也就是维吉尔和卢克莱修的时代，在英国则为德莱顿和蒲柏的时代；第四个时代为青铜时代，诗歌回归朴实无华的时代，即新古典主义衰落时代，在英国则为华兹华斯、司各特、拜伦等人所在之时代。皮考克还认为，随着文明的进步和自然科学的发展，诗歌的社会功能将日趋萎缩，才智之士必将投身于自然科学或社会科学，不想在诗歌领域浪费时间。

在选文略去的那一部分中，雪莱认为，广义而言，诗歌是想象的表现；狭义而言，诗歌表现了语言的组合，尤其是有韵律的语言的编排组合，这种语言的编排组合是想象力作用的结果。为了回应皮考克所说的科学思想和政治思想（它们也是想象的产物）会后来居上的看法，雪莱极力证实，诗歌是想象力最高级和最有用的表现，因为，与自然界的其他材料——雕塑家的石头、科学家的化学药品、艺术家的颜料——相比，语言能够更直接、更忠实地表现想象。换句话说，语言能够更有效地沟通观念和表现，所以说诗人的地位自然高过雕刻家、画家和音乐家。至于说立法者和宗教创始人，看似高过诗人，可是，如果抛开因群小阿谀奉承而致获之盛名和他们固有的诗人品质，很难说他们比诗人更加高明。

第 1 段至 19 段为选文主体，在这一部分，雪莱从荷马时代以来欧洲文学发展史的宏观视角出发，论述文学与社会之间的关系，提出两个观点：文学向各种社会力量作出反应；诗人的职责在于襄助人类的进步。这是对他此前所作《改良的哲学观》一文思想主旨的引申和发挥。在他看来，在史诗中，荷马将当时道德理想的最高境界具体地表现在人物性格中，从而诱发读者立志模仿英雄人物的道德品质。雪莱讨厌专事道德说教的教谕诗，但他也坚信文学有其社会功用。诗人固然不可堂而皇之地为道德戒律鸣锣开道，不过，他还是可以通过人物塑造或讲故事来寄托自己的理想，间接帮助道德的改进和提高。雪莱暗示，在荷马时代，唯一可行的途径是个人的理想化，因为推动整个人类走向平等的伟大思想尚未产生。然而，事易时移，到了当今时代，这些伟大思想俯拾皆是，不但可用于个人道德的改进，也可用于改良世界。诗歌从中发挥的作用是间接的，诗人在创作中越隐蔽其道德目的，效果就越好。雪莱相信，诗人可用他如椽之笔为政治鼓噪呼号，他本人的那些政论文章和小册子即为此例。当然，诗人也可以写诗言志，鼓励民众对抗反动势力，他的名篇《暴政的假面游行》和《希腊》皆在此列。诗人还可以揭露当前社会的邪恶无道，揭示未来社会的新方向，《麦布女王》、《伊斯兰的反叛》和《解放了的普罗米修斯》即属此类。

在选文的第二部分，雪莱论述了古往今来戏剧与社会的关系。在他看来，诗与社会福祉之间的关联在戏剧当中表现得最为显著。在雅典时代，戏剧成就登峰造极，提高了观众的思想道德境界，强烈激发了他们的想象力，所以当时的社会道德和知识也是成绩斐然。当社会生活开始堕落腐化，戏剧也随之步入衰落时代，英国王政复辟时期的戏剧即为显例。雪莱用力挞伐复辟时期的戏剧，是因为，它们充盈着贵族气息，漠视普通人，拿下层民众插科打诨。自荷马之后，雪莱认为，西西里和埃及的后希腊化时期的田园诗人（如公元前二三世纪的Theocritus 忒奥克里斯，Bion 彼翁和 Moschus 马楚斯）既缺乏思想的深度，也没有达到一定的艺术高度。至于罗马时代的大诗人，在他眼里，只有共和时代思想激进的哲理诗人卢克莱修才算得上最有成就的创造者。虽说维吉尔也是有成就的创造者，可他遣词设句过于纤巧。至于维吉尔时代的其他大家，例如贺拉斯和奥维德等辈，只不过以模仿希腊人为能事。总的说来，雪莱不大将罗马人放在眼里，因为他们的文学缺乏创新。他说，罗马的诗歌无法与其完美的社会组织和家庭组织相提并论。罗马时代之后，文学在中世纪复兴，受到多种因素的推动和影响：个人奴役和家庭奴役遭废除，妇女部分获得解放，基督教里某些宣扬人人平等的教义开始散布开来。但丁的《神曲》将中世纪的宗教思想精华、典雅爱情的传统同文艺复兴和宗教改革运动连接起来。弥尔顿质疑陈腐的教条，同时又保存了古典时代和基督教传统遗留的富于想象的内容，有意或无意地为启蒙运动充当了先锋。雪莱还给荷马、但丁和弥尔顿排了座次，荷马为第一位史诗诗人，但丁第二，弥尔顿第三。其他如维吉尔、塔索、斯宾塞（Herbert Spencer）等辈都不配史诗诗人的称号。

在选文的第三部分，雪莱反驳了皮考克提出的自然科学与社会科学将取代诗歌至尊地位的看法。雪莱承认，自然科学和社会科学固然可以提高劳动的效率；然而，它们的副作用也极大：加剧了贫富的分化，使国家陷入无政府和专制政治两个极端。在答复科学高于诗歌这一论调时，雪莱认为诗可以囊括一切知识，包含一切科学，是一切思想体系的来源和升华；没有诗性的创造想象，科学也就成为"机械师"所凭恃的种种枯燥无味的客观事实。在这一部分，雪莱想表达的核心观点是反驳皮考克所说当代诗歌处在"青铜时代"这一提法。他畅言英国文学正高歌猛进，现代的许多哲学家和诗人超过17世纪英国革命以来的任何哲学家和诗人。他暗示，当前英国正处在与伊丽莎白时代相似的时代，处于一场革命的前夜。当一个伟大民族觉醒，为争取思想和制度的改进而奋争时，诗歌是这项宏伟事业最坚定的先驱、同伴和追随者。诗人是光照未来的明镜，是"未经公认的立法者。"

诗人是"未经公认的立法者"一说发端于塞缪尔·约翰逊《拉塞拉斯》（*Rasselas*）一书。约翰逊说诗人的作用相当于"自然的阐释者，人类的立法者"，这句话经过雪莱巧妙化用，遂成名句。需要说明的是，雪莱文章中说的"诗人"，泛指一切有创意的思想者，包括柏拉图和卢梭。雪莱说诗人是立法者，并不是说，诗人真的在为世人制定道德准则或起草法律；他真正想说的是，诗人可以为崭新的政治和司法制度的产生营造思想氛围。在这种意义上，诗人才是"立法者"，而且经常得不到认可。显然，雪莱的言外之意是，包括拜伦、赫兹利特和他本人在内的这一代诗人为新的社会秩序的出现铺平了道路。他们不一定像政治家那样全面、细致地分析社会，而是发挥自己的想象去感受即将来临的社会变迁。他们通过创作，凭借语言的力量重新塑造了读者大众看待世界的方式，从而"重新创造了一个宇宙。"

Percy Bysshe Shelley (1792—1822)

From *A Defence of Poetry, or Remarks Suggested by an Essay Entitled "The Four Ages of Poetry"*

. . .

Poetry is ever accompanied with pleasure: all spirits on which it falls, open themselves to receive the wisdom which is mingled with its delight.[1] In the infancy of the world, neither poets themselves nor their auditors are fully aware of the excellence of poetry: for it acts in a divine and unapprehended manner, beyond and above consciousness; and it is reserved for future generations to contemplate and measure the mighty cause and effect in all the strength and splendor of their union.[2] Even in modern times, no living poet ever arrived at the fulness of his fame; the jury which sits in judgment upon a poet, belonging as he does to all time, must be composed of his peers:[3] it must be impaneled by Time from the selectest of the wise of many generations. A Poet is a nightingale, who sits in darkness and sings to cheer its own solitude with sweet sounds; his auditors are as men entranced by the melody of an unseen musician, who feel that they are moved and softened, yet know not whence or why. The poems of Homer and his contemporaries were the delight of infant Greece; they were the elements of that social system which is the column upon which all succeeding civilization has reposed. Homer embodied the ideal perfection of his age in human character; nor can we doubt that those who read his verses were awakened to an ambition of becoming like to Achilles, Hector and Ulysses:[4] the truth and beauty of friendship, patriotism and persevering devotion to an object, were unveiled to the depths in these immortal creations: the sentiments of the auditors must have been refined and enlarged by a sympathy with such great and lovely impersonations, until from admiring they imitated, and from imitation they identified themselves with the objects of their admiration. Nor let it be objected, that these characters are remote from moral perfection, and that they can by no means be considered as edifying patterns for general imitation. Every epoch under names more or less specious has deified its peculiar errors;[5] Revenge is the naked Idol of the worship of a semi-barbarous age; and Self-deceit is the veiled Image of unknown evil before which luxury and satiety lie prostrate.[6] But a poet considers the vices of his contemporaries as the temporary dress in which his creations must be arrayed, and which cover without concealing the eternal proportions of their beauty.[7] An epic or dramatic personage is understood to wear them around his soul, as he may the ancient armor or the modern uniform around his body; whilst it is easy to conceive a dress more graceful than either. The beauty of the internal nature cannot be so far concealed by its accidental vesture, but that the spirit of its form shall communicate itself to the very disguise, and indicate the shape it hides from the manner in which it is worn. A majestic form and graceful motions will express themselves through the most barbarous and tasteless costume. Few poets of the highest class have chosen to exhibit the beauty of their conceptions in its naked truth and splendor; and it is doubtful whether the alloy of costume, habit, etc., be not necessary to temper this planetary music[8] for mortal ears.

The whole objection however of the immorality of poetry rests upon a misconception of the manner in which poetry acts to produce the moral improvement of man.[9] Ethical science arranges the elements which poetry has created, and propounds schemes and proposes examples of civil and domestic life: nor is it for want of admirable doctrines that men hate, and despise, and censure, and deceive, and subjugate one another.[10] But Poetry acts in another and diviner manner. It awakens and enlarges the mind itself by rendering it the receptacle of a thousand unapprehended combinations of thought. Poetry lifts the veil from the hidden beauty of the world, and makes familiar objects be as if they were not familiar: it reproduces all that it represents, and the impersonations clothed in its Elysian light[11] stand thenceforward in the minds of those who have once contemplated them, as memorials of that gentle and exalted content which extends itself over all thoughts and actions with which it coexists. The great secret of morals is Love: or a going out of our own nature, and an identification of ourselves with the beautiful which exists in thought, action, or person, not our own.[12] A man, to be greatly good, must imagine intensely and comprehensively; he must put himself in the place of another and of many others; the pains and pleasures of his species must become his own. The great instrument of moral good is the imagination; and poetry administers to the effect by acting upon the cause. Poetry enlarges the circumference of the imagination by replenishing it with thoughts of ever new delight, which have the power of attracting and assimilating to their own nature all other thoughts, and which form new intervals and interstices whose void for ever craves fresh food,[13] Poetry strengthens that faculty which is the organ of the moral nature of man, in the same manner as exercise strengthens a limb. A Poet therefore would do ill to embody his own conceptions of right and wrong, which are usually those of his place and time, in his poetical creations, which participate in neither.[14] By this assumption of the inferior office of interpreting the effect, in which perhaps after all he might acquit himself but imperfectly, he would resign the glory in a participation in the cause. There was little danger that Homer, or any of the eternal poets, should have so far misunderstood themselves as to have abdicated this throne of their widest dominion. Those in whom the poetical faculty, though great, is less intense, as Euripides, Lucan, Tasso, Spenser[15], have frequently affected a moral aim, and the effect of their poetry is diminished in exact proportion to the degree in which they compel us to advert to this purpose.[16]

Homer and the cyclic poets[17] were followed at a certain interval by the dramatic and lyrical Poets of Athens, who flourished contemporaneously with all that is most perfect in the kindred expressions of the poetical faculty; architecture, painting, music, the dance, sculpture, philosophy, and, we may add, the forms of civil life. For although the scheme of Athenian society was deformed by many imperfections[18] which the poetry existing in Chivalry and Christianity have erased from the habits and institutions of modern Europe; yet never at any other period has so much energy, beauty, and virtue, been developed: never was blind strength and stubborn form so disciplined and rendered subject to the will of man, or that will less repugnant to the dictates of the beautiful and the true, as during the century which preceded the death of Socrates.[19] Of no other epoch in the history of our species have we records and fragments stamped so visibly with the image of the divinity in man. But it is Poetry alone, in form, in action, or in language, which has rendered this epoch memorable above all others, and the storehouse of examples to everlasting time. For written poetry existed at the epoch simultaneously with the other arts, and it is an idle enquiry to demand which gave and which received the light, which all as from a common focus have scattered over the darkest periods of succeeding time.[20] We know no more of cause and effect than a constant conjunction of events: Poetry is ever found to coexist with whatever other arts contribute to the happiness and perfection of man.[21] I appeal to what has already been established to distinguish between the cause and the effect.

It was at the period here adverted to, that the Drama had its birth; and however a succeeding writer may have equaled or surpassed those few great specimens of the Athenian drama which have been preserved to us, it is indisputable that the art itself never was understood or practised according to the true philosophy of it, as at Athens. For the Athenians employed language, action, music, painting, the dance, and religious institutions, to produce a common effect in the representation of the highest idealisms of passion and of power; each division in the art was made perfect in its kind by artists of the most consummate skill, and was disciplined into a beautiful proportion and unity one towards another.[22] On the modern stage a few only of the elements capable of expressing the image of the poet's conception are employed at once. We have tragedy without music and dancing; and music and dancing without the highest impersonations of which they are the fit accompaniment, and both without religion and solemnity. Religious institution has indeed been usually banished from the stage. Our system of divesting the actor's face of a mask, on which the many expressions appropriated to his dramatic character might be moulded into one permanent and unchanging expression, is favorable only to a partial and inharmonious effect; it is fit for nothing but a monologue, where all the attention may be directed to some great master of ideal mimicry. The modern practice of blending comedy with tragedy, though liable to great abuse in point of practice, is undoubtedly an extension of the dramatic circle; but the comedy should be as in King Lear,[23] universal, ideal, and sublime. It is perhaps the intervention of this principle which determines the balance in favor of King Lear against the OEdipus Tyrannus or the Agamemnon, or, if you will, the trilogies with which they are connected,[24] unless the intense power of the choral poetry, especially that of the latter, should be considered as restoring the equilibrium. King Lear, if it can sustain this comparison, may be judged to be the most perfect specimen of the dramatic art existing in the world; in spite of the narrow conditions to which the poet was subjected by the ignorance of the philosophy of the Drama which has prevailed in modern Europe. Calderón[25] in his religious Autos has attempted to fulfill some of the high conditions of dramatic representation neglected by Shakespeare; such as the establishing a relation between the drama and religion, and the accommodating them to music and dancing; but he omits the observation of conditions still more important, and more is lost than gained by a substitution of the rigidly-defined and ever-repeated idealisms of a distorted superstition for the living impersonations of the truth of human passion.[26]

But we digress.—The Author of the *Four Ages of Poetry* has prudently omitted to dispute on the effect of the Drama upon life and manners. For, if I know the knight by the device of his shield, I have only to inscribe Philoctetes[27] or Agamemnon or Othello upon mine to put to flight the giant sophisms which have enchanted him, as the mirror of intolerable light, though on the arm of one of the weakest of the Paladins[28], could blind and scatter whole armies of necromancers and pagans.[29] The connection of scenic exhibitions with the improvement or corruption of the manners of men, has been universally recognized: in other words, the presence or absence of poetry in its most perfect and universal form has been found to be connected with good and evil in conduct and habit. The corruption which has been imputed to the drama as an effect, begins, when the poetry employed in its constitution, ends: I appeal to the history of manners whether the periods of the growth of the one and the decline of the other have not corresponded with an exactness equal to any other example of moral cause and effect.[30]

The drama at Athens, or wheresoever else it may have approached to its perfection, coexisted with the moral and intellectual greatness of the age. The tragedies of the Athenian poets are as mirrors in which the spectator beholds himself, under a thin disguise of circumstance, stript of all but that ideal perfection and energy which every one feels to be the internal type of all that he loves, admires, and would become. The imagination is enlarged by a sympathy with pains and passions so mighty, that they distend in their conception the capacity of that by which they are conceived; the good affections are strengthened by pity, indignation, terror and sorrow;[31] and an exalted calm is prolonged from the satiety of this high exercise of them into the tumult of familiar life; even crime is disarmed of half its horror and all its contagion by being represented as the fatal consequence of the unfathomable agencies of nature; error is thus divested of its wilfulness; men can no longer cherish it as the creation of their choice. In a drama of the highest order there is little food for censure or hatred; it teaches rather self-knowledge and self-respect. Neither the eye nor the mind can see itself, unless reflected upon that which it resembles. The drama, so long as it continues to express poetry, is as a prismatic and many-sided mirror, which collects the brightest rays of human nature and divides and reproduces them from the simplicity of these elementary forms, and touches them with majesty and beauty, and multiplies all that it reflects, and endows it with the power of propagating its like wherever it may fall.[32]

But in periods of the decay of social life, the drama sympathizes with that decay. Tragedy becomes a cold imitation of the form of the great masterpieces of antiquity, divested of all harmonious accompaniment of the kindred arts; and often the very form misunderstood: or a weak attempt to teach certain doctrines, which the writer considers as moral truths; and which are usually no more than specious flatteries of some gross vice or weakness with which the author in common with his auditors are infected. Hence what has been called the classical and domestic drama. Addison's *Cato*[33] is a specimen of the one; and would it were not superfluous to cite examples of the other! To such purposes poetry cannot be made subservient. Poetry is a sword of lightning, ever unsheathed, which consumes the scabbard that would contain it.[34] And thus we observe that all dramatic writings of this nature are unimaginative in a singular degree; they affect sentiment and passion: which, divested of imagination, are other names for caprice and appetite. The period in our own history of the grossest degradation of the drama is the reign of Charles II[35] when all forms in which poetry had been accustomed to be expressed became hymns to the triumph of kingly power over liberty and virtue. Milton stood alone illuminating an age unworthy of him.[36] At such periods the calculating principle pervades all the forms of dramatic exhibition, and poetry ceases to be expressed upon them. Comedy loses its ideal universality: wit succeeds to humor; we laugh from self-complacency and triumph instead of pleasure; malignity, sarcasm and contempt, succeed to sympathetic merriment; we hardly laugh, but we smile. Obscenity, which is ever blasphemy against the divine beauty in life, becomes, from the very veil which it assumes, more active if less disgusting: it is a monster for which the corruption of society for ever brings forth new food, which it devours in secret.

The drama being that form under which a greater number of modes of expression of poetry are susceptible of being combined than any other,[37] the connection of poetry and social good is more observable in the drama than in whatever other form: and it is indisputable that the highest perfection of human society has ever corresponded with the highest dramatic excellence; and that the corruption or the extinction of the drama in a nation where it has once flourished, is a mark of a corruption of manners, and an extinction of the energies which sustain the soul of social life. But, as Machiavelli says of political institutions, that life may be preserved and renewed, if men should arise capable of bringing back the drama to its principles. And this is true with respect to poetry in its most extended sense: all language, institution and form, require not only to be produced but to be sustained: the office and character of a poet participates in the divine nature as regards providence, no less than as regards creation.

Civil war, the spoils of Asia, and the fatal predominance first of the Macedonian[38], and then of the Roman arms were so many symbols of the extinction or suspension of the creative faculty in Greece. The bucolic writers[39], who found patronage under the lettered tyrants of Sicily and Egypt, were the latest representatives of its most glorious reign. Their poetry is intensely melodious: like the odor of the tuberose, it overcomes and sickens the spirit with excess of sweetness; whilst the poetry of the preceding age was as a meadow-gale of June which mingles the fragrance of all the flowers of the field, and adds a quickening and harmonizing spirit of its own which endows the sense with a power of sustaining its extreme delight. The bucolic and erotic delicacy in written poetry is correlative with that softness in statuary, music, and the kindred arts, and even in manners and institutions which distinguished the epoch to which we now refer. Nor is it the poetical faculty itself, or any misapplication of it, to which this want of harmony is to be imputed. An equal sensibility to the influence of the senses and the affections is to be found in the writings of Homer and Sophocles: the former especially has clothed sensual and pathetic images with irresistible attractions. Their superiority over these succeeding writers consists in the presence of those thoughts which belong to the inner faculties of our nature,[40] not in the absence of those which are connected with the external; their incomparable perfection consists in a harmony of the union of all. It is not what the erotic writers have, but what they have not, in which their imperfection consists. It is not inasmuch as they were Poets, but inasmuch as they were not Poets, that they can be considered with any plausibility as connected with the corruption of their age. Had that corruption availed so as to extinguish in them the sensibility to pleasure, passion and natural scenery, which is imputed to them as an imperfection, the last triumph of evil would have been achieved. For the end of social corruption is to destroy all sensibility to pleasure; and therefore it is corruption. It begins at the imagination and the intellect as at the core, and distributes itself thence as a paralyzing venom, through the affections into the very appetites, until all become a torpid mass in which sense hardly survives. At the approach of such a period, Poetry ever addresses itself to those faculties which are the last to be destroyed, and its voice is heard, like the footsteps of Astraea[41], departing from the world. Poetry ever communicates all the pleasure which men are capable of receiving: it is ever still the light of life; the source of whatever of beautiful, or generous, or true can have place in an evil time. It will readily be confessed that those among the luxurious citizens of Syracuse and Alexandria who were delighted with the poems of Theocritus, were less cold, cruel and sensual than the remnant of their tribe. But corruption must have utterly destroyed the fabric of human society before Poetry can ever cease. The sacred links of that chain have never been entirely disjoined, which descending through the minds of many men is attached to those great minds, whence as from a magnet the invisible effluence is sent forth, which at once connects, animates and sustains the life of all. It is the faculty which contains within itself the seeds at once of its own and of social renovation. And let us not circumscribe the effects of the bucolic and erotic poetry within the limits of the sensibility of those to whom it was addressed. They may have perceived the beauty of those immortal compositions, simply as fragments and isolated portions: those who are more finely organized, or born in a happier age, may recognize them as episodes to that great poem, which all poets, like the co-operating thoughts of one great mind, have built up since the beginning of the world.

The same revolutions within a narrower sphere had place in ancient Rome; but the actions and forms of its social life never seem to have been perfectly saturated with the poetical element. The Romans appear to have considered the Greeks as the selectest treasuries of the selectest forms of manners and of nature, and to have abstained from creating in measured language, sculpture, music or architecture, anything which might bear a particular relation to their own condition, whilst it should bear a general one to the universal constitution of the world. But we judge from partial evidence; and we judge perhaps partially. Ennius, Varro, Pacuvius, and Accius,[42] all great poets, have been lost. Lucretius is in the highest, and Virgil in a very high sense, a creator. The chosen delicacy of the expressions of the latter is as a mist of light which conceals from us the intense and exceeding truth of his conceptions of nature. Livy[43] is instinct with poetry. Yet Horace, Catullus[44], Ovid, and generally the other great writers of the Virgilian age, saw man and nature in the mirror of Greece. The institutions also and the religion of Rome were less poetical than those of Greece, as the shadow is less vivid than the substance. Hence poetry in Rome, seemed to follow rather than accompany the perfection of political and domestic society. The true Poetry of Rome lived in its institutions; for whatever of beautiful, true and majestic they contained could have sprung only from the faculty which creates the order in which they consist. The life of Camillus, the death of Regulus; the expectation of the Senators,[45] in their godlike state, of the victorious Gauls; the refusal of the Republic to make peace with Hannibal after the battle of Cannae[46], were not the consequences of a refined calculation of the probable personal advantage to result from such a rhythm and order in the shews of life, to those who were at once the poets and the actors of the immortal dramas. The imagination beholding the beauty of this order, created it out of itself according to its own idea: the consequence was empire, and the reward everliving fame. These things are not the less poetry, *quia carent vate sacro*[47]. They are the episodes of the cyclic poem written by Time upon the memories of men. The Past, like an inspired rhapsodist, fills the theater of everlasting generations with their harmony.

At length the ancient system of religion and manners had fulfilled the circle of its revolution. And the world would have fallen into utter anarchy and darkness, but that there were found poets among the authors of the Christian and Chivalric systems of manners and religion, who created forms of opinion and action never before conceived; which, copied into the imaginations of men, became as generals to the bewildered armies of their thoughts.[48] It is foreign to the present purpose to touch upon the evil produced by these systems: except that we protest, on the ground of the principles already established, that no portion of it can be imputed to the poetry they contain.[49]

It is probable that the astonishing poetry of Moses, Job, David, Solomon and Isaiah had produced a great effect upon the mind of Jesus and his disciples.[50] The scattered fragments preserved to us by the biographers of this extraordinary person, are all instinct with the most vivid poetry.[51] But his doctrines seem to have been quickly distorted. At a certain period after the prevalence of a system of opinions founded upon those promulgated by him, the three forms into which Plato had distributed the faculties of mind[52] underwent a sort of apotheosis, and became the object of the worship of the civilized world. Here it is to be confessed that "Light seems to thicken," and

> The crow makes wing to the rooky wood,
> Good things of day begin to droop and drowse,
> And night's black agents to their preys do rouse.[53]

But mark how beautiful an order has sprung from the dust and blood of this fierce chaos! how the World, as from a resurrection, balancing itself on the golden wings of knowledge and of hope, has reassumed its yet unwearied flight into the Heaven of time. Listen to the music, unheard by outward ears, which is as a ceaseless and invisible wind, nourishing its everlasting course with strength and swiftness.

The poetry in the doctrines of Jesus Christ, and the mythology and institutions of the Celtic conquerors[54] of the Roman empire, outlived the darkness and the convulsions connected with their growth and victory, and blended themselves into a new fabric of manners and opinion. It is an error to impute the ignorance of the dark ages to the Christian doctrines or the predominance of the Celtic nations. Whatever of evil their agencies may have contained sprung from the extinction of the poetical principle, connected with the progress of despotism and superstition. Men, from causes too intricate to be here discussed, had become insensible and selfish: their own will had become feeble, and yet they were its slaves, and thence the slaves of the will of others: lust, fear, avarice, cruelty and fraud, characterised a race amongst whom no one was to be found capable of *creating* in form, language, or institution. The moral anomalies of such a state of society are not justly to be charged upon any class of events immediately connected with them, and those events are most entitled to our approbation which could dissolve it most expeditiously. It is unfortunate for those who cannot distinguish words from thoughts, that many of these anomalies have been incorporated into our popular religion.

It was not until the eleventh century that the effects of the poetry of the Christian and Chivalric systems began to manifest themselves. The principle of equality had been discovered and applied by Plato in his Republic[55], as the theoretical rule of the mode in which the materials of pleasure and of power produced by the common skill and labor of human beings ought to be distributed among them. The limitations of this rule were asserted by him to be determined only by the sensibility of each, or the utility to result to all. Plato, following the doctrines of Timaeus[56] and Pythagoras, taught also a moral and intellectual system of doctrine comprehending at once the past, the present, and the future condition of man. Jesus Christ divulged the sacred and eternal truths contained in these views to mankind, and Christianity, in its abstract purity, became the exoteric expression of the esoteric doctrines of the poetry and wisdom of antiquity.[57] The incorporation of the Celtic nations with the exhausted population of the south, impressed upon it the figure of the poetry existing in their mythology and institutions. The result was a sum of the action and reaction of all the causes included in it; for it may be assumed as a maxim that no nation or religion can supersede any other without incorporating into itself a portion of that which it supersedes. The abolition of personal and domestic slavery, and the emancipation of women from a great part of the degrading restraints of antiquity were among the consequences of these events.

The abolition of personal slavery is the basis of the highest political hope that it can enter into the mind of man to conceive. The freedom of women produced the poetry of sexual love. Love became a religion, the idols of whose worship were ever present. It was as if the statues of Apollo and the Muses[58] had been endowed with life and motion and had walked forth among their worshippers;[59] so that earth became peopled by the inhabitants of a diviner world. The familiar appearance and proceedings of life became wonderful and heavenly; and a paradise was created as out of the wrecks of Eden. And as this creation itself is poetry, so its creators were poets; and language were the instrument of their art: "Galeotto fù il libro, e chi lo scrisse."[60] The Provençal Trouveurs[61], or inventors, preceded Petrarch, whose verses are as spells, which unseal the inmost enchanted fountains of the delight which is in the grief of Love. It is impossible to feel them without becoming a portion of that beauty which we contemplate: it was superfluous to explain how the gentleness and the elevation of mind connected with these sacred emotions can render men more amiable, more generous, and wise, and lift them out of the dull vapors of the little world of self.[62] Dante understood the secret things of love even more than Petrarch. His *Vita Nuova*[63] is an inexhaustible fountain of purity of sentiment and language: it is the idealized history of that period, and those intervals of his life which were dedicated to love. His apotheosis of Beatrice in Paradise and the gradations of his own love and her loveliness, by which as by steps he feigns himself to have ascended to the throne of the Supreme Cause, is the most glorious imagination of modern poetry[64]. The acutest critics have justly reversed the judgment of the vulgar, and the order of the great acts of the "Divine Drama," in the measure of the admiration which they accord to the Hell, Purgatory and Paradise.[65] The latter is a perpetual hymn of everlasting love. Love, which found a worthy poet in Plato alone of all the ancients, has been celebrated by a chorus of the greatest writers of the renovated world; and the music has penetrated the caverns of society, and its echoes still drown the dissonance of arms and superstition. At successive intervals, Ariosto, Tasso, Shakespeare, Spenser, Calderon, Rousseau, and the great writers of our own age, have celebrated the dominion of love, planting as it were trophies in the human mind of that sublimest victory over sensuality and force. The true relation borne to each other by the sexes into which human kind is distributed has become less misunderstood; and if the error which confounded diversity with inequality of the powers of the two sexes has become partially recognized in the opinions and institutions of modern Europe, we owe this great benefit to the worship of which Chivalry was the law, and poets the prophets.

The poetry of Dante may be considered as the bridge thrown over the stream of time, which unites the modern and ancient world. The distorted notions of invisible things which Dante and his rival Milton have idealized, are merely the mask and the mantle in which these great poets walk through eternity enveloped and disguised. It is a difficult question to determine how far they were conscious of the distinction which must have subsisted in their minds between their own creeds and that of the people. Dante at least appears to wish to mark the full extent of it by placing Riphaeus, whom Virgil calls *justissimus unus*, in Paradise,[66] and observing a most heretical caprice in his distribution of rewards and punishments. And Milton's poem contains within itself a philosophical refutation of that system of which, by a strange and natural antithesis, it has been a chief popular support.[67] Nothing can exceed the energy and magnificence of the character of Satan as expressed in Paradise Lost. It is a mistake to suppose that he could ever have been intended for the popular personification of evil. Implacable hate, patient cunning, and a sleepless refinement of device to inflict the extremest anguish on an enemy, these things are evil; and although venial in a slave are not to be forgiven in a tyrant; although redeemed by much that ennobles his defeat in one subdued, are marked by all that dishonors his conquest in the victor.[68] Milton's Devil as a moral being is as far superior to his God as one who perseveres in some purpose which he has conceived to be excellent in spite of adversity and torture, is to one who in the cold security of undoubted triumph inflicts the most horrible revenge upon his enemy, not from any mistaken notion of inducing him to repent of a perseverance in enmity, but with the alleged design of exasperating him to deserve new torments. Milton has so far violated the popular creed (if this shall be judged to be a violation) as to have alleged no superiority of moral virtue to his God over his Devil. And this bold neglect of a direct moral purpose is the most decisive proof of the supremacy of Milton's genius. He mingled as it were the elements of human nature, as colors upon a single pallet, and arranged them into the composition of his great picture according to the laws of epic truth; that is, according to the laws of that principle by which a series of actions of the external universe and of intelligent and ethical beings is calculated to excite the sympathy of succeeding generations of mankind. The Divina Commedia and Paradise Lost have conferred upon modern mythology a systematic form; and when change and time shall have added one more superstition to the mass of those which have arisen and decayed upon the earth, commentators will be learnedly employed in elucidating the religion of ancestral Europe, only not utterly forgotten because it will have been stamped with the eternity of genius.[69]

Homer was the first, and Dante the second epic poet: that is, the second poet the series of whose creations bore a defined and intelligible relation to the knowledge, and sentiment, and religion, and political conditions of the age in which he lived, and of the ages which followed it, developing itself in correspondence with their development. For Lucretius had limed the wings of his swift spirit in the dregs of the sensible world; and Virgil, with a modesty which ill became his genius, had affected the fame of an imitator even whilst he created anew all that he copied; and none among the flock of mock-birds, though their notes were sweet, Apollonius Rhodius, Quintus Calaber, Nonnus, Lucan, Statius, or Claudian,[70] have sought even to fulfil a single condition of epic truth. Milton was the third Epic Poet. For if the title of epic in its highest sense be refused to the AEneid, still less can it be conceded to the Orlando Furioso, the Gerusalemme Liberata, the Lusiad, or the Fairy Queen.[71]

Dante and Milton were both deeply penetrated with the ancient religion of the civilized world; and its spirit exists in their poetry probably in the same proportion as its forms survived in the unreformed worship of modern Europe. The one preceded and the other followed the Reformation at almost equal intervals. Dante was the first religious reformer, and Luther[72] surpassed him rather in the rudeness and acrimony, than in the boldness of his censures of papal usurpation. Dante was the first awakener of entranced Europe: he created a language, in itself music and persuasion, out of a chaos of inharmonious barbarisms.[73] He was the congregator of those great spirits who presided over the resurrection of learning; the Lucifer[74] of that starry flock which in the thirteenth century shone forth from republican Italy, as from a heaven, into the darkness of the benighted world. His very words are instinct with spirit; each is as a spark, a burning atom of inextinguishable thought; and many yet lie covered in the ashes of their birth, and pregnant with a lightning which has yet found no conductor. All high poetry is infinite; it is as the first acorn, which contained all oaks potentially. Veil after veil may be undrawn, and the inmost naked beauty of the meaning never exposed. A great Poem is a fountain for ever overflowing with the waters of wisdom and delight; and after one person and one age has exhausted all its divine effluence which their peculiar relations enable them to share, another and yet another succeeds, and new relations are ever developed, the source of an unforeseen and an unconceived delight.

The age immediately succeeding to that of Dante, Petrarch, and Boccaccio, was characterized by a revival of painting, sculpture, music, and architecture. Chaucer caught the sacred inspiration, and the superstructure of English literature is based upon the materials of Italian invention.

But let us not be betrayed from a defence into a critical history of Poetry and its influence on Society. Be it enough to have pointed out the effects of poets, in the large and true sense of the word, upon their own and all succeeding times and to revert to the partial instances cited as illustrations of an opinion the reverse of that attempted to be established in the Four Ages of Poetry.

But poets have been challenged to resign the civic crown to reasoners and mechanists on another plea.[75] It is admitted that the exercise of the imagination is most delightful, but it is alleged that that of reason is more useful. Let us examine as the grounds of this distinction, what is here meant by Utility.[76] Pleasure or good in a general sense, is that which the consciousness of a sensitive and intelligent being seeks, and in which when found it acquiesces. There are two kinds of pleasure, one durable, universal, and permanent; the other transitory and particular. Utility may either express the means of producing the former or the latter. In the former sense, whatever strengthens and purifies the affections, enlarges the imagination, and adds spirit to sense, is useful. But the meaning in which the Author of the Four Ages of Poetry seems to have employed the word utility is the narrower one of banishing the importunity of the wants of our animal nature, the surrounding men with security of life, the dispersing the grosser delusions of superstition, and the conciliating such a degree of mutual forbearance among men as may consist with the motives of personal advantage.

Undoubtedly the promoters of utility in this limited sense, have their appointed office in society. They follow the footsteps of poets, and copy the sketches of their creations into the book of common life. They make space, and give time. Their exertions are of the highest value so long as they confine their administration of the concerns of the inferior powers of our nature within the limits due to the superior ones. But whilst the sceptic destroys gross superstitions, let him spare to deface, as some of the French writers have defaced, the eternal truths charactered upon the imaginations of men.[77] Whilst the mechanist abridges, and the political economist combines, labor, let them beware that their speculations, for want of correspondence with those first principles which belong to the imagination, do not tend, as they have in modern England, to exasperate at once the extremes of luxury and want.[78] They have exemplified the saying, "To him that hath, more shall be given; and from him that hath not, the little that he hath shall be taken away."[79] The rich have become richer, and the poor have become poorer; and the vessel of the state is driven between the Scylla and Charybdis of anarchy and despotism.[80] Such are the effects which must ever flow from an unmitigated exercise of the calculating faculty.

It is difficult to define pleasure in its highest sense; the definition involving a number of apparent paradoxes. For, from an inexplicable defect of harmony in the constitution of human nature, the pain of the inferior is frequently connected with the pleasures of the superior portions of our being. Sorrow, terror, anguish, despair itself are often the chosen expressions of an approximation to the highest good. Our sympathy in tragic fiction depends on this principle; tragedy delights by affording a shadow of the pleasure which exists in pain. This is the source also of the melancholy which is inseparable from the sweetest melody. The pleasure that is in sorrow is sweeter than the pleasure of pleasure itself. And hence the saying, "It is better to go to the house of mourning, than to the house of mirth."[81] Not that this highest species of pleasure is necessarily linked with pain. The delight of love and friendship, the ecstasy of the admiration of nature, the joy of the perception and still more of the creation of poetry is often wholly unalloyed.

The production and assurance of pleasure in this highest sense is true utility. Those who produce and preserve this pleasure are Poets or poetical philosophers.

The exertions of Locke, Hume, Gibbon, Voltaire, Rousseau,[82] and their disciples, in favor of oppressed and deluded humanity, are entitled to the gratitude of mankind. Yet it is easy to calculate the degree of moral and intellectual improvement which the world would have exhibited, had they never lived.[83] A little more nonsense would have been talked for a century or two; and perhaps a few more men, women, and children, burnt as heretics. We might not at this moment have been congratulating each other on the abolition of the Inquisition in Spain[84]. But it exceeds all imagination to conceive what would have been the moral condition of the world if neither Dante, Petrarch, Boccaccio, Chaucer, Shakespeare, Calderón, Lord Bacon, nor Milton, had ever existed; if Raphael and Michael Angelo had never been born; if the Hebrew poetry had never been translated; if a revival of the study of Greek literature had never taken place; if no monuments of ancient sculpture had been handed down to us; and if the poetry of the religion of the ancient world had been extinguished together with its belief. The human mind could never, except by the intervention of these excitements, have been awakened to the invention of the grosser sciences, and that application of analytical reasoning to the aberrations of society, which it is now attempted to exalt over the direct expression of the inventive and creative faculty itself.

We have more moral, political and historical wisdom, than we know how to reduce into practice; we have more scientific and economical knowledge than can be accommodated to the just distribution of the produce which it multiplies. The poetry in these systems of thought, is concealed by the accumulation of facts and calculating processes.There is no want of knowledge respecting what is wisest and best in morals, government, and political economy, or at least, what is wiser and better than what men now practise and endure.[85] But we let "*I dare not* wait upon *I would*, like the poor cat in the adage."[86] We want[87] the creative faculty to imagine that which we know; we want the generous impulse to act that which we imagine; we want the poetry of life: our calculations have outrun conception; we have eaten more than we can digest. The cultivation of those sciences which have enlarged the limits of the empire of man over the external world, has, for want of the poetical faculty, proportionally circumscribed those of the internal world; and man, having enslaved the elements, remains himself a slave. To what but a cultivation of the mechanical arts in a degree disproportioned to the presence of the creative faculty, which is the basis of all knowledge, is to be attributed the abuse of all invention for abridging and combining labor, to the exasperation of the inequality of mankind? From what other cause has it arisen that the discoveries which should have lightened, have added a weight to the curse imposed on Adam?[88] Poetry, and the principle of Self, of which money is the visible incarnation, are the God and the Mammon of the world.

The functions of the poetical faculty are two-fold; by one it creates new materials of knowledge, and power and pleasure; by the other it engenders in the mind a desire to reproduce and arrange them according to a certain rhythm and order which may be called the beautiful and the good. The cultivation of poetry is never more to be desired than at periods when, from an excess of the selfish and calculating principle, the accumulation of the materials of external life exceed the quantity of the power of assimilating them to the internal laws of human nature. The body has then become too unwieldy for that which animates it.

Poetry is indeed something divine.[89] It is at once the center and circumference of knowledge; it is that which comprehends all science, and that to which all science must be referred.[90] It is at the same time the root and blossom of all other systems of thought; it is that from which all spring, and that which adorns all; and that which, if blighted, denies the fruit and the seed, and withholds from the barren world the nourishment and the succession of the scions of the tree of life. It is the perfect and consummate surface and bloom of things; it is as the odor and the color of the rose to the texture of the elements which compose it, as the form and the splendor of unfaded beauty to the secrets of anatomy and corruption. What were Virtue, Love, Patriotism, Friendship—what were the scenery of this beautiful Universe which we inhabit—what were our consolations on this side of the grave—and what were our aspirations beyond it—if Poetry did not ascend to bring light and fire from those eternal regions where the owl-winged faculty of calculation dare not ever soar?[91] Poetry is not like reasoning, a power to be exerted according to the determination of the will. A man cannot say, "I will compose poetry." The greatest poet even cannot say it: for the mind in creation is as a fading coal which some invisible influence, like an inconstant wind, awakens to transitory brightness: the power arises from within, like the color of a flower which fades and changes as it is developed, and the conscious portions of our natures are unprophetic either of its approach or its departure.[92] Could this influence be durable in its original purity and force, it is impossible to predict the greatness of the results; but when composition begins, inspiration is already on the decline, and the most glorious poetry that has ever been communicated to the world is probably a feeble shadow of the original conception of the poet. I appeal to the greatest Poets of the present day, whether it be not an error to assert that the finest passages of poetry are produced by labor and study. The toil and the delay recommended by critics can be justly interpreted to mean no more than a careful observation of the inspired moments, and an artificial connection of the spaces between their suggestions by the intertexture of conventional expressions; a necessity only imposed by a limitedness of the poetical faculty itself. For Milton conceived the Paradise Lost as a whole before he executed it in portions. We have his own authority also for the Muse having "dictated" to him the "unpremeditated song,"[93] and let this be an answer to those who would allege the fifty-six various readings of the first line of the Orlando Furioso. Compositions so produced are to poetry what mosaic is to painting. This instinct and intuition of the poetical faculty is still more observable in the plastic and pictorial arts: a great statue or picture grows under the power of the artist as a child in the mother's womb, and the very mind which directs the hands in formation is incapable of accounting to itself for the origin, the gradations, or the media of the process.

Poetry is the record of the best and happiest moments of the happiest and best minds. We are aware of evanescent visitations of thought and feeling sometimes associated with place or person, sometimes regarding our own mind alone and always arising unforeseen and departing unbidden, but elevating and delightful beyond all expression; so that even in the desire and the regret they leave, there cannot but be pleasure, participating as it does in the nature of its object.[94] It is as it were the interpenetration of a diviner nature through our own; but its footsteps are like those of a wind over the sea, which the coming calm erases, and whose traces remain only as on the wrinkled sand which paves it. These and corresponding conditions of being are experienced principally by those of the most delicate sensibility and the most enlarged imagination; and the state of mind produced by them is at war with every base desire. The enthusiasm of virtue, love, patriotism, and friendship is essentially linked with these emotions; and whilst they last, self appears as what it is, an atom to a Universe. Poets are not only subject to these experiences as spirits of the most refined organization, but they can color all that they combine with the evanescent hues of this ethereal world; a world, a trait in the representation of a scene or a passion, will touch the enchanted chord, and reanimate, in those who have ever experienced these emotions, the sleeping, the cold, the buried image of the past. Poetry thus makes immortal all that is best and most beautiful in the world; it arrests the vanishing apparitions which haunt the interlunations[95] of life, and veiling them or in language or in form sends them forth among mankind, bearing sweet news of kindred joy to those with whom their sisters abide—abide, because there is no portal of expression from the caverns of the spirit which they inhabit into the universe of things.[96] Poetry redeems from decay the visitations of the divinity in man.

Poetry turns all things to loveliness; it exalts the beauty of that which is most beautiful, and it adds beauty to that which is most deformed: it marries exultation and horror, grief and pleasure, eternity and change; it subdues to union under its light yoke all irreconcilable things. It transmutes all that it touches, and every form moving within the radiance of its presence is changed by wondrous sympathy to an incarnation of the spirit which it breathes;[97] its secret alchemy turns to potable gold the poisonous waters which flow from death through life; it strips the veil of familiarity from the world, and lays bare the naked and sleeping beauty which is the spirit of its forms.

All things exist as they are perceived: at least in relation to the percipient. "The mind is its own place, and of itself can make a heaven of hell, a hell of heaven."[98] But poetry defeats the curse which binds us to be subjected to the accident of surrounding impressions. And whether it spreads its own figured curtain or withdraws life's dark veil from before the scene of things, it equally creates for us a being within our being. It makes us the inhabitants of a world to which the familiar world is a chaos. It reproduces the common universe of which we are portions and percipients, and it purges from our inward sight the film of familiarity which obscures from us the wonder of our being.[99] It compels us to feel that which we perceive, and to imagine that which we know. It creates anew the universe after it has been annihilated in our minds by the recurrence of impressions blunted by reiteration.[100] It justifies that bold and true word of Tasso—*Non merita nome di creatore, se non Iddio ed il Poeta.*[101]

A Poet, as he is the author to others of the highest wisdom, pleasure, virtue and glory, so he ought personally to be the happiest, the best, the wisest, and the most illustrious of men. As to his glory, let Time be challenged to declare whether the fame of any other institutor of human life be comparable to that of a poet. That he is the wisest, the happiest, and the best, inasmuch as he is a poet, is equally incontrovertible: the greatest poets have been men of the most spotless virtue, of the most consummate prudence, and, if we could look into the interior of their lives, the most fortunate of men: and the exceptions, as they regard those who possessed the poetic faculty in a high yet inferior degree, will be found on consideration to confirm rather than destroy the rule.[102] Let us for a moment stoop to the arbitration of popular breath, and usurping and uniting in our own persons the incompatible characters of accuser, witness, judge and executioner, let us decide without trial, testimony, or form, that certain motives of those who are "there sitting where we dare not soar"[103] are reprehensible. Let us assume that Homer was a drunkard, that Virgil was a flatterer, that Horace was a coward, that Tasso was a madman, that Lord Bacon was a peculator[104], that Raphael was a libertine, that Spenser was a poet laureate. It is inconsistent with this division of our subject to cite living poets, but Posterity has done ample justice to the great names now referred to. Their errors have been weighed and found to have been dust in the balance; if their sins "were as scarlet, they are now white as snow"; they have been washed in the blood of the mediator and the redeemer Time. Observe in what a ludicrous chaos the imputations of real or fictitious crime have been confused in the contemporary calumnies against poetry and poets; consider how little is, as it appears—or appears, as it is: look to your own motives, and judge not, lest ye be judged.[105]

Poetry, as has been said, in this respect differs from logic, that it is not subject to the control of the active powers of the mind, and that its birth and recurrence has no necessary connection with consciousness or will. It is presumptuous to determine that these are the necessary conditions of all mental causation, when mental effects are experienced insusceptible of being referred to them.[106] The frequent recurrence of the poetical power, it is obvious to suppose, may produce in the mind a habit of order and harmony correlative with its own nature and with its effects upon other minds. But in the intervals of inspiration, and they may be frequent without being durable, a poet becomes a man, and is abandoned to the sudden reflux of the influences under which others habitually live. But as he is more delicately organized than other men, and sensible to pain and pleasure, both his own and that of others, in a degree unknown to them, he will avoid the one and pursue the other with an ardor proportioned to this difference. And he renders himself obnoxious to calumny, when he neglects to observe the circumstances under which these objects of universal pursuit and flight have disguised themselves in one another's garments.

But there is nothing necessarily evil in this error, and thus cruelty, envy, revenge, avarice, and the passions purely evil, have never formed any portion of the popular imputations on the lives of poets.

I have thought it most favorable to the cause of truth to set down these remarks according to the order in which they were suggested to my mind by a consideration of the subject itself, instead of following that of the treatise that excited me to make them public. Thus although devoid of the formality of a polemical reply; if the view they contain be just, they will be found to involve a refutation of the Four Ages of Poetry, so far at least as regards the first division of the subject. I can readily conjecture what should have moved the gall of the learned and intelligent author of that paper;[107] I confess myself like him unwilling to be stunned by the Theseids of the hoarse Codri[108] of the day. Bavius and Maevius[109] undoubtedly are, as they ever were, insufferable persons. But it belongs to a philosophical critic to distinguish rather than confound.

The first part of these remarks has related to Poetry in its elements and principles; and it has been shown, as well as the narrow limits assigned them would permit, that what is called poetry, in a restricted sense, has a common source with all other forms of order and of beauty according to which the materials of human life are susceptible of being arranged, and which is poetry in a universal sense.

The second part[110] will have for its object an application of these principles to the present state of the cultivation of Poetry, and a defence of the attempt to idealize the modern forms of manners and opinion, and compel them into a subordination to the imaginative and creative faculty. For the literature of England, an energetic development of which has ever preceded or accompanied a great and free development of the national will, has arisen as it were from a new birth. In spite of the low-thoughted envy which would undervalue contemporary merit, our own will be a memorable age in intellectual achievements, and we live among such philosophers and poets as surpass beyond comparison any who have appeared since the last national struggle for civil and religious liberty[111]. The most unfailing herald, companion, and follower of the awakening of a great people to work a beneficial change in opinion or institution, is Poetry. At such periods there is an accumulation of the power of communicating and receiving intense and impassioned conceptions respecting man and nature. The persons in whom this power resides, may often, as far as regards many portions of their nature, have little apparent correspondence with that spirit of good of which they are the ministers. But even whilst they deny and abjure, they are yet compelled to serve, the Power which is seated upon the throne of their own soul. It is impossible to read the compositions of the most celebrated writers of the present day without being startled with the electric life which burns within their words. They measure the circumference and sound the depths of human nature with a comprehensive and all-penetrating spirit, and they are themselves perhaps the most sincerely astonished at its manifestations, for it is less their spirit than the spirit of the age. Poets are the hierophants[112] of an unapprehended inspiration, the mirrors of the gigantic shadows which futurity casts upon the present, the words which express what they understand not; the trumpets which sing to battle, and feel not what they inspire: the influence which is moved not, but moves. Poets are the unacknowledged legislators of the World.

注释

1. 贺拉斯在《诗艺》中提出，诗人的目的在于寓教于乐。
2. 大意为：诗人与读者见解一致所产生的全部力量和绽放的光彩，其中非凡的因果关系，还有待后人去审视和衡量。
   文中对诗歌娱乐功能的强调，附和了锡德尼《诗辩，1595》中的观点。另见威廉·华兹华斯《〈抒情歌谣集〉序，1800》："也不要把直接给人愉快这种必要性当做诗人艺术的退化。事实上绝非如此。"
3. 大意为：评判诗人的那些评论家，要想同该诗人一样，为万世景仰，其才华必须与该诗人不相上下。
4. Achilles, Hector and Ulysses：这三位都是荷马史诗中的英雄人物。
5. 大意为：每个时代都以某些貌似有理的名义将它特有的谬误加以神化。
6. 大意为：自欺是被掩饰的无名恶行，奢侈和餍足都对它顶礼膜拜。
7. 大意为：不过诗人却认为，他的同时代人的种种恶行是一时的行头，他笔下人物必须穿上的一时的行头，而这套行头却丝毫不会掩盖那些人物身上永恒的美。
8. planetary music：据说是由星体运动所形成的美妙音响。
9. 大意为：然而，所有指责诗歌不道德的反对之声均源于对诗歌改进人类道德所采用的方式的误解。
10. 大意为：人类之所以相互敌视、鄙视、指责、欺骗和压迫，也不是因为缺乏那些可敬的学说（即上文所说的 ethical science）。

11. Elysian light：天国乐园的光辉。根据古典神话，受神祇保佑的人在死后都住在天国乐园（Elysian Fields）。
这句话的大意为：诗歌重现了它所表明的一切，沐浴在天国光辉之中的诗歌人物留在了曾经欣赏他们的读者的头脑中，作为优雅与高贵内容的象征；这内容影响到并同时存在于思想和行动中。

12. 大意为：道德的大秘密是爱，也就是摆脱自己的天性，主动去认同那些存在于别人的思想、行动或人格中的美的东西。

13. 大意为：诗歌利用新鲜有趣的思想去充实想象，从而扩大想象的范围；这些新鲜有趣的思想有能力吸收和消化其他思想，并形成新的间隙；为了填补这段空白，永远需要新材料。

14. 大意为：如果诗人把他受时空限制的是非观念表现在通常不受时空限制的诗歌创作中，那他可就错了。

15. Spenser：斯宾塞（Edmund Spenser, 1552—1599），英国诗人，以长篇寓言诗《仙后》著称。

16. 最后一句大意为：他们越是强迫我们注意诗中的道德目的，他们诗作的影响、效果就越差。

17. cyclic poet：组诗诗人，指荷马之后以特洛伊战争为主题创作史诗的诗人。

18. imperfections：是指奴隶制和妇女卑微的社会地位。

19. 即公元前5世纪，雅典政治和艺术全盛时期（苏格拉底死于公元前399年）。

20. 大意为：在那一时期，以文字形式出现的诗歌与其他艺术并存。要是有人问，究竟哪门艺术有烛照之功，哪门艺术接受其光辉的照耀，这是徒劳之举；因为光辉都来自一个共同的焦点，散布在此后最为黑暗的时期。

21. 大意为：凡是有助于人类幸福和完善的艺术，诗歌总是与之共存。

22. 大意为：艺术的各组成部分，在技巧无比高明的艺术家手里，都会臻于完美，而且各个组成部分也被整合为美的均衡与统一体。

23.《李尔王》（King Lear）中有两个疯子相会这样的喜剧性场面。

24. 索福克勒斯的三部曲有《俄狄浦斯王》（Oedipus Tyrannus）、《俄狄浦斯在科罗诺斯》（Oedipus Coloneus）和《安提戈涅》（Antigone）；埃斯库罗斯（Aeschylus）的三部曲有《阿伽门农》（Agamemnon）、《奠酒人》（The Libation Bearers）和《降福女神》（Eumenides）。

25. Calderón：卡尔德隆（Pedro Calderón de la Barca, 1600—1681），西班牙

戏剧作家和诗人。他 1651 年成为教士后，只写 autos sacramentales（只有一幕的宗教短剧，通常具有讽喻意义）。

26. 大意为：卡尔德隆在他的宗教短剧中试图弥补被莎士比亚忽视的戏剧表现中的某些重要条件，例如，确立戏剧与宗教之间的关系，给戏剧配上音乐和舞蹈。不过，他忽视了更为重要的条件，从而得不偿失。那就是，他用一种曲解的迷信当中搬出的中规中矩、千篇一律的理想主义去替代那些具有人类真实情感的活人。

27. Philoctetes：菲罗克忒忒斯，特洛伊战争中的希腊英雄。他的事迹成为许多悲剧的主题。

28. Paladin：帕拉丁，查理大帝（Charlemagne, 742—814）帐下十二武士之一。

29. 大意为：因为，如果我单凭盾上的标记就知道骑士是谁，那么我只需把菲罗克忒忒斯或阿伽门农或奥赛罗的名字记在我的盾上，就足以驱走纠缠他的种种谬见。这正如光芒耀眼刺目的明镜，即使拿在最软弱的武士帕拉丁斯手里，也会驱散那些成群结队的巫师和异教徒。

30. 大意为：我要诉诸风格史以做出判断，诗歌的兴衰与道德兴衰的对应程度是否如同所有道德上的因果关系事例那样准确。

31. 这是对亚里士多德《诗学》中提出的"净化"观念的一种解释。

32. 大意为：只要戏剧继续表现诗意，它就是一面多棱镜，镜面上集中了人性最灿烂的光辉。然后根据其基本形式加以分门别类，予以再现，赋予它们端庄和美丽，让其所反映的内容更加丰富，使所照之处同类事物衍生不息。

33. Cato：《加图》，英国诗人和小品文作家约瑟夫·艾迪生创作的一部新古典主义风格的戏剧。

34. 大意为：诗是一柄闪耀电光的宝剑，它永远是出鞘的，因为电光会损耗剑鞘。

35. Charles II：查理二世，英国国王（1660—1685）。他在位时期就是所谓王政复辟时期，以统治者骄奢淫逸、世风轻浮浅薄著称。

36. 弥尔顿是清教徒革命的支持者，曾为议会处死英王查理一世辩护。

37. 大意为：与其他艺术形式相比，戏剧更易于综合众多的诗的表现形式……

38. 这里所说的马其顿人，是指马其顿国王亚历山大大帝，他将统治疆域扩展到埃及和印度。

39. 田园诗作家们，指古希腊的田园诗人，著名的有忒奥克里托斯（约前310—约前250），后来有马楚斯（大约生活在公元前150）和彼翁（大约生活在公元前100）。

40. 大意为：他们之所以胜过后来的这些作家，是因为，他们的思想属于我们天性中固有的能力。

41. Astraea：阿斯脱利亚，古希腊神话中的正义女神。在人类的黄金时代，她居住在人间；可是在黑暗时代，人类恶行肆虐，她重返天上。

42. 这几位都是前奥古斯丁时代的作家。Varro，瓦罗（Marcus Terentius Varro, 前116—前27），罗马时代最伟大的学者，编、著作达620卷；Pacuvius，帕库维乌（Marcus Pacuvius，前220—约前130），罗马悲剧家和讽刺作家；Accius，阿克齐乌斯（Lucius Accius, 前170—约前86），罗马悲剧作家，曾被同时代人目为最伟大的罗马悲剧诗人。

43. Livy：李维（前59—17），罗马历史学家，著罗马史142卷，大部分佚失。

44. Catullus：卡图卢斯（Gaius Valerius Catullus, 约前84—约前54），古罗马抒情诗人。

45. Camillus：卡米卢斯（Marcus Furius Camillus，约死于公元前365），罗马军人、政治家，在高卢人于公元前387年劫掠罗马城后加强城防，重整政局，被尊崇为罗马城的第二个奠基人。Regulus，雷古卢斯（Marcus Atilius Regulus, 生活在公元前3世纪），古罗马政治家、将军（第一次布匿战争中被迦太基人俘虏，被假释送回罗马。可他敦促元老院拒绝赎回自己和其他战俘，假释期满返回迦太基后被拷打致死）。

46. Battle of the Cannae：坎尼战役，公元前216年罗马军队与迦太基军队在意大利东南部阿普利亚的坎尼村大会战，罗马军队大败。

47. 拉丁文，大意为：因为他们没有神圣的诗人。语出贺拉斯诗。

48. 大意为：在描写基督教和骑士制度的风俗和宗教方面的作家当中涌现了一些诗人，他们创造出前人从未构想过的种种形式的言行。这些言行的形式一旦进入人们的想象，就得以仿效，就好像乱军有了主将，纷乱的思想有了头绪。要不是有了这些诗人，整个世界就会陷入彻头彻尾的无政府状态和黑暗之中。

49. 大意为：讲述基督教和骑士制度造成的罪恶与我们论述的主旨无关。不过，我们根据既定的原则发表反对意见，说那些罪恶中没有任何一点可归咎于这些制度下产生的诗歌。

50. 约伯（Job）和以赛亚（Isaiah）曾被当做《约伯记》和《以赛亚书》的作者。传统上，摩西被认为是摩西五经的作者。一般认为，《圣经》大部分诗篇为大卫所作；《传道书》、《箴言》和《雅歌》则归于所罗门名下。

51. 大意为：这位非凡人物的传记作家们给我们留下的断简残篇，无不充满最为生动的诗意。

52. 柏拉图在《理想国》中将人的灵魂分为三部分：欲望部分、理性部分和精神部分。

53. 语出《麦克白》（*Macbeth*），引文略有出入。"乌鸦/飞去了昏黑的巢林。白天的好事开始萎顿了，瞌睡了，黑夜的黑爪牙起来要扑食生物了。"（卞之琳译）。

54. Celtic conqueror：凯尔特人，北欧日耳曼部落。

55. 即柏拉图所著《理想国》。

56. Timaeus：蒂迈欧，毕达哥拉斯派信徒，或许仅是虚拟的人物，是柏拉图对话集《蒂迈欧》一文中的主要对话人。

57. 大意为：基督教通俗地表现了古代诗歌和智慧的神秘教诲。

58. the Muses：缪斯，希腊神话中司文艺和科学的九位女神，都是宙斯和记忆女神之女。

59. 大意为：这就好像阿波罗和缪斯的雕像都有了生命，可以行动，在他们的崇拜者中间行进。

60. 意大利文，意为："加罗多就是这本书，也是这本书的作者。"语出但丁《地狱》第 5 篇 137 行。加罗多为"圆桌骑士故事"中骑士朗赛罗之友，朗赛罗爱上了亚瑟王之妻，加罗多助成骑士和王后的恋爱。

61. the Provençal Trouveur：普罗旺斯的吟游诗人，12 世纪至 13 世纪法国东南部诗人，是最早颂扬骑士爱情和典雅爱情的诗人。

62. 大意为：我们感受这些爱情诗的时候，自会变成我们敛心默祷的美丽的一部分。温文尔雅和高尚庄严的心灵与这些神圣的情感相结合，如何使人变得更加和蔼可亲，更加慷慨和明智，将他们从笼罩着晦暗迷雾的自我小世界里拉出来，这一点不必解释。

63. Vita Nuora：《新生》（约 1293）。但丁在这部诗歌与散文夹杂并置的作品中讲述了他对贝雅特丽齐（Beatrice）的单相思过程。

64. 但丁在《神曲·天堂篇》中将贝雅特丽齐置于天国的顶端。

65. 即《神曲》的《地狱篇》、《炼狱篇》和《天堂篇》。

66. 大意为：但丁使特洛伊武士里菲亚斯成为天堂中唯一的异教徒。*justissimus unus*：（特洛伊人当中）最正直的人，语出维吉尔《伊尼特》，第2卷，第426—427行。

67. 大意为：弥尔顿诗歌（这里指《失乐园》）的一些内容从哲理上驳斥了基督教制度。那些内容是通过一种既让人感到匪夷所思而又合乎情理的对比，以通俗的形式来捍卫基督教的。

68. 大意为：（以上种种罪恶），虽说在虽败犹荣的被征服者一方可以救赎，但更加凸显征服者一方胜得不够光彩。

69. 大意为：《神曲》和《失乐园》赋予现代神话一个系统的形式；随着时代变迁和时间流逝，在世上经历过兴衰变化的诸多迷信中将再多上一种，就需要评论家发挥他们的聪明才智去阐发古代欧洲的宗教。这派古代宗教之所以没有被完全忘记，只是因为它被打上了天才的永恒烙印。

70. 这里提到的几位作者都是希腊和罗马时代的史诗诗人，其作品质量参差不齐，前三位用希腊语创作，后几位用拉丁文创作。

71. 《疯狂的奥兰多》《被解放的耶路撒冷》《鲁西亚德》《仙后》的作者分别是阿里奥斯托、塔索、葡萄牙诗人卡蒙斯（Luis Vaz de Camöes）和英国大诗人斯宾塞。

72. Luther：路德（Martin Luther, 1483—1546），德国神学家和宗教改革者。

73. 大意为：但丁是第一位将欧洲从沉迷状态中唤醒的人，他从混乱的粗鄙的方言中创造出一种既有音乐性又有说服力的语言。

74. Lucifer：字面意义为"光明的携带者"，即晨星。在弥尔顿的《失乐园》中，他是反叛上帝的众天使的领袖，他堕落后被称为撒旦。

75. 大意为：可是有人却以另一种借口向诗人提出挑战，要求诗人将桂冠送给社会科学理论家和机械师。

76. 雪莱在此回应英国社会改良者、哲学家、功利主义创始人边沁这一派人士的观点。边沁声称，一切社会行为和立法应以绝大多数人的最大幸福为目的，而且他还制定了一套计算快乐的方法。皮考克在《诗歌的四个时代》中认为："（诗歌）既不能造就哲学家，也不能造就政治家，也不能在任何一种生活中造就一名有用的或有理性的人。它与生活中的任何一种慰藉或功用毫无关系。"

77. 大意为：然而，既然怀疑论者已经毁灭了粗俗的迷信，就请他就此罢手，不要像某些法国作家那样，去铲平根据人类想象所表现的永恒真理。

78. 大意为：虽说机械师减少了人类劳动，政治经济家（优化）组合了人类劳动，可是需要提请他们注意的是，他们的思考缺乏与想象的首要原则的联系，并不会触怒奢侈和贫困这两端，就像在英国那样。

79. 语出《新约·马可福音》第 4 卷 25 节，"有的，还要给他；没有的，连他所有也要夺去。"

80. 在古希腊神话中，锡拉岩礁上栖居女妖，对面是卡斯布狄斯大漩涡，给往返于意大利和西西里岛的水手造成了极大的危害。雪莱用这个典故喻指处于无政府状态和专制主义这两种极端。

81. 语出《旧约·传道书》第 7 章 2 节。"往遭丧的家去，强如往宴乐的家去。"

82. 雪莱原注为："我依据《诗歌的四个时代》的作者进行的分类。不过卢梭本质上是诗人。其他人，甚至伏尔泰，都是纯粹的理论家。"

83. 大意为：然而，即便上述人等没有生存于世，计算这个世界所体现出的道德和知识进步程度也是容易做到的。

84. Inquisition in Spain：西班牙的宗教裁判所，是天主教为了严厉镇压异端而设置的法庭，建于 1478 年，直到 1820 年改良派军官发动革命才最终取消。

85. 大意为：在道德、政府和政治经济上，哪些是最明智和最优秀的办法，或者说哪些比目前人们正在实行的和承受的更高明，这方面的知识并不缺乏。

86. 语出《麦克白》第 1 章，第 7 场，44—45 行，"'我不敢'来伺候'我要'像老话所说的那只可怜猫。"麦克白的夫人鼓励麦克白谋杀邓肯，借用西方古谚"猫要吃鱼，又怕湿爪。"

87. want：这里是"缺少"之意。

88. the curse imposed on Adam：为谋生而付出的辛劳。根据《旧约·创世记》第 3 章 19 节，亚当和夏娃因食禁果而受罚终生辛劳："你必汗流满面才得糊口，直到你归了土。"

89. 锡德尼在《诗辩》中说，诗是 "a divine gift"。

90. 大意为：诗歌既是知识的圆心又是知识的圆周；诗包括一切科学，所有科学都起源于诗。

91. 大意为：如果诗没有扶摇直上，飞到（理智的）精打细算未敢振翅前往的永恒地域，拿来光明和火焰，那么，美德、爱、爱国主义、友谊是什么？我们栖居的美丽的宇宙的景致是什么？我们在今世的慰藉是什么？我们对来世的期盼又是什么？

92. 大意为：因为，在创作过程中，作者的心宛如渐渐黯淡的煤火，某种无形的影响，例如突如其来的一阵风，都会使它暂时发出光亮：这股力量萌生于内部，就像花朵的颜色，随着花开花落而黯淡而变化。我们靠天生的意识既无法预知它何时来，也无法预知它何时去。

93. 语出弥尔顿《失乐园》第 9 卷，第 20—24 行。这句话大意为：我们以他自己的话为证，他说缪斯曾"口授"给他"以前未曾想到的诗歌"。

94. 大意为：因此，即使在它们（指上文所说的"思想和情感的短暂眷顾"）所留下的向往和惆怅中，也不能没有快乐，快乐构成了它影响的对象的本质。

95. interlunation：黑暗时期。

96. 大意为：因为，在他们居住的魂灵的洞穴，没有一扇表现之门可以通到万物的宇宙。

97. 大意为：诗歌改变了它所触及的一切，在诗歌光辉下活动的每一种形式都会出于一种奇妙的同感，而成为诗歌精神的化身。

98. 语出《失乐园》第 1 卷第 254—255 行，引文略有出入，这是撒旦的狂悖之言。

99. 雪莱在此呼应柯勒律治在《文学传记》第 14 章中的说法。

100. 在这句话中，第一个 it 指"诗歌"，第二个 it 指"宇宙"。大意为：因重复而失去吸引力的印象不断重现，破坏了宇宙在我们心目中的形象。然而，此后诗歌又重新创造了宇宙。

101. 拉丁文，大意为：除了上帝和诗人之外，无人能荣获创造者这一尊号。语出皮兰多尼奥·塞拉西的《塔索传》（1785）。

102. 全句大意为：一个人只要是诗人，那么他就是最明智、最幸福、最出色的人。同样没有异议的是：最伟大的诗人都是品质高洁、毫无瑕疵的人，是最能深谋远虑之人。而且，假如我们能够洞察他们生活内幕，就会发现，他们还是最幸运的人；那些诗才虽高而名位靠后的诗人，在他们看来属于例外；然而，仔细考虑一下，这些例外证实了而不是毁坏了这条常规。

103. 语出《失乐园》第 4 卷 829 行，引文略有出入。

104. peculator：盗用公款之人。

105. 在这段文字中，雪莱一再重复《圣经》中的语言："Their errors have been weighed"出自《但以理书》（Daniel）第 5 章 27 节；"dust of the balance"出自《以赛亚书》第 40 卷 15 节；"were as scarlet"出自《以赛亚书》第 1 章 18 节；"washed in the blood"出自《启

示录》（Revelation）第 7 章 14 节；"the mediator" 出自《希伯来书》（Hebrews）第 9 章 15 节，第 12 章 24 节；"Judge not"，出自《马太福音》（Matthew）第 7 章 1 节。

106. 大意为：断定意识或意志是一切心理因果关系的必要条件，只不过是臆断，意识和意志其实难以影响我们体验的心理效应。

107. 大意为：我很容易猜测到，究竟是什么东西触怒了这位博学而多智的作者（指皮考克）。

108. 古罗马讽刺诗人维纳利斯在《讽刺诗》第 1 篇中抱怨过 "粗鲁的 codrus" 的《忒西德》。这部史诗讲述的是古希腊传说中阿提卡（Attica）地方的英雄忒修斯的故事。该诗已亡佚，作者不可考，想必是一首劣诗。

109. 这两人都是很平庸的拉丁诗人，遭到维吉尔和贺拉斯的嘲笑。

110. 本文的第二部分始终没有完成。如果第二部分写完，可能看到雪莱对同时代作家的评论。

111. the last national struggle for civil and religious liberty：即英国内战（1642—1651）。

112. hierophant：解释宗教秘义的大师。

阿诺德　　《批评在目前的作用》

马修·阿诺德（1822—1888）

马修·阿诺德，19 世纪英国维多利亚时代杰出的诗人、评论家。1857 年至 1867 年任牛津大学教授，讲授诗歌。1851 年起任督学，直至去世前两年。他的诗作有《新诗集》（*New Poems*）等，创作的剧本有《梅罗珀，一出悲剧》（*Merope, a Tragedy*, 1867）。他的诗多忧伤、惋惜和怀旧之情。他认为诗应该反映时代的要求，重视道德和智慧。

他在文论方面的著名作品是《论荷马的翻译》（*On Translating Homer*, 1861）、《凯尔特文学研究》（*The Study of Celtic Literature*, 1867）、《文化与无政府状态》（*Culture and Anarchy*, 1869）、《批评在目前的作用》等。他的论述抨击了当时英国批评界的狭隘和庸俗，拓宽了英国文学批评的视野和范围。

他的文论观点使人觉得他属于亚里士多德派。他认为，人的行动而不是诗人的个人意识，才应该是诗的题材。在他的《诗集》（*Poems*, 1853）的序言中，他写道，"What are the eternal objects of poetry, among all nations and at all times? They are actions; human actions; possessing an inherent interest in themselves, and which are to be communicated in an interesting manner the art of the poet"。

但是，实际上，阿诺德对文学的看法与亚里士多德在《诗学》中所论述的观点是不同的。如，亚里士多德关注诗的形式胜于诗的内容，而阿诺德几乎没有论述诗的形式问题，他关心的主要是诗的内容。

阿诺德所说的"批评"不限于文学批评。他把文学称作"对生活的评论"。他认为文学和文学批评均全面地评论整个文化。他指出，文学之所以有趣主要是因为它是社会的产物，并反映社会。他强调文学的社会功能。他说，"More and more mankind will discover that we have to turn to poetry to interpret life for us, to console us, to sustain us. Without poetry, our science will appear incomplete; most of what now passes with us for religion and philosophy will be replaced by poetry"。

他使英国文坛看到欧洲文学和文学批评的发展。《文化与无政府状态》作为阿诺德的一部重要论著,抨击了维多利亚时代英国人的自满、庸俗和拜金主义。这种庸俗和拜金主义使英国社会失去了行为的准则和社会发展的方向感,从而使社会陷入无政府主义。

阿诺德在批评中强调道德。在《批评在目前的作用》一文中,他把文学批评作为一般批评的一个分支来看待。无论是什么领域的批评,批评的目的是一样的,即"呈现事物的真实面目。这就要求批评者努力学习和宣扬世界上公认的最优秀的东西。"

他主张用有学识的智慧精神和公正无私的态度研究文学、神学、历史、艺术、科学、社会学和政治学。阿诺德生活的时代是历史批评开始兴起的年代。他在《诗歌研究》("The Study of Poetry")一文中不赞成对诗作历史性评论,也反对以个人的好恶对诗进行评论。他认为文学是文化的基础,而文学则应该展示人类最崇高的理想。

内容提要

阿诺德在文章一开始就指出,在所有的知识领域,不管是文学,还是神学、哲学、历史、艺术和科学,批评的目的都是要弄清批评对象的真实面目。英国人轻视批评,而欧洲人却十分看重批评。不少人认为他强调批评的重要性过了头,他们认为创作比批评重要。华兹华斯便是一例。他认为批评才能低于创作才能,并且说,如果把写评论的时间用于创作富有新意的文章,就会好得多。其实,华兹华斯本人不仅是个伟大的诗人,还是个杰出的批评家。他写的《〈抒情歌谣集〉序》(1800 年第 2 版)就是文学批评的上品。还有歌德,他既是伟大的诗人和戏剧家,也是个了不起的批评家。塞缪尔·约翰逊也是个出色的批评家。我们并不希望他能多写点像《爱里尼斯》(Irenes)这样的悲剧,而是喜欢看到他能写出更多的像《英国诗人传》(1779—1781)这样的文学评论。

的确,批评才能低于创作才能,因为自由的创作活动是人的最高级的功能。人从自己的创作活动中得到极大的愉快。但是,这种极大的愉快不仅来自创作文学艺术的佳作。如果是这样,不从事文学艺术创作的人就不可能享受极大的愉快了。从批评中也同样可以得到这种愉快。

世界和现代生活是复杂的。现代诗人要写出好诗,也必须有批评能力;不然，写出的诗就贫乏，枯燥无味，也没有生命力。正因为如此，拜伦的诗就不如歌德的诗。拜伦和歌德均有巨大的创作才能，但是歌德却富有批评、判断才能，因此能为他的诗作提供真实的素材。与拜伦相比，歌德对生活世界以及诗人应该写什么题材，有更全面、深刻的了解。

在品达、索福克勒斯生活的古希腊，在莎士比亚生活的英国伊丽莎白时代，新的思潮给诗人提供了丰富生动的创作源泉。歌德所生活的时代也是德国思想活跃、各个领域的知识十分发达的时代。也正是这样的时代和环境培养了富有创造力的一代文豪歌德。而19世纪的前25年，英国却缺乏伊丽莎白时代所具有的那种生活和思想的光彩，也没有歌德时代德国的学识和批评。因此，这一时期的英诗就显创造力不足。

真正的批评在本质上是应用人性中的好品质，例如好奇心。好奇心在其他语言中是褒义，而在英语中却含有贬义。好奇心驱使人们不考虑政治、实践和其他此类因素，去了解世界上公认的最好的东西。英国的批评应该明确自己的规则和走向，以便在未来取得好成绩。

所谓规则可以归纳为一个词——公正。批评中的"公正"就是批评者要摆脱政治和实用的观点去观察、评论事物，充分发挥自己的想象力。英国批评界之所以落后于欧洲大陆，症结就在于此。批评必须保持自己的独立性，不要受实用观念的影响。欧洲人如此重视批评是因为批评能促进智能和精神的提高。批评将有助于英国未来的发展。

从事创造性的活动给人以极大的愉快，从事批评同样能给人带来极大的愉快。但是批评必须真诚、简洁、灵活、充满热情，不断地扩充知识。唯如此，批评才能成为一种愉快的创作活动。

Matthew Arnold (1822—1888)

The Function of Criticism at the Present Time

Many objections have been made to a proposition which, in some remarks of mine on translating Homer, I ventured to put forth; a proposition about criticism and its importance at the present day. I said: "Of the literature of France and Germany, as of the intellect of Europe in general, the main effort, for now many years, has been a critical effort; the endeavor, in all branches of knowledge, theology, philosophy, history, art, science, to see the object as in itself it really is." I added, that owing to the operation in English literature of certain causes, "almost the last thing for which one would come to English literature is just that very thing which now Europe most desires—criticism;" and that the power and value of English literature was thereby impaired. More than one rejoinder declared that the importance I here assigned to criticism was excessive, and asserted the inherent superiority of the creative effort of the human spirit over its critical effort. And the other day, having been led by a Mr. Shairp's[1] excellent notice of Wordsworth to turn again to his biography, I found, in the words of this great man, whom I, for one, must always listen to with the profoundest respect, a sentence passed on the critic's business, which seems to justify every possible disparagement of it. Wordsworth says in one of his letters: "The writers in these publications [the reviews], while they prosecute their inglorious employment, cannot be supposed to be in a state of mind very favorable for being effected by the finer influences of a thing so pure as genuine poetry." And a trustworthy reporter of his conversation quotes a more elaborate judgment to the same effect:

> Wordsworth holds the critical power very low, infinitely lower than the inventive; and he said today that if the quantity of time consumed in writing critiques on the works of others were given to original composition, of whatever kind it might be, it would be much better employed; it would make a man find out sooner his own level, and it would do infinitely less mischief. A false or malicious criticism may be much injury to the minds of others, a stupid invention, either in prose or verse, is quite harmless.[2]

It is almost too much to expect of poor human nature, that a man capable of producing some effect in one line of literature, should, for the greater good of society, voluntarily doom himself to impotence and obscurity in another. Still less is this to be expected from men addicted to the composition of the "false or malicious criticism," of which Wordsworth speaks. However, everybody would admit that a false or malicious criticism had better never have been written. Everybody, too, would be willing to admit, as a general proposition, that the critical faculty is lower than the inventive. But is it true that criticism is really, in itself, a baneful and injurious employment; is it true that all time given to writing critiques on the works of others would be much better employed if it were given to original composition, of whatever kind this may be? Is it true that Johnson[3] had better have gone on producing more *Irenes*[4] instead of writing his *Lives of the Poets*[5]; nay, is it certain that Wordsworth himself was better employed in making his Ecclesiastical Sonnets than when he made his celebrated "Preface"[6], so full of criticism, and criticism of the works of others? Wordsworth was himself a great critic, and it is to be sincerely regretted that he has not left us more criticism; Goethe was one of the greatest of critics, and we may sincerely congratulate ourselves that he has left us so much criticism. Without wasting time over the exaggeration which Wordsworth's judgment on criticism clearly contains, or over an attempt to trace the causes—not difficult, I think, to be traced—which may have led Wordsworth to this exaggeration, a critic may with advantage seize an occasion for trying his own conscience, and for asking himself of what real service at any given moment the practice of criticism either is or may be made to his own mind and spirit, and to the minds and spirits of others.

The critical power is of lower rank than the creative. True; but in assenting to this proposition, one or two things are to be kept in mind. It is undeniable that the exercise of a creative power, that a free creative activity, is the highest function of man; it is proved to be so by man's finding in it his true happiness. But it is undeniable, also, that men may have the sense of exercising this free creative activity in other ways than in producing great works of literature or art; if it were not so, all but a very few men would be shut out from the true happiness of all men. They may have it in well-doing, they may have it in learning, they may have it even in criticizing. This is one thing to be kept in mind. Another is, that the exercise of the creative power in the production of great works of literature or art, however high this exercise of it may rank, is not at all epochs and under all conditions possible; and that therefore labor may be vainly spent in attempting it, which might with more fruit be used in preparing for it, in rendering it possible. This creative power works with elements, with materials; what if it has not those materials, those elements, ready for its use? In that case it must surely wait till they are ready. Now, in literature—I will limit myself to literature, for it is about literature that the question arises—the elements with which the creative power works are ideas; the best ideas on every matter which literature touches, current at the time. At any rate we may lay it down as certain that in modern literature no manifestation of the creative power not working with these can be very important or fruitful. And I say *current* at the time, not merely accessible at the time; for creative literary genius does not principally show itself in discovering new ideas, that is rather the business of the philosopher. The grand work of literary genius is a work of synthesis and exposition, not of analysis and discovery; its gift lies in the faculty of being happily inspired by a certain intellectual and spiritual atmosphere, by a certain order of ideas, when it finds itself in them; of dealing divinely with these ideas, presenting them in the most effective and attractive combinations—making beautiful works with them, in short. But it must have the atmosphere, it must find itself amidst the order of ideas, in order to work freely; and these it is not so easy to command. This is why great creative epochs in literature are so rare, this is why there is so much that is unsatisfactory in the productions of many men of real genius; because, for the creation of a masterwork of literature two powers must concur, the power of the man and the power of the moment, and the man is not enough without the moment; the creative power has, for its happy exercise, appointed elements, and those elements are not in its own control.

Nay, they are more within the control of the critical power. It is the business of the critical power, as I said in the words already quoted, "in all branches of knowledge, theology, philosophy, history, art, science, to see the object as in itself it really is." Thus it tends, at last, to make an intellectual situation of which the creative power can profitably avail itself. It tends to establish an order of ideas, if not absolutely true, yet true by comparison with that which it displaces; to make the best ideas prevail. Presently these new ideas reach society, the touch of truth is the touch of life, and there is a stir and growth everywhere; out of this stir and growth come the creative epochs of literature.

Or, to narrow our range, and quit these considerations of the general march of genius and of society—considerations which are apt to become too abstract and impalpable—everyone can see that a poet, for instance, ought to know life and the world before dealing with them in poetry; and life and the world being in modern times very complex things, the creation of a modern poet, to be worth much, implies a great critical effort behind it; else it must be a comparatively poor, barren, and short-lived affair. This is why Byron's poetry had so little endurance in it, and Goethe's so much; both Byron and Goethe had a great productive power, but Goethe's was nourished by a great critical effort providing the true materials for it, and Byron's was not; Goethe knew life and the world, the poet's necessary subjects, much more comprehensively and thoroughly than Byron. He knew a great deal more of them, and he knew them much more as they really are.

It has long seemed to me that the burst of creative activity in our literature, through the first quarter of this century, had about it in fact something premature; and that from this cause its productions are doomed, most of them, in spite of the sanguine hopes which accompanied and do still accompany them to prove hardly more lasting than the productions of far less splendid epochs. And this prematureness comes from its having proceeded without having its proper data, without sufficient materials to work with. In other words, the English poetry of the first quarter of this century, with plenty of energy, plenty of creative force, did not know enough. This makes Byron so empty of matter, Shelley so incoherent, Wordsworth even, profound as he is, yet so wanting in completeness and variety. Wordsworth cared little for books, and disparaged Goethe. I admire Wordsworth, as he is, so much that I cannot wish him different; and it is vain, no doubt, to imagine such a man different from what he is, to suppose that he *could* have been different. But surely the one thing wanting to make Wordsworth an even greater poet than he is—his thought richer, and his influence of wider application—was that he should have read more books, among them, no doubt, those of that Goethe whom he disparaged without reading him.

. . .

It is noticeable that the word *curiosity*, which in other languages is used in a good sense, to mean, as a high and fine quality of man's nature, just this disinterested love of a free play of the mind on all subjects, for its own sake—it is noticeable, I say, that this word has in our language no sense of the kind, no sense but a rather bad and disparaging one. But criticism, real criticism is essentially the exercise of this very quality. It obeys an instinct prompting it to try to know the best that is known and thought in the world, irrespectively of practice, politics, and everything of the kind; and to value knowledge and thought as they approach this best, without the intrusion of any other considerations whatever. This is an instinct for which there is, I think, little original sympathy in the practical English nature, and what there was of it has undergone a long benumbing period of blight and suppression in the epoch of concentration which followed the French Revolution.

. . .

It is of the last importance that English criticism should clearly discern what rule for its course, in order to avail itself of the field now opening to it, and to produce fruit for the future, it ought to take. The rule may be summed up in one word—*disinterestedness*. And how is criticism to show disinterestedness? By keeping aloof from what is called "the practical view of things;" by resolutely following the law of its own nature, which is to be a free play of the mind on all subjects which it touches. By steadily refusing to lend itself to any of those ulterior, political, practical considerations about ideas, which plenty of people will be sure to attach to them, which perhaps ought often to be attached to them, which in this country at any rate are certain to be attached to them quite sufficiently, but which criticism has really nothing to do with. Its business is, as I have said, simply to know the best that is known and thought in the world, and by in its turn making this known, to create a current of true and fresh ideas. Its business is to do this with inflexible honesty, with due ability; but its business is to do no more, and to leave alone all questions of practical consequences and applications, questions which will never fail to have due prominence given to them.

· · ·

What then is the duty of criticism here? To take the practical point of view, to applaud the liberal movement and all its works—its New Road religions of the future into the bargain—for their general utility's sake? By no means; but to be perpetually dissatisfied with these works, while they perpetually fall short of a high and perfect ideal.

For criticism, these are elementary laws; but they never can be popular, and in this country they have been very little followed, and one meets with immense obstacles in following them. That is a reason for asserting them again and again. Criticism must maintain its independence of the practical spirit and its aims. Even with well-meant efforts of the practical spirit it must express dissatisfaction, if in the sphere of the ideal they seem impoverishing and limiting. It must not hurry on to the goal because of its practical importance. It must be patient, and know how to wait; and flexible, and know how to attach itself to things and how to withdraw from them. It must be apt to study and praise elements that for the fullness of spiritual perfection are wanted, even though they belong to a power which in the practical sphere may be maleficent. It must be apt to discern the spiritual shortcomings or illusions of powers that in the practical sphere may be beneficent.

· · ·

If I have insisted so much on the course which criticism must take where politics and religion are concerned, it is because, where these burning matters are in question, it is most likely to go astray. I have wished, above all, to insist on the attitude which criticism should adopt towards things in general; on its right tone and temper of mind. But then comes another question as to the subject matter which literary criticism should most seek. Here, in general, its course is determined for it by the idea which is the law of its being; the idea of a disinterested endeavor to learn and propagate the best that is known and thought in the world, and thus to establish a current of fresh and true ideas.

· · ·

I am bound by my own definition of criticism: "a disinterested endeavor to learn and propagate the best that is known and thought in the world." How much of current English literature comes into this "best that is known and thought in the world?" Not very much I fear; certainly less, at this moment, than of the current literature of France or Germany. Well, then, am I to alter my definition of criticism, in order to meet the requirements of a number of practicing English critics, who, after all, are free in their choice of a business? That would be making criticism lend itself just to one of those alien practical considerations, which, I have said, are so fatal to it. One may say, indeed, to those who have to deal with the mass—so much better disregarded—of current English literature, that they may at all events endeavor, in dealing with this, to try it, so far as they can, by the standard of the best that is known and thought in the world; one may say, that to get anywhere near this standard, every critic should try and possess one great literature, at least, besides his own; and the more unlike his own, the better. But, after all, the criticism I am really concerned with—the criticism which alone can much help us for the future, the criticism which, throughout Europe, is at the present day meant, when so much stress is laid on the importance of criticism and the critical spirit—is a criticism which regards Europe as being, for intellectual and spiritual purposes, one great confederation, bound to a joint action and working to a common result; and whose members have, for their proper outfit, a knowledge of Greek, Roman, and Eastern antiquity, and of one another. Special, local, and temporary advantages being put out of account, that modern nation will in the intellectual and spiritual sphere make most progress, which most thoroughly carries out this program. And what is that but saying that we too, all of us, as individuals, the more thoroughly we carry it out, shall make the more progress?

There is so much inviting us! What are we to take? What will nourish us in growth towards perfection? That is the question which, with the immense field of life and of literature lying before him, the critic has to answer; for himself first, and afterwards for others. In this idea of the critic's business the essays brought together in the following pages have had their origin; in this idea, widely different as are their subjects, they have, perhaps, their unity.

I conclude with what I said at the beginning: to have the sense of creative activity is the great happiness and the great proof of being alive, and it is not denied to criticism to have it; but then criticism must be sincere, simple, flexible, ardent, ever widening its knowledge. Then it may have, in no contemptible measure, a joyful sense of creative activity; a sense which a man of insight and conscience will prefer to what he might derive from a poor, starved, fragmentary, inadequate creation. And at some epochs no other creation is possible.

Still, in full measure, the sense of creative activity belongs only to genuine creation; in literature we must never forget that. But what true man of letters ever can forget it? It is no such common matter for a gifted nature to come into possession of a current of true and living ideas, and to produce amidst the inspiration of them, that we are likely to underrate it. The epochs of Aeschylus and Shakespeare make us feel their pre-eminence. In an epoch like those is, no doubt, the true life of literature; there is the promised land, towards which criticism can only beckon. That promised land it will not be ours to enter, and we shall die in the wilderness: but to have desired to enter it, to have saluted it from afar, is already, perhaps, the best distinction among contemporaries; it will certainly be the best title to esteem with posterity.

注释

1. Mr. Shairp：J. C. Shairp，苏格兰批评家，曾写《华兹华斯：其人，其诗》（"Wordsworth：The Man and Poet"，载《北英评论》[*North British Review*]，XLI, 1864)。

2. 此段文字引自威廉·奈特（William Knight）所写的《华兹华斯传》(*Life of Wordsworth*, 3：438 [ED.])。

3. Johnson：指塞缪尔·约翰逊。

4. *Irenes*：《爱里尼斯》，塞缪尔·约翰逊所写的悲剧。

5. *Lives of the Poets*：塞缪尔·约翰逊的评论名著。

6. "Preface"：《〈抒情歌谣集〉序》（ "Preface to the *Lyrical Ballads*")。

佩特 　　《〈文艺复兴史研究〉前言和结论》

沃尔特·佩特（1839—1894）

沃尔特·佩特，英国批评家、散文作家、唯美主义运动的重要人物。出生于医生家庭，幼年丧父，少年丧母，两个姐姐被亲戚带到国外受教育；惨痛的人生经历对他内向性格的形成不无影响，加剧了他的孤独感。他早年（1858—1862）就读于牛津大学女王学院，受教于著名古典学者本杰明·乔伊特（Benjamin Jowett），写过几篇关于古希腊哲学的短论，深得乔伊特的赏识。大学毕业后做了两年私人教师，1864 年当选为牛津大学的研究员，开始了他在牛津 30 多年的舌耕和笔墨生涯。他在学生中很受追捧，可他的思想与维多利亚时代的礼法格格不入，因而饱受同侪的排挤和当局的嫉视。依他们之见，佩特容易诱导青年误入歧途。尽管他行事低调，处处谨慎，时时压抑内心的隐秘情感，他的同性恋传闻还是差点让他身败名裂。佩特羞于交结新友，却热衷于旅游。1865 年夏，他游历了意大利。佛罗伦萨等城市遗存的文艺复兴时期绚丽多彩的绘画让他大开眼界，感慨颇多，从而对那段历史的兴趣大增。在 1866 和 1868 年，他以笔名先后发表了两篇文章评论柯勒律治和温克尔曼（Johann Joachim Winckleman），在牛津学界和伦敦文坛引起了一场小小的轰动。待到 1869 年，他以实名发表论列奥那多·达·芬奇的文章，更是好评如潮。前拉菲尔派的领袖罗塞蒂（Dante Rossetti）击节赞赏，史文朋（Algernon Swinburne）也引他为同道。1877 年，他把这篇文章连同已发表的其他几篇放在一起，以《文艺复兴史研究》（*Studies in the History of the Renaissance*）为题，结集付梓。因此，这本书不是一部以首尾贯通、体系严谨为特征，以辨章学术、考镜源流为主旨的历史著作，而是一系列人物专论的集合。作者以饱含深情的笔触、敏锐细致的鉴赏力，阐释了波提切利（Botticelli）、米开朗琪罗等先贤人物；有人（温克尔曼）虽属 18 世纪，但也厕身其中，理由是，他们都是文艺复兴精神的体现。

这本书出版后，赞扬之声鹊起，漫骂声也不绝于耳，可谓毁誉参半。王尔德称它为"金子般的书"、"美的诏书";对于最为惊世骇俗的结论部分,他居然熟能成诵。书中表露的无视道德和宗教的倾向,招来了敌视,佩特不得不在第二版中删掉结论部分。不管怎样,佩特名声大噪,他的"为艺术而艺术"主张成为英国唯美主义运动的不二原则,被王尔德等人发展到极端,他本人则被奉为一代宗师。虽说佩特与他们在精神上声气相同,但行事内敛得多,甚至南辕北辙。他终生未婚,艺术、文学和哲学是他寄托情感的世界。

除《文艺复兴史研究》之外,他生前还有 4 本书问世,皆有声于时。它们是《伊壁鸠鲁信徒马里乌斯》(*Marius the Epicurean*, 1885),《想象的画像》(*Imaginary Portraits*, 1887),《欣赏集》(*Appreciations, with an Essay on Style*, 1889),《柏拉图与柏拉图主义》(*Plato and Platonism*, 1893)。在他去世的第二年,《希腊研究》(*Greek Studies*, 1895) 出版,生前尚未完成的小说《加斯通·德·拉图尔》(*Gaston de Latour*, 1896) 也是他去世后才问世的。在晚年,佩特还打算写一部 3 卷本的神学著作,以回应马修·阿诺德的宗教和文学观。可惜未及动笔,他就因心脏病突发,于 1894 年撒手归西。

《伊壁鸠鲁信徒马里乌斯》以公元 2 世纪罗马皇帝、斯多噶派哲学家马可·奥勒利乌斯(Marcus Aurelius)时代为背景,描述了一位罗马青年的精神之旅。这位秉性善良的青年是罗马传统宗教的忠实信徒,他先是倾心于伊壁鸠鲁主义,后又为斯多噶主义所吸引,最后,他接触到基督教。虽说他冒充基督教徒替友人殉难,且以基督教仪式安葬,但他始终是伊壁鸠鲁主义者。研究享乐主义哲学之后,马里乌斯得出结论,知识就是通过感官所获取的经验。他认为,唯有大量的感官体验,才能达到智慧的最高境界。这本小说自传色彩浓厚,主人公身上有作者本人的影子,他在借他人的酒杯浇自家的块垒。《想象的画像》是一部短篇小说集,共计 4 篇。《欣赏集》收录了 1866 年以来他在各式文学杂志上发表的一系列评论,评论对象有华兹华斯、柯勒律治、莎士比亚的《一报还一报》(*Measure for Measure*)以及罗塞蒂的诗歌。其中两篇为批评史上的佳作,一篇论文风,一篇辨析古典主义与浪漫主义。《柏拉图与柏拉图主义》根据课堂讲稿写成,为他得意之作。这本书别开洞天,在英语世界较早地表现出历史相对论倾向。佩特以为,他的职事不在于演绎出典型的柏拉图式学说,也不在于判断它们的真伪和内涵;他研究的是柏拉图这个具体的人,研究他所在的世界,进而证明,如此之人在如此之时代自会生发如此之思想。

佩特既是学识渊博、识力精到的学者，也是讲求文字风格的作家。大部分时间里，他都在苦吟推敲，酝酿佳句，颇有语不惊人死不休的韧劲。这正是他"唯美是举"思想的具体写照。不过，这种不懈努力的效果往往背离初衷。按照有的文学史家的说法，他遣词设句过于雕琢藻饰，久之易让读者审美疲劳，反应麻木；他叙事过于舒缓，致使行文拖沓；他苦心孤诣追求精确又使句子冗长，句法过于复杂，意义晦暗不明；他在字里行间偶尔还流露出对暴力和残忍的病态欣赏。总之，他的文风因浓墨重彩而略显滞重，不似前辈阿诺德、后辈王尔德那般轻盈舒展。对于此二者的笔法，他虽心向往之，惜未能躬身实践。

哈罗德·布鲁姆曾感言，19 世纪的批评大家，柯勒律治、兰姆、赫兹利特、德·昆西、罗斯金，都有一个显著特征：他们的批评建树不在于评判具体作家和作品的高下，他们凭借独特的感受力为读者提供一种艺术观，他们的批评文字常常模糊批评和创作之间的界限。此类批评家在 20 世纪凤毛麟角，在 19 世纪则是司空见惯。佩特即是其中一员，他的批评妙笔不但让评论对象生发出新意，还让目光敏锐的读者更新自家的文学观念。

内容提要

与以往的文艺复兴史研究不同，佩特的这本书绝不是那种以不偏不倚的态度、平实无奇的语言，展现时代整体风貌和思想潮流的艺术史。毋宁说，它以高度个人化的态度、诗意的语言、人物专论的形式，提供了那段历史的一幅幅横断面。

现代人回顾文艺复兴时期，总是带着诗意的眼光，抱着审美的态度，把它理想化，以它为黄金时代。同以往在小说、诗歌、历史和文学批评中触及这段历史的歌德、布克哈特、泰纳、布朗宁、罗塞蒂、乔治·艾略特一样，佩特也带着几分怀旧情绪看待它。文艺复兴时期的种种优点，例如激情奔放、活力四射、思想自由，一直为 19 世纪人所推重和期许。特别是当他们环顾四周，发现社会现实与文艺复兴理想相距甚远之时就更是如此。与大部分文艺复兴研究者一样，佩特一再强调，文艺复兴是现代时期的开端；因此，书中常常突出这两段历史时期之间的延续和关联。他意在说明，它们只是同一历史时期的两个阶段。例如，他从 12 世纪的法国文学入手追溯浪漫派和抒情诗传统，发现了雨果、戈蒂耶和波德莱尔等人的抒情风格和浪漫主义思想的根源。他还发现，16世纪有人将达·芬奇当做星相学家，与19世纪他被看做浮士德式的人物，二者之间有一定的联系。

《文艺复兴史研究》中影响最巨、争议最大的不是正文内容，而是该书的结论。这短短的5段文字是英国唯美主义运动的宣言、维多利亚时代盛名卓著的文献。佩特也因此而被奉为唯美主义的领袖，虽说他本人不愿膺此虚衔。

唯美主义主要观点是，艺术应当遗世独立，追求自身的完美和精进；它不必做道德说教、政治宣传，也不应该根据非审美标准来判断它（例如看它是否有利于世道人心）。唯美主义的源头可追溯到德国浪漫主义时期的几位巨擘，尤以康德、谢林、歌德和席勒的影响最大。他们都认为，艺术必须自主，艺术家应当与众不同。用丁尼生的话说，诗人要高出芸芸众生。19世纪后期的唯美主义艺术家造就出一副特立独行、放浪形骸的形象，与浪漫主义这种崇尚个体自我不无关系。德国浪漫派的思想通过柯勒律治和卡莱尔得以风行英国。康德有言，审美判断的无功利性意味着，我们为美本身而欣赏美，而不是为美的道德和功用而欣赏美。佩特相应提出"为艺术而艺术"的口号，暗示艺术自有其内在价值而无道德说教义务。这句口号并非始于佩特，它最早出现于莱辛（Gotthold Ephraim Lessing）的《拉奥孔》(*Laokoon*, 1766)，后来戈蒂耶在《莫班小姐》(*Mademoisselle de Maupin*)的序言中又制造了它的法文版。

《文艺复兴史研究》大受攻击和谩骂，主要有两个原因，首先是佩特的享乐主义审美观念所致。他在结论部分大声疾呼，"永远和这强烈的、宝石般的火焰一起燃烧吧，保持这种心醉神迷的状态才是人生的成功"。像这样孤注一掷追求感官刺激和享受，有悖维多利亚时代禁欲修德、端庄体面的功用伦理。在马修·阿诺德的道德批评居主流的时代，这绝对是异数。另外，他不但没把宗教当做慰藉情感、指导人生的工具，反而把艺术当做智慧的最高境界。

在《文艺复兴史研究》的前言中，佩特提出了印象式文学批评的原则。他首先明确反对笼统地、抽象地给美下定义，因为美是相对的，批评家就应当具体谈它。接下来，他修正了阿诺德所规定的文学批评的目标。阿诺德说，"按照其本来面目看待事物"；他则认为，"在审美批评中，按照其本来面目看待事物的第一步，就是了解自己印象的本来面目，对其加以辨析，明确把握。"批评家的任务是辨析艺术产生的强烈印象，而不必纠缠诸如美是什么、美与真理有何联系等形而上的问题。艺术因其优美而使人产生美感，批评家应去分析其优美之处，指出美感源于何处，犹如化学家之于化学元素。

《文艺复兴史研究》的结论以一句古希腊文作引言，这是苏格拉底转述赫拉克利特的话。佩特直接援引古希腊文，利用古代大哲的只言片语来诠释下文所说的现代思想。这样做，一方面有炫学之意，显示他对整个西方哲学史了然于胸，他本人即为这一脉思想的传人；另一方面，意在暗示，以下内容便是赫拉克利特的思想主旨在19世纪英国得到的回应；现代思想并非全新，只是古典传统的现代化。

"将万事万物以及事物的原则看作变动不居的样式和风尚，这种看法日益成为现代思想的趋向，"这句话是点题之笔。接下来，作者从两方面进行解说。第一段讲人类生理过程中的瞬息万变。按照科学的观点，这些变动不居的生理过程是简单的和基本的力作用的结果，这些力作用于人体的诸种构成元素；我们的生命如同火焰，是多种力交汇组合的结果；这些组合时时更新，而那些力终归会消散。

第二段讲心理世界的稍纵即逝。思想感情等内心世界看似风平浪静，实际却如中流之水，怒涛起伏。我们眼前所见，心中所想，胸中的激情，无不瞬息万变。当我们反思眼前之物的时候，它们在我们心目中呈现的只是一组印象；摆在我们面前的是一个由印象组成的世界。由于印象受时间的制约，而时间又是可以无限分割的，因此印象也可以无限分割。它在我们脑海中的存在只是一瞬间，待到我们捕捉它时，它已飞身离去，了无踪影。因此，与其说它存在，不如说它不再存在更确切。正是因为印象、形象和感觉不断流逝，我们才无从分析内心世界不可名状、不断进行的组合和分解过程。

在第三段中，佩特援引诺瓦利斯的话，说明哲学或思辨文化的作用在于鼓舞人的精神，悉心观察生活。在第四段中提出了审美的具体要求，那就是，捕捉审美经验中的感官刺激，保持心醉神迷的状态，沉醉于审美的愉悦之中。在这种状态下，我们无暇从理论上演绎我们的见闻，假如哲学理论遮蔽我们的亲身体验，就不要理会它们。在最后一段，佩特借用雨果的话慨叹人生短暂，而大智大慧之人将有限的人生投入到艺术和诗歌当中。正因为人生短促，我们只好努力延长生命，在既定的期限内尽量增加脉搏的跳动。只有激情才能让我们脉搏加快，赋予我们爱情的狂喜和悲伤，而诗歌的激情、对美的热爱、为艺术本身而热爱艺术是智慧的最高境界；艺术会在瞬息之间给你带来高品质美的享受。

Walter Pater (1839—1894)

From *Studies in the History of the Renaissance*

Preface

Many attempts have been made by writers on art and poetry to define beauty in the abstract, to express it in the most general terms, to find some universal formula for it. The value of these attempts has most often been in the suggestive and penetrating things said by the way. Such discussions help us very little to enjoy what has been well done in art or poetry, to discriminate between what is more and what is less excellent in them, or to use words like beauty, excellence, art, poetry, with a more precise meaning than they would otherwise have.[1] Beauty, like all other qualities presented to human experience, is relative; and the definition of it becomes unmeaning and useless in proportion to its abstractness.[2] To define beauty, not in the most abstract but in the most concrete terms possible, to find, not its universal formula, but the formula which expresses most adequately this or that special manifestation of it, is the aim of the true student of aesthetics.

"To see the object as in itself it really is,"[3] has been justly said to be the aim of all true criticism whatever; and in aesthetic criticism the first step towards seeing one's object as it really is, is to know one's own impression as it really is, to discriminate it, to realize it distinctly. The objects with which aesthetic criticism deals—music, poetry, artistic and accomplished forms of human life—are indeed receptacles of so many powers or forces: they possess, like the products of nature, so many virtues or qualities. What is this song or picture, this engaging personality presented in life or in a book to me? What effect does it really produce on me? Does it give me pleasure? and if so, what sort or degree of pleasure? How is my nature modified by its presence, and under its influence? The answers to these questions are the original facts with which the aesthetic critic has to do; and, as in the study of light, of morals, of number, one must realize such primary data for one's self, or not at all. And he who experiences these impressions strongly, and drives directly at the discrimination and analysis of them, has no need to trouble himself with the abstract question what beauty is in itself, or what its exact relation to truth or experience—metaphysical questions, as unprofitable as metaphysical questions elsewhere. He may pass them all by as being, answerable or not, of no interest to him.

The aesthetic critic, then, regards all the objects with which he has to do, all works of art, and the fairer forms of nature and human life, as powers or forces producing pleasurable sensations, each of a more or less peculiar or unique kind. This influence he feels, and wishes to explain, by analyzing and reducing it to its elements. To him, the picture, the landscape, the engaging personality in life or in a book, *La Gioconda*, the hills of Carrara, Pico of Mirandola,[4] are valuable for their virtues, as we say, in speaking of a herb, a wine, a gem; for the property each has of affecting one with a special, a unique, impression of pleasure. Our education becomes complete in proportion as our susceptibility to those impressions increases in depth and variety. And the function of the aesthetic critic is to distinguish, to analyze, and separate from its adjuncts, the virtue by which a picture, a landscape, a fair personality in life or in a book, produces this special impression of beauty or pleasure, to indicate what the source of that impression is, and under what conditions it is experienced. His end is reached when he has disengaged that virtue, and noted it, as a chemist notes some natural element, for himself and others; and the rule for those who would reach this end is stated with great exactness in the words of a recent critique of Sainte-Beuve:— *De se borner à connaître de près les belles choses, et à s'en nourrir en exquis amateurs, en humanistes accomplis.*[5]

What is important, then, is not that the critic should possess a correct abstract definition of beauty for the intellect, but a certain kind of temperament, the power of being deeply moved by the presence of beautiful objects. He will remember always that beauty exists in many forms. To him all periods, types, schools of taste, are in themselves equal. In all ages there have been some excellent workmen, and some excellent work done. The question he asks is always: —In whom did the stir, the genius, the sentiment of the period find itself? where was the receptacle of its refinement, its elevation, its taste? "The ages are all equal," says William Blake, "but genius is always above its age."[6]

Often it will require great nicety to disengage this virtue from the commoner elements with which it may be found in combination. Few artists, not Goethe or Byron even, work quite cleanly, casting off all *débris*, and leaving us only what the heat of their imagination has wholly fused and transformed.[7] Take, for instance, the writings of Wordsworth. The heat of his genius, entering into the substance of his work, has crystallized a part, but only a part, of it; and in that great mass of verse there is much which might well be forgotten. But scattered up and down it, sometimes fusing and transforming entire compositions, like the Stanzas on *Resolution and Independence*, or the *Ode on the Recollections of Childhood*,[8] sometimes, as if at random, depositing a fine crystal here or there, in a matter it does not wholly search through and transmute, we trace the action of his unique, incommunicable faculty, that strange, mystical sense of a life in natural things, and of man's life as a part of nature, drawing strength and color and character from local influences, from the hills and streams, and from natural sights and sounds. Well! that is the *virtue*, the active principle in Wordsworth's poetry; and then the function of the critic of Wordsworth is to follow up that active principle, to disengage it, to mark the degree in which it penetrates his verse.

The subjects of the following studies are taken from the history of the *Renaissance*, and touch what I think the chief points in that complex, many-sided movement. I have explained in the first of them what I understand by the word, giving it a much wider scope than was intended by those who originally used it to denote that revival of classical antiquity in the fifteenth century which was only one of many results of a general excitement and enlightening of the human mind, but of which the great aim and achievements of what, as Christian art, is often falsely opposed to the Renaissance, were another result.[9] This outbreak of the human spirit may be traced far into the middle age itself, with its motives already clearly pronounced, the care for physical beauty, the worship of the body, the breaking down of those limits which the religious system of the middle age imposed on the heart and the imagination. I have taken as an example of this movement, this earlier Renaissance within the middle age itself, and as an expression of its qualities, two little compositions in early French; not because they constitute the best possible expression of them, but because they help the unity of my series, inasmuch as the Renaissance ends also in France,[10] in French poetry, in a phase of which the writings of Joachim du Bellay are in many ways the most perfect illustration. The Renaissance, in truth, put forth in France an aftermath, a wonderful later growth, the products of which have to the full that subtle and delicate sweetness which belongs to a refined and comely decadence, as its earliest phases have the freshness which belongs to all periods of growth in art, the charm of *ascêsis*, of the austere and serious girding of the loins in youth.[11]

But it is in Italy, in the fifteenth century, that the interest of the Renaissance mainly lies,—in that solemn fifteenth century which can hardly be studied too much,[12] not merely for its positive results in the things of the intellect and the imagination, its concrete works of art, its special and prominent personalities, with their profound aesthetic charm, but for its general spirit and character, for the ethical qualities of which it is a consummate type.[13]

The various forms of intellectual activity which together make up the culture of an age, move for the most part from different starting-points, and by unconnected roads. As products of the same generation they partake indeed of a common character, and unconsciously illustrate each other; but of the producers themselves, each group is solitary, gaining what advantage or disadvantage there may be in intellectual isolation. Art and poetry, philosophy and the religious life, and that other life of refined pleasure and action in the conspicuous places of the world, are each of them confined to its own circle of ideas, and those who prosecute either of them are generally little curious of the thoughts of others. There come, however, from time to time, eras of more favorable conditions in which the thoughts of men draw nearer together than is their wont, and the many interests of the intellectual world combine in one complete type of general culture. The fifteenth century in Italy is one of these happier eras, and what is sometimes said of the age of Pericles is true of that of Lorenzo[14]—it is an age productive in personalities, many-sided, centralized, complete. Here, artists and philosophers and those whom the action of the world has elevated and made keen, do not live in isolation, but breathe a common air, and catch light and heat from each other's thoughts. There is a spirit of general elevation and enlightenment in which all alike communicate. The unity of this spirit gives unity to all the various products of the Renaissance; and it is to this intimate alliance with mind, this participation in the best thoughts which that age produced, that the art of Italy in the fifteenth century owes much of its grave dignity and influence.

I have added an essay on Winckelmann[15], as not incongruous with the studies which precede it, because Winckelmann, coming in the eighteenth century, really belongs in spirit to an earlier age. By his enthusiasm for the things of the intellect and the imagination for their own sake, by his Hellenism, his life-long struggle to attain to the Greek spirit, he is in sympathy with the humanists of a previous century. He is the last fruit of the Renaissance, and explains in a striking way its motive and tendencies.

Conclusion

Λέγει που 'Ηράκλειτος ὅτι πάντα χωρεῖ καὶ οὐδὲν μένει[16]

To regard all things and principles of things as inconstant modes or fashions has more and more become the tendency of modern thought. Let us begin with that which is without[17]—our physical life. Fix upon it in one of its more exquisite intervals, the moment, for instance, of delicious recoil from the flood of water in summer heat. What is the whole physical life in that moment but a combination of natural elements to which science gives their names? But those elements, phosphorus and lime and delicate fibers, are present not in the human body alone: we detect them in places most remote from it. Our physical life is a perpetual motion of them—the passage of the blood, the waste and repairing of the lenses of the eye, the modification of the tissues of the brain under every ray of light and sound—processes which science reduces to simpler and more elementary forces. Like the elements of which we are composed, the action of these forces extends beyond us: it rusts iron and ripens corn. Far out on every side of us those elements are broadcast, driven in many currents; and birth and gesture and death and the springing of violets from the grave[18] are but a few out of ten thousand resultant combinations. That clear, perpetual outline of face and limb is but an image of ours, under which we group them—a design in a web, the actual threads of which pass out beyond it. This at least of flame-like our life has, that it is but the concurrence, renewed from moment to moment, of forces parting sooner or later on their ways.

Or if we begin with the inward world of thought and feeling, the whirlpool is still more rapid, the flame more eager and devouring. There it is no longer the gradual darkening of the eye, the gradual fading of color from the wall—movements of the shore-side, where the water flows down indeed, though in apparent rest—but the race of the midstream, a drift of momentary acts of sight and passion and thought. At first sight experience seems to bury us under a flood of external objects, pressing upon us with a sharp and importunate, reality, calling us out of ourselves in a thousand forms of action. But when reflexion begins to play upon those objects they are dissipated under its influence; the cohesive force seems suspended like some trick of magic; each object is loosed into a group of impressions—color, odor, texture—in the mind of the observer. And if we continue to dwell in thought on this world, not of objects in the solidity with which language invests them, but of impressions, unstable, flickering, inconsistent, which burn and are extinguished with our consciousness of them, it contracts still further: the whole scope of observation is dwarfed into the narrow chamber of the individual mind. Experience, already reduced to a group of impressions, is ringed round for each one of us by that thick wall of personality through which no real voice has ever pierced on its way to us, or from us to that which we can only conjecture to be without. Every one of those impressions is the impression of the individual in his isolation, each mind keeping as a solitary prisoner its own dream of a world. Analysis goes a step further still, and assures us that those impressions of the individual mind to which, for each one of us, experience dwindles down, are in perpetual flight; that each of them is limited by time, and that as time is infinitely divisible, each of them is infinitely divisible also; all that is actual in it being a single moment, gone while we try to apprehend it, of which it may ever be more truly said that it has ceased to be than that it is. To such a tremulous wisp constantly re-forming itself on the stream, to a single sharp impression, with a sense in it, a relic more or less fleeting, of such moments gone by, what is real in our life fines itself down. It is with this movement, with the passage and dissolution of impressions, images, sensations, that analysis leaves off—that continual vanishing away, that strange, perpetual, weaving and unweaving of ourselves.

Philosophiren, says Novalis, *ist dephlegmatisiren, vivificiren*.[19] The service of philosophy, of speculative culture, towards the human spirit, is to rouse, to startle it to a life of constant and eager observation. Every moment some form grows perfect in hand or face; some tone on the hills or the sea is choicer than the rest; some mood of passion or insight or intellectual excitement is irresistibly real and attractive to us,—for that moment only. Not the fruit of experience, but experience itself, is the end. A counted number of pulses only is given to us of a variegated, dramatic life. How may we see in them all that is to be seen in them by the finest senses? How shall we pass most swiftly from point to point, and be present always at the focus where the greatest number of vital forces unite in their purest energy? [20]

To burn always with this hard, gem-like flame, to maintain this ecstasy, is success in life. In a sense it might even be said that our failure is to form habits: for, after all, habit is relative to a stereotyped world, and meantime it is only the roughness of the eye that makes any two persons, things, situations, seem alike.[21] While all melts under our feet, we may well grasp at any exquisite passion, or any contribution to knowledge that seems by a lifted horizon to set the spirit free for a moment, or any stirring of the senses, strange dyes, strange colors, and curious odors, or work of the artist's hands, or the face of one's friend. Not to discriminate every moment some passionate attitude in those about us, and in the very brilliancy of their gifts some tragic dividing of forces on their ways, is, on this short day of frost and sun, to sleep before evening.[22] With this sense of the splendor of our experience and of its awful brevity, gathering all we are into one desperate effort to see and touch, we shall hardly have time to make theories about the things we see and touch. What we have to do is to be for ever curiously testing new opinions and courting new impressions, never acquiescing in a facile orthodoxy, of Comte[23], or of Hegel, or of our own. Philosophical theories or ideas, as points of view, instruments of criticism, may help us to gather up what might otherwise pass unregarded by us. "Philosophy is the microscope of thought."[24] The theory or idea or system which requires of us the sacrifice of any part of this experience, in consideration of some interest into which we cannot enter, or some abstract theory we have not identified with ourselves, or of what is only conventional, has no real claim upon us.

One of the most beautiful passages of Rousseau is that in the sixth book of the *Confessions*[25], where he describes the awakening in him of the literary sense. An undefinable taint of death had clung always about him, and now in early manhood he believed himself smitten by mortal disease. He asked himself how he might make as much as possible of the interval that remained; and he was not biassed by anything in his previous life when he decided that it must be by intellectual excitement, which he found just then in the clear, fresh writings of Voltaire.[26] Well! we are all *condamnés*[27], as Victor Hugo says: we are all under sentence of death but with a sort of indefinite reprieve—*les hommes sont tous condamnés à mort avec des sursis indéfinis*:[28] we have an interval, and then our place knows us no more. Some spend this interval in listlessness, some in high passions, the wisest, at least among "the children of this world,"[29] in art and song. For our one chance lies in expanding that interval, in getting as many pulsations as possible into the given time. Great passions may give us this quickened sense of life, ecstasy and sorrow of love, the various forms of enthusiastic activity, disinterested or otherwise, which come naturally to many of us. Only to be sure it is passion—that it does yield you this fruit of a quickened, multiplied consciousness. Of such wisdom, the poetic passion, the desire of beauty, the love of art for its own sake, has most. For art comes to you proposing frankly to give nothing but the highest quality to your moments as they pass, and simply for those moments' sake.

注释

1. 这几句话大意为：试图抽象地给美下定义，以最为笼统的方式表述美是什么，为它找到放之四海皆准的公式，由此产生的真知灼见是旁出的。这样做无益于赏析艺术或诗歌的匠心所在，无益于辨析其优劣高下，也无益于我们更精确地运用美、优秀、艺术、诗歌等词语的意义。

2. 这句话大意为：给美下的定义越抽象，就越不明确，越无用处。

3. 马修·阿诺德语。最早见于《论荷马的翻译》（1862）一书，亦可见于他的名篇《批评在目前的作用》开篇部分。

4. *La Gioconda*：《蒙娜丽莎》。据说达·芬奇创作《蒙娜丽莎》时，以乔康达（Francesco del Gioconda）的妻子为原型。Carrara，卡拉拉，意大利一地区，以盛产白色大理石著称。Pico of Mirandola，即乔万尼·皮科（Giovanni Pico, 1463—1494），米兰德拉公国的伯爵，意大利人文主义者和新柏拉图主义哲学家。《文艺复兴史研究》中有一篇他的专论。

5. 法文，大意为：熟悉这些美丽的东西，利用它们将自己培养成目光敏锐的爱好者和造诣深厚的人文主义者。
   这句话出自圣伯夫（St. Beuve, 1804—1869）1867 年评论法国诗人和人文主义者倍雷（Joachim du Bellay, 1522—1560）的一篇文章。《文艺复兴史研究》中有一篇他的专论。

6. 出自英国浪漫派诗人布莱克为《约舒亚·雷诺兹文集》（*The Works of Sir Joshua Reynolds*）第 6 卷所作的评注。

7. 大意为：几乎没有作家能在自己的作品中把平庸的残渣清理得一干二净，只给我们留下他们炽热的想象力所熔化和改变的东西，即便是歌德和拜伦也不能做到。

8. 斜体部分为华兹华斯的两首诗。

9. 大意为：文艺复兴一词最早暗指 15 世纪古典文化的复兴。其实，文艺复兴只是人类心智普遍奋进和启蒙的诸多结果之一，通常被当做文艺复兴对立面的基督教艺术，它的伟大目标和成就则是另一个结果。

10. 《文艺复兴史研究》以探讨两篇法国故事为开端。与以往认为文艺复兴源于意大利的说法不同，佩特在本书中认为，文艺复兴结束于法国，也始于法国。

11. 大意为：文艺复兴在法国成熟较晚，法国文艺复兴时期的作品完全具备优雅考究的衰颓阶段所特有的精致细腻，就像它在初始阶段具有艺术成长过程的那种清新活泼和刻苦修行（ascêsis）的魅力，也就是青年时代蓄势待发所具有的严肃和庄重的魅力。

12. 大意为：15 世纪的意大利才是人们研究文艺复兴的兴趣所在，对于这个世纪的研究怎么多也不过分。

13. 这句话里有黑格尔时代精神的影子。

14. Lorenzo：美地奇家族的罗伦佐（1449—1492），佛罗伦萨统治者、艺术保护人。他本人也是诗人。

15. Winckelmann：温克尔曼（Johann Joachim Winckelmann, 1717—1768），德国考古学家和艺术史家。

16. 古希腊文，大意为：赫拉克利特说，万物流变不息，无物永恒不变。赫拉克利特，前苏格拉底时代古希腊哲学家。

17. which is without：外在的东西。

18. 在《哈姆雷特》第5幕，莱欧提斯（Laertes）在奥菲利娅（Ophelia）墓前说，"愿她洁白无瑕的肉体上开出来／紫罗兰鲜花吧！"

19. 文中所引德文出自诺瓦利斯（德国诗人和小说家，本名为哈登贝格［Friedrich von Hardenberg, 1772—1801］的散文诗《夜颂》（*Hymns to the Night*, 1800）。大意为：进行哲学思考就要摈弃惰性，奋发向上。

20. 大意为：虽说生活丰富多彩、激动人心，然而生命短暂。在有限的生命中，我们怎样以最敏锐的感觉观看生命中应该看到的东西呢？我们应该怎样去把握每一瞬间，总能够感受为数众多的生命力劲头十足凝聚在一起？

21. 大意为：在某种意义上，甚至可以说，形成习性就是失败。毕竟，习性是同一个固定不变的世界联系在一起的。另外，只有眼光不够细致的人才把两个人、两件事、两种情境看成彼此相似。

22. 大意为：如果不能在每一瞬间分辨出周围人的热情态度，在他们出色的才华中分辨出悲剧的成分，就相当于在昼短夜长、霜露已降的日子，我们在日暮之前就昏然睡去。

23. Comte：孔德（Auguste Comte, 1789—1857），法国实证主义哲学家。

24. 语出雨果《悲惨世界》。

25. 这里提到的 *Confessions*，指卢梭的《忏悔录》，该书曾以12卷本形式出版。

26. 有研究者曾指出，卢梭在《忏悔录》中没有提到过他曾读过伏尔泰的作品。

27. condamné：法文，意为"被判了死刑"。

28. 法文，大意为：人都是被判了死刑的，只不过是无限期地缓期执行。

29. 语出《圣经·路加福音》（Luke）第16章第8节，意为"今世之子"。

王尔德 《作为艺术家的批评家》

奥斯卡·王尔德（1854—1900）

1900 年，"龙阳才子"奥斯卡·王尔德穷困潦倒，在巴黎的一家小客店抑郁而终，结束了他短暂而跌宕的一生。消息传到国内，一家很有名气的报纸发出讣告，替他盖棺论定："他的作品中没有流传后世的力量"，大有尔曹身与名俱灭之意。这一预言并未成真。百年之后，王尔德不但没有成为明日黄花，反倒繁花似锦：他的戏剧照演，小说照印，童话有人看，唯美主义的印象式批评也没绝迹，若干理念甚至与读者反映理论、精神分析批评有暗合之处；至于他的那段不堪回首的经历，方兴未艾的同性恋批评正在细细咀嚼回味。

王尔德 1854 年出生在都柏林的一个富裕的中产阶级家庭。他的父亲是著名的外科医生；母亲是小有名气的诗人，主持过文学沙龙。王尔德从小就受艺术熏陶。他先就学于都柏林的三一学院，后来考取了奖学金进入牛津大学，结识了沃尔特·佩特，接受了唯美主义思想。此后，他以佩特的弟子自居，尊奉"为艺术而艺术"的信条。除佩特外，他还受到艺术史家约翰·罗斯金（John Ruskin）、先拉斐尔派诗人和画家的影响。1881 年，他出版了第一部诗集，显示了济慈、史文朋、佩特以及先拉斐尔派的思想痕迹。

王尔德性喜招摇，好奇装异服，以玩世不恭自炫，频繁出入公共场合，每有乖张之举。他言谈诙谐，妙语连珠，嘲讽维多利亚时代的森严礼法、中产阶级的行为规范，宣扬唯美主义的信条，成为英国唯美主义运动的领袖。诗集出版之后，他应邀到美国巡回演出。海关人员询问报关物品，他大喇喇地回应，"除了天才，我没有什么可申报的。"恃才傲物，可见一斑。1884 年，他娶了爱尔兰一位著名律师的女儿，婚后育有二子。而在此之前，他已有断袖的经历。1888 年，他出版了著名童话集《快乐王子》（*The Happy Prince and Other Tales*），这是专为儿子写的。1891 年，他出版了自己唯一的一部长篇小说《道林·格雷的画像》（*The Picture of Dorian Gray*）。这部小说此前曾在报纸上连载，为了这次出版，他扩充了小说的内容。这部哥特式小说宣扬艺术高于生活这个主题。在序言中，王尔德以格言的形式总结了他对艺术的总体看法：艺术家是各种美的东西的创造者，他的任务不是模仿世象万态，也不是作道德训诫；他只需要专注形式和风格；艺术不应有实用目的，艺术家不应有道德倾向；如果有，那将是一种不可原谅的矫饰；文学作品没有什么道德与不道德之分，只有高下之分。这些大胆直白、蔑视社会礼法的言论引起了轩然大波；而这正是王尔德所要达到的目的。

王尔德才华横溢，涉笔成趣，在每一个创作领域都有不凡的成就。他的几部讽刺剧最为脍炙人口：《温德米尔夫人的扇子》（*Lady Windermere's Fan*, 1892）、《一个无足轻重的女人》（*A Woman of No Importance*, 1893）、《理想丈夫》（*An Ideal Husband*, 1895）以及《不可儿戏》（*The Importance of Being Earnest*, 1895）。这些讽刺性喜剧结构巧妙，悬念迭出，对话幽默，妙语连珠——"我什么都能抵挡得住，就是抵挡不住诱惑"；"公众极能容忍，除了天才，他们什么都能原谅"。这都是对虚伪的社会道德的尖锐讽刺。

1895年，在声誉登峰之际，王尔德突遭厄运。他被一纸诉状告上法庭，起诉者是他的同性恋伙伴、美男子阿尔弗雷德勋爵的父亲。法庭对质过程中，阿尔弗雷德勋爵念及父子之情，不肯替他开脱。王尔德被判罚苦役二年，罪名是有伤风化。在雷丁监狱服刑期间，王尔德备尝苦楚，一时悲愤中来，无法自已，写了一封长信给阿尔弗雷德勋爵。这就是他的那部著名的忏悔录《自深深处》（*De Profundis*, 1895）。

1897年出狱后，他离婚破产，身败名裂，无处容身。他只好自我流放，去了法国，别无所长，仍以卖文为生。1898年出版的《雷丁监狱之歌》（*The Ballad of Reading Gaol*）描写了他在监中的痛苦经历。1900年，他在巴黎的一家小客店去世，死前还念念有词："如果我活到20世纪，那英国人可就真受不了。"落难如此，还要语出惊人，真可谓将唯美主义进行到底了。

王尔德的批评文章主要收录在1891年出版的《臆度集》（*Intentions*）中，其中《谎言的衰落》（"*The Decay of Lying*"）和《作为艺术家的批评家》（"*The Critic as Artist*"）已经成为批评史上的名篇。

内容提要

19 世纪的文学大家，多能左手创作，右手批评；此辈人士多以创作为文学正道，以批评为创作之余的副业，更以批评家为寄生人物。那时候，虽有马修·阿诺德倡言文学批评的重要性，但还不足以转变世风，况且，阿诺德本人也承认，批评能力还是低于创造能力的。王尔德却一反流俗之见，认为批评能力也是创造能力，足与后者相颉颃。在这篇对话体的长文中，作者通过恩斯特和吉尔伯特这两位虚构人物的交谈辩论，阐述了自己对艺术与批评关系的见解。吉尔伯特是王尔德的代言人，恩斯特是论辩对手，批评的靶子。

文章伊始，恩斯特提出当时常见的看法：创造力高于批评能力，二者无法相提并论。吉尔伯特则反驳说：这种对立过于武断，因为，倘若没有批评能力，货真价实的艺术创作便无从谈起；艺术家向读者表现生活时，必然对笔下的材料有取舍，这种巧妙的选择便是批评能力的典型体现；没有这种批评能力，艺术创造就无从实现。他还以阿诺德的文学定义——文学是人生的批评——为例，申说批评因素在文学创作中的重要性。

不唯如此，批评本身也是一门创造性艺术。它巧妙处理了原材料，使之新颖怡人，而诗歌创作过程也不过如此。批评还是"创造之中的创造"。从古希腊的荷马与埃斯库罗斯，直到莎士比亚和济慈，这一干伟大的创造型艺术家，在创作时，并非直接取材于生活，而是间接地取材于神话、传说和古代故事。批评家何尝不是如此，他所处理的材料，别人（作家）已经替他提炼过，已经赋予这些东西以想象的形式和色彩。最高境界的批评无需参照外在的标准，不受亚里士多德的模仿论的局限，描述沉闷乏味的生活中可能发生的事情；它只描述批评家个人的印象，品藻作品的精神气韵，记述自身的思想状况。它之所以比历史更吸引人，是因为它不枝不蔓，只关心自家事物；它之所以比哲学更令人心怡，是因为它的主题具体而不抽象，实实在在，绝不含糊其辞。

对于同时代的批评大家马修·阿诺德的见解，王尔德颇有非议。阿诺德在他的批评名篇《批评在目前的作用》中提出，文学批评的目的是观察事物的本来面目。王尔德认为，这种客观化追求没有认识到，最上乘的批评本质上是主观的；它不把艺术当做作者意图的表现，而是当做批评家纯粹的个人印象。接下来，他援引沃尔特·佩特对达芬奇名作《蒙娜丽莎》的诠释，借以说明，真正的批评不局限于追溯作者的真实意图，并以其为定论。他给出的理由是，作品完成后，就有了自己的生命，它在读者（或观众）那里生发出的意义，可能与作者原有的打算大不相同。在这里，王尔德预示了 20 世纪读者反映理论的观点。用他的话说，美好的形式有一个特点，那就是，人们可以按照自己的意愿去打造它，从中看出自己想要看的东西。

Oscar Wilde (1854—1900)

From The Critic as Artist

From *Part* 1

Ernest. · · · I am quite ready to admit that I was wrong in what I said about the Greeks. They were, as you have pointed out, a nation of art critics. I acknowledge it, and I feel a little sorry for them. For the creative faculty is higher than the critical. There is really no comparison between them.

Gilbert. The antithesis between them is entirely arbitrary. Without the critical faculty, there is no artistic creation at all worthy of the name.[1] You spoke a little while ago of that fine spirit of choice and delicate instinct of selection by which the artist realizes life for us, and gives to it a momentary perfection. Well, that spirit of choice, that subtle tact of omission, is really the critical faculty in one of its most characteristic moods[2], and no one who does not possess this critical faculty can create anything at all in art. Arnold's definition of literature as a criticism of life,[3] was not very felicitous in form, but it showed how keenly he recognized the importance of the critical element in all creative work.

Ernest. I should have said that great artists worked unconsciously, that they were "wiser than they knew,"[4] as, I think, Emerson remarks somewhere.

Gilbert. It is really not so, Ernest. All fine imaginative work is self-conscious and deliberate. No poet sings because he must sing. At least, no great poet does. A great poet sings because he chooses to sing. It is so now, and it has always been so. We are sometimes apt to think that the voices that sounded at the dawn of poetry were simpler, fresher, and more natural than ours, and that the world which the early poets looked at, and through which they walked, had a kind of poetical quality of its own, and almost without changing could pass into song. The snow lies thick now upon Olympus, and its steep, scarped sides are bleak and barren, but once, we fancy, the white feet of the Muses brushed the dew from the anemones in the morning, and at evening came Apollo to sing to the shepherds in the vale. But in this we are merely lending to other ages what we desire, or think we desire, for our own.⁵ Our historical sense is at fault.⁶ Every century that produced poetry is, so far, an artificial century, and the work that seems to us to be the most natural and simple product of its time is always the result of the most self-conscious effort. Believe me, Ernest, there is no fine art without self-consciousness, and self-consciousness and the critical spirit are one.⁷

Ernest. I see what you mean, and there is much in it. But surely you would admit that the great poems of the early world, the primitive, anonymous collective poems, were the result of the imagination of races, rather than of the imagination of individuals?

Gilbert. Not when they became poetry. Not when they received a beautiful form.⁸ For there is no art where there is no style, and no style where there is no unity, and unity is of the individual. No doubt Homer had old ballads and stories to deal with, as Shakespeare had chronicles and plays and novels from which to work, but they were merely his rough material. He took them and shaped them into song. The longer one studies life and literature, the more strongly one feels that behind everything that is wonderful stands the individual, and that it is not the moment that makes the man, but the man who creates the age.⁹ Indeed, I am inclined to think that each myth and legend that seems to us to spring out of the wonder, or terror, or fancy of tribe and nation, was in its origin the invention of one single mind. The curiously limited number of the myths seems to point to this conclusion. But we must not go off into questions of comparative mythology.¹⁰ We must keep to criticism. And what I want to point out is this. An age that has no criticism is either an age in which art is immobile, hieratic, and confined to the reproduction of formal types, or an age that possesses no art at all. There have been critical ages that have not been creative, in the ordinary sense of the word, ages in which the spirit of man has sought to set in order¹¹ the treasures of his treasure-house, to separate the gold from the silver, and the silver from the lead, to count over the jewels, and to give names to the pearls. But there has never been a creative age that has not been critical also. For it is the critical faculty that invents fresh forms. The tendency of creation is to repeat itself. It is to the critical instinct that we owe each new school that springs up, each new mould that art finds ready to its hand.¹² There is really not a single form that art now uses that does not come to us from the critical spirit of Alexandria[13], where these forms were either stereotyped, or invented, or made perfect. I say Alexandria, not merely because it was there that the Greek spirit became most self-conscious, indeed ultimately expired in skepticism and theology, but because it was to that city, and not to Athens, that Rome turned for her models, and it was through the survival, such as it was, of the Latin language that culture lived at all. When, at the Renaissance, Greek literature dawned upon Europe, the soil had been in some measure prepared for it. But to get rid of the details of history, which are always wearisome, and usually inaccurate, let us say generally that the forms of art have been due to the Greek critical spirit. To it we owe the epic, the lyric, the entire drama in every one of its developments, including burlesque, the idyll, the romantic novel, the novel of adventure, the essay, the dialogue, the oration, the lecture, for which perhaps we should not forgive them, and the epigram, in all the wide meaning of that word. In fact, we owe it everything, except the sonnet, to which, however, some curious parallels of thought movement may be traced in the Anthology[14], American journalism, to which no parallel can be found anywhere, and the ballad in sham Scotch dialect, which one of our most industrious writers[15] has recently proposed should be made the basis for a final and unanimous effort on the part of our second-rate poets to make themselves really romantic. Each new school, as it appears, cries out against criticism, but it is to the critical faculty in man that it owes its origin. The mere creative instinct does not innovate, but reproduces.

Ernest. You have been talking of criticism as an essential part of the creative spirit, and I now fully accept your theory. But what of criticism outside creation? I have a foolish habit of reading periodicals, and it seems to me that most modern criticism is perfectly valueless.

Gilbert. So is most modern creative work, also.[16] Mediocrity weighing mediocrity in the balance,[17] and incompetence applauding its brother—that is the spectacle which the artistic activity of England affords us from time to time. And yet, I feel I am a little unfair in this matter. As a rule, the critics—I speak, of course, of the higher class, of those, in fact, who write for the sixpenny papers—are far more cultured than the people whose work they are called upon to review.[18] This is, indeed, only what one would expect, for criticism demands infinitely more cultivation than creation does.

Ernest. Really?

Gilbert. Certainly. Anybody can write a three-volumed novel.[19] It merely requires a complete ignorance of both life and literature. The difficulty that I should fancy the reviewer feels is the difficulty of sustaining any standard. Where there is no style a standard must be impossible. The poor reviewers are apparently reduced to be the reporters of the police court of literature, the chronicles of the doings of the habitual criminals of art. It is sometimes said of them that they do not read all through the works they are called upon to criticize. They do not. Or at least they should not. If they did so, they would become confirmed misanthropes[20]; or, if I may borrow a phrase from one of the pretty Newnham[21] graduates, confirmed womanthropes[22] for the rest of their lives. Nor is it necessary. To know the vintage and quality of a wine one need not drink the whole cask.[23] It must be perfectly easy in half an hour to say whether a book is worth anything or worth nothing. Ten minutes are really sufficient, if one has the instinct for form.[24] Who wants to wade through a dull volume?[25] One tastes it, and that is quite enough—more than enough, I should imagine. I am aware that there are many honest workers in painting as well as in literature who object to criticism entirely. They are quite right. Their work stands in no intellectual relation to their age. It brings us no new element of pleasure. It suggests no fresh departure of thought, or passion, or beauty. It should not be spoken of. It should be left to the oblivion that it deserves.[26]

Ernest. But, my dear fellow—excuse me for interrupting you—you seem to me to be allowing your passion for criticism to lead you a great deal too far. For, after all, even you must admit that it is much more difficult to do a thing than to talk about it.

Gilbert. More difficult to do a thing than to talk about it? Not at all. That is a gross popular error. It is very much more difficult to talk about a thing than to do it. In the sphere of actual life that is, of course, obvious. Anybody can make history. Only a great man can write it. There is no mode of action, no form of emotion, that we do not share with the lower animals. It is only by language that we rise above them, or above each other—by language, which is the parent, and not the child, of thought. Action, indeed, is always easy, and when presented to us in its most aggravated, because most continuous form, which I take to be that of real industry, becomes simply the refuge of people who have nothing whatsoever to do. No, Ernest, don't talk about action. It is a blind thing, dependent on external influences, and moved by an impulse of whose nature it is unconscious. It is a thing incomplete in its essence, because limited by accident, and ignorant of its direction, being always at variance with its aim. Its basis is the lack of imagination. It is the last resource of those who know not how to dream.

Ernest. Gilbert, you treat the world as if it were a crystal ball. You hold it in your hand, and reverse it to please a willful fancy.[27] You do nothing but rewrite history.

Gilbert. The one duty we owe to history is to rewrite it. That is not the last of the tasks in store for the critical spirit. When we have fully discovered the scientific laws that govern life we shall realize that one person who has more illusions than the dreamer is the man of action. He, indeed, knows neither the origin of his deeds nor their results. From the field in which he thought that he had sown thorns we have gathered our vintage, and the fig-tree that he planted for our pleasure is as barren as the thistle, and more bitter.[28] It is because Humanity has never known where it was going that it has been able to find its way.

Ernest. You think, then, that in the sphere of action a conscious aim is a delusion?

Gilbert. It is worse than a delusion. If we lived long enough to see the results of our actions, it may be that those who call themselves good would be sickened with a dull remorse, and those whom the world calls evil stirred by a noble joy. Each little thing that we do passes into the great machine of life, which may grind our virtues to powder and make them worthless, or transform our sins into elements of a new civilization, more marvelous and more splendid than any that has gone before. · · ·

Ernest. · · · But, surely, the higher you place the creative artist, the lower must the critic rank.

Gilbert. Why so?

Ernest. Because the best that he can give us will be but an echo of rich music, a dim shadow of clear-outlined form. It may, indeed, be that life is chaos, as you tell me that it is; that its martyrdoms are mean and its heroisms ignoble; and that it is the function of Literature to create, from the rough material of actual existence, a new world that will be more marvelous, more enduring, and more true than the world that common eyes look upon, and through which common natures seek to realize their perfection. But surely, if this new world has been made by the spirit and touch of a great artist, it will be a thing so complete and perfect that there will be nothing left for the critic to do. I quite understand now, and indeed admit most readily, that it is far more difficult to talk about a thing than to do it. But it seems to me that this sound and sensible maxim, which is really extremely soothing to one's feelings, and should be adopted as its motto by every Academy of Literature all over the world, applies only to the relations that exist between Art and Life, and not to any relations that there may be between Art and Criticism.

Gilbert. But, surely, Criticism is itself an art. And just as an artistic creation implies the working of the critical faculty,[29] and, indeed, without it cannot be said to exist at all, so Criticism is really creative in the highest sense of the word.[30] Criticism is, in fact, both creative and independent.

Ernest. Independent?

Gilbert. Yes; independent. Criticism is no more to be judged by any low standard of imitation or resemblance than is the work of poet or sculptor. The critic occupies the same relation to the work of art that he criticizes as the artist does to the visible world of form and color, or the unseen world of passion and of thought. He does not even require for the perfection of his art the finest materials. Anything will serve his purpose. And just as out of the sordid and sentimental amours of the silly wife of a small country doctor in the squalid village of Yonville-L'Abbaye, near Rouen, Gustave Flaubert was able to create a classic, and make a masterpiece of style, so from subjects of little or of no importance, such as the pictures in this year's Royal Academy, or in any year's Royal Academy, for that matter, Mr. Lewis Morris's poems, M. Ohnet's novels, or the plays of Mr. Henry Arthur Jones, the true critic can, if it be his pleasure so to direct or waste his faculty of contemplation, produce work that will be flawless in beauty and instinct with intellectual subtlety.[31] Why not? Dullness is always an irresistible temptation for brilliancy, and stupidity is the permanent *Bestia Trionfans*[32] that calls wisdom from its cave. To an artist so creative as the critic, what does subject-matter signify? No more and no less than it does to the novelist and the painter. Like them, he can find his motives everywhere. Treatment is the test. There is nothing that has not in it suggestion or challenge.

Ernest. But is Criticism really a creative art?

Gilbert. Why should it not be? It works with materials, and puts them into a form that is at once new and delightful. What more can one say of poetry? Indeed, I would call criticism a creation within a creation. For just as the great artists, from Homer and AEschylus, down to Shakespeare and Keats, did not go directly to life for their subject-matter, but sought for it in myth, and legend, and ancient tale, so the critic deals with materials that others have, as it were, purified for him, and to which imaginative form and color have been already added. Nay, more, I would say that the highest Criticism, being the purest form of personal impression, is, in its way, more creative than creation, as it has least reference to any standard external to itself, and is, in fact, its own reason for existing, and, as the Greeks would put it, in itself, and to itself, an end. Certainly, it is never trammeled by any shackles of verisimilitude. No ignoble considerations of probability, that cowardly concession to the tedious repetitions of domestic or public life, affect it ever. One may appeal from fiction unto fact. But from the soul there is no appeal.[33]

Ernest. From the soul?

Gilbert. Yes, from the soul. That is what the highest Criticism really is, the record of one's own soul. It is more fascinating than history, as it is concerned simply with oneself. It is more delightful than philosophy, as its subject is concrete and not abstract, real and not vague. It is the only civilized form of autobiography, as it deals not with the events, but with the thoughts of one's life; not with life's physical accidents of deed or circumstance, but with the spiritual moods and imaginative passions of the mind. I am always amused by the silly vanity of those writers and artists of our day who seem to imagine that the primary function of the critic is to chatter about their second-rate work. The best that one can say of most modern creative art is that it is just a little less vulgar than reality, and so the critic, with his fine sense of distinction and sure instinct of delicate refinement, will prefer to look into the silver mirror or through the woven veil, and will turn his eyes away from the chaos and clamor of actual existence, though the mirror be tarnished and the veil be torn. His sole aim is to chronicle his own impressions. It is for him that pictures are painted, books written, and marble hewn into form.

Ernest. I seem to have heard another theory of Criticism.

Gilbert. Yes: it has been said that the proper aim of Criticism is to see the object as in itself it really is.[34] But that is a very serious error, and takes no cognizance of Criticism's most perfect form, which is in its essence purely subjective, and seeks to reveal its own secret and not the secret of another. For the highest Criticism deals with art not as expressive, but as impressive, purely.

Ernest. But is that really so?

Gilbert. Of course it is. Who cares whether Mr. Ruskin's views on Turner[35] are sound or not? What does it matter? That mighty and majestic prose of his, so fervid and so fiery-colored in its noble eloquence, so rich in its elaborate, symphonic music, so sure and certain, as its best, in subtle choice of word and epithet, is at least as great a work of art as any of those wonderful sunsets that bleach or rot on their corrupted canvases in England's Gallery; greater, indeed, one is apt to think at times, not merely because its equal beauty is more enduring, but on account of the fuller variety of its appeal, soul speaking to soul in those long-cadenced lines, not through form and color alone, though through these, indeed, completely and without loss, but with intellectual and motional utterance, with lofty passion and with loftier thought, with imaginative insight, and with poetic aim; greater, I always think, even as Literature is the greatest art. Who, again, cares whether Mr. Pater has put into the portrait of Monna Lisa something that Lionardo never dreamed of? The painter may have been merely the slave of an archaic smile, as some have fancied, but whenever I pass into the cool galleries of the Palace of the Louvre, and stand before that strange figure "set in its marble chair in that cirque of fantastic rocks, as in some faint light under sea," I murmur to myself, "She is older than the rocks among which she sits; like the vampire, she has been dead many times, and learned the secrets of the grave; and has been a diver in deep seas, and keeps their fallen day about her; and trafficked for strange webs with Eastern merchants; and, as Leda, was the mother of Helen of Troy, and, as St. Anne, the mother of Mary; and all this has been to her but as the sound of lyres and flutes, and lives only in the delicacy with which it has moulded the changing lineaments, and tinged the eyelids and the hands." And I say to my friend, "The presence that thus so strangely rose beside the waters is expressive of what in the ways of a thousand years man had come to desire"; and he answers me, "Here is the head upon which all 'the ends of the world are come,' and the eyelids are a little weary." [36]

And so the picture becomes more wonderful to us than it really is, and reveals to us a secret of which, in turn, it knows nothing, and the music of the mystical prose is as sweet in our ears as was that flute-player's music that lent to the lips of La Gioconda those subtle and poisonous curves. Do you ask me what Lionardo would have said had any one told him of this picture that "all the thoughts and experience of the world had etched and moulded there in that which they had of power to refine and make expressive the outward form, the animalism of Greece, the lust of Rome, the reverie of the Middle Age with its spiritual ambition and imaginative loves, the return of the Pagan world, the sins of the Borgias [37]?" He would probably have answered that he had contemplated none of these things, but had concerned himself simply with certain arrangements of lines and masses, and with new and curious color-harmonies of blue and green. And it is for this very reason that the criticism which I have quoted is criticism of the highest kind. It treats the work of art simply as a starting-point for a new creation. It does not confine itself—let us at least suppose so for the moment—to discovering the real intention of the artist and accepting that as final. And in this it is right, for the meaning of any beautiful created thing is, at least, as much in the soul of him who looks at it as it was in his soul who wrought it. [38] Nay, it is rather the beholder who lends to the beautiful thing its myriad meanings, and makes it marvelous for us, and sets it in some new relation to the age, so that it becomes a vital portion of our lives, and a symbol of what we pray for or perhaps of what, having prayed for, we fear that we may receive. The longer I study, Ernest, the more clearly I see that the beauty of the visible arts is, as the beauty of music, impressive primarily, [39] and that it may be marred, and indeed often is so, by any excess of intellectual intention on the part of the artists. For when the work is finished it has, as it were, an independent life of its own, and may deliver a message far other than that which was put into its lips to say. Sometimes, when I listen to the overture to *Tannhäuser*[40], I seem indeed to see that comely knight treading delicately on the flower-strewn grass, and to hear the voice of Venus calling to him from the caverned hill. But at other times it speaks to me of a thousand different things, of myself, it may be, and my own life, or of the lives of others whom one has loved and grown weary of loving, or of the passions that man has known, or of the passions that man has not known, and so has sought for. To-night it may fill one with that *ΕΡΩΣ ΤΩΝ ΑΔΥΝΑΤΩΝ*, that Amour de l'Impossible,[41] which falls like a madness on many who think they live securely and out of reach of harm, so that they sicken suddenly with the poison of unlimited desire, and, in the infinite pursuit of what they may not obtain, grow faint and swoon or stumble. To-morrow, like the music of which Aristotle and Plato tell us, the noble Dorian music[42] of the Greek, it may perform the office of a physician, and give us an anodyne against pain, and heal the spirit that is wounded, and "bring the soul into harmony with all right things." And what is true about music is true about all the arts. Beauty has as many meanings as man has moods. Beauty is the symbol of symbols. Beauty reveals everything, because it expresses nothing. When it shows us itself it shows us the whole fiery-colored world.

Ernest. But is such work as you have talked about really criticism?

Gilbert. It is the highest Criticism, for it criticizes not merely the individual work of art, but beauty itself, and fills with wonder a form which the artist may have left void, or not understood, or understood incompletely.

Ernest. The highest Criticism, then, is more creative than creation, and the primary aim of the critic is to see the object as in itself it really is not;[43] that is your theory, I believe?

Gilbert. Yes, that is my theory. To the critic the work of art is simply a suggestion for a new work of his own,[44] that need not necessarily bear any obvious resemblance to the thing it criticizes. The one characteristic of a beautiful form is that one can put into it whatever one wishes, and see in it whatever one chooses to see; and the Beauty, that gives to creation its universal and aesthetic element, makes the critic a creator in his turn, and whispers of a thousand different things which were not present in the mind of him who carved the statue or painted the panel or graved the gem.

It is sometimes said by those who understand neither the nature of the highest Criticism nor the charm of the highest Art, that the pictures that the critic loves most to write about are those that belong to the anecdotage[45] of painting, and that deal with scenes taken out of literature or history. But this is not so. Indeed, pictures of this kind are far too intelligible[46]. As a class, they rank with illustrations, and, even considered from this point of view, are failures, as they do not stir the imagination, but set definite bounds to it[47]. For the domain of the painter is, as I suggested before, widely different from that of the poet. To the latter belongs life in its full and absolute entirety;[48] not merely the beauty that men look at, but the beauty that men listen to also; not merely the momentary grace of form or the transient gladness of color, but the whole sphere of feeling, the perfect cycle of thought. The painter is so far limited that it is only through the mask of the body that he can handle ideas; only through its physical equivalents that he can deal with psychology. And how inadequately does he do it then, asking us to accept the torn turban of the Moor for the noble rage of Othello, or a dotard in a storm for the wild madness of Lear! [49] Yet it seems as if nothing could stop him. Most of our elderly English painters spend their wicked and wasted lives in poaching upon the domain of the poets, marring their motives by clumsy treatment, and striving to render, by visible form or color, the marvel of what is invisible, the splendor of what is not seen. Their pictures are, as a natural consequence, insufferably tedious. They have degraded the visible arts into the obvious arts[50], and the one thing not worth looking at is the obvious. I do not say that poet and painter may not treat of the same subject. They have always done so, and will always do so. But while the poet can be pictorial or not, as he chooses, the painter must be pictorial always. For a painter is limited, not to what he sees in nature, but to what upon canvas may be seen.[51]

And so, my dear Ernest, pictures of this kind will not really fascinate the critic. He will turn from them to such works as make him brood and dream and fancy, to works that possess the subtle quality of suggestions[52], and seem to tell one that even from them there is an escape into a wilder world. It is sometimes said that the tragedy of an artist's life is that he cannot realize his ideal. But the true tragedy that dogs the steps of most artists is that they realize their ideal too absolutely.[53] For, when the ideal is realized, it is robbed of its wonder and its mystery, and becomes simply a new starting point for an ideal that is other than itself. This is the reason why music is the perfect type of art. Music can never reveal its ultimate secret. This, also, is the explanation of the value of limitations in art. The sculptor gladly surrenders imitative color, and the painter the actual dimensions of form, because by such renunciations they are able to avoid too definite a presentation of the Real, which would be mere imitation, and too definite a presentation of the Ideal, which would be too purely intellectual[54]. It is through its very incompleteness that Art becomes complete in beauty,[55] and so addresses itself, not to the faculty of recognition nor to the faculty of reason, but to the aesthetic sense alone, which, while accepting both reason and recognition as stages of apprehension, subordinates them both to a pure synthetic impression of the work of art as a whole, and, taking whatever alien emotional elements the work may possess, uses their very complexity as a means by which a richer unity may be added to the ultimate impression itself. You see, then, how it is that the aesthetic critic rejects those obvious modes of art that have but one message to deliver, and having delivered it becomes dumb and sterile, and seeks rather for such modes as suggest reverie and mood, and by their imaginative beauty make all interpretations true and no interpretation final. Some resemblance, no doubt, the creative work of the critic will have to work that has stirred him to creation, but it will be such resemblance as exists, not between Nature and the mirror that the painter of landscape or figure may be supposed to hold up to her, but between Nature and the work of the decorative artist: Just as on the flowerless carpets of Persia, tulip and rose blossom indeed, and are lovely to look on, though they are not reproduced in visible shape or line; just as the pearl and purple of the sea-shell is echoed in the church of St. Mark at Venice[56]; just as the vaulted ceiling of the wondrous chapel of Ravenna[57] is made gorgeous by the gold and green and sapphire of the peacock's tail, though the birds of Juno[58] fly not across it; so the critic reproduces the work that he criticizes in a mode that is never imitative, and part of whose charm may really consist in the rejection of resemblance, and show us in this way not merely the meaning but also the mystery of Beauty, and, by transforming each art into literature, solves once for all the problem of Art's unity.

· · ·

注释

1. 大意为：没有批评能力，就没有真正的艺术创造。

2. the critical faculty in one of its most characteristic moods：最为典型的批评才能。

3. 这是马修·阿诺德著名的文学定义，参见本书选文《批评在目前的作用》。

4. they were "wiser than they knew"：他们的聪明程度超出了他们的自我评价。

5. 大意为：但是，在上述看法当中，我们只是把自己在当下的期待强加给了远古时代。

6. 大意为：我们的这种历史意识是有问题的。

7. 这段话的核心观念是：一切伟大的艺术都是艺术家自觉努力的结果。即便那些在我们看来像是某个时代最自然、最质朴的作品，其实也是经过艺术家自觉努力的结果。

8. 这两句话的潜台词是：那些原始的、作者佚名的、集体创作的诗歌，必须经过艺术家个人想象力的提炼，赋予它优美的形式，才能成为真正的诗。

9. 大意为：不是时代创造了人，而是人创造了时代。

10. 大意为：我们千万不要扯到比较神话学那里去。

11. set in order：清理。

12. each new mould that art finds ready to its hand：艺术随时可用的新模式。

13. 创建于公元前 331 年的亚历山大城，是当时希腊世界著名的商业和文化中心。这里所说的"亚历山大批评精神"指古希腊、罗马"亚历山大学派"在文学、科学和哲学中强调的批判精神。

14. 这里提到的 *Anthology*，指的是成书于 10 世纪的希腊箴言集，其中收录的作品至少可以追溯到公元前 7 世纪。

15. one of our most industrious writers：指苏格兰作家夏普（William Sharp, 1855—1905）。

16. 大意为：绝大部分现代创作都是毫无价值的。

17. 大意为：平庸的创作与平庸的评论，半斤八两，旗鼓相当。

18. 这句话语带讥讽。大意为：一般说来，批评家——当然我指的是那种比较高明一点的，也就是替廉价报纸撰稿的批评家——总要比那些四处找人替自己写评论的作家更有学养。

19. 维多利亚时代的长篇小说多为三卷本。

20. confirmed misanthrope：坚定不移的厌世者。

21. Newnham：Newnham College，剑桥大学的女子学院，创建于1871年。

22. Womanthropes：这是作者对上面提到的 misanthropes 一词的戏仿，意为"厌女症"。

23. 大意为：如果想知道某种葡萄酒的生产年份和品质，用不着把整桶酒都喝下去。

24. 这两句话的大意为：判断一本书是否有价值，读半个小时就足矣。如果读者对形式很有直觉，读上十分钟就够了。

25. 大意为：谁愿意费那么大的劲儿去啃完一本枯燥乏味的东西呢？

26. 这几句话的大意为：在美术界和文学界，有许多诚实不欺的作者反对评论。他们是对的。他们的作品和他们所在的时代并无思想上的关联。他们的作品没有给人带来新的愉悦，没有给人带来思想上的启迪，也没有给人带来激情和美感。他们的作品不值一提，理应被遗忘。

27. 这两句话的意思是：你把世界当成了一个水晶球，拿在手里，颠来倒去，就是为了满足自己一厢情愿的幻想。

28. 这两句话的大意为：实际行动家对自己的行为既不了解前因，也不了解后果。他自以为在地里种下了荆棘，我们从那里收获到的却是葡萄酒；他们为取悦我们种下的无花果，却像蓟草一样不结果，而且味道更苦。

29. 大意为：艺术创作之中暗含批评的才能。

30. 大意为：批评是最高层次的创作。

31. 这两句话大意为：批评不受题材的限制，任何微末的素材都无碍于批评艺术的完美。正如福楼拜能以一位乡村医生妻子的婚外情创作出一部经典杰作，对于真正的批评家而言，皇家艺术学院的绘画、刘易斯·莫里斯的诗歌、乔治·奥内的小说、亨利·阿瑟·琼斯的戏剧，都可以成为他精思深辩的批评才能的用武之地，让他写出完美无缺、思想精深的批评之作。

32. Bestia Trionfans：意大利文，意为"趾高气扬的野兽"，语出意大利哲学家、天文学家布鲁诺（Giordano Bruno, 1548—1600）的哲学寓言《驱逐趾高气扬的野兽》（*Expulsion of the Triumphant Beast*）。

这句话的意思是：单调沉闷的生活总能刺激人卓越的才华，愚蠢的行径就像那"趾高气昂的野兽"，永远激发批评者的智慧。

33. 大意为：人们可能要求虚构类文学忠于事实，但不会这样去要求记录个人精神灵魂的批评。

34. 大意为：文学批评的目的是按照事物的本来面目去看待事物。
这是马修·阿诺德的名言，见本书选文《批评在目前的作用》。

35. Ruskin：罗斯金（John Ruskin, 1819—1900），英国著名散文家、艺术批评家。他对英国风景画家透纳（J. M. W. Turner, 1775—1851）的作品评价极高。

36. 作者的这段话意在论证：罗斯金的艺术评论甚至比国家美术馆收藏的艺术品更伟大，沃尔特·佩特对《蒙娜丽莎》的阐释，超出了达芬奇本人的想象。作者举这两个例子是为了说明，批评高于创作。

37. the Borgias：博尔吉亚家族，定居意大利的西班牙贵族，出过多位宗教、军事、政治领袖，以残忍、贪婪著称。

38. 大意为：任何优美的作品的意义，既存在于观众的灵魂之中，也存在于作者的灵魂之中，程度不相上下。

39. 大意为：视觉艺术之美，一如音乐之美，主要在于观众的印象之中。

40. Tannhäuser：《汤豪舍》，理查德·瓦格纳的歌剧，创作于1845年，讲述14世纪诗人汤豪舍与维纳斯之间的爱情故事。

41. 希腊文和法文，"不可能发生的爱情"。

42. Dorian Music：多利安音乐。多利安人在公元前11世纪侵入希腊。

43. 王尔德在此特意挑战马修·阿诺德。阿诺德说过，批评家的主要任务是依据事物的本来面目去看待事物（the primary aim of the critic is to see the object as in itself it really is），王尔德在后面加了一个否定词 not，反其意而用之。

44. 大意为：对批评家而言，原作只是一种启发，启发他写出自己的批评新作。

45. anecdotage：轶事集。

46. far too intelligible：过于浅显直白。

47. set definite bounds to it：限制了观众的想象。

48. 大意为：诗人笔下处理的生活更丰富、更完整。

49. 大意为：（画家）用摩尔人的破头巾来表现奥赛罗的愤怒，把暴风雨中的昏聩老汉当做李尔王的疯狂表现。

50. obvious arts：浅显（没有内涵）的艺术。

51. 大意为：画家不仅受限于他的眼界，也受限于画布的空间。

52. the subtle quality of suggestion：含义隽永。

53. 大意为：然而，对于大部分艺术家而言，真正的悲剧在于，他们过于绝对彻底地实现了自己的理想。

54. too purely intellectual：过于理智。

55. 大意为：正是因为艺术没有面面俱到，艺术才达到了完美的境界。

56. 威尼斯的圣·马可大教堂。

57. 意大利城市拉文纳的小礼拜堂。

58. the bird of Juno：孔雀。

《一间自己的屋》

弗吉尼亚·伍尔夫（1882—1941）

一战之前的英国社会，阶级壁垒森严，在学界也有明显反应。高级知识分子具有家族世袭特征，大师硕学往往出自所谓的知识贵族的家庭，伊顿、哈罗是其人生阅历的起点，牛津、剑桥是其名山事业的发端。翻看《大英百科全书》，即可发现，祖孙、父子、兄弟、舅甥、翁婿同时入选现象比比皆是，许多人都出自一些声名显赫的家族：达尔文、赫胥黎、阿诺德、斯蒂芬等等。其子弟幼承家学，涵濡教泽，允称博雅。这种文化世袭状态，正如 T. S. 艾略特在小册子《略论文化的定义》（*Notes towards the Definition of Cultur*e）中所言，可以保证传统文化一脉相承，金瓯不缺。

弗吉尼亚·伍尔夫就出生在这样的文化名门。她的父亲莱斯利·斯蒂温（Leslie Stephen）是维多利亚时代著名的文人，主编过赫赫有名的文学杂志《康希尔》（*Cornhill*），为多位英国作家写过传记。他的《18 世纪的英国思想史》（*History of the English Thought in the 18th Century*）为传世之作，他还主持过《国家名人传记大辞典》（*Dictionary of National Biograph*y）。由于自幼健康不佳，伍尔夫没有接受过正规的学校教育，丰富的家庭藏书为她自学提供了极大的便利。1904 年，在父亲去世之后，伍尔夫与志趣相投的姐姐和哥哥移居伦敦的布鲁姆斯伯里。他们同一群志同道合的朋友形成了文人圈子——"布鲁姆斯伯里集团"（Bloomsbury Group），往还人物多为文化界名流，如传记文学大家林顿·斯特拉奇（Lytton Strachey）、小说家 E. M. 福斯特（E. M. Forster）、亨利·詹姆斯（Henry James）、诗人 T. S. 艾略特、美学家罗杰·弗赖（Roger Fry）、经济学家凯恩斯（John Maynard Keynes），均为人杰俊彦。

从 1905 年起，伍尔夫就为《泰晤士报文学增刊》（*Times Literary Supplement*）写书评，直到 1941 年去世为止。1912 年，她与伍尔夫（Leonard Woolf）结婚。伦纳德早年写过多部长篇，后来转向社会问题研究和政论写作；他是费边社成员，社会改良主义者。伍尔夫幼年时代受过同母异父的两个哥哥的性骚扰，精神敏感失常。后来她一直受到这种隐疾的困扰；幸亏她婚后生活幸福，得到伦纳德无微不至的照顾。1917 年夫妻俩创办了霍加斯出版社。这家规模不大的出版社逐渐成为英国现代主义文学的出版重镇，出版过艾略特的《荒原》（*The Wasteland*）、福斯特和凯瑟琳·曼斯菲尔德（Katherine Mansfield）的长篇小说、伍尔夫的全部著作、弗洛伊德著作 24 卷本的英译。

伍尔夫以长篇小说名世，《达洛威夫人》（*Mrs. Dalloway*, 1925）、《到灯塔去》（*To the Lighthouse*, 1927）等早已成为英国现代主义文学经典。她惯用的意识流手法和内心独白为现代主义作家频频借鉴。她的小说注重刻画人物的心理，而疏于描写人物行动和社会环境；情感细腻丰富，但缺乏扣人心弦的情节；易得学识高深读者的青睐，而让普通读者望而却步。20 年代是她的创作高峰时期，她最有原创性的著作都是在这一时期完成。就在这一时期，她与作家维多利亚·萨克维尔－韦斯特（Victoria Sackville-West）发生同性恋关系。这段经历在小说《奥兰多》（*Orlando*）中有所反映。

1941 年，欧战正酣，德军空袭频仍，伍尔夫精神异常紧张。伦纳德是犹太人，对纳粹的排犹政策非常敏感。两人早有约定，一旦德军入侵，两人即自杀。在最后一部小说《幕与幕之间》（*Between the Acts*）出版不久，她精神病复发，在住所附近投河自尽。

伍尔夫也是造诣颇深的批评家，她的主要文学评论收录在《普通读者》（*The Common Reader*, 1925）一书中。1929 年面世的《一间自己的屋》是英国女性主义的开创性著作。

内容提要

《一间自己的屋》是伍尔夫根据她在剑桥大学的学术报告整理而成。作者在书中探讨了女性在社会、经济、政治和文化层面上遭受的歧视和压迫，追述了女性文学创作的传统。她认为，女性作家的天赋和才能不逊于男性，只是囿于世俗成见而无法充分发挥；女性创作成功必须有一定的物质经济条件：自己独处一室，免受生活琐事的干扰；只有这样，她才能以炽烈澄明的心境投入创作当中。

作者发现，回顾伊丽莎白时代的文学史，有一现象令人费解：在那个诗坛异常繁茂的时代，却未见女性躬逢其盛。翻开史学大家特里维廉的名著《英格兰史》(*History of England*)，不难找出答案：从 15 世纪末乔叟时代结束之后，直到 17 世纪斯图亚特王朝时代，妇女地位低下，婚姻不能自主，在家从父，出嫁从夫，这种现象无处不在。在莎士比亚等人笔下，个性鲜明的女性不时出现，可谓千姿百态；但这只是文学虚构，并不符合社会实情；女性在现实生活中的作用无足轻重。在文学作品中，她们可能倾倒了君王，支配了政局；还可能妙语连珠，思想深邃，发人深思。然而，在现实生活中，她们多半是文盲，是丈夫的财产。女性仅在文学中出现，在史乘中缺席；史书记载的女性，仅限于女王或贵妇；对于女性的生活，史家总是惜墨如金。如此说来，在伊丽莎白时代没有出现女诗人，也就不足为奇了，更不能指望她们写出与莎剧相媲美的文学作品了。

接下来，作者提出一个设想：即便莎士比亚有一个天赋惊人的妹妹，她也会受到家庭环境和社会习俗的制约，不可能像莎士比亚那样去文法学校念书，学习拉丁文，阅读古典作品，学会基本语言和逻辑；其次，她也不可能像莎士比亚那样闯荡社会，积累丰富的人生阅历；即便她桀骜不驯，逃出家庭的牢笼，跑到伦敦，追求演艺事业，也不可能像莎士比亚那样一帆风顺；无论她的天分有多高，她都很可能遭到剧院的拒绝，还可能被剧院经理诱奸，怀上他的孩子；最终，她会因为现实与理想的尖锐矛盾而精神崩溃，自杀了事。

即便到了 19 世纪，个别有天分的女性能够提笔写出杰作，也只能匿名发表——夏洛蒂·勃朗特 (Charlotte Brantë)、乔治·艾略特 (George Eliot)、乔治·桑 (George Sand) 等人的经历就是明证，这都是社会习俗使然；社会习俗认为，让女性引起公众的瞩目是一件讨厌的事情。

天才作品的产生需要静谧的写作环境，需要澄澈的心境。可是，即便在 19 世纪，让女性拥有一间自己的屋子安心写作，也是一件难事，除非家庭很富裕。但即便如此，她也很难享受到男性穷作家在其他方面的待遇，例如，出国旅行，增长见闻。如果说一些男性作家境遇不佳，经常面临世人的冷漠；女性作家的境遇就更惨了，她们面临的是世人的敌意。女性不仅在文学创作方面遇到重重障碍，她们在从政、从艺之时也面临着相同的困境：不断受到冷落、排斥和规劝。

Virginia Woolf (1882—1941)

THREE

It was disappointing not to have brought back in the evening some important statement, some authentic fact. Women are poorer than men because—this or that. Perhaps now it would be better to give up seeking for the truth, and receiving on one's head an avalanche of opinion hot as lava, discolored as dish-water[1]. It would be better to draw the curtains; to shut out distractions; to light the lamp; to narrow the enquiry and to ask the historian, who records not opinions but facts, to describe under what conditions women lived, not throughout the ages, but in England, say, in the time of Elizabeth.

For it is a perennial puzzle why no woman wrote a word of that extraordinary literature when every other man, it seemed, was capable of song or sonnet. What were the conditions in which women lived? I ask myself; for fiction, imaginative work that is, is not dropped like a pebble upon the ground, as science may be; fiction is like a spider's web, attached over so lightly perhaps, but still attached to life at all four corners. Often the attachment is scarcely perceptible; Shakespeare's plays, for instance, seem to hang there complete by themselves. But when the web is pulled askew, hooked up at the edge, torn in the middle, one remembers that these webs are not spun in mid-air by incorporeal creatures, but are the work of suffering human beings, and are attached to grossly material things, like health and money and the house we live in.[2]

I went, therefore, to the shelf where the histories stand and took down one of the latest, Professor Trevelyan's[3] HISTORY OF ENGLAND. Once more I looked up Women, found "position of" and turned to the pages indicated. "Wife-beating," I read, "was a recognized right of man, and was practiced without shame by high as well as low...Similarly," the historian goes on, "the daughter who refused to marry the gentleman of her parents' choice was liable to be locked up, beaten and flung about the room, without any shock being inflicted on public opinion. Marriage was not an affair of personal affection, but of family avarice, particularly in the 'chivalrous' upper classes...Betrothal often took place while one or both of the parties was in the cradle, and marriage when they were scarcely out of the nurses' charge." That was about 1470, soon after Chaucer's time. The next reference to the position of women is some two hundred years later, in the time of the Stuarts[4]. "It was still the exception for women of the upper and middle class to choose their own husbands, and when the husband had been assigned, he was lord and master, so far at least as law and custom could make him. Yet even so," Professor Trevelyan concludes, "neither Shakespeare's women nor those of authentic seventeenth-century memoirs, like the Verneys and the Hutchinsons, seem wanting in personality and character[5]." Certainly, if we consider it, Cleopatra must have had a way with her;[6] Lady Macbeth, one would suppose, had a will of her own; Rosalind, one might conclude, was an attractive girl.[7] Professor Trevelyan is speaking no more than the truth when he remarks that Shakespeare's women do not seem wanting in personality and character. Not being a historian, one might go even further and say that women have burnt like beacons in all the works of all the poets from the beginning of time—Clytemnestra, Antigone, Cleopatra, Lady Macbeth, Phedre, Cressida, Rosalind, Desdemona, the Duchess of Malfi, among the dramatists;[8] then among the prose writers: Millamant, Clarissa, Becky Sharp, Anna Karenina, Emma Bovary, Madame de Guermantes[9]—the names flock to mind, nor do they call women "lacking in personality and character." Indeed, if woman had no existence save in the fiction written by men, one would imagine her a person of the utmost importance; very various; heroic and mean; splendid and sordid; infinitely beautiful and hideous in the extreme; as great as a man, some think even greater. But this is woman in fiction. In fact, as Professor Trevelyan points out, she was locked up, beaten and flung about the room.

A very queer, composite being thus emerges.[10] Imaginatively she is of the highest importance; practically she is completely insignificant. She pervades poetry from cover to cover; she is all but absent from history. She dominates the lives of kings and conquerors in fiction; in fact she was the slave of any body whose parents forced a ring upon her finger. Some of the most inspired words, some of the most profound thoughts in literature fall from her lips; in real life she could hardly read, could scarcely spell, and was the property of her husband.

It was certainly an odd monster that one made up by reading the historians first and the poets afterwards—a worm winged like an eagle; the spirit of life and beauty in a kitchen chopping up suet.[11] But these monsters, however amusing to the imagination, have no existence in fact. What one must do to bring her to life was think poetically and prosaically at one and the same moment, thus keeping in touch with fact—that she is Mrs. Martin, aged thirty-six, dressed in blue, wearing a black hat and brown shoes; but not losing sight of fiction either—that she is a vessel in which all sorts of spirits and forces are coursing and flashing perpetually. The moment, however, that one tries this method with the Elizabethan woman, one branch of illumination fails; one is held up by the scarcity of facts. One knows nothing detailed, nothing perfectly true and substantial about her. History scarcely mentions her. And I turned to Professor Trevelyan again to see what history meant to him. I found by looking at his chapter headings that it meant—

"The Manor Court and the Methods of Open-field Agriculture...The Cistercians[12] and Sheep-farming...The Crusade...The University...The House of Commons...The Hundred Years' War...The Wars of the Roses... The Renaissance Scholars...The Dissolution of the Monasteries...Agrarian and Religious Strife...The Origin of English Sea-power...The Armada..."[13] and so on. Occasionally an individual woman is mentioned, an Elizabeth, or a Mary; a queen or a great lady. But by no possible means could middle-class women with nothing but brains and character at their command[14] have taken part in any one of the great movements which, brought together, constitute the historian's view of the past. Nor shall we find her in collection of anecdotes. Aubrey[15] hardly mentions her. She never writes her own life and scarcely keeps a diary; there are only a handful of her letters in existence. She left no plays or poems by which we can judge her. What one wants, I thought—and why does not some brilliant student at Newnham or Girton[16] supply it?—is a mass of information; at what age did she marry; how many children had she as a rule; what was her house like, had she a room to herself; did she do the cooking; would she be likely to have a servant? All these facts lie somewhere, presumably, in parish registers and account books; the life of the average Elizabethan woman must be scattered about somewhere, could one collect it and make a book of it. It would be ambitious beyond my daring, I thought, looking about the shelves for books that were not there, to suggest to the students of those famous colleges that they should rewrite history, though I own that it often seems a little queer as it is, unreal, lop-sided;[17] but why should they not add a supplement to history, calling it, of course, by some inconspicuous name so that women might figure there without impropriety? [18] For one often catches a glimpse of them in the lives of the great, whisking away into the back ground, concealing, I sometimes think, a wink, a laugh, perhaps a tear. And, after all, we have lives enough of Jane Austen; it scarcely seems necessary to consider again the influence of the tragedies of Joanna Baillie[19] upon the poetry of Edgar Allan Poe; as for myself, I should not mind if the homes and haunts of Mary Russell Mitford[20] were closed to the public for a century at least. But what I find deplorable, I continued, looking about the bookshelves again, is that nothing is known about women before the eighteenth century. I have no model in my mind to turn about this way and that. Here am I asking why women did not write poetry in the Elizabethan age, and I am not sure how they were educated; whether they were taught to write; whether they had sitting-rooms to themselves; how many women had children before they were twenty-one; what, in short, they did from eight in the morning till eight at night. They had no money evidently; according to Professor Trevelyan they were married whether they liked it or not before they were out of the nursery, at fifteen or sixteen very likely. It would have been extremely odd, even upon this showing, had one of them suddenly written the plays of Shakespeare, I concluded, [21] and I thought of that old gentleman, who is dead now, but was a bishop, I think, who declared that it was impossible for any woman, past, present, or to come, to have the genius of Shakespeare. He wrote to the papers about it. He also told a lady who applied to him for information that cats do not as a matter of fact go to heaven, though they have, he added, souls of a sort. How much thinking those old gentlemen used to save one![22] How the borders of ignorance shrank back at their approach! Cats do not go to heaven. Women cannot write the plays of Shakespeare.

Be that as it may, I could not help thinking, as I looked at the works of Shakespeare on the shelf, that the bishop was right at least in this; it would have been impossible, completely and entirely, for any woman to have written the plays of Shakespeare in the age of Shakespeare.[23] Let me imagine, since facts are so hard to come by, what would have happened had Shakespeare had a wonderfully gifted sister, called Judith, let us say. Shakespeare himself went, very probably—his mother was an heiress—to the grammar school, where he may have learnt Latin—Ovid, Virgil and Horace[24]—and the elements of grammar and logic. He was, it is well known, a wild boy who poached rabbits, perhaps shot a deer, and had, rather sooner than he should have done, to marry a woman in the neighborhood, who bore him a child rather quicker than was right. That escapade[25] sent him to seek his fortune in London. He had, it seemed, a taste for the theater; he began by holding horses at the stage door. Very soon he got work in the theater, became a successful actor, and lived at the hub of the universe, meeting everybody, knowing everybody, practicing his art on the boards, exercising his wits in the streets, and even getting access to the palace of the queen. Meanwhile his extraordinarily gifted sister, let us suppose, remained at home. She was as adventurous, as imaginative, as agog to see the world as he was. But she was not sent to school. She had no chance of learning grammar and logic, let alone of reading Horace and Virgil. She picked up a book now and then, one of her brother's perhaps, and read a few pages. But then her parents came in and told her to mend the stockings or mind the stew and not moon about with books and papers. They would have spoken sharply but kindly, for they were substantial people[26] who knew the conditions of life for a woman and loved their daughter—indeed, more likely than not she was the apple of her father's eye. Perhaps she scribbled some pages up in an apple loft on the sly[27] but was careful to hide them or set fire to them. Soon, however, before she was out of her tens, she was to be betrothed to the son of a neighboring wool-stapler. She cried out that marriage was hateful to her, and for that she was severely beaten by her father. Then he ceased to scold her. He begged her instead not to hurt him, not to shame him in this matter of her marriage. He would give her a chain of beads or a fine petticoat, he said; and there were tears in his eyes. How could she disobey him? How could she break his heart? The force of her own gift alone drove her to it. She made up a small parcel of her belongs, let herself down by a rope one summer's night and took the road to London. She was not seventeen. The birds that sang in the hedge were not more musical than she was. She had the quickest fancy, a gift like her brother's, for the tune of words. Like him, she had a taste for the theater. She stood at the stage door; she wanted to act, she said. Men laughed in her face. The manager—a fat, looselipped man—guffawed. He bellowed something about poodles dancing and women acting—no woman, he said, could possibly be an actress.[28] He hinted—you can imagine what. She could get no training in her craft. Could she even seek her dinner in a tavern or roam the streets at midnight? Yet her genius was for fiction and lusted to feed abundantly upon the lives of men and women and the study of their ways[29]. At last—for she was very young, oddly like Shakespeare the poet in her face, with the same grey eyes and rounded brows—at last Nick Greene[30] the actor-manager took pity on her; she found herself with child by that gentleman and so—who shall measure the heat and violence of the poet's heart when caught and tangled in a woman's body?[31]—killed herself one winter's night and lies buried at some cross-roads where the omnibuses now stop outside the Elephant and Castle[32].

That, more or less, is how the story would run, I think, if a woman in Shakespeare's day had had Shakespeare's genius. But for my part, I agree with the deceased bishop, if such he was—it is unthinkable that any woman in Shakespeare's day should have had Shakespeare's genius. For genius like Shakespeare's is not born among laboring, uneducated, servile people. It was not born in England among the Saxons and the Britons.[33] It is not born to-day among the working classes. How, then, could it have been born among women whose work began, according to Professor Trevelyan, almost before they were out of the nursery, who were forced to it by their parents and held to it by all the power of law and custom? Yet genius of a sort must have existed among women as it must have existed among the working classes. Now and again an Emily Brontë or a Robert Burns blazes out and proves its presence. But certainly it never got itself on to paper.[34] When, however, one reads of a witch being ducked, of a woman possessed by devils, of a wise woman selling herbs, or even of a very remarkable man who had a mother, then I think we are on the track of a lost novelist, a suppressed poet, of some mute and inglorious Jane Austen, some Emily Brontë who dashed her brains out on the moor or mopped and mowed about the highways crazed with the torture that her gift had put her to[35]. Indeed, I would venture to guess that Avon[36], who wrote so many poems without singing them, was often a woman. It was a woman Edward Fitzgerald[37], I think, suggested who made the ballads and the folk-songs, crooning them to her children, beguiling her spinning with them, or the length of the winter's night.

This may be true or it may be false—who can say?—but what is true in it, so it seemed to me, reviewing the story of Shakespeare's sister as I had made it, is that my woman born with a great gift in the sixteenth century would certainly have gone crazed, shot herself, or ended her days in some lonely cottage outside the village, half witch, half wizard, feared and mocked at. For it needs little skill in psychology to be sure that a highly gifted girl who had tried to use her gift for poetry would have been so thwarted and hindered by other people, so tortured and pulled asunder by her own contrary instincts, that she must have lost her health and sanity to a certainty. No girl could have walked to London and stood at a stage door and forced her way into the presence of actor-managers without doing herself a violence and suffering an anguish which may have been irrational—for chastity may be a fetish invented by certain societies for unknown reasons[38]—but were none the less inevitable. Chastity had then, it has even now, a religious importance in a woman's life, and has so wrapped itself round with nerves and instincts that to cut it free and bring it to the light of day demands courage of the rarest[39]. To have lived a free life in London in the sixteenth century would have meant for a woman who was a poet and playwright a nervous stress and dilemma which might well have killed her. Had she survived, whatever she had written would have been twisted and deformed, issuing from a strained and morbid imagination. And undoubtedly, I thought, looking at the shelf where there are no plays by women, her work would have gone unsigned. The refuge she would have sought certainly. It was the relic of the sense of chastity that directed anonymity to women even so late as the nineteenth century.[40] Currer Bell, George Eliot, Gorge Sand,[41] all the victims of inner strife as their writings prove, sought ineffectively to veil themselves by using the name of a man.

That woman, then, who was born with a gift of poetry in the sixteenth century, was an unhappy woman, a woman at strife against herself. All the conditions of her life, all her own instincts, were hostile to the state of mind which is needed to set free whatever is in the brain. But what is the state of mind that is most propitious to the act of creation? I asked. Can one come by any notion of the state that furthers and makes possible that strange activity? [42] Here I opened the volume containing the Tragedies of Shakespeare. What was Shakespeare's state of mind, for instance, when he wrote LEAR and ANTONY AND CLEOPATRA? It was certainly the state of mind most favorable to poetry that there has ever existed. But Shakespeare himself said nothing about it. We only know casually and by chance that he "never blotted a line." [43] Nothing indeed was ever said by the artist himself about his state of mind until the nineteenth century self-consciousness had developed so far that it was the habit for men of letters to describe their minds in confessions and autobiographies. Their lives also were written, and their letters were printed after their deaths. Thus, though we do not know what Shakespeare went through when he wrote LEAR, we do not know what Carlyle [44] went through when he wrote the FRENCH REVOLUTION; what Flaubert [45] went through when he wrote MADAME BOVARY; what Keats was going through when he tried to write poetry against the coming death and the indifference of the world.

And one gathers from this enormous modern literature of confession and self-analysis that to write a work of genius is almost always a feat of prodigious difficulty. [46] Everything is against the likelihood that it will come from the writer's mind whole and entire. Generally material circumstances are against it. Dogs will bark; people will interrupt; money must be made; health will break down. Further, accentuating all these difficulties and making them harder to bear is the world's notorious indifference. It does not ask people to write poems and novels and histories; it does not need them. It does not care whether Flaubert finds the right word or whether Carlyle scrupulously verifies this or that fact. Naturally, it will not pay for what it does not want. And so the writer, Keats, Flaubert, Carlyle, suffers, especially in the creative years of youth, every form of distraction and discouragement. A curse, a cry of agony, rises from those books of analysis and confession. "Mighty poets in their misery dead" [47]—that is the burden of their song. If anything comes through in spite of all this, it is a miracle, and probably no book is born entire and uncrippled as it was conceived.

But for women, I thought, looking at the empty shelves, these difficulties were infinitely more formidable. In the first place, to have a room of her own, let alone a quiet room or a sound-proof room, was out of the question, unless her parents were exceptionally rich or very noble, even up to the beginning of the nineteenth century. Since her pin money, which depended on the goodwill of her father, was only enough to keep her clothed, she was debarred from such alleviations as came even to Keats or Tennyson[48] or Carlyle, all poor men, from a walking tour, a little journey to France, from the separate lodging which, even if it were miserable enough, sheltered them from the claims and tyrannies of their families. Such material difficulties were formidable; but much worse were the immaterial. The indifference of the world which Keats and Flaubert and other men of genius have found so hard to bear was in her case not indifference but hostility. The world did not say to her as it said to them, Write if you choose;[49] it makes no difference to me. The world said with a guffaw, Write? What's the good of your writing? Here the psychologists of Newnham and Girton might come to our help, I thought, looking again at the blank spaces on the shelves. For surely it is time that the effect of discouragement upon the mind of the artist should be measured,[50] as I have seen a dairy company measure the effect of ordinary milk and Grade A milk upon the body of the rat. They set two rats in cages side by side, and of the two one was furtive, timid, and small, and the other was glossy, bold and big. Now what food do we feed women as artists upon? I asked, remembering, I suppose, that dinner of prunes and custard. To answer that question I had only to open the evening paper and to read that Lord Birkenhead is of opinion—but really I am not going to trouble to copy out Lord Birkenhead's opinion upon the writings of women. What Dean Inge[51] says I will leave in peace. The Harley Street specialist[52] may be allowed to rouse the echoes of Harley Street with his vociferations without raising a hair on my head. I will quote, however, Mr. Oscar Browning[53], because Mr. Oscar Browning was a great figure in Cambridge at one time, and used to examine the students at Girton and Newnham. Mr. Oscar Browning was wont to declare "that the impression left on his mind, after looking over any set of examination papers, was that, irrespective of the marks he might give,[54] the best woman was intellectually the inferior of the worst man". After saying that Mr. Browning went back to his rooms—and it is this sequel[55] that endears him and makes him a human figure of some bulk and majesty—he went back to his rooms and found a stable-boy lying on the sofa—a mere skeleton, his cheeks were cavernous and sallow, his teeth were black, and he did not appear to have the full use of his limbs. "That's Arthur" [said Mr. Browning]. "He's a dear boy really and most high-minded."—The two pictures always seem to me to complete each other. And happily in this age of biography the two pictures often do complete each other, so that we are able to interpret the opinions of great men not only by what they say, but by what they do.

But though this is possible now, such opinions coming from the lips of important people must have been formidable enough even fifty years ago. Let us suppose that a father from the highest motives did not wish his daughter to leave home and become writer, painter, or scholar. "See what Mr. Oscar Browning says," he would say; and there so was not only Mr. Oscar Browning; there was the SATURDAY REVIEW; there was Mr. Greg[56]—the "essentials of a woman's being," said Mr. Greg emphatically, "are that THEY ARE SUPPORTED BY, AND THEY MINISTER TO, MEN"—there was an enormous body of masculine opinion to the effect that nothing could be expected of women intellectually.[57] Even if her father did not read out loud these opinions, any girl could read them for herself; and the reading, even in the nineteenth century, must have lowered her vitality, and told profoundly upon her work. There would always have been that assertion— you cannot do this, you are incapable of doing that—to protect against, to overcome. Probably for a novelist this germ is no longer for much effect; for there have been women novelists of merit. But for painters it must still have some sting in it; and for musicians, I imagine, is even now active and poisonous in the extreme. The woman composer stands where the actress stood in the time of Shakespeare.[58] Nick Greene, I thought, remembering the story I had made about Shakespeare's sister, said that a woman acting put him in mind of a dog dancing. Johnson[59] repeated the phrase two hundred years later of women preaching. And here, I said, opening a book about music, we have the very words used again in this year of grace, 1928, of women who try to write music. 'Of Mlle. Germaine Tailleferre one can only repeat Dr. Johnson's dictum concerning, a woman preacher, transposed into terms of music.[60] "Sir, a woman's composing is like a dog's walking on his hind legs. It is not done well, but you are surprised to find it done at all."[61] So accurately does history repeat itself.

Thus, I concluded, shutting Mr. Oscar Browning's life and pushing away the rest, it is fairly evident that even in the nineteenth century a woman was not encouraged to be an artist. On the contrary, she was snubbed, slapped, lectured, and exhorted. Her mind must have been strained and her vitality lowered by the need of opposing this, of disproving that. For here again we come within range of that very interesting and obscure masculine complex which has had so much influence upon the woman's movement; that deep-seated desire, not so much that SHE shall be inferior as that HE shall be superior, which plants him wherever one looks, not only in front of the arts, but barring the way to politics too, even when the risk to himself seems infinitesimal and the suppliant humble and devoted.[62] Even Lady Bessborough, I remembered, with all her passion for politics, must humbly bow herself and write to Lord Granville Leveson-Gower[63]: "...notwithstanding all my violence in politicks and talking so much on that subject, I perfectly agree with you that no woman has any business to meddle with that or any other serious business, farther than giving her opinion (if she is ask'd)." And so she goes on to spend her enthusiasm where it meets with no obstacle whatsoever, upon that immensely important subject, Lord Granville's maiden speech[64] in the House of Commons. The spectacle is certainly a strange one, I thought. The history of men's opposition to women's emancipation is more interesting perhaps than the story of that emancipation itself. An amusing book might be made of it if some young student at Girton or Newnham would collect examples and deduce a theory, —but she would need thick gloves on her hands, and bars to protect her of solid gold.[65]

But what is amusing now, I recollected, shutting Lady Bessborough, had to be taken in desperate earnest once.[66] Opinions that one now pastes in a book labelled cock-a-doodledum[67] and keeps for reading to select audience on summer nights once drew tears. I can assure you. Among your grandmothers and great-grandmothers there were many that wept their eyes out. Florence Nightingale shrieked aloud in her agony.[68] Moreover, it is all very well for you, who have got yourselves to college and enjoying sitting-rooms—or is it only bed-sitting-rooms?—of your own to say that genius should disregard such opinions; that genius should be above caring what is said of them. Remember Keats. Remember the words he had cut on his tombstone. Think of Tennyson, think but I need hardly multiply instance of the undeniable, if very fortunate, fact that it is the nature of the artist to mind excessively what is said about him. Literature is strewn with the wreckage of men who have minded beyond reason the opinions of others.[69]

And the susceptibility of theirs is doubly fortunate, I thought, returning again to my original enquiry into what state of mind is most propitious for creative work, because the mind of an artist, in order to achieve the prodigious effort of freeing whole and entire the work that is in him, must be incandescent, like Shakespeare's mind, I conjectured, looking at the book which lay open at ANTONY AND CLEOPATRA. There must be no obstacle in it, no foreign matter unconsumed.

For though we say that we know nothing about Shakespeare's state of mind, even as we say that, we are saying something about Shakespeare's state of mind. The reason perhaps why we know so little of Shakespeare—compared with Donne or Ben Jonson or Milton—is that his grudges and spites and antipathies are hidden from us. We are not held up by some 'revelation' which reminds us of the writer.[70] All desire to protest, to preach, to proclaim an injure, to pay off a score, to make the world the witness of some hardship or grievance was fired out of him and consumed.[71] Therefore his poetry flows from him free and unimpeded. If ever a human being got his work expressed completely, it was Shakespeare. If ever a mind was incandescent, unimpeded, I thought, turning again to the bookcase, it was Shakespeare's mind.

注释

1. hot as lava, discolored as dish-water: 像岩浆一样炽热，像洗碗水一样肮脏。

2. 大意为：文学艺术始终以物质生活为基础，它们并非凭空而来，而是受苦受难者的作品，依附于健康、金钱和房屋等物质条件。

3. Trevelyan：特里维廉（George Macaulay Trevelyan, 1876—1962），英国著名史学家。

4. time of the Stuarts：斯图亚特王朝时代。

5. 大意为：好像并不缺乏气质与特性。

6. 大意为：克里奥佩特拉身上自有她的做派。

7. 这句话中提到的三位女性，都是莎士比亚作品中的人物。

8. 这句话中提到的女性，都是欧洲著名戏剧中的要角。

9. 这句话中提到的女性，都是欧洲小说中的重要人物。

10. 大意为：这样一来，女性就成了一种非常奇妙的复合体。

11. 大意为：读了史书，再读诗歌，由此而总结设想出的女性必定是一个怪物形象——就像蠕虫长着一对鹰翅，就像一个光彩照人的仙子在厨房里剁板油。

12. 天主教西多会修士。西多会创建于 1098 年，位于法国第戎。

13. 这段引文意在说明，女性在史籍中一直是缺席的。

14. 大意为：但是，除了智慧与个性之外一无所有的中产阶级女性……

15. Aubrey：奥布里（John Aubrey, 1626—1697），英国古物研究者、传记作家，终生致力于考古研究，以《名人传》（Brief Lives）一书著称于世。

16. 剑桥大学两所女子学院的名称。

17. 大意为：尽管我认为，当下的史书有些令人匪夷所思，不够真实，有失偏颇。

18. 大意为：他们为什么不去弥补史书中的缺失呢？给这段补遗部分安上一个不显山、不露水的名头，让女性也能堂而皇之地厕身于史籍之中。

19. Joanna Baillie：贝莉（1762—1851），苏格兰女戏剧家和诗人。

20. Mary Russell Mitford：米特福德（1787—1855），英国女作家，著有诗集、戏剧、小说等多种。

21. 大意为：鉴于以上情况，我可以得出结论，要是（在伊丽莎白时代）有哪位女性突然写出莎士比亚那样的剧作，那可真是一桩怪事。

22. 讽刺之语。大意为：这些老先生为了拯救人类，可真没少费心思。

23. 大意为：在莎士比亚时代，女性完全不可能写出莎士比亚笔下的剧作。

24. 自从文艺复兴时代以后，在英国的各类学校，奥维德、维吉尔和贺拉斯的作品成为男生的必读书。

25. 指上文提到的莎士比亚的妻子婚后不足十月即产子一事。

26. they were substantial people：家道殷实。

27. 大意为：她偷偷地在装苹果的阁楼里胡涂乱画。

28. 在莎士比亚时代，剧中女性通常由青年男子扮演。

29. the study of their ways：研究世上男男女女的习性。

30. 这里提到的 Nick Greene 可能是戏剧家格林（Robert Greene，约 1558—1592）。

31. 大意为：当诗人的心灵为女性的躯体所束缚，他该变得多么狂暴！

32. Elephant and Castle：酒馆名称，曾位于伦敦最繁华的一个十字路口，毁于二战。按照英国旧时风俗，自杀者被埋于十字路口，以防其鬼魂归来。

33. 在英国历史上，撒克逊人和不列颠人都曾饱受外来征服者的欺凌，其社会经济地位一如现代社会受压迫的女性。

34. 大意为：但是这种天才从来没有机会在文学创作上表现出来。

35. the torture that her gift had put her to：因怀才不遇而备受心理折磨

36. Avon：此处指无名氏。

37. Edward Fitzgerald：菲茨杰拉德（1809—1883），英国学者、翻译家，以翻译波斯文学名著《鲁拜集》（The Rubáiyát of Omar Khayyám）而驰名。

38. 大意为：贞洁可能是某些社会出于莫名其妙的原因发明的东西，让人盲目崇拜。

39. courage of the rarest：极为罕见的勇气。

40. 大意为：贞洁观的影响绵延不绝，直到 19 世纪末，还让女性作家隐姓埋名。

41. Currer Bell 是夏洛蒂·勃朗特的笔名。George Eliot，George Sand 也不是这两位女作家的本名。

42. 大意为：人们是否了解促发女性写作的那种心态？

43. 大意为：他对此只字不提。

44. Carlyle：卡莱尔（Thomas Carlyle，1795—1881），英国散文家、历史学家，著有《法国革命史》（History of the French Revolution）、《论英雄、英雄崇拜和历史上的英雄事迹》（On Heroes, Hero-Worship and the Heroic in History）等书。

45. Flaubert：福楼拜（Gustave Flaubert，1821—1880），法国大作家，

代表作《包法利夫人》(*Madame Bovary*)和《情感教育》(*L'Education Sentimentale*)最为世人称道。

46. 这里的 literature 意为"文献"。这句话大意为：要写就天才之作，几乎总是难度相当之大的壮举。关于这一点，从现代人所写的大量自我剖析的文献中可以看出来。

47. 大意为：大诗人悲惨地死去。

48. Tennyson：丁尼生（Alfred Tennyson, 1809—1892），英国诗人，华兹华斯逝世后为后继的英国桂冠诗人。其诗讲究音律，注重技巧，表现出极高的才力和修养，但有时雕琢过甚。

49. 大意为：世人对男性天才作家说，你想写就写吧，然而，他们对女性作家的态度不仅是漠然，而且是敌视。

50. 大意为：的确应当估算一下这种打击对艺术家造成的心理影响。

51. Dean Inge：英奇（William Ralph Inge, 1860—1954），圣保罗大教堂教长，有著作多种，对当时的民主、进步教育持有悲观态度而有"忧郁的教长"之称。

52. Harley：哈利是伦敦的一条街道，当年这里的住户多为医生，故文中有"哈利的专家"之说。

53. Oscar Browning：布朗宁（1837—1923），学者、传记作家，曾任剑桥大学国王学院讲师，为人虚荣、势利，为当年剑桥大学传奇人物，有关他的逸闻轶事甚多。

54. 大意为：无论他给的分数是多少。

55. sequel：指下文中 Browning 对形容枯槁、生活无着的小马倌的怜悯之语，这与他轻视女性的态度形成鲜明对比。

56. Mr. Greg：格雷格（Sir Walter Wilson Greg, 1875—1959），英国学者、目录学家。

57. 大意为：还有大量男性见解，大意是，不要对女性的智力有太多的期待。

58. 大意为：女性作曲家今日的处境，相当于莎士比亚时代女演员的处境。

59. 即 18 世纪英国文学巨匠塞缪尔·约翰逊。

60. 大意为：关于日尔曼娜·泰莱费尔小姐，我们只需重复约翰逊博士对女传道士的论断即可，只是换上一套音乐术语罢了。

61. 【作者原注】*A Survey of Contemporary Music*, Cecil Gray, p. 246.

62. 大意为：即便他允许女性参与艺术或政治不会给他自己带来什么风险，而恳求参与艺术或政治的女性又是如此谦卑、虔诚，他还是不肯放行。

63. Lord Granville Leveson-Gower：葛兰斐尔（1815—1891），英国自由党政治家、外交家。

64. maiden speech：尤指国会议员在下议院发表的首次演说。

65. 调侃之语，大意为：她需要戴上厚厚的手套，手中拿着棍子来保护自己的高贵。

66. 大意为：合上 Bessborough 女士的书，我心里想，现在看起来很好笑的东西，过去却得认真对待。

67. a book labelled cock-a-doodledum：公认为滑稽无聊的一本书。

68.【作者原注】See *Cassandra*, by Florence Nightingale, printed in *The Cause*, by R. Strachey.

69. 大意为：文学界到处都是那些过度看重别人对自己看法的受难者。

70. revelation：透露出的相关信息。

71. was fired out of him and consumed：（上述愿望）已不属于莎士比亚。

休姆　《浪漫主义与古典主义》

T. E. 休姆（1883—1917）

20世纪英国著名美学家、文学批评家、诗人。英年早逝，诗作极少（仅有八首），论著不丰（仅有两种），但影响巨大。就创作领域而言，他是意象派的创始人，影响了整个20年代英国现代主义诗歌名家，例如艾略特、庞德（Ezra Pound）、温德海姆·刘易斯（Wyndham Lewis）等人；在文学批评领域，他是英美新批评的先驱，他的作品中暗伏新批评的许多观点。他的影响大于成就，在文学界诚属异数。

1883年，休姆出生于英格兰斯塔福德郡的一个富裕的地主兼商人家庭。在文法学校就读期间，他对自然科学和数学极感兴趣，显示出过人的聪慧和桀骜不驯的个性。1902年进入剑桥大学圣约翰学院学习数学，课上喜欢与老师辩难，课下喜欢同学争论。他的兴趣逐渐从数学转移到哲学和艺术。他纠集了一伙人，成立所谓的"不和谐俱乐部"（Discord Club），倡导种种离经叛道的乖张举动。1904年，因为无理取闹、攻击警察而被开除学籍。

他在伦敦游荡了一段时间，一度就学伦敦大学。但他对学习开始失去兴趣，1906年去了加拿大。这里的山光水色和辽阔草原令他诗兴大发，他开始萌生了做诗人的念头。

告别加拿大，他又去了比利时的布鲁塞尔，一边教英文，一边自学法文；他开始倾心于亨利·柏格森的哲学思想，于是着手将柏格森的著作翻译成英文。回到英国后，他在伦敦组织了诗人俱乐部，结识了艾略特和庞德等诗坛新秀，经常聚在一起探讨文学和哲学问题。

从1909年起，他经常为《新时代》（New Age）杂志撰写文学和哲学评论，这些文章对英国现代主义文学产生了一定的影响。他反对浪漫主义浮夸、滥情的文风，力主诗歌意象明晰精确。最早的意象派诗歌就出自他的手笔，虽然庞德被奉为意象派鼻祖。1912年，《新时代》上发表了他的五首诗。这些短诗深得艾略特的推崇。艾略特称他是"我们这一代人中头脑最丰富的人"、"伟大的诗人"，并说"T. E. 休姆的诗只要大声朗读就会产生直接效果"。

在政治思想上，休姆深受法国极右翼思想家、"法兰西行动"中坚人物皮埃尔·拉塞尔（Pierre Lasserre）的影响。他是英国法西斯主义的先驱；假如他能活到动荡不安的 30 年代，说不定会闹出什么乱子来。他的朋友庞德和刘易斯后来为法西斯政权效力，与休姆当年的言传身教不无关系。

1912 年，休姆向剑桥大学当局发出申请，要求返校完成学业。在柏格森的鼎力推荐之下，剑桥当局批准了他的申请。但是时隔不久，被迫仓皇出逃。原来他想勾引一位未成年少女，结果惹恼了对方的父亲，欲杀之而后快。为躲避风头，他只好跑到德国去。

1914 年，第一次世界大战爆发。休姆主动请缨，同年 12 月开赴法国战场，与德军作战。他在军中依旧笔耕不辍，写下了一系列的"战争笔记"，攻击罗素的和平主义思想。这些文章都发表在《新时代》上面。1915 年，他作战负伤，回国休养；1916 年重返战场；1917 年 9 月战死于法国，也算是"求仁得仁"了。

1924 年，赫伯特·里德（Herbert Read）为他编辑出版了《臆度集》（*Speculations: Essays on Humanism*），这是他的第一部文集。1929 年，里德又替他编辑出版了文集《略论语言与文体》（*Notes on Language and Style*）。1955 年，S. 海因斯（S. Hynes）又编了一部《臆度集补遗》（*Further Speculations*）。

内容提要

1924 年，休姆的生前好友 T. S. 艾略特在自己主编的《标准》（*Criterion*）杂志上写道，休姆是集古典派、反动派和革命派于一身的人物，与 19 世纪末宽容的民主思想背道而驰。艾略特不愧是文字高手，只用寥寥数语就厘清了休姆的政治立场、文学主张和思想观念。说他是古典派，因为他宣扬古典主义以对抗浪漫派；说他是反动派，因为他反对 19 世纪末期的乐观主义进步论；说他是革命派，因为他提倡现代主义先锋艺术。这一切在休姆一生中最重要的文章《古典主义与浪漫主义》得到了体现。

休姆首先将浪漫主义等同于政治自由主义，将古典主义等同于政治保守主义。为了说明浪漫主义与政治之间的联系，他特意以法国发生的一场骚乱作为例证：有人在演讲中诋毁法国新古典主义戏剧家拉辛，在听众中引起了轩然大波。赞成者与反对者群情激昂，论辩不休。

原因在于，在反对者看来，反对古典主义无异于宣扬浪漫主义；而浪漫主义是引发法国革命的洪水猛兽，他们由憎恨法国革命而连带憎恨浪漫主义。休姆认为，在法国革命爆发之前，社会各阶级对革命都充满了热情，革命仿佛成了一种狂热的宗教，而它的根子就在于卢梭倡导的浪漫主义。按照卢梭的说法，人本性是善良的，只是受到不良的法律和习俗的压制；一旦取消这些消极因素，人的无限潜力就可以释放出来，人就可以走向完美。这种学说给法国人带来的启示是：人的身上蕴藏了无限的可能性（潜力）；一旦摧毁压迫人的秩序，重新整顿社会，人的潜能就会释放出来，人类社会就会取得进步。法国人之所以对革命产生宗教般的热情，原因就在于此。古典主义的看法与此正好相反，它认为人性是恒定不变的，人的潜能是有限的；只有遵循传统和秩序，人才能发挥出他身上优良的东西。在 19 世纪后期，由于达尔文进化论思想泛滥，浪漫主义的人类进步学说得以广为流传。按照达尔文的说法，新物种的出现是渐变的结果，这就为社会进步说提供了科学上的支持。总而言之，浪漫主义与古典主义的区别在于，前者认为人性本善，是环境使之变坏；后者认为人的潜能有限，但经过法律和传统的规训，可能向善。走笔至此，休姆意犹未尽，还打了一个著名的比喻，以期形象地说明二者之间的分野：对于浪漫主义者而言，人性就像一口井，里面充满了无限可能性（潜能）；对于古典主义者而言，人性就像一只水桶，里面盛的东西总是有限，固定不变的。

人性中有一种东西是恒定不变的，那就是人的宗教情结。当人性中的这部分内容受到理性主义无神论的束缚时，它就会以另一种形式表现出来。于是，当人不信上帝时，就开始相信人是神；当人不再相信天国的存在，就开始相信人间会出现天堂，而这就是浪漫主义的表现。本来属于宗教信仰领域的种种概念被浪漫主义传布开来，让原本清晰的人类体验的轮廓变得模糊起来。就此而言，浪漫主义是一种溢出的宗教（spilt religion）。

在文学方面，浪漫主义与古典主义表现出两种截然不同的气质。前者总是大谈人的无限潜质，放纵天马行空式的想象；后者不忘人的局限性，在想象之时总是有所节制，有所保留。古典派的代表作家有贺拉斯、伊丽莎白时代（17 世纪）的作家和奥古斯丁时代（18 世纪）的作家，浪漫派的代表人物是拉马丁、雨果、济慈、柯勒律治、拜伦、雪莱以及史文朋等人。就 20 世纪初的情形而言，浪漫主义已经用尽了自己的技巧，盛极而衰，势所必然。

Thomas Ernest Hulme (1883—1917)

Romanticism and Classicism

I want to maintain that after a hundred years of romanticism, we are in for a classical revival, and that the particular weapon of this new classical spirit, when it works in verse, will be fancy. And in this I imply the superiority of fancy—not superior generally or absolutely, for that would be obvious nonsense, but superior in the sense that we use the word good in empirical ethics—good for something, superior for something. I shall have to prove then two things, first that a classical revival is coming, and, secondly, for its particular purposes, fancy will be superior to imagination.

So banal have the terms Imagination and Fancy become that we imagine they must have always been in the language. Their history as two differing terms in the vocabulary of criticism is comparatively short. Originally, of course, they both meant the same thing; they first began to be differentiated by the German writers on aesthetics in the eighteenth century.

I know that in using the words 'classic' and 'romantic' I am doing a dangerous thing. They represent five or six different kinds of antitheses, and while I may be using them in one sense you may be interpreting them in another. In this present connection I am using them in a perfectly precise and limited sense. I ought really to have coined a couple of new words, but I prefer to use the ones I have used, as I then conform to the practice of the group of polemical writers who make the most use of them at the present day, and have almost succeeded in making them political catchwords. I mean Maurras, Lasserre, and all the groups connected with *L'Action Française*[1].

At the present time this is the particular group with which the distinction is most vital. Because it has become a party symbol. If you asked a man of a certain set whether he preferred the classics or the romantics, you could deduce from that what his politics were.

The best way of gliding into a proper definition of my terms would be to start with a set of people who are prepared to fight about it—for in them you will have no vagueness. (Other people take the infamous attitude of the person with catholic tastes who says he likes both.)

About a year ago, a man whose name I think was Fauchois gave a lecture at the Odéon[2] on Racine, in the course of which he made some disparaging remarks about his dullness, lack of invention and the rest of it. This caused an immediate riot: fights took place all over the house; several people were arrested and imprisoned, and the rest of the series of lectures took place with hundreds of gendarmes and detectives scattered all over the place. These people interrupted because the classical ideal is a living thing to them and Racine is the great classic. This is what I call a real vital interest in literature. They regard romanticism as an awful disease which France had just recovered.

The thing is complicated in their case by the fact that it was romanticism that made the revolution. They hate the revolution, so they hate romanticism.

I make no apology for dragging in politics here; romanticism both in England and France is associated with certain political views, and it is in taking a concrete example of the working out of a principle in action that you can get its best definition.

What was the positive principle behind all the other principles of '89[3]? I am talking here of the revolution in as far as it was an idea; I leave out material causes—they only produce the forces. The barriers which could easily have resisted or guided these forces had been previously rotted away by ideas. This always seems to be the case in successful changes; the privileged class is beaten only when it has lost faith in itself, when it has itself been penetrated with the ideas which are working against it.

It was not the rights of man—that was a good solid practical war-cry. The thing which created enthusiasm, which made the revolution practically a new religion, was something more positive than that. People of all classes, people who stood to lose by it, were in a positive ferment about the idea of liberty. There must have been some idea which enabled them to think that something positive could come out of so essentially negative a thing. There was, and here I get my definition of romanticism. They had been taught by Rousseau that man was by nature good, that it was only bad laws and customs that had suppressed him. Remove all these and the infinite possibilities of man would have a chance. This is what made them think that something positive could come out of disorder, this is what created the religious enthusiasm. Here is the root of all romanticism: that man, the individual, is an infinite reservoir of possibilities; and if you can so rearrange society by the destruction of oppressive order then these possibilities will have a chance and you will get Progress.

One can define the classical quite clearly as the exact opposite to this. Man is an extraordinarily fixed and limited animal whose nature is absolutely constant. It is only by tradition and organization that anything decent can be got out of him.

This view was a little shaken at the time of Darwin. You remember his particular hypothesis, that new species came into existence by the cumulative effect of small variations—this seems to admit the possibility of future progress. But at the present day the contrary hypothesis makes headway in the shape of De Vries's mutation theory, that each new species comes into existence, not gradually by the accumulation of small steps, but suddenly in a jump, a kind of sport, and that once in existence it remains absolutely fixed. This enables me to keep the classical view with an appearance of scientific backing.

Put shortly, these are the two views, then. One, that man is intrinsically good, spoilt by circumstance; and the other that he is intrinsically limited, but disciplined by order and tradition to something fairly decent. To the one party man's nature is like a well, to the other like a bucket. The view which regards man as a well, a reservoir full of possibilities, I call the romantic; the one which regards him as a very finite and fixed creature, I call the classical.

One may note here that the Church has always taken the classical view since the defeat of the Pelagian[4] heresy and the adoption of the same classical dogma of original sin.

It would be a mistake to identify the classical view with that of materialism. On the contrary it is absolutely identical with the normal religious attitude. I should put it in this way: That part of the fixed nature of man is the belief in the Deity. This should be as fixed and true for every man as belief in the existence of matter and in the objective world. It is parallel to appetite, the instinct of sex, and all the other fixed qualities. Now at certain times, by the use of either force or rhetoric, these instincts have been suppressed—in Florence under Savonarola[5], in Geneva under Calvin[6], and here under the Roundheads[7]. The inevitable result of such a process is that the repressed instinct bursts out in some abnormal direction. So with religion. By the perverted rhetoric of Rationalism, your natural instincts are suppressed and you are converted into an agnostic. Just as in the case of the other instincts, Nature has her revenge. The instincts that find their right and proper outlet in religion must come out in some other way. You don't believe in God, so you begin to believe that man is a god. You don't believe in heaven, so you begin to believe in a heaven on earth. In other words, you get romanticism. The concepts that are right and proper in their own sphere are spread over, and so mess up, falsify and blur the clear outlines of human experience. It is like pouring a pot of treacle over the dinner table. Romanticism then, and this is the best definition I can give of it, is spilt religion.

I must now shirk the difficulty of saying exactly what I mean by romantic and classical in verse. I can only say that it means the result of these two attitudes towards the cosmos, towards man, in so far as it gets reflected in verse. The romantic, because he thinks man infinite, must always be talking about the infinite; and as there is always the bitter contrast between what you think you ought to be able to do and what man actually can, it always tends, in its later stages at any rate, to be gloomy. I really can't go any further than to say it is the reflection of these two temperaments, and point out examples of the different spirits. On the one hand I would take such diverse people as Horace, most of the Elizabethans[8] and the writers of the Augustan age[9], and on the other side Lamartine[10], Hugo, parts of Keats, Coleridge, Byron, Shelly, and Swinburne[11].

I know quite well that when people think of classical and romantic in verse, the contrast at once comes into their mind between, say, Racine and Shakespeare. I don't mean this; the dividing line that I intend is here misplaced a little from the true middle. That Racine is on the extreme classical side I agree, but if you call Shakespeare romantic, you are using a different definition to the one I give. You are thinking of the difference between classic and romantic as being merely one between restraint and exuberance. I should say with Nietzsche that there are two kinds of classicism, the static and the dynamic. Shakespeare is the classic of motion.

What I mean by classical in verse, then, is this. That even in the most imaginative flights there is always a holding back, a reservation. The classical poet never forgets this finiteness, this limit of man. He remembers always that he is mixed up with earth. He may jump, but he always returns back; he never flies away into the circumambient gas.

You might say if you wished that the whole of the romantic attitude seems to crystallize in verse round metaphors of flight. Hugo is always flying, flying over abysses, flying up into the eternal gases. The word infinite in every other line.

In the classical attitude you never seem to swing right along to the infinite nothing. If you say an extravagant thing which does exceed the limits inside which you know man to be fastened, yet there is always conveyed in some way at the end an impression of yourself standing outside it, and not quite believing it, or consciously putting it forward as a flourish. You never go blindly into an atmosphere more than the truth, an atmosphere too rarefied for man to breathe for long. You are always faithful to the conception of a limit. It is a question of pitch; in romantic verse you move to a certain pitch of rhetoric which you know, man being what he is, to be a little high-falutin.[12] The kind of thing you get in Hugo or Swinburne. In the coming classical reaction that will feel just wrong. For an example of the opposite thing, a verse written in the proper classical spirit, I can take the song from *Cymbeline*[13] beginning with "Fear no more the heat of the sun". I am just using this as a parable. I don't quite mean what I say here. Take the last two lines:

> Golden lads and girls all must,
> Like chimney sweepers come to dust.

Now, no romantic would have ever written that. Indeed, so ingrained is romanticism, so objectionable is this to it, that people have asserted that these were not part of the original song.[14]

Apart from the pun, the thing that I think quite classical is the word lad. Your modern romantic could never write that. He would have to write golden youth, and take up the thing at least a couple of notes in pitch.[15]

I want now to give the reasons which make me think that we are nearing the end of the romantic movement.

The first lies in the nature of any convention or tradition in art. A particular convention or attitude in art has a strict analogy to the phenomena of organic life. It grows old and decays. It has a definite period of life and must die. All the possible tunes get played on it and then it is exhausted; moreover its best period is its youngest. Take the case of the extraordinary efflorescence of verse in the Elizabethan period. All kinds of reasons have been given for this—the discovery of the new world and all the rest of it. There is a much simpler one. A new medium had been given them to play with—namely, blank verse. It was new and so it was easy to play new tunes on it.

The same law holds in other arts. All the masters of painting are born into the world at a time when the particular tradition from which they start is imperfect. The Florentine tradition was just short of full ripeness when Raphael came to Florence, the Bellinesque was still young when Titian was born in Venice.[16] Landscape was still a toy or an appanage of figure-painting when Turner and Constable[17] arose to reveal its independent power. When Turner and Constable had done with landscape they left little or nothing for their successors to do on the same lines. Each field of artistic activity is exhausted by the first great artist who gathers a full harvest from it.

This period of exhaustion seems to me to have been reached in romanticism. We shall not get any new efflorescence of verse until we get a new technique, a new convention, to turn ourselves loose in.

Objection might be taken to this. It might be said that a century as an organic unity doesn't exist, that I am being deluded by a wrong metaphor, that I am treating a collection of literary people as if they were an organism or state department. Whatever we may be in other things, an objective might urge, in literature in as far as we are anything at all—in as far as we are worth considering—we are individuals, we are persons, and as distinct persons we cannot be subordinated to any general treatment. At any period at any time, an individual poet may be a classic or a romantic just as he feels like it. You at any particular moment may think that you can stand outside a movement. You may think that as an individual you observe both the classic and the romantic spirit and decide from a purely detached point of view that one is superior to the other.

The answer to this is that no one, in a matter of judgment of beauty, can take a detached standpoint in this way.[18] Just as physically you are not born that abstract entity, man, but the child of particular parents, so you are in matters of literary judgment. Your opinion is almost entirely of the literary history that came just before you, and you are governed by that whatever you may think. Take Spinoza's[19] example of a stone falling to the ground. If it had a conscious mind it would, he said, think it was going to the ground because it wanted to. So you with your pretended free judgment about what is and what is not beautiful. The amount of freedom in man is much exaggerated. That we are free on certain rare occasions,[20] both my religion and the views I get from metaphysics convince me. But many acts which we habitually label free are in reality automatic. It is quite possible for a man to write a book almost automatically. I have read several such products. Some observations were recorded more than twenty years ago by Robertson on reflex speech, and he found that in certain cases of dementia, where the people were quite unconscious so far as the exercise of reasoning went, very intelligent answers were given to a succession of questions on politics and such matters.[21] The meaning of these questions could not possibly have been understood. Language here acted after the manner of a reflex. So that certain extremely complex mechanisms, subtle enough to imitate beauty, can work by themselves—I certainly think that this is the case with judgment about beauty.

I can put the same thing in slightly different form. Here is a question of a conflict of two attitudes, as it might be of two techniques. The critic, while he has to admit that changes from one to the other occur, persists in regarding them as mere variations to a certain fixed normal, just as a pendulum might swing. I admit the analogy of the pendulum as far as movement, but I deny the further consequence of the analogy, the existence of the point of rest, the normal point.

When I say that I dislike the romantics, I dissociate two things: the part of them in which they resemble all the great poets, and the part in which they differ and which gives them their character as romantics. It is their minor element which constitutes the particular note[22] of a century, and which, while it excites contemporaries, annoys the next generation. It was precisely that quality in Pope which pleased his friends, which we detest. Now, anyone just before the romantics who felt that, could have predicted that a change was coming. It seems to me that we stand just in the same position now. I think that there is an increasing proportion of people who simply can't stand Swinburne.

When I say that there will be another classical revival I don't necessarily anticipate a return to Pope. I say merely that now is the time for such a revival. Given people of the necessary capacity, it may be a vital thing; without them we may get a formalism something like Pope. When it does come we may not even recognize it as classical. Although it will be classical it will be different because it has passed through a romantic period.[23] To take a parallel example: I remember being very surprised, after seeing the Post Impressionists, to find in Maurice Denis's[24] account of the matter that they consider themselves classical in the sense that they were trying to impose the same order on the mere flux of new material provided by the impressionist movement, that existed in the more limited materials of the painting before.[25]

There is something now to be cleared away before I get on with my argument, which is that while romanticism is dead in reality, yet the critical attitude appropriate to it still continues to exist. To make this a little clearer: For every kind of verse, there is a corresponding receptive attitude. In a romantic period we demand from verse certain qualities. In a classical period we demand others. At the present time I should say that this receptive attitude has outlasted the thing from which it was formed. But while the romantic tradition has run dry, yet the critical attitude of mind, which demands romantic qualities from verse, still survives. So that if good classical verse were to be written tomorrow very few people would be able to stand it.

I object even to the best of the romantics. I object still more to the receptive attitude. I object to the sloppiness[26] which doesn't consider that a poem is a poem unless it is moaning or whining about something or other. I always think in this connection of the last line of a poem of John Webster's[27] which ends with a request I cordially endorse:

End your moan and come away.

The thing has got so bad now that a poem which is all dry and hard, a properly classical poem, would not be considered poetry at all. How many people now can lay their hands on their hearts and say that they like either Horace or Pope? They feel a kind of chill when they read them.

The dry hardness which you get in the classics is absolutely repugnant to them. Poetry that isn't damp isn't poetry at all. They cannot see that accurate description is a legitimate object of verse. Verse to them always means a bringing in of some of the emotions that are grouped round the word infinite.

The essence of poetry to most people is that it must lead them to a beyond[28] of some kind. Verse strictly confined to the earthly and the definite (Keats is full of it) might seem to them to be excellent writing, excellent craftsmanship, but not poetry. So much has romanticism debauched us, that, without some form of vagueness, we deny the highest.[29]

In the classic it is always the light of ordinary day, never the light that never was on land or sea. It is always perfectly human and never exaggerated: man is always man and never a god.

But the awful result of romanticism is that, accustomed to this strange light, you can never live without it. Its effect on you is that of a drug.

There is a general tendency to think that verse means little else than the expression of unsatisfied emotion. People say: "But how can you have verse without sentiment?" You see what it is: the prospect alarms them. A classical revival to them would mean the prospect[30] of an arid desert and the death of poetry as they understand it, and could only come to fill the gap caused by that death. Exactly why this dry classical spirit should have a positive and legitimate necessity to express itself in poetry is utterly inconceivable to them. What this positive need is, I shall show later. It follows from the fact that there is another quality, not the emotion produced, which is at the root of excellence in verse. Before I get to this I am concerned with a negative thing,[31] a theoretical point, a prejudice that stands in the way and is really at the bottom of this reluctance to understand classical verse.

It is an objection which ultimately I believe comes from a bad metaphysic of art. You are unable to admit the existence of beauty without the infinite being in some way or another dragged in.[32]

. . .

In prose as in algebra concrete things are embodied in signs or counters which are moved about according to rules, without being visualized at all in the process. There are in prose certain type situations and arrangements of words, which move as automatically into certain other arrangements as do functions[33] in algebra. One only changes the X's and the Y's back into physical things at the end of the process.[34] Poetry, in one aspect at any rate, may be considered as an effort to avoid this characteristic of prose. It is not a counter language[35], but a visual concrete one. It is a compromise for a language of intuition, which would hand over sensations bodily. It always endeavors to arrest you, and to make you continuously see a physical thing, to prevent you gliding through an abstract process. It chooses fresh epithets and fresh metaphors, not so much because they are new, and we are tired of the old, but because the old cease to convey a physical thing and become abstract counters. A poet says a ship "coursed the seas"[36] to get a physical image, instead of the counter word "sailed." Visual meanings can only be transferred by the new bowl of metaphor; prose is an old pot that lets them leak out. Images in verse are not mere decoration, but the very essence of an intuitive language. Verse is a pedestrian taking you over the ground, prose—a train which delivers you at a destination.

I can now get on to a discussion of two words often used in this connection, "fresh" and "unexpected". You praise a thing for being "fresh". I understand what you mean, but the word besides conveying the truth, conveys a secondary something which is certainly false. When you say a poem or drawing is fresh, and so good, the impression is somehow conveyed that the essential element of goodness is freshness, that it is good because it is fresh. Now this is certainly wrong, there is nothing particularly desirable about freshness *per se*. Works of art aren't eggs. Rather the contrary. It is simply an unfortunate necessity due to the nature of language and technique that the only way the element which does constitute goodness, the only way in which its presence can be detected externally, is by freshness. Freshness convinces you, you feel at once that the artist was in an actual physical state.

You feel that for a minute. Real communication is so very rare, for plain speech is unconvincing. It is in this rare fact of communication that you get the root of aesthetic pleasure.

I shall maintain that wherever you get an extraordinary interest in a thing, a great zest in its contemplation which carries on the contemplator to accurate description in the sense of the word accurate I have just analysed, there you have sufficient justification for poetry. It must be an intense zest which heightens a thing out of the level of prose. I am using contemplation here just in the same way that Plato used it, only applied to a different subject; it is a detached interest. "The object of aesthetic contemplation is something framed apart by itself and regarded without memory or expectation, simply as being itself, as end not means, as individual not universal."[37]

注释

1. L'Action Française：法兰西行动，活跃在 19 世纪末、一战之前的法国极右翼知识分子团体。这句话中提到的莫拉斯和拉塞尔都是这一组织的重要人物。

2. Odéon：奥德翁，法国巴黎地名。

3. '89：指 1789 年法国大革命。

4. Pelagian：贝拉基主义者。贝拉基主义是 5 世纪神学家贝拉基首倡的基督教极端教义，强调人性本善以及人有自由意志。

5. Savonarola：萨沃那洛拉（Girolamo Savonarola, 1452—1498），意大利宗教、政治改革家，抨击罗马教廷和暴政，领导佛罗伦萨人民起义，建立民主政权，后被教皇推翻处死。

6. Calvin：加尔文（John Calvin, 1509—1564），法国宗教改革家、基督教新教加尔文宗的创始人，否认罗马教会的权威，著有《基督教原理》（*Institution de la Religion Chrétienne*）。

7. the Roundhead：圆颅党人，1642—1652 英国内战期间的议会派成员。因剪短发故名，为清教徒。

8. the Elizabethan：伊丽莎白时代（1558—1603）的英国诗人。

9. Augustan age：这里指英国 18 世纪的新古典主义时代。

10. Lamartine：拉马丁（Alphonse de Lamartine, 1790—1869），法国浪

漫派诗人、政治活动家。

11. Swinburne：史文朋（Algernon Charles Swinburne, 1837—1909），英国诗人、文学评论家，主张无神论，同情意大利独立运动和法国革命。其诗作技巧纯熟，色彩丰富，音调优美，有唯美主义倾向。与"先拉斐尔派"关系密切。

12. 大意为：浪漫主义诗歌多浮词虚饰，对人的潜能多有夸大之词。

13. *Cymbeline*：莎士比亚戏剧《辛白林》。

14. 大意为：这里援引的两行文字与浪漫派的写法背道而驰。浪漫派观念在人们头脑中根深蒂固，以至于人们认为，原作当中没有这两行文字。

15. 大意为：上述两行诗体现古典主义倾向的是"小伙子（lad）"一词，而现代浪漫派决不会用这个词；他很可能用"金发少年"，而且还要着重强调。

16. the Florentine tradition：指佛罗伦萨画派的传统。Raphael，拉斐尔（1483—1520），意大利文艺复兴盛期画家、建筑师。Titian，提香（1488—1576），意大利文艺复兴盛期画家，擅长肖像画、宗教和神话题材的绘画。

17. Constable：康斯特布尔（John Constable, 1776—1837），英国风景画家，追求真实再现英国农村的自然景色。

18. 大意为：在审美判断的时候，人不可能这样处于超然地位。

19. Spinoza：斯宾诺莎（Baruch Spinoza, 1632—1677），荷兰哲学家、唯理主义的代表之一，认为只有凭借理性知识才能得到可靠的知识。

20. 大意为：只有在非常罕见的情况下，人才是自由的。

21. 大意为：罗伯逊发现，某些人在精神错乱的时候，根本没有意识到自己的推理活动；面对一连串政治类问题，他会给出非常理性的回答。

22. note：基调。

23. 大意为：尽管它是古典主义的，但是，经历了浪漫主义时期之后，它已不同于往日的古典主义。

24. Maurice Denis：丹尼斯（1870—1943），法国画家。

25. 大意为：他们试图把从前绘画素材有限时使用的那套绘画规则强加给印象派运动造就的层出不穷的素材。

26. sloppiness：伤感滥情。

27. John Webster：韦伯斯特（1580?—1625?），英国剧作家，著有《白魔》（*The White Devil*）和《马尔菲公爵夫人》（*The Duchess of Malfi*）。

28. a beyond：超凡脱俗之境，与下一段中的 ordinary day 形成鲜明对比。

29. 大意为：我们否认它们是上乘之作。

30. the prospect：指上文提到的"作诗不带伤感"（have verse without sentiment）这一前景。

31. 大意为：在谈这一点之前，我先谈一谈一种消极的观点。

32. 大意为：不设法扯进"无限"（the infinite being），就没法承认美的存在。

33. function：函数。

34. 大意为：人们只需在过程结束后将 X 或 Y 换成具体的东西即可。

35. a counter language：算数语言。

36. coursed the seas：穿越大海。

37. 大意为：审美静观的对象是某种自足之物，人们看待它时，只把它当做它自身，把它看做目的而非手段，把它当做个别而非普遍。
有关想象（imagination）和幻想（fancy）之间的区分，见本书柯勒律治《文学生涯》内容提要。

艾略特　《传统与个人才能》

托马斯·斯特恩斯·艾略特（1888—1965）

在 20 世纪初，托马斯·斯特恩斯·艾略特以奇崛的诗风、别出机杼的技巧和描绘人类幽暗心灵的题材，为英美现代主义诗歌定下了标准和基调，广为现代诗人所师法，遂得一代诗宗之名。其代表作《荒原》（1922）、《四个四重奏》（"Four Quartets", 1943）已成现代主义的经典。

艾略特 1888 年出生于美国密苏里州的圣路易斯的一个商人家庭，早年受过良好的古典教育。1906 年进入哈佛大学。在校期间，他受教于新人文主义者欧文·白壁德（Irving Babbitt），学习 19 世纪法国文学批评，深受白壁德对浪漫主义的批评态度的影响，先后获得学士、硕士学位。自哈佛毕业后，在巴黎大学留学一年（1910—1911），学习文学和哲学；回到哈佛后学习印度哲学和梵文（1911—1914）。1914 年结识庞德，并接受其劝说，定居英国。1915 年发表《普鲁弗洛克情歌》（"The Love Song of J. Alfred Prufrock"）。从 1917 至 1920 年期间，在劳埃德银行任职员。1920 年创办文学评论季刊《标准》。1922 年发表《荒原》，声震诗坛。1927 年加入英国国籍。他自命为宗教上的天主教徒、政治上的保皇派、文学上的古典主义者。从 20 世纪 30 年代起，他致力于复兴古典诗剧。1948 年获得诺贝尔文学奖。

艾略特的文学成就不仅表现在他的诗歌创作，也体现在他在诗学领域的理论和批评建树。虽说他本人谦称自己的文学批评只不过是诗歌创作之余的副产品，但是，他的文学理论和批评并未受到忽视。素有"批评家的批评家"之称的雷内·韦勒克（Réne Wellek）对他极为推崇，誉之为"20 世纪英语世界至今最为重要的批评家"。此誉并不过分，他的文论贡献足以与他的诗歌成就相提并论。他的主要文学评论文集有《圣林》（*The Sacred Wood*, 1920）、《论文选》（*Selected Essays*, 1932）、《论诗与诗人》（*On Poetry and Poets*, 1957）以及《对批评家的批评：论文学八题》（*To Criticize Critics: Eight Essays on Literature*, 1965）等。虽说未见系统性的文学专著，但这些论文中若干观点，却如明珠串天，处处显眼，常能让人耳目一新。在这些文章中，他提出了所谓的"文学传统有机整体观"、"非个性化理论"以及"客观对应物说"。这些重要观点，着力批判浪漫主义文论和传记式批评，对英国的细绎派和美国的新批评深有影响。

内容提要

在名篇《传统与个人才能》一文中，艾略特主要阐述了"文学传统有机整体观"和"非个性化理论"；二者互为表里，构成了他的诗学理论的核心。前者从宏观的文学史角度为后者预设了一个前提，进行了铺垫，后者又对前者进行了引申和补充。

艾略特认为，自荷马时代以来的欧洲文学，并不是历代作品综合的简单累加，而是一个秩序井然、相互关联的有机整体；文学家的个别作品，只有以这个有机整体为参照，才能显示出其独特意义。不过，这个有机整体并非一成不变。由于带有异质性的新作品的加入，这个传统会逐渐进行自我调整，以适应这些异质性的东西。不过这些异质性的东西与既有传统始终有相近之处，因为，新作品在创作过程中需要以传统精神为依托，逐步向其靠拢，而对它并无本质上的修改；也就是说，新作品只是对老传统的发扬光大而非断然弃绝。

传统确乎重要，但传统精神的获得，殊非易事，作家必须付出辛苦来培养自己的历史感才能得到。只有具备一定的历史感，作家才能意识到，荷马时代以来的整个欧洲文学以及他所在国度的文学构成了一个共时的整体；并意识到传统中的哪些内容是永恒的，哪些内容是昙花一现的，只是一定历史阶段的产物。这种历史感也会使作家强烈地意识到，自己在文学史长河中的地位以及他在当代的价值。即，在当前的历史阶段，他应该对传统做出什么样的贡献。

文学传统影响了作家的创作，反过来，作家的创作也会改变文学传统；但是，这种改变是微不足道的。正因为这个原因，作家若想在文学史中获得一席之地，他在作品中就不能到处突出有悖于传统的个性，而应泯灭个性，适应传统。于是，一反浪漫主义文论力主抒发个人情感、突出诗人个性的见解，艾略特提出了一种"非个性化理论"："诗不是放纵情感，而是逃避情感，不是表现个性而是逃避个性"；"一位艺术家的进步意味着不断的自我牺牲，个性的不断泯灭。如果我们不抱着这种先入为主的成见去研究某位诗人，我们往往会发现，不仅他的作品中最好的部分，而且最有个性的部分，很可能正是已故诗人们，也就是他的先辈们，最有力表现他们作品之所以不朽的地方"。

为了更加形象地说明"非个性化理论"，艾略特还拿一个化学反应作比喻：把一根白金丝放进一个装有氧气和二氧化硫的箱子中，这两种气体产生化合作用，形成硫酸；在反应过程中，白金丝是不可或缺的媒介，然而，这个反应所产生的硫酸却不含白金的成分，白金的性质也始终保持不变。艾略特想要说明的是，在诗歌的创作过程中，诗人的心灵犹如白金丝，始终保持客观中正；没有诗人的心灵，诗歌无从产生，但是，即成的诗作中也不应显露诗人的心灵。

艾略特之所以如此强调文学传统对个人创作的影响，是为了抗衡浪漫主义的诗歌理论。正如 M. H. 艾布拉姆斯（M. H. Abrams）在浪漫主义的总结性著作《镜与灯》（*The Mirror and the Lamp*）中所说，以文学为作家个性的标志，是浪漫主义文论的一个特色；华兹华斯说，诗歌是（诗人）"强烈情感的自然流露"。柯勒律治的名言，"要问诗是什么，差不多等于问诗人是什么"，也被广泛征引去证明诗歌是诗人个性的展示。艾略特却以为，浪漫主义诗歌张扬情感，失之含蓄，造成情感与理智的分离。有鉴于此，他极力推崇 17 世纪英国"玄学派"诗歌，因为，后者体现了情感与理智的结合。

Thomas Stearns Eliot (1888－1965)

TRADITION AND THE INDIVIDUAL TALENT

I

In English writing we seldom speak of tradition, though we occasionally apply its name in deploring its absence.[1] We cannot refer to "the tradition" or to "a tradition"; at most, we employ the adjective in saying that the poetry of So-and-so is "traditional" or even "too traditional." Seldom, perhaps, does the word appear except in a phrase of censure. If otherwise, it is vaguely approbative, with the implication, as to the work approved, of some pleasing archaeological reconstruction.[2] You can hardly make the word agreeable to English ears without this comfortable reference to the reassuring science of archaeology.

Certainly the word is not likely to appear in our appreciations of living or dead writers. Every nation, every race, has not only its own creative, but its own critical turn of mind; and is even more oblivious of[3] the shortcomings and limitations of its critical habits than of those of its creative genius. We know, or think we know, from the enormous mass of critical writing that has appeared in the French language the critical method or habit of the French; we only conclude (we are such unconscious people) that the French are "more critical" than we, and sometimes even plume ourselves a little[4] with the fact, as if the French were the less spontaneous. Perhaps they are; but we might remind ourselves that criticism is as inevitable as breathing, and that we should be none the worse for articulating what passes in our minds when we read a book and feel an emotion about it, for criticizing our own minds in their work of criticism. One of the facts that might come to light in this process is our tendency to insist, when we praise a poet, upon those aspects of his work in which he least resembles anyone else. In these aspects or parts of his work we pretend to find what is individual, what is the peculiar essence of the man. We dwell with satisfaction upon the poet's difference from his predecessors, especially his immediate predecessors; we endeavor to find something that can be isolated in order to be enjoyed. Whereas if we approach a poet without this prejudice we shall often find that not only the best, but the most individual parts of his work may be those in which the dead poets, his ancestors, assert their immortality most vigorously. And I do not mean the impressionable period of adolescence, but the period of full maturity.

Yet if the only form of tradition, of handing down, consisted in following the ways of the immediate generation before us in a blind or timid adherence to its success, "tradition" should positively be discouraged.[5] We have seen many such simple currents soon lost in the sand; and novelty is better than repetition. Tradition is a matter of much wider significance. It cannot be inherited, and if you want it you must obtain it by great labor. It involves, in the first place, the historical sense, which we may call nearly indispensable to anyone who would continue to be a poet beyond his twenty-fifth year; and the historical sense involves a perception, not only of the pastness of the past, but of its presence; the historical sense compels a man to write not merely with his own generation in his bones, but with a feeling that the whole of the literature of Europe from Homer and within it the whole of the literature of his own country has a simultaneous existence and composes a simultaneous order. This historical sense, which is a sense of the timeless as well as of the temporal and of the timeless and the temporal together, is what makes a writer most acutely conscious of his place in time, of his own contemporaneity.[6]

No poet, no artist of any art, has his complete meaning alone. His significance, his appreciation is the appreciation of his relation to the dead poets and artists. You cannot value him alone; you must set him, for contrast and comparison, among the dead. I mean this as a principle of aesthetic, not merely historical, criticism. The necessity that he shall conform, that he shall cohere, is not one-sided; what happens when a new work of art is created is something that happens simultaneously to all the works of art which preceded it.[7] The existing monuments form an ideal order among themselves, which is modified by the introduction of the new (the really new) work of art among them. The existing order is complete before the new work arrives; for order to persist after the supervention of novelty, the *whole* existing order must be, if ever so slightly, altered; and so the relations, proportions, values of each work of art toward the whole are readjusted; and this is conformity between the old and the new. Whoever has approved this idea of order, of the form[8] of European, of English literature will not find it preposterous that the past should be altered by the present as much as the present is directed by the past. And the poet who is aware of this will be aware of great difficulties and responsibilities.

In a peculiar sense he will be aware also that he must inevitably be judged by the standards of the past. I say judged, not amputated, by them; not judged to be as good as, or worse or better than, the dead; and certainly not judged by the canons of dead critics. It is a judgment, a comparison, in which two things are measured by each other. To conform[9] merely would be for the new work not really to conform at all; it would not be new, and would therefore not be a work of art. And we do not quite say that the new is more valuable because it fits in; but its fitting in is a test of its value—a test, it is true, which can only be slowly and cautiously applied, for we are none of us infallible judges of conformity. We say: it appears to conform, and is perhaps individual, or it appears individual, and may conform; but we are hardly likely to find that it is one and not the other.[10]

To proceed to a more intelligible exposition of the relation of the poet to the past: he can neither take the past as a lump, an indiscriminate bolus[11], nor can he form himself wholly on one or two private admirations, nor can he form himself wholly upon one preferred period. The first course is inadmissible, the second is an important experience of youth, and the third is a pleasant and highly desirable supplement[12]. The poet must be very conscious of the main current, which does not at all flow invariably through the most distinguished reputation[13]. He must be quite aware of the obvious fact that art never improves, but that the material of art is never quite the same. He must be aware that the mind of Europe—the mind of his own country—a mind which he learns in time to be much more important than his own private mind—is a mind which changes, and that this change is a development which abandons nothing *en route*[14], which does not superannuate either Shakespeare, or Homer, or the rock drawing of the Magdalenian draughtsmen[15]. That this development, refinement perhaps, complication certainly, is not, from the point of view of the artist, any improvement.

Perhaps not even an improvement from the point of view of the psychologist or not to the extent which we imagine; perhaps only in the end based upon a complication in economics and machinery.[16] But the difference between the present and the past is that the conscious present is an awareness of the past in a way and to an extent which the past's awareness of itself cannot show.

Some one said: "The dead writers are remote from us because we *know* so much more than they did." Precisely, and they are that which we know.

I am alive to a usual objection to what is clearly part of my program for the *métier* of poetry.[17] The objection is that the doctrine requires a ridiculous amount of erudition (pedantry), a claim which can be rejected by appeal to the lives of poets in any pantheon.[18] It will even be affirmed that much learning deadens or perverts poetic sensibility. While, however, we persist in believing that a poet ought to know as much as will not encroach upon his necessary receptivity and necessary laziness, it is not desirable to confine knowledge to whatever can be put into a useful shape for examinations, drawing-rooms, or the still more pretentious modes of publicity. Some can absorb knowledge, the more tardy must sweat for it. Shakespeare acquired more essential history from Plutarch than most men could from the whole British Museum. What is to be insisted upon is that the poet must develop or procure the consciousness of the past and that he should continue to develop this consciousness throughout his career.

What happens is a continual surrender of himself as he is at the moment to something which is more valuable. The progress of an artist is a continual self-sacrifice, a continual extinction of personality.

There remains to define this process of depersonalization and its relation to the sense of tradition. It is in this depersonalization that art may be said to approach the condition of science. I, therefore, invite you to consider, as a suggestive analogy, the action which takes place when a bit of finely filiated platinum is introduced into a chamber containing oxygen and sulphur dioxide.[19]

II

Honest criticism and sensitive appreciation are directed not upon the poet but upon the poetry. If we attend to the confused cries of the newspaper critics and the *susurrus* of popular reputation that follows, we shall hear the names of poets in great numbers; if we seek not Blue-book knowledge but the enjoyment of poetry, and ask for a poem, we shall seldom find it.[20] I have tried to point out the importance of the relation of the poem to other poems by other authors, and suggested the conception of poetry as a living whole of all the poetry that has ever been written. The other aspect of this Impersonal theory of poetry is the relation of the poem to its author. And I hinted, by an analogy, that the mind of the mature poet differs from that of the immature one not precisely in any valuation of "personality," not being necessarily more interesting, or having "more to say," but rather by being a more finely perfected medium in which special, or very varied, feelings are at liberty to enter into new combinations.[21]

The analogy was that of catalyst. When the two gases previously mentioned are mixed in the presence of a filament of platinum, they form sulphurous acid. This combination takes place only if the platinum is present; nevertheless the newly formed acid contains no trace of platinum, and the platinum itself is apparently unaffected; has remained inert, neutral, and unchanged.[22] The mind of the poet is the shred of platinum. It may partly or exclusively operate upon the experience of the man himself; but, the more perfect the artist, the more completely separate in him will be the man who suffers and the mind which creates;[23] the more perfectly will the mind digest and transmute the passions which are its material.

· · ·

It is not in his personal emotions, the emotions provoked by particular events in his life, that the poet is in any way remarkable or interesting. His particular emotions may be simple, or crude, or flat. The emotion in his poetry will be a very complex thing, but not with the complexity of the emotions of people who have very complex or unusual emotions in life. One error, in fact, of eccentricity in poetry is to seek for new human emotions to express; and in this search for novelty in the wrong place it discovers the perverse. The business of the poet is not to find new emotions, but to use the ordinary ones and, in working them up into poetry, to express feelings which are not in actual emotions at all. And emotions which he has never experienced will serve his turn as well as those familiar to him.

Consequently, we must believe that "emotion recollected in tranquility"[24] is an inexact formula. For it is neither emotion, nor recollection, nor, without distortion of meaning[25], tranquility. It is a concentration, and a new thing resulting from the concentration, of a very great number of experiences which to the practical and active person would not seem to be experiences at all; it is a concentration which does not happen consciously or of deliberation. These experiences are not "recollected," and they finally unite in an atmosphere which is "tranquil" only in that it is a passive attending upon the event. Of course this is not quite the whole story. There is a great deal, in the writing of poetry, which must be conscious and deliberate. In fact, the bad poet is usually unconscious where he ought to be conscious, and conscious where he ought to be unconscious. Both errors tend to make him "personal." Poetry is not a turning loose of emotion, but an escape from emotion; it is not the expression of personality, but an escape from personality.[26] But, of course, only those who have personality and emotions know what it means to want to escape from these things.

III

This essay proposes to halt at the frontier of metaphysics or mysticism, and confine itself to such practical conclusions as can be applied by the responsible person interested in poetry.[27] To divert interest from the poet to the poetry is a laudable aim: for it would conduce to a juster estimation of actual poetry, good and bad. There are many people who appreciate the expression of sincere emotion in verse, and there is a smaller number of people who can appreciate technical excellence. But very few know when there is an expression of *significant* emotion, emotion which has its life in the poem and not in the history of the poet. The emotion of art is impersonal. And the poet cannot reach this impersonality without surrendering himself wholly to the work to be done. And he is not likely to know what it is to be done unless he lives in what is not merely the present, but the present moment of the past, unless he is conscious, not of what is dead, but of what is already living.

注释

1. 大意为：以传统的名义叹惋它的消逝。

2. 大意为：如果"传统"一词不是用作指责之语，便表示一种含糊其辞的认可，暗指那部得到认可的作品具有复古的韵味。

3. is even more oblivious of：更容易忘记。

4. even plume ourselves a little：甚至有点沾沾自喜。

5. 大意为：如果坚守传统只意味着盲目地或胆怯地追随前辈的成功之处，那么，"传统"也的确不值得提倡了。

6. 大意为：历史意识使作家极为敏锐地意识到自己在文学史长河中的地位，在同时代人中的地位。

7. 结合上下文，这句话暗指，新的作品面世后，先前的作品将被重新定位。

8. form：模式。

9. conform：这里指适应传统。

10. 大意为：新的艺术作品只有适应传统，才具有个性；或者说，它若想彰显个性，就得适应传统，传统与个性在此不可分离。

11. an indiscriminate bolus：没有区别的一团东西。

12. supplement：弥补。

13. the most distinguished reputation：声名最为显赫的文学大家。

14. en route：在路上。

15. Magdalenian：马格德林时代的、欧洲旧石器时代后期的。后人在法国的马格德林山洞里发现了这一时期艺术家创作的壁画。

16. 大意为：这种发展，在心理学家看来，也许算不上是一种进步，或许没有我们想象得进步大；或许最终它只是经济与机械日趋复杂产生的后果而已。

17. 大意为：我意识到我为诗歌这一行当拟就的章程常常招致反对意见。

18. 大意为：反对意见认为，我提出的博学要求竟然达到了令人发笑的炫学地步，只要考究那些大诗人的生平，就有理由拒绝这个要求。

19. platinum：白金丝。sulphur dioxide：二氧化硫。

20. 大意为：如果我们不靠社会名人录，想找首好诗来欣赏，我们很难如愿。

21. 大意为：成熟诗人的心灵迥异于不成熟诗人的心灵，二者之间的区别不在于，哪一个更重视"个性"，也不在于哪一个更有趣，或者哪一个内容更丰富；二者之间的区别在于，前者是一个完美的媒介，通过它，各种特殊的、不同的情感得以自由地组合，形成新意。

22. 大意为：只有以白金丝为媒介，氧气和二氧化硫才会发生化学反应，生成硫酸；但是，在硫酸当中却没有白金的成分。在整个化学反应过程中，白金丝始终保持中性。

23. 大意为：艺术家越是完美，他个人的感受与他创造的思维就相距越远。

24. emotion recollected in tranquility：心情平静之际回忆起来的情感。语出华兹华斯《〈抒情歌谣集〉序》。

25. without distortion of meaning：如果不歪曲词义的话。

26. 大意为：诗不是放纵情感而是逃避情感，它不是表现个性而是逃避个性。

27. 大意为：本文不打算就诗进行玄妙无稽的探讨，只想得出一些切实可行的结论，供那些有鉴赏力的诗歌爱好者来使用。
这句话旨在强调，诗人必须具有强烈的历史意识，深刻地认识到当代事物背后的传统精神。

《〈实用批评〉导言》

艾弗·阿姆斯特朗·瑞恰慈（1893—1979）

艾弗·阿姆斯特朗·瑞恰慈，20世纪著名批评家、英语教育家，英美新批评的开山人物。早年毕业于剑桥大学克里夫顿和马格德琳学院。在20世纪20年代，剑桥大学初创英文系，瑞恰慈担任英国文学讲师。一反传统的英国文学教学模式，他的文学教学不涉作家生平和逸闻轶事，也不作大而无当的社会背景解说，转而强调作品自身在文学批评的重要性，注重作品的语言分析，为剑桥大学的文学研究带来了一场革命。这套文学批评方法被称为实用批评。后来经过他的学生威廉·燕卜荪（William Empson）和 F. R. 利维斯（F. R. Leavis）发扬光大，再加上美国新批评的部分更正，成为英语世界学院派批评的主导模式，直到60年代随着结构主义等新理论的兴起，才宣告失势，但影响弥足深远。

1929年，瑞恰慈来华游历，任教于北京清华大学。1931年移讲哈佛大学，专事语言学研究和英语教学，脱离文学研究。1944年任教授，1963年正式退休，1979年重返中国，四处讲学，推行其基础英语教学理念。因旧症复发，一病不起，回国后即去世。瑞恰慈也从事诗歌创作，有多部诗集问世，但他文名过盛，终不以诗名彰显于世。

其治学范围广，横跨多个学科，著述甚丰，主要有：与人合著的《美学原理》（*The Foundations of Aesthetics*, 1922）、与查尔斯·凯·奥格登（Charles Ogden）合著的《意义之意义》（*The Meaning of Meaning*, 1923）《文学批评原理》（*Principles of Literary Criticism*, 1924）、《科学与诗》（*Science and Poetry*, 1926）、《实用批评》（*Practical Criticism*, 1929）。

在其主要文学理论著作中，他试图将心理学和现代语义学引入文学批评，使文学批评变成一门准科学式的学科。为了强调文学作品的独立地位以及语言分析在文学批评中的重要作用，他对科学语言和文学语言进行了细致的区分。按照他的说法，科学语言是一种指称性陈述，主要功能在于指称客观事实，论证指称对象的是非与真伪。它必须准确对应客观，丝丝入扣，它的真实性在日常生活或科学实验中可以得到验证。文学语言并不像科学语言那样具有指称性，它主要发挥情感的功能。换句话说，它的目的是打动读者的情感，调动读者的想象；它表达的是作者对待事物的主观，可以无关于客观事实。例如，"白发三千丈"显然严重不符生活常识，它只是诗人情感的一种表述。不过，说文学语言与客观事实无关，并不等于说文学没有真实性可言。文学的真实性在于它的"可接受性"。他举例说，《鲁滨逊漂流记》（*Robinson Crusoe*）的真实性在于，它在读者那里产生了可接受性，即读者认为它真实可靠。这种可接受性完全是作品的叙事所造成的，而不是因为它吻合于笛福小说的人物原型——流放荒岛多年的那位水手——的亲身经历。

瑞恰慈的这种区分因过于极端而饱受诟病。我们知道，文学作品中的许多语言陈述是可以经过日常生活的证实的；也就是说，它们是符合客观事实的，这在虚实相生的历史小说中体现得尤为明显；而且，即以文学性最强的诗歌而论，它的许多语言也是来自于日常生活，例如，华兹华斯的诗歌。

内容提要

在瑞恰慈的全部理论与批评论著中，《实用批评：文学判断力研究》一书对新批评的影响最大。新批评派极力推崇它的语义学分析方法，而摈弃了它的心理主义倾向。这本书为英语文学的研究和教学带来了一种新的范式。

作者在序言当中申明，此书的主要目的是为分析诗歌提供一种新的技巧，有效地提高人们的文学辨别力和理解力，从而改进文学教学的方法。作者在剑桥执教过程中，曾做了一个著名的文学批评实验，实验时间长达9年之久。他从英国文学史上遴选若干诗作，隐去作者的姓名，印在小卷子上，发给学生，让他们任意评论。入选诗歌当中，既有名篇佳作，也有平庸之作。在它们的作者中，既有名家里手，也有无名之辈。除了极个别的情况，单凭原诗看不出作者是谁。受试者男女比例相当，他们多为英文系的在读本科生，也有其他专业的学生，只有少数是研究生。受试者对卷子上的诗歌进行了比较透彻的研究，大部分人都花了很大的工夫，认认真真地写出自己对这些诗歌的评论，表现出对诗歌很感兴趣。

　　然而，这些学生的评价结果却相当令人吃惊：相当一部分人对经典之作大加痛斥，却对一些庸劣之作赞誉有加。为了解释这一令人啼笑皆非的现象，瑞恰慈精思熟虑，总结出十点原因。原因之一是，受试者对诗歌文字意义的理解不够充分，从而误解了诗中的情感、基调和意图。原因之二是，受试者对诗的感受存在障碍，没有深切地体会到诗中的情感。原因之三是，对诗中意象（imagery）把握不准，一些受试者一门心思关注诗中的意象，甚至全凭意象来判定一首诗的价值；可是，一首诗在读者头脑中引发的生动形象（image），可能与诗人心中原有的形象并不相干。原因之四是，受试者在阅读过程中容易产生一些毫不相关的思维活动（mnemonic irrelevances），受试者个人生活中的场景或奇遇、他散漫无章的联想以及他对往事的回忆给他带来的情感震荡可能与诗毫无关系，这些因素误导了读者对诗的正确理解。原因之五是习惯性反应（stock responses）的干扰，受试者读诗之时很容易受到头脑中既有观点、即成见的影响；这样一来，他对诗的反应就与诗人原有的意图脱节。原因之六是滥情（sentimentality），受试者对诗的情感反应过度。原因之七与原因之六正好相反，是情感抑制（inhibition），读者对诗的反应不够敏感。原因之八是依附教条（doctrinal adhesions），读者喜欢从诗中发掘诗人对世界的看法和信条；然而，无论这些见解或信条是否具有真理性，它们都与该诗的文学价值没有关系。原因之九是，读者对诗歌手法存在很多先入之见（technical presuppositions）；如果读者仅从技巧的细节来评判一首诗，就是把手段置于目的之上，是本末倒置之举。原因之十是，读者受到文学批评的先入之见（general critical preconditions）影响太深，文学理论对诗的本质和价值的既有之见干扰了读者的阅读和理解。

Ivor Armstrong Richards (1893—1979)

INTRODUCTORY

I have set three aims before me in constructing this book. First, to introduce a new kind of documentation to those who are interested in the contemporary state of culture whether as critics, as philosophers, as teachers, as psychologists, or merely as curious persons. Secondly, to provide a new technique for those who wish to discover for themselves what they think and feel about poetry (and cognate matters) and why they should like or dislike it. Thirdly, to prepare the way for educational methods more efficient than those we use now in developing discrimination and the power to understand what we hear and read.

For the first purpose I have used copious quotations from material supplied to me as a Lecturer at Cambridge and elsewhere. For some years I have made the experiment of issuing printed sheets of poems—ranging in character from a poem by Shakespeare to a poem by Ella Wheeler Wilcox[1]— to audiences who were requested to comment freely in writing upon them. The authorship of the poems was not revealed, and with rare exceptions it was not recognized.

After a week's interval I would collect these comments, taking certain obvious precautions to preserve the anonymity of the commentators, since only through anonymity could complete liberty to express their genuine opinions be secured for the writers. Care was taken to refrain from influencing them either for or against any poem. Four poems were issued at a time in groupings indicated in the Appendix, in which the poems I am here using will be found. I would, as a rule, hint that the poems were perhaps a mixed lot, but that was the full extent of my interference. I lectured the following week partly upon the poems, but rather more upon the comments, or protocols, as I call them.

Much astonishment both for the protocol-writers and for the Lecturer ensued from this procedure. The opinions expressed were not arrived at lightly or from one reading of the poems only. As a measure of indirect suggestion, I asked each writer to record on his protocol the number of "readings" made of each poem. A number of perusals made at one session were to be counted together as one "reading" provided that they aroused and sustained on single growing response to the poem, or alternatively led to no response at all and left the reader with nothing but the bare words before him on the paper. This description of a "reading" was, I believe, well understood. It follows that readers who recorded as many as ten or dozen readings had devoted no little time and energy to their critical endeavor.[2] Few writers gave less than four attacks to any of the poems. On the whole it is fairly safe to assert that the poems received much more thorough study than, shall we say, most anthology pieces get in the ordinary course. It is from this thorougness, prompted by the desire to arrive at some definite expressible opinion, and from the week's leisure allowed that these protocols derive their significance.

The standing of the writers must be made clear. The majority were undergraduates reading English with a view to an Honors Degree.[3] A considerable number were reading other subjects but there is no ground to suppose that these differed for this reason in any essential respect. There was a sprinkling of graduates, and a few members of the audience were non-academic. Men and women were probably included in about equal numbers, so, in what follows "he" must constantly be read as equivalent to "he or she". There was no compulsion to return protocols. Those who took the trouble to write—about 60 percent—may be presumed to have been actuated by a more than ordinary keen interest in poetry. From such comparisons as I have been able to make with protocols supplied by audiences of other types, I see no reason whatever to think that a higher standard of critical discernment can easily be found under our present cultural conditions.[4] Doubtless, could the Royal Society of Literature or the Academic Committee of the English Association be impounded for purposes of experiment we might expect greater uniformity in the comments or at least in their style, and a more wary approach as regards some of the dangers of the test. But with regard to equally essential matters occasions for surprise might still occur. The precise conditions of this test are not duplicated in our everyday commerce with literature.[5] Even the reviewers of new verse have as a rule a considerable body of the author's work to judge by. And editorial complaints are frequent as to the difficulty of obtaining good reviewing. Editors themselves will not be the slowest to agree with me upon the difficulty of judging verse without a hint as to its provenance.[6]

Enough, for the moment, about the documentation of this book. My second aim is more ambitious and requires more explanation. It forms part of a general attempt to modify our procedure in certain forms of discussion. There are subjects—mathematics, physics and the descriptive science supply some of them—which can be discussed in terms of verifiable facts and precise hypotheses. There are other subjects—the concrete affairs of commerce, law, organization and police work—which can be handled by rules of thumb and generally accepted conventions. But in between is the vast *corpus*[7] of problems, assumptions, adumbrations, fictions, prejudices, tenets; the sphere of random beliefs and hopeful guesses; the whole world, in brief, of abstract opinions and disputation about matters of feeling.[8] To this world belongs everything about which civilized man cares most. I need only instance ethics, metaphysics, morals, religion, aesthetics, and the discussions surrounding liberty, nationality, justice, love, truth, faith and knowledge to make this plain. As a subject-matter for discussion, poetry is a central and typical denizen of this world. It is so both by its own nature and by the type of discussion with which it is traditionally associated. It serves, therefore, as an eminently suitable *bait* for anyone who wishes to trap the current opinions and responses in this middle field for the purpose of examining and comparing them, and with a view to advancing our knowledge of what may be called the natural history of human opinions and feelings.[9]

In part then this book is the record of a piece of field-work in comparative ideology[10]. But I hope, not only to present an instructive collection of contemporary opinions, presuppositions, theories, beliefs, responses and the rest, but also to make some suggestions towards a better control of these tricksy components of our lives. The way in which it is hoped to do this can be briefly indicated at this point.

There are two ways of interpreting all but a very few utterances.

Whenever we hear or read any not too nonsensical opinion, a tendency so strong and so automatic that it must have been formed along with our earliest speech-habits, leads us to consider *what seems to be said* rather than the *mental operations*[11] of the person who said it. If the speaker is a recognized and obvious liar this tendency is, of course, arrested.[12] We do then neglect what he has said and turn our attention instead to the motives or mechanisms that have caused him to say it. But ordinarily we at once try to consider the objects his words seem to stand for and not the mental goings-on that led him to use the words. We say that we "follow his thought" and mean, not that we have traced what happened in his mind, but merely that we have gone through a train of thinking that seems to end where he ended.[13] We are in fact so anxious to discover whether we agree or not with what is being said that we overlook the mind that says it, unless some very special circumstance calls us back.

Compare now the attitude to speech of the alienist[14] attempting to "follow" the ravings of mania or the dream maunderings of a neurotic. I do not suggest that we should treat one another altogether as "mental cases" but merely that for some subject-matters and some types of discussion the alienist's attitude, his direction of attention, his order or plan of interpretation, is far more fruitful, and would lead to better understanding on both sides of the discussion, than the usual method that our language habits force upon us. For normal minds are easier to "follow" than diseased minds, and even more can be learned by adopting the psychologist's attitude to ordinary speech-situations than by studying aberrations.

It is very strange that we have no simple verbal means by which to describe these two different kinds of "meaning". Some device as unmistakable as the "up" or "down" of a railway signal[15] ought to be available. But there is none. Clumsy and pedantic looking psychological periphrases have to be employed instead. I shall, however, try to use one piece of shorthand consistently. In handling the piles of material supplied by the protocols I shall keep the term "statement" for those utterances whose "meaning" in the sense of what they *say*, or purport to say, is the prime object of interest. I shall reserve the term "expression" for those utterances where it is the mental operations of the writers which are to be considered.

When the full range of this distinction is realized the study of criticism takes on a new significance. But the distinction is not easy to observe. Even the firmest resolution will be constantly broken down, so strong are our native language habits. When views that seem to conflict with our own pre-possessions are set before us, the impulse to refute, to combat or to reconstruct them, rather than to investigate them, is all but overwhelming. So the history of criticism, like the history of all the middle subjects alluded to above, is a history of dogmatism and argumentation rather than a history of research. And like all such histories the chief lesson to be learnt from it is the futility of all argumentation that precedes understanding. We cannot profitably attack any opinion until we have discovered what it expresses as well as what it states; and our present technique for investigating opinions must be admitted, for all these middle subjects, to be woefully inadequate.

Therefore, the second aim of this book is to improve this technique. We shall have before us several hundreds of opinions upon particular aspects of poetry, and the poems themselves to help us to examine them. We shall have the great advantage of being able to compare numbers of extremely different opinions upon the same point. We shall be able to study what may be called the same opinion in different stages of development as it comes from different minds. And further, we shall be able in many instances to see what happens to a given opinion, when it is applied to a different detail or a different poem.

The effect of all this is remarkable. When the first dizzy bewilderment has worn off, as it very soon does, it is as though we were strolling through and about a building that hitherto we were only able to see from one or two distant standpoints. We gain a much more intimate understanding both of the poem and of the opinions it provokes. Something like a plan of the most usual approaches can be sketched and we learn what to expect when a new object, a new poem, comes up for discussion.

It is as a step towards another training and technique in discussion that I would best like this book to be regarded. If we are to begin to understand half the opinions which appear in the protocols we shall need no little mental plasticity. And in the course of our comparisons, interpretations and extrapolations something like a plan of the ways in which the likely ambiguities of any given term or opinion-formula may radiate will make itself apparent. For the hope of a new technique in discussion lies in this: that the study of the ambiguities of one term assists in the elucidation of another. To trace the meanings of "sentimentality," "truth," "sincerity," or "meaning" itself, as these terms are used in criticism, can help us with other words in other topics. Ambiguity in fact is systematic; the separate senses that a word may have are related to one another, if not as strictly as the various aspects of a building, at least to a remarkable extent. Something comparable to a "perspective"[16] which will include and enable us to control and "place" the rival meanings that bewilder us in discussion and hide our minds from one another can be worked out. Perhaps every intelligence that has ever reflected upon this matter will agree that this may be so. Every one agrees but no one does any research into the matter, although this is an affair in which even the slightest step forward affects the whole frontier line of human thought and discussion. [17]

The indispensable instrument for this inquiry is psychology. I am anxious to meet as far as may be the objection that may be brought by some psychologists, and these the best, that the protocols do not supply enough evidence for us really to be able to make out the motives of the writers and that therefore the whole investigation is superficial. But the *beginning* of every research ought to be superficial, and to find something to investigate that is accessible and detachable is one of the chief difficulties of psychology. I believe the chief merit of the experiment here made is that it gives us this. Had I wished to plumb the depths of these writers' Unconscious, where I am quite willing to agree the real motives of their likings and dislikings would be found, I should have devised something like a branch of psychoanalytic technique for the purpose. But it was clear that little progress would be made if we attempted to drag too deep a plough. However, even as it is, enough strange material is turned up.

After these explanations the reader will be prepared to find little argumentation in these pages, but much analysis, much rather strenuous exercise in changing our ground and a good deal of rather intricate navigation. Navigation, in fact—the art of knowing where we are wherever, as mental travelers, we may go—is the main subject of the book. To discuss poetry and the ways in which it may be approached, appreciated and judged is, of course, its prime purpose. But poetry itself is a mode of communication. What it communicates and how it does so and the worth of what is communicated from the subject-matter of criticism. It follows that criticism itself is very largely, though not wholly, an exercise in navigation. It is all the more surprising then that no treatise on the art and science of intellectual and emotional navigation has yet been written; for logic, which might appear to cover part of this field, in actuality hardly touches it.[18]

That the one and only goal of all critical endeavors, of all interpretation, appreciation, exhortation, praise or abuse, is improvement in communication may seem an exaggeration.[19] But in practice it is so. The whole apparatus of critical rules and principles is a means to the attainment of finer, more precise, more discriminating communication. There is, it is true, a valuation side to criticism. When we have solved, completely, the communication problem, when we have got, perfectly, the experience, *the mental condition* relevant to the poem, we have still to judge it, still to decide upon its worth. But the later question nearly always settles itself; or rather, our own inmost nature and the nature of the world in which we live decide it for us. Our prime endeavor must be to get the relevant mental condition and then see what happens. If we cannot then decide whether it is good or bad, it is doubtful whether any principles, however refined and subtle, can help us much. Without the capacity to get the experience they cannot help us at all. This is still clearer if we consider the use of critical maxims in teaching. Value cannot be demonstrated except through the communication of what is valuable.

Critical principles, in fact, need wary handling. They can never be a substitute for discernment though they may assist us to avoid unnecessary blunders. There has hardly ever been a critical rule, principle or maxim which has not been for wise men a helpful guide but for fools a will-o'-the-wisp.[20] All the great watchwords of criticism from Aristotle's "Poetry is an imitation" down to the doctrine that "Poetry is expression," are ambiguous pointers that different people follow to very different destinations. Even the most sagacious critical principles may, as we shall see, become merely a cover for critical ineptitude; and the most trivial or baseless generalisation may really mask good and discerning judgment. Everything turns upon how the principles are applied.[21] It is to be feared that critical formulas, even the best, are responsible for more bad judgment than good, because it is far easier to forget their subtle sense and apply them crudely than to remember it and apply them finely.

The astonishing variety of human responses makes irksome any too systematic scheme for arranging these extracts. I wish to present a sufficient selection to bring the situation concretely before the reader, reserving to the chapters of Part III any serious attempt to clear up the various difficulties with which the protocol-writers have been struggling. I shall proceed poem by poem, allowing the internal drama latent in every clash of opinion, of taste or temperament to guide the arrangement. Not all the poems, needless to say, raise the same problems in equal measure. In most, some one outstanding difficulty, some special occasion for a division of minds, takes precedence.

It is convenient therefore to place here a somewhat arbitrary list of the principal difficulties that may be encountered by one reader or another in the presence of almost any poem. This list is suggested by a study of the protocols themselves, and drawn up in an order which proceeds from the simplest, infant's, obstacle to successful reading up to the most insidious, intangible and bewildering of critical problems.

If some of these difficulties seem so simple as to be hardly worth discussion, I would beg my reader who feels a temptation to despise them not to leap lightly to his decision. Part of my purpose is *documentation* and I am confident of showing that the simple difficulties are those that most need attention as they are those that in fact receive least.

We soon advance, however, to points on which more doubt may be felt—where controversy, more and less enlightened, still continues—and we finish face to face with questions which no one will pretend are yet settled and with some which will not be settled till the Day of Judgment[22]. In the memorable words of Benjamin Paul Blood[23], "What is concluded that we should conclude anything about it?"

The following seem to be the chief difficulties of criticism or, at least, those which we shall have most occasion to consider here: —

A. First must come the difficulty of *making out the plain sense* of poetry. The most disturbing and impressive fact brought out by this experiment is that a large proportion of average-to-good (and in some cases, certainly, devoted) readers of poetry frequently and repeatedly *fail to understand it*, both as a statement and as an expression. They fail to make out its prose sense, its plain, overt meaning, as a set of ordinary, intelligible, English sentences, taken quite apart from any further poetic significance.

And equally, they misapprehend its feeling, its tone, and its intention. They would travesty it in a paraphrase. They fail to construe it just as a schoolboy fails to construe a piece of Caesar. How serious in its effects in different instances this failure may be, we shall have to consider with care. It is not confined to one class of readers; not only those whom we would suspect fall victims. Nor is it only the most abstruse poetry which so betrays us. In fact, to settle down, for once, the brutal truth, no immunity is possessed on any occasion, not by the most reputable scholar, from this or any other of these critical dangers.

B. Parallel to, and not unconnected with, these difficulties of interpreting the meaning are the difficulties of *sensuous apprehension*. Words in sequence have a form to the mind's ear and the mind's tongue and larynx, even when silently read. They have a movement and may have a rhythm. The gulf is wide between a reader who naturally and immediately perceives this form and movement (by a conjunction of sensory, intellectual and emotional sagacity) and other reader, who either ignores it or has to build it up laboriously with finger-counting, table-tapping, and the rest; and this difference has most far-reaching effects.

C. Next may come those difficulties that are connected with the place of *imagery*, principally visual imagery, in poetic reading. They arise in part from the incurable fact that we differ immensely in our capacity to visualize, and to produce imagery of the other senses. Also the importance of our imagery as a whole, as well as of some pet particular type of image, in our mental lives varies surprisingly. Some minds can do nothing and get nowhere without images; others seem to be able to do everything and get anywhere, reach any and every state of thought and feeling without making use of them. Poets on the whole (though by no means all poet always) may be suspected of exceptional imaging capacity, and some readers are constitutionally prone to stress the place of imagery in reading, to pay great attention to it, and even to judge the value of the poetry by the images it excites in them. But images are erratic things; lively images aroused in one mind need have on similarity to the equally lively images stirred by the same line of poetry in another, and neither set need have anything to do with any images which may have existed in the poet's mind. Here is a troublesome source of critical deviations.

D. Thirdly, more obviously, we have to note the powerful very pervasive influence of *mnemonic irrelevances*. These are misleading effects of the reader's being reminded of some personal scene or adventure, erratic associations, the interference of emotional reverberations from a past which may have nothing to do with the poem. Relevance is not an easy notion to define or to apply, though some instances of irrelevant intrusions are among the simplest of all accidents to diagnose.

E. More puzzling and more interesting are the critical traps that surround what may be called *Stock Responses*. These have their opportunity whenever a poem seems to, or does, involve views and emotions already fully prepared in the reader's mind, so that what happens appears to be more of the reader's doing than the poet's. The button is pressed, and then the author's work is done, for immediately the record starts playing in quasi- (or total) independence of the poem which is supposed to be its origin or instrument.

Whenever this lamentable redistribution of the poet's and reader's share in the labor of poetry occurs, or is in danger of occurring, we require to be especially on our guard. Every kind of injustice may be committed as well by those who just escape as by those who are caught.

F. *Sentimentality* is a peril that needs less comment here. It is a question of the due measure of response. This over-facility in certain emotional directions is the Scylla whose Charybdis is—

G. *Inhibition*. This, as much as Sentimentality, is a positive phenomenon, though less studied until recent years and somewhat masked under the title of Hardness of Heart. But neither can well be considered in isolation.

H. Doctrinal Adhesions present another troublesome problem. Very much poetry—religious poetry may be instanced—seems to contain or imply views and beliefs, true or false, about the world. If this be so, what bearing has the truth-value of the views upon the worth of the poetry?

Even if it be not so, if the beliefs are not really contained or implied, but only seem so to a non-poetical reading, what should be the bearing of the reader's conviction, if any, upon his estimate of the poetry? Has poetry anything to say; if not, why not, and if so, how? Difficulties at this point are a fertile source of confusion and erratic judgment.

I. Passing now to a different order of difficulties, the effects of *technical presuppositions* have to be noted. When something has once been well done in a certain fashion we tend to expect similar things to be done in the future in the same fashion, and are disappointed or do not recognize them if they are done differently. Conversely, a technique which has shown its ineptitude for one purpose tends to become discredited for all. Both are cases of mistaking means for ends. Whenever we attempt to judge poetry from outside by technical details we are putting means before ends, and— such is our ignorance of cause and effect in poetry—we shall be lucky if we do not make even worse blunders. We have to try to avoid judging pianists by their hair.

J. Finally, *general critical preconceptions* (prior demands made upon poetry as a result of theories—conscious or unconscious—about its nature and value), intervene endlessly, as the history of criticism shows only too well, between the reader and the poem. Like an unlucky dietetic formula they may cut him off from what he is starving for, even when it is at his very lips.

These difficulties, as will have been observed, are not unconnected with one another and indeed overlap. They might have been collected under more heads or fewer. Yet, if we set aside certain extreme twists or trends of the personality (for example, blinding narcissism or groveling self-abasement— aberrations, temporary or permanent, of the self-regarding sentiment)[24] together with undue accumulations or depletions of energy, I believe that most of the principal obstacles and causes of failure in the reading and judgment of poetry may without much straining be brought under these ten heads. But they are too roughly sketched here for this to be judged.

More by good luck than by artful design, each poem, as a rule, proved an invitation to the mass of its readers to grapple with some *one* of the difficulties that have just been indicated.[25] Thus a certain sporting interest may be felt by the sagacious critic in divining where, in each case, the dividing line of opinion will fall, and upon what considerations it will turn.[26] No attempt will be made, in the survey which follows, to do more than shake out and air these variegated opinions. Elucidations, both of the poems and the opinions, will be for the most part postponed, as well as my endeavors to adjudicate upon the poetic worth of the unfortunate subjects of debate.

A very natural suspicion may fittingly be countered in this place. Certain doubts were occasionally expressed to me after a lecture that not all the protocol extracts were equally genuine. It was hinted that I might have myself composed some of those which came in most handily to illustrate a point. But none of the protocols have been tampered with and nothing has been added. I have even left the spelling and punctuation unchanged in all significant places.

But another falsification may perhaps be charged against me, falsification through bias in selection. Space, and respect for the reader's impatience, obviously forbade my printing the whole of my material. Selected extracts alone could be ventured. With a little cunning it would be possible to make selections that would give very different impressions. I can only say that I have been on my guard against unfairness. I ought to add perhaps that the part of the material least adequately represented is the havering, non-committal, vague, sit-on-the-fence, middle-body of opinion. I would have put in more of this if it were not such profitless reading.

注释

1. Ella Wheeler Wilcox: 威尔科克斯（1850—1919），美国女诗人，诗风浪漫伤感，好作香艳绮语。
2. 大意为：那些把一首诗读了十几遍的读者，在评论上花费了大量的时间和精力。
3. 大意为：这些受试者多为英文系中想获得优等荣誉学位的本科生。
4. 大意为：在当前的文化环境下，没有比这更高的批评判断标准。
5. 大意为：这次试验的条件是我们在日常文学阅读和评论活动中所没有

的。作者暗示说，试验条件苛刻，受试者在写评论的时候没有别的
作品可以依傍。

6. 大意为：编辑们会毫不犹豫地同意说，对于一首诗，如果不知道它的
出处，评论起来的确是一件难事。

7. the vast corpus of：一大堆。

8. 大意为：简而言之，这其中是就感性事物持有的抽象见解和争论不休
的领域。

9. this middle field：指的是上文提到的处于自然科学与商法政治之间的
领域，即文中所说的 "ethics, metaphysics, morals, religion, aesthetics,
and the discussions surrounding liberty, nationality, justice, love, truth,
faith and knowledge"。

10. ideology：指思想意识。

11. mental operation：具体的心理活动。

12. 大意为：如果发现说话人显然是在撒谎，我们当然会抑制这种倾向。

13. 大意为：当我们说我们追随他的想法，并不意味着我们完全按照他
的思路进行思考，而只是说，我们在经历一番思考后，与他的想法
殊途同归。

14. alienist：精神病学家。

15. "up" or "down" of a railway signal：铁路上的 "上行"、"下行" 信号。

16. perspective：透视法。

17. 大意为：尽管大家都同意，但没有人研究这个问题。在这件事情上，
哪怕取得一点点进步，都会改变人类思想和讨论的局面。

18. 大意为：逻辑学似乎与这个领域有一定的关系，但实际上几乎没有
触及它。

19. 大意为：一切批评活动，一切阐释、赏析、劝诫、褒贬，凡此种种，
它们的唯一目标是改进文学的表达方式，这么说似乎是在夸大其词。

20. 大意为：对于智者而言，文学批评的规则、原理或法则是一种有用
的指导；对于蠢汉而言，它们是虚无缥缈的东西。

21. 一切都取决于批评原理的具体应用。

22. Day of Judgment：世界末日。

23. Benjamin Paul Blood：布拉德（1832—1919），美国哲学家、诗人。

24. 大意为：如盲目自恋或自轻自贱——即，看待自己的情绪发生偏常，
这种偏常可能是一时的，也可能是一世的。

25. 大意为：与其说是设计巧妙，不如说是凭运气，每首诗都需要读者

去克服上文提到的某个困难。

26. 大意为：目光深邃的批评家会感觉一种运动的兴致，去推测见解的分水岭在哪儿，以及什么情况下这个分水岭会变。

<table>
<tr><td>利维斯</td><td>《〈艰难时世〉：分析札记》</td></tr>
</table>

弗兰克·雷蒙德·利维斯（1895—1978）

一讲到英美形式主义文论，就很容易把 F. R. 利维斯的细绎式批评与美国的新批评相提并论，仿佛它们是大西洋两岸的一对孪生兄弟。利维斯的文学批评，无论是诗歌批评，还是小说批评，都注重文本的细读，突出语言的感受；但是，正如论者所言，他的批评思想中有明显的社会学倾向。另外，他在批评实践中，经常将具体文本放在它们所在的文学传统中去加以解说，而非就事论事，孤立地看待个别文本。在他看来，批评家在分析具体作品的过程中，要尽可能地留意一些细节，再参照其他类似作品来判断其价值高下。这种从文学史长河中淘沙沥金的做法，就视野与格局而论，远比美国新批评宏阔高远。利维斯深受马修·阿诺德所谓文学即生活批评一说的启发与影响，有意将文学阅读与社会生活联系起来，要求文学必须坚守道德价值观，必须促进社会文化的健康。这是他文学批评和教学的核心信条，与美国新批评的精神主旨也相距甚远。

利维斯 1895 年出生在剑桥镇的一个自行车商店主家庭，他一生中的大部分时光都在剑桥度过。他先是在剑桥大学学历史，后来转行读英文。在 20 世纪 20 年代，瑞恰慈在剑桥英文系革新文学教学，大讲其"实用批评"，利维斯也参加了这场著名的文学试验。利维斯于 1924 年获得博士学位，论文题目为《报刊业与文学之关系》（"The Relationship of Journalism to Literature: Studies in the Rise and Earlier Development of the Press in England"）。从 1927 年到 1931 年，利维斯在剑桥大学任见习讲师，讲授英国文学。在此期间，他开始为《剑桥评论》（Cambridge Review）撰写书评；但是，他的精力主要用于教学。1929 年，他娶了自己的学生、剑桥才女奎尼·多萝西·罗斯（Queenie Dorothy Roth）。此后夫唱妇随，开始了长达 50 年之久的文学研究合作生涯。利维斯夫人未有教职，著作仅有一本《小说与阅读公众》（Fiction and Reading Public），文章数量也寥寥可数。她把自己的精力和时间用来持家和协助利维斯办《细绎》（Scrutiny）。1936 年，利维斯始任剑桥大学唐宁学院的院士，1937 年至 1960 年任唐宁学院讲师，1960 年至 1962 年任高级讲师（Reader），退休后赴英美多所大学任客座教授。

利维斯的文学与文化观念深受马修·阿诺德和 T. S. 艾略特的影响。在 20 世纪 30 年代出版的小册子《大众文明和少数派文化》（*Mass Civilization and Minority Culture*）和《文化与环境》（*Culture and Environment*）中，利维斯认为，在 19 世纪之前，尤其在 17 世纪之前，处在农业时代的英国存在着一种生机勃勃的共同文化。这是社会各个阶层共享的文化，莎士比亚的戏剧即为显例。它既能为宫廷权贵所激赏，又能为社会底层所喜闻乐见。然而，随着工业的出现和商业的发展，这种共同的文化走向解体，一分为二：一边是少数品味高雅之士欣赏的文化，它主要体现在伟大的文学巨著；另一边是大众化文明，即广告、报纸、收音机、电影、小报、流行小说等文化产品，其消费主力是略识之无的草根大众。在这两本小册子以及后来出版的《教育与大学》（*Education and University*, 1943）当中，利维斯一再呼吁，那些情趣高雅、精于赏鉴之士承担重任，挽救文化危亡，守护传统的精华，以匡正世风。这些人的数量非常有限，而文学教学的任务就是培养一批这类具有文学心灵（literary mind）的精英，以抗衡科学技术和大众文化对传统文化的威胁。

利维斯的文学研究以诗歌批评和小说批评为主。他的诗论深受 T. S. 艾略特的影响。因此，有学者称，就某种程度而言，他的诗歌批评是艾略特诗学理论的具体阐述和应用。相比之下，他的小说研究更见独创性。他最有代表性的诗歌研究是两部评论文集：1932 年出版的《英诗新方向》（*New Bearings in English Poetry*）和 1936 年出版的《再评价》（*Revaluation*）。前者以艾略特、霍普金斯、叶芝和庞德为研究对象，旨在展示现代诗歌的新成就，同时攻击丁尼生和史文朋的诗风；后者论述内容为，上自莎士比亚时代下至 19 世纪初英国诗歌的演变。它与《英诗新方向》恰成双璧，记录了英国诗歌的流变经过。利维斯小说研究的代表作是 1948 年出版的《伟大的传统》（*The Great Tradition*），虽说颇有争议，这本书还是英国小说研究中不可回避的著作。在书中，他把以前仅用于诗歌和戏剧诗研究的细读式分析应用到长篇小说研究当中。除了本书之外，其他重要的小说研究著作还有《小说家劳伦斯》（*D. H. Lawrence: Novelist*, 1955）和《小说家狄更斯》（*Dickens the Novelist*, 1970）等。

从 1932 年到 1953 年，利维斯主编文学评论季刊《细绎》，形成了一个以他为核心的英国学院式文学批评流派——细绎派。30 年代以来，细绎派就一直以剑桥大学为大本营和文学批评试验场，这一传统如今已是根深蒂固。总的说来，细绎派自命为英国文学研究道统的维护者，注重形式分析，反对文学批评过多地掺杂历史和社会的考量。他们视经典文学为文学研究的正统，以它为改变世道人心的利器；对于战后兴起的流行文化，则视其为文化水准堕落的表征，腐蚀心灵的渊薮，一概予以否认和抹杀，故受文化保守主义之讥。在新左派学者看来，这种文学观背后隐藏的精英主义文化观未免乡曲狭隘，兼具人文主义的狂妄自大，甚至有意识形态共谋的嫌疑。当然，细绎派的出现和得势也是有它的合理性的。撇开作品的历史语境，远离作品背后的观念结构，去揣摩具体段落和语句中的语气和感受，再去微言大义，细致申说——细绎派的这种批评方式自有其纠偏对象，那就是一战之前英国大学所盛行的传记式批评。那种批评热衷于作家的生活轶事，很少具体论述作品的风格与结构，显得散漫松弛，缺乏严谨性。细绎派与此针锋相对，力主回到作品本身，让文学批评摆脱散漫的业余作风，成为一门严谨的、类似于科学的学科。在当时的背景下，细绎派的主张是有见识和道理的；否则，它也不会大受追捧，迅速跻身于文学批评的正统。

因为人际关系的缘故，利维斯在他所钟爱的剑桥大学屡遭排挤；可他的批评方法却成为剑桥英文系的官方传统，成为后世文学研究者的无意识的一部分。

内容提要

随着英国资本主义的迅速发展，资产阶级的散文体史诗——长篇小说——在18世纪异军突起，大家巨匠纷纭辈出。从开山鼻祖亨利·菲尔丁到现代主义集大成者 D. H. 劳伦斯，在众多名家作手当中，利维斯只找出五个人作为英国小说伟大传统的代表，他们是简·奥斯汀、乔治·艾略特、亨利·詹姆斯、约瑟夫·康拉德（Joseph Conrad）和 D. H. 劳伦斯。利维斯的理由是，这五位小说大家不仅让小说这门艺术生发出新意，从而更新了作家和读者对它的固有看法，他们还推动了人们探索生活的潜能。道德与生活（或人生）是利维斯在小说批评中最常使用的概念，也是他评价小说高下的最重要的标准。这几位小说家之所以跻身于经典大家行列，正是因为他们的作品中体现了强烈的道德关怀，表现出对生活的虔敬热爱。他们在形式和技巧方面进行的形式创新，都是严肃的道德热诚和深切的生活关怀所造就的。

家喻户晓的狄更斯被排除在这个伟大的传统之外，这不能不让人疑窦丛生: 在狄更斯作品中，悲天悯人的情怀是何等令人印象深刻，难道这不是强烈的道德关怀? 他对当时社会生活各方面的描述是何等逼真，难道这不是忠实于生活? 面对这些可能出现的质疑之声，利维斯的解释是，狄更斯固然是天才人物，但是，纵观他的全部作品，却很难找到一种一以贯之的严肃性: 他是娱乐性的天才。在他的所有小说中，只有《艰难时世》是例外。书中没有狄更斯其他小说中那种没完没了的夸张渲染，也没有无所不包、芜杂凌乱的内容，它具有一种臻于完美的严肃性。正因为这个原因，利维斯在《伟大的传统》的最后一章对该小说进行了细致解读。

狄更斯在他的许多小说中都在批评维多利亚时代的社会现象;但是，在其他作品中，狄更斯的批评往往是就事论事，针对具体弊端大为光火，然后了事。唯有在《艰难时世》之中，他的批评展现出一种广阔的思想视野。他敏锐地认识到，维多利亚时代的种种残酷现实肇始于当时整个社会上通行的功利主义哲学。这套高度理性化、精于算计的哲学，毫无理想的成分可言;它最讲求的是实效，一旦实行起来，丝毫不顾及道德后果。小说中的重要角色焦炭镇议员、乡绅汤玛士·葛擂硬即是这种哲学的化身。他是功利主义哲学的虔诚信奉者，实践起来一丝不苟。他严格遵照它来培养子女、教育学生和处理家庭事务。另一位功利主义哲学的化身是资本家约瑟亚·庞得贝。此人是维多利亚时代最为粗鄙的个人主义的代表，市侩气息十足，既无理想可言，也无精神追求，专以聚敛为能事，而且不择手段。与这种人为造就、阴冷残酷的理性相对立的是一种天然自发、充满温情的人性，它集中体现在西丝·朱浦身上。西丝出身马戏团，父亲离家出走，下落不明，遂为葛擂硬所收养。她是善良和活力的象征，她与葛擂硬学校培养出的"好学生"毕周形成了鲜明对比。后者工于心计、虚伪至极，为了一己私利不择手段。西丝出身的马戏团象征着人性之善和生机活力，与葛擂硬学校的冷酷无情和拘泥教条形成鲜明对照。葛擂硬的教育成就——按照他的功利主义培养方案长大的儿子，干涉公司财务，受到警方的追捕。他之所以能够逃脱法律的制裁，靠的是马戏演员史里锐的帮忙，史里锐此举正是为了报答葛擂硬领养西丝的恩情。在一系列失败案例的面前，葛擂硬反躬自省，终于认识到功利主义哲学的虚妄。

利维斯总结说，《艰难时世》的一大特点是，它表现的生活具有无比的丰富性，这种丰富性源于狄更斯非凡的感受力和表达力。狄更斯对生活有着异常敏锐的感受力，他能够在肮脏丑恶当中看到人性的美和善。论语言之丰富，狄更斯足以比肩莎士比亚；他那些精彩绝伦、丰富多彩的语句，源于他对生活的那种异常发达的敏感。

Frank Raymond Leavis (1895—1978)

CHAPTER 5

HARD TIMES

An Analytic Note

HARD TIMES is not a difficult work; its intention and nature are pretty obvious. If, then, it is the masterpiece I take it for, why has it not had general recognition? To judge by the critical record, it has had none at all. If there exists anywhere an appreciation, or even an acclaiming reference, I have missed it. In the books and essays on Dickens, so far as I know them, it is passed over as a very minor thing; too slight and insiginificant to distract us for more than a sentence or two from the works worth critical attention. Yet, if I am right, of all Dickens's works it is the one that has all the strength of his genius, together with a strength no other of them can show—that of a completely serious work of art.

The answer to the question asked above seems to me to bear on[1] the traditional approach to "the English novel." For all the more sophisticated critical currency of the last decade or two, that approach still prevails, at any rate in the appreciation of the Victorian novelists. The business of the novelists, you gather, is to "create a world," and the mark of the master is external abundance—he gives you lots of "life." The test of life in his characters (he must above all create "living" characters) is that they go on living outside the book. Expectations as unexacting as these are not, when they encounter significance, grateful for it, and when it meets them in that insistent form where nothing is very engaging as "life" unless its relevance is fully taken, miss it altogether.[2] This is the only way in which I can account for the neglect suffered by Henry James's[3] *The Europeans*, which may be classed with *Hard Times* as a moral fable—though one might have supposed that James would enjoy the advantage of being approached with expectations of subtlety and closely calculated relevance. Fashion, however, has not recommended his earlier work, and this (whatever appreciation may be enjoyed by *The Ambassadors*) still suffers from the prevailing expectation of redundant and irrelevant "life".

I need say no more by way of defining the moral fable than that in it the intention is peculiarly insistent[4], so that the representative significance of everything in the fable—character, episode, and so on—is immediately apparent as we read. Intention might seem to be insistent in Dickens, without its being taken up in any inclusive significance that informs and organizes a coherent whole; and, for lack of any expectation of an organized whole, it has no doubt been supposed that in *Hard Times* the satiric irony of the first two chapters is merely, in the large and genial Dickensian way, thrown together with melodrama, pathos, and humor—and that we are given these ingredients more abundantly and exuberantly elsewhere. Actually, the Dickensian vitality is there, in its varied characteristic modes, which have the more force because they are free of redundance: the creative exuberance is controlled by a profound inspiration.

The inspiration is what is given in the grim clinch of the title, *Hard Times*. Ordinarily Dickens's criticisms of the world he lives in are casual and incidental—a matter of including among the ingredients of a book som indignant treatment of a particular abuse. But in *Hard Times* he is for once possessed by a comprehensive vision, one in which the inhumanities of Victorian civilization are seen as fostered and sanctioned by a hard philosophy, the aggressive formulation of an inhuman spirit.[5] The philosophy is represented by Thomas Gradgrind, Esquire, Member of Parliament for Coketown, who has brought up his children on the lines of the experiment recorded by John Stuart Mill[6] as carried out on himself. What Gradgrind stands for is, though repellent, nevertheless respectable; his Utilitarianism is a theory sincerely held and there is the intellectual disinterestedness in its application. But Gradgrind marries his eldest daughter to Josiah Bounderby, "banker, merchant, manufacturer," about whom there is no disinterestedness whatver, and nothing to be respected. Bounderby is Victorian "rugged individualism" in its grossest and most intransigent form. Concerned with nothing but self-assertion and power, and material success, he has no interest in ideals or ideas—except the idea of being the completely self-made man (since, for all his brag, he is not that in fact)[7]. Dickens here makes a just observation about the affinities and practical tendency of Utilitarianism, as, in his presentment of the Gradgrind home and the Gradgrind elementary school, he does about the Utilitarian spirit in Victorian education.

All this is obvious enough. But Dickens's art, while remaining that of the great popular entertainer, has in *Hard Times*, as he renders his full critical vision, a stamina, a flexibility combined with consistency, and a depth that he seems to have had little credit for. Take that opening scene in the school-room:

> "Girl number twenty," said Mr. Gradgrind, squarely pointing with his square forefinger, "I don't know that girl. Who is that girl?"
>
> "Sissy Jupe, sir," explained number twenty, blushing, standing up, and curtsying.
>
> "Sissy is not a name," said Mr. Gradgrind. "Don't call yourself Sissy. Call yourself Cecilia."
>
> "It's father as call me Sissy, sir." returned the young girl in a trembling voice, and with another curtsy.
>
> "Then he has no business to do it," said Mr. Gradgrind. "Tell him he mustn't. Cecilia Jupe. Let me see. What is your father?"
>
> "He belongs to the horse-riding, if you please, sir."
>
> Mr. Gradgrind frowned, and waved off the objctional calling with his hand.
>
> "We don't want to know anything about that here. You mustn't tell us about that here. Your father breaks horses, don't he?"
>
> "If you please, sir, when they can get any to break, they do break horses in the ring, sir."
>
> "You mustn't tell us about the ring here. Very well, then. Describe your father as a horse-breaker. He doctors sick horses, I dare say?"
>
> "Oh, yes, sir!"
>
> "Very well, then. He is a veterinary surgeon, a farrier, and a horse-breaker. Give me your definition of a horse."
>
> (Sissy Jupe thrown into the greatest alarm by this demand.)
>
> "Girl number twenty unable to define a horse!" said Mr. Gradgrind, for the general benefit of all the little pitchers. "Girl number twenty

possessed of no facts in reference to one of the commonest animals! Some boy's definition of a horse. Bitzer, yours."...

"Quadruped. Graminivorous. Forty teeth, namely, twenty-four grinders, four eye-teeth, and twelve incisive. Sheds coat in the spring; in marshy countries, sheds hoofs too. Hoofs hard, but requiring to be shod with iron. Age known by marks in mouth." Thus (and much more) Bitzer.

Lawrence[8] himself, protesting against harmful tendencies in education, never made the point more tellingly. Sissy has been brought up among horses, and among people whose livelihood depends upon understanding horses but "we don't want to know anthing about that here." Such knowledge isn't real knowledge. Bitzer, the model pupil, on the button's being pressed, promptly vomits up the genuine article, "Quadruped. Graminivorous," etc.; and "Now, girl number twenty, you know what a horse is." The irony, pungent enough locally, is richly developed in the subsequent action. Bitzer's aptness has its evaluative comment in his career. Sissy's incapacity to acquire this kind of "fact" or formula, her unaptness for education, is manifested to us, on the other hand, as part and parcel of her sovereign and indefeasible humanity: it is the virtue that makes it impossible for her to understand, or acquiesce in, an ethos for which she is "girl number twenty," or to think of any other human being as a unit for arithmetic[9].

This kind of ironic method might seem to commit the author to very limited kinds of effect.[10] In *Hard Times*, however, it associates quite congruously, such is the flexibility of Dickens's art, with very different methods; it cooperates in a truly dramatic and profoundly poetic whole. Sissy Jupe, who might be taken here for a merely conventional *persona*, has already, as a matter of fact, been established in a potently symbolic role: she is part of the poetically-creative operation of Dickens's genius in *Hard Times*. Here is a passage I omitted from the middle of the excerpt quoted above.

The square finger, moving here and there, lighted suddenly on Bitzer, perhaps because he chanced to sit in the same ray of sun-light which, darting in at one of the bare windows of the intensely whitewashed room, irradiated Sissy. For the boys and girls sat on the face of an inclined plane in two compact bodies, divided up the center by a narrow interval;

and Sissy, being at the corner of a row on the sunny side, came in for the beginning of a sunbeam, of which Bitzer, being at the corner of a row on the other side, a few rows in advance, caught the end. But, whereas the girl was so dark-eyed and dark-haired that she seemed to receive a deeper and more lustrous color from the sun when it shone upon her, the boy was so light-eyed and light-haired that the self-same rays appeared to draw out of him what little color he ever possessed. His cold eyes would hardly have been eyes, but for the short ends of lashes which by bringing them into immediate contrast with something paler than themselves, expressed their form. His short-cropped hair might have been a mere continuation of the sandy freckles on his forehead and face. His skin was so unwholesomely deficient in the natural tinge, that he looked as though, if he were cut, he would bleed white.

There is no need to insist on the force—representative of Dickens's art in general in *Hard Times*—with which the moral and spiritual differences are rendered here in terms of sensation,[11] so that the symbolic intention emerges out of metaphor and the vivid evocation of the concrete. What may, perhaps, be emphasized is that Sissy stands for vitality as well as goodness—they are seen, in fact, as one; she is generous, impulsive life, finding self-fulfilment in self-forgetfulness—all that is the antithesis of calculating self-interest. There is an essentially Laurentian[12] suggestion about the way in which 'the dark-eyed and dark-haired' girl, contrasting with Bitzer, seemed to receive a "deeper and more lustrous color from the sun," so opposing the life that is lived freely and richly from the deep instinctive and emotional springs to the thin-blooded, quasi-mechanical product of Gradgrindery.

Sissy's symbolic significance is bound up with that of Sleary's Horse-riding where human kindness is very insistently associated with vitality.

The way in which the Horse-riding takes on its significance illustrates beautifully the poetic-dramatic nature of Dickens's art. From the utilitarian schoolroom Mr. Gradgrind walks towards his utilitarian abode, Stone Lodge, which, as Dickens evokes it, brings home to us concretely the model regime that for the little Gradgrinds (among whom are Malthus and Adam Smith) is an inescapble prison. But before he gets there he passes the back of a circus booth, and is pulled up by the sight of two palpable offenders.[13] Looking more closely, "What did he behold but his own metallurgical Louisa peeping through a hole in a deal board, and his own mathematical Thomas abasing himself on the ground to catch but a hoof of the grateful equestrian Tyrolean flower act!" The chapter is called "A Loophole," and Thomas "gave himself up to be taken home like a machine."

Representing human spontaneity, the circus-athletes represent at the same time highly-developed skill and deftness of kinds that bring poise, pride, and confident ease—they are always buoyant, and ballet-dancer-like, in training:

> There were two or there handsome young women among them, with two or three husbands, and their two or three mothers, and their eight or nine little children, who did the fairy business when required. The father of one of the families was in the habit of balancing the father of another of the families on the top of a great pole; the father of the third family often made a pyramid of both those fathers, with Master Kidderminster for the apex, and himself for the base; all the fathers could dance upon rolling casks, stand upon bottles, catch knives and balls, twirl hand-basins, ride upon anything, jump over everything, and stick at nothing. All the mothers could (and did) dance upon the slack wire and the tight-rope, and perform rapid acts on bare-backed steeds; none of them were at all particular in respect of showing their legs; and none of them were at all particular in respect of showing their legs; and one of them, alone in a Greek chariot, drove six-in-hand into every town they came to. They all assumed to be mighty rakish and knowing, they were not very tidy in their private dresses, they were not at all orderly in their domestic arrangements, and the combined literature of the whole company would have produced but a poor letter on any subject. Yet there was a remarkable gentleness and childishness about these people, a spcial inaptitude for any kind of sharp practice, and an untiring readiness to help and pity one another, deserving often of as much respect, and always of as much generous construction, as the every-day virtues of any class of people in the world.

Their skills have no value for the Utilitarian calculus, but they express vital human impulse, and they minister to vital human needs. The Horse-riding, frowned upon as frivolous and wasteful by Gradgrind and malignantly scorned by Bounderby, brings the machine-hands of Coketown (the spirit-quenching hideousness of which is hauntingly evoked) what they are starved of. It brings to them, not merely amusement, but art, and the spectale of triumphant activity that, seeming to contain its end within itself, is, in its easy mastery, joyously self-justified. In investing a traveling circus with this kind of symbolic value Dickens expresses a profounder reaction to industrialism than might have been expected of him. It is not only pleasure and relaxation the Coketowners stand in need of; he feels the dreadful degradation of life that would remain even if they were to be given a forty-four-hour week, comfort, security, and fun.

· · ·

Here an objection may be anticipated—as a way of making a point. Coketown, like Gradgrind and Bounderby, is real enough; but it can't be contended that the Horse-riding is real in the same sense. There would have been some athletic skill and perhaps some bodily grace among the people of a Victorian traveling circus, but surely so much squalor, grossness, and vulgarity that we must find Dickens's symbolism sentimentally false? And "there was a remarkable gentleness and childishness about these people, a special inaptitude for any kind of sharp practice"—that, surely, is going ludicrously too far?

If Dickens, intent on an emotional effect, or drunk with moral enthusiasm, had been deceiving himself (it couldn't have been innocently) about the nature of the actuality, he would then indeed have been guilty of sentimental falsity, and the adverse criticism would have held. But the Horse-riding presents no such case. The virtues and qualities that Dickens prizes do indeed exists, and it is necessary for his critique of Utilitarianism and industrialism, and for (what is the same thing) his cretaive purpose, to evoke them vividly. The book can't, in my judgment, be fairly charged with giving a misleading representation of human nature. And it would plainly not be intelligent criticism to suggest that anyone could be misled about the nature of circuses by *Hard Times*. The critical question is merely one of tact: was it well-judged of Dickens to try to do *that*—which had to be done somehow—with a traveling circus?

Or, rather, the question is: by what means has he succeeded? For the success is complete. It is conditioned partly by the fact that, from the opening chapters, we have been tuned for the reception of a highly conventional art—though it is a tuning that has no narrowly limiting effect. To describe at all cogently the means by which this responsiveness is set up would take a good deal of "practical criticism" analysis—analysis that would reveal an extraordinary flexibility in the art of *Hard Times*. This can be seen very obviously in the dialogue. Some passages might come from an ordinary novel. Others have the ironic pointedness of the school-room scene in so insistent a form that we might be reading a work as stylized as Jonsonian comedy[14]: Gradgrind's final exchange with Bitzer (quoted below) is a supreme instance. Others again are "literary", like the conversation between Gradgrind and Louisa on her flight home for refuge from Mr. James Harthouse's attentions.

To the question how the reconciling is done—there is much more diversity in *Hard Times* than these references to dialogue suggest—the answer can be given by pointing to the astonishing and irresistible richness of life that characterizes the book everywhere. It meets us everywhere, unstrained and natural, in the prose. Out of such prose a great variety of presentations can arise congenially with equal vividness. There they are, unquestionably "real." It goes back to an extraordinary energy of perception and registration in Dickens. "When people say that Dickens exaggerates" says Santayana[15], "it seems to me that they can have no eyes and no ears. They probably only have *notions* of what things and people are; they accept them conventionally, at their diplomatic value."[16] Setting down as we read to an implicit recognition of this truth, we don't readily and confidently apply any criterion we suppose ourselves to hold for distinguishing varieties of relation between what Dickens gives us and a normal "real." His flexibility is that of a richly poetic art of the world. He doesn't write "poetic prose;" he writes with a poetic force of evocation, registering with the responsiveness of a genius of verbal expression what he so sharply sees and feels. In fact, by texture, imaginative mode, symbolic method, and the resulting concentration,

Hard Times affects us as belonging with formally poetic works.

There is, however, more to be said about the success that attends Dickens's symbolic intention of the Horse-riding; there is an essential quality of his genius to be emphasized. There is no Hamlet in him, and he is quite unlike Mr. Eliot[17].

> The red-eyed scavengers are creeping
> From Kentish Town and Golders Green

—there is nothing of that in Dickens's reaction to life. He observes with gusto the humanness of humanity as exhibited in the urban (and suburban) scene. When he sees, as he sees so readily, the common manifestations of human kindness, and the essential virtues, asserting themselves in the midst of ugliness, squalor, and banality, his warmly sympathetic response has no disgust to overcome. There is no suggestion, for instance, of recoil—or of distance-keeping—from the game-eyed, brandy-soaked, flabby-surfaced Mr. Sleary, who is successfully made to figure for us a humane, anti-Utilitarian positive. This is not sentimentality in Dickens, but genius, and a genius that should be found peculiarly worth attention in an age when, as D. H. Lawrence (with, as I remember, Wyndham Lewis[18] immediately in view) says, "My God! they stink" tends to be an insuperable and final reaction.

Dickens, as everyone knows, is very capable of sentimentality. We have it in *Hard Times* (though not to any seriously damaging effect) in Stephen Blackpool, the good, victimized working-man, whose perfect patience under infliction we are expected to find supremely edifying and irresistibly touching as the agonies are piled on for his martyrdom. But Sissy Jupe is another matter. A general description of her part in the fable might suggest the worst, but actually she has nothing in common with Little Nell: she shares in the strength of the Horse-riding. She is wholly convincing in the function Dickens assigns to her. The working of her influence in the Utilitarian home is conveyed with a fine tact, and we do really feel her as a growing potency. Dickens can even, with complete success, give her the stage for a victorious tête-à-tête[19] with the well-bred and languid elegant, Mr. James Harthouse, in which she tells him that his duty is to leave Coketown and cease troubling Lousia with his attentions:

> She was not afraid of him, or in any way disconcerted; she seemed
> to have her mind entirely preoccupied with the occasion of her visit, and
> to have substituted that consideration for herself.

The quiet victory of disinterested goodness is wholly convincing.

At the opening of the book Sissy establishes the essential distinction between Gradgrind and Bounderby.[20] Gradgrind, by taking her home, however ungraciously, shows himself capable of humane feeling, however unacknowledged. We are reminded, in the previous school-room scene, of the Jonsonian affinities of Dickens's art, and Bounderby turns out to be consistently a Jonsonian character in the sense that he is incapable of change.[21] He remains the blustering egotist and braggart and responds in character to the collapse of his marriage:

> "I'll give *you* to understand, in reply to that, that there unquestionably
> is an incompatibility of the first magnitude—to be summed up in this—
> that your daughter don't properly know her husband's merits, and is not
> impressed with such a sense as would become her, by George! of the
> honor of his alliance. That's plain speaking, I hope."

He remains Jonsonianly consistent in his last testament and death. But Gradgrind, in the nature of the fable, has to *experience* the confutation of his philosophy, and to be capable of the change involved in admitting that life has proved him wrong. (Dickens's art in *Hard Times* differs from Ben Jonson's not in being inconsistent, but in being so very much more flexible and inclusive—a point that seemed to be worth making because the relation between Dickens and Jonson has been stressed of late, and I have known unfair conclusions to be drawn from the comparison, notably in rspect of *Hard Times*.)

The confutation of Utilitarianism by life is conducted with great subtlety. That the conditions for it are there in Mr. Gradgrind he betrays by his initial kindness, ungenial enough, but properly rebuked by Bounderby, to Sissy.[22] "Mr. Gradgrind," we are told, "though hard enough, was by no means so rough a man as Mr. Bounderby. His character was not unkind, all things considered; it might have been very kind indeed if only he had made some mistake in the arithmetic that balanced it years ago." The inadequacy of the calculus is beautifully exposed when he brings it to bear on the problem of marriage in the consummate scene with his eldest daughter:

> He waited, as if he would have been glad that she said something. But she said never a word.
>
> "Louisa, my dear, you are the subject of a proposal of marriage that has been made to me."
>
> Again he waited, and again she answered not one word. This so far surprised him as to induce him gently to repeat, "A proposal of marriage, my dear." To which she returned, without any visible emotion whatever:
>
> "I hear you, father. I am attending, I assure you."
>
> "Well!" said Mr. Gradgrind, breaking into a smile, after being for the moment at a loss, "you are even more dispassionate than I expected, Louisa. Or, perhaps, you are not unprepared for the announcement I have it in charge to make?"
>
> "I cannot say that, father, until I hear it. Prepared or unprepared, I wish to hear it all from you. I wish to hear you state it to me, father."
>
> Strange to relate, Mr. Gradgrind was not so collected at this moment as his daughter was. He took a paper knife in his hand, turned it over, laid it down, took it up again, and even then had to look along the blade of it, considering how to go on.
>
> "What you say, my dear Louisa, is perfectly reasonable. I have undertaken, then, to let you know that—in short, that Mr. Bounderby..."

His embarrassment—by his own avowal—is caused by the perfect rationality with which she receives his overture. He is still more disconcerted when, with a completely dispassionate matter-of-factness that does credit to his régime,[23] she gives him the opportunity to state in plain terms precisely what marriage should mean for the young Houyhnhnm[24]:

> Silence between them. The deadly statistical clock very hollow. The distant smoke very black and heavy.
>
> "Father," said Louisa, "do you think I love Mr. Bouderby?"
>
> Mr. Gradgrind was extremely discomforted by this unexpected

question. "Well, my child," he returned, "I—really—cannot take upon myself to say."

"Father," pursued Louisa in exactly the same voice as before, "do you ask me to love Mr. Bounderby?"

"My dear Louisa, no. I ask nothing."

"Father," she still pursued, "does Mr. Bounderby ask me to love him?"

"Really, my dear," said Mr. Gradgrind, "it is difficult to answer your question—"

"Difficult to answer it, Yes or No, father?"

"Certainly, my dear. Because"—here was something to demonstrate, and it set him up again—"because the reply demands so materially, Louisa, on the sense in which we use the expression. Now, Mr. Bounderby does not do you the injustice, and does not do himself the injustice, of pretending to anything fanciful, fantastic, or (I am using synonymous terms) sentimental. Mr. Bounderby would have seen you grow up under his eye to very little purpose, if he could so far forget what is due to your good sense, not to say to his, as to address you from any such ground. Therefore, perhaps, the expression itself—I merely suggest this to you, my dear—may be a little misplaced."

"What would you advise me to use in its stead, father?"

"Why, my dear Louisa," said Mr. Gradgrind, completely recovered by this time, "I would advise you (since you ask me) to consider the question, as you have been accustomed to consider every other question, simply as one of tangible Fact. The ignorant and the giddy may embarrass such subjects with irrelevant fancies, and other absurdities that have no existence, properly viewed—really no existence—but it is no compliment to say that you know better. Now, what are the Facts of this case? You are, we will say in round numbers, twenty years of age; Mr. Bounderby is, we will say in round numbers, fifty. There is some disparity in your respective years, but ..."

—And at this point Mr. Gradgrind seizes the chance for a happy escape into statistics. But Louisa brings him firmly back:

"What do you recommend, father," asked Louisa, her reserved composure not in the least affected by these gratifying results, "that I should substitute for the term I used just now? For the misplaced expression?"

"Louisa," returned her father, "it appears to me that nothing can be plainer. Confining yourself rigidly to Fact, the question of Fact you state to yourself is: Does Mr. Bounderby ask me to marry him? Yes, he does. The sole remaining question then is: Shall I marry him? I think nothing can be plainer than that."

"Shall I marry him?" repeated Louisa with great deliberation.

"Precisely."

It is a triumph of ironic art. No logical analysis could dispose of the philosophy of fact and calculus with such neat finality. As the issues are reduced to algebraic formulation they are patently emptied of all real meaning. The instinct-free rationality of the emotionless Houyhnhnm is a void. Louisa proceeds to try and make him understand that she is a living creature and therefore no Houyhnhnm, but in vain ("to see it, he must have overleaped at a bound the artificial barriers he had for many years been erecting between himself and all those subtle essences of humanity which will elude the utmost cunning of algebra, until the last trumpet ever to be sounded will blow even algebra to wreck").

Removing her eyes from him, she sat so long looking silently towards the town, that he said at length: "Are you consulting the chimneys of the Coketown works, Louisa?"

"There seems to be nothing there but languid and monotonous smoke. Yet, when the night comes, Fire bursts out, father!" she answered, turning quickly.

"Of course I know that, Louisa. I do not see the application of the remark." To do him justice, he did not at all.

She passed it away with a slight motion of her hand, and concentrating her attention upon him again, said, "Father, I have often thought that life is very short."—This was so disinctly one of his subjects that he interposed:

"It is short, no doubt, my dear. Still, the average duration of human life is proved to have increased of later years. The calculations of various life assurance and annuity offices, among other figures which cannot go wrong, have established the fact."

"I speak of my own life, father."

"Oh, indeed! Still," said Mr. Gradgrind, "I need not point out to you, Louisa, that it is governed by the laws which govern lives in the aggregate."

"While it lasts, I would wish to do the little I can, and the little I am fit for. What does it matter?"

Mr. Gradgrind seemed rather at a loss to understand the last four words; replying, "How, matter? What matter, my dear?"

"Mr. Bounderby," she went on in a steady, straight way, without regarding this, "asks me to marry him. The question I have to ask myself is, shall I marry him? That is so, father, is it not? You have told me so, father. Have you not?"

"Certainly, my dear."

"Let it be so."

The psychology of Louisa's development and of her brother Tom's is sound. Having no outlet for her emotional life except in her love for her brother, she lives for him, and marries Bounderby—under pressure from Tom—for Tom's sake ("What does it matter?"). Thus, by the constrictions and starvations of the Gradgrind régime, are natural affection and capacity for disinterested devotion turned to ill.[25] As for Tom, the régime has made of him a bored and sullen whelp, and "he was becoming that not unprecedented triumph of calculation which is usually at work on number one"—the Utilitarian philosophy has done that for him. He declares that when he goes to live with Bounderby as having a post in the bank, "he'll have his revenge."—"I mean, I'll enjoy myself a little, and go about and see something and hear something. I'll recompense myself for the way in which I've been brought up." His descent into debt and bank-robbery is natural. And it is natural that Louisa, having sacrificed herself for this unrepaying objection of affection, should be found not altogether unresponsive when Mr. James Harthouse, having seized up the situation, pursues his opportunity with well-bred and calculating tact. His apologia for genteel cynicism is a shrewd thrust at the Gradgrind philosophy:

> "The only difference between us and the professors of virtue or benevolence, or philanthrophy—never mind the name—is, that we know it is all meaningless, and say no; while they know it equally, and will never say so."
>
> Why should she be shocked or warned by this reiteration? It was not so unlike her father's principles, and her early training, that it need startle her.

When, fleeing from temptation, she arrives back at her father's house, tells him her plight, and, crying, "All I know is, your philosophy and your teaching will not save me," collapses, he sees "the pride of his heart and the triumph of his system lying an insensible heap at his feet." The fallacy now calamitously demonstrated can be seen focused in that "pride," which brings togetehr in an illusory oneness the pride of his system and his love for his child. What that love is Gradgrind now knows, and he knows that it matters to him more than the system, which is thus confuted (the educational failure as such being a lesser matter). There is nothing sentimental here; the demonstration is impressive, because we are convinced of the love, and because Gradgrind has been made to exist for us as a man who has "meant to do right":

> He said it earnestly, and, to do him justice, he had. In gauging fathomless deeps with his little mean excise rod, and in staggering over the universe with his rusty stiff-legged compasses, he had meant to do great things. Within the limits of his short tether he had tumbled about, annihilating the flowers of existence with greater singleness of purpose than many of the blatant personages whose company he kept.

The demonstration still to come, that of which the other "triumph of his system," Tom, is the center, is sardonic comedy, imagined with great intensity and done with the sure touch of genius. There is the pregnant scene in which Gradgrind, in the deserted ring of a third-rate traveling circus, has to recognize his son in a comic Negro servant; and has to recognize that his son owes his escape from Justice to a peculiarly disinterested gratitude—to the opportunity given him to assume such a disguise by the non-Utilitarian

Mr. Sleary, grateful for Sissy's sake:

In a preposterous coat, like a beadle's, with cuffs and flaps exaggerated to an unspeakable extent; in an immense waistcoat, knee breeches, buckled shoes, and a mad cocked-hat; with nothing fitting him, and everything of coarse material, moth-eaten, and full of holes; with seams in his black face, where fear and heat had started through the greasy composition daubed all over it; anything so grimly, detestably, ridiculously shameful as the whelp in his comic livery, Mr. Gradgrind never could by any other means have believed in, weighable and measurable fact though it was. And one of his model children had come to this!

At first the whelp would not draw any nearer but persisted in remaining up there by himself. Yielding at length if any concession so sullenly made can be called yielding, to the entreaties of Sissy—for Louisa he disowned altogether—he came down, bench by bench, until he stood in the sawdust, on the verge of the circle, as far as possible, within its limits, from where his father sat.

"How was this done?" asked the father.

"How was what done?" moodily answered the son.

"This robbery," said the father, raising his voice upon the word.

"I forced the safe myself overnight, and shut it up ajar before I went away. I had had the key that was found made long before. I dropped it that morning, that it might be supposed to have been used. I didn't take the money all at once. I pretended to put my balance away every night, but I didn't. Now you know all about it."

"If a thunderbolt had fallen on me," said the father, "it would have shocked me less than this!"

"I don't see why," grumbled the son. "So many people are employed in situations of trust; so many people, out of so many, will be dishonest. I have heard you talk, a hundred times, of its being a law. How can I help laws? You have comforted others with such things, father. Comfort yourself!"

The father buried his face in his hands, and the son stood in his disgraceful grotesqueness, biting straw: his hands, with the black partly worn away inside, looking like the hands of a monkey. The evening was fast closing in; and, from time to time, he turned the whites of his eyes restlessly and impatiently towards his father. They were the only parts of his face that showed any life or expression, the pigment upon it was so thick.

Something of the rich complexity of Dickens's art may be seen in this passage. No simple formula can take account of the various elements in the whole effect, a sardonic-tragic in which satire consorts with pathos. The excerpt in itself suggests the justification for saying that *Hard Times* is a poetic work. It suggests that the genius of the writer may fairly be described as that of a poetic dramatist, and that, in our preconceptions about "the novel," we may miss, within the field of fictional prose, possibilities of concentration and flexibility in the interpretation of life such as we associate with Shakespearean drama.

The note, as we have it above in Tom's retort, of ironic-satiric discomfiture of the Utilitarian philosopher by the rebound of his formulae upon himself is developed in the ensuing scene with Bitzer, the truly successful pupil, the real triumph of the system. He arrives to intercept Tom's flight:

Bitzer, still holding the paralysed culprit by the collar, stood in the Ring, blinking at his old patron through the darkness of the twilight.

"Bitzer," said Mr. Gradgrind, broken down and miserably submissive to him, "have you a heart?"

"The circulation, sir," returned Bitzer, smiling at the oddity of the question, "couldn't be carried on without one. No man, sir, acquainted with the facts established by Harvey relating to the circulation of the blood, can doubt that I have a heart."

"Is it accessible," cried Mr. Gradgrind, "to any compassionate influence?"

"It is accessible to Reason, sir," returned the excellent young man. "And to nothing else."

They stood looking at each other; Mr. Gradgrind's face as white as the pursuer's.

"What motive—even what motive in reason—can you have for preventing the escape of this wretched youth," said Mr. Gradgrind, "and crushing his miserable father? See his sister here. Pity us!"

"Sir," returned Bitzer in a very business-like and logical manner, "since you ask me what motive I have in reason for taking young Mr. Tom back to Coketown, it is only reasonable to let you know...I am going to take young Mr. Tom back to Coketown, in order to deliver him over to Mr. Bounderby. Sir, I have no doubt whatever that Mr. Bounderby will then promote me to young Mr. Tom's situation. And I wish to have his situation, sir, for it will be a rise to me, and will do me good."

"If this is solely a question of self-interest with you—" Mr. Gradgrind began.

"I beg your pardon for interrupting you, sir," returned Bitzer, "but I am sure you know that the whole social system is a question of self-interest. What you must always appeal to is a person's self-interest. It's your only hold. We are so constituted. I was brought up in that catechism when I was very young, sir, as you are aware."

"What sum of money," said Mr. Gradgrind, 'will you set against your expected promotion?"

"Thank you, sir," returned Bitzer, "for hinting at the proposal; but I will not set any sum against it. Knowing that your clear head would propose that alternative, I have gone over the calculations in my mind; and I find that to compound a felony, even on very high terms indeed, would not be as safe and good for me as my improved prospects in the Bank."

"Bitzer," said Mr. Gradgrind, stretching out his hands as though he would have said, See how miserable I am! "Bitzer, I have but one chance left to soften you. You were many years at my school. If, in rememberance of the pains bestowed upon you there, you can persuade yourself in any degree to disregard your present interest and release my son, I entreat and pray you to give him the benefit of that rememberance."

"I really wonder, sir," rejoined the old pupil in an argumentative manner, "to find you taking a position so untenable. My schooling was paid for; it was a bargain; and when I came away, the bargain ended."

It was a fundamental principle of the Gradgrind philosophy, that everything was to be paid for. Nobody was ever on any account to give anybody anything, or render anybody help without purchase. Gratitude was to be abolished, and the virtues springing from it were not to be. Every inch of the existence of mankind, from birth to death, was to be a bargain across the counter. And if we didn't get to Heaven that way, it was not a politico-economical place, and we had no business there.

"I don't deny," added Bitzer, "that my schooling was cheap. But that comes right, sir. I was made in the cheapest market, and have to dispose of myself in the dearest."

. . .

But the packed richness of *Hard Times* is almost incredibly varied, and not all the quoting I have indulged in suggests it adequately. The final stress may fall on Dickens's command of word, phrase, rhythm, and image: in ease and range there is surely no greater master of English except Shakespeare. This comes back to saying that Dickens is a great poet: his endless resource in felicitously varied expression is an extraordinary responsiveness to life. His senses are charged with emotional energy, and his intelligence plays and flashes in the quickest and sharpest perception. That is, his mastery of "style" is of the only kind that matters—which is not to say that he hasn't a conscious interest in what can be done with words; many of his felicities could plainly not have come if there had not been, in the background, a habit of such interest. Take this, for instance:

> He had reached the neutral ground upon the outskirts of the town,
> which was neither town nor country, but either spoiled ...

But he is no more a stylist than Shakespeare; and his mastery of expression is most fairly suggested by stressing, not his descriptive evocations (there are some magnificent ones in *Hard Times*—the varied décor of the action is made vividly present, you can feel the velvety dust trodden by Mrs. Sparsit in her stealth, and feel the imminent storm), but his strictly dramatic felicities. Perhaps, however, "strictly" is not altogether a good pointer, since Dickens is a master of his chosen art, and his mastery shows itself in the way in which he moves between less direct forms of the dramatic and the direct rendering of speech.

注释

1. to bear on：和……有关。

2. 大意为：既然读者心中的这些期待可以轻易满足，所以，即使他们看出作品蕴藉深厚，也不会有所感激。除非读者充分考虑到作品意蕴的重要性，否则无从发现里面有像生活那样诱人的东西。假如作品的意蕴坚持以这种形式出现，那么，读者根本看不出它的存在。

3. 这段当中提到的亨利·詹姆斯的两部小说，表现了欧洲与美国新旧文化之间的冲突。

4. 大意为：作者的意图在道德寓意中尤为执着。

5. 这两句话的大意为：一般来说，狄更斯对当时英国社会的种种批评都是偶然之笔、顺势而为——针对某种弊端抒发愤慨之情，这是他在书中常有之情。但是，在《艰难时世》之中，他却打破常例，表现出一种宏观全面的眼光。在他看来，维多利亚文明的种种惨无人道之举，得到了一种残酷哲学的培养和支持，这种哲学肆无忌惮地演绎出一种非人道的精神。

6. John Stuart Mill：穆勒（1806—1873），英国哲学家和经济学家、功利主义者，主要著作有《政治经济学原理》(*Principles of Political Economy*)、《论自由》(*Liberty*)、《功利主义》(*Utilitarianism*)等。

7. 大意为：不管庞得贝如何吹嘘自己白手起家，他都不是依靠自我奋斗而成功的人士。

8. Lawrence：指 D. H. 劳伦斯。

9. a unit for arithmetic：算数单位。

10. 大意为：作者使用这种反讽手法所取得的效果似乎很有限。

11. 大意为：作者通过感觉描写凸显了西丝与毕周的道德和精神差异。

12. Laurentian：劳伦斯式的。
    利维斯在此暗指，狄更斯对西丝进行外表描写的笔法与劳伦斯相似。

13. and pulled up by the sight of two palpable offenders：看到两个明显违背校规的人，他停下了脚步。

14. Jonsonian comedy：本·琼生式的喜剧。

15. Santayana：桑塔雅那（George Santayana, 1863—1952），西班牙哲学家、文学家。1872 年移居美国。

16. 大意为：他们（对于人和事）采取了圆滑的态度，约定成俗地接受下来。

17. 这里的 Mr. Eliot，指 T. S. 艾略特，下文引用的是他的两行诗。

18. Wyndham Lewis：刘易斯（1882—1957），英国画家、作家、文艺批评家，创立旋涡画派。

19. tête-à-tête：法文，面对面地。

20. 大意为：小说开篇伊始，西丝就分辨出葛擂硬与庞得贝之间的不同。

21. 大意为：庞得贝始终酷似本·琼生戏剧中的人物，因为他为人行事没有任何变化。

22. 大意为：反对功利主义思想的条件体现在葛擂硬身上，他最初对西丝表露出的那番善意固然不够和蔼可亲，但仍然遭到庞得贝的斥责。

23. 大意为：带着一股心闲气定、就事论事的神态，这正是他家教之所赐。

24. Houyhnhnm：斯威夫特在《格列佛游记》中所描写的具有理性和人性的马，与卑鄙下流的 yahoo（暗指人类）形成了鲜明对比。

25. 大意为：葛擂硬家教严厉，让露易莎无处释放情感。结果是，她的手足之情和奉献能力都变了质（为了弟弟汤姆的前程，她嫁给了比她大三十岁的庞得贝）。

燕卜荪 《含混的七种形式》

威廉·燕卜荪（1906—1984）

在英美新批评的发展过程中，威廉·燕卜荪与瑞恰慈都是开风气之先的人物。20 世纪 20 年代，瑞恰慈最早在剑桥倡导细读式批评，一时应者云从。此前盛行的传记式批评、印象派批评、考据式批评和社会历史批评顿时失势，风光不再。不过，瑞恰慈本人的著作多为理论的阐述，没有提出一套具体可行的操作手法作为细读式分析的范例。这项艰巨的任务是他的得意门生威廉·燕卜荪来完成的，他的成名作《含混的七种形式》是细读式文本解读的开山之作。书中主要分析的是文本自身，而毫不牵涉作者生平和社会环境，对后来新批评的发展极具启蒙意义。不过，燕卜荪本人并不是一个纯粹的新批评家，他对美国新批评的一些极端做法并不赞同。他后来的几部著作，例如《田园诗的几种形式》（*Some Versions of Pastoral*, 1938）、《复杂词的结构》（*The Structure of Complex Words*, 1951）和《弥尔顿的上帝》（*Milton's God*, 1965），都论证说，不应孤立地去研究文本。

燕卜荪早年在剑桥大学学习数学专业，在即将完成学业的最后一年，他转攻文学，受业于瑞恰慈。据瑞恰慈回忆，燕卜荪读过的英国文学作品的数量在自己之上，而且，他对新作品的熟悉程度也超过了自己。这个智力异常发达的青年在瑞恰慈的鼓励之下，将自己的一份作业扩充成《含混的七种形式》这部名作，并于 1930 年付梓出版，时年 24 岁。

自 1931 至 1934 年，燕卜荪任教于日本东京大学，讲授英国文学。1937 年应北京大学之聘来华任教，旋因抗战爆发，随校迁徙至湖南长沙；再迁至云南，任教于北大、清华和南开三校合一的西南联大，直至 1939 年。二战期间，曾供职于英国广播公司，任中文部编辑。1947 年，再度来华任教，1952 年回国。燕卜荪记忆力惊人，学识渊博、教学认真，深得学生敬佩。他为中国培养了一大批英语语言和文学专家，许国璋、王佐良、李赋宁等人就是其中的佼佼者。自 1953 年起，他一直任教于谢菲尔德大学，直到 1971 年退休为止。因其学术上的巨大贡献，晚年获得"爵士"（Sir）勋位。除了从事文学评论之外，他也是一位诗人，有三部诗集行世。他的诗作对 50 年代英国"运动派"（Movement）诗人很有影响。

内容提要

　　燕卜荪从英国文学史上的诸多诗人、剧作家和散文家的作品中采撷了大量例证，用以说明，含混是诗歌的一种重要表现手段，是一切优秀文学作品的基本特征。不过，对于这个术语，他在书中始终未能给出一个全面而明确的定义。若想弄清这个词的确切含义，必须结合他在这本书以及后来评论著作中的说明。综合来看，含混指的是，作品中的词语同时向读者释放出两种或两种以上的意义，让读者产生多种解读，而且每一种解读都言之成理。这种数义并存、彼此结合、意义并不定于一尊的现象就是含混。例如，在南唐后主李煜的名句"独自莫凭栏，无限江山。别时容易见时难"中，即存在含混现象。这里的"江山"既可以指南唐故国的山光水色，也可以指作者丢掉的"江山社稷"——政权。其实，早在燕卜荪之前，瑞恰慈就发现了并论述过含混问题。他认为，诗歌中的词语大多含混不清，意义芜杂；读者读诗之时，必须在其中选择一个最合适的意义。瑞恰慈不同于燕卜荪之处在于，他认为读者在诸多歧义当中只会选择出一种；而燕卜荪则认为，诸多歧义可以同时存在。燕卜荪的著作深得瑞恰慈的激赏，他最终还是认可燕卜荪的观点。

　　选文出自《含混的七种形式》（1947 年修订版）的第一章，主要解说了第一种含混形式——隐喻造成的含混。作者开篇伊始，先对含混进行了初步界定："任何词语的精妙涵义，不管其间的差别如何细微，只要让读者对同一句话产生不同的理解，就称得上是含混。"而最简单的含混是由隐喻引起的。用赫伯特·里德的话说，隐喻把人对事物的多方面观察和见解融汇综合成一个主导形象；它表达复杂思想的方式，既不是细致分析，也不是平铺直叙，而是利用顿悟来参透两种事物之间的客观联系。当我们说一物与另一物相似之时，那就意味着，它们各自的性质令它们彼此相似。接下来，作者以莎士比亚十四行诗的第 73 首中的一行为例，来说明这种最基本的含混形式。在"荒废的唱诗坛，再也不闻百鸟歌唱"这句话中，莎士比亚将百鸟嘤鸣的树林比作教堂中的唱诗坛。这个比喻之所以成立，就是因为唱诗坛与树林有很多相似的地方：树林中有百鸟鸣叫，唱诗坛上曾有人唱诗；唱诗班成员与百鸟都是排着队唱歌；唱诗坛是木制的，百鸟鸣唱其中的树林也是林木葱茏；先前，唱诗坛四周有建筑物，仿佛树林遮蔽四周，教堂上的彩色玻璃和壁画就像树林中的红花与绿叶；因为现在教堂已经荒废，唯余四壁高墙，尽染寒天的铅灰色，类似冬日树林灰暗之色；因为唱诗班少年冷漠的深情与顾影自怜的媚态正是莎士比亚对自己赠诗的那位（可能与他有分桃断袖关系的）青年男子的心理感受；另外还有各种社会和历史原因（新教徒捣毁修道院；对清教主义的恐惧等等）。上述诸种因素合在一起赋予这行诗以美感，正因为读者弄不清究竟是哪一种因素从中发挥主导作用，含混之感油然而生。

William Empson (1906 — 1984)

SEVEN TYPES OF AMBIGUITY

An ambiguity, in ordinary speech, means something very pronounced, and as a rule witty or deceitful. I propose to use the word in an extended sense, and shall think relevant to my subject any verbal nuance, however slight, which gives room for alternative reactions to the same piece of language.[1] Sometimes, especially in this first chapter, the word may be stretched absurdly far, but it is descriptive because it suggests the analytical mode of approach, and with that I am concerned.

In a sufficiently extended sense any prose statement could be called ambiguous. In the first place it can be analysed. Thus, "The brown cat sat on the red mat" may be split up into a series: "This is a statement about a cat.The cat the statement is about is brown." and so forth. Each such simple statement may be translated into a complicated statement which employs other terms: thus you are now faced with the task of explaining what a "cat" is: and each such complexity may again be analysed into a simple series; thus each of the things that go to make up a "cat" will stand in some spatial relation to the "mat." "Explanation," by choice of terms, may be carried in any direction the explainer wishes; thus to translate and analyse the notion of "sat" might involve a course of anatomy; the notion of "on" a theory of gravitation. Such a course, however, would be irrelevant not only to my object in this essay but to the context implied by the statement, the person to whom it seems to be addressed, and the purpose for which it seems to be addressed to him; nor would you be finding out anything very fundamental about the sentence by analysing it in this way; you would merely be making another sentence, stating the same fact, but designed for a different purpose, context, and person. Evidently, the literary critic is much concerned with implications of this last sort, and must regard them as a main part of the meaning. There is a difference (you may say that between thought and feeling) between the fact stated and the circumstance of the statement, but very often you cannot know one without knowing the other,[2] and an apprehension of the sentence involves both without distinguishing between them. Thus I should consider as on the same footing the two facts about this sentence, that it is about a cat and that it is suited to a child. And I should only isolate two of its "meanings," to form an ambiguity worth notice; it has contradictory associations, which might cause some conflict in the child who heard it, in that it might come out of a fairy story and might come out of *Reading without Tears*[3].

In analysing the statement made by a sentence (having, no doubt, fixed on the statement by an apprehension of the implications of the sentence)[4], one would continually be dealing with a sort of ambiguity due to metaphors, made clear by Mr. Herbert Read[5] in *English Prose Style*; because metaphor, more or less far-fetched[6], more or less complicated, more or less taken for granted (so as to be unconscious), is the normal mode of development of a language. "Words used as epithets are words used to analyse a direct statement," whereas "metaphor is the synthesis of several units of observation into one commanding image,[7] it is the expression of a complex idea, not by analysis, nor by direct statement, but by a sudden perception of an objective relation." One thing is said to be like another, and they have several different properties in virtue of which they are alike. Evidently this, as a verbal matter, yields more readily to analysis than the social ambiguities I have just considered; and I shall take it as normal to the simplest type of ambiguity, which I am considering in this chapter. The fundamental situation, whether it deserves to be called ambiguous or not, is that a word or a grammatical structure is effective in several ways at once. To take a famous example, there is no pun, double syntax, or dubiety of feeling, in

Bare ruined choirs, where late the sweet birds sang,

but the comparison holds for many reasons; because ruined monastery choirs are places in which to sing, because they involve sitting in a row, because they are made of wood, are carved into knots and so forth, because they used to be surrounded by a sheltering building crystallised out of the likeness of a forest, and colored with stained glass and painting like flowers and leaves, because they are now abandoned by all but the grey walls colored like the skies of winter, because the cold and Narcissistic charm suggested by choirboys suits well with Shakespeare's feeling for the object of the Sonnets, and for various sociological and historical reasons (the protestant destruction of monasteries; fear of puritanism), which it would be hard now to trace out in their proportions; these reasons, and many more relating the simile to its place in the Sonnet,[8] must all combine to give the line its beauty, and there is a sort of ambiguity in not knowing which of them to hold most clearly in mind.[9] Clearly this is involved in all such richness and heightening of effect, and the machinations of ambiguity are among the very roots of poetry.

Such a definition of the first type of ambiguity covers almost everything of literary importance, and this chapter ought to be my longest and most illuminating, but it is the most difficult. The important meanings of this sort, as may be seen from the example about the cat, are hard to isolate, or to be sure of when you have done so; and there is a sort of meaning, the sort that people are thinking of when they say "this poet will mean more to you when you have had more experience of life," which is hardly in reach of the analyst at all.[10] They mean by this not so much that you will have more information (which could be given at once) as that the information will have been digested; that you will be more experienced in the apprehension of verbal subtleties or of the poet's social tone; that you will have become the sort of person that can feel at home in, or imagine, or extract experience from, what is described by the poetry; that you will have included it among the things you are prepared to apprehend.[11] There is a distinction here of the implied meanings of a sentence into what is to be assimilated at the moment and what must already be part of your habits; in arriving at the second of these the educator (that mysterious figure) rather than the analyst would be helpful.[12] In a sense it cannot be explained in language, because to a person who does not understand it any statement of it is as difficult as the original one, while to a person who does understand it a statement of it has no meaning because no purpose.

Meanings of this kind,[13] indeed, are conveyed, but they are conveyed much more by poets than by analysts; that is what poets are for, and why they are important. For poetry has powerful means of imposing its own assumptions, and is very independent of the mental habits of the reader; one might trace its independence to the ease with which it can pass from the one to the other of these two sorts of meaning.[14] A single word, dropped where it comes most easily, without being stressed, and as if to fill out the sentence, may signal to the reader what he is meant to be taking for granted,[15] if it is already in his mind the word will seem natural enough and will not act as an unnecessary signal. Once it has gained its point,[16] on further readings, it will take for granted that you always took it for granted; only very delicate people are as tactful in this matter as the printed page.[17] Nearly all statements assume in this way that you know something but not everything about the matter in hand, and would tell you something different if you knew more; but printed commonly differ from spoken ones in being intended for a greater variety of people, and poetical from prosaic ones in imposing the system of habits they imply more firmly or more quickly.[18]

As examples of the things that are taken for granted in this way, and assume a habit, rather than a piece of information, in the reader,[19] one might give the fact that a particular section of the English language is being used; the fact that English is being used, which you can be conscious of if you can use French; the fact that a European language is used, which you can be conscious of if you can use Chinese. The first of these "facts" is more definite than it sounds; a word in a speech which falls outside the expected vocabulary will cause an uneasy stir in all but the soundest sleepers; many sermons use this with painful frankness. Evidently such a section[20] is defined by its properties rather than by enumeration, and so alters the character of the words it includes; for instance, one would bear it in mind when considering whether the use of a word demands that one should consider its derivation. Regional or dialect poets are likely to use words flatly from that point of view. No single example of so delicate and continuous a matter can be striking; I shall take one at random out of the Synge[21] *Deirdre*, to make clear that a word need not be unpoetical merely because its meaning has been limited:

> Deirdre...It should be a sweet thing to have what is best and richest,
> if it's for a short space only.[22]
> Naisi. And we've a short space only to be triumphant and brave.[23]

The language here seems rich in implications; it certainly carries much feeling and conveys a delicate sense of style. But if one thinks of the Roman or medieval associations of *triumphant*, even of its normal use in English, one feels a sort of unexplained warning that these are irrelevant; the word here is a thin counter standing for a notion not fully translated out of Irish; it is used to eke out that alien and sliding speech-rhythm, which puts no weight upon its single words.[24]

The process of becoming accustomed to a new author is very much that of learning what to exclude in this way, and this first of the three "facts," hard as it may be to explain in detail, is one with which appreciative critics are accustomed to deal very effectively. But the other two are more baffling; one can say little about the quality of a language, if only because the process of describing it in its own language is so top-heavy, and the words of another language will not describe it. The English prepositions, for example, from being used in so many ways and in combination with so many verbs, have acquired not so much a number of meanings as a body of meaning continuous in several dimensions; a tool-like quality, at once thin, easy to the hand, and weighty, which a mere statement of their variety does not convey. In a sense all words have a body of this sort; none can be reduced to a finite number of points, and if they could the points could not be conveyed by words.

Thus a word may have several distinct meanings; several meanings connected with one another; several meanings which need one another to complete their meaning; or several meanings which unite together so that the word means one relation or one process. This is a scale[25] which might be followed continuously. "Ambiguity" itself can mean an indecision as to what you mean, an intention to mean several things, a probability that one or other or both of two things has been meant, and the fact that a statement has several meanings.[26] It is useful to be able to separate these if you wish, but it is not obvious that in separating them at any particular point you will not be raising more problems than you solve. Thus I shall often use the ambiguity of "ambiguity," and pronouns like "one," to make statements covering both reader and author of a poem, when I want to avoid raising irrelevant problems as to communication. To be less ambiguous would be like analysing the sentence about the cat into a course of anatomy. In the same way the words of the poet will, as a rule, be more justly words, what they represent will be more effectively a unit in the mind, than the more numerous words with which I shall imitate their meaning so as to show how it is conveyed.[27]

And behind this notion of the word itself, as a solid tool rather than as a collection of meanings, must be placed a notion of the way such a word is regarded as a member of the language; this seems still darker and less communicable in any terms but its own. For one may know what has been put into the pot, and recognize the objects in the stew, but the juice in which they are sustained must be regarded with a peculiar respect because they are all in there too, somehow, and one does not know how they are combined or held in suspension. One must feel the respect due to a profound lack of understanding for the notion of a potential, and for the poet's sense of the nature of a language.

These examples of the "meanings" of an English sentence should make clear that no explanation, certainly no explanation written in English, can be conceived to list them completely; and that there may be implications (such as I should call meanings) of which a statement would be no use.[28] Neither of these are objections to my purpose, because I can assume that my readers already understand and enjoy the examples I shall consider, and I am concerned only to conduct a sufficient analysis of their enjoyment to make it seem more understandable.

It is possible that there are some writers who write very largely with this sense of a language as such, so that their effects would be almost out of reach of analysis.[29] Racine always seems to me to write with the whole weight of the French language, to remind one always of the latent assumptions of French, in a way that I am not competent to analyse in any case, but that very possibly could not be explained in intelligible terms. Dryden is a corresponding English figure in this matter; Miss Gertrude Stein[30], too, at this point, implores the passing tribute of a sigh.[31] To understand their methods one might have to learn a great deal about the mode of action of language which is not yet known, and it might always be quicker to use habit than analysis, to learn the language than to follow the explanation.

注释

1. 大意为：我是在使用含混一词的引申意义，任何微妙的语义差别，只要它能使一句话产生不同的反应，我就认为它与含混有关。

2. 大意为：如果不知其一就不知其二。

3. reading without tears：浅近读物。

4. 大意为：当然，先是理解句子含义，再确定句子的陈述。

5. Herbert Read：里德（1893—1968），英国诗人、文艺评论家，著有《赤膊的战士》（*Naked Warriors*）等多种诗集和论著《现代诗的形式》（*Form in Modern Poetry*）、《艺术和工业》（*Art and Industry*）等。

6. far-fetched：牵强的。

7. 大意为：隐喻就是将若干观察结果综合成一个主要形象。

8. 大意为：有许多理由可以证明这句诗中的比拟是成立的。

9. 大意为：在上述原因当中，不知哪一种是最想清楚表达的。

10. which is hardly in reach of the analyst at all：（这位诗人的意思）只可意会，不可言传。

11. 大意为：由于你有理解潜质，早晚能弄明白。

12. 大意为：一个句子的各种隐含意义，有的是读了这个句子后才消化吸收的，有的则早已纳入你的阅读习性，是不言而喻的东西；做到后一点，以往无形当中受教育的经历比现时的解释分析更有帮助。

13. 指的是句子里的隐含意义。

14. 大意为：诗歌有强大的力量，让别人接受自己的见解，并且不受读者心理习惯的束缚；它能在两种意义之间轻松自如地转移，足以说明它不受读者心理习惯的束缚。

15. 大意：一个词所处的位置，不令人感到突兀和牵强或仿佛让句子完整无缺，这就提醒读者，他必须把这个词看做天经地义的东西。

16. 大意为：一旦这个词在读者那里产生意义。

17. 大意为：在这方面，只有非常敏锐的人才能灵活地把握一个词的多种含义，就像印刷出来的文字可以灵活地表现多种含义一样。

18. 大意为：诗歌语言与散文语言不同之处在于，它能用自己暗含的习惯系统更坚定有力或更加迅速地影响别人。

19. 大意为：像这样被当成理所当然的事物，与其说是向读者传达某种信息，不如说帮助读者养成一种习惯，这方面的例子很多。

20. such a section：指的是牧师使用的那种英文。

21. Synge：辛格（John Millington Synge, 1871—1909），爱尔兰剧作家、爱尔兰文艺复兴代表人物，作品有悲剧《骑马下海的人》（*Riders to the Sea*）、喜剧《峡谷阴影》（*In the Shadow of the Glen*）、《西方世界的花花公子》（*The Playboy of the Western World*）等。

22. 大意为：哪怕只是在片刻之间（拥有）。

23. 大意为：然而，我们的胜利和勇敢也只是一时之快。

24.【作者原注】Not a clear example, and I am not sure that what I said is true; but a borderline example was needed here to show that fine shades can be concerned.

25. scale：阶梯。

26.【作者原注】It would seem pedantic to alter the phrase "has several meanings," but it is treacherous. If the simplest statement has a subject and a predicate it may be said to include two meanings. There would be no point in calling it ambiguous unless it gave room for alternative reactions.

27. 大意为：同样地，诗人使用的词语一般来说是比较恰当、精确的，更能有效地表现思想整体，而我为了表达同样的意义，可能需要更多的词语。

28. 大意为：这些例子说明，一个英文句子的含义不一而足，没有哪一种解释能够把它们网络殆尽；对于一个句子的各种隐含意义，即便加以陈述说明，也无济于事。

29. 大意为：有些作家在写作的时候，在很大程度上持有这种语言观；这样一来，他们笔下文字的效果几乎无法分析。

30. Gertrude Stein：斯泰因（1874—1946），美国女作家，"迷惘的一代"一词的首创者。

31. 这里暗指，斯坦因的文字也是意蕴丰富，令人无从下手加以细致分析，只能叹为观止。

克里斯托弗·考德威尔（1907—1937）

在 20 世纪 30 年代，一方面，由于英国国内的经济危机加剧；另一方面，国外法西斯主义势力甚嚣尘上，许多青年知识分子担心人类文明将毁于一旦。他们当中有相当多的人开始倾心于共产主义，认为这是拯救人类文明的良方。他们发出要求社会变革的呼声，一场激进的文学运动由此而生，其代表人物有奥登（W. H. Auden）、休·麦克德米德（Hugh MacDiarmid）、C. D. 刘易斯（C. D. Lewis）、斯蒂温·斯彭德（Stephen Spender）等人。20 年代盛行的艾略特式玄妙古奥的诗风黯然隐退，一种清新刚健、带有强烈社会批判意识的文学风格开始出现。随着文学创作的左倾主义渐成风气，文学批评领域出现了马克思主义性质的文学理论和批评实践，有代表性的批评家有克里斯托弗·考德威尔、拉尔夫·福克斯（Ralph Fox）以及艾里克·韦斯特（Alick West）。在这三人当中，考德威尔的成就最高，堪称 30 年代英国马克思主义文学理论的代表。此人天分极高，才华横溢，有"英国的卢卡奇"之美誉。

克里斯托弗·考德威尔原名克里斯托弗·圣·约翰·斯皮格，出生于中产阶级家庭。他的父亲是职业报人，母亲是一位天分很高的画家。他早年受教于一所天主教学校。可能因为家庭经济状况不佳，他中学毕业后没上大学，年纪轻轻就步入社会，进入他父亲供职的《约克郡观察家报》，开始了记者生涯，当时不过 15 岁。1925 年，这位早慧的少年记者跑到伦敦，在一家报社当编辑。当时航空业方兴未艾，这类书籍很抢手，他和长兄一道创办了一家航空工业出版社。他立志打通文理以成一家之言。一有时间，他就泡在大英图书馆里饱览群籍。他阅读范围广泛得惊人，不仅包括文史哲，还涉及物理学、人类学、心理学、神经学。考德威尔下笔迅疾，产出惊人，从 24 岁到 29 岁，短短的五年之中，出版了七部侦探小说、五本航空方面的科普读物，一部长篇小说，还有大量的未刊手稿。

在 1934 年末，在英国共产党的一些知识分子的影响下，他开始倾心于马克思主义，研读马克思的著作。到了 1935 年夏天，他已经读过马克思、恩格斯、列宁、布哈林和斯大林等人的许多著作，对经典马克思主义有了相当程度的了解。就在这一年，他加入了英国共产党。他为人低调，在党内籍籍无名，从事普通知识分子党员例行的工作：贴标语、写口号、街头言说。1935 年 9 月，他完成了《幻想与现实》(*Illusion and Reality: A Study of the Source of Poetry*) 一书的初稿，寄给著名的 Allen & Unwin 出版公司，遭到退稿；再寄麦克米伦出版公司，终被接受，但迟至 1937 年春才付梓问世。此时考德威尔已经战死西班牙，不及亲见了。1936 年，他出版了严肃小说《这是我的手》(*This My Hand*)。这一次，他用了克里斯托弗·考德威尔这个笔名，以示告别侦探作家的生涯。1936 年 12 月，他响应英国共产党的号召，开着英共募捐买来的救护车，开赴西班牙战场；加入国际旅，抗击佛朗哥的叛军，捍卫西班牙共和国政府。1937 年 2 月，这位知行合一的党员知识分子在马德里保卫战中牺牲，年仅 29 岁。在他的遗著当中，最为重要的是两部文学理论和批评著作：《幻想与现实》和《传奇与现实主义》(*Romance and Realism*)。前者于 1937 年出版，后者于 1970 年出版。《幻想与现实》是英国首部严肃的马克思主义文学理论著作。由于时代的局限，考德威尔的著作深受经济决定论的影响，有些论断显得简单粗糙、教条生硬，经常是后来的马克思主义批评家批判的靶子。假以天年，以他的才智和勤奋，他定能与时俱进，克服教条的羁绊，旁采众家之长，为英国马克思主义文论创造一个新的格局。

内容提要

　　《幻想与现实》全书 12 章，其内容大致可以分为两部分。前 6 章重在论述诗歌的社会起源和历史演变，后 6 章旨意在阐述诗学的基本原理。在考德威尔看来，诗（广义上的文学）的本质与社会的经济活动息息相关，诗的发展与社会的劳动分工同步进行。就起源而论，诗诞生于部落的节庆活动，是集体劳动的产物。

　　这篇选文论述了诗歌在资本主义发展的不同阶段所表现出的不同精神风貌。从 15 世纪开始，英国逐渐步入了资本主义时代。在资本主义原始积累时期，资产阶级崇尚绝对自由的意识形态，这反映出资产阶级的一种精神诉求：希望自己的经济活动不受任何约束。资产阶级的这种不受任何约束的自由理念，催生了马洛笔下的那些追求个人绝对意志的人物：浮士德和帖木儿；在同时代的文学巨匠莎士比亚的笔下，李尔王、麦克白和哈姆雷特等人物，也都带着豪迈不羁之情不顾一切去完成自我实现。到了18世纪新古典主义时代，资产阶级的文学表现出土地贵族与工业资本家相妥协的精神。这一时期的资产阶级有一种普遍心态：人的要求必须适度，生活在向上发展，但步伐不可能太快；外在的约束是必要的，也是可以接受的。与此相呼应的是蒲柏的诗歌。蒲柏推崇理性、讲求文字优美、韵律谨严、对仗工整，反映出当时的资产阶级对自由的诉求还受到一定程度的限制这一历史事实。到了工业革命时期，社会经济力量的对比开始有利于工业无产阶级。英国政府为了捍卫土地贵族的利益而推行《谷物法》，遭到工业资产阶级的强烈反抗。工业资产阶级号召社会各阶级站在自己的麾下，它以全社会的代言人身份自居，要求社会改革，提出人性本善、人生而自由、但又处处受到禁锢的观念，号召人们起来反对现存的法律、成规、形式和传统。在文学上，与这种激烈的资产阶级革命意识形态相对应的是拜伦、雪莱、济慈和华兹华斯掀起的浪漫主义革命。拜伦意识到自己所在的贵族阶级不可避免地没落下去，转投资产阶级阵营。这类人物背叛自己的阶级投靠另一阶级，并不是出于对历史发展必然性的认识，而是为了反抗于己不利的社会环境。他们在一种利己主义的无政府心态的驱使下，迎合资产阶级的愿望，充当他们的战斗武器。拜伦笔下的唐璜即是他本人的思想写照。他既嘲笑世间的种种荒唐可笑，又十分伤感、自怨自艾，埋怨社会在虐待一个伟大的天才。雪莱以一切受苦人的代言人而自居。在这一时期的资产阶级诗人当中，他的革命性最强，他的《解放的普罗米修斯》不是在翻历史的旧案，而是当前革命的纲领。被缚的普罗米修斯象征着在重商主义时期受到严重束缚的工业资产阶级，让他获得自由，整个世界也就自由了。这正是当时工业资产阶级的普遍心声。华兹华斯受法国的卢梭影响甚深，喜欢从"自然人"中寻找自由和美；这些东西在现实的人的身上中找不到。他的那些颂扬自然的诗篇也反映出法国革命时期资产阶级的一种普遍心态。激烈的法国大革命让英国资产阶级深为恐惧，他们对自由的追求出现了倒退的色彩。他们再也不想借助于反抗而得到自由，而是想回到自然中寻找自由。济慈出身于小资产阶级家庭，经常为现实生活中的经济难题所困扰。他对现实认识比较清楚，他为资产阶级文学定下一个基调："革命"就是逃避现实。他在诗中回避日常生活中真实而残酷的世界，创造了一个浪漫美好的世界。这个新世界因其可爱美好，与现实世界形成巨大反差；所以说，它是对冷酷现实世界的无言谴责。

Christopher Caudwell (1907—1937)

English Poets at the Time of the Industrial Revolution

I

The bourgeois illusion now passes to another stage, that of the Industrial Revolution, the "explosive" stage of capitalism. Now the growth of capitalism transforms all idyllic patriarchal relations—including that of the poet to the class whose aspirations he voices—into "callous" cash-nexus.

Of course this does not make the poet regard himself as a shopkeeper and his poems as cheeses. To suppose this is to overlook the compensatory and dynamic nature of the connection between illusion and reality. In fact it has the opposite effect. It has the effect of making the poet increasingly regard himself as a man removed from society, as an individualist realizing only the instincts of his heart and not responsible to society's demands[1]— whether expressed in the duties of a citizen, a fearer of God, or a faithful servant of Mammon[2]. At the same time his poems come increasingly to seem worthy ends-in-themselves.[3]

This is the final explosive movement of the bourgeois contradiction. The bourgeois illusion has already swayed from antithesis to antithesis, but as a result of this last final movement it can only pass, like a whirling piece of metal thrown off by an exploding flywheel, out of the orbit of the bourgeois categories of thought altogether.

As a result of the compromise of the eighteenth century, beneath the network of safeguards and protections which was characteristic of the era of manufacture, bourgeois economy developed to the stage where by the use of the machine, the steam-engine, and the power-loom it acquired an enormous power of self-expansion. At the same time the "factory" broke away from the farm of which it was the handicraft adjunct[4] and challenged it as a mightier and opposed force.

On the one hand organized labor inside the factory progressively increased, on the other hand the individual anarchy of the external market also increased. On the one hand there was an increasingly public form of production, on the other hand an increasingly private form of appropriation. At the one pole was an increasingly landless and toolless proletariat, at the other an increasingly wealthy bourgeoisie. This self-contradiction in capitalist economy provided the terrific momentum of the Industrial Revolution.

The bourgeoisie, who had found its own revolutionary-puritan ideals of liberty "extreme," and returned to the compromise of mercantilist good taste that seemed eternal reason, now again found its heart had been right, and reason wrong.[5]

This revealed itself first of all as a cleavage between the former landed aristocracy and the industrial bourgeoisie, expressing the rise of the factory to pre-dominance over the farm. The landed aristocracy, and the restrictions it demanded for its growth, was now confronted by industrial capital and its demands. Capital had found an inexhaustible self-expansive power in machinery and outside sources of raw material. So far from any of the earlier forms being of value to it, they were so many restraints. The cost of labor power could safely be left to fall to its real value, for the machine by its competition creates the proletariat it requires to serve it. The real value of labor power in turn depends on the real value of wheat, which is less in the colonies and America than in England because there it embodies less socially necessary labor. The Corn Laws,[6] which safeguard the agricultural capitalist, therefore hamper the industrialist. Their interests—reconciled during the period of wage-labor shortage—are now opposed. All the forms and restraints that oppose this free expansion of the industrial bourgeoisie must be shattered. To accomplish this shattering, the bourgeoisie called to its standard all other classes, precisely as in the time of the Puritan Revolution. It claimed to speak for the people as against the oppressors. It demanded Reform and the Repeal of the Corn Laws. It attacked the Church, either as Puritan (Methodist) or as open sceptic. It attacked all laws as restrictive of equality. It advanced the conception of the naturally good man, born free but everywhere in chains.[7] Such revolts against existing systems of laws, canons, forms, and traditions always appear as a revolt of the heart against reason, a revolt of feeling and the sentiments against sterile formalism and the tyranny of the past. Marlowe, Shelley, Lawrence, and Dali[8] have a certain parallelism here; each expresses this revolt in a manner appropriate to the period.

We cannot understand this final movement of poetry unless we understand that at every step the bourgeois is revolutionary in that he is revolutionizing his own basis. But he revolutionizes it only to make it consistently more bourgeois. In the same way each important bourgeois poet is revolutionary, but he expresses the very movement which brings more violently into the open the contradiction against which his revolutionary poetry is a protest.[9] They are "mirror revolutionaries." They attempt to reach an object in a mirror, only to move farther away from the real object. And what can that object be but the common object of man as producer and as poet—freedom? The poignancy of their tragedy and pessimism derives its bite from this perpetual recession of the desired object as they advance to grasp it. "La Belle Dame Sans Merci" has them all in thrall. They wake up on the cold hillside.[10]

II

Blake, Byron, Keats, Wordsworth, and Shelley express this ideological revolution, each in their different ways, as a Romantic Revolution.

Byron is an aristocrat—but he is one who is conscious of the break-up of his class as a force, and the necessity to go over to the bourgeoisie. Hence his mixture of cynicism and romanticism.

These deserters[11] are in moments of revolution always useful and always dangerous allies. Too often their desertion of their class and their attachment to another, is not so much a "comprehension of the historical movement as a whole" as a revolt against the cramping circumstances imposed on them by their own class's dissolution, and in a mood of egoistic anarchy they seize upon the aspirations of the other class as a weapon in their private battle. They are always individualistic, romantic figures with a strong element of the *poseur*[12]. They will the destruction of their own class but not the rise of the other, and this rise, when it becomes evident and demands that they change their merely destructive enmity to the dying class to a constructive loyalty to the new, may, in act if not in word, throw them back into the arms of the enemy. They become counter-revolutionaries. Danton[13] and Trotsky are examples of this type. Byron's death at Missolonghi[14] occurred before any such complete development, but it is significant that he was prepared to fight for liberty in Greece rather than England. In him the revolt of the heart against the reason appears as the revolt of the hero against circumstances, against morals, against all 'pettiness'[15] and convention. This Byronism is very symptomatic, and it is also symptomatic that in Byron it goes with a complete selfishness and carelessness for the sensibilities of others. Milton's Satan has taken on a new guise, one far less noble, petulant even.

Byron is most successful as a mocker—as a Don Juan. On the one hand to be cynical, to mock at the farce of human existence, on the other hand to be sentimental, and complain of the way in which the existing society has tortured one's magnificent capabilities—that is the essence of Byronism. It represents the demoralization in the ranks of the aristocracy as much as a rebellion against the aristocracy.[16] These men are therefore always full of death-thoughts: the death-thoughts of Fascism fighting in the last ditch, the death-thought of Jacobites; the glorification of a heroic death justifying a more dubious life. The same secret death-wishes are shown by these aristocrats if they turn revolutionary, performing deeds of outstanding individual heroism—sometimes unnecessary, sometimes useful, but always romantic and singlehanded. They cannot rise beyond the conception of the desperate hero of revolution.

Shelley, however, expresses a far more genuinely dynamic force. He speaks for the bourgeoisie who, at this stage of history, feel themselves the dynamic force of society and therefore voice demands not merely for themselves but for the whole of suffering humanity. It seems to them that if only *they* could realize themselves, that is, bring into being the conditions necessary for their own freedom, this would of itself ensure the freedom of all. Shelley believes that he speaks for all men, for all sufferers, calls them all to a brighter future. The bourgeois trammeled by the restraints of the era of mercantilism is Prometheus, bringer of fire, fit symbol of the machine-wielding capitalist. Free him and the world is free. A Godwinist[17], Shelley believed that man is naturally good—institutions debase him. Shelley is the most revolutionary of the bourgeois poets of this era because *Prometheus Unbound* is not an excursion into the past, but a revolutionary program for the present. It tallies with Shelley's own intimate participation in the bourgeois-democratic revolutionary movement of his day.

Although Shelley is an atheist, he is not a materialist. He is an idealist. His vocabulary is, for the first time, consciously idealist—that is, full of words like "brightness," "truth," "beauty," "soul," "aether," "wings," "fainting," "panting," which stir a whole world of indistinct emotions. Such complexes, because of their numerous emotional associations, appear to make the word indicate one distinct concrete entity, although in fact no such entity exists, but each word denotes a variety of different concepts.

This idealism is a reflection of the revolutionary bourgeois belief that, once the existing social relations that hamper a human being are shattered, the "natural man will be realized"—his feelings, his emotions, his aspirations, will all be immediately bodied forth as material realities. Shelley does not see that these shattered social relations can only give place to the social relations of the class strong enough to shatter them and that in any case these feelings, aspirations, and emotions are the product of the social relations in which he exists and that to realize them a social act is necessary, which in turn has its effect upon a man's feelings, aspirations, and emotions.[18]

The bourgeois illusion is, in the sphere of poetry, a revolt. In Wordsworth the revolt takes the form of a return to the natural man, just as it does in Shelley. Wordsworth, like Shelley profoundly influenced by French Rousseauism, seeks freedom, beauty—all that is not now in man because of his social relations—in "Nature." The French Revolution now intervenes. The bourgeois demand for freedom has now a regressive tinge. It no longer looks forward to freedom by revolt but by return to the natural man.

Wordsworth's "Nature" is of course a Nature freed of wild beasts and danger by aeons of human work, a Nature in which the poet, enjoying a comfortable income, lives on the products of industrialism even while he enjoys the natural scene "unspoilt" by industrialism. The very division of industrial capitalism from agricultural capitalism has now separated the country from the town. The division of labor involved in industrialism has made it possible for sufficient surplus produce to exist to maintain a poet in austere idleness in Cumberland. But to see the relation between the two, to see that the culture, gift of language and leisure which distinguish a Nature poet from a dumb subhuman[19] are the product of economic activity—to see this would be to pierce the bourgeois illusion and expose the artificiality of "Nature" poetry. Such poetry can only arise at a time when man by industrialism has mastered Nature—but not himself.

Wordsworth therefore is a pessimist. Unlike Shelley, he revolts regressively—but still in a bourgeois way—by demanding freedom from social relations, the specific social relations of industrialism, while still retaining the products, the freedom, which these relations alone make possible.

With this goes a theory that "natural," i.e. *conversational* language is better, and therefore more poetic than "artificial," i.e. *literary* language. He does not see that both are equally artificial—i.e. directed to a social end—and equally natural, i.e. products of man's struggle with Nature. They merely represent different spheres and stages of that struggle and are good or bad not in themselves, but in relation to this struggle. Under the spell of this theory some of Wordsworth's worst poetry is written.

Wordsworth's form of the bourgeois illusion has some kinship with Milton's. Both exalt the natural man, one in the form of Puritan "Spirit," the other in the more sophisticated form of pantheistic "Nature." One appeals to the primal Adam as proof of man's natural innocence, the other to the primal child. In the one case original sin, in the other social relations, account for the fall from grace. Both therefore are at their best when consciously noble and elevated. Milton, reacting against primitive accumulation and its deification of naïve princely desire and will, does not, however—as Wordsworth does—glorify the wild element in man, the natural primitive. Hence he is saved from a technical theory that conduces to "sinking" in poetry.

Keats is the first great poet to feel the strain of the poet's position in this stage of the bourgeois illusion, as producer for the free market. Wordsworth has a small income; Shelley, although always in want, belongs to a rich family and his want is due simply to carelessness, generosity, and the impracticability which is often the reaction of certain temperaments to a wealthy home.[20] But Keats comes of a small bourgeois family and is always pestered by money problems. The sale of his poems is an important consideration to him.

For Keats therefore freedom does not lie, like Wordsworth, in a return to Nature; his returns to Nature were always accompanied by the uncomfortable worry, where was the money coming from? It could not lie, as with Shelley, in a release from the social relations of this world, for mere formal liberty would still leave the individual with the problem of earning a living. Keats's greater knowledge of bourgeois reality therefore led him to a position which was to set the keynote for future bourgeois poetry: "revolution" as a flight *from* reality. Keats is the banner-bearer of the Romantic Revival. The poet now escapes upon the "rapid wings of poesy" to a world of romance, beauty, and sensuous life separate from the poor, harsh, real world of everyday life, which it sweetens and by its own loveliness silently condemns.[21]

This world is the shadowy enchanted world built by Lamia for her lover or by the Moon for Endymion. It is the golden-gated upper world of Hyperion, the word-painted lands of the nightingale, of the Grecian urn, of Baiae's isle.[22] This other world is defiantly counterpoised to the real world:

> "Beauty is truth, truth beauty"—that is all
> Ye know on earth, and all ye need to know.

And always it is threatened by stern reality in the shape of sages, rival powers or the drab forces of everyday. Isabella's world of love is shattered by the two money-grubbing brothers.[23] Even the wild loveliness of *The Eve of St. Agnes*[24] is a mere interlude between storm and storm, a colored dream snatched from the heart of cold and darkness—the last stanzas proclaim the triumph of decay. "La Belle Dame Sans Merci" gives her knight only a brief delight before he wakes. The flowering basil sprouts from the rotting head of Isabella's lover, and is watered with her tears.

> The fancy cannot cheat so well
> As she is famed to do, deceiving elf! ...
> Was it a vision or a waking dream?
> Fled is that music—do I wake or sleep? [25]

Like Cortes[26], Keats gazes entranced at the New World of poetry, Chapman's[27] realms of gold, summoned into being to redress the balance of the old, but however much voyaged in, it is still only a world of fancy.

A new vocabulary emerges with Keats, the dominating vocabulary of future poetry. Not Wordsworth's—because the appeal is not to the unspoilt simplicity of the country. Not Shelley's—because the appeal is not to the "ideas" that float on the surface of real material life and can be skimmed off like froth. The country is a part of the real material world, and the froth of these metaphysical worlds is too unsubstantial and therefore is always a reminder of the real world which generated it. A world must be constructed which is more real precisely because it is more unreal and has sufficient inner stiffness to confront the real world with the self-confidence of a successful conjuring trick.[28]

Instead of taking, like Wordsworth and Shelley, what is regarded as the most natural, spiritual, or beautiful part of the real world, a new world is built up out of words, as by a mosaic artist, and these words therefore must have solidity and reality. The Keatsian vocabulary is full of words with a hard material texture, like tesserae, but it is an "artificial" texture—all crimson, scented, archaic, stiff, jeweled, and anti-contemporary. It is as vivid as missal painting. Increasingly this world is set in the world of feudalism, but it is not a feudal world. It is a bourgeois world—the world of the Gothic cathedrals and all the growing life and vigor of the bourgeois class under late feudalism. Here too poetic revolution has a strong regressive character, just as it had with Wordsworth, but had not with the most genuinely revolutionary poet, Shelley.

The bourgeois, with each fresh demand he makes for individualism, free competition, absence of social relations, and more equality, only brings to birth greater organization, more complex social relations, higher degrees of trustification and combination, more inequality. Yet each of these contradictory movements revolutionizes his basis and creates new productive forces. In the same way the bourgeois revolution, expressed in the poetry of Shelley, Wordsworth, and Keats, although it is contradictory in its movement, yet brings into being vast new technical resources for poetry and revolutionizes the whole apparatus of the art.

The basic movement is in many ways parallel to the movement of primitive accumulation which gave rise to Elizabethan poetry. Hence there was at this era among poets a revival of interest in Shakespeare and the Elizabethans. The insurgent outburst of the genetic individuality which is expressed in Elizabethan poetry had a collective guise, because it was focused on that collective figure, the prince. In romantic poetry it has a more artificial air as an expression of the sentiments and the emotions of the individual figure, the "independent" bourgeois. Poetry has separated itself from the story, the heart from the intellect, the individual from society; all is more artificial, differentiated, and complex.

The poet now begins to show the marks of commodity-production. We shall analyze this still further when, as in a later date, it sets the whole key for poetry. At present the most important sign is Keats's statement, that he could write for ever, burning his poems afterwards. The poem has become already an end in itself.

But it is more important to note the air of tragedy that from now on looms over all bourgeois poetry that is worth the adjective "great." Poetry has become pessimistic and self-lacerating. Byron, Keats, and Shelley die young. And though it is usual to regret that they died with their best works unwritten, the examples of Wordsworth, Swinburne, and Tennyson make fairly clear that this is not the case, that the personal tragedy of their deaths, which in the case of Shelley and Byron at least seemed sought, prevented the tragedy of the bourgeois illusion working itself out impersonally in their poetry. For the contradiction which secures the movement of capitalism was now unfolding so rapidly that it exposed itself in the lifetime of a poet and always in the same way. The ardent hopes, the aspirations, the faiths of the poet's youth melted or else were repeated in the face of a changed reality with a stiffness and sterility that betrayed the lack of conviction and made them a mocking caricature of their youthful sincerity. True, all men grow old and lose their youthful hopes—but not in this way. A middle-aged Sophocles can speak with searching maturity of the tragedy of his life, and at eighty he writes a drama that reflects the open-eyed serenity of wisdom's child grown aged. But mature bourgeois poets are not capable of tragedy or resignation, only of a dull repetition of the faiths of youth—or silence. The movement of history betrays the contradiction for what it is, and yet forces the bourgeois to cling to it. From that moment the lie has entered his soul, and by shutting his eyes to the consciousness of necessity, he has delivered his soul to slavery.

In the French Revolution the bourgeoisie, in the name of liberty, equality, and fraternity, revolted against obsolete social relations. They claimed, like Shelley, to speak in the name of all mankind; but then arose, at first indistinctly, later with continually increasing clarity, the claim of the proletariat also demanding liberty, equality, and fraternity. But to grant these to the proletariat means the abolition of the very conditions which secure the existence of the bourgeois class and the exploitation of the proletariat. Therefore the movement for freedom, which at first speaks largely in the voice of mankind, is always halted at a stage where the bourgeoisie must betray its ideal structure expressed in poetry, forget that it claimed to speak for humanity, and crush the class whose like demands are irreconcilable with its own existence. Once robbed of its mass support, the revolting bourgeoisie can always be beaten back a stage by the forces of reaction. True, these forces have learned "a sharp lesson" and do not proceed too far against the bourgeoisie who have shown their power. Both ally themselves against the proletariat. Ensues an equillibrium when the bourgeoisie have betrayed their talk of freedom, and compromised their ideal structure, only themselves to have lost part of the ideal fruit of their struggle to the more reactionary forces—feudal forces, if the struggle is against feudalism, landowning, and big financial forces, if the struggle is between agricultural and industrial capitalism.

Such a movement was that from Robespierre to the Directory[29] and the anti-Jacobin movement which as a result of the French Revolution swept Europe everywhere. The whole of the nineteenth century is a record of the same betrayal, which in the life of the poets expresses itself as a betrayal of youthful idealism. 1830, 1848 and, finally, 1871 are the dates which make all bourgeois poets now tread the path of Wordsworth, whose revolutionary fire, as the result of the proletarian content of the final stage of the French Revolution, was suddenly chilled and gave place to common sense, respectability, and piety.

It was Keats who wrote:

> "None can usurp this height," the shade returned,
>
> "Save those to whom the misery of the world
>
> Is misery and will not let them rest."[30]

The doom of bourgeois poets in this epoch is precisely that the misery of the world, including their own special misery, will not let them rest, and yet the temper of the time forces them to support the class which causes it. The proletarian revolution has not yet advanced to a stage where "some bourgeois ideologists, comprehending the historical movement as a whole," can ally themselves with it and really speak for suffering humanity and for a class which is the majority now and the whole world of men tomorrow. They speak only for a class that is creating the world of tomorrow willy-nilly, and at each step draws back and betrays its instinctive aspirations because of its conscious knowledge that this world of tomorrow it is creating, *cannot include itself.*

注释

1. 大意为：工业资本主义的发展使诗人越来越倾向于认为，自己可以遗世独立，做一个只需实现内心本能天性而罔顾社会需求的个体主义者。
2. Mammon：拜金偶像。
3. worthy ends-in-themselves：价值在于自身。
4. the handcraft adjunct：辅助农业的手工业。
5. 大意为：资产阶级发现自己的革命清教徒式的自由理想"太极端"，就回过头来采取折中的办法，服膺重商主义的高雅文学欣赏品味；后者似乎就是永恒的理性，现在却发现，自己的心灵是正确的，理性是错误的。
6. Corn Laws：《谷物法》，指英国历史上管理粮食进出口的规章。虽然早在 12 世纪就有《谷物法》实施，但直到 18 世纪末和 19 世纪前半叶，英国由于人口不断增加和拿破仑战争的封锁，粮食短缺，《谷物法》才具有政治意义。1839 年在曼彻斯特成立的反谷物法同盟发动工业资产阶级反对地主。1846 年《谷物法》被废除。
7. born free but everywhere in chains：人生而自由，但处处受限制。这是卢梭的名言。

8. Dali：达里（Salvador Dali, 1904—1989）：西班牙超现实主义画家。

9. 大意为：同样地，每一位重要的资产阶级诗人都是革命的，但是，他表现的这场运动却把他的革命诗篇所反抗的矛盾，更加强烈地暴露出来。

10. 语出济慈的名诗《无情的少女》（"La Belle Dame Sans Merci"）。

11. deserter：叛逃者。

12. poseur：装腔作势之徒。

13. Danton：丹东（Georges Jacques Danton, 1759—1794），法国大革命期间雅各宾派领导人。

14. Missolonghi：希腊城市迈索隆吉翁，拜伦在此去世。

15. pettiness：猥琐。

16. 大意为：拜伦主义既体现了贵族阶级的堕落，又体现了对贵族阶级的反叛。

17. William Godwin：戈德温（1756—1836），英国哲学家、作家、无神论者，著有政治思想名著《政治正义论》（*Enquiry Concerning Political Justice*），具有无政府主义色彩。娶妻玛丽·沃尔斯通克拉夫特，生女玛丽·雪莱。

18. 大意为：雪莱没有看到，这些被破坏的社会关系只能让位于另一阶级的社会关系，后者的力量强大，足以破坏先前的社会关系；不管怎样，这些感觉、愿望和情感都是他所处的社会关系的产物；为了实现这些社会关系，有必要采取社会行动，而社会行动也会影响人的感觉、愿望和情感。

19. a dumb subhuman：不会说话的弱智。

20. which is often the reaction of certain temperaments to a wealthy home：这常常是某些很有性情的富家子弟反叛家庭之举。

21. 大意为：这个浪漫世界本身可爱，这对严酷的现实世界是一种无声的谴责。

22. 这里提到的 Lamia、Endymion 和 Hyperion 都是济慈诗中的人物。Baiae's isle 则为济慈诗中地名。

23. 大意为：伊莎贝拉的爱情世界毁于两个贪财的兄弟之手。事见济慈名诗《伊莎贝拉》（"Isabella"）。

24. The Eve of St. Agnes：济慈的诗歌《圣艾格尼丝之夜》。

25. 幻想，这骗人的妖童，
    不能老要弄它盛传的伎俩。

············

噫，这是个幻觉，还是梦寐？

那歌声去了：——我是睡？是醒？（查良铮译文）

26. Cortes：科尔特斯（Hernando Cortes, 1485—1547），西班牙冒险家、墨西哥的征服者。济慈在十四行诗 "On First Looking into Chapman's Homer" 中提到过他。

27. Chapman：查普曼（George Chapman, 1559—1634），英国诗人、剧作家、荷马史诗的英译者。

28. 大意为：他必须打造一个因为不真实而显得更有现实意义的世界；这个世界带着一种志在必得的自信坚忍不拔地对抗现实世界。

29. Directory：1795—1799，法兰西第一共和国的督政府时期。

30. 大意为："没有谁能侵占这块高地"，阴影回答说，"除了那些承受了世人的痛苦、不得安生的人"。

霍加特

《"真实的"大众世界：
通俗文艺举例》

理查·霍加特（1918—）

理查·霍加特 1918 年出生在英国利兹的一个工人阶级家庭。中学毕业后，考取了国家奖学金进入利兹大学，学习英国文学专业。二战期间应征入伍，转战北非和意大利。服役期间即表现出文化组织才能，在军中创建了"三艺俱乐部"（Three Arts Club），为参战人士主编了四本文集；此外，还在意大利的那不勒斯大学兼职授课。

从 1946 年到 1959 年，霍加特投身于英国工人阶级协会的成人教育工作，在赫尔大学的成人教育系担任文学导师。1951 年出版专著《奥登》（Auden）一书，发表了一些有关 19 世纪和 20 世纪英国文学以及教学法方面的论文。1959 年起，任莱斯特大学高级讲师，1962 年任伯明翰大学英文教授，1964 年在伯明翰大学创建了当代文化研究中心（Center for Contemporary Cultural Studies），使该校成为英国文化研究的重镇。与此同时，霍加特还曾在英国的教育、艺术等委员会任职。1970 年，他出任联合国教科文组织副总干事。

在霍加特的大力倡导下，当代文化研究中心于 1964 年在伯明翰大学成立。该中心在行政上隶属于英文系，霍加特为中心的首任主任。中心只招收研究生，学生主要来自文学、史学、哲学和社会学等专业。霍加特在就职演说中表明了研究中心成立的初衷：利用文学批评方法去评判和阐释大众文化，文化研究要肩负起三大领域的任务，一个大致相当于历史和哲学，一个是社会学，最后一个是文学批评，后者最为重要。这样做有一个好处，那就是，可以把大众文化放在一个更加全面的历史和社会背景下加以理解。一言以蔽之，对待大众文化，要有历史的眼光，当代的意识和文学批评的方法。但是，这种博观约取的态度却遭到两面夹击。英文系有一些经典文学的坚定支持者，对大众文化研究很不以为然；在他们看来，劳神费力去研究大众文化，实在不值得。社会学家则说，文化研究不够科学；而且，他们在私下里还认为，这是在侵犯自家的研究领地。

霍加特对文化研究有两大贡献：第一，他克服重重困难，创建了当代文化研究中心，为文化研究领域培养了大量的人才；当代英美学界的文化研究学者，其治学经历多与中心渊源颇深，要么曾在那里读过学位，要么曾在那里进修。第二，他的代表作《识字的用途》(*The Use of Literacy*) 为早期的英国文化研究确立了一种研究范式，以文学分析为文化研究的主要方法；在结构主义进入英国之前，这种批评模式一直支配着英国文化研究。

内容提要

选文出自霍加特的代表作《识字的用途》。一般认为，霍加特的《识字的用途》与雷蒙·威廉斯（Raymond Williams）的《文化与社会》(*Culture and Society*, 1780—1950) 和《漫长的革命》(*The Long Revolution*) 以及 E.P. 汤普森（E. P. Thompson）的《英国工人阶级的形成》(*The Making of the English Working Class*) 被并称为英国文化研究的奠基之作，它们为早期的英国文化研究提供了思想资源和批评范例。威廉斯和汤普森是英国新左派的先驱，英国马克思主义思想与学术的代表人物；霍加特则是具有民粹思想的自由派知识分子。他对马克思主义不感兴趣，与新左派没有什么瓜葛，虽说他也出身于工人阶级家庭，而且留恋 30 年代的工人阶级生活方式。

在《识字的用途》这部笔带深情、自传色彩浓厚的著作中，作者勾勒出 20 世纪 30 年代至 50 年代英国城市工人阶级日常生活的历史变迁；笔调感伤幽怨，怀旧之情跃然纸上。该书上半部分采用了人类学中常见的参与性观察方法，叙述了作者在幼年时代（20 世纪 30 年代）耳濡目染的工人阶级文化：他们的休闲方式、生活态度、业余爱好栩栩如生地展现在读者面前。在娓娓而谈、态度亲切的语调下，作者每每流露出美化和揄扬之意。在该书的第二部分，霍加特利用文学批评的细读方法分析了二战后涌现的大众文化。他一反先前的礼赞态度，对这些新型文化侵蚀和取代旧有文化忧心忡忡。

在选文中，霍加特从工人阶级经常阅读的报刊当中援引了大量例证，以便说明，工人阶级所喜闻乐见的通俗文艺，并不是像一些文化精英主义者所认为的那样内容粗俗不堪，败坏人心。作者开篇伊始，即总括出工人阶级艺术的主要特征：工人阶级的艺术总是立足于现实生活，它们表现的内容都是读者所熟悉的东西，而且其中贯穿了一些简单而又牢固的道德准则。工人阶级经常阅读的报刊刊载一些耸人听闻的小说，但这些作品对生活细节的描写十分真实；大多数作品并不鼓励人们逃避日常生活，反倒认为日常生活充满了情趣。

工人阶级在日常生活中阅读的报刊杂志大多遵循《佩格报》（*Peg's Paper*）的传统：纸张粗糙、封面色调单一，价格低廉，目标读者几乎都是工人阶级自身。除了刊载日常生活用品的广告之外，这些报刊主要刊登长短篇小说。与资产阶级经常阅读的报刊相比，这些杂志上的通俗小说反映出工人阶级更加重视社会道德观。同样是描写通奸偷情，在中产阶级经常阅读的通俗作品中，坏人最后虽然未能获胜，但他在感情上总是占据上风。因为这类作品一直在暗示，从"精神上"讲，情人总是胜过妻子。而在工人阶级阅读的这类通俗小说中，通奸者总是被妖魔化，全无英雄气息。在这类小说中，如果出现少女失贞或妻子外遇的情节，随后出现的就是女主人公真诚而深切的自责。例如"所以那天晚上，我堕落了"或"我犯下了大罪"，其道德的严肃性显而易见。这类小说反映了工人阶级传统的价值观："以爱情、忠诚和幸福为基础的婚姻和家庭是女性生活的正当目的。"于是，在描写女性失贞的作品的常见结尾，"要么让姑娘发现那个男人变得愿意承担责任，终于跟她结了婚；要么让她另外找一个男人，他虽然了解真相，但仍然爱她们母子两人，愿意娶她为妻并充当那个孩子的父亲。"

Richard Hoggart (1918—   )

The "Real" World of People: Illustrations from Popular Art
—*Peg's Paper*

This overriding interest in the close detail of the human condition is the first pointer to an understanding of working-class art. To begin with, working-class art is essentially a "showing" (rather than an "exploration"), a presentation of what is known already. It starts from the assumption that human life is fascinating in itself. It has to deal with recognizable human life[1], and has to begin with the photographic[2], however fantastic it may become; it has to be underpinned by a few simple but firm moral rules.

Here is the source of the attraction, the closely, minutely domestic attraction, of *Thomson's Weekly News*. It is this, more than a vicarious snobbery, which makes radio serials with middle-class settings popular with working-class people, since these serials reflect daily the minutiae of everyday life. It is this which helps to ensure that the news-presentation of most popular newspapers belongs to the realms of imaginative or fictional writing of a low order. Those special favorites of working-class people, the Sunday gossip-with-sensation papers[3], the papers for the free day, assiduously collect from throughout the British Isles all the suitable material they can find, for the benefit of almost the whole of the adult working-class population. It is true that their interest, whether in news-reporting or in fiction, is often increased by the "ooh-aah" element—a very "ordinary" girl is knocked down by a man who proves to be a film-star; an attractive young widow proves to have disposed of two husbands with arsenic and popped them under the cellar-flagstones—and it is easy to think that most popular literature is of the "ooh-aah" kind. One should think first of the photo-graphically detailed aspect; the staple fare is not something which suggests an escape from ordinary life, but rather it assumes that ordinary life is intrinsically interesting. The emphasis is initially on the human and detailed, with or without the "pepping-up"[4] which crime or sex or splendor gives. De Rougemont[5] speaks of millions (though he has in mind particularly the middle classes) who "breathe in...a romantic atmosphere in the haze of which passion seems to be the supreme test." As we shall see, there is much in working-class literature too which gives support to this view; but it is not the first thing to say about the more genuinely working-class publications which persist. For them passion is no more interesting than steady home life.[6]

Some BBC programs underline the point. Notice how popular the "homely" programs are, not simply such programs as *Family Favorites* ("for Good Neighbors") nor simply the family serials and feature-programs such as *Mrs. Dale's Diary, The Archers, The Huggetts, The Davisons, The Grove Family, The Hargreaves*; but the really ordinary homely programs, often composed, rather like the more old-fashioned papers, of a number of items linked only by the fact that they all deal with the ordinary lives of ordinary people. I have in mind programs like Wilfred Pickles's *Have a Go* and Richard Dimbleby's *Down Your Way*. They have no particular shape; they do not set out to be "art" or entertainment in the music-hall sense; they simply "present the people to the people" and are enjoyed for that. So are the programs which still make use of the music-hall "comic's" tradition of handling working-class life, programs like Norman Evans's *Over the Garden Wall* and Al Read's superb sketches. It is not necessary, for success, that the programs should be a form of professional art; if it is really homely and ordinary it will be interesting and popular.[7]

I have suggested that it is commonly thought that some magazines—for example, those predominantly read by working-class women and usually spoken of as "*Peg's Paper*[8] and all that"—provide little other than undiluted fantasy and sensation. This is not true; in some ways the more genuinely working-class magazines are preferable to those in the newer style. They are in some ways crude, but often more than that; they still have a felt sense of the texture of life in the group they cater for. I shall refer to them as "the older magazines" because they carry on the *Peg's Paper* tradition, and reflect the older forms of working-class life: in fact, most of them, under their present titles, are between ten and twenty years old.

Almost all are produced by the three large commercial organizations: Amalgamated Press, the Newnes Group, and Thomson and Leng. But the authors and illustrators seem to have a close knowledge of the lives and attitudes of their audience[9]. One wonders whether the publishers take in much of their material piecemeal from outside, rather as the stocking-makers of Nottingham once did. Most of the material is conventional—that is, it mirrors the attitudes of the readers; but those attitudes are by no means as ridiculous as one might at first be tempted to think. In comparison with these papers, some of those more recently in the front are as a smart young son with a quick brain and a bundle of up-to-date opinions beside his sentimental, superstitious, and old-fashioned mother.

These older magazines can often be recognized by their paper, a roughly textured newsprint which tends to have a smell—strongly evocative to me now, because it is also that of the old boys' magazines and comics—of something slightly damp and fungoid. They can be recognized also by their inner lay-out, in which only a few kinds of type are likely to be used; by their covers, which are usually "flat"[10] and boldly colored in a limited range—almost entirely of black with strong shades of blue, red, and yellow, with few intermediates. They usually sell at threepence each, and have such titles as *Secrets*, *Red Star weekly*, *Lucky Star* (which now incorporates *Peg's Paper*), *The Miracle*, *The Oracle*, *Glamor*, *Red Letter*, and *Silver Star*. They are apparently designed for adolescent girls and young married women in particular; thus, two in three of the readers of *Red Letter* are under thirty-five. There is some provision for older readers. The number of their readers varies between one-third and three-quarters of a million each, with most of them above the half-million. There will be much overlapping, but the total number of readers remains considerable, and they are almost entirely from the working-classes.

In composition they are all much alike. There are many advertisements, scattered throughout in penny packets, on the back cover and over large parts of the last couple of text-pages; there are usually no advertisements on the front cover pages and first text-pages. After the colored cover, the inner cover page is generally given to some regular editorial feature;[11] or the main serial, or the week's "dramatic long complete novel", begins there. The advertisements, regularly recurring throughout the whole group of magazines, cover a narrow range of goods. Some cosmetics still use an aristocratic appeal, with photographs of titled ladies dressed for a ball.

The same ailments appear so often in the advertisements for proprietary remedies that a hasty generalizer might conclude from them that the British working-classes are congenitally both constipated and "nervy." There are many announcements of cures for disabilities which are likely to make a girl a "wallflower." The "scientists tell us" approach is there, but so still is its forerunner, the "gypsy told me" approach. Thus, there are occasionally esoteric Indian remedies in this manner—"Mrs. Johnson learned this secret many years ago from her Indian nurse in Bombay. Since then, many thousands have had cause to be glad that they reposed confidence in her system." For married women there are washing-powder advertisements, and those for headache powders or California Syrup of Figs for children. But, in general, the assumption is that the married women readers are young enough to want to keep up with the unmarried by the use of cosmetics and hair-shampoos. Mail-order firms advertise fancy wedge-shoes, nylon underwear for—I suppose—the young women, and corsets for the older. For all groups, but especially, it appears, for the youngish married women with little money to spare, there are large advertisements (much the biggest in these magazines) inviting them to become agents for one of the great Clothing or General Credit Clubs, which proliferate, chiefly from the Manchester area, and usually give their agents two shillings in the pound, a fat catalogue, and free notepaper.[12]

Stories make up the body of the text pages, but interspersed are the regular and occasional features[13]. There are no politics, no social questions, nothing about the arts. This is neither the world of the popular newspapers which still purport to be alive to events[14], nor that of those women's magazines which have an occasional flutter with "culture." There are beauty hints, often over the signature of a well-known film-star: and some very homely home hints; there is a half-page of advice from an "aunt" or a nurse on personal problems—the kind of thing laughed at as "Aunt Maggie's advice;" in fact, it is usually very sensible. I do not mean, though this is true, that there is never a breath which is not firmly moral. But the general run of the advice is practical and sound, and when a problem arises whose answer is beyond the competence of the journalist, the inquirer is told to go to a doctor or to one of the advisory associations. There is a fortune-teller's section, based on the stars or birthday dates.

. The stories divide easily into serials, the long complete story of the week, and the short stories (probably only one page in length). The long stories and the serials often have startling surprises, as a young man proves to be really wealthy or a girl finds she wins a beauty competition, even though she has always thought of herself as a plain Jane[15]. This is particularly the case with the serials, which must be "dramatic" and mount their accumulated series of suspended shocks as week follows week. So they tend to deal in what are called wild passions and in murder. There are handsome men on the loose, usually called Rafe. But much more interesting; because much more obviously feared, are the "fascinating bitches," the Jezebels,[16] as most advance trailer[17] dub them. These are the women who set up in provincial towns and fail to report[18] that they have a "dreadful past" or that a "dreadful secret" lies in their previous home a hundred miles away; or they get rid of pretty young girls by whom the man they are after is really attracted, by tipping them overboard from a rowing-boat, trussed in a cabin-trunk; or they convert an electric kettle into a lethal weapon: "She did not look evil—yet her presence was like a curse"—"She was a woman fashioned by the Devil himself into the mould of the fairest of angels."

The strong case against this kind of literature is well known, and I do not mean to take that case lightly. It applies, one should remember, to popular literature for all classes. When one has said that some of these stories supply the thrill of the wicked or evil, can one go further? Can one distinguish them from the general run of this kind of popular writing?[19] Denis de Rougemont points out that this type of story, especially when it is written for the middle classes, usually manages to have things both ways, that though the villains never triumph in fact, they do triumph emotionally; that where, for instance, adulterous love is the subject, these stories imply an emotional betrayal. They "hold the chains of love to be indefeasible and [imply] the superiority from a 'spiritual' standpoint of mistress over wife." "Therefore," M. de Rougemont continues, "the institution of marriage comes off rather badly, but that does not matter...since the middle-class (especially on the Continent) is well aware that this institution is no longer grounded in morality or religion, but rests securely upon financial foundations." M. de

Rougemont also emphasizes the fascination of the love/death theme, of an adulterous love-relationship which can find some sort of resolution only in death.

There seems to me a difference between this and most of the "thrilling" stories in these "older" magazines. There seems to be little emotional betrayal of the explicit assumptions here; the thrill comes because the villain is striking—"making passes at"—some things still felt underneath to be important, at a sense of the goodness of home and married life, above individual relations of passion. Thus there is no use of the love/death theme, since that would be to kill altogether the positive and actual home/marriage theme. The villain, inviting an adulterous relationship, seems to be found interesting less because he offers a vicarious enjoyment of a relationship which, though forbidden, is desired, as because he makes a shocking attack on what is felt to count greatly[20]. He is a kind of bogy-man rather than a disguised hero. He does not usually triumph emotionally in the way he does in that more sophisticated literature which I take M. de Rougemont to be describing; this is, in fact, an extremely uncomplicated kind of literature.

These stories differ yet more obviously from many later versions of the sex-and-violence tale, from the kind of tale which is serialized in some of the Sunday papers. In those the author tries—while the rape or violence is being committed—to give a mild thrill and then laps the whole in hollow moral triteness. They are even further from the two-shilling sex-and-violence novelettes. They have no sexual excitement at all, and no description aiming to arouse it; and this, I think, is not only because women are not usually as responsive as men to that kind of stimulus, but because the stories belong to different worlds. These stories from the working-class women's magazines belong neither to the middle-class world, nor to that of the more modern Sunday papers, nor to that of the later novelettes, nor, even less, to an environment in which illicit relations can be spoken of as "good fun," as "smart" or "progressive." If a girl does lose her virginity here, or a wife commit adultery, you hear, "And so that night I fell," or "I committed the great sin": and though a startled thrill is evident there, you feel that the sense of a fall and a sin is real also.

The strongest impression, after one has read a lot of these stories, is of their extraordinary fidelity to the detail of the readers's lives. The short stories take up as much space as the serial or long story, and they seem to be mainly faithful transcripts of minor incidents, amusing or worrying, from ordinary life. The serials may erupt into the startlingly posh world of what are still called "the stately homes of England"[21], or present a Rajah[22] or a Sheik: but often the world is that the readers live in, with a considerable accuracy in its particulars. A fair proportion of the crime is of that world too—the distress when Mrs. Thompson is suspected of shoplifting, and so on. I open *Silver Star*: on the inner front cover the complete long novel, *Letters of Shame*, begins:

> As Stella Kaye unlatched the gate of number 15, the front door opened and her mother beckoned agitatedly.
>
> "Whatever's made you so late?" she whispered. "Did you remember the sausages? Oh, good girl!"
>
> Stella looked at her mother's flushed face and best flowered apron.
>
> Visitors! Just when she was bursting to spring her news on them all!
>
> It would have to keep.

A typical copy of *Secrets* has as its week's verse, "Mother's Night Out," about the weekly visit by Father and Mother to the pictures: "It's Monday night and at No. 3, Mother and Dad are hurrying tea. In fact, poor Dad has scarcely done before Mother's urging, 'Fred, come on!'"

A short story at the back of the *Oracle*, "Hero's Homecoming," opens: "Most of the women who dealt at the little general store on the corner of Roper's Road were rather tired of hearing about Mrs. Bolsom's boy, but they couldn't very well tell her so because she was so obliging and so handy to run to at times of emergency."[23] A typical *Lucky Star* one-page story starts: "Lilian West glanced at the clock on the kitchen wall. 'My goodness,' she thought. 'How quickly I get through the housework these days!'" It goes on to tell how, after deciding to leave her married children alone so as not to be thought a nuisance, she found fresh happiness in realizing how much she was still needed. "Mary was an ordinary girl doing an ordinary job in a factory," another story begins, and incidentally epitomizes the points of departure for almost all of them.

The illustrations help to create the same atmosphere. Some of the newer magazines specialize in photographic illustrations of the candid camera kind[24]. The "older" ones still use black-and-white drawings in an unsophisticated style. There exist, particularly in more modern publications, black-and-white line drawings which are very sophisticated: compared with them the cartoons still to be found in some provincial newspapers, drawn by a local man, belong to thirty years ago. So it is with most of the drawings here (the main illustration to the serial or the long complete novel is sometimes an exception); they are not smart in their manner, and their detail is almost entirely romanticized. The girls are usually pretty (unless the burden[25] is that even a plain girl can find a good husband), but they are pretty in an unglamorous way, in the way working-class girls are often very pretty. They wear blouses and jumpers with skirts, or their one dance-dress. The factory chimney can be seen sticking up in one corner and the street of houses with intermittent lamp-posts stretches behind; there are the buses and the bikes and the local dance-halls and the cinemas.

Such a nearness to the detail of the lives of readers might be simply the prelude to an excursion into the wish-fulfilment story about the surprising things that can happen to someone from that world. Sometimes this is so, and there is occasionally a stepping-up of the social level[26] inside the stories, so that people can feel how nice it would be to be a member of the villa or good-class housing groups. But often what happens is what might happen to anyone, and the environment is that of most readers.

If we look more closely at the stories we are reminded at once of the case against "stock responses"[27]: every reaction has its fixed counter for presentation.[28] I run through the account of a trial: the mouths are "set," the faces "tense with excitement;" tremors run down spines; the hero exhibits "iron control" and faces his captors with a "stony look;" his watching girl-friend is the victim of an "agonized heart" as "suspense thickens in the air." But what does this indicate? That the writers use cliché, and that the audience seems to want cliché, that they are not exploring experience, realizing experience through language? That is true. But these are first, I repeat, statements; picture presentations of the known[29]. A reader of them is hardly likely to tackle anything that could be called serious literature;

but there are worse diets, especially today. If we regard them as faithful but dramatized presentations of a life whose form and values are known, we might find it more useful to ask what are the values they embody. There is no virtue in merely laughing at them: we need to appreciate first that they may in all their triteness speak for a solid and relevant way of life. So may the tritest of Christmas and birthday card verses; that is why those cards are chosen with great care, usually for the "luvliness" and "rightness" of their verse. The world these stories present is a limited and simple one, based on a few accepted and long-held values. It is often a childish and garish world, and the springs of the emotions work in great gushing.[30] But they do work; it is not a corrupt or a pretentious world. It uses boldly words which serious writers for more sophisticated audiences understandably find difficulty in using today, and which many other writers are too knowing to be caught using. It uses, as I noted in another connection, words like "sin," "shame," "guilt," "evil," with every appearance of meaningfulness. It accepts completely, has as its main point of reference, the notion that marriage and a home, founded on love, fidelity, and cheerfulness, are the right purpose of a woman's life. If a girl "sins" the suggestion is—and this reinforces what I said earlier about the ethical emphasis in working-class beliefs—not that the girl has "sinned against herself," as another range of writers would put it, or that she has fallen short in some relationship other than the human and social, but that she has spoiled her chances of a decent home and family. One of the commoner endings to this kind of serial is for the girl either to find again the man responsible, and marry him, or to find another man who, though he knows all, is prepared to marry her and be a father to the child, loving them both. One can appreciate the force of the mistrust of "the other woman," the Jezebel, the home-breaker, the woman who sets out to wreck an existing marriage or one just about to start. Even the man with a roving eye gets short shrift[31] if he goes in for marriage-breaking; before that he comes under dispensations more indulgent than those accorded to women on the loose.[32]

It is against this ground-pattern that the thrills throw their bold reliefs, and to which they are indissolubly bound. I do not think that the thrills tempt the readers to imitate them, or much to dream of them in a sickly way. They bear the same relation to their lives as the kite to the solid flat common from which it is flown. The ground-pattern of ordinary life weaves its strands in and out through the serials and the short stories, in all the magazines. It is the pattern of the main assumptions:

> Don't spoil today because some friend has left you; you cannot say
> of ALL God has bereft you. Life is too brief for anger or for sorrow...

or:

> Happiness is made up
> Of a million tiny things
> That often pass unnoticed...

In its outlook, this is still substantially the world of Mrs. Henry Wood (*East Lynne*; *Danesbury House*; *Mrs. Haliburton's Troubles*), of Florence L. Barclay (one million copies of *The Rosary* sold), of Marie Corelli (*The Sorrows of Satan*—a "classic" to my aunts), of Silas K. Hocking (*Ivy*; *Her Benny*; *His Father*), of Annie S. Swan (A *Divided House*), of Ruth Lamb (A *Wilful Ward*; *Not Quite a Lady*; *Only a Girl Wife*; *Thoughtful Joe and How He Gained His Name*), and of a great number of others, often published by the Religious Tract Society and given as prizes in the upper classes of Sunday schools[33]. It is being ousted now by the world of the newer kind of magazine. I wonder, incidentally, whether it is resisting longer in Scotland: a very plain but attractive three-penny weekly, *People's Friend*, is still published there; a similar magazine, the *Weekly Telegraph* from Sheffield, died only a few years ago, I believe. Some of the "older" magazines are trying to preserve themselves by producing the glamour of the newer magazines, often linked to an inflated form of the older thrills. Tense and gripping new serials are announced on the placards, with large illustrations compounded of the old-style ordinariness and the new-style close-up.

But a few of the newer kind of magazines continue to increase their already phenomenal circulations. In many ways they embody the same attitudes as the "older" magazines, though they aim at too large an audience to be able to identify themselves with one social class. They are considerably smarter in presentation and presumably can provide more specialized articles on home problems than the "older" magazines. There are crudities in the "older" magazines whose removal ought not to be regretted. I have not stressed these qualities because I have been concerned to show the better links with working-class life. But the smartness of the newer magazines often extends, it seems to me, to their attitudes, and the change is not always for the good. The smartness easily becomes a slickness; there is an emphasis on money-prestige (figures of salaries or winnings are given in brackets after the names of people in the news), much "fascinated" attention is given to public personalities such as the gay wives[34] of industrial magnates, or radio and film-stars; there is a kittenish domesticity and a manner predominantly arch or whimsical.

The "glossies" are aiming, successfully, to attract the younger women who want to be smart and up to date, who do not like to seem old-fashioned. The "older" magazines would perhaps like to catch up with the "glossies," but that would be very costly; and there is still presumably a large enough audience for them to be profitably produced in much their old form. When that ceases to be the case they will, I suppose, either make really radical changes in the direction indicated by the "glossies," or die.

注释

1. recognizable human life：人们所熟知的社会生活。
2. photographic：忠实（于社会生活）的。
3. Sunday gossip-with-sensation paper：刊载流言蜚语、耸人听闻内容的星期日报纸。
4. pepping-up：让人兴奋的东西。
5. 【作者原注】Denis de Rougement, *Passion and Society*（1940）.
6. 这两句话的大意为：描写浪漫激情并非工人阶级出版物的首要内容。它们更感兴趣的是平平常常的家庭生活。
7. 作者在这段文字中力求证明：表现普通人生活的广播节目备受欢迎。
8. *Peg's Paper*：《佩格报》，以青年女性为阅读对象的流行杂志，在 20 世纪初风行一时，内容以小说为主。
9. audience：这里指读者。
10. flat：单调。

11. editorial feature：编者按。

12. 这段文字主要介绍了老式工人阶级读物中的广告。

13. the regular and occasional features：定期和不定期的特写。

14. be alive to events：追踪时事。

15. a plain Jane：意指相貌平平的女人。《简·爱》中的女主人公简（Jane）是一个姿色平常的女性。

16. Jezebel：耶洗别，以色列王亚哈（Ahab）之妻，以淫荡著称。

17. advance trailer：电影预告片。

18. fail to report：隐瞒。

19. 大意为：我们能否将它们与通俗文学的主流区分开来呢？

20. what is felt to count greatly：指读者非常看重的正常婚姻、家庭生活。

21. the stately home of England：（供人参观的）豪华宅邸。

22. Rajah：阿拉伯的酋长。

23. 大意为：因为她古道热肠，能急人所难。

24. the candid camera kind：如照相机一般准确真实。

25. the burden：主题，要旨。

26. a stepping-up of the social level：向社会上一个层次的攀爬。

27. stock response：语出瑞恰慈《实用批评》，意为"固定的反应"。

28. 大意为：在这些小说中，人物的每一种反应都有固定不变的表述方式。下一句话中的引文即是例证。

29. the known：工人阶级耳熟能详的事物。

30. 大意为：情感喷薄而出。

31. 大意为：心怀不轨的男子遭到冷遇。

32. women on the loose：放荡的女人。

33. Sunday school：主日学校，在星期日对儿童进行宗教教育的学校。

34. the gay wife：衣着艳丽的太太。

威廉斯　　　《工业小说》

雷蒙·威廉斯（1921—1988）

　　20世纪英国最重要的马克思主义文化理论家、文学批评家、英国新左派的精神导师。出生在威尔士一个工人家庭，祖父和父亲都是工人运动的活跃分子。受家庭影响，他从少年时代就积极参加工党的政治选举。1939年秋，他凭借国家奖学金，就学于剑桥大学英文系。在校期间，他参加了英国共产党。在20世纪30年代，他受到两种对立思想的影响：以克里斯多夫·考德威尔等人为代表的马克思主义文化理论和批评和F. R.利维斯为代表的细绎派的文学批评。1941年夏，威廉斯应征入伍，转战欧洲大陆。二战结束后，返回剑桥继续中断的学业。1946年，他以一篇研究易卜生戏剧的论文获得优等学士学位。大学毕业后，他谢绝了剑桥大学的研究职位，参加英国工人阶级教育协会主办的成人教育工作。从1946年到1961年，他主要讲授英国文学和国际时事方面的课程。他始终认为，文化教育是唤起民主意识、争取民主权利的有效手段。为了很好地达到这一目的，他总是把传统的人文主义教育思想与左派政治思想结合起来。在从事成人教育的同时，他还与好友合办了两份水准很高的刊物《批评家》（*Critics*）和《政治与文学》（*Politics and Letters*）。1961年，威廉斯回到剑桥大学任教，1974年就任戏剧教授，1982年从剑桥大学退休，1988年1月因病去世。

　　在40年左右的写作和学术生涯中，威廉斯出版了30多部著作，发表了几百篇文章，这当中有五部长篇小说和四部剧本。他的论著内容汪洋恣肆、旁征博引，涉及文化研究、文学批评、文化理论、文化人类学和社会学、传播学等学科，并在每一个领域都不乏独到之见。他以学院内部文化左派的身份，毕生坚持对当代资本主义社会的批判立场，始终不懈地关注社会底层争取民主权利的斗争。从40年代末到50年代初，他致力于工人阶级教育协会的成人教育工作；从50年代末发起新左派运动，积极参与核裁军运动。在1967年他与E. P.汤普森、斯图亚特·霍尔（Stuart Hall）联名发表《五一宣言》（*May*

Day Manifesto），赞同学生的造反行动。在七八十年代，他又投身于英国的反越战运动、女权主义和民主社会主义运动。他最具代表性的论著是：《文化与社会》（1958）、《漫长的革命》（1961）、《乡村与城市》（The Country and the City, 1973）、《马克思主义与文学》（Marxism and Literature, 1977）等。

《文化与社会》发掘和整理了18世纪至20世纪中叶英国社会思想史上"文化与社会"的传统及处在这一传统中的人物，包括这一百多年间大部分思想家、作家、社会改良者，从英国现代保守派的始祖、以《法国革命论》（Reflections on the Revolution in France）一书而驰名的爱德蒙·伯克（Edmund Burke）开始，直到20世纪的左翼作家乔治·奥韦尔（George Orwell）。这本书汇总了一百多年来英国思想人物对于工业资本主义的反思。它对工业革命以来英国社会思想的归纳和总结，使其成为一部出色的思想史著作。该书已被视为英国文化研究的奠基之作，任何追溯文化研究发展历程的学术性探讨，都不可避免地由它入手。当然，其影响和意义远逾文化研究和文学批评领域。

《漫长的革命》一书最有创意的地方在于，它提出了一种具体的、可操作的文化分析模式。在他看来，高头讲章式的文化史有一大缺陷：编撰者在选材落笔之际，难免受到当时意识形态的制约；行文立论、材料取舍具有高度的选择性，有维护现存社会阶级结构的嫌疑。而且，后人去分析先前历史时期的文化，仅仅依赖文化史记录也有失偏颇。为了比较完整地认识过去的文化，就必须把握住时人的社会体验和真实感受。他提出，分析一个时期的文化，一定要去分析当时人们的情感结构。在《漫长的革命》一书中，他从情感结构入手，分析了19世纪40年代以及20世纪60年代英国社会的心理。这一部分是全书的精华所在。

《乡村与城市》堪称威廉斯文学批评的代表作。自从中世纪以来，直到20世纪，英国文学中一直存在着田园忆旧文学的传统。这个传统中的诗人、作家都极力美化乡村生活。在他们笔下，安闲静谧的田园风光与丑陋粗俗的城市面目形成了有力的对比，乡村生活被理想化为人类纯真的童年——伊甸园时代。在整个19世纪，乡村一直被文人学者用来批判唯利是图、道德堕落的资本主义工业社会。可是威廉斯却独具慧眼地指出，这实际上是一种误解。资本主义通常被等同于工业生产，英国的情况则不同。英国的资本主义不是从城市而是从农村开始的。它初始于16世纪，在17世纪和18世纪出现了高度发达和现代化的农业，为工业生产提供了基础。事实上，那种田野牧歌似的乡村生活景象，不过是反资本主义的贵族人士、中世纪情结严重的浪漫文人一厢情愿的幻想产物。在此书的后几章，他利用城市与乡村的对立模式去解释宗主国与前殖民地国家。这一视角颇有新意，也有很强的预见性，它与后来兴起的后殖民主义批评有殊途同归之处。

有学者曾经这样评说，威廉斯死后留给英国思想文化界三笔丰厚的思想遗产：一是他对利维斯的高雅文化传统提出了另类解读方式，二是马克思主义的或后马克思主义的文化唯物论，三是他创建了一门新学科——文化研究。综合威廉斯三十多年思想生涯的全部成果，我们不妨得出如下结论：这三笔不菲的遗产其实是一个整体的组成部分，这个整体就是威廉斯的马克思主义文化理论。威廉斯于利维斯精英主义文化观（只有伟大的文学作品才算作文化）之外，另辟蹊径，扩大文化的范围，为流行文化正了名，认为它们也体现出社会意义，承载着社会的价值观念。这种另类的思想举措是文化研究诞生的前提，取得合法地位的基础。文化唯物论一方面是对利维斯派专注文本轻视社会历史背景的批评方式的反动，另一方面它也是对正统马克思主义文化理论的扬弃。其唯物之处在于，它强调社会生产、历史语境对于文化生产的重要性。文化唯物论经过后人的演绎，在80年代中后期逐渐生发出自己的一套批评原则，发展成为一个以文艺复兴研究为主体的批评流派，在牛津、剑桥以外的英国大学中占据了相当大的势力。

内容提要

一个时期的情感结构，多出现在官方的意识形态与民众实际社会体验发生冲突之时。在《文化与社会》中，威廉斯在分析19世纪工业题材小说之时，发现当时社会的主要情感结构，集中体现在中产阶级意识形态与小说家实际生活感受的对立之处。一方面，小说家对残酷粗俗、唯利是图的工业资本主义持有强烈的批判态度；他们充分认识到这种社会制度不公正、不人道。另一方面，他们在灵魂深处又惧怕社会变革，反对激烈改变社会现状，显得又畏手畏尾，摇摆不定。

一个时期的文学往往记录了时人对世事沧桑的直接体悟。工业革命的横空出世、社会的剧烈变化，造就了彷徨无依、矛盾丛生、焦躁不安的社会心态，这在当时的文学作品中均有所体现。在《文化与社会》中，威廉斯分析了19世纪中叶出版的六部以工业社会的阶级矛盾为题材的长篇小说，去揭示和展露这种普遍的社会心态。这六部小说分别是盖斯凯尔夫人（Mrs. Elizabeth Gaskell）的《玛丽·巴顿》（*Mary Barton*, 1948）、《南方与北方》（*North and South*, 1855），狄更斯的《艰难时世》（*Hard Times*, 1854）、本杰明·狄斯累利（Benjamin Disraeli）的《西比尔》（*Sybil*, 1845），金斯利（Charles Kinsley）的《奥尔顿·洛克》（*Alton Locke*, 1850）和乔治·艾略特（George Eliot）的《费立克斯·霍尔特》（*Felix Holt*, 1866）。

《玛丽·巴顿》描写了19世纪40年代的工业资本主义造就的阶级对立、社会贫困，感人至深。按照威廉斯的分析，作者原想以书中小人物约翰·巴顿的名字为此书命名，以他为核心人物。其意在说明，一个原本善良纯正之人因生活困顿、情绪绝望，铤而走险，犯下杀人大罪。可是，在盖斯凯尔夫人所处时代，上层阶级患上了一种"暴力恐惧症"，对于那些危及本阶级统治的政治谋杀异常恐惧。正是因为这种"暴力恐惧症"的思想渗透，限制了作者对约翰·巴顿的想象同情。于是，作者改变了初衷，转而以玛丽·巴顿为核心人物，书名当然也就因此而改变，而且特意突出约翰·巴顿杀人系工会所指使。作者既同情城市贫民的可怜境遇，同时又害怕他们铤而走险，暴力反抗。这种情感结构让作者无法适从，为摆脱困局，她只好给故事安排这样一个结局：杀人者在忏悔中了却残生，仇家则悔不该报复，并着手改善阶级关系，争取相互谅解。显然，这样的结局缺乏可信度。为了给读者提供虚幻的希望，在小说结束之际，作者将玛丽·巴顿等主要人物打发到美洲大陆；这片新开发的土地尚未受到工业社会的染指，充满新的希望，将给他们带来新的生活。

这种解决（更确切地说，是回避）社会矛盾的无奈之举，也被《南方与北方》照搬不误。这部小说的情节大致如下：一位崇尚实利的北方工业资本家，遇到一位富有人道主义精神的南方少女。在她的思想感化之下，这位资本家甘愿破产来解决劳资矛盾。然而，就在他举步维艰之际，那位南方少女突然获得了一笔意外的遗产。结果工业家人财两得，故事在皆大欢喜中结束。因不期而至的遗产而脱困，这种故事套路在维多利亚时代的小说中屡见不鲜。这种小说结局恰恰反映出作者对社会问题的无所适从。

维多利亚时代著名政客、数度出任英国首相的本杰明·狄斯雷利也以为文著称。他写过一本说教气味浓厚的政治小说《西比尔》，在当时还颇有影响。作者以小说为政论，从保守党的立场出发，攻击工业主义和自由党的政治改革。他解决社会问题的办法是开明的贵族政治。于是，在小说的结尾，尖锐贫富的冲突变成了一场喜剧大团圆：男主人公"开明贵族"与女主人公"人民女儿"欢天喜地结为一体。威廉斯评论说，这种贫富的结合象征着一个崭新国家的诞生。这正是狄斯雷利本人的政治理想的体现。

基督教社会主义者金斯利的小说《奥尔顿·洛克》也是一部政治小说，寄托着作者的社会理想。作品的主人公是一名工人，他在劳动繁重、生计困难之时，想去参加宪章运动；但经人劝说，他转而投入基督教社会主义事业。作者对宪章运动充满同情，可并不赞同宪章运动的实际行动。本书的主人公也是在矛盾无法解决之际被作者打发到了美国，最后客死他乡。

乔治·艾略特小说《菲立克斯·霍尔特》的结构与前几部小说颇为类似。小说情节以财产继承之纠葛为主线，女主人公身处贫困环境，但具有很高的思想教养。小说的男主角是一位激进的劳工，鼓吹社会变革，但不主张改变现行的阶级结构，其经历类似金斯利笔下的奥尔顿·洛克。两人都卷入一场暴乱，因涉嫌为主谋，被判刑入狱。对于这些形式结构上的雷同，威廉斯并不认为是作者因袭的结果；其真正原因是，就心理而言，这几位作者有着相同的情感结构：他们对下层阶级的悲惨遭遇充满同情之心，对于社会现状均有改良之意；可是，他们又对群众暴力改变现实充满恐惧之情。

至于狄更斯的《艰难时世》，威廉斯认为，它对工业主冷酷行径的探索很有创建，对于工业主义意识形态——功利哲学的认识和批判尤为全面；但狄更斯的解决方式不是社会改革，更不是反抗，而是求助最不牢靠的人性，"个人的仁慈、同情以及宽厚克己"来解决社会冲突。因此，这部小说没有写出值得师法的英雄人物。读罢全书，读者感受的也只有参透世事玄机的苍凉。《艰难时世》渗透了工业革命时期人们无力改变现状的普遍情感，活话出时人独特的社会体验。

分析完这几部小说后，威廉斯总结说，这几部小说反映了19世纪中期英国中产阶级一种普遍的情感结构：一方面，他们因新兴的工业社会剥削残酷、有悖人道而反感日增，对其强烈批判，并对这个社会制度的邪恶有相当直接的认识；但是，在另一方面，他们又恐惧激烈的社会变革会带来巨大的动荡。

Raymond Henry Williams (1921—1988)

THE INDUSTRIAL NOVELS

Our understanding of the response to industrialism would be incomplete without reference to an interesting group of novels, written at the middle of the century, which not only provide some of the most vivid descriptions of life in an unsettled industrial society, but also illustrate certain common assumptions within which the direct response was undertaken. There are the facts of the new society, and there is this structure of feeling, which I will try to illustrate from *Mary Barton*, *North and South*, *Hard Times*, *Sybil*, *Alton Locke*, and *Felix Holt*.

Mary Barton (1848)

Mary Barton, particularly in its early chapters, is the most moving response in literature to the industrial suffering of the 1840s. The really impressive thing about the book is the intensity of the effort to record, in its own terms, the feel of everyday life in the working-class homes. The method, in part, is that of documentary record, as may be seen in such details as the carefully annotated reproduction of dialect, the carefully included details of food prices in the account of the tea-party, the itemized description of the furniture of the Barton's living-room, and the writing-out of the ballad (again annotated) of *The Oldham Weaver*[1]. The interest of this record is considerable, but the method has, nevertheless, a slightly distancing effect. Mrs. Gaskell could hardly help coming to this life as an observer, a reporter, and we are always to some extent conscious of this. But there is genuine imaginative re-creation in her accounts of the walk in Green Heys Fields, and of tea at the Bartons's house, and again, notably, in the chapter *Poverty and Death* Where John Barton and his friend find the starving family in the cellar. For so convincing a creation of the characteristic feelings and responses of families of this kind (matters more determining than the material details on which the reporter is apt to concentrate) the English novel had to wait, indeed, for the early writing of D. H. Lawrence.[2] If Mrs. Gaskell never quite manages the sense of full participation which would finally authenticate this, she yet brings to these scenes an intuitive recognition of feelings which has its own sufficient conviction.³ The chapter *Old Alice's History* brilliantly dramatizes the situation of that early generation brought from the villages and the countryside to the streets and cellars of the industrial towns. The account of Job Legh, the weaver and naturalist, vividly embodies that other kind of response to an urban industrial environment: the devoted, lifelong study of living creatures—a piece of amateur scientific work, and at the same time an instinct for living creatures which hardens, by its very contrast with its environment, into a kind of crankiness. In the factory workers walking out in spring into Green Heys Fields; in Alice Wilson, remembering in her cellar the ling-gathering for besoms in the native village that she will never again see; in Job Legh, intent on his impaled insects—these early chapters embody the characteristic response of a generation to the new and crushing experience of industrialism. The other early chapters movingly embody the continuity and development of the sympathy and cooperative instinct which were already establishing a main working-class tradition.

The structure of feeling from which *Mary Barton* begins is, then, a combination of sympathetic observation and of a largely successful attempt at imaginative identification.⁴ If it had continued in this way, it might have been a great novel of its kind. But the emphasis of the method changes, and there are several reasons for this. One reason can be studied in a curious aspect of the history of the writing of the book. It was originally to be called *John Barton*. As Mrs. Gaskell wrote later:

> Round the character of John Barton all the others formed themselves; he was my hero, *the* person with whom all my sympathies went.

And she added:

> The character, and some of the speeches, are exactly a poor man I know.⁵

The change of emphasis which the book subsequently underwent, and the consequent change of title to *Mary Barton*, seem to have been made at the instance of her publishers,⁶ Chapman and Hall. The details of this matter are still obscure, but we must evidently allow something for this external influence on the shape of the novel. Certainly the John Barton of the later parts of the book is a very shadowy figure. In committing the murder, he seems to put himself not only beyond the range of Mrs. Gaskell's sympathy (which is understandable), but, more essentially, beyond the range of her powers. The agony of conscience is there, as a thing told and sketched, but, as the crisis of "my hero, *the* person with whom all my sympathies went," it is weak and almost incidental. This is because the novel as published is centered on the daughter—her indecision between Jem Wilson and "her gay lover, Harry Carson;" her agony in Wilson's trial; her pursuit and last-minute rescue of the vital witness; the realization of her love for Wilson: all this, the familiar and orthodox plot of the Victorian novel of sentiment, but of little lasting interest. And it now seems incredible that the novel should ever have been planned in any other way. If Mrs. Gaskell had written "round the character of Mary Barton all the others formed themselves," she would have confirmed our actual impression of the finished book.

Something must be allowed for the influence of her publishers, but John Barton must always have been cast as the murderer, with the intention perhaps of showing an essentially good man driven to an appalling crime by loss, suffering and despair. One can still see the elements of this in the novel as we have it, but there was evidently a point, in its writing, at which the flow of sympathy with which she began was arrested,[7] and then, by the change of emphasis which the change of title records, diverted to the less compromising figure of the daughter. The point would be less important if it were not characteristic of the structure of feeling within which she was working.[8] It is not only that she recoils from the violence of the murder, to the extent of being unable even to enter it as the experience of the man conceived as her hero. It is also that, as compared with the carefully representative character of the early chapters, the murder itself is exceptional. It is true that in 1831 a Thomas Ashton, of Pole Bank, Werneth, was murdered under somewhat similar circumstances, and that the Ashton family appear to have taken the murder of Carson as referring to this. Mrs. Gaskell, disclaiming the reference in a letter to them, turned up some similar incidents in Glasgow at about the same time. But in fact, taking the period as a whole, the response of political assassination is so uncharacteristic as to be an obvious distortion. The few recorded cases only emphasize this.

Even when one adds the cases of intimidation, and the occasional vitriol-throwing[9] during the deliberate breaking of strikes, it remains true, and was at the time a subject of surprised comment by foreign observers, that the characteristic response of the English working people, even in times of grave suffering, was not one of personal violence. Mrs. Gaskell was under no obligation to write a representative novel; she might legitimately have taken a special case. But the tone elsewhere is deliberately representative, and she is even, as she says, modeling John Barton on "a poor man I know." The real explanation, surely, is that John Barton, a political murderer appointed by a trade union, is a dramatization of the *fear of violence* which was widespread among the upper and middle classes at the time, and which penetrated, as an arresting and controling factor, even into the deep imaginative sympathy of a Mrs. Gaskell. This fear that the working people might take matters into their own hands was widespread and characteristic, and the murder of Harry Carson is an imaginative working-out of this fear, and of reactions to it, rather than any kind of observed and considered experience.

The point is made clearer when it is remembered that Mrs. Gaskell planned the murder herself, and chose, for the murderer, "my hero, *the* person with whom all my sympathies went." In this respect the act of violence, a sudden aggression against a man contemptuous of the sufferings of the poor, looks very much like a projection, with which, in the end, she was unable to come to terms. The imaginative choice of the act of murder and then the imaginative recoil from it have the effect of ruining the necessary integration of feeling in the whole theme.[10] The diversion to Mary Barton, even allowing for the publishers's influence, must in fact have been welcome.

Few persons felt more deeply than Elizabeth Gaskell the sufferings of the industrial poor. As a minister's wife in Manchester, she actually saw this, and did not, like many other novelists, merely know it by report or occasional visit. Her response to the suffering is deep and genuine, but pity cannot stand alone in such a structure of feeling. It is joined, in *Mary Barton*, by the confusing violence and fear of violence, and is supported, finally, by a kind of writing-off, when the misery of the actual situation can no longer be endured. John Barton dies penitent, and the elder Carson repents of his vengeance and turns, as the sympathetic observer wanted the employers to turn, to efforts at improvement and mutual understanding. This was the characteristic humanitarian conclusion, and it must certainly be respected. But it was not enough, we notice, for the persons with whom Mrs. Gaskell's sympathies were engaged. Mary Barton, Jem Wilson, Mrs. Wilson, Margaret, Will, Job Legh—all the objects of her real sympathy—end the book far removed from the situation which she had set out to examine. All are going to Canada; there could be no more devastating conclusion. A solution within the actual situation might be hoped for, but the solution with which the heart went was a canceling of the actual difficulties and the removal of the persons pitied to the uncompromised New World.

North and South (1855)

Mrs. Gaskell's second industrial novel, *North and South*, is less interesting, because the tension is less. She takes up here her actual position, as a sympathetic observer. Margaret Hale, with the feelings and up-bringing of the daughter of a Southern clergyman, moves with her father to industrial Lancashire, and we follow her reactions, her observations, and her attempts to do what good she can. Because this is largely Mrs. Gaskell's own situation, the integration of the book is markedly superior. Margaret's arguments with the mill-owner Thornton are interesting and honest, within the political and economic conceptions of the period. But the emphasis of the novel, as the lengthy inclusion of such arguments suggests, is almost entirely now on attitudes to the working people, rather than on the attempt to reach, imaginatively, their feelings about their lives. It is interesting, again, to note the manner of the working-out. The relationship of Margaret and Thornton and their eventual marriage serve as a unification of the practical energy of the Northern manufacturer with the developed sensibility of the Southern girl: this is stated almost explicitly, and is seen as a solution. Thornton goes back to the North

> to have the opportunity of cultivating some intercourse with the hands beyond the mere "cash nexus."[11]

Humanized by Margaret, he will work at what we now call "the improvement of human relations in industry." The conclusion deserves respect, but it is worth noticing that it is not only under Margaret's influence that Thornton will attempt this, but under her patronage. The other manufacturers, as Thornton says, "will shake their heads and look grave" at it. This may be characteristic, but Thornton, though bankrupt, can be the exception, by availing himself of Margaret's unexpected legacy. Money from elsewhere, in fact—by that device of the legacy which solved so many otherwise insoluble problems in the world of the Victorian novel—will enable Thornton, already affected by the superior gentleness and humanity of the South, to make his humanitarian experiment. Once again Mrs. Gaskell works out her reaction to the insupportable situation by going—in part adventitiously—outside it.[12]

Hard Times (1854)

Ordinarily Dickens's criticisms of the world he lives in are casual and incidental[13]—a matter of including among the ingredients of a book some indignant treatment of a particular abuse. But in *Hard Times* he is for once possessed by a comprehensive vision, one in which the inhumanities of Victorian civilization are seen as fostered and sanctioned by a hard philosophy, the aggressive formulation of an inhumane spirit.[14]

This comment by F. R. Leavis on *Hard Times* serves to distinguish Dickens's intention from that of Mrs. Gaskell in *Mary Barton*. *Hard Times* is less imaginative observation than an imaginative judgment. It is a judgment of social attitudes, but again it is something more than *North and South*. It is a thorough-going and creative examination of the dominant philosophy of industrialism—of the hardness that Mrs. Gaskell saw as little more than a misunderstanding, which might be patiently broken down. That Dickens could achieve this more comprehensive understanding is greatly to the advantage of the novel.[15] But against this we must set the fact that in terms of human understanding of the industrial working people Dickens is obviously less successful than Mrs. Gaskell: his Stephen Blackpool, in relation to the people of Mary Barton, is little more than a diagrammatic figure.[16] The gain in comprehension, that is to say, has been achieved by the rigors of generalization and abstraction; *Hard Times* is an analysis of Industrialism, rather than experience of it.

The most important point, in this context, that has to be made about *Hard Times* is a point about Thomas Gradgrind. Josiah Bounderby, the other villain of the piece, is a simple enough case. He is, with rough justice, the embodiment of the aggressive money-making and power-seeking ideal which was a driving force of the Industrial Revolution. That he is also a braggart, a liar, and in general personally repellant is of course a comment on Dickens's method. The conjunction of these personal defects with the aggressive ideal is not (how much easier things would be if it were) a necessary conjunction. A large part of the Victorian reader's feelings against Bounderby (and perhaps a not inconsiderable part of the twentieth-century intellectual's) rests on the older and rather different feeling that trade, as such, is gross[17]. The very name (and Dickens uses his names with conscious and obvious effect), incorporating *bounder*[18], incorporates this typical feeling. The social criticism represented by *bounder* is, after all, a rather different matter from the question of aggressive economic individualism. Dickens, with rough justice, fuses the separate reactions, and it is easy not to notice how one set of feelings is made to affect the other.

The difficulty about Thomas Gradgrind is different in character. It is that the case against him is so good, and his refutation by experience so masterly, that it is easy for the modern reader to forget exactly *what* Gradgrind is. It is surprising how common is the mistake of using the remembered name, Gradgrind, as a class-name for the hard Victorian employer. The valuation which Dickens actually asks us to make is more difficult. Gradgrind is a Utilitarian[19]: seen by Dickens as one of the *feeloosofers* against whom Cobbett thundered,[20] or as one of the *steam-engine* intellects described by Carlyle.[21] This line is easy enough, but one could as easily draw another: say, Thomas Gradgrind, Edwin Chadwick, John Stuart Mill.[22] Chadwick, we are told, was "the most hated man in England," and he worked by methods, and was blamed for "meddling," in terms that are hardly any distance from Dickens's Gradgrind. Mill is a more difficult instance (although the education of which he felt himself a victim will be related, by the modern reader, to the Gradgrind system.[23]) But it seems certain that Dickens has Mill's *Political Economy* (1849) very much in mind in his general indictment of the ideas which built and maintained

Coketown. (Mill's reaction, it may be noted, was the expressive "that creature Dickens."[24] It is easy now to realize that Mill was something more than a Gradgrind. But we are missing Dickens's point if we fail to see that in condemning Thomas Gradgrind, the representative figure, we are invited also to condemn the kind of thinking and the methods of inquiry and legislation which in fact promoted a large measure of social and industrial reform.[25] One wonders, for example, what a typical Fabian[26] feels when he is invited to condemn Gradgrind, not as an individual but as a type. This may, indeed, have something to do with the common error of memory about Gradgrind to which I have referred. Public commissions, Blue Books, Parliamentary legislation—all these, in the world of *Hard Times*—are Gradgrindery.

For Dickens is not setting Reform against Exploitation. He sees what we normally understand by both as two sides of the same coin, Industrialism. His positives[27] do not lie in social improvement, but rather in what he sees as the elements of human nature—personal kindness, sympathy, and forbearance. It is not the model factory against the satanic mill, nor is it the humanitarian experiment against selfish exploitation. It is, rather, individual persons against the System. In so far as it is social at all, it is the Circus against Coketown.[28] The schoolroom contrast of Sissy Jupe and Bitzer is a contrast between the education, practical but often inarticulate, which is gained by living and doing, and the education, highly articulated, which is gained by systemization and abstraction. It is a contrast of which Cobbett would have warmly approved; but in so far as we have all (and to some extent inevitably) been committed to a large measure of the latter,[29] it is worth noting again what a large revaluation Dickens is asking us to make. The instinctive, unintellectual, unorganized life is the ground, here, of genuine feeling, and of all good relationship.[30] The Circus is one of the very few ways in which Dickens could have dramatized this, but it is less the Circus that matters than the experience described by Sleary:

> that there ith a love in the world, not all Thelf-interetht after all, but thomething very different... it hath a way of ith own of calculating or not calculating, which thomehow or another ith at leatht ath hard to give a name to, ath the wayth of the dogth ith.[31]

It is a characteristic conclusion, in a vitally important tradition which based its values on such grounds. It is the major criticism of Industrialism as a whole way of life, and its grounds in experience have been firm. What is essential is to recognize that Dickens saw no social expression of it, or at least nothing that could be "given a name to." The experience is that of individual persons. Almost the whole organization of society, as Dickens judges, is against it. The Circus can express it because it is not part of the industrial organization. The Circus is an end in itself, a pleasurable end, which is instinctive and (in certain respects) anarchic. It is significant that Dickens has thus to go outside the industrial situation to find any expression of his values. This going outside is similar to the Canada in which *Mary Barton* ends, or the legacy of Margaret Hale. But it is also more than these, in so far as it is not only an escape but a positive assertion of a certain kind of experience, the denial of which was the real basis (as Dickens saw it) of the hard times.

It was inevitable, given the kind of criticism that Dickens was making, that his treatment of the industrial working people should have been so unsatisfactory. He recognizes them as objects of pity, and he recognizes the personal devotion in suffering of which they are capable. But the only conclusion he can expect them to draw is Stephen Blackpool's:

Aw a muddle![32]

This is reasonable, but the hopelessness and passive suffering are set against the attempts of the working people to better their conditions. The trade unions are dismissed by a stock Victorian reaction, with the agitator Slackbridge. Stephen Blackpool, like Job Legh, is shown to advantage because he will not join them. The point can be gauged by a comparison with Cobbett, whose criticism of the System[33] is in many ways very similar to that of Dickens, and rests on so many similar valuations, yet who was not similarly deceived, even when the trade unions came as a novelty to him. The point indicates a wider comment on Dickens's whole position.

The scathing analysis of Coketown and all its works, and of the supporting political economy and aggressive utilitarianism, is based on Carlyle. So are the hostile reactions to Parliament and to ordinary ideas of reform. Dickens takes up the hostility,[34] and it serves as a comprehensive vision, to which he gives all his marvellous energy. But his identification with Carlyle is really negative. There are no social alternatives to Bounderby and Gradgrind: not the time-serving aristocrat Harthouse; not the decayed gentlewoman Mrs. Sparsit; nowhere, in fact, any active Hero. Many of Dickens's social attitudes cancel each other out, for he will use almost any reaction in order to undermine any normal representative position. *Hard Times*, in tone and structure, is the work of a man who has "seen through" society, who has found them all out. The only reservation is for the passive and the suffering, for the meek who shall inherit the earth but not Coketown, not industrial society. This primitive feeling, when joined by the aggressive conviction of having found everyone else out, is the retained position of an adolescent. The innocence shames the adult world, but also essentially rejects it. As a whole response, *Hard Times* is more a symptom of the confusion of industrial society than an understanding of it, but it is a symptom that is significant and continuing.

Sybil, or The Two Nations (1845)

Sybil can be read now as the production of a future Conservative Prime Minister,[35] and hence in the narrow sense as a political novel. The elements of political pleading are indeed evident in any reading of it. Their curiosity, their partisanship, and their opportunitism are matched only by their brilliance of address[36]. The novel would be fascinating if it were only political. The stucco elegance of Disraeli's writing has a consonance with one kind of political argument. What is intolerable in his descriptions of persons and feelings becomes in his political flights a rather likeable panache. The descriptions of industrial squalor are very like those of Dickens on Coketown: brilliant romantic generalizations—the view from the train, from the hustings, from the printed page—yet often moving, like all far-seeing rhetoric. There are similar accounts of the conditions of the agricultural poor which need to be kept in mind against the misleading contrasts of *North and South*. Again, in a quite different manner, there is in *Sybil* the most spirited description of the iniquities of the tommy-shop, and of the practical consequences of the system of truck, to be found anywhere.

Disraeli's anger—the generalized anger of an outsider making his way—
carries him often beyond his formal text. The hostile descriptions of London
political and social life are again generalization, but they have, doubtless, the
same rhetorical significance as those of the forays among the poor. Anyone
who is prepared to give credit to Disraeli's unsupported authority on any
matter of social fact has of course mistaken his man, as he would similarly
mistake Dickens. But Disraeli, like Dickens, is a very fine generalizing
analyst of cant, and almost as fine a generalizing rhetorician of human
suffering. Both functions, it must be emphasized, are reputable.

In terms of ideas, *Sybil* is almost a collector's piece. There is this, for
instance, from Coleridge:

> But if it have not furnished us with abler administration or a more
> illustrious senate, the Reform Act may have exercised on the country at
> large a beneficial influence? Has it? Has it elevated the tone of the public
> mind? Has it cultured the popular sensibilities to noble and ennobling
> ends? Has it proposed to the people of England a higher test of national
> respect and confidence than the debasing qualification universally
> prevalent in this country since the fatal introduction of the system of
> Dutch finance? Who will pretend it? If a spirit of rapacious covetousness,
> desecrating all the humanities of life, has been the besetting sin of England
> for the last century and a half, since the passing of the Reform Act the altar
> of Mammon has blazed with triple worship. To acquire, to accumulate,
> to plunder each other by virtue of philosophic phrases, to propose a
> Utopia to consist only of wealth and toil, this has been the breathless
> business of enfranchised England for the last twelve years, until we are
> startled from our voracious strife by the wail of intolerable serfage.[37]

It is true that this is political, a part of the grand assaulton Whiggery[38]. But
the terms of the assault are familiar, as part of a much wider criticism. Or
again this, which was to reappear in our own century with an air of original
discovery:

> "...There is no community in England; there is aggregation, but
> aggregation under circumstances which make it rather a dissociating than

a uniting principle...It is a community of purpose that constitutes society...
without that, men may be drawn into contiguity, but they still continue
virtually isolated."

"And is that their condition in cities?"

"It is their condition everywhere; but in cities that condition is
aggravated. A density of population implies a severer struggle for
existence, and a consequent repulsion of elements brought into too close
contact. In great cities men are brought together by the desire of gain.
They are not in a state of cooperation, but of isolation, as to the making
of fortunes; and for all the rest they are careless of neighbors. Christianity
teaches us to love our neighbors as ourself; modern society acknowledges
no neighbor."[39]

These views of the Chartist Stephen Morley were the common element in
a number of varying political positions. They have remained the terms of a
basic criticism of Industrialism.

The two nations, of rich and poor, have of course become famous.
The basis of the attempt to make one nation of them is the restoration to
leadership of an enlightened aristocracy. For,

"There is a change in them, as in all other things,"... said Egremont.

"If there be a change," said Sybil, "it is because in some degree the
people have learnt their strength."

"Ah! dismiss from your mind those fallacious fancies," said
Egremont. "The people are not strong; the people never can be strong.
Their attempts at self-vindication will end only in their suffering and
confusion."

It is, of course, the familiar injunction, in Cobbett's words, to "be quiet," and
the familiar assumption of the business of regeneration by others—in this
case "the enlightened aristocracy." Disraeli shared the common prejudices
about the popular movement: his account of the initiation of Dandy Mick
into a Trade Union—

"...you will execute with zeal and alacrity...every task and
injunction that the majority of your brethren[40]...shall impose upon you,

in furtherance of our common welfare, of which they are the sole judges: such as the chastisement of Nobs[41], the assassination of oppressive and tyrannical masters, or the demolition of all mills, works and shops that shall be deemed by us incorrigibl."[42]

—is characteristically cloak-and-dagger. This must be acknowledged alongside the shrewder assessment:

> The people she found was not that pure embodiment of unity of feeling, of interest, and of purpose which she had pictured in her abstractions. The people had enemies among the people: their own passions; which made them often sympathize, often combine, with the privileged.[43]

This shrewdness might well have been also applied to some of Disraeli's other abstractions, but perhaps that was left for later, in the progress of his political career.[44]

The passages quoted are near the climax of that uniting of Egremont, "the enlightened aristocrat," and Sybil, "the daughter of the People," which, in the novel, is the symbolic creation of the One Nation. This, again, is the way the heart goes,[45] and it is the novel's most interesting illustration. For Sybil, of course, is only theoretically "the daughter of the People." The actual process of the book is the discovery that she is a dispossessed aristocrat, and the marriage bells ring, not over the achievement of One Nation, but over the uniting of the properties of Marney and Mowbray, one agricultural, the other industrial: a marriage symbolical, indeed, of the political development which was the actual issue. The restored heiress stands, in the general picture with Margaret Thornton's legacy, with Canada, and with the Horse-Riding. But it is significant of Disraeli's shrewdness that, through the device, he embodied what was to become an actual political event.[46]

Alton Locke, Tailor and Poet (1850)

In part, *Alton Locke* is in the orthodox sense an "exposure": an informed, angry, and sustained account of sweated labor in the "Cheap and Nasty" clothing trade. Much of it can still be read in these terms, with attention and sympathy. It is fair to note, however, that in respect of this theme the Preface is more effective than the novel, and for the unexpected reason that it is more specific.

The wider intention of the book is rather different. It is really a story of conversion: of the making of a Chartist in the usual sense, and of his remaking in Kingsley's sense. This is the basic movement in a book which is extremely discursive in mood[47]. The earlier chapters are perhaps the most effective: the caricature of the Baptist home; the indignant realism of the apprenticeship in the sweating-rooms; the generalized description of the longing from the "prison-house of brick and iron" for the beauty apprehended as knowledge and poetry. The beginnings of Alton Locke in political activity are also, in general outline, convincing. With them, however, begins also the major emphasis on argument, on prolonged *discussion* of events, which is evidently Kingsley's motive and energy. Often this discussion is interesting, particularly as we recognize the familiar popularization of Carlyle and of the ideas which Carlyle concentrated. This merges, from the time of the conversion (the curious chapter *Dreamland*), into the Christian Socialist arguments with which Kingsley's name is commonly identified. It is doubtful whether much attention of a different kind, attention, that is, other than to the genealogy of ideas, can be given to all these parts of the book.[48] A very large part of it is like reading old newspapers, or at least old pamphlets. The issues are there, but the terms are arbitrary and the connexions mechanical. The book is not an "autobiography" but a tract.[49]

We need note here only the conclusion, alike of the story and of the argument. Once again, the motive to Chartism[50], to a working-class political movement, has been sympathetically set down (it was on this score that Kingsley and others were thought of as "advanced" or "dangerous" thinkers). But again the effort is seen finally as a delusion: in effect—"we understand and sympathize with your sufferings which drove you to this, but what you are doing is terribly mistaken":

> "Ay," she went on, her figure dilating, and her eyes flashing, like
> an inspired prophetess, "that is in the Bible! What would you more than
> that? That is your charter; the only ground of all charters. You, like all

mankind, have had dim inspirations, confused yearnings after your future destiny, and, like all the world from the beginning, you have tried to realize, by self-willed methods of your own, what you can only do by God's inspiration, God's method...Oh! look back, look back, at the history of English Radicalism for the last half-century, and judge by your own deeds, your own words; were you fit for those privileges which you so frantically demanded? Do not answer me, that those who had them were equally unfit; but thank God, if the case be indeed so, that your incapacity was not added to theirs, to make confusion worse confounded. Learn a new lesson. Believe at last that you are in Christ, and become new creatures. With those miserable, awful farce tragedies of April and June, let old things pass away, and all things become new. Believe that your kingdom is not of this world, but of One whose servants must not fight."[51]

It is not surprising after this that the destiny of the hero is—once again—emigration. Alton Locke dies as he reaches America, but his fellow-Chartist, Crossthwaite, will come back after seven years.

The regeneration of society, according to Kingsley's Cambridge preface to the book, will meanwhile proceed under the leadership of a truly enlightened aristocracy. It will be a movement towards democracy, but not to that "tyranny of numbers" of which the dangers have been seen in the United States. For:

> As long, I believe, as the Throne, the House of Lords, and the Press, are what, thank God, they are, so long will each enlargement of the suffrage be a fresh source not of danger, but of safety; for it will bind the masses to the established order of things by that loyalty which springs from content; from the sense of being appreciated, trusted, dealt with not as children, but as men.[52]

Felix Holt (1866)

We are interested in Mrs. Gaskell or Kingsley or Disraeli because of what they testified; with George Eliot there is another interest, because of the quality of the witness.

This quality is evident in *Felix Holt*, which as a novel has a quite different status from those previously discussed. It has also, however, much in common with them. The formal plot turns on the familiar complications of inheritance in property, and Esther, with her inherited breeding showing itself in poor circumstances, has something in common with Sybil. As with Sybil, her title to a great estate is proved, but there the comparison with Disraeli ends. Harold Transome is, like Egremont, a second son; like him, he turns to the reforming side in politics. But George Eliot was incapable of resting on[53] the image of an Egremont, the figurehead of the enlightened gentleman. Harold Transome is a coarser reality, and it is impossible that Esther should marry him. She renounces her claim and marries Felix Holt. It is as if Sybil had renounced the Mowbray estates and married Stephen Morley. I do not make any claim for the superior reality of George Eliot's proceedings.[54] The thing is as contrived, in the service of a particular image of the desirable,[55] as Disraeli's very different dénouement. George Eliot works with a rather finer net, but it is not in such elements of the novel that her real superiority is apparent.

Nor again is there much superiority in her creation of Felix Holt himself. He is shown as a working-man radical, determined to stick to his own class, and to appeal solely to the energies of "moral force". He believes in sobriety and education, argues for social rather than merely political reform, and wants to be

> a demagogue of a new sort; an honest one, if possible, who will tell
> the people they are blind and foolish, and neither flatter them nor fatten
> on them.[56]

It is not easy, at any time, to say whether a character "convinces". We are all apt, in such questions, to impose our own conceptions both of the probable and the desirable. But one can usually see, critically, when a character comes to existence in a number of aspects, forming something like the image of a life; and, alternatively, when a character is fixed at a different and simpler stage: in the case of Felix Holt, at a physical appearance and a set of opinions. Mrs. Gaskell could conceive the early John Barton in much these terms, but, because other substance was lacking, she had virtually to dismiss him as a person when the course of action found necessary on other grounds went beyond the limits of her sympathy. Felix Holt, like Alton Locke, is conceived as a more probable hero: that is to say, as one whose general attitude is wholly sympathetic to the author, and who is detached from him only by a relative immaturity. Like Alton Locke, Felix Holt becomes involved in a riot; like him, he is mistaken for a ring leader; like him, he is sentenced to imprisonment. This recurring pattern is not copying, in the vulgar sense. It is rather the common working of an identical fear, which was present also in Mrs. Gaskell's revision of John Barton. It is at root the fear of a sympathetic, reformist-minded member of the middle classes at being drawn into any kind of mob violence.[57] John Barton is involved in earnest, and his creator's sympathies are at once withdrawn, to the obvious detriment of the work as a whole[58]. Sympathy is transferred to Jem Wilson, mistakenly accused, and to Margaret's efforts on his behalf, which have a parallel in Esther's impulse to speak at the trial of Felix Holt. But the basic pattern is a dramatization of the fear of being involved in violence: a dramatization made possible by the saving clause of innocence and mistaken motive, and so capable of redemption. What is really interesting is that the conclusion of this kind of dramatization is then taken as proof of the rightness of the author's original reservations. The people are indeed dangerous, in their constant tendency to blind disorder. Anyone sympathizing with them is likely to become involved. Therefore (a most ratifying word) it can be sincerely held that the popular movements actually under way are foolish and inadequate, and that the only wise course is dissociation from them.

Of course, that there is inadequacy in any such movement is obvious, but the discriminations one would expect from a great novelist are certainly not drawn in *Felix Holt*. Once again Cobbett is a touchstone, and his conduct at his own trial after the laborers' revolts of 1830 is a finer demonstration of real maturity than the fictional compromises here examined. Cobbett, like nearly all men who have worked with their hands, hated any kind of violent destruction of useful things. But he had the experience and the strength to enquire further into violence. He believed, moreover, what George Eliot so obviously could not believe, that the common people were something other than a mob, and had instincts and habits something above drunkenness, gullibility and ignorance. He would not have thought *Felix Holt* an "honest demagogue" for telling the people that they were "blind and foolish." He would have thought him rather a very convenient ally of the opponents of reform. George Eliot's view of the common people is uncomfortably close to that of Carlyle in *Shooting Niagara*: "blockheadism, gullibility, bribeability, amenability to beer and balderdash." This was the common first assumption, and was the basis for the distinction (alike in her 1848 comment and in *Felix Holt*) between "political" and "social" reform. The former is only "machinery;" the latter is seen as substance. The distinction is useful, but consider this very typical speech by Felix Holt:

> The way to get rid of folly is to get rid of vain expectations, and of thoughts that don't agree with the nature of things. The men who have had true thoughts about water, and what it will do when it is turned into steam and under all sorts of circumstances, have made themselves a great power in the world: they are turning the wheels of engines that will help to change most things. But no engines would have done, if there had been false notions about the way water would act. Now, all the schemes about voting, and districts, and annual Parliaments, and the rest, are engines, and the water or steam—the force that is to work them—must come out of human nature—out of men's passions, feelings, and desires. Whether the engines will do good work or bad depends on these feelings. [59]

But the "engines" mentioned are, after all, particular engines, proposed to do different work from the engines previously employed. It is really mechanical to class[60] all the engines together and to diminish their importance, when in fact their purposes differ. The new proposals are an embodiment of "passions, feelings, and desires": alternative proposals, supported by alternative feelings, so that a choice can properly be made. The real criticism, one suspects, is of "thoughts that don't agree with the nature of things," and this "nature of things" can either be a supposedly permanent "human nature", or else, as probably, the supposedly immutable "laws of society." Among these "laws", as Felix Holt's argument continues, is the supposition that among every hundred men there will be thirty with "some soberness, some sense to choose", and seventy, either drunk or "ignorant or mean or stupid." With such an assumption it is easy enough to "prove" that a voting reform would be useless. George Eliot's advice, essentially, is that the workingmen should first make themselves "sober and educated," under the leadership of men like Felix Holt, and then reform will do some good. But the distinction between "political" and "social" reform is seen at this point at its most arbitrary. The abuses of an unreformed Parliament are even dragged in as an argument against parliamentary reform—it will only be more of the same sort of thing.[61] The winning through political reform of the means of education, of the leisure necessary to take such opportunity, of the conditions of work and accommodation which will diminish poverty and drunkenness: all these and similar aims, which were the purposes for which the "engines" were proposed, are leftout of the argument[62]. Without them, the sober responsible educated working man must, presumably, spring fully armed from his own ("drunken, ignorant, mean and stupid") head.

It has passed too long for a kind of maturity and depth in experience to argue that politics and political attachments are only possible to superficial minds;[63] that any appreciation of the complexity of human nature necessarily involves a wise depreciation of these noisy instruments[64]. The tone—"cold reservations and incredulities to save their credit for wisdom"[65]—is often heard in *Felix Holt*:

> Crying abuses— "bloated paupers," "bloated pluralists," and other corruptions hindering men from being wise and happy—had to be fought against and slain. Such a time is a time of hope. Afterwards, when the corpses of those monsters have been held up to the public wonder and abhorrence, and yet wisdom and happiness do not follow, but rather a more abundant breeding of the foolish and unhappy, comes a time of doubt and despondency....Some dwelt on the abolition of all abuses, and on millennial blessedness generally; others, whose imaginations were less suffused with exhalations of the dawn, insisted chiefly on the ballot-box.[66]

The wise shake of the head draws a complacent answering smile.[67] But what I myself find in such a passage as this, in the style ("suffused with exhalations of the dawn;" "millennial blessedness generally") as in the feeling ("a more abundant breeding of the foolish and unhappy"), is not the deep and extensive working of a generous mind, but rather the petty cynicism of a mind that has lost, albeit only temporarily, its capacity for human respect.

Felix Holt's opinions are George Eliot's opinions purged of just this element, which is a kind of intellectual fatigue. It is the mood of the 'sixties of—*Shooting Niagara and Culture and Anarchy*[68]—holding an incompetent post-mortem on the earlier phases of Radicalism. Felix Holt himself is not so much a character as an impersonation[69]: a role in which he again appears in the *Address to Working Men*, by *Felix Holt*, which George Eliot was persuaded to write by her publisher. Here the dangers of active democracy are more clearly put:

> The too absolute predominance of a class whose wants have been of a common sort, who are chiefly struggling to get better and more food, clothing, shelter, and bodily recreation, may lead to hasty measures for the sake of having things more fairly shared which, even if they did not fail . . . would at last debase the life of the nation.[70]

Reform must proceed

> not by any attempt to do away directly with the actually existing class distinctions and advantages... but by the turning of Class Interests into Class Functions. ... If the claims of the unendowed multitude of working men[71] hold within them principles which must shape the future, it is not less true that the endowed classes, in their inheritance from the past, hold the precious material without which no worthy, noble future can be moulded.[72]

George Eliot, in this kind of thinking, is very far from her best. Her position, behind the façade of Felix Holt, is that of a Carlyle without the energy, of an Arnold without the quick practical sense, of an anxiously balancing Mill without the intellectual persistence. Yet it is clear that, inadequate as her attempt at a position may be, it proceeds, though not fruitfully, from that sense of society as a complicated inheritance[73] which is at the root of her finest work. In *Felix Holt*, this sense is magnificently realized at the level of one set of personal relationships—that of Mrs. Transome, the lawyer

Jermyn, and their son Harold Transome. In *Middlemarch*, with almost equal intensity, this realization is extended to a whole representative section of provincial society. Always, at her best, she is unrivaled in English fiction in her creation and working of the complication and consequence inherent in all relationships. From such a position in experience she naturally sees society at a deeper level than its political abstractions indicate, and she sees her own society, in her own choice of word, as "vicious." Her favorite metaphor for society is a network: a "tangled skein;" a "tangled web;" "the long-growing evils of a great nation are a tangled business." This, again, is just; it is the ground of her finest achievements. But the metaphor, while having a positive usefulness in its indication of complexity, has also a negative effect. For it tends to represent social—and indeed directly personal—relationships as passive: acted upon rather than acting. "One fears," she remarked, "to pull the wrong thread, in the tangled scheme of things."[74] The caution is reasonable, but the total effect of the image false. For in fact every element in the complicated system is active: the relationships are changing, constantly, and any action—even abstention; certainly the impersonation of Felix Holt—affects, even if only slightly, the tensions, the pressures, the very nature of the complications. It is a mark, not of her deep perception, but of the point at which this fails, that her attitude to society is finally so negative: a negativeness of detail[75] which the width of a phrase like "deep social reform" cannot disguise. The most important thing about George Eliot is her superb control of particular complexities, but this must not be stated in terms of an interest in "personal" relationships as opposed to "social" relationships. She did not believe, as others have tried to do, that these categories are really separate: "there is no private life which has not been determined by a wider public life," as she remarks near the beginning of *Felix Holt*. Yet it is a fact that when she touches, as she chooses to touch, the lives and the problems of working people, her personal observation and conclusion surrender, virtually without a fight, to the general structure of feeling about these matters which was the common property of her generation, and which she was at once too hesitant to transcend, and too intelligent to raise into any lively embodiment. She fails in the extension which she knows to be necessary, because indeed there seems "no right thread to pull." Almost any kind of social action is ruled out, and the most that can be hoped for, with a hero like Felix Holt, is that he will in the widest sense keep his hands reasonably clean. It is indeed the mark of a deadlock in society when so fine an intelligence and so quick a sympathy can conceive no more than this.[76] For patience and caution, without detailed intention,[77] are very easily converted into acquiescence, and there is no right to acquiesce if society is known to be "vicious."[78]

These novels, when read together, seem to illustrate clearly enough not only the common criticism of industrialism, which the tradition was establishing, but also the general structure of feeling which was equally determining. Recognition of evil was balanced by fear of becoming involved. Sympathy was transformed, not into action, but into withdrawal. We can all observe the extent to which this structure of feeling has persisted, into both the literature and the social thinking of our own time.

注释

1. The Oldham Weaver:《奥尔丹织工之歌》。见《玛丽·巴顿》第四章。奥尔丹是曼彻斯特东北的一个纺织工业中心。这首民歌以贫苦织布工人的口吻哀叹织布工人生活困顿，控诉官府的横暴。
2. 大意为：在英国小说中，如此令人信服地写出这类贫困家庭特有的感受和反应，还有待于劳伦斯早期小说的面世。
3. 大意为：若要写出这类贫困家庭特有的感受和反应，需要有一种身临其境之感。虽说盖斯凯尔夫人始终未能做到这一点，但是，她凭直觉从生活场景当中认出了这类感受，她的这种认识自有可信之处。
4. 大意为：《玛丽·巴顿》开始时的情感结构是，作者同情性观察与想象性认同的结合。
5.【作者原注】cit. *Elizabeth Gatskell: her life and work*; A.B. Hopkins; 1952; p.77.
6. at the instance of her publishers：是出版商怂恿的结果。
7. 大意为：她开始写作时的那种同情心在写作过程中遇到阻碍。
8. 大意为：这一点之所以重要，恰恰是因为，它表现了作者创作时的情感结构。
9.vitriol-throwing：泼硫酸。
10. 大意为：作者凭借想象选取谋杀案例作为着重描写对象，后来又单

凭想象，掉转笔锋，弃之不顾。这就破坏了小说整个主题所必需的
情感一致。

11.【作者原注】 *North and South*; E. Gaskell（1889 edn); p.459.
cash nexus：现金关系。

12. by going... outside it：回避困局。

13. 大意为：狄更斯对他所生活的世界的批评，通常是缺乏条理的，只
是就事论事，信笔由之。

14.【作者原注】 *The Great Tradition*; F. R. Leavis ; London, 1948 ; p.228.

15. 大意为：狄更斯对工业主义的认识更加全面，这是《艰难时世》的
一大优点。

16. a diagrammatic figure：一个脸谱式的人物。

17. gross：粗俗的。

18. bounder：暴发户。

19. utilitarian：功利主义者。

20. feeloosofer：即 philosopher。William Cobbett，科贝特（1763—1835），
英国政治评论家、新闻记者。1802 年创办《政治纪事》（*Political
Register*）周刊，谴责英国政府无视工人阶级的利益，鼓吹议会改
革。作有名著《乡村漫游》。

21. steam-engine intellects：思想机械的知识人。

22. Thomas Gradgrind（托马斯·葛擂硬）是《艰难时世》当中的重
要人物，是作者着力批判的功利主义思想的化身；Edwin Chadwick
（艾德温·查德威克）是卡莱尔批评的人物。

23. 穆勒幼年在他父亲那里受过极为严苛的教育。

24.【作者原注】 cit. *Life of John Stuart Mill*; M. St. J. Packe; 1954; p.311.

25. 穆勒是当时社会与工业改良的呼吁者。

26. Fabian：费边社成员。费边社于 1884 年成立于英国，主张用迂回渐
进的方式实现社会主义。

27. positives：正面肯定的东西。

28. 此处指：小说中充满人情味的马戏团，与象征着残酷无情的工业资
本主义的焦炭镇形成了鲜明对比。

29. 大意为：鉴于我们在某种程度上不可避免地受到那种系统化、抽象
化教育的重要影响。

30. 这里指的是马戏团里的人所过的生活：行事全凭本能的人性；没有
任何理性算计，也没有任何严密的组织约束。

31.【作者原注】*Hard Times*; C. Dickens; Book the Third—Garnering; Ch. viii.

32. Aw a muddle：一团糟。

33. the System：残酷的工业资本主义制度。

34. 大意为：狄更斯采取了（卡莱尔对议会和一般改良观念的）敌视态度。

35. *Sybil, or The Two Nations*：《两国记》，是本杰明·迪斯累利出任英国首相之前的作品。所谓"两国"，就是穷人和富人这两个截然不同的世界。

36. address：措辞。

37.【作者原注】*Sybil, or the Two Nations*; B. Disraeli; repr. Penguin edn, 1954 ; p.40.

38. Whiggery：辉格党人是自由放任政策、工业主义的支持者，也是以迪斯累利为首的保守党的主要政治对手。

39.【作者原注】*Sybil, or the Two Nations*; B. Disraeli; repr. Penguin edn, 1954 ; p.71-72.

40. brethren：同道们。

41. nob：权贵。

42.【作者原注】*Sybil*. pp. 216-217.

43.【作者原注】*Sybil*, pp. 280.

44. 这句话后半部分暗指：最能体现迪斯累利这份精明的是，他后来爬上了首相的高位。

45. 大意为："开明贵族"与"人民的女儿"的结合，是作者心中最向往的结局。

46. 大意为：通过这种手法，他表现出了未来现实生活中发生的事件（工业统治集团与农业统治集团联手共治）。

47. discursive in mood：以议论为基调。

48. 大意为：在小说的这几部分，除了思想谱系之外，是否还有值得读者注意的地方，这大可值得怀疑。

49. 大意为：这本书不是"自传"，而是一本政治宣传小册子。

50. Chartism：宪章运动（1838—1848）。英国无产阶级为争取《人民宪章》而采取的革命行动。

51.【作者原注】*Alton Locke: Tailor and Poet: an Autobiography*; C. Kingsley（1892 edn); Ch. xxxvii; pp. 285-287.

52.【作者原注】*ibid., Preface to the Undergraduates of Cambridge*, p.xxxiv.

53. rest on：停留。

54. 大意为：我不是想说艾略特的情节处理比狄更斯更高超、更贴近现实。

55. 大意为：这个情节是精心设计出来的，是为了创造作者心目中的理想形象。

56. *Felix Holt the Radical*; G. Eliot (1913 edn), 2 vols; Vol. 2; p.41 (Ch. xxvii).

57. 大意为：归根到底，这是资产阶级当中一位具有同情心和改良头脑的成员，因为害怕卷入群众暴力而萌生恐惧之情。

58. 大意为：显然对整部小说造成损害。

59. *Felix Holt the Radical*; G. Eliot (1913 edn), 2 vols; Vol. 2; p.89. (Ch. xxx).

60. class：分类。

61. 大意为：改良前国会的种种弊端，甚至被生搬硬套用作反对国会改良的依据——国会改良只能产生更多的弊端。

62. are left out of the argument：（通过政治改良获得的好处）不在作者的论据之内。

63. 大意为：一个经验老到、体验深刻的人决不会认为，只有那些头脑肤浅的人才会参与政治并执迷不悟。

64. this noisy instrument：指积极参与政治的人士。

65. 大意为：为了维护他们睿智明断的声誉而表现出的那种冷漠的保留态度和不轻信人言的做派。

66.【作者原注】*ibid.*, Vol. I; pp.266-267 (Ch. xvi).

67. 大意为：这种明智的否定态度得到的回应是得意洋洋的会心微笑。

68. 前者是卡莱尔的作品，后者是马修·阿诺德的文化批评名著。

69. impersonation：（艾略特的）化身。

70.【作者原注】*Address to Working Men: by Felix Holt*; George Eliot; Blackwood's, 1868; repr. *Essays and Leaves from a Notebook*, 1884; pp.341-342.
在这段话中，艾略特反对工人阶级积极主动采取措施寻求社会公正。

71. the unendowed multitude of working man：无产阶级。

72.【作者原注】*Address to Working Men: by Felix Holt*; George Eliot; Blackwood's, 1868; repr. *Essays and Leaves from a Notebook*, 1884; pp.341-342.

73. that sense of society as a complicated inheritance：把社会当做一笔复杂的遗产。下文出现的比喻性说法，即，把社会当做盘根错节、纠缠成一团的网络，都与这种见解有关。

74. to pull the wrong thread, in the tangled scheme of things：在纷乱如麻

的事物规划中拉错了线。

75. a negativeness of detail：对社会复杂系统中的具体部分持有消极看法。

76. 大意为：凭着艾略特这样优秀的头脑、敏锐的同情心，竟然找不出问题的其他解决之道。由此可见这个社会陷入了多么严重的僵局。

77. detailed intention：（改变社会的）具体意图。

78. 大意为：既然知道社会是邪恶的，那就没有理由去默认这一社会现实。

霍尔　《编码，解码》

斯图亚特·霍尔（1932—2014）

　　斯图亚特·霍尔英国著名的新左派学人，二战之后英国人文社科学界最有名的黑人知识分子，也是英国文化研究领域最有代表性的理论家。其治学思想灵活多变，与时俱进。他的论著反映了英国文化研究在各个发展阶段所依据的理论框架：20世纪五六十年代英国本土的文化马克思主义（以雷蒙·威廉斯为代表）、70年代风行一时的阿尔都塞的结构论马克思主义、安东尼奥·葛兰西（Antonio Gramsci）的文化霸权理论、稍后引进的福柯（Michel Foucault）的后结构主义、80年代的女性主义以及90年代盛行的种族理论。可以说，霍尔本人的学术思想历程，正是英国文化研究发展史的记录。

　　霍尔于1932年出生在加勒比海牙买加的金斯顿，1951年获得罗德斯奖学金，进入牛津大学英文系读本科。英国新左派运动方兴未艾，一些激进的大学生开始倾心于社会主义。霍尔与佩里·安德森（Perry Anderson）（当代马克思主义思想大家）、查尔斯·泰勒（Charles Taylor）（著名社会学家、社群主义的领军人物）以及阿莱斯蒂尔·麦金泰尔（Alasdir MacIntyre，当代著名伦理学家），同为新左派中的青年才俊。他们要求更新社会主义理论和实践，创设民主社会主义；既反对西式的资本主义，又反对苏联式的社会主义。霍尔原计划在牛津读完博士学位，由于参与政治活动过多，始终未完成博士论文。大学毕业之后，一度任教中学。1960年，《新左派评论》（*New Left Review*）创刊，他出任首任主编。两年之后，由于不堪编务的繁重，以及内部的思想分歧，辞去主编职务，由佩里·安德森继任。

　　1964年，在理查德·霍加特的大力倡导之下，当代文化研究中心（Center for Contemporary Cultural Studies）在伯明翰大学成立，这是英国文化研究制度化的开端。中心隶属英文系，专职人员只有两位，中心主任霍加特和主任助理霍尔。中心成立之初，倡导使用文学批评的方式研究流行文化。霍尔与友人合作的《流行艺术》（*Popular Arts*）一书成为研究中心在当时推出的代表作。流行艺术向来难登大雅之堂，难得为学术界所重视，这本书是首部以同情态度审视流行文化的著作。作者对高雅文化和流行文化进行了比较分析，认为前者的美学价值在后者之上。不过，他们还是主张，不应以孰优孰劣的标准来判断它们，因为二者追求的目标不同，产生的效果也是大相异趣。在方法上，他们认为，可以针对流行文化演绎出一套分析和评介标准，这套标准可与文学批评的标准并行不悖。正如一些研究者所说，与后来出版的许多同类著作相比，这本书还是有很多不尽如人意之处。其中最为明显的是，它过多地纠缠于流行文化的美学价值，没有着力探讨它们的社会意义。

1969 年，霍加特辞去中心主任的职务，就任联合国教科文组织副总干事。霍尔临危受命，主持中心工作，表现出非凡的学术组织能力。在他主事的十年间（1969—1979），正是当代文化研究中心发展的黄金时代。一方面，中心出版了很多堪称经典的著作；另一方面，中心培养了相当多的研究人才。目前，在英国、美国、加拿大和澳大利亚等国的文化研究领域，很多颇有声望的学者都与中心有着深厚的历史渊源，要么在那里读过学位，要么曾在那里进修。其中霍尔的组织与指导之功不可埋没。总体而言，在 60 年代，中心重视研究工人阶级的文化趣味和生活方式；在 70 年代，主要致力于媒体研究和青年亚文化研究；80 年代以来，女性问题和种族研究成为关注焦点。

霍尔本人从未独立出版过一本专著。他的作品多为与人合编的论文集，他的论文散见其中。这些论文集主要有：《仪式的抵抗》（ *Resistance through Rituals: Youth Subculture in Post-war Britain*, 1976 ）、《监控危机》（ *Policing the Crisis: Mugging, the State, and Law and Order*, 1978 ）、《文化、媒体、语言》（ *Culture, Media, Language: Working Papers in Cultural Studies*, 1980 ）、《新时代》（ *New Times: The Changing Face of Politics in the 1990s*, 1990 ）和《再现》（ *Representation: Cultural Representations and Signifying Practices*, 1997 ）等。在这些著作中，尤以《仪式的抵抗》最为重要和突出。它是 70 年代英国文化研究的代表作，是当代文化研究中心师生通力合作的产物。它从社会历史变迁入手，探讨了青年亚文化得以产生的经济和文化背景，认为它们的出现与以下因素有关：经济繁荣带来了消费资本主义，其思想影响巨大无比；传统的工人阶级社团开始瓦解，他们一贯持有的清教式思想开始崩溃；工人阶级生活的中心——家庭——对子女的约束作用逐渐降低；一些工人阶级青年一边向主导文化作出挑战的姿态，一边与传统工人阶级的"父辈文化"产生代沟冲突。可是，他们的反抗举止只是仪式性的，仅具象征意义，对于资本主义社会没有实质性的颠覆作用。

在一部评传中，作者是这样评价霍尔的，他不是很有原创性的理论家，但他具有很强的综合辨析能力。他对欧洲大陆新理论在英国的普及功不可没，他本人的一些文章也很有启发意义。确为公允持平之论。

内容提要

霍尔的《电视话语中的编码与解码》(*Encoding and Decoding in Television Discourse*, 1973) 是媒体研究中的一篇重要理论文章，对于当时英国文化研究的发展，具有一定的指导意义。它是英国文化研究从文化论研究走向结构论研究的标志。这篇文章着重论证，观众对媒体的接受，是一个相当复杂的过程。所谓编码，就是电视节目在制作过程中对所传递信息的编排设计；所谓解码，就是观众在收视过程中对电视所传递信息的自家解读。霍尔在写作这篇文章之际，英国的媒体研究领域正盛行一种美国的传媒理论，其要义为，电视节目制作者所发出的信息很容易被观众全盘接受。霍尔的文章就是对这种观点的反驳。霍尔认为，观众的实际接受情况是复杂多变的，研究者切切不可执一以驭百。社会总是由不同利益群体组成，并非铁板一块。电视观众绝不是步履相同、口味一致的大众。对于相同的信息，他们的理解和阐释不一而足，有时甚至大相径庭，有的可能与制作人的意图吻合无间，有的则形同霄壤。霍尔罗列了三种典型的解读立场："主导—霸权式立场"、"商讨式立场"和"对立式立场"。所谓"主导—霸权式立场"，就是观众不折不扣地遵照主导意识形态去解读电视报道的主要信息。这种情况在日常生活中出现的几率极小，在很大程度上，它只是一种理论上的假设。不过，在极端封闭的专制政权统治下，由于愚民政策肆虐，像这样唯唯诺诺的观众当然不在少数。在多数情况下，观众奉行的都是"商讨式解读立场"。他们固然要承认，某些电视报道在大的方面可能不太离谱，但是，它们是否丝毫不差、绝对真实，还有待于检验。以电视播放的药品广告为例，我们一般不会全然视其为江湖术士的鬼蜮伎俩，但多少还是怀疑其功效是否果如其言。"对立式立场"，是针对主导意识形态的一种逆向式解读，是一种见着拆着手法。

Stuart Hall (1932—2014)

Encoding, decoding

It was argued earlier that since there is no necessary correspondence[1] between encoding and decoding, the former can attempt to "prefer" but cannot prescribe or guarantee the latter, which has its own conditions of existence. Unless they are wildly aberrant, encoding will have the effect of constructing some of the limits and parameters within which decodings will operate. If there were no limits, audiences could simply read whatever they liked into any message. No doubt some total misunderstandings of this kind do exist. But the vast range must contain *some* degree of reciprocity between encoding and decoding moments, otherwise we could not speak of an effective communicative exchange at all. Nevertheless, this "correspondence" is not given but constructed. It is not "natural" but the product of an articulation between two distinct moments[2]. And the former cannot determine or guarantee, in a simple sense, which decoding codes will be employed. Otherwise communication would be a perfectly equivalent circuit, and every message would be an instance of "perfectly transparent communication." We must think, then, of the variant articulations in which encoding/decoding can be combined. To elaborate on this, we offer a hypothetical analysis of some possible decoding positions, in order to reinforce the point of "no necessary correspondence."

We identify *three* hypothetical positions from which decodings of a televisual discourse may be constructed. These need to be empirically tested and refined. But the argument that decodings do not follow inevitably from encodings, that they are not identical, reinforces the argument of "no necessary correspondence." It also helps to deconstruct the common-sense meaning of "misunderstanding" in terms of a theory of "systematically distorted communication."

The first hypothetical position is that of the *dominant-hegemonic position*. When the viewer takes the connoted meaning from, say, a television newscast or current affairs program full and straight, and decodes the message in terms of the reference code in which it has been encoded, we might say that the viewer *is operating inside the dominant code*. This is the ideal-typical case of "perfectly transparent communication"—or as close as we are likely to come to it "for all practical purposes." Within this we can distinguish the positions produced by the *professional code*. This is the position (produced by what we perhaps ought to identify as the operation of a "metacode") which the professional broadcasters assume when encoding a message which has *already* been signified in a hegemonic manner. The professional code is "relatively independent" of the dominant code, in that it applies criteria and transformational operations of its own, especially those of a technico-practical nature. The professional code, however, operates *within* the "hegemony" of the dominant code. Indeed, it serves to reproduce the dominant definitions precisely by bracketing their hegemonic quality and operating instead with displaced professional codings which foreground such apparently neutral-technical questions as visual quality, news and presentational values, televisual quality, "professionalism" and so on. The hegemonic interpretations of, say, the politics of Northern Ireland, or the Chilean *coup*[3] or the Industrial Relations Bill[4] are principally generated by political and military elites: the particular choice of presentational occasions and formats, the selection of personnel, the choice of images, the staging of debates are selected and combined through the operation of the professional code. How the broadcasting professionals are able *both* to operate with "relatively autonomous" codes of their own *and* to act in such a way as to reproduce (not without contradiction) the hegemonic signification of events is a complex matter which cannot be further spelled out here. It must suffice to say that the professionals are linked with the defining elites not only by the institutional position of broadcasting itself as an "ideological apparatus," but also by the structure of *access* (that is, the systematic "over-accessing" of selective elite personnel and their "definition of the situation" in television). It may even be said that the professional codes serve to reproduce hegemonic definitions specifically by *not overtly* biasing their operations in a dominant direction: ideological reproduction therefore takes place here inadvertently, unconsciously, "behind men's backs." Of course, conflicts, contradictions and even misunderstandings regularly arise between the dominant and the professional significations and their signifying agencies.

The second position we would identify is that of the *negotiated code* or position. Majority audiences probably understand quite adequately what has been dominantly defined and professionally signified. The dominant definitions, however, are hegemonic precisely because they represent definitions of situations and events which are "in dominance" (*global*). Dominant definitions connect events, implicitly or explicitly, to grand totalizations, to the great syntagmatic views-of-the-world: they take "large views" of issues: they relate events to the "national interest" or to the level of geo-politics, even if they make these connections in truncated, inverted or mystified ways. The definition of a hegemonic viewpoint is (a) that it defines within its terms the mental horizon, the universe, of possible meanings, of a whole sector of relations in a society or culture; and (b) that it carries with it the stamp of legitimacy—it appears coterminous with what is "natural," "inevitable," "taken for granted" about the social order. Decoding within the *negotiated version* contains a mixture of adaptive and oppositional elements: it acknowledges the legitimacy of the hegemonic definitions to make the grand significations (abstract), while, at a more restricted, situational (situated) level, it makes its own ground rules—it operates with exceptions to the rule. It accords the privileged position to the dominant definitions of events while reserving the right to make a more negotiated application to "local conditions," to its own more *corporate* positions. This negotiated version of the dominant ideology is thus shot through with contradictions, though these are only on certain occasions brought to full visibility. Negotiated codes operate through what we might call particular or situated logics: and these logics are sustained by their differential and unequal relation to the discourses and logics of power. The simplest example of a negotiated code is that which governs the response of a worker to the notion of an Industrial Relations Bill limiting the right to strike or to arguments for a wages freeze. At the level of the "national interest" economic debate the decoder may adopt the hegemonic deftnition, agreeing that "we must all pay ourselves less in order to combat inflation." This, however, may have little or no relation to his/her willingness to go on strike for better pay and conditions or to oppose the Industrial Relations Bill at the level of shop-floor or union organization. We suspect that the great majority of so-called "misunderstandings" arise from the contradictions and disjunctures between hegemonic-dominant encodings and negotiated-corporate decodings. It is just these mismatches in the levels which most provoke defining elites and professionals to identify a "failure in communications."

Finally, it is possible for a viewer perfectly to understand both the literal and the connotative inflection given by a discourse but to decode the message in a *globally* contrary way. He/she detotalizes the message in the preferred code in order to retotalize the message within some alternative framework of reference. This is the case of the viewer who listens to a debate on the need to limit wages but "reads" every mention of the "national interest" as "class interest." He/she is operating with what we must call an *oppositional code.* One of the most significant political moments (they also coincide with crisis points within the broadcasting organizations themselves, for obvious reasons) is the point when events which are normally signified and decoded in a negotiated way begin to be given an oppositional reading. Here the "politics of signification"—the struggle in discourse—is joined.

注释

1. correspondence：一一对应关系。
2. moment：阶段。
3. the Chilean coup：智利政变。1973 年 9 月，在美国政府的支持下，以皮诺切特为首的军人集团发动政变，推翻了智利民选总统萨尔瓦多·阿连德的民选政府。
4. Industrial Relations Bill：《劳资关系法案》。

辛菲尔德	《〈麦克白〉：历史、意识形态与知识分子》

艾伦·辛菲尔德（1941— ）

　　艾伦·辛菲尔德英国文化唯物论批评的创始人之一，著名左派文学批评家，现任教于苏塞克斯大学英文学院。他涉猎广博，著述将近二十余种，涉及莎士比亚研究、同性恋研究、现代戏剧以及当代英国政治与文化等诸多领域和问题。1985 年，他与乔纳森·多利莫尔（Jonathan Dollimore）合编、雷蒙·威廉斯作序的论文集《政治莎士比亚》（*Political Shakespeare*），开创了英国文化唯物论批评的先河，与同一时期美国出现的新历史主义比肩而立。

　　在此之后，他在一些大学的英文系声望日隆、受众激增，大大改变了先前形式主义主宰学院派文学批评的格局。文化唯物论强调，社会历史语境对于文学创作和接受十分重要，同时它又突出文学对于社会意识具有重要的塑造作用。在具体的批评中，它直接切入当时的社会历史语境，大量征引不为正统文学批评所重视的生僻文献，一方面揭示作品中渗透的主导意识形态，另一方面不遗余力地挖掘作品中隐含的、与主导意识形态相对立的内容，因而能够钩沉稽古，洞隐烛微，多有发明。

　　20 世纪 30 年代之后的西方文论，从英美新批评到解构主义，几乎为形式主义所垄断；所以文化唯物论重申对历史与社会的关注，往往会给人耳目一新的感受。但是，这种重申却不是对先前社会历史批评和马克思主义批评的简单重复。无论是对文学与社会历史关系的理解，还是具体的批评策略，它都有不同于前者的地方。

　　文化唯物论认为，作家无法超越他所在的时代。无论他的个人生活，还是他的文学创作，都发生在当时主导意识形态的氛围之下。这正如马克思所说，统治阶级思想就是这一历史时期的主导思想。主导意识形态悄无声息地渗入作家头脑中的无意识层面。他们的作品不可避免地变成主导意识形态的载体，发挥文化霸权作用，诱导读者默认现存的统治秩序，并促进全社会达成思想共识。因此，传统人文主义批评所标榜的客观中正的境界, 是无法实现的。文化唯物论的批评家还发现, 在现代英国社会, 从中学到大学, 大力倡导阅读经典作品, 并以其为授课和考试准绳。此种举措, 目的在于增强民族认同感, 培养奉公守法的臣民, 其意识形态的用意颇为深刻。为此, 揭示经典作品中暗含的主导意识形态, 也就成为批评家的当务之急。要做到这一步, 必须联系当时社会历史状况, 进行全面考察, 才能确定主导意识形态的主要内容。

以往的社会历史批评, 在处理作品与社会历史语境的关系方面, 一般都把社会历史看成作品得以产生的背景陪衬, 而把作品本身视为背景陪衬的表征。社会历史背景的主要作用是为作品分析提供旁证, 帮助批评家了解作者的生平和思想脉络, 以说明作者的用意和作品的主旨, 揭示作品所表现的那个时代的精神风貌。文化唯物论取消了社会历史背景与社会历史表征之间的区分。它的理由是, 文学塑造了当时的社会意识, 因此是社会历史的一部分。即使在进行文学分析的时候, 也不能出于权宜之计, 将它从社会历史当中剥离出去。打个比方说, 这就仿佛从啤酒当中提炼出麦粒那样徒劳。

文化唯物论并不满足于揭示作品中意识形态和权力运行的机制。正如威廉斯所说, 没有哪一种思想能够笼罩一切社会体验。文学作品中总是要暗藏一些与主导意识形态相对立的因素, 而这些对立性的、颠覆性的思想内容, 也正是当时社会矛盾和冲突所造成的。文化唯物论批评还要去揭示这些颠覆性的内容。

20 世纪 80 年代以来, 文化唯物论批评家不断推出专著和论文集, 迅速在批评界和大学内部站稳了脚跟。这一时期的文化唯物论批评, 以英国文学研究的重头戏——文艺复兴时代的文学为主攻对象, 特别以莎士比亚为关注焦点。相继出版的研究专著和论文集有乔纳森·多利莫尔的《激进的悲剧》(*Radical Tragedy: Religion, Ideology and Power in the Drama of Shakespeare and His Contemporaries,* 1984)、凯瑟琳·贝尔西(Catherine Belsey)的《悲剧的主体》(*The Subject of Tragedies: Identity and Difference in Renaissance Drama,* 1985)、约翰·德拉卡基斯(John Drakakis)主编的《另读莎士比亚》(*Alternative Shakespeare*)、乔纳森·多利莫尔与艾伦·辛菲尔德合编的《政治莎士比亚》。在90 年代以后, 除了继续重视文艺复兴时代的文学之外, 同性恋与后殖民问题也相继纳入文化唯物论批评的研究视线。尤其是同性恋问题, 得到好几本专著的热切关注, 譬如乔纳森·多利莫尔的《性别歧视》(*Sexual Dissidence: Augustine to Wilde, Freud to Foucault*, 1991)、艾伦·辛菲尔德的《王尔德的世纪》(*The Wilder Century: Effeminacy, Oscar Wilde and Queer Moment*, 1994) 和《文化政治》(*Cultural Politics——Queer Reading*, 1994)。

内容提要

　　苏格兰大将麦克白功高盖世，深得君王宠信。他因耽于迷信，遂生不臣之心，在烛影斧声中弑君篡位，其累累暴行惹得天怒人怨。最后，他在诸侯的声讨中伏诛逊位，先王之子承继大统，统治秩序恢复如初。据说，这出戏是莎士比亚献给英王詹姆士一世的，有揣摩上意、曲意逢迎之嫌。在英国历史上，詹姆士一世以宣扬"君权神授"、推行绝对中央集权著称，他的种种专制举措为后人查理一世亡国削首埋下祸根。他还发明了一套理论，为绝对主义意识形态张目。这位专制君主本人把君主分为两类：僭主暴君和合法即位的君王；只有谋逆篡位的乱臣贼子才可能变成暴君，而对于合法继位的君主，则不必有此担心。这样一来，他就回避了所谓"合法明君"是否会倒行逆施，滥用暴行这一问题。按照他的说法，破坏现行权力关系结构的行为都是反上帝反人民，而维护现行利益的任何暴力行为都是可以接受的。

　　显然，《麦克白》一剧涉嫌为詹姆士一世的绝对君权论鸣锣开道。作者千方百计去否定麦克白的谋逆，并把他的殒命说成是天意。而剧中对蓓奈姆森林的移动、麦克白不寻常出生方式之解释，都是为了证明弑君谋逆终得恶报。辛菲尔德认为，文学批评家的任务即在于揭露这种国家意识形态。可是，如果仔细留意一下剧情，读者还会惊奇地发现，剧中还暗含着与主导意识形态不甚和谐、甚至针锋相对的内容。麦克达夫与玛尔柯姆之间有一段对话，二人试探对方的想法。麦克达夫表示自己愿意拥戴玛尔柯姆为王，因为他是先王邓肯之子、苏格兰王位的合法继承人。玛尔柯姆不明对方虚实，何敢贸然应允，就虚与委蛇，假意推托，说自己德行有疵，不配为万民之主；倘若登上王位，难免声色犬马，做出许多不道之举。对于这些担忧，麦克达夫很不以为然。他在话里话外暗示说，玛尔柯姆既然有合法权利继承大统，那么，只要他的荒唐行径不危及江山社稷，他自会得到接受和宽容。

　　在观众那里，这段对话却透露出这样的弦外之音：即便是合法即位的国王，也完全有可能成为暴君，合法君王与僭主暴君心理攸同、道术未裂。这段对话显然强烈质疑了"合法君主的权威不容挑战"这种意识形态。辛菲尔德说，听了这段充满矛盾的对话，"詹姆士一世时期的一些观众完全可能把《麦克白》当成反詹姆士一世的。"可以说，合法贤君与僭主暴君的对立被打破，绝对主义意识形态的矛盾暴露无遗。

Alan Sinfield (1941—)

Macbeth: History, Ideology, and Intellectuals

It is often said that Macbeth is about "evil," but we might draw a more careful distinction: between the violence the state considers legitimate and that which it does not. Macbeth, we may agree, is a dreadful murderer when he kills Duncan. But when he kills Macdonwald—"a rebel" (1.2.10)—he has Duncan's approval:

> For brave Macbeth (well he deserves that name),
> Disdaining Fortune, with his brandish'd steel,
> Which smok'd with bloody execution,
> Like Valor's minion, carv'd out his passage,
> Till he fac'd the slave;
> which ne'er shook hands, nor bade farewell to him,
> Till he unseam'd him from the nave to th' chops,
> And fix'd his head upon our battlements.
> DUNCAN. O valiant cousin! worthy gentleman!
>
> (1.2.16-24) [1]

Violence is good, in this view, when it is in the service of the prevailing dispositions of power; when it disrupts them, it is evil. A claim to a monopoly of legitimate violence is fundamental in the development of the modern state;[2] when that claim is successful, most citizens learn to regard state violence as qualitatively different from other violence, and perhaps they don't think of state violence as violence at all (consider the actions of police, army, and judiciary as opposed to those of pickets, protesters, criminals, and terrorists). *Macbeth* focuses major strategies by which the state asserted its claim at one conjuncture.

Generally in Europe in the sixteenth century, the development was from feudalism to the absolutist state. Under feudalism, the king held authority among his peers, his equals, and his power was often little more than nominal; authority was distributed also among over-lapping non-national institutions such as the church, estates, assemblies, regions, and towns. In the absolutist state, power became centralized in the figure of the monarch, the exclusive source of legitimacy. The movement from one to the other was, of course, contested, not only by the aristocracy and the peasantry, whose traditional rights were threatened, but also by the gentry and urban bourgeoisie, who found new space for power and influence within more elaborate economic and governmental structures. The absolutist state, I have argued, was never fully established in England. Probably the peak of the monarch's personal power was reached by Henry VIII; the attempt of Charles I to reassert that power led to the English Civil War. In between, Elizabeth and James I, and those who believed their interests to lie in the same direction, sought to sustain royal power and to suppress dissidents. The latter category was broad; it comprised aristocrats like the Earls of Northumberland and Westmorland, who led the Northern Rising of 1569, and the Duke of Norfolk, who plotted to replace Elizabeth with Mary Queen of Scots in 1571; clergy who refused the state religion; gentry who supported them and who tried to raise awkward matters in Parliament; writers and printers who published criticism of state policy; the populace when it complained about food prices, enclosures, or anything. The exercise of state violence against such dissidents depended upon the achievement of a degree of legitimation, and hence the ideology of absolutism, which represented the English state as a pyramid, any disturbance of which would produce general disaster, and which insisted increasingly on the "divine right" of the mortarch.[3] This system was said to be "natural" and ordained by "God"; it was "good," and disruptions of it were "evil." This is what some Shakespeareans have celebrated as a just and harmonious "world picture."[4] Compare Perry Anderson's[5] summary: "Absolutism was essentially just this: *a redeployed and recharged apparatus of feudal domination*, designed to clamp the peasant masses back into their traditional social position."[6]

The reason why the state needed violence and propaganda was that the system was subject to persistent structural difficulties. *Macbeth*, like very many plays of the period, handles anxieties about the violence exercised under the aegis of absolutist ideology. Two main issues come into focus. The first is the threat of a split between legitimacy and actual power—when the monarch is not the strongest person in the state. Shakespeare's Richard

II warns Northumberland, the king-maker, that Northumberland is bound, structurally, to disturb the rule of Bolingbroke:

> thou shalt think,
> Though he [Bolingbroke] divide the realm and give thee half,
> It is too little, helping him to all.[7]

Jonathan Dollimore and I have argued that the potency of the myth of Henry V in Shakespeare's play, written at the time of Essex's[8] ascendancy, derives from the striking combination in that monarch of legitimacy and actual power. At the start of *Macbeth*, the manifest dependency of Duncan's state upon its best fighter sets up a dangerous instability (this is explicit in the sources). In the opening soliloquy of act 1 scene 7, Macbeth freely accords Duncan entire legitimacy: he is Duncan's kinsman, subject, and host, the king has been "clear in his great office," and the idea of his deposition evokes religious imagery of angels, damnation, and cherubim. But that is all the power the king has that does not depend upon *Macbeth*; against it is ranged "vaulting ambition," Macbeth's impetus to convert his actual power into full regal authority.

LAWFUL GOOD KING / USURPING TYRANT

The split between legitimacy and actual power was always a potential malfunction in the developing absolutist state. A second problem was less dramatic but more persistent. It was this: what is the difference between absolutism and tyranny?—having in mind contemporary state violence such as the Massacre of St. Bartholomew's Day in France in 1572[9], the arrest of more than a hundred witches and the torturing and killing of many of them in Scotland in 1590-91, and the suppression of the Irish by English armies. The immediate reference for questions of legitimate violence in relation to *Macbeth* is the Gunpowder Plot of 1605[10]. This attempted violence against the state followed upon many years of state violence against Roman Catholics: the absolutist state sought to draw religious institutions entirely within its control, and Catholics who actively refused were subjected to fines, imprisonment, torture, and execution. Consider the sentence passed upon Jane Wiseman in 1598:

> The sentence is that the said Jane Wiseman shall be led to the prison of the Marshalsea of the Queen's Bench, and there naked, except for a linen cloth about the lower part of her body, be laid upon the ground, lying directly on her back: and a hollow shall be made under her head and her head placed in the same; and upon her body in every part let there be placed as much of stones and iron as she can bear and more; and as long as she shall live, she shall have of the worst bread and water of the prison next her; and on the day she eats, she shall not drink, and on the day she drinks she shall not eat, so living until she die.[11]

This was for "receiving, comforting, helping, and maintaining priests," refusing to reveal, under torture, who else was doing the same thing, and refusing to plead. There is nothing abstract or theoretical about the state violence to which the present essay refers. Putting the issue succinctly in relation to Shakespeare's play, what is the difference between Macbeth's rule and that of contemporary European monarchs?

In *Basilikon Doron*[12] (1599), King James tried to protect the absolutist state from such pertinent questions by asserting an utter distinction between "a lawful good King" and "a usurping Tyran":

> The one acknowledgeth himself ordained for his people, having received from God a burthen of government, where of he must be countable: the other thinketh his people ordained for him, a prey to his passions and inordinate appetites, as the fruits of his magnanimity: And therefore, as their ends are directly contrary, so are their whole actions, as means whereby they press to strain to their ends.[13]

Evidently James means to deny that the absolutist monarch has anything significant in common with someone like Macbeth. Three aspects of James's strategy in this passage are particularly revealing. First, he depends upon an utter polarization between the two kinds of rulers. Such antitheses are characteristic of the ideology of absolutism: they were called upon to tidy the uneven apparatus of feudal power into a far neater structure of the monarch versus the rest, and protestantism tended to see "spiritual" identities in similarly polarized terms. James himself explained the function of demons like this: "Since the Devil is the very contrary opposite to God, there can be no better way to know God, than by the contrary."[14] So it is with the two kinds of rulers: the badness of one seems to guarantee the goodness of the other. Second, by defining the lawful good king against the usurping tyrant, James refuses to admit the possibility that a ruler who has not usurped will be tyrannical. Thus he seems to cope with potential splits between legitimacy and actual power by insisting on the unique status of the lawful good king, and to head off questions about the violence committed by such a ruler by suggesting that all his actions will be uniquely legitimate. Third, we may notice that the whole distinction, as James develops it, is cast in terms, not of the *behavior* of the lawful good king and the usurping tyrant, respectively, but of their *motives*. This seems to render vain any assessment of the actual manner of rule of the absolute monarch. On these arguments, any disturbance of the current structure of power relations is against God and the people, and consequently any violence in the interest of the status quo is acceptable. Hence the legitimate killing of Jane Wiseman. (In fact, the distinction between lawful and tyrannical rule eventually breaks down even in James's analysis, as his commitment to the state leads him to justify even tyrannical behavior by established monarchs.)

It is often assumed that *Macbeth* is engaged in the same project as King James: attempting to render coherent and persuasive the ideology of the absolutist state.[15] The grounds for a Jamesian reading are plain enough—to the point where it is often claimed that the play was designed specially for the king. At every opportunity, Macbeth is disqualified ideologically and his opponents are ratified. An entire antithetical apparatus of nature and supernature—the concepts through which a dominant ideology most commonly seeks to establish itself—is called upon to witness against him as usurping tyrant. The whole strategy is epitomized in the account of Edward's alleged curing of "the Evil"—actually scrofula—"A most miraculous work in this good King" (4.3.146-147). James himself knew that this was a superstitious practice, and he refused to undertake it until his advisers persuaded him that it would strengthen his claim to the throne in the public eye. "As Francis Bacon observed, notions of the supernatural help to keep people acquiescent (e.g. the man in pursuit of power will do well to attribute his success "rather to divine Providence and felicity, than to his own virtue or policy").[16] *Macbeth* draws upon such notions more than any other play by Shakespeare. It all suggests that *Macbeth* is an extraordinary eruption in a good state—obscuring the thought that there might be any proneness to structural malfunctioning in the system. It suggests that Macbeth's violence is wholly bad, whereas state violence committed by legitimate monarchs is quite different.

Such maneuvers are even more necessary to a Jamesian reading of the play in respect of the deposition and killing of Macbeth. Absolutist ideology declared that even tyrannical monarchs must not be resisted, yet Macbeth could hardly be allowed to triumph. Here the play offers two moves. First, the fall of Macbeth seems to result more from (super)natural than human agency: it seems like an effect of the opposition of good and evil ("Macbeth/Is ripe for shaking, and the Powers above/Put on their instruments" [4.3.237-39]).[17] Most cunningly, although there are material explanations for the moving of Birnam Wood and the unusual birth of Macduff, the audience is allowed to believe, at the same time, that these are (super)natural effects (thus the play works upon us almost as the Witches work upon Macbeth). Second, insofar as Macbeth's fall is accomplished by human agency, the play is careful to suggest that he is hardly in office before he is overthrown. The years of successful rule specified in the chronicles are erased, and, as Henry Paul points out, neither Macduff nor Malcolm has tendered any allegiance to Macbeth. The action rushes along, he is swept away as if he had never truly been king.[18] Even so, the contradiction can hardly vanish altogether. For the Jamesian reading, it is necessary for Macbeth to be a complete usurping tyrant in order that he shall set off the lawful good king, and also, at the same time, for him not to be a ruler at all in order that he may properly be deposed and killed. Macbeth kills two people at the start of the play: a rebel and the king, and these are apparently utterly different acts of violence. That is the ideology of absolutism. Macduff also, killing Macbeth, is killing both a rebel and a king, but now the two are apparently the same person. The ultimate intractability of this kind of contradiction disturbs the Jamesian reading of the play.

Criticism has often supposed, all too easily, that the Jamesian reading of *Macbeth* is necessary on historical grounds—that other views of state ideology were impossible for Shakespeare and his contemporaries.[19] But this was far from being so: there was a well-developed theory allowing for resistance by the nobility, and the Gunpowder Plotters were manifestly unconvinced by the king's arguments. Even more pertinent is the theory of the Scotsman George Buchanan[20], as we may deduce from the fact that James tried to suppress Buchanan's writings in 1584 after his assumption of personal rule; in *Basilikon Doron*, James advises his son to "use the Law upon the keepers" of "such infamous invectives" (p.40). With any case so strenuously overstated and manipulative as James's, we should ask what alternative position it is trying to put down. Arguments in favor of absolutism constitute one part of *Macbeth*'s ideological field—the range of ideas and attitudes brought into play by the text; another main part may be represented by Buchanan's *De jure regni* (1579) and *History of Scotland* (1582). In Buchanan's view, sovereignty derives from and remains with the people; the king who exercises power against their will is a tyrant and should be deposed. The problem in Scotland is not unruly subjects, but unruly monarchs: "Rebellions there spring less from the people than from the rulers, when they try to reduce a kingdom which from earliest times had always been ruled by law to an absolute and lawless despotism." Buchanan's theory is the virtual antithesis of James's; it was used eventually to justify the deposition of James's son.

Buchanan's *History of Scotland* is usually reckoned to be one of the sources of *Macbeth*. It was written to illustrate his theory of sovereignty and to justify the overthrow of Mary Queen of Scots in 1567. In it the dichotomy of true, lawful king and usurping tyrant collapses, for Mary is the lawful ruler *and* the tyrant, and her deposers are usurpers *and yet* lawful also.[21] To her are attributed many of the traits of Macbeth: she is said to hate integrity in others, to appeal to the predictions of witches, to use foreign mercenaries, to place spies in the households of opponents, and to threaten the lives of the nobility; after her surrender, she is humiliated in the streets of Edinburgh as Macbeth fears to be. It is alleged that she would not have shrunk from the murder of her son if she could have reached him. This account of Mary as arch-tyrant embarrassed James,[22] and that is perhaps why just eight kings are shown to Macbeth by the Witches (4.1.119). Nevertheless, it was well established in protestant propaganda and in Spenser's *Faerie Queene*, and the Gunpowder Plot would tend to revivify it. Any recollection of the alleged tyranny of Mary, the lawful ruler, prompts awareness of the contradictions in absolutist ideology, disturbing the customary interpretation of *Macbeth*.[23] Once we are alert to this disturbance, the Jamesian reading of the play begins to leak at every joint.

One set of difficulties is associated with the theology of good, evil, and divine ordination that purports to discriminate Macbeth's violence from that legitimately deployed by the state. I write later of the distinctive attempt of Reformation Christianity[24] to cope with the paradoxical conjunction in one deity of total power and goodness. There is also a sequence of political awkwardnesses. These are sometimes regarded as incidental, but they amount to an undertow of circumstances militating against James's binary. Duncan's status and authority are in doubt, he is imperceptive, and his state is in chaos well before Macbeth's violence against it (G. K. Hunter in the introduction to his Penguin edition [1967] registers unease at the "violence and bloodthirstiness" of Macbeth's killing of Macdonwald [pp.9-10]). Nor is Malcolm's title altogether clear, since Duncan's declaration of him as "Prince of Cumberland" (1.4.35-42) suggests what the chronicles indicate—namely that the succession was not necessarily hereditary. Macbeth seems to be elected by the thanes (2.4.29-32). Although *Macbeth* may be read as working to justify the overthrow of the usurping tyrant, the *awkwardness* of the issue is brought to the surface by the uncertain behavior of Banquo.[25] In the sources, he collaborates with Macbeth, but to allow that in the play would taint King James's line and blur the idea of the one monstrous eruption.[26] Shakespeare compromises and makes Banquo do nothing at all. He fears Macbeth played "most foully for't" (3.1.3)[27] but does not even communicate his knowledge of the Witches' prophecies. Instead, he wonders if they may "set me up in hope" (3.1.10). If it is right for Malcolm and Macduff, eventually, to overthrow Macbeth, then it would surely be right for Banquo to take a clearer line.

Furthermore, the final position of Macduff appears quite disconcerting, once we read it with Buchanan's more realistic, political analysis in mind:

Macduff at the end stands in the same relation to Malcolm as Macbeth did to Duncan in the beginning. He is now the king-maker on whom the legitimate monarch depends, and the recurrence of the whole sequence may be anticipated (in production this might be suggested by a final meeting of Macduff and the Witches).[28] The Jamesian reading requires that Macbeth be a distinctively "evil" eruption in a "good" system; awareness of the role of Macduff in Malcolm's state alerts us to the fundamental instability of power relations during the transition to absolutism, and consequently to the uncertain validity of the claim of the state to the legitimate use of violence.[29] Certainly Macbeth is a murderer and an oppressive ruler, but he is one version of the absolutist ruler, not the polar opposite.

Malcolm himself raises very relevant issues in the conversation in which he tests Macduff: specifically tyrannical qualities are invoked. At one point, according to Buchanan, the Scottish lords "give the benefit of the doubt" to Mary and her husband, following the thought that "more secret faults" may be tolerated "so long as these do not involve a threat to the welfare of the state" (*Tyrannous Reign*, p.88). Macduff is prepared to accept considerable threats to the welfare of Scotland:

> Boundless intemperance
> In nature is a tyranny; it hath been
> Th' untimely emptying of the happy throne,
> And fall of many kings. But fear not yet
> To take upon you what is yours: you may
> Convey your pleasures in a spacious plenty,
> And yet seem cold—the time you may so hoodwink:
> We have willing dames enough; there cannot be
> That vulture in you, to devour so many
> As will to greatness dedicate themselves,
> Finding it so inclin'd.[30]

(4.3.66-76)

Tyranny in nature means disturbance in the metaphorical kingdom of a person's nature but, in the present context, one is likely to think of the effects of the monarch's intemperance on the literal kingdom.[31] Macduff suggests that such behavior has caused the fall not just of usurpers but of kings, occupants of "the happy throne." Despite this danger, he encourages Malcolm to "take upon you what is yours"—a sinister way of putting it, implying either Malcolm's title to the state in general or his rights over the women he wants to seduce or assault. Fortunately, the latter will not be necessary, there are "willing dames enough": Macduff is ready to mortgage both the bodies and (within the ideology invoked in the play) the souls of women to the monster envisaged as lawful good king. It will be all right, apparently, because people can be hoodwinked: Macduff allows us to see that the virtues James tries to identify with the absolutist monarch are an ideological strategy, and that the illusion of them will probably be sufficient to keep the system going.

Nor is this the worst: Malcolm claims more faults,[32] and according to Macduff "avarice / Sticks deeper"[33] (lines 84-85): Malcolm may corrupt not merely people but also property relations. Yet this too is to be condoned. Of course, Malcolm is not actually like this, but the point is that he could well be, as Macduff says many kings have been, and that would all be acceptable. And even Malcolm's eventual protestation of innocence cannot get round the fact that he has been lying. He says "my first false speaking / Was this upon myself"[34] (lines 130-31) and that may indeed be true, but it nevertheless indicates the circumspection that will prove useful to the lawful good king, as much as to the tyrant. In Holinshed[35] the culminating vice claimed by Malcolm is lying, but Shakespeare replaces it with a general and rather desperate evocation of utter tyranny (lines 91-100); was the original self-accusation perhaps too pointed? The whole conversation takes off from the specific and incomparable tyranny of Macbeth, but in the process succeeds in suggesting that there may be considerable overlap between the qualities of the tyrant and the true king.

Macbeth allows space for two quite different interpretive organizations: against a Jamesian illustration of the virtues of absolutism, we may produce a disturbance of that reading, illuminated by Buchanan. This latter makes visible the way religion is used to underpin state ideology, and undermines notions that established monarchs must not be challenged or removed and that state violence is utterly distinctive and legitimate. It is commonly assumed that the function of criticism is to resolve such questions of interpretation—to go through the text with an eye to sources, other plays, theatrical convention, historical context, and so on, deciding on which side the play comes down and explaining away contrary evidence. However, this is neither an adequate program nor an adequate account of what generally happens.

Let us suppose, to keep the argument moving along, that the Jamesian reading fits better with *Macbeth* and its Jacobean[36] context, as we understand them at present. Two questions then offer themselves: what is the status of the disturbance of that reading, which I have produced by bringing Buchanan into view? And what are the consequences of customary critical insistence upon the Jamesian reading?

On the first question, I would make three points. First, the Buchanan disturbance *is in the play*, and inevitably so. Even if we believe that Shakespeare was trying to smooth over difficulties in absolutist ideology, to do this significantly, he must deal with the issues that resist convenient inclusion. Those issues must be brought into visibility in order to be handled, and once exposed, they are available for the reader or audience to seize and focus upon, as an alternative to the more complacent reading. Even James's writings are vulnerable to such analysis—for instance, when he brings up the awkward fact that the prophet Samuel urgently warns the people of Israel against choosing a king, because he will tyrannize over them. This prominent biblical example could hardly be ignored, so James cites it and says that Samuel was preparing the Israelites to be obedient and patient. Yet once James has brought Samuel's pronouncement into visibility, the reader is at liberty to doubt the king's tendentious interpretation of it.[37] It is hardly possible to deny the reader this scope: even the most strenuous closure can be repudiated as inadequate.

Second, the Buchanan disturbance has been activated, in the present essay, as a consequence of the writer's skepticism about Jamesian ideological strategies and his concern with current political issues. It is conceivable that many readers of *Macbeth* will come to share this outlook. Whether this happens or not, the theoretical implication may be taken: if such a situation should come about, the terms in which *Macbeth* is customarily discussed would shift, and eventually the Buchanan disturbance would come to seem an obvious, natural way to consider the play. That is how notions of appropriate approaches to a text get established. We may observe the process, briefly, in the career of the Witches. For many members of Jacobean audiences, witches were a social and spiritual reality: they were as real as Edward the Confessor[38], perhaps more so. As belief in the physical manifestation of supernatural powers, and especially demonic powers, weakened, the Witches were turned into an operatic display,[39] with new scenes singing and dancing, fine costumes, and flying machines. In an adaptation by Sir William Davenant,[40] this was the only stage form of the play from 1674 to 1744, and even after Davenant's version was abandoned the Witches' divertissements were staged, until 1888. Latterly we have adopted other ways with the Witches—being still unable, of course, to contemplate them, as most of Shakespeare's audience probably did, as phenomena one might encounter on a heath. Kenneth Muir comments: "With the fading of belief in the objective existence of devils, they and their operations can yet symbolize the workings of evil in the hearts of men" (New Arden *Macbeth*, p. lxx). Recent critical accounts and theatrical productions have developed all kinds of strategies to make the Witches "work" for our time. These successive accommodations of one aspect of the play to prevailing attitudes are blatant, but they illustrate the extent to which critical orthodoxy is not the mere response to the text it claims to be: it is remaking it within currently acceptable parameters. The Buchanan disturbance may not always remain a marginal gloss to the Jamesian reading.

Third, we may assume that the Buchanan disturbance was part of the response of some among the play's initial audiences. It is in the nature of the matter that it is impossible to assess how many people inclined towards Buchanan's analysis of royal power. That there were such may be supposed from the multifarious challenges to state authority—culminating, of course, in the Civil War.[41] *Macbeth* was almost certainly read against James by some Jacobeans. This destroys the claim to privilege of the Jamesian reading on the ground that it is historically valid: we must envisage diverse original audiences, activating diverse implications in the text.[42]

With these considerations about the status of the Buchanan disturbance in mind, the question about the customary insistence on the Jamesian reading appears as a question about the politics of criticism. Like other kinds of cultural production, literary criticism helps to influence the way people think about the world; that is why the present study seeks to make space for an oppositional understanding of the text and the state. It is plain that most criticism has not only reproduced but also endorsed Jamesian ideology, so discouraging scrutiny, which *Macbeth* may promote, of the legitimacy of state violence.[43] That we are dealing with live issues is shown by the almost uncanny resemblances between the Gunpowder Plot and the bombing in 1984 by the Irish Republican Army of the Brighton hotel where leading members of the British government were staying, and in the comparable questions about state and other violence that they raise. My concluding thoughts are about the politics of the prevailing readings of *Macbeth*. I distinguish conservative and liberal positions; both tend to dignify their accounts with the honorific term *tragedy*.

The conservative position insists that the play is about "evil." Kenneth Muir offers a string of quotations to this effect: it is Shakespeare's "most profound and mature vision of evil"; "the whole play may be writ down as a wrestling of destruction with creation"; it is "a statement of evil"; "it is a picture of a special battle in a universal war"; and it "contains the decisive orientation of Shakespearean good and evil." This is little more than Jamesian ideology writ large: killing Macdonwald is "good" and killing Duncan is "evil," and the hierarchical society envisaged in absolutist ideology is identified with the requirements of nature, supernature, and the "human condition." Often this view is elaborated as a sociopolitical program, allegedly expounded by Shakespeare, implicitly endorsed by the critic. So Muir writes of "an orderly and close-knit society, in contrast to the disorder consequent upon Macbeth's initial crime [i.e., killing Duncan, not Macdonwald]. The naturalness of that order, and the unnaturalness of its violation by Macbeth, is emphasized" (New Arden *Macbeth*, p. li). Irving Ribner says Fleance, Banquo's son, is "symbolic of a future rooted in the acceptance of natural law, which inevitably must return to reassert God's harmonious order when evil has worked itself out."

This conservative endorsement of Jamesian ideology is not intended to ratify the modern state. Rather, like much twentieth-century literary criticism, it is backward-looking, appealing to an imagined earlier condition of society. Roger Scruton comments: "If a conservative is also a restorationist[44], this is because he lives close to society, and feels in himself the sickness which infects the common order. How, then, can he fail to direct his eyes towards that state of health from which things have declined? This quotation is close to the terms in which many critics write of *Macbeth* and their evocation of the Jamesian order allegedly restored at the end of the play constitutes a wistful gesture towards what they would regard as a happy ending for our troubled society. However, because this conservative approach is based on an inadequate analysis of political and social process, it gains no purchase on the main determinants of state power.

A liberal position hesitates to endorse any state power so directly, finding some saving virtue in Macbeth: "To the end he never totally loses our sympathy"; "we must still not lose our sympathy for the criminal." In this view there is a flaw in the state; it fails to accommodate the particular consciousness of the refined individual. Macbeth's imagination is set against the blandness of normative convention[45], and for all his transgressions, perhaps because of them, he transcends the laws he breaks. In John Bayley's version: "His superiority consists in a passionate sense for ordinary life, its seasons and priorities, a sense which his fellows in the play ignore in themselves or take for granted. Through the deed which tragedy requires of him he comes to know not only himself; but what life is all about." I call this view "liberal" because it is anxious about a state, absolutist or modern, that can hardly take cognizance of the individual sensibility, and it is prepared to validate to some degree the recalcitrant individual. But it will not undertake the political analysis that would press the case. Hence there is always in such criticism a reservation about Macbeth's revolt and a sense of relief that it ends in defeat: nothing could have been done anyway; it was all inevitable, written in the human condition. This retreat from the possibility of political analysis and action leaves the state virtually unquestioned, almost as fully as the conservative interpretation.[46]

Shakespeare, notoriously, has a way of anticipating all possibilities. The idea of literary intellectuals identifying their own deepest intuitions of the universe in the experience of the "great" tragic hero who defies the limits of the human condition is surely a little absurd; we may sense delusions of grandeur. *Macbeth* includes much more likely models for its conservative and liberal critics in the characters of the two doctors. The English Doctor has just four and a half lines (4.3.141-45), in which he says that King Edward is coming and that sick people whose malady conquers the greatest efforts of medical skill await him, expecting a heavenly cure for "evil." Malcolm, the king to be, says, "I thank you, Doctor." This doctor is the equivalent of conservative intellectuals who encourage respect for mystificatory images of ideal hierarchy that have served the state in the past, and who invoke "evil," "tragedy," and "the human condition" to produce, in effect, acquiescence in state power.[47]

The Scottish Doctor, in act 5 scenes 1 and 3, is actually invited to cure the sickness of the rulers and by implication the state: "If thou couldst, Doctor, cast / The water of my land, find her disease" (5.3.50-51). But this doctor, like the liberal intellectual, hesitates to press an analysis. He says: "This disease is beyond my practice" (5.1.56); "I think, but dare not speak" (5.1.76); "Therein the patient / Must minister to himself" (5.3.45-46); "Were I from Dunsinane away and clear, / Profit again should hardly draw me here" (5.3.61-62). He wrings his hands at the evidence of state violence and protects his conscience with asides. This is like the liberal intellectual who knows there is something wrong at the heart of the system but will not envisage a radical alternative and, to ratify this attitude, discovers in Shakespeare's plays "tragedy" and "the human condition" as explanations of the supposedly inevitable defeat of the person who steps out of line.[48]

By conventional standards, this chapter is perverse. But an oppositional criticism is bound to appear thus: its task is to work across the grain of customary assumptions and, if necessary, across the grain of the text, as it is customarily perceived. Of course, literary intellectuals don't have much influence over state violence; their therapeutic power is very limited. Nevertheless, writing, teaching, and other modes of communicating all contribute to the steady, long-term formation of opinion, to the establishment of legitimacy. This contribution King James himself did not neglect.

注释

1. 【作者原注】*Macbeth*, ed. K. Muir,（London, 1962）, I, ii, 16-24.
   译文: 因为英勇的麦克白不以命运的喜怒为意; 挥舞着他的血腥的宝剑, 一路砍杀过去, 直到那奴才的面前, 也不打一句话, 就挺剑从他的肚脐刺了进去, 把他的胸膛划破, 一直划到下巴; 他的头已经割下来挂在我们的城楼上了
   邓肯: 啊, 英勇的表弟! 了不起的壮士!
   (《麦克白》的引文, 以朱生豪先生译文为主, 有的地方采用了卞之琳先生的译文。)

2. 大意为: 在现代国家发展进程中, 国家对垄断合法暴力的要求至关重要。

3. 这两句话的大意为: 用国家暴力来对付这些持不同政见者, 需要获得一定程度的合法性, 因此也需要绝对主义意识形态。绝对主义意识形态把英国看作一座金字塔, 对这座金字塔的任何破坏行为都会给社会带来灾难, 并且, 绝对主义意识形态变本加厉地坚持"君权神授"。

4. 语出英国莎学名家 E. M. W. 蒂利亚德（E. M. W. Tillyard）的名作《伊丽莎白时代的世界图景》(*The Elizabethan World Picture*, 1942) 一书。

5. Perry Anderson: 佩里·安德森（1939—）: 英国新左派历史学家, 著有《绝对主义国家的系谱》(*Lineages of the Absolutist State*) 等书。

6. 大意为: 绝对主义本质就是: 重新调整和装配封建统治机器, 以便把为数众多的农民固定在他们传统的社会地位上。

7. 译文: 你的心里这样想, 虽然他 [博林布鲁克] 把国土一分为二, 把一半给了你, 可你有帮助他君临天下的大功, 这样的报酬还嫌太轻。

8. Essex: 埃塞克斯伯爵, 伊丽莎白的宠臣兼面首, 后以谋反罪伏诛。

9. Massacre of St. Bartholomew's Day in France in 1572: 1572 年在法国发生的针对新教徒的圣巴多罗马大屠杀。

10. the Gunpowder Plot of 1605: 1605 年英国天主教徒企图炸毁议会大厦、炸死国王的火药阴谋案。

11. 大意为: 判决的结果是, 简·怀斯曼被投入王座法院的马夏尔西监狱。在狱中, 除了允许她用一块亚麻布遮住下体外, 让她赤身露体、仰面朝天地躺在地上。在地上挖一个坑, 把她的头放在里面; 在她身上压上她能承受的石头和铁块。只要她活一天, 就得吃监狱里最粗劣的面包, 喝最差的水; 她吃饭的那一天, 不让她喝水; 让她喝

水的那一天，不让她吃饭，直到把她折磨死为止。

12. Basilikon Doron：拉丁文，詹姆士一世为他的儿子写给的如何治理国家的教诲。英文意为"Royal Gift"，似可译为"皇室箴言"。

13. 大意为：前者（合法贤君）承认自己命定为臣民造福，他从上帝手中接过管理国家的重担，他对此成竹在胸；后者（僭主暴君）视臣民为皇恩浩荡下的草芥，命定为他服务，受他恣意摆弄，满足他的骄奢淫逸。正因为二者的目的背道而驰，他们为达到目的所采取的手段、他们的所作所为也是南辕北辙。

14. 大意为：既然邪恶与上帝完全对立，那么认识上帝最好的办法就是从认识邪恶入手。

15. 大意为：经常有人这样去推断：《麦克白》的主旨与詹姆士一世的思想有异曲同工之处，即，提供逻辑谨严和令人信服的绝对主义国家意识形态。

16. 大意为：正如弗朗西斯·培根所见，超自然观念有助于让人默认现状（例如，追逐权力的人往往把自己的成功"不是归因于自身的美德或政策，而是归因于天意和福分"）。

17. 译文：麦克白烂熟了，经不起一摇，上天准备好装备 / 就要诛伐了。

18. 大意为：随着作者的笔锋所及，他被撂在了一边，好像从未当过国王似的。

19. 大意为：文学批评经常轻易地预设，基于历史原因，对《麦克白》进行的詹姆士一世式的解读是非常必要的，莎士比亚和他的同时代人对国家意识形态不可能有别的看法。

20. George Buchanan：乔治·布凯南（1506—1582），苏格兰人文主义者、教育家和作家。他以对话形式写的《论苏格兰的王权》，即文中提到的《君权论》（"De jure regni"）是一篇坚决主张限制王权的文章。

21. 大意为：布凯南的《苏格兰史》打破了合法君主与僭主暴君这种二分法，因为玛丽女王既是合法即位的君主，同时又是暴君。废黜她的那些人固然是谋逆贰臣，但他们的行为是合法的。

22. 詹姆士一世为玛丽女王之子。在英格兰的伊丽莎白一世去世后，他承继英格兰王位大统。

23. 大意为：只要想到统治者玛丽女王的所谓暴政，就会让人意识到绝对主义意识形态的矛盾，从而破坏了读者对《麦克白》的习惯性阐释。

24. Reformation Christianity：宗教改革后的基督教。

25. 大意为：有人会认为，《麦克白》的作用在于证明，推翻僭主暴君是合理之举。然而，班柯的行为交代不清，暴露出剧本在这个问题的尴尬。

26. 大意为：在《苏格兰史》当中，班柯与麦克白有过合作；但是，如果剧本这样写的话，就会越过詹姆士规定的界线，掩盖了麦克白是邪恶力量的迸发这一观念。

27. 译文：为此干得太肮脏了。

28. 大意为：麦克达夫与女巫的最后一次谋面可能暗示出这一点。

29. 大意为：认识到麦克达夫在马尔柯姆政权中的角色，我们会看到，向绝对主义过渡的过程中，权力关系根本不稳定。这最终让我们看到，国家对合法使用暴力的要求缺乏正当的理由。

30. 译文：

无限的放纵，

本质上是暴虐。这曾经

促使幸福的宝座太早出空、

许多国王的垮台。可是也不要怕

取得你应有的东西。你可以设法

充分享受丰富多彩的欢乐

而取得一本正经，掩人耳目。

我们这里有的是情愿的女子。

你的一张饿鹰的馋嘴也吞不了

那么多向富贵尊荣竞来献身的

国色天香哪。

31. the monarch's intemperance on the literal kingdom：君主在现实生活中的放纵。

32. 大意为：马尔柯姆可能还会犯下更多的罪过。

33. 译文：这一种贪欲 / 扎根就更深了。

34. 译文：第一次说假话 / 就是我这次骂自己。

35. Holinshed：这里指的是霍林希德的《英格兰、苏格兰、爱尔兰编年史》(*Chronicles of England, Scotland and Ireland*)。

36. Jacobean：詹姆士一世时代的。

37. 大意为：一旦詹姆士一世将撒母耳的见解公之于众，读者就有权怀疑国王对它的解释有倾向性。

38. Edward the Confessor：忏悔者爱德华（1003—1066），英格兰国王，

因笃信宗教，获"忏悔者"称号。在位期间，兴建了伦敦威斯敏斯特大教堂。

39. operatic display：歌剧表演。

40. William Davenant：戴夫南特（1606—1668），英国诗人、剧作家和剧院经理，被封为桂冠诗人。莎士比亚是他的教父，据传还可能是他的父亲。

41. 大意为：倾向于布凯南式王权分析的还是大有人在，国家权威经受了各种挑战这个事实可以证明。当然，这种挑战在内战期间达到了顶峰（指英国内战期间查理一世被处决一事）。

42. 大意为：这就打破了詹姆士一世式解读独尊的局面，因为这是有历史依据的：我们一定要想到早年那些立场各异的观众，他们激活了文本中的各种隐含意义。

43. 大意为：不难看出，大多数批评家不仅重复而且支持詹姆士一世式的意识形态，从而压制了人们对国家暴力合法性的详细考察，而这种考察正是《麦克白》一剧可能促发的。

44. restorationist：众生复位说信徒。

45. the blandness of normative convention：枯燥乏味的成规。

46. 大意为：像这样回避政治分析以及政治行动的做法，同保守主义的阐释一样，并未对国家提出异议。

47. 大意为：这位医生相当于保守主义知识分子，他鼓励人们尊重那些令人困惑的理想的等级制形象，而这些形象正是为过去的国家服务的。他引出了"邪恶"和"人类状况"等话，实际上产生了默认国家权力的效果。

48. 大意为：这很像自由派知识分子，明知道现行制度在根子上出了毛病，但也不肯设想一个激进的替代方案；而且，为了证明自己的态度正确，他从莎剧中找来"悲剧"和"人类状况"等词语，用来解释越轨者必然失败的命运。

伊格尔顿 《英文研究的兴起》

特里·伊格尔顿（1943— ）

　　特里·伊格尔顿是继雷蒙·威廉斯之后英国最负盛名的马克思主义批评家。在当代英美文学理论与批评界，能与他相提并论的只有詹明信（Fredric Jameson）；但他在读书界明星般的人气，则非后者所能比肩。

　　伊格尔顿于1943年出生在英国萨福郡的一个工人家庭，祖上为爱尔兰人，全家信奉天主教。无论从经济地位上讲，还是从宗教信仰上讲，这个家庭在英国社会都处于边缘位置。在当地一家天主教学校毕业后，获得奖学金，进入剑桥英文系读本科。大学期间，他受知于雷蒙·威廉斯，走上了马克思主义文学批评的道路。他于1964年获得学士学位，1968年获得文学博士学位，后来长期任教于牛津大学。1992年至2001年，任牛津大学托马斯·华顿讲座教授。这是英语文学界数一数二的大讲座，为许多人觊觎的目标。然而，伊格尔顿颇嫌此间的学术思想空气保守，于2002年移讲曼彻斯特大学。2009年9月，任美国圣母大学访问教授。

　　伊格尔顿天资聪颖，思想早慧，成名甚早。在30岁之前，他就出版了好几本书，在批评界崭露头角。读博士期间，受到当时的激进神学家的影响，积极参加了天主教左翼运动，写了一本神学著作《新左派教会》（New Left Church）。这场运动的主力是剑桥的一群青年知识分子，他们周旋于天主教和马克思主义之间，创办了自己的刊物，伊格尔顿任主编。在此时期，伊格尔顿还加入了当时英国著名的托洛茨基派组织"工人社会主义同盟"（Workers Socialist League）。

　　1967年，他出版了第一本文学研究专著《莎士比亚与社会》（Shakespeare and Society），着重描述个人与社会之间的冲突。在方法上，这本书有威廉斯《文化与社会》影响的痕迹，从书名中不难看出。在1970年出版的《流放与移民作家》（Exile and Emigré）是一部英国现代主义文学研究专著。书中提出的一个重要观点是，在20世纪英国本土小说家当中，没有哪一位有着当年狄更斯和艾略特的气魄，对于英国社会进行总体审视，描述其整体风貌；做到这一点的，只有约瑟夫·康拉德等移民作家。就方法而言，作者没有申明自己使用了马克思主义的理论框架；他用的是利维斯派的细读式分析方法，以自由人文主义的语言进行激进的社会批判。1975 年出版的《权力的神话：勃朗特姐妹的马克思主义研究》(*Myths of Power: A Marxist Study of the Brontës*)，在副标题中径直打出马克思主义的旗号，这是伊格尔顿转向马克思主义理论的重要标志。书中利用发生学结构主义方法来分析勃朗特姐妹的小说，显示出欧陆西方马克思主义理论家吕西安·戈德曼（Lucien Goldmann）的思想影响。1976 年出版的《批评与意识形态》(*Criticism and Ideology: A Study in Marxist Literary Theory*) 是他在 70 年代最重要的理论著作，反映出他当时力图以皮埃尔·马谢雷（Pierre Macherey）的文学生产理论解决文学问题的雄心。他在书中还尖锐批评了英国文学的批评传统，并从意识形态角度分析了几部英国小说。在他看来，文学的主要功能并非像传统的人文主义批评所认为的那样，在于产生审美的愉悦，也不像传统的马克思主义文学批评所认为的那样，反映了统治阶级的意识形态。他认为，文学本身就是一种意识形态，文学批评的主要任务就是发现"文学作为一种意识形态话语的规律"。同年出版的另一部短论《马克思主义与文学批评》(*Marxism and Literary Criticism*) 相当于一部马克思主义文学理论与批评简史，它以夹叙夹议的手法概述了从 19 世纪马恩等经典理论家到 20 世纪 70 年代的阿尔都塞（Louis Althusser）和皮埃尔·马谢雷这一系列马克思主义理论家的思想路途和论争。1981 年出版的《瓦尔特·本雅明；或走向一种革命批评》(*Walter Benjamin; or Towards a Revolutionary Criticism*) 为那些有志于激进政治的批评家制定了批评策略，要求他们摆脱狭隘的文本分析，扩大分析对象的范围，探讨文化生产和文学政治功用等问题。1983 年出版的《文学理论导论》(*Literary Theory: An Introduction*) 是伊格尔顿最负盛名的著作，是难得一见的学术畅销书，对于当代文论的普及居功厥伟。如果说韦勒克和奥斯汀·沃伦（Austin Warren）的《文学理论》是新批评的圣经，这本书可以说是 20 世纪西方文论的圣经。全书围绕着一个主题展开：文学理论就是意识形态的体现。1996 年问世的第二版基本保持初版的原貌，只增加了一篇后记。由于成书较早，内容相对有限，只覆盖了 20 世纪西方文论的半壁江山：英美新批评、现象学和阐释学、结构主义、后结构主义和精神分析。

假如读者想去了解伊格尔顿对新历史主义、文化研究、后结构主义和西方马克思主义的详尽论述，只能从后记中去领略作者的零星见解了。1985 年出版的《文学批评的功能》(*The Function of Criticism: From the "Spectator" to Post-Structualism*) 是一部英国文学批评的社会史。作者在这本薄薄的小书（仅有 133 页）中提出一个观点，自从 18 世纪以来，英国文学批评的社会功能不断退化，当代文学批评已经不具备任何实质性的社会功能；文学批评要么成为文学产业的公关手段，要么完全学院化，文学批评家成了一伙自弹自唱、彼此欣赏的学究。1986 年出版的论文集《格格不入》(*Against the Grain: Essays 1975—1985*) 记录了作者在这十年当中理论视线的转移和演变。

进入 20 世纪 90 年代后，伊格尔顿尤为关注现代文学批评的发展和演变。1990 年出版的《审美意识形态》(*The Ideology of the Aesthetic*) 论述了 18 世纪已降直至 20 世纪中叶，从大卫·休谟直到西奥多·阿多诺 (Theodor Adorno)，这段时期西方美学史上的重要人物和思想，追溯当代理论与批评的现状的历史根源。在同一年出版的演讲集《理论的意义》(*Significance of Theory*) 中，作者提出，理论的意义在于，它防止统治阶级将激进思想从人们头脑中抹去。1991 年出版的《意识形态导论》(*Ideology: An Introduction*) 梳理整理了"意识形态"概念的历史演变和理论论争，以及当代理论就后现代主义和后马克思主义问题而发生的论战。在 90 年代后期，伊格尔顿还完成了几部爱尔兰文学文化研究之作：1995 年出版的《希斯克利夫与大饥荒》(*Heathcliff and the Great Hunger*)、1998 年出版的《疯狂的约翰与主教》(*Crazy John and the Bishop and Other Essays*)、1999 年出版的《19 世纪爱尔兰的学者与反叛者》(*Scholars and Rebels in Nineteenth-Century Ireland*)等。在这些作品中，作者试图从马克思主义视角重新书写爱尔兰文化史。1996 年出版的《后现代主义的幻象》(*The Illusions of Postmodernism*) 批判了后现代主义过于突出去中心化的倾向以及它与资本主义的政治共谋。

进入 21 世纪后，伊格尔顿笔耕不辍，其研究范围进一步扩大。除了当代批评理论外，他的关注视线兼及神学、伦理学、悲剧史、文学史、文化理论等多个理论。近十年以来，他的主要著作有：《文化的观念》(*The Idea of Culture*)、自传《守门人》(*Gatekeeper*)、《理论之后》(*After Theory*)、《甜蜜的暴力》(*Sweet Violence*)、《异见人物》(*Dissent Figures*)、《英国小说》(*English Novel*)、《如何读诗》(*How to Read a*

Poem)、访谈录《批评家的任务》(*The Task of a Critic*) 等多种，反思当代批评理论的得失，探索激进政治的文化策略。

内容提要

本文选自伊格尔顿的《文学理论导论》第一章。伊格尔顿着力论述的是，在 19 世纪末期，随着宗教的社会影响力逐渐式微，英国文学研究迅速崛起，填补了宗教留下的意识形态空白，成为英国大学的常设学科。

对于统治阶级而言，宗教一直是维系其统治的有效意识形态。与一切成功的意识形态一样，宗教活动主要依靠的不是明确的概念或系统的学说，而是意象、象征、习惯、仪式和神话。它在人的无意识层面发挥作用，塑造社会共识。作为一股社会安抚力量，它致力于培养民众的服从、奉献、内省的精神。维多利亚时代中期，由于科学的进步和社会历史的变迁，宗教的社会作用开始变弱。在这种形势之下，英国文学研究就被当做一门学科，取代了宗教的位置，承担起宗教曾经发挥的意识形态功能。在这个过程中，文学批评家、教育家、学者马修·阿诺德发挥过重要作用。阿诺德敏锐地意识到，贵族阶级已经无力担当英国的统治阶级，而这个国家的新主人——资产阶级——又缺乏一种精致细微的意识形态来巩固自己的政治经济权力，他们只好求救于传统贵族的生活方式。利用文学文化来教化粗鄙的资产阶级已经成为当务之急。与此同时，倡导文学文化还有另一个政治效果，那就是控制和同化工人阶级。英国文学研究通过淡化阶级冲突，认可民族和谐，间接地发挥了创造社会共识的政治作用；与宗教一样，文学主要依靠情感和体验来发挥作用；因此，它非常适宜完成宗教遗留下的意识形态任务。文学宣扬永恒的真理，可以转移群众的视线，使他们不去关注眼前的实际困境；文学还可以制造各种虚无缥缈的幻象，让群众沉浸其中，替代性地满足现实生活中的物质需要。

在英国，文学研究这门学科不是出现在牛津、剑桥这样的统治阶级生长的摇篮，而是在工人阶级子弟就读的"技工学院、工人院校和大学附属夜校"。英国文学实际上是穷人的古典文学。自诞生之日起，这门学科就强调社会各个阶级之间的团结，强调培养同情心，灌输民族自豪感，传播道德价值的标准。也就是说，文学开始更加微妙和生动地传达统治阶级的道德价值标准了。

　　文学这门学科也成为英帝国殖民事业的组成部分。正如克里斯·鲍迪克（Chris Baldick）在《英国文学批评的社会使命》（*The Social Mission of English Criticism*）一书中所指出的那样，英国文学在维多利亚时代被纳入文官考试的范围，这一举措极为重要。一旦经过文学文化的包装，大英帝国的官员就可以带着对本民族的认同感冲向海外，向殖民地人民炫耀这种文化的优越性。

　　在牛津和剑桥这两个老牌大学，文学研究在相当长的一段时间之后才成为常设课程；而且，在创设之初，它就遭到传统学科（例如语文学）的排斥。一战的爆发大大改变了英文研究的地位，战时强烈的民族主义情绪使英国文学研究的老对手——语文学——处于不利地位；因为，古典语文学与德国学术渊源颇深，而此时德国恰好是英国的对手。第一次世界大战给英国人带来了巨大精神创伤。战后，文学又成为医治统治阶级精神创伤的良方。

The Rise of English

To speak of "literature and ideology" as two separate phenomena which can be interrelated is, as I hope to have shown, in one sense quite unnecessary. Literature, in the meaning of the word we have inherited, is an ideology. It has the most intimate relations to questions of social power. But if the reader is still unconvinced, the narrative of what happened to literature in the later nineteenth century might prove a little more persuasive.

If one were asked to provide a single explanation for the growth of English studies in the later nineteenth century, one could do worse than reply: "the failure of religion."[1] By the mid-Victorian period, this traditionally reliable, immensely powerful ideological form was in deep trouble. It was no longer winning the hearts and minds of the masses, and under the twin impacts of scientific discovery and social change its previous unquestioned dominance was in danger of evaporating. This was particularly worrying for the Victorian ruling class, because religion is for all kinds of reasons an extremely effective form of ideological control. Like all successful ideologies, it works much less by explicit concepts or formulated doctrines than by image, symbol, habit, ritual and mythology.[2] It is affective and experiential, entwining itself with the deepest unconscious roots of the human subject; and any social ideology which is unable to engage with such deep-seated a-rational fears and needs, as T. S. Eliot knew, is unlikely to survive very long. Religion, moreover, is capable of operating at every social level: if there is a doctrinal inflection of it for the intellectual elite, there is also a pietistic brand of it for the masses.[3] It provides an excellent social "cement," encompassing pious peasant, enlightened middle-class liberal and theological intellectual in a single organization. Its ideological power lies in its capacity to "materialize" beliefs as practices: religion is the sharing of the chalice and the blessing of the harvest, not just abstract argument about consubstantiation or hyperdulia. Its ultimate truths, like those mediated by the literary symbol, are conveniently closed to rational demonstration, and thus absolute in their claims. Finally religion, at least in its Victorian forms, is a pacifying influence, fostering meekness, self-sacrifice and the contemplative inner life. It is no wonder that the Victorian ruling class looked on the threatened dissolution of this ideological discourse with something less than equanimity.

Fortunately, however, another, remarkably similar discourse lay to hand: English literature. George Gordon[4], early Professor of English Literature at Oxford, commented in his inaugural lecture that "England is sick, and... English literature must save it. The Churches (as I understand) having failed, and social remedies being slow, English literature has now a triple function: still, I suppose, to delight and instruct us, but also, and above all, to save our souls and heal the State."[5] Gordon's words were spoken in our own century, but they find a resonance everywhere in Victorian England. It is a striking thought that had it not been for this dramatic crisis in mid-nineteenth-century ideology, we might not today have such a plentiful supply of Jane Austen casebooks and bluffer's guides to Pound[6]. As religion progressively ceases to provide the social "cement," affective values and basic mythologies by which a socially turbulent class-society can be welded together, "English" is constructed as a subject to carry this ideological burden from the Victorian period onwards. The key figure here is Matthew Arnold, always preternaturally sensitive to the needs of his social class, and engagingly candid about being so. The urgent social need, as Arnold recognizes, is to "Hellenize"[7] or cultivate the philistine middle class, who have proved unable to underpin their political and economic power with a suitably rich and subtle ideology. This can be done by transfusing into them something of the traditional style of the aristocracy, who as Arnold shrewdly perceives are ceasing to be the dominant class in England, but who have something of the ideological wherewithal to lend a hand to their middle-class masters. State-established schools, by linking the middle class to "the best culture of their nation," will confer on them "a greatness and a noble spirit, which the tone of these classes is not of itself at present adequate to impart."[8]

The true beauty of this manoeuver, however, lies in the effect it will have in controling and incorporating the working class:

> It is of itself a serious calamity for a nation that its tone of feeling and grandeur of spirit should be lowered or dulled. But the calamity

appears far more serious still when we consider that the middle classes, remaining as they are now, with their narrow, harsh, unintelligent, and unattractive spirit and culture, will almost certainly fail to mould or assimilate the masses below them, whose sympathies are at the present moment actually wider and more liberal than theirs. They arrive, these masses, eager to enter into possession of the world, to gain a more vivid sense of their own life and activity. In this their irrepressible development, their natural educators and initiators are those immediately above them, the middle classes. If these classes cannot win their sympathy or give them their direction, society is in danger of falling into anarchy.[9]

Arnold is refreshingly unhypocritical: there is no feeble pretence that the education of the working class is to be conducted chiefly for their own benefit, or that his concern with their spiritual condition is, in one of his own most cherished terms, in the least "disinterested." In the even more disarmingly candid words of a twentieth-century proponent of this view: "Deny to working-class children any common share in the immaterial, and presently they will grow into the men who demand with menaces a communism of the material."[10] If the masses are not thrown a few novels, they may react by throwing up a few barricades.

Literature was in several ways a suitable candidate for this ideological enterprise. As a liberal, "humanizing" pursuit, it could provide a potent antidote to political bigotry and ideological extremism. Since literature, as we know, deals in universal human values rather than in such historical trivia as civil wars, the oppression of women or the dispossession of the English peasantry, it could serve to place in cosmic perspective the petty demands of working people for decent living conditions or greater control over their own lives, and might even with luck come to render them oblivious of such issues in their high-minded contemplation of eternal truths and beauties.[11] English, as a Victorian handbook for English teachers put it, helps to "promote sympathy and fellow feeling among all classes;" another Victorian writer speaks of literature as opening a "serene and luminous region of truth where all may meet and expatiate in common," above "the smoke and stir, the din and turmoil of man's lower life of care and business and debate."[12]

Literature would rehearse the masses in the habits of pluralistic thought and feeling, persuading them to acknowledge that more than one viewpoint than theirs existed—namely, that of their masters. It would communicate to them the moral riches of bourgeois civilization, impress upon them a reverence for middle-class achievements, and, since reading is an essentially solitary, contemplative activity, curb in them any disruptive tendency to collective political action. It would give them a pride in their national language and literature: if scanty education and extensive hours of labor prevented them personally from producing a literary masterpiece, they could take pleasure in the thought that others of their own kind—English people—had done so. The people, according to a study of English literature written in 1891, "need political culture, instruction, that is to say, in what pertains to their relation to the State, to their duties as citizens; and they need also to be impressed sentimentally by having the presentation in legend and history of heroic and patriotic examples brought vividly and attractively before them."[13] All of this, moreover, could be achieved without the cost and labor of teaching them the Classics: English literature was written in their own language, and so was conveniently available to them.

Like religion, literature works primarily by emotion and experience, and so was admirably well-fitted to carry through the ideological task which religion left off. Indeed by our own time literature has become effectively identical with the opposite of analytical thought and conceptual enquiry: whereas scientists, philosophers and political theorists are saddled with these drably discursive pursuits, students of literature occupy the more prized territory of feeling and experience. Whose experience, and what kinds of feeling, is a different question. Literature from Arnold onwards is the enemy of "ideological dogma," an attitude which might have come as a surprise to Dante, Milton and Pope; the truth or falsity of beliefs such as that blacks are inferior to whites is less important than what it feels like to experience them. Arnold himself had beliefs, of course, though like everybody else he regarded his own beliefs as reasoned positions rather than ideological dogmas. Even so, it was not the business of literature to communicate such beliefs directly—to argue openly, for example, that private property is the bulwark of liberty.[14] Instead, literature should convey timeless truths, thus distracting the masses from their immediate commitments, nurturing in them a spirit of tolerance and generosity, and so ensuring the survival of private property. Just as Arnold attempted in *Literature and Dogma* and *God and the Bible* to dissolve away the embarrassingly doctrinal bits of Christianity into poetically suggestive sonorities, so the pill of middle-class ideology was to be sweetened by the sugar of literature.

There was another sense in which the "experiential" nature of literature was ideologically convenient. For "experience" is not only the homeland of ideology, the place where it takes root most effectively; it is also in its literary form a kind of vicarious self-fulfilment. If you do not have the money and leisure to visit the Far East, except perhaps as a soldier in the pay of British imperialism, then you can always "experience" it at second hand by reading Conrad or Kipling.[15] Indeed according to some literary theories this is even more real than strolling round Bangkok. The actually impoverished experience of the mass of people, an impoverishment bred by their social conditions, can be supplemented by literature: instead of working to change such conditions (which Arnold, to his credit, did more thoroughly than almost any of those who sought to inherit his mantle),[16] you can vicariously fulfil someone's desire for a fuller life by handing them *Pride and Prejudice*.

It is significant, then, that 'English' as an academic subject was first institutionalized not in the Universities, but in the Mechanics' Institutes, working men's colleges and extension lecturing circuits.[17] English was liter-ally the poor man's Classics—a way of providing a cheapish "liberal" education for those beyond the charmed circles of public school[18] and Oxbridge. From the outset in the work of "English" pioneers like F. D. Maurice[19] and Charles Kingsley, the emphasis was on solidarity between the social classes, the cultivation of "larger sympathies," the instillation of national pride and the transmission of "moral" values. This last concern—still the distinctive hallmark of literary studies in England, and a frequent source of bemusement to intellectuals from other cultures—was an essential part of the ideological project; indeed the rise of "English" is more or less concomitant with a historic shift in the very meaning of the term "moral,"[20] of which Arnold, Henry James and F. R. Leavis are the major critical exponents. Morality is no longer to be grasped as a formulated code or explicit ethical system: it is rather a sensitive preoccupation with the whole quality of life itself, with the oblique, nuanced particulars of human experience.[21] Somewhat rephrased, this can be taken as meaning that the old religious ideologies have lost their force, and that a more subtle communication of moral values, one which works by "dramatic enactment" rather than rebarbative abstraction, is thus in order. Since such values are nowhere more vividly dramatized than in literature, brought home to "felt experience" with all the unquestionable reality of a blow on the head, literature becomes more than just a handmaiden of moral ideology: it is moral ideology for the modern age, as the work of F. R. Leavis was most graphically to evince.

The working class was not the only oppressed layer of Victorian society at whom "English" was specifically beamed. English literature, reflected a Royal Commission witness in 1877, might be considered a suitable subject for "women... and the second- and third-rate men who... become school-masters."[22] The "softening" and "humanizing" effects of English, terms recurrently used by its early proponents, are within the existing ideological stereotypes of gender clearly feminine. The rise of English in England ran parallel to the gradual, grudging admission of women to the institutions of higher education; and since English was an untaxing sort of affair, concerned with the finer feelings rather than with the more virile topics of *bona fide*[23] academic "disciplines," it seemed a convenient sort of non-subject to palm off on the ladies, who were in any case excluded from science and the professions. Sir Arthur Quiller Couch[24], first Professor of English at Cambridge University, would open with the word "Gentlemen" lectures addressed to a hall filled largely with women. Though modern male lecturers may have changed their manners, the ideological conditions which make English a popular University subject for women to read have not.

If English had its feminine aspect, however, it also acquired a masculine one as the century drew on. The era of the academic establishment of English is also the era of high imperialism in England. As British capitalism became threatened and progressively outstripped by its younger German and American rivals, the squalid, undignified scramble of too much capital chasing too few overseas territories, which was to culminate in 1914 in the first imperialist world war, created the urgent need for a sense of national mission and identity. What was at stake in English studies was less English literature than English literature: our great "national poets" Shakespear and Milton, the sense of an "organic" national tradition and identity to which new recruits could be admitted by the study of humane letters. The reports of educational bodies and official enquiries into the teaching of English, in this period and in the early twentieth century, are strewn with nostalgic back-references to the "organic" community of Elizabethan England in which nobles and groundlings found a common meeting-place in the Shakespearian theater, and which might still be reinvented today. It is no accident that the author of one of the most influential Government reports in this area, *The Teaching of English in England* (1921), was none other than Sir Henry Newbolt[25], minor jingoist poet and perpetrator of the immortal line "Play up! play up! and play the game!" Chris Baldick has pointed to the importance of the admission of English literature to the Civil Service examinations in the Victorian period: armed with this conveniently packaged version of their own cultural treasures, the servants of British imperialism could sally forth overseas secure in a sense of "their national identity, and able to display that cultural superiority to their envying colonial peoples."[26]

It took rather longer for English, a subject fit for women, workers and those wishing to impress the natives, to penetrate the bastions of ruling-class power in Oxford and Cambridge. English was an upstart, amateurish affair as academic subjects went, hardly able to compete on equal terms with the rigors of Greats[27] or philology; since every English gentleman read his own literature in his spare time anyway, what was the point of submitting it to systematic study? Fierce rearguard actions were fought by both ancient Universities against this distressingly dilettante subject: the definition of an academic subject was what could be examined, and since English was no more than idle gossip about literary taste it was difficult to know how to make it unpleasant enough to qualify as a proper academic pursuit. This, it might be said, is one of the few problems associated with the study of English which have since been effectively resolved. The frivolous contempt for his subject displayed by the first really "literary" Oxford professor, Sir

Walter Raleigh, has to be read to be believed.[28] Raleigh held his post in the years leading up to the First World War; and his relief at the outbreak of the war, an event which allowed him to abandon the feminine vagaries of literature and put his pen to something more manly—war propaganda—is palpable in his writing. The only way in which English seemed likely to justify its existence in the ancient Universities was by systematically mistaking itself for the Classics; but the classicists were hardly keen to have this pathetic parody of themselves around.

If the first imperialist world war more or less put paid to Sir Walter Raleigh, providing him with a heroic identity more comfortingly in line with that of his Elizabethan namesake[29], it also signaled the final victory of English studies at Oxford and Cambridge. One of the most strenuous antagonists of English—philology—was closely bound up with Germanic influence; and since England happened to be passing through a major war with Germany, it was possible to smear classical philology as a form of ponderous Teutonic nonsense with which no self-respecting Englishman should be caught associating.[30] England's victory over Germany meant a renewal of national pride, an upsurge of patriotism which could only aid English's cause; but at the same time the deep trauma of the war, its almost intolerable questioning of every previously held cultural assumption, gave rise to a "spiritual hungering," as one contemporary commentator described it, for which poetry seemed to provide an answer. It is a chastening thought that we owe the University study of English, in part at least, to a meaningless massacre. The Great War, with its carnage of ruling-class rhetoric, put paid to some of the more strident forms of chauvinism on which English had previously thrived: there could be few more Walter Raleighs after Wilfred Owen[31]. English Literature rode to power on the back of wartime nationalism; but it also represented a search for spiritual solutions on the part of an English ruling class whose sense of identity had been profoundly shaken, whose psyche was ineradicably scarred by the horrors it had endured. Literature would be at once solace and reaffirmation, a familiar ground on which Englishmen could regroup both to explore, and to find some alternative to, the nightmare of history.

注释

1. 大意为：英国文学研究之所以兴起于 19 世纪末，原因之一是宗教的衰落。

2. 大意为：宗教发挥意识形态作用，主要依靠的是意象、象征、习惯、仪式和神话，而不是依靠明确的概念或系统的教义。

3. 大意为：宗教在社会各个阶层发挥作用，如果说它有适合思想精英口味的变种，那它也有适合普通民众口味的虔诚品牌。

4. George Gordon：乔治·戈登（1881—1947），牛津教授、批评家。

5.【作者原注】Quoted by Chris Baldick, "The Social Mission of English Studies" (unpublished D.Phil. thesis, Oxford 1981), p.156. I am considerably indebted to this excellent study, published as *The Social Mission of English Criticism* (Oxford, 1983).

6. bluffer's guide to Pound：炫学者使用的庞德作品指南。

7. Hellinize：希腊化。阿诺德在《文化与无政府》一书中区分了希腊精神和希伯来精神。所谓"希腊化"，就是希腊精神的培养。

8.【作者原注】"The Popular Education of France," in *Democratic Education*, ed. R. H. Super (Ann Arbor, 1962), p.22.

9.【作者原注】Ibid., p.26.

10.【作者原注】George Sampson, *English for the English* (1921), quoted by Baldick, "The Social Mission of English Studies," p.153.

11. 这句话暗含反讽意味。大意为：它有助于人们从宇宙的视角去看待劳动人民提出的那些琐碎的要求，即，体面的生活条件或更多地支配自己的生活。

12.【作者原注】H. G. Robinson, "On the Use of English Classical Literature in the Work of Education," *Macmillan's Magazine* 11 (1860), quoted by Baldick, "The Social Mission of English Studies," p.103.

13.【作者原注】J. C. Collins, *The Study of English Literature* (1891), quoted by Baldick, "The Social Mission of English Studies," p.100.

14. 大意为：即便如此，直接传达这类信念——例如公开主张私有财产是捍卫自由的堡垒——并不是文学的分内之事。

15. 康拉德和吉卜林都写过以远东为背景的小说。

16. 大意为：值得表扬的是，阿诺德在这方面倒是做得非常深入、扎实，超过那些想继承他衣钵的批评家。

17.【作者原注】See Lionel Gossman, "Literature and Education," *New Literary History*, vol. XIII, no. 2, winter 1982, pp.341-371. See also D. J. Palmer, *The Rise of English Studies* (London, 1965).

18. 大意为：英国文学实际上成了穷人的古典文学，它为那些无缘进入公学的人提供了廉价的人文教育（在 19 世纪，公学的课程以讲授古典科目为主）。

19. F. D. Maurice：毛里斯（1805—1872），英国神学家、作家。

20. 大意为：英国文学研究的兴起与道德一词含义的历史变迁同步进行。

21. the oblique, nuanced particulars of human experience：人类经验中那些间接的、细微的具体情形。

22.【作者原注】Quoted by Gossman, "Literature and Education," pp.341-342.

23. *bona fide*：拉丁文，意为"真诚的"。

24. Sir Arthur Quiller Couch：考奇（1863—1944），英国文学批评家。

25. Sir Henry Newbolt：纽波特（1862—1938），英国诗人、历史学家。

26.【作者原注】See Baldick, "The Social Mission of English Studies,"pp.108-111.

27. Greats：牛津大学的古典人文学科课程。

28.【作者原注】See ibid., pp.117-23.

29. his Elizabethan namesake：指的是文艺复兴时期的瓦特·雷利爵士。

30.【作者原注】See Francis Mulhern, *The Moment of* "*Scrutiny*" (London, 1979), pp.20-22.

31.Wilfred Owen：欧文（1893—1918），英国战地诗人，死于一战期间。

赫布迪 《从文化到霸权》

狄克·赫布迪（1951— ）

狄克·赫布迪 1951 年出生在伦敦的一个工人阶级家庭。在 20 世纪 70 年代，他受教于英国文化研究的重镇——伯明翰大学当代文化研究中心。赫布迪在学期间，正值当代文化研究中心的黄金时代。1979年，赫布迪出版了他的代表作《亚文化：风格的意义》(*Subculture: The Meaning of Style*)。这本书连同斯图亚特·霍尔等人合编的《仪式的抵抗》、保罗·威利斯（Paul Willis）的《学习劳动》(*Learning to Labor*)，被认为是青年亚文化研究的代表性著作。这本书出版后，被翻译成多种语言，几乎每年都有重印。从 1984 年至 1992 年，赫布迪任教于伦敦大学戈德史密斯学院；1991 年后移居美国，现任教于加州大学圣巴巴拉校区。

青年亚文化研究是 20 世纪 70 年代英国文化研究的重头戏，是赫布迪当时所在的伯明翰大学当代文化研究中心最为主要的研究课题。"青年亚文化"现象出现在 20 世纪 60 年代。当时英美世界的一些青年因苦闷厌世，挑战中产阶级循规蹈矩的价值观，故作种种惊世骇俗之举：奇装异服，举止轻佻，满嘴脏话，一口俚语，情迷摇滚乐，流连酒吧间。他们被冠以各式各样的"尊号"：光头仔（skinhead）、男阿飞（Teddy）、摩登派（moderns）和朋克（punks）。这就是所谓的青年亚文化现象；这些人的种种偏常举止就是赫布迪书名中所说的"风格"。在美国，这些游手好闲、四处惹事的浮浪子弟多为中产阶级家庭出身的在校大学生。在英国，这类人多为游离于大学之外的工人阶级子弟。他们对社会现状非常不满，感觉向上流动无望，故而放浪形骸，抒发愤懑；末流所至，竟有殴打同性恋、施暴南亚移民的粗野举动。对于他们的行为，赫布迪等文化批评家在研究过程中总是抱有一种同情性理解，力图深入他们的心灵世界，探索和构建他们反抗行为背后暗藏的文化和社会意义。

内容提要

本文选自赫布迪的名作《亚文化：风格的意义》，它以时间为序，简要地概述了从 20 世纪 50 年代到 70 年代英国文化研究所奉行的研究范式：雷蒙·威廉斯的人文主义文学式分析、罗兰·巴特（Roland Barthes）的符号学分析、路易·阿尔都塞的意识形态理论和安东尼奥·葛兰西的文化霸权理论。

雷蒙·威廉斯在《文化与社会》一书的基本内容可以大致转述如下：18 世纪中期以来，也就是工业革命后，近代英国思想史中出现了所谓"文化与社会"的传统。其核心观点是，工业革命之前，在农业时代的英国，存在着一种自然和谐、自成一体的有机文化（organic culture）。可是，自从工业革命勃兴以来，这种有机和谐的社会文化却遭到了人为造就的工业文明的侵蚀，整个社会开始唯利是图，道德缺失，文化欣赏水准也江河日下，社会精神危机由此产生。若想摆脱这种危机，只有两条出路。一条是保守派的解决方案，重建等级分明的有机社会，重申文化的重要性，对抗机械性的资本主义文明。另一种是政治激进派的方案，推翻工业资本主义，另建新的文化和社会形态。在这个传统中，文化保守派占据多数。激进和保守之间的对立催生出两种不同的文化定义。一种是经典的、保守的文化定义：文化是高雅的文学和艺术（歌剧、芭蕾、戏剧、文学），体现出高超的审美标准。用阿诺德的话说，它是"思想和言论的精华"。文化的另一种定义来自人类学，按照这种定义，文化指的是某种特定的生活方式。它的范围十分广泛，远远超出文学和思想的范围。如果根据这个定义去从事文化分析，就是要澄清某种生活方式显示或暗含的意义和价值观，以便揭示日常生活表象背后的一般性原因和广阔的历史潮流。这两种相互冲突的文化定义在文化研究出现之际就一同存在。无论在威廉斯的著作中，还是在霍加特的著作中，都是如此。威廉斯为大众文化确立了审美和道德标准，霍加特则强调要用精妙的文学感受力去解读社会。

罗兰·巴特借鉴了结构主义语言学的分析方法。他像语言学者分析语言那样，去揭示文化现象的任意性，去发掘日常生活现象背后隐藏的意义。与霍加特不同，巴特并不去区分现代大众文化的优劣。他意在说明，在当代资产阶级社会之中，那些看似自然而然产生的形式和仪式，实际上是经过系统地扭曲之后才出现的；它们随时可能被"自然化"、去历史化，被奉为永恒不变的东西，进而成为一种神话。巴特在《神话学》一书中主要考察，某一社会集团（例如掌权者）的价值观和意义阐释是如何变成整个社会共有的意义阐释。巴特利用语言分析的方法去分析语言系统以外的其他话语系统，例如服装、电影、广告等等，为当代文化研究开辟了一个新天地。

从 20 世纪 60 年代后期开始，路易·阿尔都塞的结构主义马克思主义风靡英国左翼学界，他的意识形态理论为这一阶段的英国文化研究提供了理论框架。按照传统马克思主义的说法，意识形态是一套虚假的观念，是统治者刻意经营的思想骗术；它阻碍人们正确地认识社会的真相，掩盖现实生活中的矛盾。阿尔都塞却另辟蹊径，提出一套新的意识形态理论。在他看来，意识形态并非意识，而是无意识，是人们在无意识之中"体验"这个世界的方式。它是一套再现系统，通常表现为形象（image），偶尔表现为概念。我们都是意识形态治下的"主体"，我们的思想和行动必然受到它的影响和渗透。一方面，意识形态是我们思考问题的框架，我们需要通过它来感受和认识世界；另一方面，意识形态通过意识形态国家机器，渗透到社会生活的方方面面。所谓意识形态国家机器，就是诸如家庭、学校、语言、媒体等社会机制，它们约束我们按照一定的社会规范去思考行事。这些规范经常以常识的面貌出现，体现的却是统治阶级的利益。正是因为意识形态从中作祟，我们对统治集团的种种举措往往居之不疑，以为天经地义。在相当长的一段时间之内，英国文化研究的重要内容——媒体研究——都是以阿尔都塞的意识形态理论为圭臬，发掘媒体产生的意识形态后果和影响。但是，阿尔都塞的意识形态理论也有很大的缺陷，它夸大了意识形态的思想控制力度，忽视了人的主观能动作用，低估了人在主导意识形态面前的抗争力量。所以从 70 年代开始，英国文化研究又从欧洲大陆引进了葛兰西的文化霸权理论，来匡正阿尔都塞理论的偏颇。

葛兰西所说的文化霸权，指的是统治阶级将于己有利的价值观和信仰普遍推行给社会各个阶级的过程。这个过程的实现主要依靠的不是暴力，而是精神和道德领导，依靠大部分社会成员的自动认同。正如有的批评家所指出的那样，葛兰西还特意强调，霸权不是一成不变的，它既可以得到，也可能失去。这就不同于阿尔都塞的意识形态观念。阿尔都塞认为，意识形态贯穿整个社会，无所不在，无往而不胜。

Dick Hebdige (1951—)

From Culture to Hegemony

Culture

> Culture: cultivation, tending, in Christian authors, worship; the
> action or practice of cultivating the soil; tillage, husbandry; the cultivation
> or rearing of certain animals (e. g. fish); the artificial development
> of microscopic organisms, organisms so produced; the cultivating
> or development (of the mind, faculties, manners), improvement or
> refinement by education and training; the condition of being trained or
> refined; the intellectual side of civilization; the prosecution or special
> attention or study of any subject or pursuit. (*Oxford English Dictionary*)

Culture is a notoriously ambiguous concept as the above definition
demonstrates.[1] Refracted through centuries of usage, the word has acquired a
number of quite different, often contradictory, meanings. Even as a scientific
term, it refers both to a process (artificial development of microscopic
organisms) and a product (organisms so produced). More specifically,
since the end of the eighteenth century, it has been used by English
intellectuals and literary figures to focus critical attention on a whole range
of controversial issues. The "quality of life", the effects in human terms of
mechanization, the division of labor and the creation of a mass society have
all been discussed within the larger confines of what Raymond Williams
has called the "Culture and Society" debate.[2] It was through this tradition
of dissent and criticism that the dream of the "organic society"—of society
as an integrated, meaningful whole—was largely kept alive. The dream had
two basic trajectories. One led back to the past and to the feudal ideal of a
hierarchically ordered community. Here, culture assumed an almost sacred
function. Its "harmonious perfection" was posited against the Wasteland of
contemporary life.

The other trajectory, less heavily supported, led towards the future,
to a socialist Utopia where the distinction between labor and leisure
was to be annulled. Two basic definitions of culture emerged from this

tradition, though these were by no means necessarily congruent with the two trajectories outlined above. The first—the one which is probably most familiar to the reader—was essentially classical and conservative. It represented culture as a standard of aesthetic excellence: "the best that has been thought and said in the world,"[3] and it derived from an appreciation of "classic" aesthetic form (opera, ballet, drama, literature, art). The second, traced back by Williams to Herder[4] and the eighteenth century, was rooted in anthropology. Here the term "culture" referred to a

> ...particular way of life which expresses certain meanings and values not only in art and learning, but also in institutions and ordinary behavior. The analysis of culture, from such a definition, is the clarification of the meanings and values implicit and explicit in a particular way of life, a particular culture. [5]

This definition obviously had a much broader range. It encompassed, in T. S. Eliot's words:

> ...all the characteristic activities and interests of a people. Derby Day, Henley Regatta, Cowes, the 12th of August, a cup final, the dog races, the pin table, the dartboard, Wensleydale cheese, boiled cabbage cut into sections, beetroot in vinegar, 19th century Gothic churches, the music of Elgar...[6]

As Williams noted, such a definition could only be supported if a new theoretical initiative was taken. The theory of culture now involved the "study of relationships between elements in a whole way of life". The emphasis shifted from immutable to historical criteria, from fixity to transformation:

> ...an emphasis [which] from studying particular meanings and values seeks not so much to compare these, as a way of establishing a scale, but by studying their modes of change to discover certain general causes or "trends" by which social and cultural developments as a whole can be better understood.[7]

Williams was, then, proposing an altogether broader formulation of the relationships between culture and society, one which through the analysis of "particular meanings and values" sought to uncover the conceived fundamentals of history; the "general causes" and broad social "trends" which lie behind the manifest appearances of an "everyday life".

In the early years, when it was being established in the Universities, Cultural Studies sat rather uncomfortably on the fence between these two conflicting definitions—culture as a standard of excellence, culture as a "whole way of life"—unable to determine which represented the most fruitful line of enquiry. Richard Hoggart and Raymond Williams portrayed working-class culture sympathetically in wistful accounts of pre-scholarship boyhoods but their work displayed a strong bias towards literature and literacy and an equally strong moral tone. Hoggart deplored the way in which the traditional working-class community—a community of tried and tested values despite the dour landscape in which it had been set—was being undermined and replaced by a "Candy Floss World" of thrills and cheap fiction which was somehow bland *and* sleazy. Williams tentatively endorsed the new mass communications but was concerned to establish aesthetic and moral criteria for distinguishing the worthwhile products from the "trash"; the jazz—"a real musical form" —and the football— "a wonderful game"— from the "rape novel, the Sunday strip paper and the latest Tin Pan drool". In 1966 Hoggart laid down the basic premises upon which Cultural Studies were based:

> First, without appreciating good literature, no one will really understand the nature of society, second, literary critical analysis can be applied to certain social phenomena other than "academically respectable" literature (for example; the popular arts, mass communications) so as to illuminate their meanings for individuals and their societies.[8]

The implicit assumption that it still required a literary sensibility to "read" society with the requisite subtlety, and that the two ideas of culture could be ultimately reconciled was also, paradoxically, to inform the early work of the French writer, Roland Barthes, though here it found validation in a method—semiotics—a way of reading signs.

Barthes: Myths and Signs

Using models derived from the work of the Swiss linguist Ferdinand de Saussure Barthes sought to expose the *arbitrary* nature of cultural phenomena, to uncover the latent meanings of an everyday life which, to all intents and purposes, was "perfectly natural". Unlike Hoggart, Barthes was not concerned with distinguishing the good from the bad in modern mass culture, but rather with showing how *all* the apparently spontaneous forms and rituals of contemporary bourgeois societies are subject to a systematic distortion, liable at any moment to be dehistoricized, "naturalized", converted into myth:

> The whole of France is steeped in this anonymous ideology: our press, our films, our theater, our pulp literature, our rituals, our Justice, our diplomacy, our conversations, our remarks about the weather, a murder trial, a touching wedding, the cooking we dream of, the garments we wear, everything in everyday life is dependent on the representation which the bourgeoisie *has and makes us have* of the relations between men and the world.[9]

Like Eliot, Barthes's notion of culture extends beyond the library, the opera-house and the theater to encompass the whole of everyday life. But this everyday life is for Barthes overlaid with a significance which is at once more insidious and more systematically organized. Starting from the premise that "myth is a type of speech", Barthes set out in *Mythologies* to examine the normally hidden set of rules, codes and conventions through which meanings particular to specific social groups (i. e. those in power) are rendered universal and "given" for the whole of society. He found in phenomena as disparate as a wrestling match, a writer on holiday, a tourist guide-book, the same artificial nature, the same ideological core. Each had been exposed to the same prevailing rhetoric (the rhetoric of common sense) and turned into myth, into a mere element in a "second-order semiological system". (Barthes uses the example of a photograph in *Paris-Match*[10] of a Negro soldier saluting the French flag, which has a first and second order connotation. (1) a gesture of loyalty, but also (2) "France is a great empire, and all her sons, without color discrimination, faithfully serve under her flag".)

Barthes's application of a method rooted in linguistics to other systems of discourse outside language (fashion, film, food, etc.) opened up completely new possibilities for contemporary cultural studies. It was hoped that the invisible seam between language, experience and reality could be located and prised open through a semiotic analysis of this kind: that the gulf between the alienated intellectual and the "real" world could be rendered meaningful and, miraculously, at the same time, be made to disappear. Moreover, under Barthes's direction, semiotics promised nothing less than the reconciliation of the two conflicting definitions of culture upon which Cultural Studies so ambiguously posited—a marriage of moral conviction (in this case, Barthes's Marxist beliefs) and popular themes: the study of a society's total way of life.

This is not to say that semiotics was easily assimilable within the Cultural Studies project. Though Barthes shared the literary preoccupations of Hoggart and Williams, his work introduced a new Marxist "problematic" which was alien to the British tradition of concerned and largely untheorized "social commentary". As a result, the old debate seemed suddenly limited. In E. P. Thompson's words it appeared to reflect the parochial concerns of a group of "gentlemen amateurs". Thompson sought to replace Williams's definition of the theory of culture as "a theory of relations between elements in a whole way of life" with his own more rigorously Marxist formulation: "the study of relationships in a whole way of *conflict*".[11] A more analytical framework was required; a new vocabulary had to be learned. As part of this process of theorization, the work "ideology" came to acquire a much wider range of meanings than had previously been the case. We have seen how Barthes found an "anonymous ideology" penetrating every possible level of social life, inscribed in the most mundane of rituals, framing the most casual social encounters. But how can ideology be "anonymous", and how can it assume such a broad significance? Before we attempt any reading of subcultural style, we must first define the term "ideology" more precisely.

Ideology: a *Lived* Relation

In the *German Ideology*, Marx shows how the basis of the capitalist economic structure (surplus value, neatly defined by Godelier as "Profit...is unpaid work") is hidden from the consciousness of the agents of production. The failure to see through appearances to the real relations which underlie them does not occur as the direct result of some kind of masking operation consciously carried out by individuals, social groups or institutions. On the contrary, ideology by definition thrives *beneath* consciousness. It is here, at the level of "normal common sense", that ideological frames of reference are most firmly sedimented and most effective, because it is here that their ideological nature is most effectively concealed. As Stuart Hall puts it:

> It is precisely its "spontaneous" quality, its transparency, its "naturalness", its refusal to be made to examine the premises on which it is founded, its resistance to change or to correction, its effect of instant recognition, and the closed circle in which it moves which makes common sense, at one and the same time, "spontaneous", ideological and *unconscious*. You cannot learn, through common sense, *how things are*: you can only discover *where they fit* into the existing scheme of things. In this way, its very taken-for-grantedness is what establishes it as a medium in which its own premises and presuppositions are being rendered invisible by its apparent transparency.

Since ideology saturates everyday discourse in the form of common sense, it cannot be bracketed off from everyday life as a self-contained set of "political opinions" or "biased views". Neither can it be reduced to the abstract dimensions of a "world view" or used in the crude Marxist sense to designate "false consciousness". Instead, as Louis Althusser has pointed out:

> ...ideology has very little to do with "consciousness"... It is profoundly *unconscious*...Ideology is indeed a system of representation, but in the majority of cases these representations have nothing to do with "consciousness": they are usually images and occasionally concepts, but it is above all as *structures* that they impose on the vast majority of men, not via their "consciousness". They are perceived-accepted-suffered cultural objects and they act functionally on men via a process that escapes them.[12]

Although Althusser is here referring to structures like the family, cultural and political institutions, etc., we can illustrate the point quite simply by taking as our example a physical structure. Most modern institutes of education, despite the apparent neutrality of the materials from which they are constructed (red brick, white tile, etc.) carry within themselves implicit ideological assumptions which are literally structured into the architecture itself. The categorization of knowledge into arts and sciences is reproduced in the faculty system which houses different disciplines in different buildings, and most colleges maintain the traditional divisions by devoting a separate floor to each subject. Moreover, the hierarchical relationship between teacher and taught is inscribed in the very layout of the lecture theater where the seating arrangements—benches rising in tiers before a raised lectern—dictate the flow of information and serve to "naturalize" professorial authority. Thus, a whole range of decisions about what is and what is not possible within education have been made, however unconsciously, before the content of individual courses is even decided.

These decisions help to set the limits not only on what is taught but on how it is taught. Here the buildings literally *reproduce* in concrete terms prevailing (ideological) notions about what education is and it is through this process that the educational structure, which can, of course, be altered, is placed beyond question and appears to us as a "given" (i.e. as immutable). In this case, the frames of our thinking have been translated into actual bricks and mortar.

Social relations and processes are then appropriated by individuals only through the forms in which they are represented to those individuals. These forms are, as we have seen, by no means transparent. They are shrouded in a "common sense" which simultaneously validates and mystifies them. It is precisely these "perceived-accepted-suffered cultural objects" which semiotics sets out to interrogate and decipher. All aspects of culture possess a semiotic value, and the most taken-for-granted phenomena can function as signs: as elements in communication systems governed by semantic rules and codes which are not themselves directly apprehended in experience. These signs are, then, as opaque as the social relations which produce them and which they represent. In other words, there is an ideological dimension to every signification.

To uncover the ideological dimension of signs we must first try to disentangle the codes through which meaning is organized. "Connotative" codes are particularly important. As Stuart Hall has argued, they "cover the face of social life and render it classifiable, intelligible, meaningful". He goes on to describe these codes as "maps of meaning" which are of necessity the product of selection. They cut across a range of potential meaning, making certain meaning available and ruling others out of court. We tend to live inside these maps as surely as we live in the "real" world: they "think" us as much as we "think" them, and this in itself is quite "natural". All human societies *reproduce* themselves in this way through a process of "naturalization". It is through this process—a kind of inevitable reflex of all social life—that *particular* sets of social relations, *particular* ways of organizing the world appear to us as if they were universal and timeless. This is what Althusser means when he says that "ideology has no history" and that ideology in this general sense will always be an "essential element of every social formation".

However, in highly complex societies like ours, which function through a finely graded system of divided (i. e. specialized) labor, the crucial question has to do with which specific ideologies, representing the interests of which specific groups and classes will prevail at any given moment, in any given situation. To deal with this question, we must first consider how power is distributed in our society. That is, we must ask which groups and classes have how much say in defining, ordering and classifying out the social world. For instance, if we pause to reflect for a moment, it should be obvious that access to the means by which ideas are disseminated in our society (i. e. principally the mass media) is *not* the same for all classes. Some groups have more say, more opportunity to make the rules, to organize meaning, while others are less favorably placed, have less power to produce and impose their definitions of the world on the world.

Thus, when we come to look beneath the level of "ideology-in-general" at the way in which specific ideologies work, how some gain dominance and others remain marginal, we can see that in advanced Western democracies the ideological field is by no means neutral. To return to the "connotative" codes to which Stuart Hall refers we can see that these "maps of meaning" are charged with a potentially explosive significance because they are traced and re-traced along the lines laid down by the *dominant* discourses about reality, the *dominant* ideologies. They thus tend to represent; in however obscure and contradictory a fashion, the interests of the *dominant* groups in society.

To understand this point we should refer to Marx:

> The ideas of the ruling class are in every epoch the ruling ideas, i.e. the class which is the ruling *material* force of society is at the same time its ruling *intellectual* force. The class which has the means of material production at its disposal, has control at the same time over the means of mental production, so that generally speaking, the ideas of those who lack the means of mental production are subject to it. The ruling ideas are nothing more than the ideal expression of the dominant material relationships grasped as ideas; hence of the relationships which make the one class the ruling class, therefore the ideas of its dominance.

This is the basis of Antonio Gramsci's theory of *hegemony* which pro- vides the most adequate account of how dominance is sustained in advanced capitalist societies.

Hegemony: the Moving Equilibrium

> Society cannot share a common communication system so long as it is split into warring classes.
>
> (Brecht, *A Short Organum for the Theater*)

The term hegemony refers to a situation in which a provisional alliance of certain social groups can exert "total social authority" over other subordinate groups, not simply by coercion or by the direct imposition of ruling ideas, but by "winning and shaping consent so that the power of the dominant classes appears both legitimate and natural". Hegemony can only be maintained so long as the dominant classes "succeed in framing all competing definitions within their range", so that subordinate groups are, if not controlled, then at least contained within an ideological space which does not seem at all "ideological": which appears instead to be permanent and "natural", to lie outside history, to be beyond particular interests.

This is how, according to Barthes, "mythology" performs its vital function of naturalization and normalization and it is in his book *Mythologies* that Barthes demonstrates most forcefully the full extension of these normalized forms and meanings. However, Gramsci adds the important proviso that hegemonic power, precisely *because* it requires the consent of the dominated majority, can never be permanently exercised by the same alliance of "class fractions". As has been pointed out, "Hegemony...is not universal and 'given' to the continuing rule of a particular class. It has to be won, reproduced, sustained. Hegemony is, as Gramsci said, a 'moving equilibrium' containing relations of forces favorable or unfavorable to this or that tendency."

In the same way, forms cannot be permanently normalized. They can always be deconstructed, demystified, by a "mythologist" like Barthes. Moreover commodities can be symbolically "repossessed" in everyday life, and endowed with implicitly oppositional meanings, by the very groups who originally produced them. The symbiosis in which ideology and social order, production and reproduction, are linked is then neither fixed nor guaranteed. It can be prised open. The consensus can be fractured, challenged, overruled, and resistance to the groups in dominance cannot always be lightly dismissed or automatically incorporated. Although, as Lefebvre[13] has written, we live in a society where "objects in practice become signs and signs objects and a second nature takes the place of the first—the initial layer of perceptible reality", there are, as he goes on to affirm, always "objections and contradictions which hinder the closing of the circuit" between sign and object, production and reproduction.

We can now return to the meaning of youth subcultures, for the emergence of such groups has signaled in a spectacular fashion the breakdown of consensus in the post-war period. It is precisely objections and contradictions of the kind which Lefebvre has described that find expression in subculture. However, the challenge to hegemony which subcultures represent is not issued directly by them. Rather it is expressed obliquely, in style. The objections are lodged, the contradictions displayed (and "magically resolved") at the profoundly superficial level of appearances, that is, at the level of signs. For the signcommunity, the community of myth-consumers, is not a uniform body. As Volosinov[14] has written, it is cut through by class.

Class does not coincide with the sign community, i.e. with the totality of users of the same set of signs of ideological communication. Thus various different classes will use one and the same language. As a result, differently oriented accents intersect in every ideological sign. Sign becomes the arena of the class struggle.

The struggle between different discourses, different definitions and meanings within ideology is therefore always, at the same time, a struggle within signification, a struggle for possession of the sign which extends to even the most mundane areas of everyday life. "Humble objects" can be magically appropriated; "stolen" by subordinate groups and made to carry "secret" meanings: meanings which express, in code, a form of resistance to the order which guarantees their continued subordination.

Style in subculture is, then, pregnant with significance. Its transformations go "against nature", interrupting the process of "normalization". As such, they are gestures, movements towards a speech which offends the "silent majority", which challenges the principle of unity and cohesion, which contradicts the myth of consensus. Our task becomes, like Barthes's, to discern the hidden messages inscribed in code on the glossy surfaces of style, to trace them out as "maps of meaning" which obscurely represent the very contradictions they are designed to resolve or conceal.

注释

1. 雷蒙·威廉斯认为，"文化"是英语中最复杂的两三个词之一。他在《漫长的革命》和《关键词》等书中为文化归纳出三种定义：文化表示人类走向完美的一种状态或过程；文化是思想性和想象性作品的总和；文化是日常生活方式。英国文化研究采用的是文化的第三种定义。

2. 即雷蒙·威廉斯在《文化与社会》中首次揭示和提炼出的"文化与社会"的传统。这个传统的核心内容可归纳如下：在工业革命之前，英国社会文化浑然一体、有机和谐，社会各个阶层都奉行志趣高尚、品味高雅的文化标准。可是，自工业革命以来，这种有机和谐的社会文化，却遭到了人为造就的工业文明的侵蚀，举国上下唯利是图，致使道德缺失，人的心灵机械麻木，文化水准江河日下，文化欣赏品位今不如昔，社会精神陷入危机之中。摆脱危机的出路只有两个。

一个是遵循文化保守派的方案，重申传统文化的价值，借以对抗资本主义工业文明；另一个是政治激进派的方案，推翻工业资本主义，建立新的文化和社会形态，塑造新型阶级关系。

3. 意为"思想和言论的精华"。语出马修·阿诺德的文化批评名著《文化与无政府》。

4. Herder：赫尔德（Johann Gottfried von Herder, 1744—1803），德国思想家、作家、狂飙运动的先锋。

5. 这是威廉斯在《文化与社会》一书中提出的文化定义和文化分析的内容。

6. 这是艾略特在著名的小册子《略论文化的定义》（*Notes towards the Definition of Culture*）中罗列的文化内容。艾略特将文化定义为某种生活方式，把文化的内涵扩大到文学和艺术的范围之外。这一定义给威廉斯以及后来的英国文化研究批评家们以极大的启发。

7. 语出威廉斯的名著《漫长的革命》（1961）。

8. 早期的英国文化研究，尤其是在霍加特担任当代文化研究中心主任期间，采用了文学研究中实用批评的方法来分析日常生活中的诸种现象。

9. 语出罗兰·巴特的《神话》（1972）。

10. 法国杂志《巴黎竞赛》。巴特从符号学角度分析黑人青年向法国国旗敬礼的文章题目为《现代神话》，该文被收入《神话》一书中。

11. 英国新左派历史学家 E. P. 汤普森在一篇评论文章中批评威廉斯的文化定义忽略了日常生活中的阶级冲突。威廉斯在访谈录《政治与文学》（*Politics and Letters*）中对此进行过辩解。

12. 引文出自阿尔都塞的名著《保卫马克思》（*For Marx*）。阿尔都塞将意识形态视为一个再现系统，认为它处于人的无意识心理层面。

13. Lefebvre：列斐伏尔（Henri Lefebvre, 1901—1991），法国著名马克思主义哲学家，著有《日常生活批判》（*The Critique of Everyday Life*, 1947）和《现代世界的日常生活》（*Everyday Life in the Modern World*, 1968）等书。

14. Volosinov：沃洛希诺夫，应为巴赫金（Mikhail Bakhtin, 1895—1975）。由于政治原因，巴赫金的好几部作品都是以别人的名字出版的，其中包括这里引用的《马克思主义与语言哲学》（*Marxism and the Philosophy of Language*）。直到 20 世纪 60 年代，他才开始以自己的名字发表作品。